Engaging the Reader

Activities that are tied to each skill level offer students multiple opportunities to engage with the reading and receive immediate feedback.

Steps in Evaluating an Author's Argument: Activity

Choose a highlight color:

| None | Either-Or | Personal Attack | Appeal to Ignorance |

I have not seen one study to prove that these new social programs will not work.

How can you argue for more funding for Child Protective Services when I have seen you spank your own son?

Anyone who does not support the current homeland security policy supports terrorism.

Buy our anti-aging moisturizer or continue to watch your wrinkles grow.

If you yourself have to wear makeup, then why should I believe that your skin

You have added 2 out of 5 highlights.   Instructions   Submit

Identifying, Marking, and Annotating Supporting Details: Activity

Choose a highlight color:

| None | Supporting Details |

flying. These dreams sometimes became myths, stories, and art. In a Greek myth, a king trapped Daedalus and his son, Icarus, in a maze. Daedalus made wings of wax so that they could fly away, but Icarus flew too close to the sun. His wings melted, and he fell into the sea. A coin of ancient Babylonia showed the king flying on an eagle's back. The Inca claimed that one of their ancestors had wings and could fly.

Perhaps the first people to get off the ground were the Chinese. In about 1000 B.C. they made large kites that carried men to spy on enemy troops. In about 1100, in Turkey, a man made wings of pleated fabric. He jumped from a tower and fell to his death. Centuries later, a man in France built wings that flapped

You have added 2 out of 11 highlights.   Instructions   Submit

"Connect Reading gives [students] more study options and a fresh perspective to listen and learn from."
—Yvette Daniel, Central Georgia Tech.

Reading Critically

LiveInk, a research-based technology, increases the reader's comprehension, which leads to improved synthesis and understanding of information, the foundation of critical reading and critical thinking.

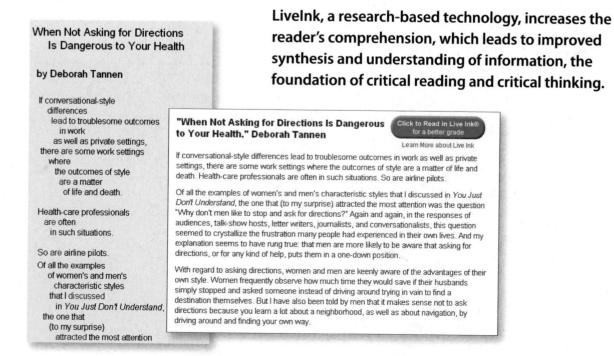

When Not Asking for Directions Is Dangerous to Your Health

by Deborah Tannen

If conversational-style
differences
    lead to troublesome outcomes
    in work
    as well as private settings,
there are some work settings
    where
        the outcomes of style
        are a matter
        of life and death.

Health-care professionals
    are often
        in such situations.

So are airline pilots.

Of all the examples
    of women's and men's
        characteristic styles
        that I discussed
        in *You Just Don't Understand,*
    the one that
        (to my surprise)
        attracted the most attention

"When Not Asking for Directions Is Dangerous to Your Health," Deborah Tannen

Click to Read in Live Ink®
for a better grade

Learn More about Live Ink

If conversational-style differences lead to troublesome outcomes in work as well as private settings, there are some work settings where the outcomes of style are a matter of life and death. Health-care professionals are often in such situations. So are airline pilots.

Of all the examples of women's and men's characteristic styles that I discussed in *You Just Don't Understand,* the one that (to my surprise) attracted the most attention was the question "Why don't men like to stop and ask for directions?" Again and again, in the responses of audiences, talk-show hosts, letter writers, journalists, and conversationalists, this question seemed to crystallize the frustration many people had experienced in their own lives. And my explanation seems to have rung true: that men are more likely to be aware that asking for directions, or for any kind of help, puts them in a one-down position.

With regard to asking directions, women and men are keenly aware of the advantages of their own style. Women frequently observe how much time they would save if their husbands simply stopped and asked someone instead of driving around trying in vain to find a destination themselves. But I have also been told by men that it makes sense not to ask directions because you learn a lot about a neighborhood, as well as about navigation, by driving around and finding your own way.

Reading and All That Jazz

Tuning Up Your Reading, Thinking, and Study Skills

FIFTH EDITION

Peter Mather

Retired from Glendale Community College
Glendale, Arizona

Rita McCarthy

Glendale Community College
Glendale, Arizona

The McGraw-Hill Companies

Mc Graw Hill

Connect
Learn
Succeed™

Published by McGraw-Hill, an imprint of The McGraw-Hill Companies, Inc., 1221 Avenue of the Americas, New York, NY 10020. Copyright © 2012, 2010, 2007, 2003, 1999. All rights reserved. No part of this publication may be reproduced or distributed in any form or by any means, or stored in a database or retrieval system, without the prior written consent of The McGraw-Hill Companies, Inc., including, but not limited to, in any network or other electronic storage or transmission, or broadcast for distance learning.

This book is printed on acid-free paper.

1 2 3 4 5 6 7 8 9 0 QDB/QDB 1 0 9 8 7 6 5 4 3 2 1

ISBN: 978-0-07-340728-9 (student edition)
MHID: 0-07-340728-3 (student edition)
ISBN: 978-0-07-741149-7 (instructor's edition)
MHID: 0-07-741149-8 (instructor's edition)

Senior Sponsoring Editor: *John Kindler*
Senior Marketing Manager: *Jaclyn Elkins*
Developmental Editor: *Merryl Maleska Wilbur*
Production Editor: *Jasmin Tokatlian*
Manuscript Editor: *Carole Crouse*
Senior Design Manager: *Allister Fein*
Text Designer: *Lisa Buckley*
Cover Designer: *Brian Salisbury*
Photo Research: *Natalia Peschiera*
Senior Buyer: *Sherry Kane*
Media Project Manager: *Jennifer Barrick*
Composition: *10/13 Palatino by Aptara®, Inc.*
Printing: *45# New Era Matte Thin, Quad/Graphics Dubuque*

Vice President Editorial: *Michael Ryan*
Publisher: *David Patterson*
Senior Director of Development: *Dawn Groundwater*

Cover: *Guitar, Book and Palette (1990) by Gerald Bustamante. Medium: Cardboard/acrylic/spray paint collage.* © *Gerald Bustamante/Getty Images*

Credits: The credits section for this book begins on page C-1 and is considered an extension of the copyright page.

Library of Congress Cataloging-in-Publication Data

Mather, Peter.
  Reading and all that jazz / Peter Mather, Rita McCarthy.—5th ed.
    p. cm.
  Includes bibliographical references and index.
  ISBN-13: 978-0-07-340728-9 (acid-free paper)
  ISBN-10: 0-07-340728-3 (acid-free paper) 1. Reading (Higher education)—
  United States. 2. English language—Rhetoric. 3. Critical thinking—Study
  and teaching (Higher)—United States. 4. Study skills—United States.
  I. McCarthy, Rita. II. Title.
  LB2395.3.M28 2011
  428.4071'1—dc23

2011037360

The Internet addresses listed in the text were accurate at the time of publication. The inclusion of a website does not indicate an endorsement by the authors or McGraw-Hill, and McGraw-Hill does not guarantee the accuracy of the information presented at these sites.

Printed in the USA

www.mhhe.com

Copyright © 2012 by The McGraw-Hill Companies, Inc.

Peter dedicates this book to his late parents,
Carl and Dorothy; and his brother and sister-in-law,
John and Peggy.

Rita dedicates this book to her sons, Ryan and Steve;
her daughters-in-law, Bonnie and Raquel; her grandchildren,
Zachary, Kate, and Dylan; and especially her husband, Greg.

Letter from the Authors

Dear Colleagues,

Thank you for taking the time to consider *Reading and All That Jazz*, our textbook that precedes *The Art of Critical Reading*. We wrote this book with the goal of helping students become better at reading, understanding, and evaluating college-level materials. With this in mind, we have designed this book so that it has the following four attributes. First, we expose students to the sorts of readings they will encounter in their college courses, including excerpts from college textbooks, literature, newspapers, and popular fiction and non-fiction. In selecting this material, we have favored readings that the students will find both interesting and challenging. Second, we discuss the reading skills that students need to succeed in college and beyond, and give them many opportunities to practice and develop these skills. The review tests and quizzes give both student and teacher a tool for assessing progress. Third, we want students to develop their vocabularies, and so we examine potentially troublesome words and phrases taken from the readings and discuss context clues and word parts as techniques for uncovering the meanings of words. Finally, to improve our students' chances for success in college and life more generally, we discuss the need to manage time and give them techniques that will aid them in becoming more effective as students, readers, and individuals.

Students are more likely to read when they have confidence in themselves as readers, find reading interesting and even exciting or entertaining, and understand its importance in enriching life and affording opportunities for greater success. Our hope is that students will come away from working in this book with both a desire to read and an ability to do so effectively and well.

Rita McCarthy

About the Authors

Peter Mather—earned his BA in government from the University of Redlands; his first MA, in African studies, from the University of California, Los Angeles; his second MA, in reading, from California State University, Los Angeles; and his EdD in curriculum and instruction from the University of Southern California. Before recently retiring from Glendale Community College, he taught at the secondary, adult-education, and community-college levels for over 30 years. While at Glendale Community College, he taught both developmental reading and critical and evaluative reading. He also taught American government and was the college director of the America Reads/Counts Program. In addition to being coauthor of *The Art of Critical Reading*, now in its third edition, and *Racing Ahead with Reading*, he has published articles in the *Journal of Reading*.

Rita Romero McCarthy—earned a BA in sociology and history from the University of California, Berkeley, and an MA in education from Arizona State University. She has taught at the elementary, secondary, adult-education, and community-college levels. For the past 23 years, she has taught ESL, college preparatory reading, and college critical reading at Glendale Community College. Ms. McCarthy has published articles in professional journals and other media on the use of bibliotherapy. She has also published reading lists for beginning and remedial readers and is a reading specialist. In addition to this textbook, she is coauthor of *The Art of Critical Reading* and *Racing Ahead with Reading*.

Brief Contents

Contents

Preface

Reading and All That Jazz allows students to take control of their study plan while providing engaging and diverse reading selections, multiple assessment opportunities, and in-context and essential vocabulary content in an integrated print and digital program designed to prepare students for reading in college and beyond.

ENGAGING AND DIVERSE READING SELECTIONS

Reading selections were chosen for their excellence, their contemporary relevance and interest, and their overall diversity.

The fifth edition of **Reading and All That Jazz** includes new reading selections with accompanying exercises.

Powered by Connect, Reading and All That Jazz uses the research-based LiveInk technology to increase the student's reading comprehension, which leads to improved synthesis of information.

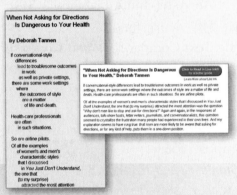

MULTIPLE ASSESSMENTS

Multiple assessment opportunities in the book and online help students test their knowledge to understand what their next steps will be in advancing their reading skills. Assessments are placed after each reading and at the end of chapters giving students the opportunity to understand what they know and don't know.

Each chapter contains a series of exercises arranged sequentially progressing from easy to difficult. Review Tests are included throughout the book.

Connect Reading places reading in the hands of the students giving them the opportunity to judge for themselves what they know and what they need to still learn.

IN-CONTEXT AND ESSENTIAL VOCABULARY

Two units present key vocabulary development techniques and provide context practice. Eight additional units introduce a set of Latin or Greek word parts or homonyms. Students learn college-level words associated with these word parts and then practice the key words through context exercises and crossword puzzles.

To further vocabulary development, each end-of-chapter vocabulary unit lists additional college-level words in a new section titled "Expanding Your Word Power." These words draw on and exemplify the unit's word parts.

McGraw Hill connect | READING

Connect Reading brings three levels of vocabulary to students.

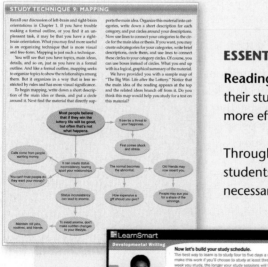

ESSENTIAL STUDY TECHNIQUES

Reading and All That Jazz shows students how to take control of their study plan through integral study skills, helping students study more effectively and manage their schedules throughout the term.

Through multiple activities contained within the book, students are given an opportunity to learn the key skills necessary to be successful in school and life.

McGraw Hill connect | READING

In **Connect Reading** students are given hands-on training in learning how to effectively manage their study time, preparing them for their next classes.

Hallmarks of *Reading and All That Jazz*

*"Reading furnishes the mind only with materials of knowledge;
it is thinking that makes what we read ours."*—John Locke

In 1999, we published the first edition of *Reading and All That Jazz*. Over the ensuing years, we have been extremely gratified by *Jazz's* success. Teachers and students alike have complimented us on the outstanding reading selections and engaging exercises, which have all been classroom-tested.

We initially selected the theme of jazz to emphasize a positive, exciting, personally involved approach to reading and learning. Just as jazz relies on improvisation, we want teachers to feel free to improvise in their use of this book so that it becomes an effective learning tool for classes of varying skill levels and areas of interest. And just as jazz musicians bring their individual backgrounds to bear on the music they play, we encourage our students to draw from their individual backgrounds when they read and interpret the selections in the book. Jazz, an American art form, grew from many diverse influences—African, Spanish, European. Similarly, we have tried to reflect the cultural diversity and varying interests of our students by having our textbook highlight the influence and contributions of various peoples and cultures.

In this edition, while continuing to include the jazz music form, we have broadened the music theme to include several different kinds of music and musicians. We believe this expanded music focus even better reflects the varying interests of our students. This greater range of topics and perspectives will, we believe, further enable students to clarify their own values and experience events through the eyes of others.

Organization of the Text

This book is organized along two dimensions. First, the successive parts of the book focus on different skills that an effective learner and reader must master. Second, the book begins with a narrow perspective focusing on the student as learner and then moves to increasingly broader perspectives, focusing in turn on interpersonal, social, national, and then global issues.

Part 1 Is Designed to Capture Students' Attention and Interest by Helping Them Discover More about Themselves as Learners

The goals in Part 1 are to introduce students to the study techniques likely to lead to a successful college experience and to help students recognize the individual strengths and weaknesses they bring to the learning process. The mood of the selections is "upbeat" in the sense of being positive and encouraging. The Introduction in Part 1 is meant to be completed in the first week of class. The reading selections and the short written assignments that follow the selections are designed so that the instructor can use them for quickly assessing the skills of individual students and classes as a whole. The theme of Part 1 is the student as learner.

- New: Introduction to the Study Techniques of Skimming, Scanning, Marking Written Material, and SQ3R

- New: Excerpt from *Power Learning*—"Motivation"
- New: Excerpt from *Step Out on Nothing* by Byron Pitts—"Keep Your Head Up"
- New: "Warren Buffett Offers Advice to Students"
- New: Excerpt from *Interpersonal Communication*—"Naming Defines and Differentiates Us"
- New: Student Stress Scale
- New: Excerpt from *First Things First* by Kurt and Brenda Warner—"Strive to Be the Best You Can Be"

Part 2 Is Directed at Developing the Basic Skills Needed to Make Reading Easier and More Productive

The focus is on the process and structure of reading. Skills emphasized include identifying the topic, main idea, and supporting details; determining the author's purpose; and transition words and patterns of organization. Themes touched on in Part 2 include communication, anger, and work.

- New: Inclusion of the "Spatial Order" and "Addition" patterns of organization
- New: Exercises on Relationships within and between Sentences
- New: Exercises on Identifying Transition Words and Predicting the Pattern

Part 3 Emphasizes Reading as an Interpretive Process

The goal of Part 3 is to enable students to become proficient at "reading between the lines." Topics introduced in Part 3 include inference, figurative language, and author's tone.

- New: Excerpt from *Wouldn't Take Nothing for My Journey Now* by Maya Angelou—"Complaining"
- New: Excerpt from *Core Concepts in Health*—"El Día de los Muertos"
- New: Excerpt from *Farmworker's Daughter: Growing Up Mexican in America* by Rosa Castillo Guilbault—"The Conveyor Belt Ladies"

Part 4 Focuses on Modes of Writing and of Organization

Chapter 8 introduces students to the primary modes of narrative, descriptive, expository, and persuasive writing. This chapter features the theme of relationships. Chapter 9 familiarizes students with the various modes of organization, including cause and effect, categories, and chronological order. This chapter features the topic of happiness. In addition, Part 4 introduces several new study techniques and provides further practice in study techniques introduced previously.

- New: Introduction to the Study Techniques of creating Venn diagrams, maps, time lines, outlines, and summaries
- New: Increased application of Study Techniques to reading selections
- New: "The Jacket" by Gary Soto

Part 5 Concentrates on Developing Critical Reading and Thinking Skills

Topics discussed include fact and opinion, bias, propaganda techniques, argument, and evaluation of the evidence. The theme of Part 5 focuses on social issues such as public opinion, advertisers promoting smoking by women and children, the

Hallmarks of *Reading and All That Jazz*

prevalence of violence on television and in video games, and the medical use of marijuana.

- New: "Ties That Bind" and "The Blind Side"
- New: Exercise on Writing Opposing Claims
- New: Exercise on Identifying the Evidence That Supports the Claim
- New: Exercise on Identifying the Assumptions
- New: Exercises on Valid or Invalid Arguments
- New: Excerpt from *Your Health Today*—"Cannabinoids"

Part 6 Is Devoted to Becoming Ready for Content-Area Classes

Material covered includes skimming and scanning, study techniques, and visual aids. Part 6 has the environment as a theme.

- New: Scanning a Nutritional Content Chart from a Fast-Food Restaurant
- New: Scanning a Food Label
- New: Completing a Comparison-Contrast Chart
- New: Visual Aids exercises on a table, diagram, flow chart, pie graph, line graph, and bar graph

The Appendices

Focus on the specific skills of reading rate, using a dictionary, and test-taking techniques. Sample assignment sheets and sample student summaries are also included.

- New: Timed Reading Rate Information

Additional New Features and Revisions

- Six new part openers that can be used as timed readings, featuring Louis Armstrong, Johnny Cash, Elvis Presley, Carlos Santana, *American Idol*, and Esperanza Spalding
- New feature focused on study skills—Study Techniques
- More and better-focused Review Tests throughout the book
- New cartoons, full-color photographs, and visual aids
- More in-depth questions for In Your Own Words and Written Assignments
- Updated Internet Activity sections
- Additional vocabulary words for the eight Vocabulary Units

Popular Continuing Features

- **A vocabulary unit on homonyms,** which includes practice exercises and a crossword puzzle.
- **Eight independent vocabulary units emphasizing Latin and Greek word parts.** Each unit includes practice exercises and a crossword puzzle.
- **Thorough coverage of each chapter's topic.** Each chapter contains a series of exercises arranged sequentially, progressing from the relatively easy to the quite difficult. Exercises are designed so that the instructor can have the students work either individually or in groups. Exercises appear in many different formats to maintain student interest.

Copyright © 2012 by The McGraw-Hill Companies, Inc.

- **A wealth of quality material to choose from**. The textbook is designed to enable the instructor to select the material that best fits each class.
- **Formatting that shows the reading selections as they would appear in their original forms**. For instance, selections from magazines have the look of magazine articles, and selections from textbooks look like textbook material. This not only gives the text a more varied and interesting appearance but also smooths students' transition to readings in other classes and outside the classroom.
- **A standardized format for presenting the pre-reading material for the reading selections**. A section titled "Tuning In to Reading" contains questions designed to actively engage the student with the subject of the upcoming selection. A "Bio-sketch" provides information about each author's background. "Notes on Vocabulary" offers a discussion of unusual words that appear in the selection.
- **A standardized format for "Comprehension Checkup" sections**. Objective questions, written in the style of those found on many standardized tests, come first, followed by "Vocabulary in Context" questions designed to test knowledge of vocabulary used in the selection. This is followed by a series of open-ended questions for critical thinking titled "In Your Own Words." A section titled "Written Assignment" that calls for more in-depth writing on the students' part is next, and finally "Internet Activity" asks students to do Internet research on topics or issues raised by the selection.
- **Quotations in the margins** for student journal writing, discussion, and extra credit.

Teaching and Learning Aids

- *PowerPoint Slides.* The instructional content of each chapter is summarized for overhead projection on PowerPoint slides.
- *Multiple-Choice Quiz.* A multiple-choice quiz on the instructional content is provided for each chapter of the text.
- *Comprehension Exercises.* Comprehension exercises are provided for all the substantive reading selections.
- *Merriam-Webster's Notebook Dictionary.* A compact word resource conveniently designed for three-ring binders, *Merriam-Webster's Notebook Dictionary* includes 40,000 entries for widely used words with concise, easy-to-understand definitions and pronunciations.
- *The Merriam-Webster Dictionary.* This handy paperback dictionary contains over 75,000 definitions, yet is small enough to carry around in a backpack, so it's always there when it's needed.
- *Random House Webster's College Dictionary.* This authoritative dictionary includes over 160,000 entries and 207,000 definitions. The most commonly used definitions are always listed first, so students can find what they need quickly.
- *Merriam-Webster's Collegiate Dictionary & Thesaurus* CD-ROM. This up-to-the-minute electronic dictionary and thesaurus offers 225,000 definitions, 340,000 synonyms and related words, and 1,300 illustrations.
- *Merriam-Webster's Notebook Thesaurus.* Conveniently designed for three-ring binders, this thesaurus provides concise, clear guidance for over 157,000 word choices.

- *Merriam-Webster Thesaurus.* This compact thesaurus offers over 157,000 word choices, and includes concise definitions and examples to help students choose the correct word for the context.

Novel Ideas

These Random House and HarperCollins paperbacks are available at a low cost when packaged with the text: *The Monkey Wrench Gang* (Abbey); *Things Fall Apart* (Achebe); *The Lone Ranger and Tonto* (Alexie); *Integrity* (Carter); *The House on Mango Street* (Cisneros); *Heart of Darkness* (Conrad); *Pilgrim at Tinker Creek* (Dillard); *Love Medicine* (Erdrich); *Their Eyes Were Watching God* (Hurston); *Boys of Summer* (Kahn); *Woman Warrior* (Kingston); *One Hundred Years of Solitude* (García Márquez); *Clear Springs* (Mason); *All the Pretty Horses* (McCarthy); *House Made of Dawn* (Momaday); *Joy Luck Club* (Tan); and *Essays of E. B. White* (White).

Acknowledgments

No textbook can be created without the assistance of many people. First, we relied on the thoughtful reactions and suggestions of our colleagues across the country, who reviewed this project at various stages.

Jesus Adame, *El Paso Community College*

Edith Alderson, *Joliet Junior College*

Bonnie Arnett, *Washtenaw Community College*

Ellen Bagby, *Midlands Technical College*

Doralee Brooks, *Community College of Allegheny County*

Charlotte Brown, *Norfolk State University*

Helen Carr, *San Antonio College*

Diane Cole, *Pensacola Junior College*

Gertrude Coleman, *Middlesex County College*

Barbara Culhane, *Nassau Community College*

Elizabeth Earle, *Valencia Community College*

Jan Eveler, *El Paso Community College*

Vicci Fox, *Pima Community College*

Dennis Gabriel, *Cuyahoga Community College West*

Robert Gibson, *Truman College*

Amy Girone, *Arizona Western College*

Suzanne Gripenstraw, *Butte College*

Kevin Hayes, *Essex Community College*

James R. Henson, *Northeast State Community College*

Rita L. Higgins, *Essex County College*

Sue M. Hightower, *Tallahassee Community College*

Glenda Jackson, *Gaston College*

Mahalia H. Johnson, *Greenville Technical College*

Lorna Keebaugh, *Taft College*

Julie Kelly, *St. Johns River Community College*

J. C. Kissinger, III, *Cy-Fair College*

Sandi Komarow, *Montgomery College*

Patty Kunkel, *Santa Fe College*

Jeanne Mauzy, *Valencia Community College West*

Margaret McClain, *Arkansas State University*

Sherry Mosher, *University of Akron*

Debbie Naquin, *Northern Virginia Community College*

Elizabeth Nelson, *Tidewater Community College Thomas Moss Campus*

Cynthia Ortega, *Phoenix College*

Aida Pavese, *Suffolk Community College*

Bethany Plett, *Seattle University*

Peggy Porter, *Houston Community College System Northwest*

Elizabeth Ragsdale, *Darton College*

Keflyn Reed, *Bishop State College*

Karen Reilly, *Ivy Tech Community College, Fort Wayne*

Mitye Jo Richey, *Community College of Allegheny County*

Kathleen Riehle, *Sinclair Community College*

Jackie Roberts, *Richland Community College*

Alan Rosati, *Oakton Community College*

Deirdre Rowley, *Imperial Valley College*

Joanne Russell, *Wright State University*

Victoria Sarkisian, *Marist College*

Lisa Schuemer, *College of DuPage*

Carole Shaw, *Northeast State Technical Community College*

Margaret Sims, *Midlands Technical College*

Sharon Smallwood, *St. Petersburg Junior College*

Katie Smith, *Riverside Community College*

Anne G. Solomon, *South Plains College*

Diane Starke, *El Paso Community College*

Marsha Stowe, *Ivy Tech Community College*

Peggy Strickland, *Gainesville College*

Marjorie Susman, *Miami-Dade Community College*

Shirey VanHook, *Ozarks Technical Community College*

Judith M. Walter, *New York City College of Technology—CUNY* (Emerita)

Carole Widsor, *Santa Fe Community College*

Barbara Wilan, *Northern Virginia Community College*

Anne Willekens, *Antelope Valley College*

Andrea Williams, *Purdue University*

Nancy Wood, *University of Arkansas*

We owe a special thanks to the honest and valuable criticism from our colleagues in the Maricopa Community College District. In particular, we would like to thank Cindy Ortega, Mary Jane Onnen, Gwen Worthington, Viva Henley, and Karen Irwin. Others who helped us with the fifth edition of this book are Cindy Gilbert, Marilyn Brophy, Nancy Edwards, Arlene Lurie, Carol Jones, Lynda Svendsen, Lucy Ehlers, and Tom Mather.

We'd also like to thank all of those at McGraw-Hill who have helped us in the production of the fifth edition of *Reading and All That Jazz*. We owe a special debt of gratitude to our first editor, Sarah Touborg, who shepherded our first unwieldy manuscript into something close to its present form. We are especially grateful to Dawn Groundwater, Senior Director of Development, and John Kindler, Senior Sponsoring Editor, for always being willing to discuss our ideas and concerns and give us valuable feedback. In addition, we are grateful to Merryl Maleska Wilbur, Development Editor, for her diligence, Jesse Hassenger, Editorial Coordinator, for his able assistance, Marketing Manager Kevin Colleary, Production Editor Jasmin Tokatlian, Permissions Editor Marty Moga, and Review Coordinator Zachary Norton. We have been especially fortunate in having Sherree DeAmico, as our local McGraw-Hill sales representative. Whenever we wanted to look at a book, Sherree magically obtained it for us.

We also wish to thank our students, who in addition to reading the selections and completing the exercises, made many helpful suggestions.

Reading and All That Jazz

Getting a Handle on College

CHAPTERS IN PART 1

LOUIS ARMSTRONG

Louis Armstrong (1901–1971) was born in New Orleans and from infancy heard the many forms of black music in that city. When he was 12, he was sent to the Colored Waifs' Home for Boys for shooting a pistol during New Year's festivities. It was at the home that Louis took up the bugle—later the cornet—and upon leaving at the age of 16, he began playing professionally. Joe Oliver, Kid Ory, and the other elders of the jazz scene gave young Armstrong guidance and employment. After Oliver's travels brought him to Chicago to form his Creole Jazz Band, he sent for Armstrong to play second cornet. Armstrong married the group's pianist, Lillian Hardin, who prepared him to leave Oliver and go out on his own as a freelance artist. From 1924 on, Armstrong appeared with many bands. During this period, Armstrong became the Johnny Appleseed of jazz, profoundly influencing his fellow musicians wherever he went. Armstrong had a rare technical and creative talent, which emerged in his trumpet playing performances. He was also a formidable force in American popular singing and influenced many popular singers. In 1964, at the height of Beatlemania in the United States, Armstrong's recording of "Hello Dolly" was the only American popular recording to compete with the Beatles for the top spot on the *Billboard* charts. His 1968 recording of "What a Wonderful World" is still popular today. Armstrong is truly a timeless musician and entertainer, honored even today by both the world of jazz artists and the popular audience. (David Lee Joyner, *American Popular Music*, 3/e, 2009)

TIMED READING If you wish to use "Louis Armstrong" as a timed reading, please turn to page A-2 in the Appendices.

I Your First Week in Class

In this chapter, you will

- Learn how to keep track of assignments.
- Learn how to skim written material.
- Examine your motivation for attending college.
- Learn techniques for discovering the meanings of words.
- Learn how to scan material quickly to locate specific information.

"There are no secrets to success. It is the result of preparation, hard work, and learning from failure."

—Colin Powell

Some of you just recently graduated from high school. Others have been out in the "real world" and now realize the importance of a college education. Each of you decides what is important in your life, and you have decided that going to college is important. Besides investing your time, you are investing money, and so you want to get as much benefit as you can out of college. In high school, perhaps many of you did well in your classes without trying very hard. This won't happen in college, because college is more demanding. Whether you succeed in college is up to you. It is your responsibility to attend class, study, and turn in your work on time. No one else can do it for you.

Reading and studying will be an important part of your college career. You can't expect to do well in college without having good reading and studying skills. In this book, we will provide you with techniques for improving these skills. Using these techniques will make the time you spend in college more enjoyable and productive.

Assignment Sheets

Success in college requires an organized and disciplined approach. So, one of the first things you need to think about is how to organize yourself as a serious student. Perhaps the easiest way to improve your college performance is to take charge of your assignments. Many of your assignments will be listed in the class syllabi, while other assignments will be announced in class. In some classes, late assignments will receive less credit, and in others, they will not be accepted at all—no excuses!

The best way to keep a record of your classroom assignments is by using assignment sheets. Developing the habit of carefully recording your assignments is crucial not only in this class but in your other classes as well. On the next page are samples of three types of assignment sheets. The first sample shows a weekly format, the second a monthly format, and the third a "continuous log" format. You

2

Weekly Assignment Sheet

ASSIGNMENTS
MONDAY
TUESDAY
WEDNESDAY
THURSDAY
FRIDAY
OTHER ASSIGNMENTS, TESTS, ETC.

Monthly Assignment Sheet

MONTH _____						
SUNDAY	MONDAY	TUESDAY	WEDNESDAY	THURSDAY	FRIDAY	SATURDAY

Continuous Log Assignment Sheet

ASSIGNMENT SHEET			
Subject(s) _____			
Date	Assignments	Due	Finished

can find a copy of each type of assignment sheet in the Appendices. Whichever format you prefer, be sure to make additional copies of it for future use.

Your First Assignment

Now you can write down your first assignment for this class. This assignment will be due the next class session. Below you will find a crossword puzzle that will introduce you to the material covered in this book. Read the clues, use the table of contents and index to find the answers in the book, and record the answers in the puzzle. Bring your completed puzzle the next time class meets.

Introduction Crossword Puzzle

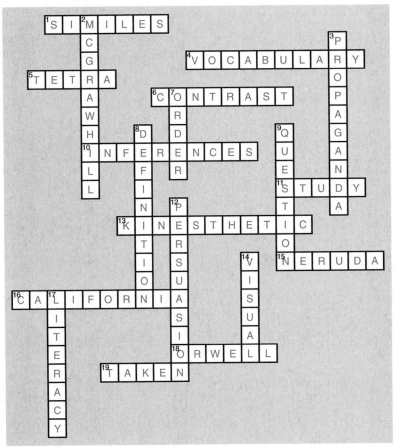

ACROSS CLUES

1. _____ are one type of figure of speech. They use words such as *like* and *as*.

4. "Notes on _____" will introduce you to difficult words in the reading selections.

5. A word part meaning "four." (Vocabulary Unit 2 in Chapter 3)

6. One type of pattern of organization in Chapter 4 is the comparison-_____ pattern.

10. Chapter 5 contains information about _____ (s).

11. In the Introduction, you will be introduced to _____ Skills Technique 1: Skimming.

13. One type of learning style discussed in Chapter 1.

15. The author of "Ode to the Present" is Pablo _____.

16. Both authors of this textbook attended colleges in _____.

18. The author of "A Hanging" is George _____.

19. A Robert Frost poem in Chapter 6 is titled "The Road Not _____."

DOWN CLUES

2. The publisher of this book is _____. (Don't use a hyphen.)

3. Chapter 12 discusses _____ techniques.

7. Chapter 4 introduces you to the spatial _____ pattern of organization.

8. The first type of context clue discussed in "Vocabulary: Words in Context" in Chapter 1.

9. The "Q" in SQ3R stands for _____.

12. In the table of contents "TV" by Mary Pipher is listed as Reading _____.

14. Chapter 14 covers _____ aids.

17. A reading by Fred T. Hofstetter in Chapter 1 is titled "Internet _____."

STUDY TECHNIQUE 1: SKIMMING

Skimming (sometimes called previewing or surveying) is a means of familiarizing yourself with the content and organization of reading material before you begin to read it carefully.

The following assignment provides an example of how to skim. On pages 5–6, read only the material that is underlined, which includes the pre-reading sections (Tuning In to Reading, Bio-Sketch, and Notes on Vocabulary), the title of the selection, the headings and subheadings, the first sentence of each paragraph, and the print in bold and italics. Then answer the true-or-false questions in the Comprehension Checkup at the end of the reading.

READING

"Effort produces success."

TUNING IN TO READING Did you know that approximately half of those who begin taking classes at a community college will drop out by the end of the first year? Notice how many cars there are in the parking lot now. As the days and weeks pass, you will see more empty parking spaces as students drop out for one reason or another. You are the one who decides whether you are going to be a survivor. *Decide to be a survivor!*

BIO-SKETCH The author of the following selection, Robert S. Feldman, remembers being overwhelmed when he first started college. He wondered whether he was capable of meeting the challenges of college, and he realized he had no idea what it took to be successful. Feldman, the author of numerous books, went on to receive a doctorate in psychology and today teaches at the University of Massachusetts.

NOTES ON VOCABULARY
swollen head an exaggerated sense of self-importance. If someone has a *swollen head*, they think they are more intelligent or more important than they actually are.

MOTIVATION
Robert S. Feldman

Finding the Motivation to Work

"If only I could get more motivated, I'd do so much better with my _____" (insert *schoolwork, diet, exercising,* or the like—you fill in the blank).

All of us have said something like this at one time or another. We use 2 the concept of **motivation**—or its lack—to explain why we just don't work hard at a task. But when we do that, we're fooling ourselves. We all have some motivation, that inner power and psychological energy that directs and fuels our behavior. Without any motivation, we'd never get out of bed in the morning.

We've all seen evidence about how strong our motivation can be. Perhaps 3 your love of music helped you learn to play the guitar, making practicing for hours a pleasure rather than a chore. Or perhaps you're a single mother, juggling work, school, and family. Because you are highly motivated, you get up early every morning to make breakfast for your kids before they go off to school.

All of us are motivated. The key to success in and out of the classroom is to 4 *tap into, harness, and direct that motivation.* But there's a key concept that underlies the control of motivation—viewing success as a consequence of effort.

Effort produces success. Suppose, for example, you've gotten a good grade 5 on your mid-term. The instructor smiles at you as she hands back your test. How do you feel?

You will undoubtedly be pleased, of course. But at the same time you might 6 think to yourself, "Better not get a swollen head about it. It was just luck. If she'd asked other questions I would have been in trouble." Or perhaps you explain your success by thinking, "Pretty easy test."

If you often think this way, you're cheating yourself. Using this kind of 7 reasoning when you succeed, instead of patting yourself on the back and think-ing with satisfaction, "All my hard work really paid off," is sure to undermine your future success.

A great deal of psychological research has shown that thinking you have 8 no control over what happens to you sends a powerful and damaging message to your self-esteem—that you are powerless to change things. Just think of how different it feels to say to yourself, "Wow, I worked at it and did it," as com-pared with "I lucked out" or "It was so easy that anybody could have done well."

In the same way, we can delude ourselves when we try to explain our 9 failures. People who see themselves as the victims of circumstance may tell themselves, "I'm just not smart enough" when they don't do well on an aca-demic task. Or they might say, "Those other students don't have to work five hours a day."

The way in which we view the causes of success and failure is, in fact, 10 directly related to our success. Students who generally see effort and hard work as the reason behind their performance usually do better in college. It's not hard to see why: When they are working on an assignment, they feel that the greater the effort they put forth, the greater their chances of success. So they work harder. They believe that they have control over their success, and if they fail, they believe they can do better in the future.

Here are some tips for keeping your motivation alive: 11

- **Take responsibility for your failures—and successes.** When you do poorly on a test, don't blame the teacher, the textbook, or a job that kept you from studying. Analyze the situation and see how you could have changed what you did to be more successful in the future. At the same time, when you're successful, think of the things you did to bring about that success.

- **Think positively.** Assume that the strengths that you have will allow you to succeed, and that, if you have difficulty, you can figure out what to do.

- **Accept that you can't control everything.** Seek to understand which things can be changed and which cannot. You might be able to get an extension on a paper due date, but you are probably not going to be excused from a college-wide requirement.

(Robert S. Feldman, *Power Learning,* 4/e, 2009)

COMPREHENSION CHECKUP

True or False

Directions: Without referring back to the reading, answer the following questions. Write **T** or **F** in the space provided.

____T____ 1. To stay motivated, it is important to remain positive.

____T____ 2. You are harming your self-esteem when you think you have no control over your future.

____F____ 3. The amount of effort you put into something has very little to do with your eventual success.

____F____ 4. Professor Feldman never had any doubts about whether or not he would be successful in college.

____T____ 5. To stay motivated, you must learn to accept responsibility for your failures as well as your successes.

Was your previewing successful? How many of the true-or-false questions did you get right? You likely discovered that you were able to acquire a great deal of information about the topic of motivation and the organization of the reading excerpt in a short amount of time. Now go back and read "Motivation" carefully. Drawing on your broader understanding of the reading, fill in the blanks below with an appropriate phrase or sentence.

Fill in the Blanks

1. Of the three tips presented by Robert Feldman, which one do you find the most helpful? Why?

   _____

   _____

   _____

2. What are your motivators—the things that will get you going when things become difficult? Try to list at least three things below.

   _____

   _____

   _____

In Your Own Words

Explain the following quotations.

1. "Many of life's failures are people who did not realize how close they were to success when they gave up."—Thomas Alva Edison, inventor

2. "Opportunity is missed by most people because it is dressed in overalls and looks like work."—Thomas Alva Edison, inventor

Written Assignment

On the next page is a quiz for assessing how difficult it may be for you to stay in college. This quiz is just for you and is not to be turned in. Place a check mark beside each statement that applies to you.

Motivational Quiz

_____ 1. I have not yet really decided what my career objective is. Or it is difficult for me to visualize what I will be doing in five years.

_____ 2. High school was easy for me, and I never really had to study to get good grades. Or I never really studied in high school and got average or above-average grades.

_____ 3. My main reason for being here is athletics.

_____ 4. I have small children at home I must take care of.

_____ 5. I need to stay in school so that I can remain on my parents' health insurance.

_____ 6. My parents want me to go to college, and I want to please them.

_____ 7. I am working 30 to 40 hours a week and taking 12 to 15 units. (Consider unpaid activities such as athletics as part of those 30 to 40 hours.)

_____ 8. I am living with two or more roommates and plan to do most of my studying at home or in my dorm room.

_____ 9. I need to work part-time to pay for my car, clothes, stereo, etc.

_____ 10. This is the first time I have been away from home on my own.

_____ 11. I plan to get married soon. Or I am going through a divorce.

Now take a look at the number of statements you checked. The more you checked, the greater your chances of not making it. If you checked a lot, this does not mean that you will drop out. But it does mean that you need to do some thinking about your priorities and goals. Your chances of not making it are greater if you are here for the wrong reasons or if you have too many other commitments.

Now write a short paragraph giving your assessment of whether you will be able to complete college.

The following reading features CBS correspondent Byron Pitts. Pitts accepted the many adversities in his life as challenges. He is an example of a person who refused to be defeated.

READING

"I'm sorry, Mr. and Mrs. Pitts. Byron is functionally illiterate."

TUNING IN TO READING   CBS *60 Minutes* correspondent Byron Pitts did not learn to read until he was 12 years old, and he had a debilitating stutter until he was 20. He was bullied throughout elementary and junior high school and placed in remedial classes. As a result of those circumstances, he had problems with anger and suffered from low self-esteem. And yet today, after a great deal of hard work, he has a career that many aspire to and very few achieve.

BIO-SKETCH   In his memoir, *Step Out on Nothing,* Pitts describes how, with faith and the help of family, friends, and mentors, he overcame illiteracy to become an award-winning correspondent. As a correspondent for CBS News, Pitts has interviewed five presidents of the United States, reported from 33 countries, and covered three wars. He won an Emmy Award for his coverage of the 9/11 attacks. Pitts graduated from Ohio Wesleyan University with a B.A. in journalism.

READING *(continued)*

NOTES ON VOCABULARY

finagled obtained or achieved by indirect, usually devious, methods

warehoused placed or stored. The author is referring to the practice of placing people where they receive only minimal care and opportunities.

sheepish meek. Sheep are noted for their tendency to follow others in the flock and for their fearfulness.

Keep Your Head Up

BYRON PITTS

THE ST. KATHARINE'S STAFF MEMBER AND I, along with my parents, were all sitting in our living room. He asked to speak to my parents privately, but Mother assured him that whatever he had to say was fine to say in front of me. He had brought the results of some tests my parents had not yet seen. His words will always ring in my ears.

"I'm sorry, Mr. and Mrs. Pitts. Byron is functionally illiterate." 2

My father frowned, my mother raised her hand to her mouth, and I looked 3 puzzled. What does "functionally illiterate" mean? My parents were finding out that in all the years in school I hadn't learned to read. I'd faked and finagled. It wasn't that I couldn't do the math: I could not read the directions. All these years and no one had noticed. Sweet, polite, quiet Byron could not read. I could recognize some words, identify names of certain locations, remember the words I'd memorized at the kitchen table, the name of my school on the side of the building, and the names of my siblings attached to magnets on the refrigerator. I could function, but I could not read. My mother would say years later that it was one of the few nights she cried herself to sleep. Usually knowing is better than not knowing, but initial shock has a pain all its own. She'd been asked on more than a few occasions, why didn't you know sooner that Byron couldn't read? The short answer: when did she have time? Two jobs, three kids, night school, and a cheating husband usually made for a very full day.

The anger and tension that often curled through our house like smoke 4 up a chimney was suddenly replaced by sadness. Everyone felt it. Everyone dealt with it in different ways. My brother treated me like his best friend. My mother, whom I used to follow around the house, was now following me. This went on for weeks. As we searched for some resource, some long-term solution, my mother set out the short-term course.

"Okay, honey, if we've spent two hours on homework, we'll try four 5 hours. We will pray when we start. We'll pray when we get tired. And we'll pray when we're done."

Just the idea of working longer hours seemed to make her happy. As sad 6 as I was at the time, I remember the joy I felt in anticipating the journey. I had no control over how poorly I read at the time, but I did have control over how hard I worked. That's what you do if you're Clarice Pitts's child. You work hard.

"Smart people can think their troubles to the ground, honey," she'd say. 7 "We have to wrestle ours."

Soon my father seemed disengaged from the process. He worked more 8 overtime, or at least that's what he told my mother, and stayed away from the house for longer hours. I don't recall a single conversation we ever had after my diagnosis. Maybe he really was embarrassed. Relatives had long teased me, "You're a Momma's boy." From that moment and every day since, I've been proud to be a Momma's boy.

These were the darkest days of my life. It wasn't simply the shame of not 9 knowing how to read: it was not knowing where to start. Unsure where the bottom was, it felt as if I was falling. My mother was holding my hand, but we were both just falling. How easy it would have been for her to give up. Give up on me, give up on her abilities or responsibilities as a parent. That was a vulnerable time for both of us. A working-class family, we lacked the resources to do much more than pray and look to others for help. There wasn't much help around, but the power of prayer was immeasurable. It created comfort where none existed. It revealed a path when earthly avenues seemed closed. And it provided strength that could be explained in no other way.

As the family prayed and looked for answers, a decision was made in 10 school. I was removed from a regular classroom and placed in all remedial classes. I was about to spend fifth grade as one of "the basement boys." Smart kids were taught aboveground; children like me were sent to the basement.

When I had taken classes aboveground, there were those giant glass win- 11 dows to look through to the street below. The kids in the basement looked up at a window and saw only the feet of people passing by. Deep in my heart, I knew I didn't belong there, or at the very least I had to escape. But I didn't know how. The classroom size was smaller, and these were kids with whom I had rarely spent time. Many often seemed angry, some were violent, and none seemed hopeful. In my regular class, my friends talked and dreamed of becoming teachers, doctors, lawyers, or sports stars. In my new class, the answer was always "I 'ont know." I don't know. It's the slogan for those without dreams or a path to follow.

For all the gloom of being a basement boy, this time also proved to be 12 one of life's great teachable moments. I truly believe that it is possible to find good in every moment, especially the difficult ones. Until this point, my academic life was mostly one failure after another. Each day the new challenge had been to find a way to hide. Once I was assigned to the basement, the days of hiding were finally just about over. I can still remember the glance from classmates in the morning. The bright kids, or at the very least, the normal kids walked upstairs, and my kind headed to the basement. I could feel the looks of disdain at the back of my head. Worse still, I could sometimes hear the whispers of pity or contempt. "There go the dummies . . ."

I once overheard two adults in the basement chatting in the hallway. 13 "Today the basement, tomorrow prison." It was clear the basement wasn't a place you went to learn. It's where you were warehoused until fate or the legal system had a place for you.

Many of those in the basement doubted their future, and so did many 14 of those who were paid to be there to help us. Hopelessness breeds more hopelessness. It was the same for many of us in the basement. We tried covering up our academic deficiencies with attitude and bravado. At about five feet four and ninety pounds, thank God I was never able to pull off the tough guy act. My grandmother always said, "The good Lord gives us what we need." I guess He knew I needed to remain skinny and sheepish until He got me through middle school.

There was a whole new look, language, and protocol in the basement. 15 And there was a different approach to learning. We rarely had homework; assignments were completed in the classroom as a group. Even blackboard assignments were done as a group. Upstairs, I always dreaded going to the blackboard alone, now we would go up two or three at a time.

Unlike many of my classmates, I still had an optimistic spirit. I still 16 believed that, with hard work, success was possible. Upstairs my optimism was met with skepticism and the clear sense I was naïve or even stupid, but oddly, in the basement, at least some of my new friends welcomed me. Though shy and frequently bullied, I was mostly cheerful and could keep people entertained with humor or encouragement. Classmates often chose to work with me because I could make them laugh or lift their spirits. A favorite line from childhood on a ball field was always "We got this." In other words, we can win. Upstairs I was always alone and afraid at the blackboard, but here I could be the encourager.

"If John went to the store with three dollars and bought cereal for a 17 dollar forty and gum for fifty cents, how much money would he have left?" the teacher would ask. We were to write out her question and answer it on the blackboard.

"We got this," I'd say through a ragged smile. 18

One boy would write; the other two would repeat the teacher's sen- 19 tence and help with spelling. I treated those exercises like a sporting event. We were a team. The question was the opponent. It was easier to rally the group around a sports challenge than an academic problem. We often got the answer wrong, but I took joy in the effort. Upstairs, success was almost always measured by achievement (getting the right answer; passing the test), but here, at least in my heart, success could be measured by effort. No one can always know the right answer, but you can always give your best effort.

Those days in the basement were an early lesson on how to redefine suc- 20 cess. Take life in small bites, until you can take on more. Find your own pace and stick to it. In a regular classroom, I was a kid on a tricycle trying to keep pace with cars on a highway. In the basement, some of us had tricycles and some had even less. Admittedly, I had one major advantage over most of my classmates. I had Clarice Pitts. Life has taught me there is a fast-moving river that separates success from failure. It's called giving up. Too many people drown in that river. As a boy in the basement, I was often caught in its undertow, but my mother was always nearby, screaming, encouraging, threatening, praying, and on occasion she'd dive in and pull me out.

Regardless of the obstacles in your way, one of the great wedges to get 21 you past an obstacle is hard work. There's almost a renewable fuel you get from working hard. The harder you push, the further you realize you can go. As I see it, success is just your work made public. Through the years I've come to enjoy the hard work on the way to success more than the actual achievement. It's the joy of being in the midst of it. It's like a great glass of ice water. Water's good for the body almost any day, but after you've worked hard in the sun, is there anything better than a cold glass of ice water?

Hard work never lies. It may not always reward you in the ways and 22 in the time you'd like, but it's always honest. When you've worked hard, you know where you stand. You know what you've given. I've always believed that someone else could outthink me or outmaneuver me, but I only feared the person who could outwork me. Fortunately, I haven't come across that person too often. It's actually a pretty small fraternity: hard workers. Look at almost any successful person in any field, and you'll find at least this one trait: an ability and willingness to work hard. It's the great equalizer. It's the one gift we can give to ourselves, too often overlooked as we "trade up" for a sexier approach. It's not a shortcut; rather, it's the straightest line to success. It's also a great building block for acquiring other important life skills.

Every door that's ever opened for me in life started by my knocking hard 23 and sometimes even kicking, putting my shoulder against it, and if not patiently, then prayerfully, waiting for it to open or fall off its hinges. Even as a kid who couldn't read, I knew I was fortunate. I had the gift. I knew how to work hard because my mother taught me.

And so it began. The first steps to overcoming my childhood shame of 24 illiteracy. Pure, raw, uncomplicated hard work. Except for a few school administrators and teachers, no one outside my immediate family ever knew I couldn't read. Most days I was deathly afraid of failure, but I refused to let the outside world see it. The mask was coming off . . . but ever so slowly.

Years later after that horrible diagnosis, I can still remember my mother's 25 words: "Keep your head up, son. . . . We'll pray about it. Work our way through it." She rubbed the top of my head, pulled at my chin, and then took my hand. I've never walked with my head down since that day.

(Byron Pitts, "Keep Your Head Up," 2009)

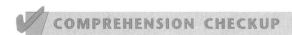

Multiple Choice

Directions: For each item, write the letter corresponding to the best answer.

__b__   1. The author's primary reason for writing this selection is
    a. to encourage those who are unable to read well to seek professional help.
    b. to share a personal story in order to motivate others to tackle their own personal difficulties.
    c. to focus attention on the staggering rate of illiteracy in the United States.
    d. to thank his mother, family members, and friends for their unwavering support.

__c__   2. The key point of the selection is that
    a. Byron Pitts pulled himself up by his own bootstraps to achieve great things.
    b. Byron Pitts owes a huge debt of gratitude to his mother.
    c. through hard work and the assistance of others, Byron Pitts overcame illiteracy.
    d. mentors provide a valuable service.

__a__   3. Based on the information in the selection, the author would agree with which of the following statements?
    a. Believing in yourself is an important key to success.
    b. Slow learners can't become successful.
    c. His difficulties with reading should have been recognized by his mother much earlier.
    d. Reading is unimportant in many endeavors in life.

__d__   4. All the following statements demonstrate that Byron Pitts is an optimistic person *except* for which one?
    a. He frequently used the phrase "we got this" to indicate to his fellow classmates that they can solve problems.
    b. He thinks good can be found in even difficult moments.
    c. He believes that success is possible with enough hard work.
    d. He measures success by achievement rather than by effort.

__d__   5. Byron Pitts did all the following *except*
    a. hide his illiteracy from his closest family members.
    b. confront his father over his lack of support and encouragement.
    c. refuse to attend remedial classes.
    d. both b and c.

True or False

Directions: Indicate whether each statement is true or false by writing **T** or **F** in the space provided.

__F__   6. After Byron Pitts's diagnosis, the family reacted with anger.

__F__   7. The encouragement of Byron Pitts's father helped Byron to overcome illiteracy.

__T__   8. Byron Pitts's mother endorsed the value of working hard to achieve a goal.

___T___ 9. Byron Pitts is proud to be a so-called Momma's boy.

___F___ 10. The students in the basement had twice as much homework as those upstairs.

___T___ 11. Byron Pitts's mother never gave up on him.

___T___ 12. Byron Pitts fears only the person who can outwork him.

Vocabulary in Context

Directions: Without consulting a dictionary, write a definition in the blank for each of the following phrases.

1. always ring in my ears (paragraph 1) always be in my thoughts

2. disengaged from the process (paragraph 8) detached; ignored what was happening

3. darkest days of my life (paragraph 9) worst or bleakest time of his life

4. pull off the tough guy act (paragraph 14) pretend to be hard and mean

5. lift their spirits (paragraph 16) make them feel better

6. a ragged smile (paragraph 18) an uncertain or meek smile

7. redefine success (paragraph 20) give a new definition of success

8. great equalizer (paragraph 22) something that has a leveling effect and makes people more the same

Understanding the Words in the Selection

Directions: In the blanks below, write the word from the list that best completes the sentence. Use each word only once.

assured	initial	protocol
bravado	obstacle	skepticism
disdain	outmaneuvered	vulnerable
immeasurable		

1. Irving's ___initial___ desire to be a pilot faded when he discovered he didn't like to fly.

2. Because Andrea didn't know how to swim, she felt very ___vulnerable___ whenever she was around a swimming pool.

3. Maria has done so much for me; her kindness is ___immeasurable___.

4. Teresa has complete ___disdain___ for those who are mean to children.

5. The young bullfighter was very nervous, but he faced the bull with swaggering ___bravado___.

6. Jon ___assured___ his mother that he intended to visit his sister in the hospital in the next couple of days.

7. There is a specific ___protocol___ for storing and displaying the American flag.

8. When someone says that astrologists can predict the future, I feel only ___skepticism___.

9. A lack of a good education can be a large ___obstacle___ to success.

10. Eduardo ___outmaneuvered___ me and scored the winning goal.

In Your Own Words

Explain the meaning of each of the following quotes.

1. "Smart people can think their troubles to the ground, honey," she'd say. "We have to wrestle ours."

2. "Today the basement, tomorrow prison."

3. "Take life in small bites, until you can take on more."

4. "Success is just your work made public."

5. "Hard work never lies."

Written Assignment

1. What advice would you give someone who is having difficulty learning how to read? What are some concrete steps an individual can take to solve reading problems? Write a short letter giving your advice.

2. Byron Pitts had an "optimistic spirit." According to Alan McGinnis, author of *The Power of Optimism,* pessimists may be overwhelmed by their problems, whereas optimists are challenged by them. "Optimists think of themselves as problem-solvers, as trouble-shooters," he says. This does not mean they see everything through rose-colored glasses. Rather, they have several traits that help them have a positive attitude while still remaining realistic and tough-minded.

Optimists . . .

1. Look for partial solutions.

2. Believe they have control over their future.

3. Interrupt their negative trains of thought.

4. Heighten their powers of appreciation.

5. Are cheerful even when they can't be happy.

6. Like to swap good news.

7. Accept what cannot be changed.

Write a few paragraphs describing how these traits helped Byron Pitts overcome his challenges.

Internet Activity

Visit the Literacy Volunteers of America Web site at

http://www.literacyvolunteers.org/conference

Write a paragraph describing what you learned about the organization.

A Short Poem for You to Analyze

Pablo Neruda (1904–1973), widely regarded as the greatest Latin American poet of the 20th century, received the Nobel Prize for Literature in 1971. Neruda, whose real name is Ricardo Eliezer Neftali Reyes y Basoalto, was born in Parral, Chile, the son of a railroad worker. He began to write poetry as a young teenager and later studied to be a teacher. At one point in his life, he was forced into exile because of his political beliefs. The movie *Il Postino* is based on this period of his life. In addition to being a poet, he served as a Chilean diplomat in various foreign countries, including Burma, Ceylon, Argentina, Mexico, and France. The following is the last stanza from one of Neruda's poems, which was translated from Spanish by Professor Maria Jacketti and appears in *Neruda's Garden: An Anthology of Odes.*

"ODE TO THE PRESENT"
BY PABLO NERUDA

You	Tú
are	eres tu presente,
your present,	tu manzana:
your own apple.	tómala
Pick it from	de tu árbol,
your tree.	levántala
Raise it	en tu mano,
in your hand.	brilla
It's gleaming,	como una estrella,
rich with stars.	tócala,
Claim it.	híncale el diente y ándate
Take a luxurious bite out	silbando en el camino.
of the present,	
and whistle along the road	
of your destiny.	

(Pablo Neruda, "Oda al presente," 2008)

1. Explain the meaning of the poem in your own words.

   _____

   _____

   _____

   _____

2. How does this poem relate to the previous reading by Byron Pitts?

   _____

   _____

   _____

   _____

Internet Activity

Type in Pablo Neruda's name in a search engine such as Google, MSN, or Yahoo!; find a Web site about Neruda; and write down five things you learned.

VOCABULARY   Introduction

One purpose of this book is to help you improve your reading and writing skills by expanding your vocabulary. Vocabulary and reading are like the chicken and the egg—which comes first? Your reading is made easier if you know more words; and the more reading you do, the more words you will learn. Is there an effortless way to learn more words and become a better reader? The answer is no. But there are some techniques that can help. Some of those techniques follow:

Context: When you come across an unfamiliar word in your reading, the first step you should take toward finding its meaning is to look for context clues. The context of a word is what surrounds it, which includes the sentence it appears in, nearby sentences, and even the whole article. Try placing your finger over the unfamiliar word, and see if you can supply another word that gives the sentence meaning, or at least enough meaning for your purposes. Remember that if you are reading a light novel for enjoyment, the exact meaning of a word may not be as important as when you are reading your psychology textbook.

Let's try a sentence with a word you may not know. See if you can figure out the meaning of the word from the context of the sentence.

Imagine Sue's *chagrin* when she realized that all of the other women at the office party were wearing long dresses and she was wearing shorts.

You could go to the dictionary to look up the definition of *chagrin*, but you can probably guess from context clues that *chagrin* in this sentence means "embarrassment."

We use context clues all the time when we read cartoons. The following cartoon uses the word *tranquility*. What do you think the word means?

Hagar © 2009 King Features Syndicate.

Structure: Word structure gives you a way to discover the meaning of a word by breaking it down into its parts. Knowing the meaning of a word's parts should help you decipher the word's meaning. Let's try an example:

Synchronized diving is a new Olympic sport that requires tremendous precision.

The word *synchronized* has in it the word parts *syn* and *chron*. *Syn* means "same" and *chron(o)* means "time." So, *synchronized* divers must leave the diving board at the same time, mirror each other's movements, and then enter the water in unison.

The eight vocabulary units inserted throughout the book will give you practice in using over 75 word parts. A complete list of these word parts is located at the end of Chapter 14.

Dictionary: Often when people come across a word they don't know, their first thought is to look it up in the dictionary. But this should be your last way of determining the meaning of a word. It's best to try first to use context clues and word structure. If these methods don't give you an accurate enough definition, then go to the dictionary.

"The first book of the nation is the dictionary of its language."

—Contanitin, Conte Volney

Before you grab the dictionary, it helps to know a little bit about the meaning of the word you are looking up. This is because the dictionary, which is a vast resource with much information (sometimes too much), may give several meanings, and you have to be able to select the appropriate one. For example, suppose in your reading you come across the following sentence and don't know what the word *annual* means:

The man decided to buy *annual* plants for his front yard.

You look up *annual* in your dictionary and find two definitions. The first definition may be "something happening once every year," and the second may be "a plant that lasts for one season or year." You can see that the second definition is the one that fits this sentence. If the man buys annual plants, let's hope that he doesn't expect them to bloom again.

We have placed the dictionary section in the Appendices. Your instructor may decide to have you work through that section as a class, or you can complete the exercises on your own.

Combination: In trying to determine the meaning of an unfamiliar word, you can use all of these techniques in combination. Take the following example:

Brian Williams is a *contemporary* of many of your instructors.

You may be thinking that *contemporary* means "modern or recent," but that meaning doesn't make sense in this context. *Con* means "with" and *temp* means "time or moderate." Now you are getting closer to the meaning in this sentence. The word *contemporary* as used here means "with time." Now go to the dictionary. You will find the definition "modern," but you will also find the definition "same time period or age group." So, Brian Williams is approximately the same age as many of your teachers.

Homonyms: As part of our vocabulary study, we also will be covering homonyms. Although homonyms are not a technique for discovering the meanings of unfamiliar words, we have included them because misuse of homonyms is a common mistake. *Homo* means "same" and *nym* means "name," so homonyms are words with the same "name," or pronunciation, but different spellings or meanings.

Look at the following sentence:

Your grandfather *passed* away.

A common mistake when writing such a sentence is to use the word *past* instead of *passed*. Because "passing away" is an action, it is a verb, and you need to use the word *passed*. In the section on homonyms, you will learn how to use many homonyms correctly.

STUDY TECHNIQUE 2: SCANNING

Scanning is a technique for reviewing reading material quickly to find answers to specific questions. When you scan, you run your eyes rapidly over the material to find the information that you need. Most of us use scanning techniques when we search the telephone book for a number or the TV guide for the time and channel of a show we want to watch.

Continued

STUDY TECHNIQUE 2: SCANNING *Continued*

Now scan "Warren Buffett Offers Advice to Students," pages 19–20, to find answers to the following questions.

1. Scan the first paragraph. What kind of advice does Warren Buffett offer students?
   <u>life-changing</u>

2. Scan paragraph 2. Whom does Buffett advise students to invest in? <u>themselves (yourselves)</u>

3. Scan paragraph 3. According to Buffett, what sort of people should students surround themselves with? <u>people who love them</u>

4. Scan paragraph 6. What course was valuable to Buffett? <u>public speaking</u>

5. Scan paragraph 7. What kind of person does Buffett advise students to strive to become? <u>a nice one</u>

6. Scan paragraph 8. What does Buffett encourage students to use? <u>all their horsepower</u>

READING

Buffett encourages students to "use all their horsepower."

TUNING IN TO READING Do you ever wonder what advice a very successful person would offer to a student such as yourself? In the following reading, Warren Buffett, who has been very successful not only financially but also as a person, offers his advice.

BIO-SKETCH Warren Buffett started his business career delivering newspapers and working at his grandfather's grocery store. Today, the chairman of Berkshire Hathaway is known not only for his investments but also for his philanthropy, primarily with the Gates Foundation.

NOTES ON VOCABULARY

oracle a person or thing regarded as an infallible authority or guide. In the ancient world, people seeking advice would go to oracles, who were believed to speak for particular gods or goddesses.

Warren Buffett Offers Advice to Students

WARREN BUFFETT, THE BILLIONAIRE CEO of Berkshire Hathaway, is a philanthropist and one of the wealthiest people in the world. Referred to as the "Oracle of Omaha," Buffett has made a habit of offering "life-changing" advice to students.

At a time when many college graduates face uncertain futures and are struggling to find jobs, Buffett advises students that "investing in yourself is the best thing you can do—anything that improves your talents." He advises parents that "investing in your children is, in some ways, investing in yourself." 2

"No matter what happens in the economy, if you have true talent yourself, and you have maximized your talent, you have a terrific asset."

Speaking with students at Rice University's Graduate School of Business, he offered the following advice: "Unconditional love is more valuable than any amount of wealth." He urged the students to surround themselves with people who love them, and to give love in return. When asked what he thought about the correlation between wealth and happiness, he explained that "success is getting what you want, and happiness is wanting what you get." 3

When speaking at Columbia University, Buffett said: "Find what turns you on . . . do what you would do if . . . the money meant nothing to you. . . . You'll have more fun and be more successful." 4

Speaking with Emory University students, he offered the following advice: "I enjoy what I do. I tap dance to work every day. I work with people I love, doing what I love. I spend my time thinking about the future, not the past. The future is exciting. . . . To focus on what you don't have is a terrible mistake." 5

At Notre Dame, Buffett told students that his taking a public speaking course had been extremely helpful and that the ability to communicate is a very valuable skill that played a critical role in his success. 6

On a more general note, Buffett advised one MBA student to "be a nice person. It's so simple that it's almost too obvious to notice. Look around at the people you like. Isn't it a logical assumption that if you like certain traits in other people, then other people would like you if you developed those same traits?" 7

Buffett encourages students to "use all their horsepower." "How big is your engine and how efficiently do you put it to work?" Buffett suggests that "many people have 400 horsepower engines, but 100 horsepower of output." According to Buffett, the person who gets full output from a 200-horse-power engine is a lot better off. 8

(InLikeMe.com, 2010)

 COMPREHENSION CHECKUP

Directions: Answer the questions below. If you're not sure about the answers, go back and find the information you need.

1. What does Buffett mean when he says that "success is getting what you want, and happiness is wanting what you get?"

2. What does Buffett mean when he says, "I tap dance to work every day?"

3. What does Buffet mean when he says, "Many people have 400 horsepower engines, but 100 horsepower of output?"

 Internet Activity

Do a search to find out more about Warren Buffett. Then use the information you collect to write a short biography of him.

Chapter Summary and Review

In this chapter, you were given an introduction to college. You learned how to keep track of your assignments, analyzed your motivation for attending college, learned some ways to expand vocabulary, and practiced the study techniques of skimming and scanning.

Short Answer

Directions: Answer the questions briefly, in a few sentences or paragraphs.

1. Which type of assignment sheet works best for you? Explain what you like about it. If you want to use another method of keeping track of your assignments, describe the method you are going to use.

2. What are some ways for improving your vocabulary?

Vocabulary in Context

Directions: Choose one of the following words to complete the sentences below. Use each word only once.

    dictionary   homonyms   scan   skimming   structure

3. _Skimming_ (surveying) is a study technique that helps you become familiar with reading material before you begin to read it carefully.

4. If you want to find a specific piece of information, such as a date or a person's name, you can _scan_ the material.

5. Understanding word _structure_ helps you unlock the meanings of words.

6. A good way to confirm the meaning of a word is to use your _dictionary_ .

7. _Homonyms_ are pronounced the same but have different meanings and are usually spelled differently.

Becoming an Effective Learner

Finding Out about Ourselves

CHAPTER PREVIEW

In this chapter, you will

- Practice marking written material.
- Discover your preferred learning style.
- Learn techniques for using context to discover the meanings of new words.
- Assess your stress level and learn ways of dealing with stress.
- Develop a study schedule compatible with your learning style.
- Become familiar with homonyms and other confusing words.
- Practice using SQ3R techniques.
- Become familiar with Internet etiquette.

How You Learn

"In Jazz the essential quality is the right to be an individual."

—Ornette Coleman

In this chapter, you are going to discover a little more about yourself so that you may become a better learner. Are you the kind of person who works best at night or during the day? Are you a visual learner or an auditory one? What kinds of things are most likely to cause stress in your life? We will be trying to answer these and many other questions in the pages that follow.

As you work through this book, you will be introduced to techniques to improve your studying. The first two techniques, skimming and scanning, were discussed in the Introduction.

Now we're going to show you another study technique.

STUDY TECHNIQUE 3: MARKING WRITTEN MATERIAL— UNDERLINING, HIGHLIGHTING, AND ANNOTATING

The common ways of marking written material are underlining, highlighting, and making notes in the margins (called annotating). Marking is something you may want to begin doing the first time you read a selection.

When marking, keep in mind that less is often better. If you underline, highlight, or annotate too much, you're defeating your purpose, because then the important material that you've marked no longer stands out.

One reason for marking is that it gets you involved right away in the material you are reading by requiring you to think about what is important. Strive to underline or highlight key ideas or concepts, or ones that you have questions about or may want to refer to later. Do you strongly agree or disagree with something you've read? Say so in the margin. Do you have a specific question about something? Put your question in the margin. In this way, you're beginning to develop your thoughts and feelings about the material.

The following is a list of techniques for marking written material. These are only suggestions. You can adapt them to suit your own purposes or create your own abbreviations and symbols to make a personal system of marking.

- Underline or highlight important terms and concepts.
- Write **MI** in the margin next to main ideas.
- Circle definitions and meanings or write **Def.** (definition) in the margin.
- Write key words and definitions in the margin or write **KV** (key vocabulary) beside important words.
- Use **EX** to indicate an example.
- Signal in the margin where important information can be found with an **IMP** or a symbol such as an asterisk (*).
- Signal summaries with **SUM** or write your own short summaries in the margin.
- Use a question mark (?) in the margin to indicate a point that needs further explanation.
- Indicate where the answers to particular questions in the text can be found by writing **ANS** (answer).

"A human being's name is a principal component in his person, perhaps a piece of his soul."

—Sigmund Freud

Look at the following reading, titled "Naming Defines and Differentiates Us," and note the markings we have supplied for the "Naming and Identity" section. Try your hand at marking the rest of the material ("Naming Practices") as if you are preparing for a test. There is no single correct way to mark, but try to identify the key ideas or concepts and avoid overmarking. Compare your work with that of a fellow student. In your opinion, which one would be more helpful for you in preparing for a test?

READING

"To an extent, then, your name tells your story."

TUNING IN TO READING In the next couple of weeks, most of your instructors will be trying hard to learn the names of their students. They do this not only for convenience but also out of politeness—they know your name is important to your sense of identity. Think about how annoyed you become when your name is forgotten or mispronounced by someone who should know better. Many of you were given your name by a close relative who chose it because it had some personal significance. Perhaps it was the relative's name, or the name of a movie star or an athlete the relative admired. Some people are even named after special places or the day of the week on which they were born. How did you get your special name?

READING (continued)

BIO-SKETCH   Kory Floyd is a professor of communication at Arizona State University. His primary research focuses on the communication of affection in families.

NOTES ON VOCABULARY
demographics   the statistical data of a group of people arranged according to such factors as age, income, and education
surname   the family name, or last name

NAMING DEFINES AND DIFFERENTIATES US
Kory Floyd

What's something that belongs to you yet is constantly used by others? The answer to this riddle is: *your name.* A name is simply a linguistic Def device that identifies something or someone. Your <u>name</u> does more, however, than just differentiate you from others—it's also <u>an important component of your sense of self</u>. Naming is <u>one way we represent ourselves to others</u> and <u>one way we gain information about other people.</u>

Naming and Identity

First impressions are often critical to the perception we form of someone. 2 Although impressions are influenced by factors such as a person's appearance or behaviors, they can also be shaped by his or her name. A <u>person's first name</u>, for instance, <u>frequently suggests information about the person's demographic characteristics</u>. One such characteristic is <u>the person's sex</u>. In Western societies, for instance, we usually assign names such as <u>Jeff, Wesley</u>, and <u>Ian</u> EX only to males and names such as Kimberly, Laura, and Monique to females.   EX

   <u>Names can also provide clues about a person's ethnicity</u>. For example, you 3 might infer that LaKeisha is African American, Huong is Asian, and <u>Santiago is</u> EX <u>Latino. Some names even suggest a person's age group</u>, so you might assume that Emma, Madison, and Hannah are younger than Edna, Mildred, and Bertha. EX

   In addition to demographic information, <u>names can suggest information</u> 4 <u>about our disposition and sense of self</u>. For instance, we might perceive an adult man who goes by the name <u>William</u> differently than one who goes by <u>Billy</u>, even though those are two forms of the same name. Indeed, <u>research shows that we</u> EX <u>do make assumptions about people</u>—whether accurately or not—<u>on the basis of their names</u>. Perhaps as a result, <u>people sometimes adopt completely different names to project a different identity</u>. Internet screen names, for instance, allow people to create their own identities for the purpose of interacting online. To EX enhance their distinctiveness, some <u>celebrities</u> have adopted the practice of being EX known by a single name, such as Bono, Cher, Madonna, Sting, and Oprah.

Naming Practices

In the United States, the Social Security Administration keeps track of the most 5 popular first names given to newborns throughout the country. Some names have remained fashionable for quite some time. Beginning in 1880, for example, Mary and John were the most popular female and male first names nearly every year until 1926, when Robert took over the top spot for boys. Mary dominated the list for girls until 1947, when it was replaced with Linda. As times change, though, so do naming preferences. By 1985, Jessica and Michael were the most popular first names. Emily and Jacob topped the list in 2006.

Practices of naming also vary according to culture and religion. In pre- 6 dominantly Catholic communities around the world, for instance, males are often given a feminine middle name, such as Marie or Maria. Among the Sikh of India, boys are given the surname *Singh* and girls the surname *Kaur,* although adults of both sexes often take these as middle names instead. This practice of giving common surnames to all boys and girls is meant to symbolize the abolition of class inequalities. In many parts of the world, it is also traditional for women to adopt their husband's last name when they marry, or at least to add his name to hers. So, when marrying George Rogers, Jean Levitt might become Jean Rogers, or Jean Levitt Rogers, or Jean Levitt-Rogers.

To an extent, then, your name tells your story. Like your clothes or your 7 hairstyle, it is a part of how you present yourself to others and how others relate to you.

(Kory Floyd, *Interpersonal Communication,* 2008)

COMPREHENSION CHECKUP

"Names" Group Exercise

Almost all English and Continental surnames (last names) fall into four basic categories: place names, patronyms, occupational names, personal descriptions. Place names derive from names of actual places or descriptions of places close to where an ancestor lived. Patronyms are derived from the name of a father or some other ancestor. Patronyms are often created by adding a suffix or prefix indicating descent, as in Johnson (son of John) or McDonald (son of Donald). Occupational names derive from the occupations of the ancestor. Thus, if someone was called Baker, that person probably made bread. If a person's last name was Smith, that person was probably a blacksmith. Personal description names derive from physical characteristics of ancestors such as height. For example, John Long probably had a tall ancestor. Following are several other examples.

Place Names	Patronyms	Occupational Names	Personal Descriptions
Winston Churchill (church on a hill)	Ronald McDonald	Anne Archer, Karen Carpenter	Henry Wadsworth Longfellow, Martin Short

Directions: Go through this list of well-known individuals, and place each surname under the appropriate heading in the chart on page 26.

Betty White	George W. Bush	Martin Luther King, Jr.
Bill Gates	Harry Truman	Michael Jackson
Chris Rock	Holly Hunter	Pamela Anderson

Christina Applegate   John McCain   Paul Newman
Clint Eastwood   John Goodman   Taylor Swift
Conan O'Brian   Justin Timberlake   Tiger Woods
David Letterman   Lance Armstrong   Will Smith
Faith Hill

NAME CATEGORY CHART

Place Names	Patronyms	Occupational Names	Personal Description
_____	_____	_____	_____
_____	_____	_____	_____
_____	_____	_____	_____
_____	_____	_____	_____
_____	_____	_____	_____
_____	_____	_____	_____
_____			

In Your Own Words

1. What are some reasons that last names might change?

2. How do people go about choosing an Internet screen name?

Written Assignment

Directions: Choose one of the following activities to complete.

1. Do you ever wish that you had a different name? Choose a new name for yourself, and explain in a paragraph the reasons behind your choice. For instance, you might choose the name Dawn because that is your favorite part of the day.

2. What are your feelings about nicknames? Do you like or dislike them? Did you have any nicknames while you were growing up? Did they affect you in any way? If you could choose your own nickname, what would it be, and why? Write a paragraph on this issue.

3. In your culture, how do you address people to show respect? How do you address people who are older than you? People in positions of authority? When do you address people by their first name only? Their last name? Using personal examples as illustrations, write a paragraph in which you discuss these issues.

4. Use the Internet to explore the meaning of your name and then write a paragraph describing your findings. Go to a search engine and type in "names and meanings." There are a variety of Web sites devoted to the meanings of names. One of the more complete Web sites related to names is www.behindthename .com. See if you can locate your name and its meaning. Did the people who named you take the meaning of your name into account when they gave it to you? If not, what were their reasons for giving you your name?

Internet Activity

Do you want to find out how popular your first name is? Visit www.babynamewizard .com/voyager and click on "NameVoyager." Has your name become more or less fashionable over time? What year was your name the most popular? Write a short paragraph discussing your results.

Auditory, Visual, or Kinesthetic

What Is Your Learning Style?

Each of us is an individual with particular strengths and weaknesses. If you want to do better in school, you must learn how to use your strengths and minimize your weaknesses. Research is beginning to demonstrate that most of us have a learning style that will work best for us.

Your learning style is partially dependent on whether you are a visual, auditory, or kinesthetic learner. The following test will help you determine your learning style. Keep in mind that there are no right or wrong answers.

ADULT LEARNING STYLES INVENTORY

Directions: Read each question and place a check mark on the appropriate line. If the question doesn't directly apply to you, think of a similar situation that might apply to you.

	Often	Sometimes	Seldom
1. I need to see a map or written directions to drive to someone's house.	_____	_____	_____
2. I remember material from a lecture without studying, or I have to tape the lecture and play the tape.	_____	_____	_____
3. I feel comfortable touching others, shaking hands, etc.	_____	_____	_____
4. I would rather learn a new recipe from a TV show than from a recipe book.	_____	_____	_____
5. When I watch sports on TV, I pay more attention to the play than to the explanation of the play by the announcers.	_____	_____	_____
6. I enjoy sewing, cooking, gardening, or working with tools.	_____	_____	_____
7. I remember a news event best by reading about it in a newspaper or magazine.	_____	_____	_____
8. I am good at making and interpreting graphs and charts.	_____	_____	_____
9. In order to learn material, I write notes over and over again.	_____	_____	_____
10. Without writing them down, I remember oral directions for assignments well.	_____	_____	_____

	Often	Sometimes	Seldom
11. I smoke, chew gum, or play with coins or keys in my pockets.	_____	_____	_____
12. In order to learn material, I read notes out loud to myself.	_____	_____	_____
13. When taking a trip, I would rather drive than be responsible for giving directions or reading a map.	_____	_____	_____
14. When I encounter a new word while I am reading, I usually sound it out.	_____	_____	_____
15. When I am trying to learn something, I form pictures in my mind.	_____	_____	_____
16. When I am studying for a test, I can visualize my notes on the page.	_____	_____	_____
17. When I study, I tend to tap my pencil or my pen.	_____	_____	_____
18. When oral introductions are made at a party, I am likely to remember the names of people I have not met before.	_____	_____	_____

Score your test below. For each question, give yourself 5 points if you answered "often," 3 points if you answered "sometimes," and 1 point if you answered "seldom." For example, if you answered "often" to question 1, you would place a 5 on the line next to that question. When you have finished, add up the points for each column.

Visual	Auditory	Kinesthetic
1. _____	2. _____	3. _____
5. _____	4. _____	6. _____
7. _____	10. _____	9. _____
8. _____	12. _____	11. _____
15. _____	14. _____	13. _____
16. _____	18. _____	17. _____
Totals _____	_____	_____

Now look at the differences between the totals for each learning style. A small difference—say, less than 4 points—doesn't mean much, but larger differences do. The larger the difference, the more dominant your learning style. For example, if your total for visual learning far exceeds the other two totals, this would be a good indication that you are basically a visual learner.

You just finished marking "Naming Defines and Differentiates Us." You are now going to annotate (place notes in the margins of the text) the information on visual, auditory, and kinesthetic learners. Look at the sample margin notes for visual learners and then fill in the blanks for the other two types of learners.

EYE SMART

Visual Learner
Definition: learns best by seeing
Application: highlights key points, and recopies notes

What does it mean to be a visual learner? A **visual learner** is one who learns best by seeing. Visual learners like to use textbooks, course outlines, maps, diagrams, charts, and pictures. Their goal is to be able to visualize the subject they are trying to learn. Visual learners prefer teachers who use a whiteboard, an overhead projector, or PowerPoint slides over ones who primarily talk. Visual learners often have a superior ability to visualize pages of print. They learn material well by highlighting key points and by copying and recopying their notes. Most people are visual learners.

EAR SMART

Auditory Learner
Definition: _____
_____
Application: _____
_____
_____
_____
_____

What does it mean to be an auditory learner? An **auditory learner** is one who learns best through hearing. Auditory learners have a superior ability to hear and remember sounds in their mind. Auditory learners like to listen, and they prefer teachers who lecture and encourage discussion. They learn material well by talking to themselves and repeating words and phrases out loud. If you are an auditory learner, you might learn best by reading your textbook out loud or by studying with a friend and talking through the key points. Auditory learners might do very well in class group activities. Many people are auditory learners.

ACTION SMART

Kinesthetic Learner
Definition: _____
_____
Application: _____
_____
_____
_____
_____

What does it mean to be a kinesthetic learner? **Kinesthetic learners,** who are the smallest group, learn best by doing and performing. They are hands-on, or tactile, learners. They have a superior ability to remember their actions. Kinesthetic learners like to be in movement while learning. Their special talent is in associating ideas and concepts with motion. When learning material, they may prefer to gesture or walk around. These students need to take frequent short study breaks. It is a good idea for kinesthetic learners to take notes and underline key points as they read. Kinesthetic learners might benefit from taking part in classroom skits and role-playing activities.

Keep in mind, though, that even if one of your scores was way above the other two, all that the test results show is a *tendency* on your part. For example, if you have a high score for auditory learning, this just means that you tend to be an auditory learner, but you are still likely to have a significant ability to learn in visual and kinesthetic ways. Most of us learn best by using some combination of all three learning styles. Suppose, for example, you want to learn how to ski. You might attend a lecture where someone discusses how to ski (auditory). Or you might watch a video in which someone demonstrates skiing techniques (visual). Or you might strap on a pair of skis and go down the beginner slope (kinesthetic). But the person who involves all three learning styles by doing all three things might learn to ski faster. The trick is to find the combination that works best for you.

VOCÁBULARY Words in Context

A technique for discovering the meaning of an unfamiliar word is to examine its context, the words surrounding it. In many instances, the neighboring words provide clues to help decipher the meaning.

There are several different kinds of context clues you can use, and it is worthwhile to become familiar with all of them. Familiarizing yourself with these techniques will go a long way to helping you study your college textbooks without having to interrupt your reading to look up a specific word. When having a precise definition is not necessary, the use of context clues can be sufficient and save you time. Of course, if a precise definition is necessary, consulting a dictionary is essential.

A good strategy is to underline or circle the words you are unfamiliar with as you move through the text. Use context clues to come up with a definition that seems to make sense and continue your reading. When you complete the reading, go back and look up in a dictionary any word for which you need a more precise definition.

Here are some common techniques for using context to determine the meaning of new words.

Definition: Sometimes a writer simply provides us with a definition of a word somewhere within the sentence, especially if the word is one that we are unlikely to be familiar with:

> A *thesaurus,* or dictionary that lists synonyms, antonyms, and other related words, can help you express your ideas more clearly and effectively.

You can see that the author defines a *thesaurus* as a special type of dictionary.

Synonym: A synonym, which is another word with a similar meaning, may be used elsewhere in the sentence.

> Four types of objects *revolve* around the sun; however, the planets are the largest objects that circle our fiery star.

If you did not know the meaning of *revolve,* you could determine its meaning from the word *circle.* To circle and to revolve mean approximately the same thing.

Antonym: Sometimes you can determine the meaning of a word by finding an antonym, a word with an opposite meaning, somewhere in the sentence.

> Gustavo was a very skillful soccer player, but Pedro was *inept.*

You can see that the writer is making a contrast, and that skillful is the opposite of *inept.*

Examples: Sometimes examples illustrate the meaning of a word.

> In a *brazen* act of defiance, Marco lit his cigarette while standing in front of a "No Smoking" sign and then refused to put it out when asked to do so.

This example suggests to you that a *brazen* act is one that is bold and shameless.

Explanation: Sometimes a writer simply gives an explanation of what a word means.

> In your communications class, you will probably have to give an *impromptu* speech. For this type of speech, you will be given a topic and only a few minutes to prepare your talk.

The writer is telling you that an *impromptu* speech is one that is given with very little preparation.

Experience: This way of discovering the meaning of a word draws on your personal experience.

> Have your efforts to complete a paper for a class ever been *thwarted* because your computer broke down?

Perhaps you have experienced this or a similar situation, and you remember that your efforts were "hindered" or "frustrated" at least for the time being.

Knowledge of Subject: In this technique, you have just enough familiarity with the subject the writer is discussing to enable you to figure out the meaning of the unknown word.

Although many Americans often diet, many have difficulty maintaining a *svelte* shape for more than a few months.

You know that people often diet to make themselves "slim" or "slender."

Combination: Can you use a number of these techniques at the same time to detect the meaning of a word? You bet!

The man at the party was a real *extrovert*. He acted like a clown and had everyone laughing the whole evening.

Here you probably used explanation, experience, and familiarity with the subject to determine that an *extrovert* is a very outgoing person.

Now work with a partner on the following exercises. Remember, no peeking at your dictionary.

Context Clue Practice 1

Directions: On the first line, write your own definition for the italicized word. Then on the second line, note the technique you used to arrive at the definition. The first item is done for you. Answers will vary.

1. Everyone in the family was *elated* to discover that Howard had the winning million-dollar lottery ticket in his pocket.

   Definition: jubilant; overjoyed

   Technique(s) used: knowledge of subject, explanation, maybe experience

2. Believing the 12-year-old offender to be *contrite*, the judge decided to give him another chance before putting him in juvenile detention.

   Definition: filled with a sense of guilt

   Technique(s) used: explanation

3. Should football games be canceled because of *inclement* weather?

   Definition: severe or stormy

   Technique(s) used: knowledge of subject, experience

4. Should sexually *explicit* scenes be deleted from movies when they are shown on television?

   Definition: obvious, leaving nothing to the imagination

   Technique(s) used: experience

5. Carol was extremely relieved to discover that her tumor was *benign* rather than malignant and so she would require no further treatment.

   Definition: not malignant

   Technique(s) used: antonym

6. Her house was so *immaculate* that you could literally eat off the floor.

   Definition: free from spot or stain

   Technique(s) used: experience

7. Many boys in high school *aspire* to be professional athletes, but very few are actually good enough to make it to the professional ranks.

   Definition: to long for, aim for, or seek ambitiously

   Technique(s) used: explanation

8. The FBI conducted *covert,* or secret, operations to find out information about the drug-smuggling ring.

   Definition: <u>concealed or secret</u>

   Technique(s) used: <u>definition—synonym</u>

9. Many students are not *affluent* enough to attend college without working part-time or receiving some type of financial assistance.

   Definition: <u>wealthy</u>

   Technique(s) used: <u>knowledge of subject</u>

Context Clue Practice 2

Directions: Use the context clues in the second sentence to define the italicized word in the first. Circle the clue word (or words) in the second sentence that provided the clue(s).

1. "Yes, this computer is *obsolete,*" said Matt. "But (out of date) or not, it's too expensive to replace."

2. "I can't accept any *remuneration* for taking care of your dog while you were in the hospital," said Carrie. "Nonsense dear," said Mrs. Watson, "you should (get paid) for doing a good deed."

3. It would be *presumptuous* to accuse him of the crime. Taking him in for questioning without solid evidence would simply be too (bold).

4. Mountain climbing is full of *hazards.* However, the adventure is worth all of the (risks).

5. He considered it an *indignity* for his parents to ignore his college graduation. He couldn't envision a worse (insult).

6. Martha complained that she was getting tired of *goading* her son to do his homework. At his age, he should be able to finish it without her (urging).

7. Some people *feign* injuries after their car is rear-ended. They don't stop (pretending) until they have received a cash settlement.

8. Todd, the pilot of our small airplane, seemed very *apprehensive* about taking off during the storm. His (anxious) behavior was upsetting the passengers.

9. I was certain he was *despondent* because he hadn't smiled all week. Perhaps he had good reason to be so (depressed).

10. The teacher was *cognizant* of the difficulties involved in learning a new language. Her (awareness) was based on the fact that she too had once emigrated from her homeland.

11. In the United States, many families celebrate Thanksgiving with a *sumptuous* meal. However, after the (lavish) feast, many Americans begin dieting in earnest.

Context Clue Practice 3

Directions: Use the context clues in each sentence to help determine the missing word. Briefly describe the clue or clues that helped you.

1. If you believe that you control your own destiny, you have an internal locus of control; however, if you believe that your fate is determined by chance or outside forces, you have an <u>external</u> locus of control.

   Clue: <u>"internal"—antonym</u>

2. Successful students are naturally __optimistic__ because they have a hopeful attitude and believe that effort, good study habits, and self-discipline will make their grades go up. "They can because they think they can."

   Clue: explanation

3. Students exhibit what is called self-serving bias. When they get an exam grade back, if they did well they tend to accept personal credit. They consider the exam to be a valid indication of their abilities. However, if they did very poorly, they are much more likely to __blame__ the teacher or the exam.

   Clue: "accept"—antonym

4. Interestingly enough, teachers do the same thing. They are likely to take credit for whatever success is associated with their students and blame the student for any __failure__. "Teachers, it seems, are likely to think, 'With my help, Maria graduated with honors. Despite all my help, Melinda flunked out.'"

   Clue: "success"—antonym

5. College students need to be especially careful about those with whom they associate. Researchers have verified that students learn more from their friends and other students than they do from their __classes/teachers__ or from books. Out-of-class relationships are clearly the major influence in a student's life.

   Clue: "experience"

(David G. Myers, *Social Psychology*, 8/e, 2005)

Day versus Night People

Are You More of a Morning Lark or a Night Owl?

You probably already have some idea whether you are more alert in the morning, afternoon, or evening. The following test is intended to determine whether you are a morning person or a night person. Answer the questions and then add up your points to determine your score.

	Points Possible	Points Earned
1. I feel best if I get up around		
5–6:30 A.M.	5	
6:30–7:30 A.M.	4	
7:30–9:30 A.M.	3	
9:30–11 A.M.	2	
11–noon	1	_____
2. If I had to describe how easy it is for me to get up in the morning, I would say		
it is not easy at all!	1	
it is not very easy.	2	
it is fairly easy.	3	
it is very easy.	4	_____
3. The way I feel for the first half-hour after I wake up is		
very tired.	1	
fairly tired.	2	
fairly refreshed.	3	
very refreshed.	4	_____

	Points Possible	Points Earned
4. If I could choose the best time to take a difficult test, it would be		
8–10 A.M.	4	
10 A.M.–1 P.M.	3	
1–5 P.M.	2	
7–9 P.M.	1	_____

5. If my job would require that I work from 4 to 6 A.M. one day, I would choose to

not go to bed until after I worked.	1	
take a nap before and sleep after.	2	
sleep before work and nap after.	3	
get all the sleep I need before work.	4	_____

6. If someone asked me to jog with them at 7 A.M. one morning, I would perform

well.	4	
reasonably well.	3	
not very well.	2	
not well at all.	1	_____

7. If I have to wake up at a specific time each morning, I

don't depend on my alarm at all.	4	
depend on my alarm slightly.	3	
depend on my alarm quite a lot.	2	
depend on my alarm desperately.	1	_____

8. I am usually tired and wanting to go to bed by

8–9 P.M.	5	
9–10:30 P.M.	4	
10:30 P.M.–12:30 A.M.	3	
12:30–2 A.M.	2	
2–3 A.M.	1	_____

Total Number of Points Earned   _____

An average score would be 17. The higher the score, the more of a morning or day person you are; the lower the score, the more of an evening person you are.

(Gary Funk and Jan Bradley, *Thrills, Spills, and Study Skills,* 1992)

In another section, we will show you how to use this information in making a study schedule. If at all possible, you should plan the activities that require the most concentration when you are the most alert. For example, if math is a difficult subject for you and you are a morning person, plan to take that class in the morning and do your homework while you are still fresh.

READING

"By understanding our body clocks, we can improve our health and continue to foster our survival."

TUNING IN TO READING   Before we see how your circadian cycle might affect how you set up your class and study schedule, read the following article from *Reader's Digest*. The article describes our circadian, or daily, cycles, and how these cycles affect us.

READING *(continued)*

BIO-SKETCH Lowell Ponte currently hosts a national talk radio show on the Genesis Communication Network and writes for FrontPageMag.com. He was formerly the roving science and technology editor for *Reader's Digest*. He has written essays for the *New York Times*, the *Los Angeles Times*, and the *Wall Street Journal* and has been a correspondent in 32 countries.

NOTES ON VOCABULARY

circadian rhythm A person's *circadian rhythm*, popularly known as one's "body clock," is a biological rhythm that governs our routine of working, eating, and sleeping through a 24-hour period. *Circadian* is derived from the Latin words *circa*, meaning "about," and *dies*, meaning "day."

dexterity skill in using the body or hands; cleverness. The word *dexterity* is derived from the Latin word *dexter*, meaning "right." The origin suggests a bias in favor of right-handed people. In the 15th century, you were not considered "skillful" unless you were right-handed.

endurance ability to bear pain, hardship, or adversity. *Endurance* is derived from the French word *endurer*, meaning "harden" or "make hard." The meaning has changed little over time. Today we talk about *enduring* pain and about *endurance* training for long-distance runners.

THE TWO MOST DANGEROUS HOURS OF YOUR DAY BY LOWELL PONTE

You awaken after a good night's sleep and start to climb out of bed. Take care! You are beginning the most dangerous time of your day.

2　For the next two hours or so, you are two to three times more likely to suffer a heart attack or a stroke than you are in the late evening, the safest cardiovascular time of your day. According to a study headed by Merrill Mitler of Scripps Clinic and Research Foundation in La Jolla, California, 6 A.M. to 10 A.M. is the average peak time for many other major causes of death: ischemic heart disease, cancer, bronchitis, emphysema and asthma.

3　Until recently doctors were taught that the human body lives in homeostasis, changing little during the day. The science of chronobiology—the study of how time affects life—is sparking a medical revolution by revealing how much our bodies change through circadian (daily) rhythms.

4　"These natural biological rhythms are as vital as our heartbeat," says Lawrence E. Scheving of the University of Arkansas for Medical Sciences in Little Rock. "By learning their secrets, we are discovering new ways to prevent and cure illness. There isn't a function in your body that doesn't have its own rhythm. The absence of rhythm is death."

While you sleep, your blood pressure 5 falls, your temperature drops more than a degree from its daily afternoon high, and some blood pools in your body's extremities. Come morning, the body has to "jump start" itself from its sleeping to waking stages with a surge of excitation chemicals called catecholamines. Heart rate increases and blood vessels constrict, raising blood pressure and reducing blood flow to the heart muscle; this might cause ischemia, or angina, as well as sudden death from myocardial infarction. If hardened plaques of cholesterol coat arteries, fragments may break loose, causing the clots that lead to heart attacks.

Also, your blood swims with cell gran- 6 ules called platelets that are most likely to stick together during these morning hours. When a leap from bed and a surge of catecholamines combine to "get your blood moving," your blood is near its daily peak in thickness and tendency to clot. Packing kids off to school and rushing to get ready for work add emotional tension to the physical stress.

This circadian cardiovascular risk comes 7 not from your bedside clock but from your interior biological clock. "Whatever hour you get up," says Dr. James Muller, chief of cardiology for New England Deaconess

Hospital in Boston, "your peak risk of myocardial infarction will come within two to three hours after awakening."

8   The master timekeepers in our bodies help synchronize us with such outside cycles as day and night. Like orchestra conductors, they coordinate hundreds of functions inside us. Our body dances through the day to complex inner rhythms of rising and falling tides of hormones, immune cells, electrolytes and amino acids.

9   The long-held belief that some of us are "larks," or morning people, and others are "owls," or evening people, has now been confirmed. Measurements of circadian rhythms in morning people show heart rates peaking between 1 and 2 P.M., while evening people peak between 5 and 6:30 P.M. Larks produce more of the stimulating hormone adrenaline during the morning hours, followed by decreasing levels of performance through the day. Owls start the day more slowly, produce more nearly level amounts of adrenaline, and improve performance through the day and into early evening.

10   Most people enjoy a peak in short-term memory and mental quickness in the late-morning hours until shortly after noon. Then a measurable dip in energy and efficiency begins around 1 P.M. In some Mediterranean cultures, shops close during the afternoon for a period of siesta.

11   In the afternoon, exercise endurance, reaction time and manual dexterity are at their highest. Some research indicates that from then until early evening, athletes put in their best performances. From 6:30 P.M. until 8:30 P.M. is the sharpest time of day for long-term memory, an optimal time to study.

12   Our daily rhythms can bring a dark side to the early evening, however. These hours include a second daily peak in heart attacks, although smaller than the morning's. Around 7 P.M., alcohol takes longer to be cleared by your liver, and hence can be more intoxicating and performance-impairing than at other times of day—except 11 P.M., which brings a second peak of high ethanol susceptibility.

13   Students often cram during late-night and early-morning hours. Research, however, shows this is the time of the circadian cycle when long-term memory, comprehension and learning are at their worst.

14   Sensitivity to pain has generally increased throughout the day; it reaches its peak late at night. But by early morning the body may have almost doubled its nighttime levels of beta endorphins, which help relieve pain. Researchers theorize that this is what increases the body's pain tolerance during the hours after awakening.

15   For most of us, sleep is a time of life's renewal. Within the first 90 minutes or so of sleep, we reach our daily peak of growth hormone, which may help regenerate our bodies. And among pregnant women, the hours between midnight and 4 A.M. most commonly mark the start of labor. "Early morning labor and birth may be part of our genetic inheritance and may have had some survival value for the species," speculates chronobiologist Michael Smolensky of the University of Texas Health Science Center in Houston.

16   By understanding our body clocks, we can improve our health and continue to foster our survival. Without grasping, for instance, that our natural temperature rises one to two degrees from morning until evening, we could misjudge thermometer readings. A temperature of 99 degrees might signal perfect health at 5 P.M. but augur illness at 7 A.M.

17   The effects of drugs are also subject to our rhythms. For instance, many doctors are learning to give powerful cancer drugs with the patient's biological clocks in mind. A given chemotherapy drug may be highly toxic to the kidneys at one time of day, for example, and far less harmful at another. "For every one of more than 20 anti-cancer drugs, there is an optimal time of day," says Dr. William Hrushesky of the Stratton Veterans Administration Medical Center in Albany, New York.

18   Some prescription drugs can reduce morning heart-attack risk, as can aspirin. One major study found that taking an aspirin *every other day* reduced overall incidence of heart attack in men by almost 45 percent and morning risk by more than 59 percent. You should, of course, consult your doctor about the use of aspirin.

19   Aside from using medicine, there are ways to make your mornings less stressful

and, perhaps, less risky. Set the alarm clock a bit earlier to give yourself time to stretch arms and legs slowly while still lying down, the way your dog or cat does. This gets the pooled blood in your extremities moving. Move slowly. Don't subject yourself to the thermal shock of a very hot or cold shower, which could boost blood pressure. Then eat breakfast. Dr. Renata Cifkova at Memorial University of Newfoundland at St. John's says, "Skipping breakfast apparently increases platelet activity and might contribute to heart attacks and stroke during morning hours."

20   To avoid the "Monday morning blues," don't change your schedule on weekends. Your body's clock naturally runs on a cycle of about 25 hours. During the week, your body uses mechanical clocks, mealtimes, work schedules and other cues to reset itself to 24 hours each day. On weekends it is tempting to let the clock "free run" forward by staying up late Friday and Saturday, then sleeping late Saturday and Sunday. This action will leave you "jet-lagged," an unnecessary stress.

21   By turning the cycles of your biological clock in your favor, you may reduce your daily danger and increase your days of life.

(Lowell Ponte, "The Two Most Dangerous Hours of Your Day," 1992)

 COMPREHENSION CHECKUP

Multiple Choice

Directions: For each item, write the letter corresponding to the best answer.

_____a_____ 1. Your circadian rhythm is
    a. a daily cycle.
    b. a 1-hour cycle.
    c. a 1-month cycle.
    d. none of the above.

_____d_____ 2. Which of the following statements is true based on paragraph 9?
    a. Owls are awake at night.
    b. Larks are more lively during the morning.
    c. Some people are morning people and some are evening people.
    d. All of the above.

_____c_____ 3. When do you think you would be least likely to suffer a heart attack or stroke?
    a. just after you wake up
    b. early evening
    c. late evening
    d. 2 hours after you wake up

_____b_____ 4. Which of the following statements is true based on the information in the article?
    a. Orchestra conductors can help coordinate the functions of our body.
    b. Babies are most likely to be born in the early morning hours.
    c. It's best to sleep in on Saturday and Sunday mornings to readjust to the 25-hour cycle.
    d. None of the above.

_____c_____ 5. The human body
    a. changes little during the day.
    b. lives in homeostasis.
    c. changes a lot through daily rhythms.
    d. has no rhythm.

True or False

Directions: Indicate whether each statement is true or false by writing **T** or **F** in the space provided.

___T___ 6. Cramming for exams late at night is unlikely to benefit most students.

___T___ 7. Most people show a decline in energy around 1 P.M.

___F___ 8. For most people, alcohol is more intoxicating in the morning.

___F___ 9. If you need to have surgery, you should plan on having it in the early evening when you are least sensitive to pain.

___T___ 10. Your body temperature increases as you go through the day.

___F___ 11. If someone *speculates* about something, he or she is sure to know the answer.

___F___ 12. If you're *sensitive* to pain, be sure to tell the dentist to avoid the use of all anesthetics.

Vocabulary in Context

Directions: In a previous section you were introduced to finding the meaning of new words by using context clues. In the following exercise, try to discover the meaning of each of the italicized words by using a technique called **scanning,** which was introduced in the Introduction. In this exercise, we have indicated the specific paragraph in which the vocabulary word is located. Quickly scan the paragraph for the context clues that will give you the answer.

1. In paragraph 2, the word *cardiovascular* refers to what specific organ of the body? heart

2. In paragraph 3, what is a synonym, or word that has a similar meaning, for *circadian?* daily

3. After scanning paragraph 3, what do you think *chronobiology* means? time/life: the study of how time affects life

4. According to the context of paragraph 3, what does *homeostasis* mean? state of balance or equilibrium; changing little

5. In paragraph 6, what is the synonym for *platelets?* cell granules

6. In paragraph 9, if something is *stimulating* to you, does it depress or energize you? energize

7. In paragraph 10, is a *peak* a high point or a low point? high point

8. In paragraph 10, what is a *siesta?* short nap

9. In paragraph 11, define *optimal.* the best

10. In paragraph 15, what do you think the prefix *re-* means? As another example, one might need to *renew* a library book. again

11. In paragraph 16, if we *misjudge,* are we judging badly or well? badly

12. In paragraph 16, what is the synonym for *augur?* signal—predict, bode, foretell

13. Use the context of paragraph 17 to define the word *toxic.* poisonous

14. According to the context of paragraph 17, if you are *anti* something, are you for it or against it? <u>against it</u>

15. After scanning paragraph 19, name some parts of your body that would be considered *extremities*. <u>arms, legs</u>

In Your Own Words

The *Zits* cartoon that follows illustrates what happens when teenagers are sleepy at the start of the school day.

As the cartoon suggests, teenagers appear to have a different circadian cycle. New research suggests that they are "wired" to stay up later at night and to sleep longer in the morning. Many prominent educators are saying that the traditional high school day is out of sync with teenagers' body clocks. These educators feel that the school day should not begin before 9 or 10 A.M. What is your opinion on this issue?

Zits

© ZITS Partnership. King Features Syndicate.

Internet Activity

Did you know that many college students have sleep patterns that are detrimental to their academic performance? Use a search engine of your choosing to find out more about the topic of "sleep and college students." Write a paragraph discussing your findings.

Left-Brain and Right-Brain Orientation

Which One Are You?

Over the past 20 years, psychologists have been studying how the two hemispheres of the brain operate. Research shows that the two sides of the brain think in quite different ways. In general, the left half is more analytical, logical, and likely to break down thoughts into parts. The right half is more likely to focus on the whole picture, to think in analogies, and to interpret things imaginatively. We use both halves of the brain together, but one side may be dominant. Being right-brain oriented or left-brain oriented has little to do with whether you are right-handed or left-handed.

Frank and Ernest

Frank & Ernest used with the permission of the Thaves and The Cartoonist Group. All rights reserved.

Take the following test to see which half of your brain is dominant.

WHICH SIDE OF YOUR BRAIN IS DOMINANT?

Directions: Check the statements that apply to you.

_____   1. When reading or watching TV, I prefer a true story to one that is fictional.

_____   2. I like to read or write poetry.

_____   3. I prefer to take tests that have no right or wrong answers rather than tests having objective and definite answers.

_____   4. I find myself solving a problem more by looking at the individual parts than by looking at the big picture.

_____   5. I usually do several tasks at once rather than one task at a time.

_____   6. I would prefer a job with a set salary over one such as sales where my income might vary considerably.

_____   7. I usually follow new directions step by step rather than improvising or taking steps out of order.

_____   8. When planning a vacation, I usually like to just go, without doing much planning in advance.

_____   9. The papers in my notebook are usually neat and orderly and not simply thrown in every which way.

_____ 10. When listening to someone else's problems, I usually become emotional instead of trying to come up with logical solutions.

To Score Your Test

To score your test, circle the number for each statement that you checked.

Right-brain hemisphere	2	3	5	8	10
Left-brain hemisphere	1	4	6	7	9

Now compare the results. Which hemisphere has the most circled numbers? The bigger the difference between the two scores, the greater your right-brain dominance or left-brain dominance. If you circled about the same number for both hemispheres, neither one of your hemispheres is dominant.

What does all this mean? One hemispheric orientation is not better than the other, but the thinking processes are different. People who are more left-brain oriented tend to be more organized, be more analytical, and use more logic. So, it is not surprising that engineers, accountants, scientists, and auto mechanics are more likely to have a dominant left hemisphere.

Those with a dominant right hemisphere, on the other hand, tend to focus on the whole more than individual parts, be imaginative, jump to conclusions, and be emotional. Poets, artists, musicians, and inventors are more likely to have a dominant right hemisphere.

We will apply this information later on when we discuss study techniques. Students with a dominant left hemisphere will probably do better organizing material by outlining, while those with a dominant right hemisphere might find mapping easier. Those who are left-brain oriented will probably find study schedules easier to stick to than those who are right-brain oriented.

Left-brain-oriented students will probably find it easier to do well in classes that require analysis and linear thinking than will students who are right-brain oriented. Examples of such classes are algebra, science, accounting, logic, computers, and engineering. Those who are more right-brain oriented might do better in classes such as art, social science, music, English, history, and geometry.

> *"Intuition becomes increasingly valuable in the new information society precisely because there is so much data."*
>
> —John Naisbitt

Multiple Intelligences

What Are Your Strengths?

Merriam Webster's Collegiate Dictionary defines intelligence as "the ability to learn or understand" and "the ability to cope with a new situation."* We have discovered in the previous sections that we are all unique individuals who learn in different ways. Some psychologists believe that intelligence can also be expressed in a variety of ways. Many of you may remember taking the Stanford-Binet IQ test. After completing the test, you were assigned a score and then evaluated based on that score. If your mental age, as measured by the test, and your age in years were the same, you had an IQ of 100. This meant that you were considered "average." The higher the score above 100, the more intelligent you were considered to be, while a score of 80 meant that you were below average.

Critics argue that one problem with this test is that it is based on the principle that our intelligence is one-dimensional. Howard Gardner, a Harvard professor, has proposed the idea that there are eight types of intelligence. His theory is based on biological research showing different parts of the brain to be the sites of different abilities. He says that "the concept of 'smart' and 'stupid' doesn't make sense. . . . You can be smart in one thing and stupid in something else." As you read a description of each type of intelligence, try to determine your own strengths and weaknesses.

> *"The art of writing is the art of discovering what you believe."*
>
> —David Hare

Practice your marking skills by highlighting (or underlining) the definition for each of the following types of intelligences. Follow the example given below for verbal/linguistic intelligence.

*By permission. From *Merriam-Webster's Collegiate® Dictionary, 11th Edition* © 2011 by Merriam-Webster, Incorporated (www.merriam-webster.com).

WORD SMART—VERBAL/LINGUISTIC INTELLIGENCE

This intelligence <u>relates to language skills</u>. It includes the <u>ability to express yourself verbally</u>, to <u>appreciate complex meanings</u>, and to <u>detect subtle differences in</u> the <u>meanings of words</u>. It is considered to be a key intelligence for success in college.

People with this type of intelligence are likely to be good writers and good spellers. For recreation, they often like to do crossword puzzles or play word games, such as Scrabble. They have good memories for names and dates. They are often good at telling stories or giving speeches. To learn best: Talk, read, or write about it.

LOGIC SMART—LOGICAL/MATHEMATICAL INTELLIGENCE

This intelligence involves the ability to reason, solve abstract problems, and understand complex relationships. Intelligence in this area is also a good predictor of academic success.

People with this type of intelligence are logical, orderly thinkers. It is easy for them to comprehend factual material. In school, they often ask a lot of questions. They like working with equations in subjects such as math and chemistry. They are often proficient with the computer. For recreation, they like board games such as Clue, Battleship, and chess, or computer games. To learn best: Think critically about it.

PICTURE SMART—VISUAL/SPATIAL INTELLIGENCE

This is the ability to think in three dimensions and to re-create experiences visually. Painters, sculptors, and architects are all able to manipulate a form in space.

People who have this type of intelligence like to visualize each step in their mind when they are given a set of directions. They are the "finders." Many can readily retrieve missing objects in the home by tapping a visual memory of where the objects were last seen. To process complex information, they like to draw pictures, graphs, or charts. They learn more in class when information is given by means of videos, movies, or PowerPoint slides. For recreation, they often like to do puzzles or mazes. To learn best: Draw, sketch, or visualize it.

MUSIC SMART—MUSICAL/RHYTHMIC INTELLIGENCE

This is the ability to hear pitch, tone, and rhythm.

People with this type of intelligence may sing or hum throughout the day. They enjoy dancing and can keep time with the music. They often need to listen to music when they study. It is very easy for them to remember the words and melodies of songs. To learn best: Sing, rap, or play music.

BODY SMART—BODILY/KINESTHETIC INTELLIGENCE

This intelligence places the emphasis on control of the body and the skillful handling of objects. The mind clearly coordinates the movements of the body. Athletes, pianists, and dancers might excel in this area.

People with this type of intelligence are often Mr. or Ms. Fix-it. They enjoy repairing things, they use many gestures when they speak, and they are good at competitive sports. For recreation, they prefer physical activities such as bicycling, rollerblading, skateboarding, and swimming. To learn best: Do hands-on activities.

PEOPLE SMART—INTERPERSONAL INTELLIGENCE

This is the ability to interact well with people. People who excel in this area are especially skillful in detecting the moods and intentions of others. Politicians might display this type of intelligence.

People with this type of intelligence are often found in leadership positions. They tend to be empathic individuals who communicate well with others. They often make good mediators and are called upon to help settle other people's problems and conflicts. To learn best: Join a group, get a study partner, or discuss the subject matter with friends.

"You're wise, but you lack tree smarts."
© Donald Reilly/The New Yorker Collection/www.cartoonbank.com

SELF SMART—INTRAPERSONAL INTELLIGENCE

This is the ability to understand one's own feelings and to use the insight gained to guide actions.

People with this type of intelligence set reasonable goals for themselves and take steps to accomplish those goals. They often study by themselves, and they need time to be alone with their thoughts. To learn best: Relate the material to your personal experiences.

ENVIRONMENT SMART—NATURALISTIC INTELLIGENCE

This is the ability to appreciate and respect the environment and nature.

People with this type of intelligence probably enjoy being outdoors and participating in hiking, camping, and gardening. They tend to notice and value diversity among plants and animals. They like studying such subjects as astronomy, zoology, and geology. Farmers or oceanographers might display this type of intelligence. To learn best: Go on field trips or walks.

Is there a relationship between these intelligences and the learning styles we have been studying? Probably, but our knowledge of how the brain functions is still in the early stages. One problem, of course, is that although we are all human beings, we are all distinctly different, making it difficult for scientists to generalize.

Another problem concerns the controversy over how much of our intelligence is fixed at birth and how much is determined by our environment. More than likely, our intelligence is a combination of these two factors, but the nature-versus-nurture debate is far from resolved. In the meantime, many educators and psychologists are not only attempting to define intelligence more broadly but also devising new methods to teach thinking skills once thought to be fixed for life.

Exercise 1: Working with Multiple Intelligences

Directions: Match the examples to the specific intelligence.

__d__ 1. Playwright William Shakespeare	a. Intrapersonal
__e__ 2. Microsoft founder Bill Gates	b. Visual/spatial
__g__ 3. Quarterback Drew Brees	c. Interpersonal
__b__ 4. Architect Maya Lin	d. Verbal
__h__ 5. Singer Beyoncé Knowles	e. Logical/Mathematical
__c__ 6. Talk show host David Letterman	f. Naturalistic
__f__ 7. Conservationist Dr. Akoi Kauadio	g. Bodily/Kinesthetic
__a__ 8. His Holiness The Dalai Lama	h. Musical/Rhythmic

Internet Activity

In this chapter, you have been trying to improve your understanding of yourself by taking various assessment tests. Go to one of the following Web sites and take one of the tests. Try to take a test that is different from one that you have already taken. What can you conclude about yourself after taking the test?

www.intelligencetest.com

www.iqtest.com

www.queendom.com

READING

"Well, then, suppose my auto repairman devised questions for an intelligence test."

TUNING IN TO READING   You are now going to read an essay by Isaac Asimov (1920–1992). This essay, written 10 years before Gardner began his research on multiple intelligences, demonstrates how we can be "smart" in many different ways. As you read the essay, try to determine which of Gardner's eight intelligences Asimov likely possessed. Which intelligences did the mechanic in the essay display? What intelligences did Asimov and the mechanic have in common?

BIO-SKETCH   According to David N. Samuelson, in *Twentieth Century Science-Fiction Writers,* Asimov is "the world's most prolific science writer" who wrote "some of the best-known science fiction ever written." In addition to science fiction, Asimov, a former professor of biochemistry, wrote many essays explaining scientific principles to the general public. The following essay, "What Is Intelligence, Anyway?" is a sample of his autobiographical writings. In these essays, Asimov recounts many incidents from his own life, both painful and pleasurable. He never forgot his early origins and often invited readers "to wonder, with him, at the rise to prominence of a bright Jewish boy brought to this country from Russia at the age of three and raised in a collection of Brooklyn candy stores." In his lengthy career, he received numerous honors and awards, including having his short story "Nightfall" chosen by the Science Fiction Writers of America as the best science fiction story of all time.

NOTES ON VOCABULARY

private   (in the Army) the lowest rank in the army. Comes from the Latin *privare,* meaning "to separate or deprive." A *private* is separated from those of higher rank and is deprived of the privileges of higher rank.

oracle   a person of great knowledge, or a wise statement or authoritative prediction. *Oracle* was originally the shrine where ancient Greeks and Romans consulted their gods and asked their advice. The *oracle* of Delphi was the most famous.

moron   fool. From the Greek word *moros,* meaning "foolish."

What Is Intelligence, Anyway?

ISAAC ASIMOV

WHAT IS INTELLIGENCE, ANYWAY? When I was in the Army, I received a kind of aptitude test that all soldiers took and, against a normal of 100, scored 160. No one at the base had ever seen a figure like that, and for two hours they made a big fuss over me. (It didn't mean anything. The next day I was still a buck private with KP—kitchen police—as my highest duty.)

All my life I've been registering scores like that, so that I have the complacent feeling that I'm highly intelligent, and I expect other people to think so, too. Actually, though, don't such scores simply mean that I am very good at answering the type of academic questions that are considered worthy of answers by the people who make up the intelligence tests—people with intellectual bents similar to mine?

2

For instance, I had an auto repairman once, who, on these intelligence ₃ tests, could not possibly have scored more than 80, by my estimate. I always took it for granted that I was far more intelligent than he was. Yet, when anything went wrong with my car I hastened to him with it, watched him anxiously as he explored its vitals, and listened to his pronouncements as though they were divine oracles—and he always fixed my car.

Well, then, suppose my auto repairman devised questions for an intelligence ₄ test. Or suppose a carpenter did, or a farmer, or, indeed, almost anyone but an academician. By every one of those tests, I'd prove myself a moron. And I'd *be* a moron, too. In a world where I could not use my academic training and my verbal talents but had to do something intricate or hard, working with my hands, I would do poorly. My intelligence, then, is not absolute but is a function of the society I live in and of the fact that a small subsection of that society has managed to foist itself on the rest as an arbiter of such matters.

Consider my auto repairman, again. He had a habit of telling me jokes ₅ whenever he saw me. One time he raised his head from under the automobile hood to say: "Doc, a deaf-and-mute guy went into a hardware store to ask for some nails. He put two fingers together on the counter and made hammering motions with the other hand. The clerk brought him a hammer. He shook his head and pointed to the two fingers he was hammering, the clerk brought him nails. He picked out the sizes he wanted, and left. Well, doc, the next guy who came in was a blind man. He wanted scissors. How do you suppose he asked for them?"

Indulgently, I lifted my right hand and made scissoring motions with my ₆ first two fingers. Whereupon my auto repairman laughed raucously and said, "Why you dumb jerk, he used his *voice* and asked for them." Then he said, smugly, "I've been trying that on all my customers today." "Did you catch many?" I asked. "Quite a few," he said, "but I knew for sure I'd catch *you*." "Why is that?" I asked. "Because you're so goddamned educated, doc, I *knew* you couldn't be very smart."

And I have an uneasy feeling he had something there. ₇

(Isaac Asimov, "What Is Intelligence, Anyway?")

 COMPREHENSION CHECKUP

Multiple Choice

Directions: For each item, write the letter corresponding to the best answer.

_____c_____ 1. While serving in the Army, Asimov was
    a. rewarded for receiving such a high score on the aptitude test.
    b. belittled and made to feel inferior.
    c. fussed over momentarily.

_____b_____ 2. The people who write the tests are emphasizing the kinds of questions
    a. they do poorly on.
    b. they do well on.
    c. they are indifferent to.

_____c_____   3. The auto repairman mentioned in the essay on a traditional aptitude test most probably would score
   a. superior.
   b. average.
   c. below average.

_____a_____   4. When Asimov says that he listened to the auto repairman's pronouncements "as though they were divine oracles," he means he listened
   a. closely.
   b. with distrust.
   c. angrily.

_____c_____   5. If a carpenter devised an aptitude test, Asimov would most probably score
   a. superior.
   b. average.
   c. below average.

_____b_____   6. When Asimov *indulgently* lifted his hand to make scissoring motions, he was indicating he
   a. felt uncertain of the correct answer.
   b. was confident he was correct.
   c. knew he was wrong.

_____b_____   7. When the auto repairman succeeded in fooling Asimov, he felt *smug*. In this context, the word *smug* most probably means
   a. frustrated.
   b. self-satisfied.
   c. silly.

_____b_____   8. Does the auto repairman have respect for Asimov's type of intelligence?
   a. most probably
   b. not likely
   c. absolutely

Vocabulary in Context

Directions: In the blanks below, write the word from the list that best completes the sentence. Use each word only once.

aptitude	arbiter	complacent	foist	fuss
hastened	indulgent	intricate	mute	raucous

1. Tara's kids weren't turning out very well because she was far too ____indulgent____ in disciplining them, letting them do whatever they felt like.

2. Sam's ____aptitude____ test indicates that he would probably do well to consider law enforcement as a possible career choice.

3. Eddie Murphy's trademark ____raucous____ laugh has been displayed in the *Shrek* movies.

4. The coffin cover of the ancient Egyptian King Tut features a(n) ____intricate____ design of gold inlaid with enamel and semiprecious stones.

5. Realizing she had forgotten to turn off the oven, Tina ____hastened____ home before her turkey dinner was ruined.

6. Darryl was feeling smug and ___complacent___ over how well he did on the last test, and so he quit working hard.

7. Whenever Cathy, the cartoon character by Cathy Guisewhite, goes home to visit her mother at the holidays, a real ___fuss___ is made over her.

8. The two sides can't agree on a deal, so Robyn has agreed to serve as a(n) ___arbiter___ in the dispute.

9. Mark gets really angry every time some of his coworkers try to ___foist___ some of their work on him.

10. Tony pushes the ___mute___ button whenever there is a loud, annoying commercial on TV.

In Your Own Words

1. What does the auto repairman mean when he says, "Because you're so goddamned educated, doc, I *knew* you couldn't be very smart"?

2. Do you think it is a good idea for people to be made aware of their score on an IQ test?

3. What does the word *intelligence* mean to you?

Written Assignment

In the book *The Learning Gap* by Harold W. Stevenson and James W. Stigler, the authors compare the Asian and American models of education. The authors believe that the American system places too much emphasis on innate abilities as measured by traditional IQ tests. In contrast, the Asian educational system is less enthusiastic about intelligence testing and instead stresses effort. While differences among people are clearly recognized, the Asian system focuses on how hard people are willing to work to develop their particular abilities. "Lack of achievement, therefore, is attributed to insufficient effort rather than lack of ability or to personal or environmental obstacles." The authors provide examples of this philosophy in proverbs such as this one from China: "The slow bird must start out early." Write a few paragraphs giving your opinion of the two different approaches to intelligence. Which approach do you think is better? Why?

Stress Inventory

How Much Stress Is There in Your Life?

Although there is no exact correlation between how well students do in college and the stress in their lives, students need to pay attention to personal stress. To be successful in college, you must be able to give full attention to your studies. This means that you must come to terms with all facets of your life, including whatever is causing you stress. If the stress in your life is controlling you, you need to do something about it. You may be able to solve the problem yourself, or you might want to consider seeking professional help. Most college campuses have a counseling center to help students deal with too much stress and other emotional problems. When we have physical problems, most of us are willing to consult a doctor. On the other hand, many of us have difficulty seeking help for other personal problems. But if you need help and help is available, why not take advantage of it?

The following test is meant to be confidential and is for your use only.

ADD IT UP: STUDENT STRESS SCALE

If you have experienced any of the events listed here in the last 12 months, check that item.

1. Death of a close family member	_____	100
2. Death of a close friend	_____	73
3. Divorce of parents	_____	65
4. Jail term	_____	63
5. Major personal injury or illness	_____	63
6. Marriage	_____	58
7. Firing from a job	_____	50
8. Failure in an important course	_____	47
9. Change in health of a family member	_____	45
10. Pregnancy	_____	45
11. Sex problems	_____	44
12. Serious argument with close friend	_____	40
13. Change of financial status	_____	39
14. Change of major	_____	39
15. Trouble with parents	_____	39
16. New girlfriend or boyfriend	_____	37
17. Increase in workload at school	_____	37
18. Outstanding personal achievement	_____	36
19. First quarter/semester in college	_____	36
20. Change in living conditions	_____	31
21. Serious argument with an instructor	_____	30
22. Lower grades than expected	_____	29
23. Change in sleeping habits	_____	29
24. Change in social activities	_____	29
25. Change in eating habits	_____	28
26. Chronic car trouble	_____	26
27. Change in the number of family get-togethers	_____	26
28. Too many missed classes	_____	25
29. Change of college	_____	24
30. Dropping of more than one class	_____	23
31. Minor traffic violations	_____	20
TOTAL	_____	

Scoring

Now total your points. A score of 300 or more is considered high and puts you at risk for developing a serious health-related stress problem. A score between 150 and 300 is considered moderately high, giving you about a 50-50 chance of developing a stress-related health problem. Even a score below 150 puts you at some risk for stress-related illness. If you do have an accumulation of stressful life events, you can improve your chances of staying well by practicing stress-management and relaxation techniques.

(Thomas H. Holmes and Richard H. Rahe, "Social Readjustment Rating Scale," 1967)

Exercise 2: Context Clue Practice Using Textbook Material (Why Students Get the Blues)

Directions: Use the context clues to determine the meaning of the italicized word, and write a definition for that word in the space provided.

1. During the school year, up to 78 percent of all college students suffer some symptoms of depression. At any given time, from 16 to 30 percent of the student population is depressed. Why should so many students be "blue"? Various factors contribute to depressive feelings. Here are some of the most *prevalent:*

   prevalent: widespread; common

2. Stresses from the increased difficulty of college work and pressures to make a career choice often leave students feeling that they are missing out on fun or that all their hard work is *for naught.*

   for naught: for nothing; worthless; useless

3. *Isolation* and loneliness are common when a student leaves his or her support group behind. In the past, family, a circle of high school friends, and often a boyfriend or girlfriend could be counted on for support or encouragement.

   isolation: state of being alone

4. Problems with studying and grades frequently trigger depression. Many students enter college with high *aspirations* and little experience with failure. At the same time, many lack *rudimentary* skills necessary for academic success.

   aspirations: goals; objectives

   rudimentary: elementary; basic

5. Another common cause of college depression is the breakup of an *intimate* relationship with a boyfriend or girlfriend.

   intimate: close; personal

6. Students who find it difficult to live up to their idealized images of themselves are especially *prone* to depression.

   prone: liable; have a tendency toward

7. Stressful events frequently *trigger* depression. An added danger is that depressed students are more likely to abuse alcohol, which is a depressant.

   trigger: initiate

(Dennis Coon, *Introduction to Psychology,* 8/e, 1998)

Internet Activity

Do a search on the Internet about how stress affects college students. Write a paragraph about what you learned.

READING

*"I just want to be the best I can be—to live up to
my fullest potential."*

TUNING IN TO READING   Inventor Thomas Alva Edison once said, "Success is 10
percent inspiration and 90 percent perspiration." In the excerpt that follows, Kurt Warner
typifies the kind of work ethic that not only leads to success on the football field, but to
success in school and life. Even for someone as successful in his chosen career as Warner,
life has not been easy. Yet, he clearly believes in trying his best and not giving up even when
the odds are stacked against him. In his case, persistence, hard work, and holding on to a
dream have paid off. Perhaps this excerpt will inspire you to take advantage of your own
opportunities in college and help you to set your own standards for excellence.

BIO-SKETCH   Kurt Warner, who was born in Iowa on June 22, 1971, graduated from the
University of Northern Iowa, where he was a backup quarterback until his senior year.
Because he was not drafted by the National Football League (NFL), Warner worked as a stock
boy in a local grocery store until the Iowa Barnstormers of the Arena Football League signed
him to a contract in 1995. Then, in 1998, the NFL's St. Louis Rams signed him. In 1999, he was
both the NFL MVP and the Super Bowl MVP. Warner became an Arizona Cardinal in 2005 and
retired after multiple injuries in 2010. Shortly thereafter he began a career in broadcasting,
working as an analyst for FOX and the NFL network. Warner competed on *Dancing with the
Stars,* coming in fifth. He has been married to his wife Brenda since 1997. Together they are
raising seven children. Kurt and Brenda are the co-authors of *First Things First,* from which
this excerpt is taken.

NOTES ON VOCABULARY

underdog   a person, team, or side that is losing or is expected to lose

benched   kept from playing in a game

stats   an abbreviated form of the word statistics

MVP   most valuable player

Strive to Be the Best You Can Be

BY KURT AND BRENDA WARNER

THE CARDINALS WERE THE WORST TEAM in NFL history. In
their sixty-year existence, they'd never been to a Super Bowl and
had played in only a handful of playoff games.

When we entered the 2008 season playoffs, no one expected much. We 2
were 9-7. People called us the worst team ever to go to the playoffs. We
were the underdogs in *every* game.

And yet we got to the Super Bowl.   3

We even had a chance to win it in the end.   4

When I was in St. Louis, the Rams were considered one of the worst 5
teams of the nineties, and yet in one year, we went from worst to first,
winning the 1999 Super Bowl. In my years as a player, I've been a part of
some real come–from–behind stories.

There have also been times in my career when I've had personal comebacks. 6
There were times when I was benched through no fault of my own, and times
when injuries prevented me from playing. Times when I did everything I could
but still got booed coming off the field. Let me just say, it's never good when
you're booed in your profession. Those were the low moments in my career.
Moments when I would ask God, *What are you doing? Why am I here?*

I had some of those same questions when I was benched two years after 7
coming to Arizona. I worried that my entire future as a player would be
limited to holding a clipboard, just waiting to see if the starter got injured.
I considered retirement in those days, but I also hoped that by working hard
I could change the situation. Before I got into the NFL, I was naïve. I
believed the best players would always play because coaches wanted to win
games. But once I got into the league, I learned it's also about other things—
money, draft picks, politics, and marketing. But despite the low times—no
matter how much the fans or coaches turned against me—I've always tried
my best, and I will continue to do my best.

That's what I want my kids to see.   8

Yes, I'm proud of my accomplishments. My quarterback rating is in the 9
top five all-time, better than some of my heroes, like Joe Montana and Roger
Staubach. I'm one of the most accurate passers in NFL history, which makes
me happy because I believe that's my greatest strength. Throughout my
career, there have been other accomplishments that have stood out, such as
fastest to throw for ten thousand yards, second fastest to a hundred touch-
downs, and second all-time to throw forty touchdown passes in a season—
with my name in the record books alongside Dan Marino's. My stats are up
there with some of the best ever to have played the game.

But beyond the statistics, I'm even more proud that I took two different 10
teams to the Super Bowl. Regardless of the odds against me, or the accolades
I've received, I've always done my best to be a leader on the field and to
inspire other players to greatness. So, on the one hand, if my career ended
today, I would be satisfied. But the truth is, I'm not done and there's more
I want to accomplish. I want to become an even better quarterback. I want
to throw more touchdown passes, break more records, and win more Super
Bowls. I want to play the perfect game.

I'm not saying I want to accomplish these things so people will look at 11
me and say, "Oh, he's the best quarterback that ever played," or whatever.
I'm not really worried about what other people think or say. I just want to
be the best I can be—to live up to my fullest potential. And I hope that in
doing so, I inspire the people who watch me to be the best at what they're
supposed to be.

After the Super Bowl, it would have been so easy to pick one of those 12
two pivotal plays—the interception to James Harrison or the touchdown to
Larry Fitzgerald—and have that define me. But those aren't the moments
that play over and over in my head. The moments I relive are the conversations I've had with people who stopped to tell me that I inspired them.

For example, I remember one of my first years in Phoenix. Larry Fitzger- 13
ald and his girlfriend were having dinner with Brenda and me. Sometime
during the main course, Larry and I got into a heated discussion about something related to football, and I said to him, "You've got to get better."

I'll never forget his response: "Kurt, I'm good enough."   14

Brenda was there, and she will tell you that I couldn't believe he'd said 15
that. It blew me away that "good enough" would be okay.

"Don't you want to be the best?" I asked.   16

That conversation stuck with me. When I disagree with someone on a 17
topic, I'm the kind of person who always asks a lot of questions—like, "Why
do you believe what you believe?" I want to understand their thinking and
how they arrived at the conclusion they did. That's what I did when Brenda
and I were dating and she kept talking about religion.

That's probably also why I still remember that conversation with Larry. 18
I had no idea why Larry would think it was okay for him just to be "good
enough."

Over the next few years, Larry and I became pretty good friends. We 19
worked closely together, both on and off the field, and I got to watch him
grow from a good player into a great player.

After the Super Bowl, Larry and I were traveling together on a plane, 20
and we had another conversation I'll never forget. He locked eyes with me
and said, "Kurt, you made me better. You made me want to be better."

That's it.   21

That's what I live for.   22

I want my life to encourage others. Whether as the leader of a football 23
team, as a husband to my wife, or as a father to my kids, I always strive to
do my best in hopes that by doing so, the people around me will strive to
do their best. I want a spirit of excellence to surround everything I do. When
my kids see me loving them, when they watch how I treat my wife, or
when they see me preparing for football, I want them to know that I'm
doing my best. I also hope that pushes them to do better in what they're
doing. I want to be great. And I hope to inspire others to want the same.

(Kurt and Brenda Warner, *First Things First*, 2009)

 COMPREHENSION CHECKUP

Multiple Choice

Directions: Write the letter of the correct answer in the blank provided.

____c____ 1. According to the selection, all of the following are important to
              Warner *except*
              a. being the best that he can be.
              b. setting a good example for his children.
              c. paying attention to what his fans think.
              d. inspiring others to be the best that they can be.

_____d_____ 2. In the selection, Kurt Warner discusses
     a. encouraging others.
     b. considering retirement.
     c. getting angry at hecklers.
     d. Both a and b.

_____c_____ 3. Which of the following is *not* discussed in the selection?
     a. Warner's success as a passer
     b. Warner's success as a motivator
     c. Warner's success as a coach
     d. Warner's success as a team leader

_____c_____ 4. Which of the following words best describe Kurt Warner now?
     a. lazy
     b. naïve
     c. motivated
     d. cautious

_____c_____ 5. The word *strive* in "I always *strive* to do my best . . ." means
     a. fight against.
     b. overexert.
     c. make every effort.
     d. bother.

True or False

Directions: Indicate whether each statement is true or false by writing **T** or **F** in the blank provided.

_____T_____ 6. A person who is *naïve* is not likely to be sophisticated.

_____F_____ 7. Kurt Warner has won two Super Bowls.

_____T_____ 8. This selection is primarily about Warner's personal philosophy of life.

_____T_____ 9. Warner has taken two different teams to the Super Bowl.

_____T_____ 10. Warner takes his profession seriously.

_____F_____ 11. Being benched was one of the high points in Warner's career.

_____F_____ 12. Warner is motivated to perform well because of public opinion.

Scanning

Directions: Scan the reading to find the word (or words) that correctly completes each statement.

1. Two of Kurt Warner's football heroes are Joe Montana and Roger Staubach.

2. Warner won the 1999 Super Bowl.

3. Warner remembers a conversation with Larry Fitzgerald about improving football skills.

4. As quarterback of the Cardinals in the 2009 Super Bowl, Warner threw an interception to James Harrison.

5. Before the 2008 playoffs, the Cardinals had a win-loss record of 9-7.

6. Prior to the Cardinals, Warner played for the St. Louis Rams.

Vocabulary in Context

Directions: Try to determine the meaning of the italicized words and then write the definition on the line provided. The paragraph in which the words appear in the reading selection is indicated in parentheses.

1. personal *comebacks* (6) <u>return to past success</u>

2. two *pivotal* plays (12) <u>of vital or critical importance; key</u>

3. have that *define me* (12) <u>describe; explain</u>

4. a *heated* discussion (13) <u>angry</u>

5. It *blew me away* (15) <u>impressed me</u>

6. conversation *stuck with me* (17) <u>unable to get rid of it</u>

In Your Own Words

1. What general statement is Warner making in this selection?

2. How does Warner describe the Cardinals before their Super Bowl performance?

3. Kurt Warner received a number of accolades throughout his lengthy career. Do you think that earning awards and recognition can also cause stress? In what ways?

4. What are some stresses that commonly affect professional athletes or their families?

Written Assignment

1. What qualities do you think Warner values in people? Write a few paragraphs giving your opinion.

2. The Warner family was featured in an article by Karen Crouse of the *New York Times*. When asked by Crouse to come up with a few rules for being a Warner daughter or son, the children quickly came up with the following:

Eight Rules for Being a Warner Daughter or Son

1. Everyone has to agree on which stranger's meal to pay for when dining at a restaurant.

2. At dinner, share the favorite part of your day.

3. Hold hands and pray before every meal.

4. After ordering at a restaurant, be able to tell Mom the server's eye color.

5. Throw away your trash at the movie theater and stack plates for the server at restaurants.

6. Spend one hour at an art museum when on the road.

7. Hold hands with a sibling for ten minutes if you can't get along.

8. If you can't get along holding hands, sit cheek to cheek. (If you can't get along cheek to cheek, then it's lips to lips!)

(Kurt and Brenda Warner, *First Things First,* pages 48–49)

What is your reaction to the Warner rules? What are the rules for your particular family? Write a short paragraph describing a few of these rules and giving the reason for each one.

Internet Activity

Karen Crouse's article, "The Rules of the Family," (September, 25, 2008) can be found at

http://www.nytimes.com/2008/09/26/sports/football/26rules.html?ref=football.

Write a paragraph reporting new information you learn about the Warners.

Study Schedules

How do you create a study schedule that makes you more efficient?

When to Study

Now let's begin to put some more of this information you have learned about yourself to practical use. Would you like to be prepared for a test two nights before the test is given? Would you like to have that paper written a day early? If so, follow along. The purpose of this section is to show you how to organize yourself so that you can take charge of your life and do better in school.

You will find a practice weekly study schedule form on page 56. Another copy is located in the Appendices.

COMPLETING A WEEKLY STUDY PLAN

Step 1: Fill in your class schedule. For example, if your math class is MWF from 9 to 10, write "math" in the three blocks for those days and times. You have no control over these items; you have to go to class.

Step 2: Now fill in your work schedule. We hope it is fairly regular, because if it is not, keeping a regular study schedule from week to week is going to be more difficult. Write "work" in the appropriate blocks. If your schedule changes from week to week, try to approximate it. If some weeks you work more than others, go to your busier weeks.

Step 3: Fill in time for school activities such as sports events, clubs, and student council.

Step 4: Fill in time for other regularly scheduled activities such as church, meetings, laundry, and grocery shopping. If it's something you do almost every week, put it in. If you do something only every once in a while, leave it out.

Step 5: Fill in time commitments to your family, spouse, and friends. These people also need your attention. Include such things as putting children to bed or doing social activities with friends. Keep in mind that it often does not work out very well to mix family or social activities with academic

"Dost thou love life? Then do not squander time; for that's the stuff life is made of."

—Benjamin Franklin

"It takes time to save time."

—Joe Taylor

WEEKLY STUDY SCHEDULE

	Monday	Tuesday	Wednesday	Thursday	Friday	Saturday	Sunday
6:00–7:00							
7:00–8:00							
8:00–9:00							
9:00–10:00							
10:00–11:00							
11:00–12:00							
12:00–1:00							
1:00–2:00							
2:00–3:00							
3:00–4:00							
4:00–5:00							
5:00–6:00							
6:00–7:00							
7:00–8:00							
8:00–9:00							
9:00–10:00							
10:00–11:00							
11:00–12:00							
12:00–1:00							

obligations. Try not to study and cook dinner simultaneously. If you can arrange things so that you can have time to concentrate solely on your school assignments, that would be better. And your friends and family may be happier too, now that they get your full attention at other moments.

Step 6: Fill in other times when you are not likely to be studying, maybe Friday and Saturday evenings, the time of your favorite TV show, or times when you exercise. Exercise is important to your health and sense of well-being, which will benefit you in many ways, including academically.

Step 7: At the bottom of the schedule sheet, list the classes you are taking. For each of the classes, estimate how much time you will need to spend working on it each week to obtain an A or a B. This number will, of course, vary from class to class, since some classes will be more difficult than others or will simply require more time to do the assignments. Generally, in college courses, you need to devote two hours outside the class to course work for each hour spent in the class. You will want to include time for reviewing notes, writing your papers, and studying for tests. If you're unsure how much time to put down, say 4 or 6 hours, go with the larger number.

Step 8: Now determine which of your classes is the most difficult and so will demand more of your time. Recall the test you took on your circadian cycle. If math is going to be your most difficult subject, try to give it your best study hours—when you have the most patience and the clearest mind. Maybe this will be early in the morning, or at noon, or in the early evening. Also keep in mind your most effective style of learning—visual, auditory, or kinesthetic. For example, if you are mostly a visual learner but have a class that emphasizes lectures, allow sufficient time for going over your lecture notes and reviewing the textbook. That way you bring your strengths into play.

Step 9: Keep in mind the limits of your attention span in setting up blocks of time to study particular courses. Some will be more interesting to you than others. Some will require more concentrated effort than others. For example, if biology is going to be difficult for you, you don't want to assign yourself a block of time for studying it that will exceed your attention span. Otherwise, you will be wasting your time. So instead of fewer, longer sessions, it may make sense for you to schedule more numerous, shorter sessions. Experiment in your academic scheduling so that your study time will be most productive.

Step 10: You now have a guide for your daily and weekly routine. You have to go to class on a regular basis, so why not study on a regular basis? What should you be doing during your scheduled study time? You can read the chapter to be covered in class, review your notes from previous days' classes, begin to study for an upcoming test, or work on a paper that is coming due. Each time you sit down to study, ask yourself how you can best use that time to master the course material or meet the course requirements. The ideal place for studying is somewhere comfortable and free of unwanted distractions. Try to come as close to this as you can.

STUDY TECHNIQUE 4: SQ3R A CLASSIC WAY TO STUDY

SQ3R (**S**urvey, **Q**uestion, **R**ead, **R**ecite, **R**eview) is a system for reading and studying textbook material that was developed by Dr. Francis P. Robinson more than 50 years ago. Most "new" study techniques are variations of this old classic.

Step 1: Survey

You survey a reading selection by looking it over before actually beginning to closely read it. When you complete your survey, you should have a general understanding of what the selection is about. Surveying is very similar to skimming. Following are some suggestions for surveying:

1. Read the title or subtitle and any information given about the author.

2. Read the first paragraph or the introduction.

3. Scan the headings or subheadings.

4. Notice any boldfaced or italicized words.

5. Read the first sentence of each paragraph.

6. Notice the charts, diagrams, pictures, or other graphical material.

7. Read the last paragraph, the conclusion, or the summary.

8. Read any questions at the end of the selection.

9. Think about what *you* already know about the topic.

Step 2: Question

After completing your survey, you should have some questions in mind about the material. If you can't think of any questions, try turning a subheading into a question. For a section with the title "SQ3R," you might ask, "What is SQ3R?" or, "Why is it a classic technique of studying?" If the material you are reading doesn't have subheadings, try turning the first sentence of every paragraph into a question. It is much easier to keep yourself actively involved in the material if you are reading to answer specific *how, why,* or *what* questions. Your attention is less likely to wander if you actually write down the questions, and their

answers, on a separate sheet of paper, or even in the textbook. You might want to try conducting an imaginary conversation with the author—talk to the author, ask her or him for answers, and keep a continuous conversation going.

Step 3: Read

Now carefully read the entire selection from beginning to end. Look for main ideas and the answers to your questions. You may also want to mark key points by underlining, highlighting, or jotting notes in the margins. Remember, most textbook material will need to be read more than once. The first reading will give you only a limited understanding of the material. If the material is particularly long, divide it into sections, read a section at a time, and perhaps take a short break between sections.

Step 4: Recite

To do this step, you must put the information you have learned into your own words, and then say it either to yourself or out loud. While it might seem odd at first, talking out loud can be a very effective technique for remembering material because it involves hearing and speaking at the same time. You might pretend someone has asked you a question about the material and then respond (out loud or to yourself) by giving the answer. Or you might pretend that you are the teacher giving a lecture on the material. Be sure you can recite the answers to *who, what, where, when, why,* and *how* questions. When you organize the material mentally and put it into your own words, you are demonstrating your understanding of the material.

Step 5: Review

In this last step, look over your questions, notes, and highlighted material. Practice giving the answers to the questions you originally posed. By now you should be able to define special terms and give relevant examples. You might want to do your review with a classmate by explaining the material to that person or by taking turns quizzing each other on the material. Review frequently so the material will stay with you.

In the following exercise, you have a chance to practice your SQ3R techniques with the excerpt from *Internet Literacy* (pages 60–65). Follow all the steps carefully. You may wish to highlight (or underline) the definitions for all the key terms. Use the margins for any notes you wish to make.

Exercise 3: SQ3R Practice

Step 1: Survey

1. Write a few sentences about what you already know about Internet etiquette.
   Answers will vary.

2. What is the title of the selection? Internet Etiquette (Netiquette)

3. What does the excerpt present? The rules for use of the Internet

4. What does *spam* refer to? Unwanted messages

5. What is the third subheading? Hoaxes

6. On the Internet, a flame is a message written in anger

7. *Shouting* means to write in capital letters

Step 2: Question

After surveying the reading selection, you should have at least two questions about it. Write your questions below.

8. Answers will vary.

9.

Step 3: Read

Now read the entire selection and answer the questions you posed previously. Then do the Comprehension Checkup following the reading.

Step 4: Recite

Can you recite the answer to the following question?

What are some commonly known netiquette rules? Answers will vary.

Step 5: Review

Now you should be able to answer your own questions from step 2. Write the answers below.

10. Answers will vary.

11.

12. What is a TLA? Three-letter acronym

13. List three TLAs you commonly use. Answers will vary.

READING

"Thou shalt always use a computer in ways that ensure consideration and respect for your fellow humans."

TUNING IN TO READING   Communication is the most popular Internet activity, and its impact cannot be overestimated. At a personal level, friends and family can stay in contact with one another even when separated by thousands of miles. At a business level, electronic communication has become a standard, and many times the preferred, way to stay in touch with suppliers, employees, and customers. The three most popular types of

READING *(continued)*

Internet communication are electronic mail (e-mail), instant messaging, and discussion groups.

In the selection that follows, you will learn techniques for communicating more effectively via *e-mail*, which is a store-and-forward method for communicating. Specifically, you will learn some "rules of the road" (Internet etiquette) for communicating effectively on the information superhighway.

BIO-SKETCH Fred T. Hofstetter, a professor in the School of Education at the University of Delaware, teaches courses in multimedia literacy. Currently, he is involved in developing a Web-based teaching and learning environment called Serf.

NOTES ON VOCABULARY

esoteric private or secret; belonging to a select few. The word *esoteric* derives from a Greek word meaning "inner." It was originally used to describe the secret doctrines that Pythagoras, a Greek philosopher and mathematician, taught to a select group of his disciples.

acronym a word formed from the initial letters or groups of letters of the words in a name or phrase, as in AIDS from "acquired immune deficiency syndrome."

jargon special words or expressions used by a profession or group that may be difficult for others to understand. The word, derived from Old French, originally meant "twittering or chattering."

newsgroup an electronic Internet site where people can read and post messages relevant to a particular topic.

listserv a mailing list service that enables users to send messages to people on a particular mailing list.

worm A program that replicates itself over a computer network and usually performs malicious actions, such as using up the computer's resources and possibly shutting down the system.

EXCERPT FROM *INTERNET LITERACY*
Fred T. Hofstetter

Internet Etiquette (Netiquette)

Netiquette is a term coined by combining the words *Internet etiquette* into a single name. **Netiquette** is the observance of certain rules and conventions that have evolved in order to keep the Internet from becoming a free-for-all in which tons of unwanted messages and junk mail would clog your inbox and make the information superhighway an unfriendly place to be. This section presents the rules for commercial and educational use of the Internet, suggests a way for you to become a good citizen of the Net (network citizens are called *Netizens*), and defines everyday terms and jargon used on the Net.

Netiquette Guidelines

The most commonly known Netiquette rules are as follows:

2

- Use business language and write professionally in all work-related messages.
- Remember that your message may be printed or forwarded to other people.
- Proofread and correct errors in your message before sending it.
- Do not use all capital letters because this connotes shouting.
- Keep in mind that your reader does not have the benefit of hearing your tone of voice and [seeing] facial clues.

- Remember that the time, date, and reply address are added automatically to your e-mail message; therefore, you do not need to type this information.
- Always include an appropriate subject line [in your] e-mail message.
- Respond promptly to e-mail.

Whenever you use the Internet, you should observe the ethics principles [3] [listed here as] the Ten Commandments of Computer Use. These principles were developed by the Computer Ethics Institute in Washington, DC.

The Ten Commandments of Computer Ethics
1. Thou shalt not use a computer to harm other people.
2. Thou shalt not interfere with other people's computer work.
3. Thou shalt not snoop around in other people's computer files.
4. Thou shalt not use a computer to steal.
5. Thou shalt not use a computer to bear false witness.
6. Thou shalt not copy or use proprietary software for which you have not paid.
7. Thou shalt not use other people's computer resources without authorization or proper compensation.
8. Thou shalt not appropriate other people's intellectual output.
9. Thou shalt think about the social consequences of the program you are writing or the system you are designing.
10. Thou shalt always use a computer in ways that ensure consideration and respect for your fellow humans.

Copyright 1991 Computer Ethics Institute. Author: Dr. Ramon C. Barquin, 1707 L. Street, NW, Suite 1030, Washington, DC 20036, Ramon C. Barquin, President, Computer Ethics Institute.

Spam

On the Internet, the term **spam** refers to unwanted messages posted to [4] newsgroups or sent to a list of users through e-mail. The term can be used either as a verb or as a noun. To *spam* means to send unwanted messages to a list of users on the Internet. Likewise, unwanted messages that you receive are called *spam.*

Perhaps the most obnoxious form of spam is unwanted commercial adver- [5] tising. The Coalition Against Unsolicited Commercial Email (CAUCE) has done the math, and the outlook is daunting. As CAUCE chairman Scott Hazen Mueller explains, "There are 24 million small businesses in the United States, according to the Small Business Administration. If just one percent of those businesses sent you just one e-mail advertisement a year, that's 657 e-mail advertisements in your inbox each day."

To prevent this from happening, Congress has enacted the CAN-SPAM Act, [6] which took effect January 1, 2004. This legislation requires that e-mailed adver- tising contain a working Unsubscribe link. Furthermore, the CAN-SPAM Act makes it illegal to falsify the From and Subject lines of an e-mail message. For violations, spammers can be jailed for up to five years and fined up to a million dollars. In practice, however, few spammers have been convicted, while the amount of spam has mounted to consume as much as 75 to 80 percent of the typical user's e-mail. As a result, ISPs are looking to technological instead of legislative means of reducing the amount of spam on the Internet. The strategy is to create e-mail authentication technology that would make it harder for spammers to falsify the origin of their messages.

There are other forms of spam besides unwanted commercial advertising. [7] A lot of chain letters, for example, are circulating on the Internet. Chain letters are spam; do not send or forward them. If you get one, you may be tempted to send a message to the originator stating that chain letters are an unethical use of the Internet, and that the sender should be ashamed of so littering the information superhighway. Be aware, however, that responding to spam lets the spammer know that your e-mail address is valid, thereby increasing the likelihood that you may receive more spam.

Hoaxes

Some pretty incredible hoaxes have been propagated across the Internet. [8] The hoaxes are designed to prey upon people's fears, desires, and sensitivities to keep the hoax spreading to other uses over the Net. An example is the Netscape-AOL giveaway hoax. It was sent all over the Internet via e-mail by the following chain letter:

> Netscape and AOL have recently merged to form the largest internet company in the world. In an effort to remain at pace with this giant, Microsoft has introduced a new e-mail tracking system as a way to keep Internet Explorer as the most popular browser on the market. This e-mail is a beta test of the new software, and Microsoft has generously offered to compensate those who participate in the testing process. For each person you send this e-mail to, you will be given $5. For every person they give it to, you will be given an additional $3. For every person they send it to, you will receive $1. Microsoft will tally all the e-mails produced under your name over a two-week period and then e-mail you with more instructions. This beta test is only for Microsoft Windows users because the e-mail tracking device that contacts Microsoft is embedded into the code of Windows 95 and 98.
>
> I know you guys hate forwards. But I started this a month ago because I was very short on cash. A week ago I got an e-mail from Microsoft asking me

"Oh no, we're being spammed!"

© Arnie Levin/The New Yorker Collection/www.cartoonbank.com

for my address. I gave it to them, and yesterday I got a check in the mail for $800. It really works. I wanted you to get a piece of the action. You won't regret it.

Sometimes you may not be sure whether a message is a hoax or not. The major hoaxes are catalogued at the U.S. Department of Energy's Computer Incident Advisory Capability (CIAC) Web site, where you can look to see whether the hoax is a recognized one. For many of the hoaxes, the CIAC will recommend what actions you can take to discourage the spreading of the hoax. At the CIAC site, you will also find links to Web pages warning you about the major chain letters and viruses that you need to watch out for on the Internet. 9

Viruses

Some of the more harmful chain letters and hoaxes have transmitted viruses across the Internet. While it is not possible for your computer to catch a virus from an e-mail address directly, the mail message may contain attachments that can give your computer a virus if you open them. One of the most harmful such e-mail viruses was the Love Bug virus. It spread as an attachment to an e-mail virus entitled "I Love you" and asked you to open the attachment, which was named LOVE-LETTER-FOR-YOU.TXT.VBS. When you opened the attachment, the virus caused computers using the Microsoft Outlook and Outlook Express e-mail programs to send copies of the message to all of the users in your computer's address book. The messages appear to come from the person who owns the computer, serving as further enticement to open the attachment, since it appeared to come from someone you knew. In addition to spreading itself to your friends, the message also deleted certain kinds of files from your computer and replaced them with more copies of the virus. 10

The best way to guard against catching a virus through e-mail is never to open an attachment to an e-mail message, especially if the attachment has an executable filename extension such as *.exe, .vbs,* or *.class.* Before you open any e-mail attachment, make very sure that . . . the message actually came from the person listed as the source. If you have any doubts, check the antivirus Web pages to see if the message you received is part of a nationally recognized virus attack. 11

A message may appear to come from a trusted acquaintance, when in fact it came from a worm. Recently, some viruses spread via e-mail that did not require the recipient to open the attachment. In addition, there are malicious virus programs that mimic the e-mail addresses of people from your address book. As a result, it is very important to keep current antivirus protection software on your computer. 12

Lurking

To **lurk** means to participate in a conversation on the Internet without responding to any of the messages. You receive and read the messages, but you do not say anything in return. Thus, you are lurking! 13

It is not unethical to lurk. To the contrary, it is often a good idea to 14 lurk at first. For example, suppose you join a listserv that has been going on for a while. Instead of jumping right in and writing something that may make you seem really out of touch with what is going on, it is smarter to lurk for a while, so you can pick up the gist of the conversation before joining in.

The same guideline applies to newsgroups. Before you begin writing mes- 15 sages in a newsgroup, spend some time looking around at what has been written previously in that newsgroup. When you write something, you want it to sound as though you know what is going on. It is inconsiderate to write messages that waste the time of other users on the Net.

Ditto for chat rooms. When you enter a chat room in which other people 16 are talking, spend some time listening to get the gist of the conversation before you chime in.

Flames

On the Internet, a **flame** is a message written in anger. The term "flame" 17 can be used as either a verb or a noun. To *flame* someone is to send them an angry message. Angry messages that people send you are known as *flames.*

You need to be careful, especially if you have a temper. Form the habit of 18 thinking carefully about what you write, and proofread several times before you send the message. Make sure the message truly conveys the emotions you want to communicate. If you are extremely mad, and send a hastily written flame, you may regret it later on. When you cool off a few minutes later, you may wish you could tone down the message a little, but it will be too late. The message has already been sent, and unfortunate damage may be done to your relationship with the receiving party.

Firefighters

Sometimes flaming can get out of hand, especially when it occurs in a 19 newsgroup or a listserv with a lot of users. People start sending hotter mes- sages, and things can get ugly. Someone has to step in and write a message intended to restore peace. Because that puts an end to the flames, such peace- makers on the Internet are known as **firefighters.**

Shouting

Messages written on the Internet are normally written in lowercase let- 20 ters, with capital letters appearing only at the start of the first word of each sentence, and on proper nouns, such as the term *Internet.* WHEN YOU WRITE IN ALL CAPS, ON THE OTHER HAND, YOU ARE SHOUTING! **Shouting** means to add emphasis to something by writing in all capital letters. Shout- ing is almost always regarded as in poor taste, however, so do it sparingly, if at all.

If you hit the <u>Caps Lock</u> key by mistake, everything you enter will be writ- 21 ten in all caps. Do not turn on the <u>Caps Lock</u> option unless you really want to shout.

An alternative to writing in all caps is to add emphasis to a word or 22 phrase by surrounding it with asterisks, such as: It is *rude* to shout on the Internet.

Smileys and Emoticons

One of the problems inherent in text messages is that you cannot see the 23 body language or facial expression of the person sending the message. Not knowing for sure whether something is said in jest can lead people to make false assumptions about the intent of a message. You need to be careful, because a miscommunication can cause serious problems.

To give the person reading your message a clue about your emotions, 24 emoticons were devised. **Emoticons** are combinations of a few characters that conjure a facial expression when turned sideways. The most common form of emoticon is the smiley, which conveys a happy facial expression. Turn your book clockwise, and you will see that the characters :) convey a happy face. The smiley often has a nose :-) and sometimes winks at you ;-).

Emoticons are not always happy. For example, :(is a frown, and :-(is a 25 frown with a nose. Someone really sad may be crying:~~ (and someone obnoxious may stick out their tongue :-P at you. You can even convey drooling :-P~~ with an emoticon.

Three-Letter Acronyms (TLAs)

To shorten the amount of keyboarding required to write a message, some 26 people use three-letter acronyms, which are appropriately known as TLAs. A **three-letter acronym (TLA)** is a way of shortening a three-word phrase such as "in my opinion" by simply typing the first letter of each word, such as *imo*. Cell phone users use TLAs to reduce the amount of keypresses required to TXT a message to another phone. Some of the more common three-letter acronyms are

brb	be right back	**j/k**	just kidding
bbl	be back later	**oic**	oh, I see
btw	by the way	**ott**	over the top (excessive, uncalled for)
imo	in my opinion	**thx**	thanks
lol	laughing out loud		

There are also two-letter acronyms, such as   27

np	no problem	**wb**	welcome back
re	hi again, as in "re hi"	**b4**	before

Some of these are more intuitive than others! There are also acronyms with 28 more than three letters, including

bbiaf	be back in a flash	**nhoh**	never heard of him/her
hhoj	ha ha, only joking	**rotfl**	rolling on the floor laughing
imho	in my humble opinion	**ttfn**	ta ta for now
morf	male or female		

(Fred T. Hofstetter, *Internet Literacy*, 4/e, 2006)

COMPREHENSION CHECKUP

Short Answer

Directions: Answer the questions briefly.

1. What is the selection about? <u>Internet communication/netiquette</u>

2. List three TLAs that you commonly use.

   <u>Answers will vary.</u>

Multiple Choice

Directions: For each item, write the letter corresponding to the best answer.

__d__ 1. Which of the following statements is true according to the information in the selection?
   a. Hoaxes work by misleading and deceiving.
   b. Many are fooled by the hoaxes they find on the Internet.
   c. There isn't any way to determine the truthfulness of Internet hoaxes.
   d. Both a and b.

__a__ 2. Which of the following is the most popular Internet activity?
   a. communication
   b. shopping
   c. searching
   d. entertainment

__a__ 3. Unwanted and unsolicited e-mails are called
   a. spam.
   b. junk.
   c. flame.
   d. lurk.

__c__ 4. According to the author, all of the following should be done before sending an e-mail message *except*
   a. proofreading and correcting errors.
   b. writing in lowercase letters, using capitals only at the beginning of a sentence and for proper nouns.
   c. typing in the time, date, and reply address.
   d. including an appropriate subject line.

__b__ 5. The author considers all of the following to be principles for computer use *except* which one?
   a. Respect other people's privacy by not reading their e-mail.
   b. The best ethical guideline is to do only what you can get away with.
   c. Stealing material from others is prohibited.
   d. Be sure to pay for what you use.

True or False

Directions: Indicate whether each statement is true or false by writing **T** or **F** in the space provided.

__F__ 6. Many spammers have been convicted and jailed.

__F__ 7. A typical computer user's e-mail consists of 50 percent spam.

_____F_____ 8. According to the author, chain letters are not considered to be spam.

_____T_____ 9. The author of the selection advises the reader not to send or forward chain letters.

_____T_____ 10. If you respond to spam, you have let the spammer know that your e-mail address is a valid one.

_____T_____ 11. A computer can't catch a virus from an e-mail directly.

_____T_____ 12. The author recommends that antivirus protection be kept current.

_____F_____ 13. According to the author, it is unethical and immoral to lurk.

_____T_____ 14. Peacemakers on the Internet are referred to as firefighters.

_____T_____ 15. In an attempt to control spam, antispam laws have been enacted.

Vocabulary Matching

Directions: Match the vocabulary words in Column A with the definitions in Column B. Place the correct letter in the space provided.

	Column A	Column B
e	1. emoticon	a. to send an e-mail message intended to insult or provoke
i	2. e-mail	b. on the Internet, typing a message IN ALL CAPITAL LETTERS to add emphasis
a	3. flame	c. Internet etiquette, which is the observance of certain rules and conventions
b	4. shouting	d. to send unwanted messages to a list of users on the Internet
j	5. smiley	e. a character combination that, when turned sideways, conjures a facial expression
d	6. spam	f. a malicious or unwanted code that installs itself on your computer without your knowledge by hiding inside other programs
h	7. firefighter	g. to participate in a conversation on the Internet without responding to any of the messages
c	8. Netiquette	h. a peacemaker who works to quell flames on the Internet
f	9. virus	i. electronic mail
g	10. lurk	j. an emoticon that conveys a happy facial expression

Vocabulary in Context

Directions: In the blanks below, write the word or phrase from the list that best completes the sentence.

compensate	daunting	deleted	enticement	free-for-all
gist	merged	prey	sensitized	tally

1. Sue gave Marie the _____gist_____ of her conversation with Mark.

2. After the president announced his resignation, the press conference deteriorated into a _____free-for-all_____.

3. The western diamondback rattlesnake's _____prey_____ is primarily small rodents, rabbits, and birds.

4. After the two airlines _____merged_____, passengers experienced higher fares and fewer flights.

5. I was advised by my boss to _____tally_____ all of my out-of-pocket expenses and submit them for reimbursement.

6. I inadvertently _____deleted_____ some important information from my computer.

7. As an _____enticement_____ for finishing my degree, my mother promised me a trip to Hawaii.

8. When her car broke down in the desert, she faced the _____daunting_____ task of hiking 10 miles to get help.

9. Nothing can _____compensate_____ for the loss of a child.

10. Some people need to be _____sensitized_____ to the effect their words have on others.

In Your Own Words

1. Patricia T. O'Conner, author of *Woe Is I*, suggests that while it's one thing to be creative with grammar, spelling, and punctuation with friends, it's quite another to use "goofy English" when writing instant messages or e-mails to teachers and people in the business community. She suggests that the audience you're writing to should influence how you write the message. What do you think?

2. Many of you post messages to blogs, bulletin boards, discussion groups, and other public forums, which are often read by complete strangers. Do you agree or disagree with the statement "You are what you write"? If you are unfamiliar with the person you're writing to, how careful should you be about what you say?

3. Your e-mail address is seen by everyone you send e-mail to. In a personal e-mail account, you often choose your own address, which says something about you in a way similar to a vanity plate on a car. How important do you think it is to avoid having an e-mail address that is too cute or too personal? Do you think people should get into the habit of using different e-mail addresses for different purposes?

4. A student turned in a term paper and, when he got it back, was surprised to see points deducted because he wrote, "In some situations, sympathy can be 2 much." Do you think shorthand expressions should be acceptable in formal papers?

5. Why has text messaging become so popular? When are you likely to use text messaging?

Written Assignment

1. The principal problem with online communication is that nonverbal communication is difficult. When you can't see or hear the other person, how can you tell what he or she is really thinking or feeling? How do you convey your feelings online to others? What clues do you rely on in determining what others are really saying to you? What kinds of problems could a nonnative speaker encounter?

2. How do you think emoticons in e-mail messages can help prevent miscommunication? How might an emoticon create a misunderstanding? Why do you think some people actively dislike the use of emoticons in written communication? When you see an emoticon in an e-mail message, what is your initial reaction?

3. Write a few short paragraphs giving your opinion of the following tips provided by *Computing Essentials*. Which tip is most valuable to you?

Tips

Are you tired of sorting through an inbox full of spam? Americans receive over 200 billion spam e-mails every year. Here are a few simple tips to help ensure that your inbox is spam-free:

- **Choose a complex address.** sally_smith@hotmail.com is much more likely to get spam than 4it3scoq2@hotmail.com. Consider using a more complicated, and less personal, user name.
- **Keep a low profile.** Many spammers collect e-mail addresses from personal Web sites, chat rooms, and message boards. Use caution when handing out your address and be sure to read the privacy policy of a site before you hand over your address.
- **Don't ever respond to spam.** Once you respond to spam, either in interest or to opt out of a list, you have confirmed the address is valid. Valid addresses are worth more to spammers, who then sell the addresses to others.
- **Use e-mail filter options.** Most e-mail programs have a filter option that screens in-coming e-mail based on a set of preferences you choose. You can set up your inbox to accept only mail from certain addresses or to block mail from others.
- **Use spam blockers.** There are plenty of programs available to help protect your inbox. For example, MailWasher provides an effective and free program available at www.mailwasher.com.

(Timothy J. O'Leary and Linda I. O'Leary, *Computing Essentials 2008,* 19/e, 2008)

4. Imagine that you are having a problem in a class. Write an e-mail to the professor about it using good Internet etiquette. In particular, be sure to begin with a proper salutation, such as "Dear Dr. Smith" or "Hello Dr. Smith." Identify yourself by referring to the class you're taking and conclude your e-mail with your full name. Be sure to avoid the use of text acronyms.

Internet Activity

Check out one of the following Web sites devoted to the topic of netiquette.

1. Take the short netiquette quiz and summarize your results:

    www.albion.com

2. This site provides good links to the Library of Congress's Guide on Copyright Basics and Citation. What information is the most relevant to writing research papers?

    www.studygs.net/netiquette.htm

3. Review the sections on the netiquette of replying to e-mails and the netiquette of confidentiality. What information is most important to you in regard to your own correspondence?

    www.livinginternet.com

Chapter Summary and Review

In Chapter 1, you learned about various learning styles and how to develop a study schedule that suits your learning style. You also learned about the theory of multiple intelligences. In addition, you learned more about how to determine the meanings of words from context. Furthermore, you learned about SQ3R and how to apply it to a reading selection. Finally, you learned some rules for effective Internet communication.

Short Answer

Directions: Answer the questions briefly, in a sentence or two.

1. What are your personal learning styles? How can you use them to do better in college?

2. What are four techniques for discovering the meanings of words from context clues?

3. Are you more of a day or night person? How will this knowledge help you prepare for your classes?

4. Which multiple intelligences are your strengths? Your weaknesses?

Vocabulary in Context

Directions: Choose one of the following words to complete the sentences below. Use each word only once.

antonyms	circadian	death	kinesthetic
left-brain	married	paragraphs	survey

5. Accountants and computer engineers are probably __left-brain__ oriented.

6. If you are a(n) __kinesthetic__ learner, you may want to take notes, highlight your textbook, or get up and walk around the room.

7. You can easily throw off your __circadian__ cycle when you get on a plane and fly to a different time zone.

8. Two of the biggest stressors for people are a(n) __death__ in the family and getting __married__.

9. A good way to __survey__ a chapter in one of your textbooks is to read the first and last __paragraphs__ and look at the headings and subheadings.

10. __Antonyms__ for homeostasis are *change* and *variation*.

VOCABULARY   Unit 1 Homonyms and Other Confusing Words

As you learned in the Introduction, homonyms are words that sound the same but may have different spellings or meanings. There are other words that could be added to our list of homonyms below, but these are the ones students most commonly have trouble with. Mastering these words will help you make a good impression in written assignments, so we have included homonyms in Chapter 1. *Affect* and *effect* are discussed in a separate box because they are especially difficult.

accept   a verb meaning "to receive, take, or hold." Did you *accept* the money given to you by your rich uncle?

U.S. Capitol

except	a preposition meaning "without." Everyone *except* you was invited to the party.
expect	a verb meaning "to look forward to an event." *Expect* is not technically a homonym, but students sometimes confuse it with *except.* I *expect* to get an A in English, but if I don't do well on the final I might end up with a B.
capitol	a noun meaning "the physical building where laws are made." From now on, you should use this word for the actual building. The *capitol* building in Washington, DC, has two branches, the Senate and the House of Representatives.
capital	a noun or an adjective meaning "most important or most serious," including the *capital* city, money, *capital* letters, *capital* punishment, and the top of a column of a building. What is the *capital* city of your state?

Think about This Sentence: Your state *capitol* building is located in the *capital* city of your state.

know	a verb meaning "to understand." Did you *know* all the important information for the test?
no	an adverb, sometimes an adjective, used to express something negative. Did you stay up all night studying for the test? *No,* you went to bed.
knew	a verb, past tense of the verb *know.* I *knew* the material for the test.
new	an adjective meaning "present, modern"; an antonym of *old.* Did you spend your money on a *new* car?
past	a noun meaning "former time." In the *past* you did not study as much as you should have.
	an adjective meaning "former." One of our *past* presidents was Thomas Jefferson.
	an adverb meaning "beyond something." Did you walk *past* the library on the way to the student union?
passed	the past tense of the verb *pass.* The quarterback *passed* the ball to the tight end, who ran for a touchdown. The student *passed* the test with an A. My father *passed* away. Each of these sentences uses the word *passed* as a verb expressing action.

Think about This Sentence: Most of our *past* presidents have *passed* away.

principal	a noun meaning "head of a school, or other person who is the main person."
	a noun meaning "sum of money." When you buy a house, you will pay on *principal* and interest.
	an adjective meaning "main" or "chief." Was the *principal* cause of the Civil War the desire to abolish slavery or the need to keep our country unified?
principle	a noun meaning "fundamental moral beliefs." Cheating people out of their money should go against the *principles* your parents taught you.
	a noun meaning "fundamental theory," as in physics. A fundamental *principle* in physics is that the atoms or molecules in gases are more widely spaced than in solids or liquids.

Think about This Sentence: Your *principal* beliefs are the *principles* you live by.

quiet	an adjective meaning "silent." Are you a *quiet* person?
quite	an adverb meaning "very" or "extremely." The line of cars trying to get into the parking lot of the football stadium was *quite* long.
quit	a verb meaning "to discontinue" or "give up." This word is not really a homonym, but is often confused with *quiet* and *quite*. The student *quit* her job at McDonald's so that she could devote more time to her studies.
their	an adjective indicating possession; the possessive form of "they." *Their* car was stolen from the parking lot.
there	an adverb indicating direction, meaning "in that position." Notice how the word *here* appears in the word *there*. The computer lab is located over *there*.
	a pronoun used to begin a sentence or phrase. *There* are a few students absent from class today.
they're	a contraction for "they are." *They're* going to the party after the game.
to	a preposition indicating direction, and meaning "toward." Are you going *to* your house after you finish class?
	part of a verb indicating an infinitive statement. Unless you are independently wealthy, you will need *to* work for a living. You may want *to* study in the library.

Think about This Sentence: You are going *to* work because you need *to* work for a living. The first *to* is a preposition indicating direction; the second *to* is part of the verb "to work."

too	an adverb meaning "also" or "excessively." He, *too*, was allowed to leave class early. She drank *too* much at the party.
two	the number 2. The baseball team scored *two* runs in the fifth inning.
threw	the past tense of the verb *throw*. The shortstop *threw* out the runner at first base.

Affect versus *Effect*

Now for the difference between *affect* and *effect*. The key to working with these words is knowing the difference between a noun and a verb. Remember that a verb indicates *action* or *state of being*. A noun is a person, place, or thing; remember that things can be intangible (for example, feelings, causes, and hopes).

action The team *won* the game last night.

state of being The team *is* excellent because its players *are* quick and play good defense.

affect a verb meaning "influence." This word will *almost always* be used as a verb. If one thing *affects* something else, it influences it. If you are using one of these words as a verb, you will use *affect* 95 percent of the time. Weather *affects* our personalities and how we feel. (The weather is influencing your personality.)

In psychology, *affect* can be used as a noun meaning "emotional response." After her mother died, Maria became depressed and had a flat *affect*.

effect Ninety-nine percent of the time this word will be a noun. *Effect* as a noun usually means "the result of an action." What will be the *effect* on you if Congress cuts back the financial aid program?

Using *effect* as a verb is very tricky, but on the positive side you will probably need to use it this way very rarely. As a verb, *effect* means "to cause or bring about." Congress may *effect* a change in the income tax laws.

through		a preposition indicating direction. The drunk driver drove *through* the red light.
		a preposition meaning "finished." When the student was *through* with the test, he took it to the instructor at the front of the class.

Finish the sentence: The boy *threw* the ball *through* the _____.

weather—Don't talk on the phone or take a shower during a thunderstorm. The electrical current of lightning can travel through phone lines and water pipes.

weather		a noun meaning "temperature, climate." The *weather* was so hot that you just had to stay inside with the air conditioner running.
whether		a conjunction similar to "if." Some people believe it really doesn't make much difference *whether* we have a Republican or a Democratic president.
were		a past tense of the verb *be*. We *were* in the mountains when the fire broke out.
we're		a contraction for *we are*. *We're* going to go to the store.
wear		a verb meaning "to have on the body" or "to diminish." What are you going to *wear* to the party on Saturday? You are going to *wear* out the carpet walking back and forth so much.
where		an adverb, a conjunction, or a noun indicating location. *Where* did I leave my books?

Now write your own sentences using *affect* and *effect*. (You may find it helpful to refer to the sample sentences above.)

_____

_____

_____

Homonym Exercise 1

Directions: For each exercise, complete the following sentences using the correct homonym.

1. Did she _____accept_____ the marriage proposal?
   accept/except

2. In the United States, the issue of _____capital_____ punishment is controversial.
   capitol/capital

3. I don't _____know_____ what to do to help you study for that quiz.
   know/no

4. That room definitely needs _____new_____ paint.
   knew/new

5. In the _____past_____, I was not available to work on Tuesdays.
   past/passed

6. My _____principles_____ include not speaking harshly of anyone.
   principals/principles

7. I want you to _____quit_____ making that very annoying noise.
   quit/quite

8. While I am the talkative one in the family, my husband is the _____quiet_____ one.
   quiet/quite

9. The noise was _____quite_____ loud and as a result gave me a headache.
   quite/quit

10. Write a sentence of your own using *capital* correctly.

_____

Homonym Exercise 2

1. People don't realize they are _____affected_____ by advertising.
   affected/effected

2. What possible _____effects_____ does drinking alcohol have on teenagers?
   affects/effects

3. Special _____effects_____ in the movie *Star Wars* look tame by today's standards.
   affects/effects

4. The teacher told me my absences _____affected_____ my grade in her class.
   affected/effected

5. The _____weather_____ forecast today shows a chance of showers in the north.
   weather/whether

6. It doesn't matter _____whether_____ I exercise or not; I still can't lose weight.
   weather/whether

7. It's not possible to _____know_____ all of the material for the quiz.
   know/no

8. I don't know _____where_____ to turn in my finished essay.
   were/where

9. They _____were_____ not able to attend the luncheon held in their honor.
   were/where

10. The babysitter wants to give the children _____their_____ lunch at noon.
    their/there

11. _____There_____ are too many people enrolled in the nine o'clock English class.
    their/there

12. Jan said that she wanted to come to the party _____too_____.
    to/too/two

13. I am not able _____to_____ visit him in the hospital today.
    to/too/two

14. Her resignation from the position was _____accepted_____ by her supervisor.
    accepted/excepted

15. The hostess _____accepted_____ my apologies when I declined the invitation.
    accepted/excepted

Vocabulary Unit 1 Crossword Puzzle

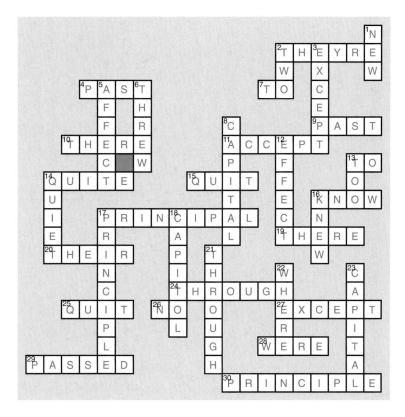

ACROSS CLUES

2. _____ on their way to class.

4. We have all done things in the _____ that we later regretted.

7. All students need _____ study several times each week for each class.

9. Did you drive your car _____ the exit on the freeway?

10. _____ is a good program on TV tonight.

11. Will you _____ your friend's invitation to the party?

13. Will you go _____ your graduation ceremony?

14. The student was _____ upset when he was withdrawn from class.

15. Many students _____ college before they graduate.

16. Do you _____ who won the game last night?

17. One of the _____ ingredients in soda is sugar.

19. Why were you over _____ when you should have been over here?

20. _____ house was broken into several times last summer.

24. You must walk _____ the hallway to get to the classroom.

25. Did you _____ your job?

26. _____, I do not want any more ice cream.

27. Everyone _____ you received an A on the test.

28. _____ you at home last night studying?

29. The elderly person _____ away.

30. One _____ of life is to do unto others as you would want them to do unto you.

DOWN CLUES

1. We went to Wal-Mart to buy _____ clothes.

2. There are _____ wheels on a typical bike.

3. All of the student's grades were A's _____ for the B on the final.

5. Studying hard should positively _____ your grade.

6. The basketball player _____ the ball out-of-bounds, by accident.

8. What is the _____ city of your state?

12. Using drugs will have a negative _____ on a person.

13. _____ little sleep will probably make you drowsy and cranky.

14. Was the room _____ while students were taking the test, or was it too noisy?

16. The student _____ all the important information for the test.

17. Religious books lay down basic _____s of life.

18. Where is the _____ building located?

21. When will you be _____ with your work and able to go home?

22. _____ is the closest McDonald's?

23. The first letter of a sentence should be a(n) _____ letter.

Discovering Meaning through Structure

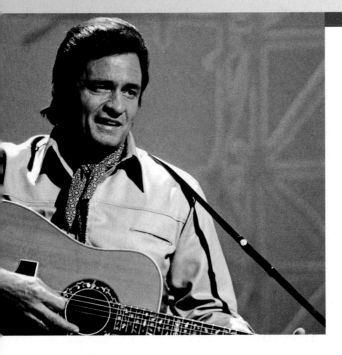

JOHNNY CASH

Johnny Cash was one of the most remarkable artists in American popular music. While always true to himself musically, he managed to stay both commercially and artistically popular for four generations. His music could be uplifting and inspiring or even hilarious—as in the case of "A Boy Named Sue."

As portrayed in the 2005 biographical film *Walk the Line*, Johnny Cash had a humble beginning, born in rural Arkansas on February 26, 1932. He established his musical image as the dark loner in 1957 with "Folsom Prison Blues" and "I Walk the Line," his first number-one country hit. He appeared at the Grand Ole Opry dressed all in black, and the image blended so well with his dark ballads that he was dubbed "the man in black."

Going into the 1960s, Cash's hectic lifestyle led him to a dependence on prescription drugs. It cost him his first marriage, his freedom, and nearly ended his career and, indeed, his life. In the meantime, he had become attracted to June Carter who co-wrote Cash's "Ring of Fire." In 1980, he became the youngest inductee into the Country Music Hall of Fame, and in 1994 was inducted into the Rock and Roll Hall of Fame. Throughout his career, Cash influenced younger artists including U2 and Bruce Springsteen. When Johnny Cash passed away in 2003, just four months after the death of his beloved wife June, he was as successful and relevant as he had ever been. (David Lee Joyner, *American Popular Music*, 3/e, 2009)

TIMED READING If you wish to use "Johnny Cash" as a timed reading, please turn to page A-3 in the Appendices.

Topics, Main Ideas, and Details

CHAPTER PREVIEW

In this chapter, you will

- Learn how to distinguish between general ideas and specific details.

- Learn how to identify the topic of a paragraph.

- Learn how to locate the stated main idea of a paragraph.

- Learn how to diagram a paragraph by identifying its main idea sentence and key details.

- Become familiar with paraphrasing.

- Learn how to formulate implied main ideas.

Description of Topics, Main Ideas, and Details

Write your own definition for each boldfaced term. Use your own words.

topic or subject:

_____

_____

main idea:

_____

_____

details:

_____

_____

Most paragraphs are about a particular **topic** or **subject.** The topic is usually a single word or phrase and is often the noun that is mentioned most frequently in a paragraph. We can identify the topic by asking ourselves "What is this all about?" or "Who is this all about?"

Paragraphs are supposed to be organized around a **main idea,** with all sentences supporting this main idea, or key point. The main idea can be identified by asking "What key point does the author want me to know about the topic?"

The main idea may be directly stated in a paragraph, usually, but not always, in the first or last sentence, or it can be implied. When trying to find a main idea that is directly stated, it helps to remember that you are looking for a general statement, not a specific one. When main ideas are implied, you, the reader, are responsible for coming up with a general statement that unites the author's key details. This general statement should be no more than one sentence long.

While all paragraphs have a topic, not all paragraphs have main ideas. Some background or descriptive paragraphs, which are meant to set the tone or mood of a piece of writing, may not have any main idea at all.

Details are supporting sentences that reinforce the main idea. While the main idea is a general statement, supporting details provide specific information such as facts, examples, or reasons that explain or elaborate on the main idea. Details answer the question words about the topic: *who, what, where, when, why,* and *how.*

Baby Blues

© Baby Blues Partnership. King Features Syndicate.

As an illustration of the difference between main ideas and details, study the *Baby Blues* cartoon. In it, Darryl provides Wanda with the main idea of the phone conversation but is unable to provide her with any of the supporting details.

major supporting details:

_____

_____

minor supporting details:

_____

_____

Those supporting sentences that directly reinforce the main idea are called **major supporting details,** and those sentences that serve only to reinforce the major supporting details are called **minor supporting details.** To gain an understanding of how main ideas and major and minor supporting details work in a paragraph, read the following paragraph on posture as body language and study the outline.

1.   Posture often indicates feelings of tension or relaxation. We take relaxed postures in non-threatening situations and tighten up in threatening situations. Based on this observation, we can tell a good deal about how others feel simply by watching how tense or loose they seem to be. For example, watching tenseness is a way of detecting status differences. The lower-status person is generally the more rigid, tense-appearing one, whereas the higher status person is more relaxed. This is the kind of situation that often happens when an employee sits ramrod straight while the boss leans back in her chair. The same principle applies to social situations, where it's often possible to tell who's uncomfortable by looking at pictures. Often you'll see someone laughing and talking as if he were perfectly at home, but his posture almost shouts nervousness. Some people never relax, and their posture shows it.

(Ronald B. Adler, Russell F. Proctor II, and Neil Towne, *Looking Out, Looking In,* 11/e, 2005)

In the outline, MI refers to the main idea, MSD to major supporting details, and msd to minor supporting details.

I.   Posture often indicates feelings of tension or relaxation. (MI)
   A. Person displays relaxed posture when not threatened. (MSD)
   B. Person displays tense posture when feeling threatened. (MSD)
   C. Tension or relaxation in posture may indicate status. (MSD)
      1. Tense-appearing person has low status. (msd)
      2. Relaxed-appearing person has high status. (msd)
   D. Posture indicates who's comfortable in a social setting. (MSD)

In the following example, the general topic is sensitivity to nonverbal communication. The format is fairly typical of information presented in college textbooks.

The main idea is given in the first sentence of the paragraph. The sentences following the main idea are all meant to serve as examples illustrating it. The last sentence concludes the paragraph and reinforces the main idea.

> 2. <u>Cultural diversity in the workplace has created a need for greater sensitivity among managers and employees regarding people's use of nonverbal communication.</u> For example, white Americans define eye contact in the course of a conversation as showing respect. But many Latinos do not, and many Americans of Asian ancestry deem eye contact with an employer to be exceedingly disrespectful behavior. Potential conflicts may arise when white supervisors consider Hispanic or Asian employees furtive or rude for casting their eyes about the room. <u>Multicultural training programs seek to teach employers and employees to look beyond their culture-bound notions about what constitutes "proper" and "improper"</u> behavior.
>
> (Michael Hughes and Carolyn J. Kroehler, *Sociology*, 7/e, 2005)

You may have experienced difficulty finding the main ideas in these two sample paragraphs. But don't be discouraged. This chapter will give you the skills you need to readily find main ideas and supporting details.

Distinguishing between General and Specific

In order to be able to recognize a main idea, you must be able to determine the difference between something that is general and something that is specific. Remember, a main idea is a general statement that is supported by specific details. In the first example below, a car is something that is general because there are more specific kinds of cars. A sedan would be one specific kind of car, and a convertible would be another. In the second example, tree is the broad category. An ash tree is a specific kind of tree, as is an elm tree.

Car	Tree
sedan	ash
convertible	elm

Exercise 1: Writing General and Specific Terms

Directions: Give two specific terms for each general category.

Example:

Professional baseball teams

Los Angeles Dodgers

New York Yankees

1. Wild animals

_____

_____

2. Countries

_____

_____

3. Weekly magazines

_____

_____

4. Universities

_____

_____

5. College courses

_____

_____

6. U.S. presidents

_____

_____

Directions: Give a general term that covers the specific items.

Example:

Jazz musicians

Louis Armstrong

Wynton Marsalis

Miles Davis

1. pain relief medication   2. artists   3. action movies

   Aleve   Picasso   *Spider-Man*

   Bayer   Van Gogh   *Avatar*

   Excedrin   Monet   *Pirates of the Caribbean*

Exercise 2: Writing Specific Sentences

Directions: A general or main idea sentence is given to you. Working in a group, try to come up with two sentences that support the main idea. Your sentences should provide specific details by giving reasons or examples.

Example: Many people do not use antibiotics properly.

   a. They stop taking the antibiotic when they start feeling better.

   b. They pass them around to their friends like candy.

1. Children today don't treat their parents with much respect.

   a. They use verbal or physical violence.

   b. They don't obey home rules.

2. Young boys are more interested in active, aggressive play than little girls.

   a. Boys play football, soccer—contact sports.

   b. Girls play house, dolls.

3. In the last 10 years, a new kind of father has emerged.

   a. Fathers now are willing to babysit kids, take them to the doctor.

   b. Fathers now change diapers, buy food for them.

4. For a student in the United States, school is just like a job.

   a. Students have to fulfill basic requirements.

   b. Students have to attend regularly.

5. Holding a part-time job can benefit students.

   a. They learn to get along with other employees.

   b. They learn to budget their money and time.

6. People are more isolated from their neighbors today than they were 50 years ago.

   a. They no longer know names of many neighbors.

   b. They no longer socialize with them.

7. The traditional family (husband as breadwinner, wife as homemaker) has all but disappeared.

   a. Today _both husband and wife work._____

   b. Today _the wife may earn more than the husband._____

Exercise 3: Identifying Topics of Paragraphs

Now apply what you have learned about general and specific to help you identify the topic of a paragraph. A good topic is comprehensive because it covers all of the ideas mentioned in the paragraph. Sometimes it helps to think of the topic as a title for the paragraph.

Directions: For each paragraph, determine the best topic and put a **T** on the line. Put a **G** on the line of the topic that is too general or broad and an **S** on the line of the topic that is too specific.

1. There is no doubt that advertisers have zeroed in on the child audience. The last few years have seen the growth of kid-specific media: Nikelodeon, websites, kid-oriented magazines, movie tie-ins, and even hamburger wrappers. From 1993 to 1999, advertising in these media increased more than 50 percent, to $1.5 billion per year. Part of the reason behind this increase is the fact that kids have become important factors in family buying decisions. First, they have more money to spend. The under-14 set gets allowances, earns money, and receives gifts to the tune of about $20 billion per year. In addition, kids probably influence another $200 billion worth of shopping decisions. Second, the increase in single-parent families and dual-career families means that kids are now making some of the purchasing decisions that were once left to Mom and Dad. It is not surprising, then, to find that companies are intensifying their efforts to reach this market segment.

    (Joseph R. Dominick, *The Dynamics of Mass Communication*, 8/e, 2005)

    Example:

    __G__ a. Audiences (This is too broad—it covers all types of audiences, not just child audiences.)

    __S__ b. A 50 percent increase in child advertising (This provides one specific detail from the paragraph.)

    __T__ c. Advertisers target child audiences (This covers all the ideas in the paragraph.)

2. Which sex is healthier: women or men? We know that women have a higher life expectancy than men and lower death rates throughout life. Women's greater longevity has been attributed to genetic protection given by the second X chromosome (which men do not have). However, factors such as men's greater propensity for risk taking and their preference for meat and potatoes rather than fruits and vegetables, also may play a part. Despite their longer life, women are more likely than men to report being in fair or poor health, go to doctors or seek outpatient or emergency room care more often, are more likely to seek treatment for minor illnesses, and report more unexplained symptoms. Men are *less* likely to seek professional help for health problems, but they have longer hospital stays, and their health problems are more likely to be chronic and life-threatening. Women's greater tendency to seek medical care does not

necessarily mean that they are in worse health than men, nor that they are imagining ailments or are preoccupied with illness. They may simply be more health conscious. Men may feel that illness is not "masculine," and seeking help means a loss of control. Research suggests that a man is least likely to seek help when he perceives a health problem as a threat to his self-esteem or if he believes his male peers would look down on him. It may well be that the better care women take of themselves helps them live longer than men.

(Diane E. Papalia, Sally Wendkos Olds, and Ruth Duskin Feldman, *Human Development*, 10/e, 2007)

_____ G _____ a. Men and women

_____ T _____ b. Which sex is healthier?

_____ S _____ c. Men and longer hospital stays

3. Engineers and inventors often appropriate their best ideas directly from the natural world. Perhaps the best example of this is the development of Velcro fasteners. Today, Velcro has hundreds of uses in diapers, running shoes, space suits, even in sealing the chambers of artificial hearts. But it all started in 1948, when George de Mestral, a Swiss hiker, observed the manner in which cockleburs clung to clothing and thought that a fastener could be designed using the pattern. Cockleburs have up to several hundred curved prickles that function in seed dispersal. These tiny prickles tenaciously hook onto clothing or the fur of animals and are thus transported to new areas. De Mestral envisioned a fastener with thousands of tiny hooks, mimicking the cocklebur prickles on one side, and on the other side thousands of tiny eyes for the hooks to lock onto. It took 10 years to perfect the original concept of the "locking tape" that has become Velcro, and is so common in modern life.

(Estelle Levetin and Karen McMahon, *Plants and Society*, 5/e, 2008)

_____ S _____ a. Velcro use in diapers and shoes

_____ G _____ b. Inventions

_____ T _____ c. The development of Velcro

4. Women absorb and metabolize alcohol differently than men do. A woman cannot metabolize much alcohol in the cells that line her stomach. Women also have less body water in which to dilute the alcohol than do men. So, when a man and a woman of similar size drink equal amounts of alcohol, a larger proportion of the alcohol reaches and remains in the woman's bloodstream. Overall, women develop alcohol-related ailments such as cirrhosis of the liver more rapidly than men do with the same alcohol consumption habits.

(Gordon Wardlaw, *Contemporary Nutrition*, 6/e, 2007)

_____ G _____ a. Alcohol

_____ S _____ b. The development of cirrhosis of the liver in women

_____ T _____ c. Gender differences in alcohol effects

5. Ethnocentrism is the belief that our own group or culture—whatever it may be—is superior to all other groups or cultures. If you were born and raised in the United States, you may find it strange that most people in India regard the cow as a sacred animal and forgo using it as a source of food. On the other hand, if you were born and raised in India, you might well be shocked at the use of cows in the United States for food, clothing, and other consumer goods. If you are a Christian, you most likely think of Sunday as the "normal" day of

worship. But if you are Jewish, you probably regard Saturday as the "correct" Sabbath. And if you are Muslim, you doubtless see both Saturday and Sunday as unusual times for worship. For you, Friday is the "right" day.

(Stephen E. Lucas, *The Art of Public Speaking*, 9/e, 2007)

___T___ a. The meaning of ethnocentrism

___S___ b. Cows as a sacred animal in Indian culture

___G___ c. Feeling superior to others

6. In a culture like ours that values time highly, waiting can be an indicator of status. "Important" people (whose time is supposedly more valuable than that of others) may be seen by appointment only, while it is acceptable to intrude without notice on lesser beings. To see how this rule operates, consider how natural it is for a boss to drop into a subordinate's office unannounced, while the employee would never intrude into the boss's office without an appointment. A related rule is that low-status people must never make high-status people wait. It would be a serious mistake to show up late for a job interview, whereas the interviewer might keep you cooling your heels in the lobby. Important people are often whisked to the head of a restaurant or airport line, while presumably less exalted people are forced to wait their turn.

(Ronald B. Adler, Russell F. Proctor II, and Neil Towne, *Looking Out, Looking In*, 11/e, 2005)

___G___ a. Waiting

___T___ b. Waiting as an indicator of status

___S___ c. Important people found at the head of the line

Exercise 4: Identifying Main Ideas

Directions: The main idea sentences are missing from the following paragraphs on nonverbal communication. Locate the letter of the main idea sentence for each paragraph in the Main Ideas box on page 87 and write it on the line provided.

1. Chinese tradition associates red with good fortune, but Korean Buddhists use red to announce death. In the United States, red is associated with a stop sign or a warning light but also symbolizes love, as in Valentine's Day. Black is the color of joy in Japan, but it is the color of death in the United States. White is the color of funerals and mourning in eastern countries, but in the United States it is the color of brides. Green is perceived to be a very lucky color in western countries like Britain, Ireland, and the United States. During the uncertain, tension-filled times following 9/11, green became a favored color. Green is perceived as being safe and serene, and it makes people feel better. Even the Department of Homeland Security put green at the bottom of the terrorist alert code, meaning we're safe. In Japan, green is associated with youth and energy.

(Kitty O. Locker and Donna S. Kienzler, *Business and Administrative Communication*, 8/e, 2008)

Main idea: ___J___

2. The intense aroma of spicy curry or barbecue may strike you differently if you are European American than if you are Arab American. At first you may find these new odors unpleasant. But as you get to know the culture and the people, you become accustomed to the new smells and may even find them inviting. People in the United States are especially concerned with body smells,

spending a great deal of money to prevent bad breath and natural body odors. In the U.S., we equate such smells with the lack of personal hygiene. Most other cultures, however, find body smell natural and are bewildered by our attempt to disguise such odors with deodorant, mouthwash, and toothpaste.

(Bethami A. Dobkin and Roger C. Pace, *Communication in a Changing World*, 2006)

Main idea: _____H_____

3. Our clothes, jewelry, cars, houses, and other objects or possessions all say something about us and are sometimes important expressions of our personalities, values, and interests. A large house, expensive car, and designer clothes all convey the nonverbal message of privilege and wealth. Military uniforms convey very precise ranks and status. Similarly, high school letter jackets convey specific ranks or awards, with a series of bars, letters, or patches. At commencement, students graduating with honors sometimes wear robes or chords, and those with PhDs wear special hoods. Objects or possessions can also communicate inclusion in or identification with a group. Students often wear caps or sports jerseys from their favorite team or school. License plates can communicate a person's home state while bumper stickers reveal a person's favorite music group, political party, religious preference, or social cause.

(Bethami A. Dobkin and Roger C. Pace, *Communication in a Changing World*, 2006)

Main idea: _____A_____

4. The handshake is the most common greeting in the United States, but in Japan people bow with hands at their waists. The depth of the bow is a sign of social status, gender, or age. The Thai, Laotians, and Khmer make a slight bow at the waist while placing their hands, palms together, under the chin. The Finnish, New Zealander, Bedouin, Polynesian, and Inuit touch noses. The tip of the nose is brought into contact with the tip of another person's nose or with another part of his or her head. Hawaiians raise their arms and wiggle the hand gently. The thumb and little finger are extended with the other fingers curled. North Africans place their index fingers side by side.

(Bethami A. Dobkin and Roger C. Pace, *Communication in a Changing World*, 2006)

Main idea: _____I_____

5. Some Muslim women wear a veil to express their strongly held convictions about gender differences and the importance of distinguishing men from women. Others wear a veil, which can cover just the head or the entire body, as a sign of disapproval of an immodest Western culture or to protect themselves from the unwanted sexual advances of men. However, the primary reason for wearing a veil is that it is believed to be commanded in the Koran and is thus a symbol of devotion to Islam.

(Mary Kay DeGenova, *Intimate Relationships, Marriages, & Families*, 7/e, 2008)

Main idea: _____C_____

6. Some years ago, during the Olympic games in Mexico, some African-American athletes raised clenched fists to protest racial discrimination and symbolize Black power. It is all too common for professional athletes to make obscene gestures at officials, members of the opposing team, or fans. Even more to the point, one college basketball player, Toni Smith, elected to symbolize her displeasure with U.S. foreign policy by turning her back on

the U.S. flag and looking down at the floor during the playing of the national anthem before games. Others in Smith's presence signaled their support for U.S. policy and expressed their patriotism by choosing to use different nonverbal cues. Some carried flags onto the court to counter Smith's actions. Others wore American flag lapel pins. Still others indicated their support for or opposition to Smith's behavior with their cheers or boos.

(Terry Kwal Gamble and Michael Gamble, *Communication Works,* 9/e, 2008)

Main idea: ___F___

7. Typically, we respond more positively to those we perceive to be well dressed than we do to those whose attire we find questionable or unacceptable. The National Basketball Association (NBA) has long had a dress code for coaches, requiring them to wear a jacket and tie during games. Now the commissioner of the NBA, David Stern, is requiring players and all other personnel to wear a jacket and tie when traveling to or from a game, home and away. The thinking is that these clothes will improve the players' image. Among the items players are prohibited from wearing are T-shirts, chains or pendants, sunglasses when indoors, headphones, and jerseys and baseball caps.

(Terry Kwal Gamble and Michael Gamble, *Communication Works,* 9/e, 2008)

Main idea: ___E___

8. In an effort to enhance the relationships between the external environment and the inner self, the Chinese, and now others, use feng shui (pronounced "fung SHWAY"), the ancient Chinese art of placement, to add harmony and balance to living spaces. Feng shui introduces the five elements in nature into design: earth, fire, water, wood, and metal. For example, it uses green plants to bring the outdoors inside, and red candles and fabrics to increase energy. The goal is to arrange space, furniture, walls, colors, and objects to promote blessings and to harness the life force (chi).

(Terry Kwal Gamble and Michael Gamble, *Communication Works,* 9/e, 2008)

Main idea: ___B___

9. The numerous signs indicating city, country, state, and national borders are examples of our strong need to communicate the boundaries of our territory. In our personal lives, we communicate boundaries by building fences around homes or putting names on office doors. National and state parks always post signs indicating their boundaries. Landscaping not only beautifies one's yard but also communicates, "This is my land." Gangs "tag" territory with graffiti or other recognizable symbols. Even universities construct elaborate entrances to identify the boundaries of campus and to restrict access from unwanted visitors. Territorial markers also extend to personal space. For example, you might place your coat or books on the chair or seat next to you at the library or on a bus. Finally, territorial markers personalize and distinguish space. For instance, many office workers mark their computer monitors with pictures, stickers, or drawings. Similarly, many university students mark their apartment or dorm room with pictures, posters, or other personal items.

(Bethami A. Dobkin and Roger C. Pace, *Communication in a Changing World,* 2006)

Main idea: ___G___

10. The voice can be used to produce a wide range of nonverbal behaviors such as sounds that are not words, laughter, pauses, silence, breathing patterns, and voice qualities. Laughter is an almost universal sign of happiness and good feelings. Pauses during a conversation can convey a variety of meanings, including confusion, concentration, thoughtful reflection, anger, nervousness, or suspense. The way you breathe often reflects your emotional state. Breathing quickly and loudly might signal arousal, physical exertion, or anxiety, whereas breathing slowly might communicate that one is relaxed or tired.

(Bethami A. Dobkin and Roger C. Pace, *Communication in a Changing World*, 2006)

Main idea: ___D___

Main Ideas

A. Objects and possessions can be forms of nonverbal communication.

B. Culture affects the treatment of space.

C. Reasons for wearing a veil (hijab) when out in public vary among Muslim women.

D. The voice itself can be used to communicate nonverbally.

E. How people dress affects how others respond to them.

F. Sometimes people deliberately use nonverbal cues to send specific messages.

G. Humans mark and defend their territory by communicating with objects or signs.

H. Culture plays a big role in determining what smells people consider pleasant and what smells they find repugnant.

I. Countries around the world have different gestures for friendly greetings.

J. Colors can have varying meanings in different cultures.

Exercise 5: Identifying Topics and Main Ideas

Directions: Now locate the topic of each paragraph and the main idea sentence. The main idea can be identified by asking, "What key point does the author want me to know about the topic?"

1. Physical motions and gestures provide signals. The "preening behavior" that accompanies courtship is a good illustration. Women frequently stroke their hair, check their makeup, rearrange their clothes, or push the hair away from the face. Men may adjust their hair, tug at their tie, straighten their clothes, or pull up their socks. These are signals that say, "I'm interested in you. Notice me. I'm an attractive person."

Topic: signals

Main idea: Physical motions and gestures provide signals.

2. Students who sit in the front rows of a classroom tend to be the most interested, those in the rear are more prone to mischievous activities, and students on the aisles are primarily concerned with quick departures. As you can see, the way we employ social and personal space also contains messages.

Topic: space—social and personal

Main idea: The way we employ social and personal space also contains messages.

3. Through physical contact such as touch, we convey our feelings to one another. However, touch can also constitute an invasion of privacy, and it can become a symbol of power when people want to make power differences visible. For example, a high-status person might take the liberty of patting a

low-status person on the back or shoulder, something that is deemed inappropriate for the subordinate.

Topic: _touch_

Main idea: _Through physical contact such as touch, we convey our feelings to one_
another.

(James W. Vander Zanden, *Sociology,* 4/e, 1996)

4. Gestures that mean approval in the United States may have different meanings in other countries. The "thumbs up" sign, which means "good work" or "go ahead" in the United States and most of western Europe, is a vulgar insult in Greece. The circle formed with the thumb and first finger that means OK in the United States is obscene in southern Italy and can mean you're worth nothing in France and Belgium. And in Japan the circle gesture is associated with money.

(Kitty O. Locker and Donna S. Kienzler, *Business and Administrative Communication,* 8/e, 2008)

Topic: _gestures of approval_

Main idea: _Gestures that mean approval in the United States may have different_
meanings in other countries.

5. Even the gestures for such basic messages as "yes" and "no," "hello" and "good-bye" are culturally based. In the United States people nod their heads up and down to signal "yes" and shake them back and forth to signal "no." In Thailand the same actions have exactly the opposite meaning! To take another example, the North American "good-bye" wave is interpreted in many parts of Europe and South America as the motion for "no," while the Italian and Greek gestures for "good-bye" is the same as the U.S. signal for "come here."

(Stephen E. Lucas, *The Art of Public Speaking,* 9/e, 2007)

Topic: _gestures for basic messages_

Main idea: _Even the gestures for such basic messages as "yes" and "no," "hello"_
and "good-bye" are culturally based.

Varying Positions for Main Ideas

In previous exercises, we saw that the main idea in a paragraph is frequently located at either the beginning or the end of the paragraph. However, the main idea also may appear in other locations within a paragraph, such as in the middle, or at both the beginning and the end. Wherever the main idea is located, it must be supported by details. Most authors provide examples, illustrations, major points, reasons, or facts and statistics to develop their main idea. While a main idea can be either directly stated somewhere in the paragraph or implied, supporting details are always directly stated. The ability to recognize supporting details is of crucial importance in the reading process. Locating supporting details will tell you whether you have correctly identified the main idea.

Paragraph Diagrams

For those of you who are visual learners, graphic organizers may be helpful. The following diagrams, a type of graphic organizer, show the development of a paragraph by indicating the position of the main idea and supporting details. The topic of each of the following paragraphs is the healing power of laughter.

(Brent Q. Hafen et al., *Mind/Body Health*, 1996)

Directions: After reading the explanation for each type of paragraph, write several key supporting details on the line provided.

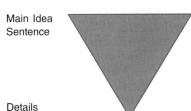

1. <u>Laughter as medicine is probably as old as humankind.</u> One of the earliest written accounts recognizing the healing power of humor is found in the Bible, in which King Solomon remarked that a "merry heart doeth good like medicine" (Proverbs 17:22). Sixteenth-century educator Richard Mulcater prescribed laughter for those afflicted with head colds and melancholy; a favorite "cure" was being tickled in the armpits. The famous seventeenth-century physician Thomas Sydenham said that "the arrival of a good clown exercises more beneficial influence upon the health of a town than twenty donkeys laden with drugs."

Main Idea Sentence

Details

In paragraph 1, the main idea is stated in the first sentence. The supporting details are a series of examples illustrating the main idea. A diagram of this type of paragraph would be a triangle with the point aiming downward. The main idea is represented by the horizontal line at the top.

Supporting detail: The healing power of humor is found in the Bible.

Supporting detail: Sixteenth-century educator Mulcater prescribed laughter for colds and melancholy.

2. Some researchers have found that a humorous outlook on life can have far-reaching benefits such as enhancing self-esteem and promoting creativity. Others suggest that humor improves negotiating and decision-making skills. Still others have found that a healthy sense of humor helps maintain a balanced outlook, improves performance, and bestows a feeling of power. At the very least, humor helps to relieve stress and improves coping abilities. <u>As you can see, a sense of humor has tremendous psychological benefits.</u>

Details

Main Idea Sentence

In paragraph 2, the author gives examples at the beginning and uses the main point to draw a conclusion. A diagram for this type of paragraph places the main idea at the bottom of the triangle.

Supporting detail: Researchers have found humor enhances self-esteem.

Supporting detail: Humor improves decision-making skills.

Details

Main Idea Sentence

Details

3. Laughter requires no special training. It requires no special equipment. You don't have to do it at the gym or on the track or on a Nautilus machine. <u>Laughter is one of the best exercises around.</u> It improves your digestion, stimulates your central nervous system, improves and tones the cardiovascular system, thereby providing what some experts have called "a total inner body workout."

In paragraph 3, the author begins with reasons explaining why laughter is one of the best exercises, states the main idea, and then concludes with additional reasons. Because the main idea is in the middle, the diagram resembles a diamond.

Supporting detail: Laughter requires no special training or equipment.

Supporting detail: Laughter improves digestion.

Main Idea
Sentence

Details

Main Idea
Sentence

4. <u>A sense of humor can give us a sense of power.</u> Anatoly Sharansky, the Russian human rights advocate, was confined for nine years in Soviet prisons. The Soviet police constantly threatened Sharansky with the *rastrel* (firing squad). Sharansky started to win the war against fear with humor. He started joking about the firing squad and talking about it on a daily basis. "You make jokes fifteen to twenty times," Sharansky remembers, "and the word becomes like any other word." <u>Humor can turn any situation around and give us a feeling of power over our circumstances.</u>

   In paragraph 4, the author begins with the main idea, provides a detailed illustration of it, and concludes with a restatement of the main idea. A diagram of this type of paragraph would have an hour-glass shape.

   Supporting detail: <u>Sharansky is threatened with the rastrel.</u>

   Supporting detail: <u>Sharansky tells jokes about it.</u>

5. In a study by University of Maryland psychologist Alice Isen, she split volunteers into two groups. One either watched a math film or did a monotonous exercise; the other group watched a clip of funny television "bloopers" or received candy.

   In paragraph 5, the main idea is not stated in any specific sentence. Instead, all of the sentences are working together to create a word picture in your mind of an experiment in progress. Because no one sentence is clearly the main idea, a diagram of this paragraph might resemble a square or a rectangle.

Exercise 6: Main Ideas, Diagrams, and Details

Directions: For additional practice, identify the main idea in each paragraph below. Then draw a diagram of the paragraph and list the supporting details.

1. Humor has been used across the span of cultures to make people feel better. A number of American Indian tribes—the Zunis, Crees, Pueblos, and Hopis among them—had ceremonial clowns whose sole purpose was to provide humor for their tribesmen. According to accounts, they were called in "to entertain and heal the sick with hilarity, frightening away the demons of ill health."

   It takes 17 muscles to smile, 43 muscles to frown.

   Diagram: ▼ _____

   Main idea: <u>Humor has been used across the span of cultures to make people feel</u>
   <u>better.</u>

   Supporting detail: <u>Many tribes had ceremonial clowns who healed the sick with</u>
   <u>humor.</u>

2. A sense of humor can actually promote good health by strengthening the immune system. Researchers subjected volunteers to a set of "hassles," situations known to invoke stress. The researchers found that people with a low sense of humor reacted strongly to the hassles causing a significant drop in their ability to withstand disease. Those who rated high on the humor scale demonstrated a strengthened immune function, even when subjected to hassles and stressors. It appears that people who tend to have a humorous outlook have greater immunity against a variety of diseases as well as increased ability to fight off infection.

   Diagram: �X _____

   Main idea: <u>(first and last sentences)</u>

Supporting details: <u>Researchers subjected volunteers to hassles; those high on the</u>

<u>humor scale had a stronger immune system.</u>

3. There are strong gender differences in laughter. Research shows that while both sexes laugh a lot, females laugh more. In male–female conversations, females laugh 126 percent more than their male counterparts. But across cultures, from early childhood on, men seem to be the main instigators of humor. Think back to your high school class clown—most likely he was a male. And so women tend to do the most laughing while males tend to do the most laugh-getting. The gender pattern of everyday laughter also suggests why there are more male than female comedians.

(Brent Q. Hafen et al., *Mind/Body Health*, 1996)

Diagram: ▼

Main idea: <u>There are strong gender differences in laughter.</u>

Supporting details: <u>Females laughed 126 percent more than males. High school</u>

<u>class clowns are usually male.</u>

4. Humor can be used inappropriately and actually cause distress. Anyone who has seen the hurt and puzzled expression on another's face in response to an ironic remark, or remembers how she or he may have felt as an object of a joke, has witnessed humor's power to cause distress. Because humor's effects are not always predictable, experts recommend that humor be used carefully when helping someone else with stress so as not to make the situation worse. However, once consideration is given to the potential negative effects of humor and they are judged to be minimal, don't hesitate to use this approach when you think it would be helpful.

(Jerrold S. Greenberg, *Comprehensive Stress Management*, 8/e, 2004)

Diagram: ▼

Main idea: <u>Humor can be used inappropriately and actually cause distress.</u>

Supporting detail: <u>hurt or puzzlement in response to an ironic remark</u>

"He deserves paradise who makes his companions laugh."

—The Koran

5. Pain reduction is one of laughter's promising benefits. Rosemary Cogan, a professor of psychology at Texas Tech University, found that subjects who laughed at a Lily Tomlin video or underwent a relaxation procedure tolerated more discomfort than other subjects. James Rotton, a professor at Florida International University, reported that orthopedic surgery patients who watched comedy videos requested fewer aspirin and tranquilizers than the group that viewed dramas. It appears that humor may help alleviate intense pain.

(Robert Provine, "The Science of Laughter," 2000)

Diagram: ▲

Main idea: <u>(first and last sentences)</u>

Supporting details: <u>Watching a Lily Tomlin video reduced discomfort; fewer</u>

<u>pain-relief medications were requested by those who watched</u>

<u>comedy videos.</u>

Exercise 7: Locating the Main Idea

Directions: The main idea sentence appears at different locations in the following paragraphs. Write the letter of the main idea sentence on the line. Then draw a diagram of the paragraph and list the supporting details.

1. (a) American males may feel uncomfortable when Middle Eastern heads of state greet the U.S. president with a kiss on the cheek. (b) A German student, accustomed to speaking rarely to "Herr Professor," considers it strange that at American colleges most faculty office doors are open and students stop by freely. (c) An Iranian student on her first visit to an American McDonald's restaurant fumbles around in her paper bag looking for the eating utensils until she sees the other customers eating their French fries with, of all things, their hands. (d) In many areas of the globe, your best manners and my best manners may be exceedingly offensive to people of different nationalities and may cause us to make a serious breach of etiquette. (e) Foreigners visiting Japan often struggle to master the rules of the social game—when to take their shoes off, how to pour the tea, when to give and open gifts, how to act toward someone higher or lower in the social hierarchy.

   Main idea sentence: <u>d</u>   Diagram: ◆_____

   Supporting details: <u>Middle Eastern heads of state greet president with kiss;</u>

   <u>foreigners visiting Japan struggle with social etiquette.</u>

2. (a) Cultures also vary in their norms for personal expressiveness and time. (b) To someone from a relatively formal northern European culture, a person whose roots are in an expressive Mediterranean culture may seem "warm, charming, inefficient, and time-wasting." (c) To the Mediterranean person, the northern European may seem "efficient, cold, and over concerned with time." (d) Latin American business executives who arrive late for a dinner engagement may be mystified by how obsessed their American counterparts are with punctuality.

   Main idea sentence: <u>a</u>   Diagram: ▼_____

   Supporting details: <u>time-wasters, Latin American executives</u>

3. (a) Adults maintain more distance from each other than children. (b) Men keep more distance from one another than do women. (c) Cultures near the equator prefer less space and more touching and hugging. (d) Thus the British and Scandinavians prefer more distance than the French and Arabs; North Americans prefer more space than Latin Americans. (e) As you can see, individuals and groups differ in their need for personal space.

   (David G. Myers, *Social Psychology*, 9/e, 2008)

   Main idea sentence: <u>e</u>   Diagram: ▲_____

   Supporting detail: <u>Cultures near equator prefer less space.</u>

4. (a) Once in Mexico I raised my hand to a certain height to indicate how tall a child was. (b) My hosts began to laugh. (c) It turned out that Mexicans have a more complicated system of hand gestures to indicate height: one for people, a second for animals, and a third for plants. (d) What had amused them was that I had ignorantly used the plant gesture to indicate the child's height.

   Main idea sentence: <u>c</u>   Diagram: ◆_____

   Supporting detail: <u>use of plant gesture to indicate child's height</u>

5. (a) To get along in another culture, then, it is important to learn the gestures of that culture. (b) If you don't, you will not only fail to achieve the simplicity of communication that gestures allow but you will also miss much of what is happening, run the risk of appearing foolish, and possibly offend people. (c) In some cultures, for example, you would provoke deep offense if you were to offer food or a gift with your left hand, because the left hand is reserved for dirty tasks, such as wiping after going to the bathroom.

(James M. Henslin, *Essentials of Sociology*, 7/e, 2007)

Main idea sentence: <u>a   </u>   Diagram: ▼<u>   </u>

Supporting details: <u>look foolish, offend people   </u>

6. (a) When Big Boy opened a restaurant in Bangkok, it quickly became popular with European and American tourists, but the local Thais refused to eat there. (b) Instead they placed gifts of rice and incense at the feet of the Big Boy statue (a chubby boy holding a hamburger) because it reminded them of Buddha. (c) In Japan, customers were forced to tiptoe around a logo painted on the floor at the entrance to an Athlete's Foot store because in Japan, it is considered taboo to step on a crest. (d) And, in Brazil, a donut shop failed because consumers felt the hole meant they were being cheated or shortchanged. (e) As these examples illustrate, many businesspeople engaged in international trade underestimate the importance of social and cultural differences.

(O. C. Ferrell, Geoffrey Hirt, and Linda Ferrell, *Business*, 5/e, 2006)

Main idea sentence: <u>a   </u>   Diagram: ▲<u>   </u>

Supporting details: <u>Big Boy, Athlete's Foot logo, donut shop   </u>

7. (a) Coor's slogan "Turn it loose" was translated into Spanish where it was read as "Suffer from diarrhea." (b) Colgate introduced Cue toothpaste in France, only to discover that Cue is a French pornographic magazine. (c) Translated into Chinese, Pepsi's "Come alive with the Pepsi generation" became "Pepsi brings back your ancestors from the grave." (d) Clairol introduced the Mist Stick curling iron in Germany where "mist" is German slang for manure. (e) These examples underscore that firms that want to market a product globally and reach consumers of varying cultures need to become thoroughly acquainted with the language, customs, prejudices, and tastes of the intended market.

Main idea sentence: <u>e   </u>   Diagram: ▲<u>   </u>

Supporting details: <u>Coor's slogan, Cue toothpaste, Clairol Mist Stick   </u>

8. (a) Even numbers have different meanings in different countries. (b) Marketers should avoid using the number four when addressing Chinese, Korean, and Japanese consumers. (c) Although advertising that says "four times the savings" would probably appeal to American consumers, it would not appeal to an Asian audience because four is the number for death in Asian numerology.

Main idea sentence: <u>a   </u>   Diagram: ▼<u>   </u>

Supporting details: <u>Avoid using the number four with Chinese, Korean consumers.</u>

9. (a) Westerners consider direct eye contact important, but many cultures see it as a personal affront, conveying a lack of respect. (b) In Japan, for example, when shaking hands, bowing, and especially when talking, it is important to glance only occasionally into the other person's face. (c) One's gaze should instead focus on fingertips, desk tops, and carpets. (d) In the words of one

American electronics representative, "Always keep your shoes shined in Tokyo. (e) You can bet a lot of Japanese you meet will have their eyes on them."

(David H. Olson and John DeFrain, *Marriage and Families*, 5/e, 2006)

Main idea sentence: <u>a_____</u>   Diagram: ▼<u>_____</u>

Supporting details: <u>In Japan, one should focus on fingertips, desk tops, or carpets.</u>

10. (a) In New York City, the party invitation may say 9:00 P.M., but nobody would think of showing up before 9:30 P.M. (b) In Salt Lake City, guests are expected to show up on time, or perhaps even a bit early. (c) Consider your own experience. (d) In school, some instructors begin and end class punctually, while others are more casual. (e) With some people you feel comfortable talking for hours in person or on the phone, while with others time seems to be precious and not "wasted." (f) As you can see, even within a culture, rules of time vary.

(Ronald B. Adler, Russell F. Proctor II, and Neil Towne, *Looking Out, Looking In*, 11/e, 2005)

Main idea sentence: <u>f_____</u>   Diagram: ▲<u>_____</u>

Supporting details: <u>Some teachers begin and end class on time while others don't.</u>

Internet Activity

To discover more about nonverbal communication, visit the following Web site sponsored by the University of California at Santa Cruz:

http://nonverbal.ucsc.edu/

You can test your skill at "reading" samples of nonverbal communication in the areas of gestures and personal space. Write a short paragraph explaining what you learned.

Exercise 8: Locating Topics, Main Ideas, and Details

Directions: In the following passages from Kitty Locker's *Business and Administrative Communication,* locate the topic of each paragraph and the main idea sentence, and write them on the designated lines. One supporting detail has been omitted from each paragraph. Look at the supporting details list at the end of the exercise, match each one to its correct paragraph, and then enter the paragraph number on the line.

1. In the United States smiling varies from region to region. Thirty years ago, Ray Birdwhistell found that "middle-class individuals" from Ohio, Indiana, and Illinois smiled more than did people from Massachusetts, New Hampshire, and Maine, who in turn smiled more than did western New Yorkers. People from cities in southern and border states—Atlanta, Louisville, Memphis, and Nashville—smiled most of all. Students from other countries who come to U.S. universities may be disconcerted by the American tendency to smile at strangers—until they realize that the smiles don't "mean" anything.

    Topic: <u>smiling</u>

    Main idea: <u>In the United States smiling varies from region to region.</u>

2. Repeated studies have shown that older people are healthier both mentally and physically if they are touched. It is well-documented that babies need to be touched to grow and thrive. Touch, while necessary for optimum health, can communicate many messages. A person who dislikes touch may seem unfriendly to someone who's used to touching. A toucher may seem overly familiar to

someone who dislikes touch. Studies in the United States have shown that touch is interpreted as power: more powerful people touch less powerful people.

Topic: <u>touch</u>

Main idea: <u>Touch, while necessary for optimum health, can communicate many messages.</u>

3. People who don't know each other well may feel more comfortable with each other if a piece of furniture separates them. For example, a group may work better sitting around a table than just sitting in a circle. Lecterns and desks can be used as barricades to protect oneself from other people. One professor normally walked among his students as he lectured. But if anyone asked a question he was uncomfortable with, he retreated behind the lectern before answering it. Spatial arrangements mean different things within a culture and between cultures. In the United States, the size, placement, and privacy of one's office connotes status. Large corner offices have the highest status. An individual office with a door that closes connotes more status than a desk in a common area. Japanese firms, however, see private offices as "inappropriate and inefficient," reports Robert Christopher. Only the very highest executives and directors have private offices in the traditional Japanese company, and even they will also have desks in the common area.

Topic: <u>spatial arrangements</u>

Main idea: <u>Spatial arrangements mean different things within a culture and between cultures.</u>

4. People in many cultures want to establish a personal relationship before they decide whether to do business with each other. For example, to do business in Mexico, you need to develop a personal relationship. Tell me about you as a person. That's very important. Then I tell you about me, and we do this sometimes not just one time, but several times. Then I will trust you and I will value your qualities. Then I will like to work with you.

Topic: <u>personal relationships and business</u>

Main idea: <u>People in many cultures want to establish a personal relationship before they decide whether to do business.</u>

5. Many North Americans measure time in five-minute blocks. Someone who's five minutes late to an appointment or a job interview feels compelled to apologize. If the executive or interviewer is running half an hour late, the caller expects to be told about the likely delay upon arriving. Some people won't be able to wait that long and will need to reschedule their appointments. But in other cultures, 15 minutes or half an hour may be the smallest block of time. To someone who mentally measures time in 15-minute blocks, being 45 minutes late is no worse than being 15 minutes late to someone who is conscious of smaller units. Different cultures also have different lead times. In some countries, you need to schedule important meetings at least two weeks in advance. In other countries, not only are people not booked up so far in advance, but a date two weeks into the future may be forgotten. Various cultures mentally measure time differently.

Topic: <u>measuring time</u>

Main idea: <u>Various cultures mentally measure time differently.</u>

6. Symbols (clothing, colors, and age) carry nonverbal meanings that vary from culture to culture. In North America, certain styles and colors of clothing are

considered more "professional" and more "credible." In Japan, clothing denotes not only status but also occupational group. Students wear uniforms. Workers wear different clothes when they are on strike than they do when they are working. In the United States, youth is valued. Some men as well as some women color their hair and even have face-lifts to look as youthful as possible. In Japan, younger people defer to older people. Americans attempting to negotiate in Japan are usually taken more seriously if at least one member of the team is noticeably gray-haired.

Topic: <u>symbols</u>

Main idea: <u>Symbols (clothing, colors, age) carry nonverbal meanings that vary from culture to culture.</u>

7. Height connotes status in many parts of the world. Executive offices are usually on the top floors; the underlings work below. Even being tall can help a person succeed. Studies have shown that employers are more willing to hire men over 6 feet tall than shorter men with the same credentials. In one study, every extra inch of height brought in an extra $1,300 a year.

Topic: <u>height</u>

Main idea: <u>Height connotes status in many parts of the world.</u>

8. Differences in eye contact can lead to miscommunication in the multicultural workplace. For example, North American whites see eye contact as a sign of honesty. But in many cultures, dropped eyes are a sign of appropriate deference to a superior. Puerto Rican children are taught not to meet the eyes of adults, and in Korea, prolonged eye contact is considered rude. The lower-ranking person is expected to look down first. Arab men in laboratory experiments looked at each other more than did two American men or two Englishmen. Eye contact is so important that Arabs dislike talking to someone wearing dark glasses or while walking side by side. It is considered impolite not to face someone directly. In Muslim countries, women and men are not supposed to make eye contact.

(Kitty O. Locker and Donna S. Kienzler, *Business and Administrative Communication*, 8/e, 2008)

Topic: <u>eye contact</u>

Main idea: <u>Differences in eye contact can lead to miscommunication in the multicultural workplace.</u>

Supporting Details

(See directions on page 94.)

___5___ In Arab countries, appointments are scheduled only three or four days in advance.

___3___ In North America, a person sitting at the head of a table is generally assumed to be the group's leader.

___4___ North Americans who believe that "time is money" are often frustrated in negotiations with people who place more emphasis on personal relationships.

___6___ Company badges indicate rank within the organization.

___8___ Superiors may feel that subordinates are being disrespectful when they look down, but the subordinate is being fully respectful—according to the norms of his or her culture.

___2___ When the toucher had higher status than the recipient, both men and women liked being touched.

___1___ Some scholars speculate that northerners may distrust the sincerity of southerners who smile a lot (like former President Jimmy Carter).

___7___ Studies of real-world executives and graduates have shown that taller men make more money.

Review Test 1: Topics, Main Ideas, and Details

Directions: Each of the following groups contains a series of related statements: One of the statements gives a topic, another gives a main idea, and the rest give supporting details. Identify the role of each statement in the space provided using the following abbreviations: **T** for Topic, **MI** for Main Idea, and **SD** for Supporting Detail.

Group 1

___SD___ a. A four-leaf clover means good luck.

___SD___ b. Red roses convey passionate love.

___T___ c. The symbolic meaning of plants.

___MI___ d. Even today, several plants have symbolic meanings.

___SD___ e. An olive branch indicates peace.

Group 2

___SD___ a. Red indicates passion.

___SD___ b. White indicates sympathy.

___T___ c. The meaning of floral colors.

___MI___ d. Floral colors also can communicate feelings.

___SD___ e. The color orange signifies friendship.

Group 3

___SD___ a. In the 1870s, an ardent suitor might have sent his beloved a bouquet of flowers that expressed a complete message.

___MI___ b. The symbolism of flowers reached its peak during the Victorian era, when almost every flower and plant had a special meaning.

___SD___ c. A bouquet of forget-me-nots conveyed the sentiment "remember me."

___SD___ d. A bouquet of jonquils, white roses, and ferns indicated that a suitor desired a return of affection, was worthy of his intended's love, and was fascinated by her.

___T___ e. The "language" of flowers.

Group 4

___SD___ a. In 1875, in Switzerland, Daniel Peter and Henri Nestle created milk chocolate by adding condensed milk to chocolate liquor.

___SD___ b. In the 1890s, the first candy bar was created by adding nuts, fruits, caramels, and other ingredients to the chocolate liquor.

___T___ c. For the love of chocolate.

___MI___ d. There have been many changes in chocolate candy since it was created in 1847.

___SD___ e. Milton Hershey modified the Peter process by adding whole milk.

Group 5

___T___ a. Food of the gods.

___SD___ b. According to Aztec mythology, the god Quetzalcoatl gave cacao beans to the Aztec people.

___SD___ c. The beans were later offered as gifts to the gods.

___MI___ d. The cacao tree, the source of chocolate, has long been cultivated by native peoples of Central and South America for religious purposes.

___SD___ e. The beans also were used to make a beverage consumed by priests on ceremonial occasions.

Group 6

___MI___ a. Originally chocolate candy bars were promoted as health foods.

___T___ b. A high energy treat.

___SD___ c. In World War I, candy bars were given to the soldiers as a source of quick energy.

___SD___ d. In the 1920s, many candy bars claimed to aid the digestion and had names like Vegetable Sandwich.

(Estelle Levetin and Karen McMahon, *Plants and Society*, 5/e, 2008)

Review Test 2: Topics, Main Ideas, and Details

Directions: The following group contains a series of related statements: One of the statements gives a topic, another gives a main idea, and four give supporting details. Identify the role of each statement in the space provided using the following abbreviations: **T** for Topic, **MI** for Main Idea, and **SD** for Supporting Detail.

Group 1

___SD___ a. Between 9 and 12 months of age, for example, Maika pointed to things to show that she wanted an object, nodded her head to mean *yes*, and shook her head to mean *no*.

___MI___ b. Babies develop a rich repertoire of nonverbal gestures before saying their first words.

___SD___ c. At 13 months, she was using representational gestures such as holding up her arms to show that she wanted to be picked up, or holding an empty cup to her mouth to show that she wanted a drink.

___T___ d. Symbolic gestures of babies.

(Diane E. Papalia, Sally Wendkos Olds, and Ruth Duskin Feldman, *Human Development*, 10/e, 2007)

Group 2

___T___ a. Demonstration of affection.

___SD___ b. For example, middle-class Brazilians teach their male and female children to kiss every adult relative they ever see.

___SD___ c. While females continue kissing throughout their lives, Brazilian men greet each other with a hearty handshake and a traditional male hug.

___MI___ d. Brazilians do not fear demonstrations of physical contact and affection.

(Conrad Phillip Kottak, Anthropology, 12/e, 2008)

Group 3

___SD___ a. In a suit brought by New Jersey importer, John Nix, tomatoes were legally declared vegetables in 1893 by the U.S. Supreme Court.

___SD___ b. The Spanish conquistadors introduced the tomato to Europe, where it was first known as the "Apple of Peru."

___T___ c. What is a fruit?

___SD___ d. Later it was known as *pomo doro,* golden apple in Italy, and *pomme d'amour,* love apple (it was believed by many to be an aphrodisiac) in France.

___MI___ e. Tomatoes, one of the most common, popular, and versatile "vegetables," is technically a fruit.

___SD___ f. Justice Horace Gray said that although tomatoes are considered to be the fruits of the vine, they are usually served at dinner, and not, like fruits, generally as dessert.

(Estelle Levetin and Karen McMahon, *Plants and Society,* 5/e, 2008)

Review Test 3: Topics, Main Ideas, and Details

Directions: The main idea sentence appears at different locations in the following paragraphs. Write the letter of the main idea sentence on the line. Then draw a diagram of the paragraph and list the supporting details by letter.

1. (a) Americans eat oysters but not snails. (b) The French eat snails but not locusts. (c) The Zulus eat locusts but not fish. (d) The Jews eat fish but not pork. (e) The Hindus eat pork but not beef. (f) The Russians eat beef but not snakes. (g) The Chinese eat snakes but not people. (h) The Jalé of New Guinea find people delicious. (i) The diversity of our customs and expressive behavior suggests that much of our behavior is socially programmed, not hardwired.

(David G. Myers, *Social Psychology,* 9/e, 2008)

Main idea sentence: ___i_____ Diagram: ▲_____

Supporting details: ___a–h_____

2. (a) Most North Americans value "fairness." (b) "You're not playing fair" is a sharp criticism calling for changed behavior. (c) In some countries, however, people expect certain groups to receive preferential treatment. (d) Most North Americans accept competition and believe that it produces better performance. (e) The Japanese, however, believe that competition leads to disharmony. (f) U.S. business people believe that success is based on individual achievement and is open to anyone who excels. (g) However, in England and in France, success is more obviously linked to social class. (h) Many people in the United States value individualism, but other countries may value the group. (i) In traditional classrooms, U.S. students are expected to complete assignments alone; if they get much help from anyone else, they're "cheating." (j) In Japan, in contrast, groups routinely work together to solve problems. (k) It appears that values and beliefs, often unconscious, affect our response to people and situations.

(Kitty O. Locker and Donna S. Kienzler, *Business and Administrative Communication*, 8/e, 2008)

Main idea sentence: k_____   Diagram: ▲_____

Supporting details: a–j_____

3. (a) The world's cultures have strikingly different notions about displays of affection and about matters of personal space. (b) "Don't touch me." (c) "Take your hands off me." (d) Such statements are not uncommon in North America, but they are virtually never heard in Brazil. (e) Brazilians like to be touched more than North Americans do. (f) When North Americans talk, walk, and dance, they maintain a certain distance from others—their personal space. (g) Brazilians, who maintain less physical distance, interpret this as a sign of coldness. (h) When conversing with a North American, the Brazilian moves in as the North American retreats. (i) Cocktail parties in international meeting places such as the United Nations can resemble an elaborate insect mating ritual as diplomats from different cultures advance, withdraw, and sidestep. (j) How people show affection and respect personal space varies greatly from culture to culture.

(Conrad Phillip Kottak, *Anthropology*, 13/e, 2009)

Main idea sentence: a, j_____   Diagram: ⧗_____

Supporting details: b–i_____

Paraphrasing

In this section, you will learn how to **paraphrase.** When you paraphrase something, you express the author's meaning in your own words. Often you will substitute synonyms for some words, but you may leave key words the same. The ability to paraphrase is important when you are trying to formulate an implied main idea.

Example: "The man who most vividly realizes a difficulty is the man most likely to overcome it." (Joseph Farrell)

Paraphrase: The man who clearly recognizes a problem is the one likely to solve it.

Exercise 9: Paraphrasing Quotations

Directions: Working in a group, paraphrase the following quotations. When you finish, check to make sure the meaning of both statements is the same.

1. Every man is the architect of his own fortune. (Anonymous)

   Each man determines his own future.

2. A life lived in fear is a life half-lived. (Spanish proverb)

   You are only half alive if you are living in fear.

3. "The crisis of yesterday is the joke of tomorrow." (H. G. Wells)

   The problems of yesterday seem funny today.

4. "I am a great believer in luck, and I find the harder I work, the more I have of it." (Thomas Jefferson)

   I believe in luck, but if I work hard I get more of it.

5. "Once you have been stung by a wasp, it is easier to tolerate a mosquito, and you can be downright friendly with a fly." (Ellen Marek)

   When you have been bitten by a wasp, it's easier to put up with a mosquito and you

   don't get upset at all with a fly.

6. "Victory finds a hundred fathers, but defeat is an orphan." (Count Galeazzo Ciano)

   Many will share in a victory, but no one wants to have anything to do with a defeat.

7. "The things which hurt, instruct." (Benjamin Franklin)

   We learn from our mistakes.

8. "Courage is resistance to fear, mastery of fear—not absence of fear." (Mark Twain)

   A courageous person recognizes and conquers fear, but doesn't pretend it doesn't exist.

A good way to begin learning how to paraphrase is to paraphrase nursery rhymes.

Exercise 10: Paraphrasing Rhymes

Directions: Working with a partner, paraphrase each of these nursery rhymes using your *own* words. Leave the key names, such as Humpty Dumpty, the same.

Example: There was an old woman who lived in a shoe,

   She had so many children she didn't know what to do;

   She gave them some broth without any bread;

   She whipped them all soundly and put them to bed.

An elderly woman, who was residing in a shoe, felt so overwhelmed by her large family that she fed all the children clear soup, spanked them, and sent them to bed.

1. Jack Sprat could eat no fat,

   His wife could eat no lean,

   And so betwixt them both, you see,

   They licked the platter clean.

2. Humpty Dumpty sat on a wall,
   Humpty Dumpty had a great fall.
   All the king's horses, and all the king's men,
   Couldn't put Humpty together again.

   _____

   _____

3. Tom, Tom, the piper's son,
   Stole a pig and away did run!
   The pig was eat, and Tom was beat,
   And Tom went howling down the street.

   _____

   _____

4. Three wise men of Gotham
   Went to sea in a bowl;
   If the bowl had been stronger
   My song had been longer.

   _____

   _____

5. Little Polly Finders
   Sat among the cinders,
   Warming her pretty little toes;
   Her mother came and caught her,
   And whipped her little daughter
   For spoiling her nice new clothes.

   _____

   _____

6. Jack and Jill
   Went up the hill,
   To fetch a pail of water;
   Jack fell down,
   And broke his crown,
   And Jill came tumbling after.

   _____

   _____

Exercise 11: Paraphrasing a Poem

Directions: Read the poem by Tran Thi Nga carefully, noting the key words and main ideas. Try to explain the meaning of the poem in your own words, and then write a paraphrase of it.

Grandmother's Fable

Once upon a time there lived a farming family.
The mother died, leaving three sons
to live with their father.

When the father became ill
and thought he was going to die, he called his children to his bedside
and handed each of them
a large bunch of chopsticks tied together.

He said, "Whoever can break this,
I will reward."
Not one was able to.

The father then handed each of them
only one set.
This they broke easily.

The father said, "If you remain united,
no one can harm you,
but if you separate, then you will be hurt.
This is the advice I leave with you.
The heritage I have for you
is in the rice fields."

After the father's death,
the three brothers stayed together
even after they married.
They did not find any golden treasures
buried in the rice fields.
They plowed and planted
and the ground gave successful harvests.
They realized working together
and working hard were life's riches.

Nga emigrated to the United States in 1975.

(Tran Thi Nga, "Grandmother's Fable")

Answers will vary. _____

_____

_____

_____

_____

Exercise 12: Paraphrasing a Fable

Directions: First, read the fable by Aesop below. Then answer the following questions. Finally, rewrite the fable in your own words.

A lion used to prowl about a field in which four oxen lived. Many a time he tried to attack them. But, whenever he came near, they turned their tails to one another, so that whichever way he approached them, he was met by the horns of one of them. At last, however, they fell to quarreling among themselves, and each went off to the pasture alone in a separate corner of the field. Then the lion attacked them one by one and soon put an end to all four.

1. How would you express the moral of this fable? _____
2. How is this fable similar to the previous fable? _____

3. In what ways are the advice of Tran Thi Nga and that of Aesop the same?

Answers will vary.

_____

_____

_____

_____

_____

Implied Main Ideas

Not all main ideas are directly stated. Sometimes you have to look closely at the details the author has provided in order to determine the main idea. Read the following paragraph from *The Art of Public Speaking* by Stephen Lucas and try to identify the implied main idea.

> 1.   It had been a long day at the office, and the going-home traffic was bumper to bumper. By the time Jason Whitehawk pulled his late-model car into the driveway at home, he was exhausted. As he trudged into the house, he routinely asked his wife, "How did things go with you at work today?"
>
> "Oh, pretty well," she replied, "except for the attack by space aliens in the morning and the outbreak of bubonic plague in the afternoon."
>
> Jason nodded his head as he made his way toward the sofa. "That's nice," he said. "At least someone had a good day. Mine was awful."
>
> (Stephen E. Lucas, *The Art of Public Speaking*, 7/e, 2001)

The topic of this paragraph is listening. The implied main idea is that sometimes without really listening, people give the appearance of being interested in what someone is saying.

In the next example, the topic could be parenting or child-rearing patterns. In order to formulate the main idea, we must mention the three categories of parents.

"Train a child in a way he should go, and when he is old, he will never depart from it."

—Proverbs 12:4

> 2.   Authoritarian parents are rigid and punitive and value unquestioning obedience from their children. They have strict standards and discourage expressions of disagreement. Permissive parents give their children lax or inconsistent direction and, although warm, require little of them. Authoritative parents are firm, setting limits for their children. As the children get older, these parents try to reason with and explain things to them. They also set clear goals and encourage their children's independence.
>
> (Robert S. Feldman, *Understanding Psychology*, 8/e, 2008)

From the details presented, we can conclude that each parent's child-rearing style is likely to have a different effect. Our implied main idea should be stated something like this:

Main idea: Three different parenting styles—authoritarian, permissive, and authoritative—shape children in different ways.

Determining an implied main idea is simply reducing all of the key information contained in the paragraph to one sentence.

It is sometimes helpful to first identify the topic and then ask *who, what, where, when, why,* and *how* about the topic.

Read the following paragraph and try to determine the main idea.

3.   In general, young males tend to be more aggressive than girls. They play more loudly; they roughhouse more and are more apt to try to dominate other children and challenge their parents. Boys argue and fight more often and are more apt to use force or threats of force to get their way, while girls try to solve conflicts by persuasion rather than confrontation. Girls are more likely to cooperate with their parents and they tend to set up rules to avoid clashes. Girls are more likely to be empathic, that is, to identify with other people's feelings.

(Diane E. Papalia and Sally Wendkos Olds, *Human Development*, 6/e, 1995)

Who: boys and girls

What: display different personality characteristics

Where: in social settings

When: during interactions with others

Why: boys are more aggressive; girls are more cooperative and empathic

How: boys dominate, fight, threaten; girls persuade, cooperate, set up rules

The topic of this paragraph appears to be personality differences between boys and girls. If we look at all the key details, our main idea will look something like this:

Main idea: Young boys are more likely to display an aggressive personality, and young girls are more likely to display an empathic, cooperative personality.

The next paragraph provides an explanation for male behavior in interpersonal relationships.

4.   Boys' play illustrates why men tend to be on the lookout for signs they are being put down or told what to do. The chief commodity that is bartered in the boys' hierarchical world is status, and the way to achieve and maintain status is to give orders and get others to follow them. A boy in a low-status position finds himself being pushed around. So boys monitor their relations for subtle shifts in status by keeping track of who's giving orders and who's taking them.

(Deborah Tannen, *You Just Don't Understand*, 1990)

Who: boys/men

What: try to achieve and keep status

Where: in settings with others

When: in relationships

Why: to avoid being pushed around

How: by monitoring who's giving and taking orders

When we put together these key details, we arrive at a main idea that looks something like this:

Main idea: Boys and men are very concerned with status, with high status going to the person who gives orders and low status going to the person who must take orders.

Baby Blues

© Baby Blues Partnership. King Features Syndicate.

Now look closely at these examples illustrating the differences in the ways men and women communicate.

5.   Two male friends share lunch at a restaurant. In the next hour they talk about sports, cars, sports cars, the *Sports Illustrated* swimsuit edition, sports, cars, and golf. (Did I mention sports and cars?) Janis, who was at a nearby table, overheard the entire conversation. Here's her summary of what the men said to each other: "Absolutely nothing!"

(Dennis Coon, *Introduction to Psychology*, 8/e, 1998)

The topic or title of the paragraph could be male-to-male conversation. The main idea is implied because no one sentence is broad enough to include all the key details.

Main idea: In their casual conversations, men like to talk about such things as sports and cars.

In the next example, there is no sentence that unites the key details of both male and female friendships.

6.   In North American culture, most male friendships are activity-based. Men tend to do things together—a pattern that provides companionship without closeness. In general, men live their friendships "side by side." On the other hand, the friendships of women are more often based on shared feelings and confidences. If two female friends spent an afternoon together and did not reveal problems, private thoughts, and feelings to one another, they would assume that something was wrong. For women, friendship is a matter of talking about shared concerns and intimate matters. Women tend to live their friendships "face to face."

(Dennis Coon, *Introduction to Psychology*, 8/e, 1998)

Main idea: While male friendships are primarily based on shared activities with little emotional closeness, women base their friendships on shared confidences and intimacy.

In the next two examples, the topic and part of the main idea are already provided for you. Complete the rest of the main idea.

7.   Nearly 50 percent of the women surveyed said they called friends at least once a week just to talk, whereas less than half as many men did

so. In fact, forty percent of the men surveyed reported that they never called another man just to chat.

(Ronald B. Adler, Russell F. Proctor II, and Neil Towne, *Looking Out, Looking In,* 11/e, 2005)

Topic: chatting

Main idea: In contrast to men, women <u>call each other just to chat.</u>

8.   Women ask more questions in mixed-sex conversations than do men—nearly three times as many, according to one study. Other research has revealed that in mixed-gender conversations, men interrupt women far more than the other way around.

(Ronald B. Adler, Russell F. Proctor II, and Neil Towne, *Looking Out, Looking In,* 11/e, 2005)

Topic: mixed-gender conversations

Main idea: In mixed-gender conversations, women <u>are interrupted more and ask more questions than men.</u>

Exercise 13: Identifying the Topic and Formulating the Main Idea

Directions: Write the topic and the main idea of each paragraph.

1.   Women are more likely than men to use *tag questions*. A tag question is a short phrase that turns a statement into a question. For example, "That was a hard test, wasn't it?" instead of simply saying, "That was a hard test." One interpretation of this is that women's tendency to use tag questions reflects uncertainty. A tag question is seen as weakening the statement being made. Another interpretation, however, is that the tag question encourages the other person to express an opinion. This view says that rather than reflecting uncertainty, a woman's use of tag questions might reflect greater sensitivity and warmth.

(Curtis O. Byer, et al., *Dimensions of Human Sexuality,* 6/e, 2002)

Topic: <u>tag questions</u>

Main idea: <u>Women, who use tag questions more often than men, are reflecting either warmth and sensitivity or uncertainty.</u>

2.   Conversational differences between men and women begin early in childhood. Deborah Tannen summarizes a variety of studies showing that boys use talk to assert control over one another, while girls' conversations are aimed at maintaining harmony. Transcripts of conversations between preschoolers aged 2 to 5 showed that girls are far more cooperative than boys. They preceded their proposals for action by saying "let's," as in "Let's go find some," or "Let's turn back." By contrast, boys gave orders like "Lie down," or "Gimme your arm."

(Ronald B. Adler, Russell F. Proctor II, and Neil Towne, *Looking Out, Looking In,* 11/e, 2005)

Topic: <u>conversational differences</u>

Main idea: <u>Conversational differences between men and women begin in childhood with girls using talk to create harmony and boys using talk to assert control.</u>

3.   According to communication researchers, women converse in e-mail messages in a manner similar to the way they speak. Their language in the

electronic medium is lavish, intimate, and intended to connect with people and build rapport. Men's e-mail messages also reflect the way they speak. Their style is brief, precise, and functional.

(Joyce Cohen, "He-Mails, She-Mails," 2001)

Topic: <u>e-mail messages</u>

Main idea: <u>Men and women converse in e-mail messages similar to the way they</u>

<u>speak.</u>

4. When it comes to public e-mail, researchers have noted that in online groups, men tend to make strong assertions, disagree with others, and use profanity, insults, and sarcasm. In contrast, women tend to ask questions, offer suggestions, and use polite expressions. They are supportive and agreeable, peppering their messages with more emoticons, such as "smiley faces," and representations of laughter like "haha," "heehee," and "lol," for "laughing out loud." Men come online to give information or give an answer, while women encourage others to engage.

(Joyce Cohen, "He-Mails, She-Mails," 2001)

Topic: <u>online groups</u>

Main idea: <u>In online groups, men tend to assert their viewpoints while women are</u>

<u>supportive and agreeable.</u>

Exercise 14: Writing General or Main Idea Sentences

Directions: Two specific detail sentences are given to you. Working in a group, try to write a main idea sentence that will cover both of the details.

Example: Dying today has become more lonely and impersonal.

   a. Today people are more likely to die in a hospital hooked up to a machine.

   b. At the time of death, people are often surrounded by strangers, such as hospital personnel, instead of loved ones.

1. <u>A nap may have many positive effects.</u>

   a. Research shows that a 15-minute nap can improve concentration.

   b. Truck drivers who pull over to the side of the road whenever they feel sleepy are less likely to have an accident on long-haul trips.

2. <u>Air bags may not be quite as beneficial as previously supposed.</u>

   a. Air bags have been responsible for the deaths of 31 young children.

   b. Air bags deploy with a 200-pound force, sometimes injuring children and small adults in minor fender-bender accidents.

3. <u>Lying appears to be a widespread habit.</u>

   a. A local minister was caught telling a lie to a member of his church.

   b. Kids as young as two years of age routinely lie to avoid punishment.

4. <u>Americans are leading unhealthy lives.</u>

   a. Americans exercise very little and watch too much TV.

   b. Americans eat far too many foods classified by nutritionists as "junk."

5. <u>Owning a pet can be good for your health.</u>

    a. Pet owners enjoy better health and have fewer visits to the doctor.

    b. Pet owners recover more quickly from surgery.

6. <u>Divorce may affect many boys adversely.</u>

    a. After a divorce, boys are more likely to be low achievers in school.

    b. After a divorce, many boys suffer from a poor self-image.

7. <u>Brushing with toothpaste may not be as healthful as many think.</u>

    a. Toothpaste contains unappetizing ingredients like chalk, detergent, seaweed, and formaldehyde.

    b. Toothpaste can actually create cavities.

8. <u>Perhaps it's time to begin compensating student-athletes.</u>

    a. College athletes spend enormous amounts of time and energy on their sport.

    b. Although individual athletic departments generate large sums from team sports, the individual student-athlete receives no compensation.

Exercise 15: Aunt Caroline—Determining the Implied Main Idea

Directions: Aunt Caroline is a fictional advice columnist who tries to help people solve personal problems. Read each paragraph below and then write the main idea. Because the main idea is not stated directly in just one sentence, you must identify the key details and unite them to form the main idea. The first one is done for you as an example.

Dear Aunt Caroline,

    Do you think my boyfriend really loves me? He gives me a present every Saturday. However, he always asks me to return the one he gave me the week before.

    Main idea: <u>My boyfriend gives me gifts but asks me to return the old ones.</u>

1. Last Saturday, my boyfriend was really furious with me for using up half a bottle of perfume in a week. I told him that I had spilled some on my floor. He took the perfume from me anyway.

    Main idea: <u>Even though I had spilled my perfume, my boyfriend angrily took it away from me.</u>

2. Yesterday, on my way to work, I eavesdropped on the conversation of the woman sitting behind me on the subway. She told her friend that her boyfriend had given her a half-empty bottle of perfume last Sunday. She told her friend that her boyfriend gives her a new gift every Sunday.

    Main idea: <u>I discovered that a woman had received a half-empty bottle of perfume from her boyfriend and that she gets a new gift every Sunday.</u>

3. I became very curious. So, before I could stop myself, I turned around and asked her if he makes her return the gifts to him the next week. She indignantly replied, "Of course not!"

    Main idea: <u>I discovered that she does not have to return her gifts to him.</u>

4. Then I asked her if he had given her a half-eaten box of candy the week before, and she replied, "How on earth did you know?" I didn't tell her, but I'm positive my boyfriend is giving my used gifts to her.

Main idea: I know that she is receiving my used gifts because the week before, she received a half-eaten box of candy.

5. What do you think, Aunt Caroline? Who does a man usually love more, the woman he gives a fresh gift to, but takes it away from, or the woman he lets keep the used gift? And how can I get my boyfriend to love only me?

Half-loved Helen

Main idea: I want to know who he loves the most and how I can get him to love just me.

(*Finding the Main Idea,* 1982)

Written Assignment

What advice would you give "Half-loved Helen"? Write a short paragraph providing Helen with an answer to her dilemma.

Exercise 16: Urban Legends—Determining the Implied Main Idea

Most of you are familiar with urban legends, those bizarre stories that are just too good to be true. Maybe you've heard the one about the man who unsuspectingly eats a fried rat at a local fast food restaurant. Or the one about the mice in Coca-Cola bottles. Or how about the one about the babysitter who receives a threatening phone call that turns out to be coming from inside the house where she's sitting. All of these stories have one thing in common: They happened to a friend of a friend's next-door neighbor's brother-in-law. Although these tales are widely believed, easily spread by word of mouth, and ever present on talk radio and the Internet, most require you to suspend all logic and just go along. And most of us are willing to suspend disbelief because the world is, after all, a scary place. The tales, many with a strong cautionary note, exploit our fears that danger lurks everywhere—even in our own homes. Like folktales, urban legends often impart real lessons by serving as warnings. The tales that follow were adapted from material by University of Utah folklorist Jan Harold Brunvand, the nation's leading expert on urban legends.

Directions: After reading each urban legend, write the lesson or moral. Then write the implied main idea. Answers will vary.

1. OLD VS. YOUNG

An older woman drives her Mercedes into a crowded parking lot. After searching in vain for a parking space she spies another car getting ready to leave, so she pulls up nearby and waits. But just as the other car pulls out a shiny blue sports car zips into the space. The young driver smiles as he gets out and shouts, "You've got to be young and fast!" The woman thinks about this a moment, then rams the sports car. She backs up and rams it again and again. The young man comes running in horror. "What are you doing?" he shouts. The woman smiles and says, "You've got to be old and rich." Then she drives away.

(Jan Harold Brunvand, *The Mexican Pet,* 1986)

Example:

Moral: It's always wise to be considerate of others.

Implied main idea: When a young man steals the parking spot of a wealthy older

woman, she retaliates by damaging his car.

2. THE KILLER IN THE BACK SEAT

Phoenix (UPI)—As the woman walked to her car in a parking lot, she noticed a man following her. She jumped in her car and tore off, only to notice to her dismay that the man was following her in his car. The woman drove through downtown Phoenix trying to elude him, passing stores, houses, and bars. When that failed, she drove across town to the home of her brother-in-law, a policeman. Horn honking, she pulled up and her brother-in-law came running out. She explained that a man was following her and "There he is, right there!" The policeman ran up to the man's car and demanded to know what he was doing. "Take it easy. All I wanted to do was tell her about the guy in her back seat," the man said. And, indeed, there was a man huddled in the woman's back seat.

(Jan Harold Brunvand, *The Mexican Pet*, 1986)

Moral: It is a good idea to lock car doors and check the back seat.

Implied main idea: The man following the woman was trying to warn her about

the man hiding in her back seat.

3. THE SOLID CEMENT CADILLAC

It seems that a man was delivering a load of wet cement to an address near his own neighborhood when he decided to detour slightly and say hello to his wife. When he came in sight of his home, he saw a shiny new Cadillac in the driveway, and he parked the ready-mix truck and walked around the house to investigate. He heard voices coming from the kitchen, and when he looked in through the window there was his wife talking to a strange, well-dressed man. Without checking any further, and without alerting the couple inside, the truck driver lowered a window of the Cadillac, and emptied the entire load of cement inside it, filling the car completely. But when he got off work that evening and returned home, his tearful wife informed him that the new (now solid-cement car) was her birthday present to him, and that the stranger was the local Cadillac dealer who had just delivered the car and was arranging the papers on it with her.

(Jan Harold Brunvand, *The Vanishing Hitchhiker*, 1981)

Moral: Don't jump to conclusions.

Implied main idea: A man seeing a strange car in his driveway mistakenly destroys

his own birthday present because he assumes his wife is having

an affair.

4. THE FATAL CAN

A couple of men walking along a stream bank to do some fishing see a little boy sitting there with his fishing line in the water and a can of bait on the ground next to him. One of them asks the lad how the fish are biting, and he replies, "Well, the fish aren't biting so well, but the worms sure are." The men chuckle about this odd answer as they continue along their way, but coming back later in the day they notice the boy slumped down in the same place he had been sitting before. He is unconscious, and they see that his hands and forearms are full of bite marks. Checking the bait can, they discover that he has been using baby rattlesnakes for bait, thinking them to be worms. They rush him to the hospital in their car but arrive there too late to save his life.

(Jan Harold Brunvand, *The Mexican Pet*, 1986)

Moral: <u>Pay attention to what children are saying.</u>

Implied main idea: <u>A young boy is using baby rattlesnakes for fishing bait, and two</u>

<u>men who could have helped him fail to save his life.</u>

5. THE BUMP IN THE RUG

A carpet layer could not find his pack of cigarettes. He had just finished laying a customer's carpet when he reached for his pack of Winstons. They were gone. He then noticed a small mound under the carpet in the middle of the room. He concluded that his pack must have slipped out of his pocket. Rather than rip up his day's work, the carpet layer hammers the lump flat and walks out to his van. To his amazement, there on the dash, are his cigarettes. Confused, he re-enters the house only to have the lady of the house ask if he had seen her precious pet parakeet that minutes ago crawled out of its cage.

(Jan Harold Brunvand, *The Choking Doberman and Other "New" Urban Legends*, 1984)

Moral: <u>Don't be lazy and take the easy way out.</u>

Implied main idea: <u>A carpet layer, assuming the lump under the carpet to be missing</u>

<u>cigarettes, inadvertently kills a pet parakeet.</u>

6. THE HOOK

A couple was dating and they went out to a place by a lake and parked. They had their radio on and heard a flash warning about a dangerous man with a hook on his arm who had escaped from prison. They sat there for a while, but the girl started getting scared. She looked over and locked her door. Then he locked his door too. Finally, he said, "This is really ridiculous getting upset about it." And she said, "Well, you know, I'm kinda scared about this thing." So they sat there for a while, and she said, "Listen, let's go back into town." and he said, "No, let's not worry about it, don't worry about it." And she said, "Listen, I'm getting kinda scared. I don't like it here anymore. Let's go into town." And so he says, "OK." So he takes her back into town, and when they drive up to her house, he gets out and he goes over to her side of the car, and on the door was a hook.

(Jan Harold Brunvand, *The Vanishing Hitchhiker*, 1981)

Moral: <u>Be cautious in strange situations.</u>

Implied main idea: <u>A couple parked by the lake hear a warning on the radio about</u>

<u>a dangerous man with a hook, and at the girl's request they</u>

<u>leave, only to discover a hook on the car door.</u>

7. THE BABY ON THE ROOF

A young couple with their baby were driving through the desert of Utah. They stopped briefly at a rest area to switch drivers so that each one could take a turn at driving and neither one would get overtired. The husband, who was driving, stayed in his seat while the wife got out on the right, placed the baby, who was asleep in her car seat, on the roof, and walked around the car to slip behind the wheel. The husband, then, just slid over and pulled the right-hand door shut, and away they went. The baby stayed on the roof. After a few miles a state police cruiser flagged them down, and the baby was rescued, still sleeping peacefully in her little plastic seat.

(Jan Harold Brunvand, *The Choking Doberman and Other "New" Urban Legends*, 1984)

Moral: Check to make sure your children are safe.

Implied main idea: In the process of changing drivers, a young couple leave their
baby on the roof, but the mistake is discovered by a police
officer.

8. THE JOGGER'S WALLET

A jogger had been running along at his customary pace early one morning in Central Park. He was surrounded by streams of others out getting their pre-work exercise, when suddenly another jogger passed by him on the path and bumped him rather hard. Checking quickly, the jogger discovered that his wallet was missing from his pocket, and he thought, "This can't happen to me; I'm not going to let it happen." So he upped his speed a bit, caught up to the other jogger, and confronted him. "Give me that wallet," he snarled, trying to sound as menacing as possible, and hoping for the best. The other jogger quickly handed it over, and our hero turned back toward his apartment for a shower and a quick change of clothes. But when he got home, there was his own wallet on the dresser, and the one he had in his pocket belonged to someone else.

(Jan Harold Brunvand, *The Choking Doberman and Other "New" Urban Legends*, 1984)

Moral: Don't jump to conclusions.

Implied main idea: A jogger bumped by another jogger assumes the other jogger
has stolen his wallet, and so he takes that man's wallet only to
discover that his own wallet is at home.

Internet Activity

Not too long ago, an alarming e-mail message showed up on computers on selected college campuses:

> Students beware!!!! My neighbor's son's best friend went to a fraternity party and was offered a cup of red punch. He thought it had alcohol in it so he drank it slowly. After a couple of sips he began to feel woozy, and he passed out. When he woke up, he found he was sitting in a hotel room bathtub full of ice. A cellular phone was next to the tub. On the mirror there was a message scrawled in lipstick, "Do not move. Call 911 immediately or you will die." He called 911 and was instructed by the operator to reach behind him and see if there was a tube coming out of his lower back. He found the tube and answered yes. The 911 operator told him to lie still and that paramedics were on the way. When the paramedics arrived, they examined him and said that both of his kidneys had been removed, probably to be sold for medical use.

(Joseph R. Dominick, *The Dynamics of Mass Communication*, 6/e, 1999)

Pretty scary, huh? Except for one thing: It never happened. Thanks to the Internet, a whole new lineup of urban legends has been circulated to millions of computer owners, most of them complete with postscripts that proclaim, "This really happened" or "This is no joke."

Find an interesting urban legend and print it. Explain why you find it interesting. Then list the topic, main idea, and a few supporting details. Finally, note the lesson or moral. A good Web site for finding urban legends is

urbanlegends.about.com

Exercise 17: Gender and Communication— Identifying the Implied Main Idea

Directions: Each of the following paragraphs from Curtis Byer's *Dimensions of Human Sexuality* deals with the topic of men's and women's communication patterns. Write the implied main idea for each paragraph.

1. Comparing the sexes, Deborah Tannen states that men's conversations are negotiations in which they try to achieve and maintain the upper hand if they can, while protecting themselves from others' attempts to put them down and push them around. Tannen says that women's conversations, on the other hand, are negotiations for closeness in which people try to seek and give confirmation and support, and to reach consensus. Women try to protect themselves from others' attempts to push them away. Life is seen as a struggle to preserve intimacy and avoid isolation.

   Implied main idea: When conversing, men try to negotiate and protect themselves, while women try to gain support and reach consensus to avoid isolation.

2. Women tend to speak and hear a language of connection and intimacy. In contrast, men tend to speak and hear a language of status and independence. As a result, the stage is set for misunderstandings and misinterpretations. Not seeing style differences for what they are, people draw faulty conclusions about each other, such as "You don't listen," "You are putting me down," or "You don't care about me."

   Implied main idea: Women speak a language of connection and intimacy, while men speak a language of status and independence, causing miscommunication.

3. Most studies have shown that, while talking, men touch women slightly more often than women touch men. Whether touching relates to power and dominance issues, sexual interest, or expression of warmth, solidarity, or caring is not always clear. One study found that women reported less positive attitudes toward other-sex touch than did men. This study also reported that men initiated touch more in casual relationships but that women initiated touch more in married relationships.

   Implied main idea: The connection between gender and touching is not always clear, but it may depend on the strength of the couple's relationship.

4. One nonverbal communication difference between the sexes is in the area of smiling. For example, women tend to smile more than men. We can only speculate on why this is, but smiling appears to be a part of the stereotypical female role. People tend to expect women to smile. A woman's smile does not necessarily reflect happiness or friendliness and can even be associated

with fear or other negative feelings. Another nonverbal communication difference is that women tend to prefer to stand or sit closer to other people while men tend to prefer a greater distance.

Implied main idea: Nonverbal communication differs between the sexes in the areas of smiling and distance.

5. One last point involves gender bias rather than gender-based communication differences. As women in many organizations have long suspected, research has shown that women's ideas can be devalued in a mixed-gender decision-making group. An idea introduced by a man has a higher probability of acceptance and use than if it were introduced by a woman. Female-introduced ideas are likely to be evaluated more stringently. If women in mixed-gender groups want their ideas to be taken seriously, they must learn to speak with authority.

Implied main idea: In mixed groups, women's ideas are not taken as seriously as men's ideas; thus, women must learn to speak with authority.

(Curtis O. Byer, et al., *Dimensions of Human Sexuality*, 6/e, 2002)

Determining Your Gender Communication Quotient

How much do you know about how men and women communicate with one another? The items in this questionnaire are based on research conducted in classrooms, private homes, businesses, offices, hospitals—places where people commonly work and socialize. The answers appear at the end.

True or False

Directions: Indicate whether each statement is true or false by writing **T** or **F** in the space provided.

_T_ 1. Men talk more than women.

_T_ 2. Men are more likely to interrupt women than they are to interrupt other men.

_T_ 3. During conversations, women spend more time gazing at their partners than men do.

_T_ 4. Nonverbal messages carry more weight than verbal messages.

_F_ 5. Female managers communicate with more emotional openness and drama than male managers.

_F_ 6. Men not only control the content of conversations, they also work harder at keeping conversations going.

_F_ 7. Women are more likely to touch others than men are.

_T_ 8. In classroom communications, male students receive more reprimands and criticism than female students.

_T_ 9. Women are more likely than men to disclose information on intimate personal concerns.

_T_ 10. Female speakers are more animated in their conversational style than are male speakers.

_T_ 11. Women use less personal space than men.

_T_ 12. When a male speaks, he is listened to more carefully than a female speaker, even when she makes the identical presentation.

_T_ 13. In general, women speak in a more tentative style than do men.

_F_ 14. Women are more likely to answer questions that are not addressed to them.

_T_ 15. Female managers are seen by both male and female subordinates as better communicators than male managers.

_F_ 16. Teachers give more verbal praise to female students than to male students.

_F_ 17. In general, men smile more often than women.

_F_ 18. When people hear generic words such as "mankind" and "he" they respond inclusively, indicating that the terms apply to both sexes.

(Hazel Rozema and John Gray, "How Wide Is Your Communication Gender Gap?")

True answers: 1–4, 8–13, 15
False answers: 5–7, 14, 16–18

Frank and Ernest

Frank & Ernest used with the permission of the Thaves and The Cartoonist Group. All rights reserved.

The topic of many of the previous exercises has been communication, both verbal and nonverbal. Some of the exercises noted the differences between male and female styles of communication. After reading the following selection by humorist Dave Barry, list the key communication differences.

READING

"A group of psychology researchers have made the breakthrough discovery that—prepare to be astounded—males and females are different."

TUNING IN TO READING   A popular advice book by John Gray is titled *Men Are from Mars, Women Are from Venus.* Do you think men and women are so different that they might as well be from different planets? Think about your own personal experiences with this issue before reading the following article.

BIO-SKETCH   Dave Barry, the Pulitzer Prize–winning columnist, is also the author of numerous best-selling books including *Dave Barry's Complete Guide to Guys,* from which this excerpt is taken. The *New York Times* calls Barry the funniest man in America. His life was featured in the hit TV show *Dave's World.* He lives in Miami with his wife, a sportswriter for the *Miami Herald,* and his two children, who, according to Barry, do not think he is funny.

NOTES ON VOCABULARY

Hindenburg   an airship (dirigible) named after the president of Germany, Paul von Hindenburg. The airship was inflated with highly flammable hydrogen gas. On May 6, 1937, the Hindenburg caught fire. The flames quickly engulfed the ship, and of the 97 people on board, 35 were killed.

Smurfs   little blue cartoon characters created by the artist Peyo. The Smurfs became a worldwide success after a television show featuring them premiered in 1981. Smurf plush toys, figurines, video games, and CDs are still popular with children and collectors.

subatomic   particles smaller than an atom.

syndrome   a pattern of behavior that tends to occur under certain circumstances; a number of symptoms that occur together to make up a particular condition.

NEITHER MAN NOR RAT CAN PROPERLY FOLD LAUNDRY BY DAVE BARRY

Are you a male or a female? To find out, take this scientific quiz:

2   Your department is on a tight deadline for developing a big sales proposal, but you've hit a snag on a key point. You want to go one way; a co-worker named Bob strongly disagrees. To break the deadlock, you:

3   a. Present your position, listen to the other side, then fashion a workable compromise.

4   b. Punch Bob.

5   Your favorite team is about to win the championship, but at the last second the victory is stolen away by a terrible referee's call. You:

6   a. Remind yourself that it's just a game, and that there are far more important things in your life.

7   b. Punch Bob again.

8   HOW TO SCORE: If you answered "b" to both questions, then you are a male. I base this statement on a recent article in *The New York Times* about the way animals, including humans, respond to stress. According to the article, a group of psychology researchers have made the breakthrough discovery that—prepare to be astounded—males and females are different.

9   The researchers discovered this by studying both humans and rats, which are very similar to humans except that they are not stupid enough to purchase lottery tickets. The studies show that when males are under stress, they respond by either fighting or running away (the so-called "fight or flight" syndrome), whereas females respond by nurturing others and making friends (the so-called "tend and befriend" syndrome).

10   This finding is big news in the psychology community, which apparently is located on a distant planet. Here on Earth, we have been aware for some time that males and females respond differently to stress. We know that if two males bump into each other, they will respond like this:

FIRST MALE: Hey, watch it!   11

SECOND MALE: No, YOU watch it!   12

FIRST MALE: Oh yeah? (They deliberately bump into each other again.)   13

Two females, in the identical situation, will respond like this: 14

FIRST FEMALE: I'm sorry!   15

SECOND FEMALE: No, it's my fault!   16

FIRST FEMALE: Say, those are cute shoes! (They go shopping.)   17

18   If the psychology community needs further proof of the difference between genders, I invite it to attend the party held in my neighborhood each Halloween. This party is attended by several hundred small children, who are experiencing stress because their bloodstreams—as a result of the so-called "trick or treat" syndrome—contain roughly the same sugar content as Cuba. Here's how the various genders respond:

19   —The females, 97 percent of whom are dressed as either a ballerina or a princess, sit in little social groups and exchange candy.

20   —The males, 97 percent of whom are dressed as either Batman or a Power Ranger, run around making martial-arts noises and bouncing violently off each other like crazed subatomic particles.

21   Here are some other gender-based syndromes that the psychology community might want to look into:

22   —The "laundry refolding" syndrome: This has been widely noted by both me and a friend of mine named Jeff. What happens is, the male will attempt to fold a piece of laundry, and when he's done, the female, with a look of disapproval, will immediately pick it up and re-fold it so that it's much neater and smaller. "My wife can make an entire bed sheet virtually disappear," reports Jeff.

23   —The "inflatable-pool-toy" syndrome: From the dawn of human civilization, the task of inflating the inflatable pool toy has always fallen to the male. It is often the

female who comes home with an inflatable pool toy the size of the Hindenburg, causing the youngsters to become very excited. But it is inevitably the male who spends two hours blowing the toy up, after which he keels over with skin the color of a Smurf, while the kids, who have been helping out by whining impatiently, leap joyfully onto the toy, puncturing it immediately.

24   I think psychology researchers should find out if these syndromes exist in other species. They could put some rats into a cage with tiny pool toys and miniature pieces of laundry, then watch to see what happens. My guess is that there would be fighting. Among the male researchers, I mean. It's a shame, this male tendency toward aggression, which has caused so many horrible problems, such as war and ice hockey. It frankly makes me ashamed of my gender.

I'm going to punch Bob.   25

(Dave Barry, "Neither Man Nor Rat Can Properly Fold Laundry," 2000)

 COMPREHENSION CHECKUP

Write the main idea of the article below.

Main idea: Males and females react to stress differently with males being more aggressive.

Why do you think Dave Barry wrote this article?

to entertain   He is poking fun at how men and women react differently in stressful

situations.

Multiple Choice

Directions: For each item, write the letter corresponding to the best answer.

____c____   1. From this article, you could conclude that
a. women do a poor job of folding the laundry.
b. girls like to be Super Heroes for Halloween.
c. many men would rather fight than compromise.
d. men and women react similarly to stress.

____c____   2. What is the meaning of the phrase *hit a snag* as used in paragraph 2?
a. encounter a problem or obstacle
b. run into an unexpected difficulty
c. both a and b
d. none of the above

____c____   3. The topic of this article is
a. the "inflatable pool toy" syndrome.
b. aggression.
c. gender differences in response to stress.
d. the problems with excessive sugar consumption.

____a____   4. The article is meant to be
a. amusing.
b. shocking.
c. serious.
d. grim.

_____b_____ 5. From this article, you could assume that the author
   a. thinks buying lottery tickets is a good idea.
   b. disapproves of buying lottery tickets.
   c. thinks buying lottery tickets is fun.
   d. thinks rats should learn to purchase lottery tickets.

_____d_____ 6. The author would agree that
   a. males and females are different.
   b. scientists spend too much time investigating the obvious.
   c. males are likely to respond more aggressively to stress than females.
   d. all of the above.

_____b_____ 7. The author ends the article with
   a. examples of the male tendency to nurture.
   b. examples of the male tendency to settle disagreements by fighting.
   c. praise of male aggressiveness.
   d. examples of female cooperation.

_____a_____ 8. According to the author, after two males bump into each other, they
   a. deliberately bump each other again.
   b. settle their differences with fists.
   c. apologize profusely.
   d. go watch a hockey game together.

_____c_____ 9. An antonym for the word _befriend_ as used in paragraph 9 is
   a. assist.
   b. support.
   c. antagonize.
   d. counsel.

_____c_____ 10. An antonym for the word _dawn_ as used in paragraph 23 is
   a. daybreak.
   b. daydream.
   c. sunset.
   d. midnight.

True or False

Directions: Indicate whether each statement is true or false by writing **T** or **F** in the space provided.

_____T_____ 11. According to the author, flight is the same as running away.

_____F_____ 12. The author's quiz to determine if someone is male or female is well-respected by the scientific community.

_____T_____ 13. The author is exaggerating the amount of sugar consumption by young children at the neighborhood Halloween party.

_____F_____ 14. The young boys at the Halloween party behave in a docile fashion.

_____F_____ 15. The "laundry refolding" syndrome has been researched by the scientific community.

_____T_____ 16. The author is exaggerating when he asserts that only men blow up inflatable pool toys.

Vocabulary in Context

Directions: Look at the italicized words in the following sentences. Do these sentences make sense (**S**) or are they nonsense (**N**)?

___S___ 1. In a major medical *breakthrough,* doctors at Johns Hopkins discovered a new treatment for early stage lung cancer.

___N___ 2. *Puncturing* a balloon will cause it to inflate rapidly.

___S___ 3. The vice president's vote broke a Senate *deadlock* so that the bill could pass.

___S___ 4. The teacher was *astounded* that so many of her past students attended her retirement party.

___N___ 5. Marla did such a good job *nurturing* her plants that all of them died.

___S___ 6. A new day *dawned* with the invention of the printing press.

___N___ 7. All was smooth sailing once the merger hit a *snag.*

___S___ 8. Miriam's grade for the research paper dropped because she turned it in past the *deadline.*

___S___ 9. They *compromised* by agreeing to take turns driving the car to work.

___S___ 10. Marco has to stay in bed for long periods of time because of chronic fatigue *syndrome.*

In Your Own Words

1. Although Barry is humorously overstating his case, do you think his position has any validity? Are men and women really as different as he portrays them to be? Base your answers on your own personal experiences.

2. In previous exercises, we saw studies asserting that in social groups boys tend to talk to attempt to exert control over others, while girls tend to talk to create harmony and generate empathy. Can you think of examples from your own life that either support or counter these claims?

Written Assignment

Dave Barry includes many examples of pretend syndromes such as the "trick or treat" syndrome, the "laundry refolding" syndrome, and the "inflatable pool toy" syndrome. However, "fight or flight" and "tend and befriend" are actual syndromes. Do some research on both of these and write a few paragraphs discussing your findings.

Internet Activity

Most of Dave Barry's articles were originally written for the *Miami Herald* and then syndicated (sold) to other newspapers around the country. Go to the Web site for the *Miami Herald,* www.miami.com/herald/, find an article by Dave Barry, print it, and write the main idea.

You might want to check out Dave Barry's Official Web site at www.davebarry .com.

Barry also has a blog (short for *weblog*), an online journal that he updates regularly. You can check out his blog at http://blogs.herald.com/dave_barrys_blog/.

READING

*"Getting a job, keeping it, and excelling in your work all
depend on knowing how to communicate clearly with others."*

TUNING IN TO READING   The workplace today is often rife with stress. Many employees work long hours and have long commutes. They don't feel their jobs are secure and as a result worry about downsizing, layoffs, budget cuts, pay freezes, and outsourcing. Burnout is commonplace. All too frequently we hear about workers losing their tempers, screaming, cursing, and even assaulting their fellow employees. This type of behavior is known as "desk rage." The people most likely to experience it are those who have the least power. Most psychologists agree that desk rage is a serious and growing phenomenon in the workplace. Have you ever seen it? Or, more to the point, have you ever been a recipient of it? In addition to desk rage, many employees have to contend with rudeness, gossip, depression, and irritability in the workplace. The following reading selection discusses specific ways to help improve communication in the workplace

BIO-SKETCH   Dennis Coon was a professor of psychology at Santa Barbara City College for over 22 years. He has since retired and is living in Tucson, Arizona, where he continues to write and edit college textbooks.

NOTES ON VOCABULARY

bottom line   the crucial factor; the main point. The term was originally used in accounting to refer to the earnings figures that appear on the last line of a statement.

goes belly-up   fails; goes bankrupt. The term originally referred to the way a dead fish looks in the water.

ASAP   as soon as possible.

circle the wagons   to take defensive action; prepare for an attack. In the American West, groups of people traveled in wagon caravans for safety. The circling of the wagons was a defensive action used to provide the best defense against attackers. The defenders could keep their women and children, livestock, and valuables within the ring of wagons. Today, the term *circle the wagons* is used in a business or political sense. It means that when a group in a corporation, a government, or a political faction is under attack (sometimes when it has done something wrong), its members must stick together and defend the group as a whole.

bean counter   a person whose job it is to keep statistics; an accountant.

HIGHLIGHTING AND ANNOTATING EXERCISE   *Directions:* For this selection, you will be asked to underline or highlight the directly stated main ideas for some of the paragraphs. For other paragraphs, which do not contain directly stated main ideas, you will be asked to formulate the implied main idea. Some examples are provided for you. Do the rest on your own.

COMMUNICATION AT WORK—GETTING THE MESSAGE ACROSS

Dennis Coon

Survey Question: *What Can Be Done to Improve Communication at Work?*

"The bottom line is we've got to round-file this puppy ASAP before it goes 1 belly-up. Stan says we're talking mouth-breather here. Copy Monica, Steve, and the bean-counters with your input and let's circle the wagons in the A.M."

"I was just, like, totally embarrassed. I mean, like abso-double-lutely totally 2 incinerated, you know? I mean, to the max. I'm all, I'm just totally sorry, Mr. Thomson. And he's all, If this is the way you do business, I'm not interested."

The people just quoted probably intended to express their ideas clearly. As 3 you can see, however, their efforts are less than a model of clarity.

<u>Effective communication is crucial in many work settings.</u> When communi- 4 cation is muddled, important messages may get lost. Feelings can be crushed. Trust may be damaged. Poor decisions are made. Almost always, group effectiveness is impaired.

Effective Communication

Getting a job, keeping it, and excelling in your work all depend on know- 5 ing how to communicate clearly with others. To improve your communication skills, or to keep them sharp, remember the following points.

- **State your ideas clearly and decisively.** News reporters learn to be precise 6 about the "who, what, when, where, how, and why" of events. At work, the same list is a good guide when you are making a request, giving instructions, or answering a question. Rather than saying, "I need someone to give me a hand sometime with some stuff," it would be better to say, "Blake, would you please meet me in the storeroom in 5 minutes? I need help lifting a box." Notice that the second request answers all of these questions: Who? Blake. What? Could you help me? How? By lifting a box. When? In 5 minutes. Where? In the storeroom. Why? It takes two people.

- As you speak, avoid overuse of ambiguous words and phrases ("wiggle 7 words") such as *I guess, I think, kinda, sort of, around, some, about, you know,* and *like.* Here's an example: "Basically, I sort of feel like we should kinda pause. I mean, and, let's see, maybe reconsider, you know, rethink some of this stuff." It would be better to say: "I believe we should revise our plans immediately." Ambiguous messages leave others in doubt as to your true thoughts and wishes.

- Also, try not to overuse intensifiers (*very, really, absolutely, extra, super,* 8 *awesome, ultimate, completely,* and so on). Super extra frequent use of such awesome words really causes them to completely lose their ultimate effectiveness.

- **Eschew the meretricious utilization of polysyllabic locutions. (In other** 9 **words, don't overuse big words.)** Overuse of obscure vocabulary is often a sign of insecurity. Big words may make you sound important, but they can also blur your message. Which of the following two statements is clearer—"Pulchritude possesses solely cutaneous profundity" or "Beauty is only skin deep"?

- Trendy, overused "buzz words" or phrases should also be avoided. Often 10 they are just a way of *sounding like* you are saying something: "Personally, I feel we've got to be more synergistically proactive and start networking in a programmatic fashion if we want to avoid being negatively impacted by future megatrends in the client-purveyor interface." Translation: I don't have any worthwhile thoughts on the topic."

- **Avoid excessive use of jargon or slang.** Most professions have their own 11 specialized terminology. Here's an example of some printer's jargon: "TR the last two lines but STET the leading." (Reverse the order of the last two lines but don't change the spacing between them.) Jargon can provide a quick, shorthand way of expressing ideas. However, jargon and technical lingo should be avoided unless you are sure the others are

Example: Underline the directly stated main idea of paragraph 4.

first sentence

Underline the directly stated main idea of paragraph 6.

first sentence

Example: Write the implied main idea of paragraph 7. <u>Avoid overusing ambiguous words and phrases because others might mistake your true meaning.</u>

Write the implied main idea of paragraph 8. Try combining the first and last sentences.

<u>Try not to overuse intensifiers so that they don't lose their effectiveness.</u>

Underline the directly stated main idea of paragraph 10.

first sentence

Write the implied main idea of paragraph 11. Try combining two sentences in the middle of the paragraph.

Jargon can be a quick way to express ideas, but it should be avoided unless the listeners are familiar with it.

familiar with it. Otherwise, people may misunderstand you or feel left out. Using slang can have the same effect as jargon. Slang that excludes people from a conversation makes them feel belittled. (The quotations at the beginning of this section [are] full of slang.)

- **Avoid loaded words.** Words that have strong emotional meanings (loaded 12 words) can have unintended effects on listeners. For example, the observation "What a stupid-looking tie" implies that anyone who likes the tie is stupid. In the same way, saying "I think the supervisor's new schedule is a *dumb* idea" brands anyone who agrees with the schedule as foolish. Good decision-making and problem-solving require an atmosphere in which people feel that their ideas are respected, even when they disagree.

- **Use people's names.** Work relationships go more smoothly when you 13 learn names and use them. An impersonal request such as "Hey you, could you make five copies of this for me?" is not likely to promote future cooperation. Of course, whether you use a first or last name will depend on how formal your relationship to a person is. In any case, learning names is well worth the effort.

- **Be polite and respectful.** Being polite is important, but don't be artificially 14 servile or stilted. Overuse of expressions such as *sir, madam, with your permission, if you would be ever so kind,* and so on can actually be insulting. True politeness puts others at ease. Phony politeness makes people feel they are being made fun of, or manipulated, or that you are faking it to win approval.

Underline the directly stated main idea of paragraph 15.

second sentence

- Being polite can be difficult when tempers flare. If you have a dispute with 15 someone at work, remember to be self-assertive, rather than aggressive. Self-assertion is a direct, honest expression of feelings and desires. In contrast to assertive behavior, aggression doesn't take into account the feelings or rights of others. It's an attempt to get one's own way no matter what. Assertion techniques emphasize firmness, not attack. Remember, you have the right to refuse, to request, and to right a wrong. Self-assertion involves standing up for these rights by speaking out in your own behalf.

Be aware that your behavior sends messages, too. Actions can parallel, 16 amplify, contradict, or undermine what you are saying. For example, being late for a meeting tells others that they are not very important to you. Likewise, your manner of dress, personal grooming—even the way you decorate your personal work space—all send messages. Think about the message you want to send and be sensitive to non-verbal channels of information.

The art of effective communication is well worth cultivating. The points 17 made here are basic, but they can go a long way toward ensuring your success at work—like, totally, abso-double-lutely, you know what I mean?

(Dennis Coon, *Psychology,* 10/e, 2006)

✔ **COMPREHENSION CHECKUP**

Short Answer

Directions: Answer the questions briefly.

1. What is the topic of this selection? communication at work

2. What is the selection's main idea? Effective communication is crucial in many work settings.

3. List three details supporting the author's main idea. <u>Answers will vary.</u>

4. The statement "If it's appropriate for the beach or the bedroom, don't wear it to work" supports the information in which paragraph of the reading selection? <u>16</u>

5. Which sentence is the main idea of paragraph 16? <u>first</u>

Multiple Choice

Directions: For each item, write the letter corresponding to the best answer.

<u>d</u>   1. Harry tells a group of employees that they must shift their paradigm so they can become more synergistically proactive. Harry has violated which principle(s) of effective communication?
a. Be polite and respectful.
b. Use people's names.
c. Avoid loaded words.
d. Don't overuse big words.

<u>b</u>   2. Which of the following is true according to the selection?
a. It's a good idea to be candid and call your coworkers' ideas "dumb" or "stupid" when you don't agree with them.
b. Most professions have their own jargon.
c. It's a good idea to use slang to show that you know what you're talking about.
d. Choose big words to demonstrate your feeling of confidence.

<u>c</u>   3. From the selection, you could conclude that ineffective communication in the workplace could result in all of the following *except*
a. messages being lost.
b. trust being damaged.
c. workplaces being made more fun.
d. group effectiveness being reduced.

<u>c</u>   4. According to the selection, all of the following are true *except* for which?
a. Actions send messages too.
b. Actions can undermine what you're saying.
c. Actions have little effect on what you're saying.
d. Actions can amplify what you're saying.

<u>c</u>   5. According to information presented in the selection,
a. it's a good idea to use intensifiers to make your feelings known.
b. your speech should be full of trendy words to demonstrate that you are "with it."
c. you should try to avoid the use of wiggle words.
d. the use of ambiguous messages is a good idea so that people are kept uninformed.

True or False

Directions: Indicate whether each statement is true or false by writing **T** or **F** in the space provided.

<u>T</u>   6. The author recommends paying attention to nonverbal forms of communication.

<u>F</u>   7. If you are habitually late to group meetings, you are telling your fellow employees that they are important to you.

___T___ 8. How you decorate your cubicle can send a message to your fellow employees.

___F___ 9. In the workplace, being self-assertive and being aggressive are the same thing.

___F___ 10. In the workplace, it makes little sense to learn your coworkers' names.

Vocabulary in Context 1

Directions: Use the context clues from the paragraph indicated to determine the meaning of the italicized words. (Remember, no looking in the dictionary.)

1. Paragraph 3: *clarity*

   Definition: clearness; lucidity

2. Paragraph 4: *crucial*

   Definition: extremely important; vital

3. Paragraph 4: *muddled*

   Definition: confused

4. Paragraph 8: *overuse*

   Definition: use too often; use excessively

5. Paragraph 11: *excludes*

   Definition: bars; keeps out

6. Paragraph 13: *promote*

   Definition: encourage

7. Paragraph 15: *dispute*

   Definition: argument; disagreement

8. Paragraph 16: *sensitive*

   Definition: aware; responsive

9. Paragraph 17: *cultivating*

   Definition: promoting; fostering; nurturing

10. Paragraph 17: *basic*

    Definition: elementary; simple

Vocabulary in Context 2

Directions: Choose one of the following words to complete each of the sentences below. Use each word only once. Be sure to pay close attention to the context clues provided.

ambiguous	amplify	belittles	contradicted	impair
obscure	revise	servile	stilted	undermined

1. The earthquake __undermined__ the main support to the bridge.

2. His stiff and __stilted__ speech made him appear arrogant.

3. Marla ___belittles___ her son's attempts to swim by calling him names. If she keeps it up, he soon won't want to be in the water.

4. A microphone will ___amplify___ her voice.

5. The doctor worried that frequent ear infections would ___impair___ the young child's ability to hear.

6. We had a great deal of trouble locating the student union because we were given unclear, ___ambiguous___ directions.

7. Instructors need to periodically ___revise___ their classroom material to keep it relevant.

8. I said my dress was blue, but my friend ___contradicted___ me when she said that it was black.

9. He did not want to be employed in a ___servile___ position; instead, he wanted to be in charge.

10. Although the assignment was to research someone famous or well-known, the teacher allowed Martha to give her report on an ___obscure___ inventor.

In Your Own Words

1. If you have a clash with a coworker, what do you think is the best way to handle it? What steps do you take to smooth ruffled feelings?

2. How common do you think desk rage is? Do you know anyone who has personally experienced it? What was the outcome? Do you think workplace outbursts are rising? If so, why?

3. Have you ever worked in an office where someone has damaged the office equipment? Why did the incident occur? Could it have been prevented?

4. Many incidents of desk rage occur among people who work in cubicles. Why do you think it is difficult to work in a cubicle? How can people make the experience of working in a cubicle better?

5. How common are yelling and verbal abuse in your workplace? Do you think anger is contagious? Do you think many people bring their problems from home to work with them? Do you think long commutes add to the tension at work?

6. Do you ever fear for your physical safety at work?

Written Assignment

1. Write a short paragraph explaining the meaning of the first paragraph of this selection in your own words.

2. Write a short essay discussing the six suggestions for effective communication and explain how these suggestions could improve communication within an organization.

Internet Activity

Do a search using the following key words: "office manners" or "office etiquette." Write a paragraph summarizing the most useful information you learn.

Chapter Summary and Review

In Chapter 2, you learned about the structure of paragraphs and how to identify topics, main ideas, and details. You also learned how to paraphrase directly stated main ideas and short paragraphs and how to formulate implied main ideas. Based on the material in Chapter 2, answer the following questions.

Short Answer

Directions: In a few words or a sentence, define each of the following terms.

1. Topic <u>the subject of the paragraph, often a single word or phrase</u>

2. Main idea <u>the key point of the paragraph</u>

3. Major supporting details <u>supporting sentences that directly reinforce the main idea</u>

4. Minor supporting details <u>sentences that reinforce the major supporting details</u>

Paragraph Diagramming

Directions: Insert the shape from pages 89–90 that best depicts the paragraph development described.

5. No sentence clearly expresses the main idea. _____■_____

6. The main idea is expressed in both the first and last sentences. _____⧗_____

7. The main idea is expressed in the last sentence. _____▲_____

Vocabulary in Context

Directions: Choose one of the following words to complete the sentences below. Use each word only once.

implied   last   paraphrasing   specific

8. When you put a sentence or paragraph into your own words, you are <u>paraphrasing</u>.

9. Sometimes paragraphs have a main idea that is not explicitly stated in any one sentence. Such a main idea is <u>implied</u>.

10. Main ideas are supported by <u>specific</u> details.

11. The main idea is usually found in the first or <u>last</u> sentence.

3

Determining
an Author's Purpose

CHAPTER PREVIEW

In this chapter, you will

- Learn the difference between a general and a specific purpose.
- Learn how to determine whether the author's purpose is to entertain, inform, or persuade.
- Learn how to summarize short articles.

Entertain, Inform, or Persuade?

Most writers create a story, essay, article, or poem with at least one **general purpose** in mind. Because most writers do not directly state their general purpose, readers must use indirect clues to determine it. We can identify the general purpose by asking "Why did the author write this?" or "What did the author want to accomplish?" Usually, this purpose will fall into one of three broad categories: to entertain, to inform, or to persuade.

To Entertain

Highlight or underline several words that define each boldfaced term.

An author whose purpose is to **entertain** will tell a story or describe someone or something in an interesting way. A piece of writing meant to entertain will often make an appeal to readers' imagination or sense of humor. If the writing is humorous, the author might say things in an exaggerated fashion or use understatement. Witty, unusual, dramatic, or exciting stories usually have entertainment as their purpose. A romance, suspense, or mystery novel is usually meant to entertain. Writing meant to entertain may be either fiction or nonfiction. The following is an example of a paragraph whose purpose is to entertain:

1. I assume you are on the Internet. If you are not, then pardon my French, but *vous êtes un big loser.* Today EVERYBODY is on the Internet, including the primitive Mud People of the Amazon rain forest. In the old days, when the Mud People needed food, they had to manually throw spears at wild boars, whereas today they simply get on the Internet, go to www.spearaboar.com and click their mouse a few times (the Mud People use actual mice). Within three business days, a large box (containing a live boar) is delivered to them by a UPS driver, whom they eat.

(Dave Barry, *Dave Barry Is Not Taking This Sitting Down,* 2000).

To Inform

An author whose purpose is to **inform** will explain something to readers or provide them with knowledge they did not possess before. Ordinarily, the material will be presented in an objective, unemotional fashion. Authors who write textbooks presenting factual material usually have this purpose in mind. Encyclopedias, research studies, and articles in newspapers are usually meant to inform. The following is an example of a paragraph whose purpose is to inform:

> 2.   In the United States, the most "wired" nation in the world, only 65 percent of Americans have Internet access at home. In many developing countries almost no one has Internet access. According to a recent report by the United Nations, 88 percent of all Internet users live in industrialized countries. One of the major barriers to Internet use in developing countries is the cost. In 1999 it cost $10.50 an hour to use the Internet in the African nation of Chad, where the average annual income was $187. The Web is also largely limited to people who read English, since 80 percent of the world's websites are in English. Another barrier in many countries is that there is no way to log on. Consider that in the industrialized nations there are about 50 phone lines for every 100 people, while developing nations average 1.4 phone lines per 100 people. According to the United Nations, half the world's population has yet to make a phone call, much less log on to the Internet.
>
> (Ralph E. Hanson, *Mass Communication*, 1/e, 2005)

To Persuade

Finally, the author's purpose may be to **persuade.** Persuasion goes beyond merely entertaining or providing information. This kind of writing tries to change readers' opinions by appealing to their emotions or intellect. If the author is making an emotional argument, vivid descriptive passages may be used to manipulate readers' feelings. If the author is making an appeal to intelligence, a rational or logical argument may be used. Political literature is a common example of writing meant to persuade. While articles in newspapers are usually meant to inform, newspaper editorials ordinarily have persuasion as their purpose. The following is an example of a paragraph whose purpose is to persuade:

POP-UPS AND SPAM: THE EVIL TWINS OF INTERNET ADVERTISING

> 3.   Suppose you are doing online research when all of a sudden an ad appears: Order DVDs by mail! You close that one but another pops up: Find low fares! Get rid of that and there is another: Lower your mortgage rates! Click to close it and there is another. And another. Pretty soon you are doing the cyber equivalent of swatting flies as you try to get rid of those intrusive pop-up and pop-under ads. Pop-up ads are bad enough, but they pale in comparison to spam. The Internet is literally stuffed full of junk e-mail for low-cost prescription drugs, debt consolidation plans, schemes that will make you a millionaire in only six months, and various treatments to enlarge certain body parts. What, if anything, can you do about it? The ultimate solution might be a legal one. It's time for Congress to pass legislation to create a national Do-Not-Spam list that resembles the Do-Not-Call list that limited telemarketers.
>
> (Joseph R. Dominick, *The Dynamics of Mass Communication*, 8/e, 2005). Reprinted with permission.

General and Specific Purposes

To determine whether the author's general purpose is to entertain, inform, or persuade, look for clues in the title, in headings and subheadings, and in the introduction or conclusion. Also, pay attention to the source of the article.

Authors also take into account their **audience**—those they are writing for—when they choose their general purpose. Writers of fiction usually want to entertain readers by creating interesting characters and stories. If an author writes an article for a wellness magazine, the general purpose probably will be to provide information promoting good health. If an author writes a letter to solicit campaign contributions for a political candidate, the general purpose will be to persuade, because the author is trying to persuade people to give money.

In addition to a general purpose, authors usually have a **specific purpose,** which gives more information about the article than the general purpose does. Take the previous "wellness" example. The general purpose is to "inform." The specific purpose might be "to inform people about foods that protect against cancer."

Multiple Purposes

Sometimes an author may have more than one purpose in mind. For instance, an author might want to both entertain and persuade. Or the author might write an entertaining article that also provides information about something important. When an author has more than one purpose in mind, usually one of the author's purposes will be primary. To determine the author's primary purpose, first identify the main idea and the key details that support the idea. Then note the source of the article or passage. Often the publication that the article or passage appears in will help you identify the author's primary purpose. Finally, note the author's choice of words. Is the vocabulary neutral and unbiased? Is it meant to influence your judgment in some way? These steps should help you identify the author's primary purpose.

Read the paragraph below and identify the writer's topic, main idea, and general and specific purposes.

4.   One of the reasons that occupational stress has been receiving so much attention lately is that businesses are genuinely beginning to care about employee welfare. You don't buy that? Well, how about this? Work stress is costing businesses billions of dollars. Sounds more plausible doesn't it? It is estimated by the International Labor Organization that stress on the job costs businesses over $200 billion per year. These costs include salaries for sick days, costs of hospitalization and outpatient care, and costs related to decreased productivity. Other stress-related factors are catching the eyes of business leaders. For example, health benefit costs to employers have increased dramatically. Employees trained over a long period of time, at great cost, may break down when stressed on the job. They may make poor decisions, miss days of work, begin abusing alcohol and other drugs, or die and have to be replaced by other workers who need training. All of this is costly. These effects of occupational stress have caused companies to give high priority to stress management programs.

(Jerrold S. Greenberg, *Comprehensive Stress Management*, 8/e, 2004)

Topic: occupational stress

Main idea: businesses giving high priority to stress management programs because of the high costs of employee occupational stress

General purpose: to inform

Specific purpose: informing readers about why businesses are paying attention to employee stress

The following exercises will give you some practice in determining an author's general purpose.

Exercise 1: Determining the General Purpose

Directions: Label each sentence according to its general purpose: to inform (**I**), to entertain (**E**), or to persuade (**P**).

_E_ 1. I have been thinking a lot about food lately. This is because I am not getting any. My wife, you see, recently put me on a diet. It is an interesting diet of her own devising that essentially allows me to eat anything I want so long as it contains no fat, cholesterol, sodium, calories, and isn't tasty. In order to keep me from starving altogether, she went to the grocery store and bought everything that had "bran" in its title. I am not sure, but I believe I had bran cutlets for dinner last night. I am very depressed.

(Bill Bryson, *I'm a Stranger Here Myself,* 1999)

_P_ 2. Most sharks are harmless—at least to humans. Actually we threaten the survival of sharks more than they threaten us. They reproduce slowly, and their numbers are already being depleted by overfishing in many areas. This attitude toward sharks may be shortsighted, because they play an important role in marine communities. Some people catch shark only for the shark's fins or jaws. Others practice shark hunting for sport, leaving the meat to waste. A magnificent predator, the shark may soon be exterminated by humans, the fiercest predator of them all.

(Peter Castro and Michael E. Huber, "Sharks," 2007)

_I_ 3. The idea of a family consisting of a wage-earning husband and a wife who stays at home has largely given way to the dual-income household. Among married people between the ages of 25 and 34, 92 percent of the men and 75 percent of the women are in the labor force. Why has there been such a rise in the number of dual-income couples? A major factor is economic need. In 2003, the median income for households with both partners employed was 99 percent more than in households in which only one person was working outside the home. Of course, because of such work-related costs as child care, not all of a family's second wage is genuine additional income.

(Richard T. Schaefer, *Sociology,* 10/e, 2007)

Exercise 2: Determining the Primary Purpose and Main Ideas

Directions: Read each of the following paragraphs to determine if the author's primary purpose is to entertain, persuade, or inform. Indicate the clues that enabled you to make your decision. In the space provided, write the directly stated or implied main idea.

1. Most crimes are committed in large urban areas rather than in small cities, suburbs, or rural areas. National Crime Victimization Survey data tell us the safest place to be is at home, although we are likely to be victimized when we are in familiar territory. In 2004, only one-quarter of violent crimes took place near or at the victim's home. Almost three-quarters of violent crimes occurred within five miles of home. Common locations for violent crimes are streets other than those near the victim's home (15 percent), at school (14 percent), or at a commercial establishment (8 percent).

    (Freda Adler et al., *Criminology*, 6/e, 2007)

    Purpose: <u>inform</u>   Clues: <u>factual data</u>

    Main idea: <u>Most crimes don't take place at home, but rather close to home.</u>

2. You know how when you buy your pants, there's a piece of paper in one of the pockets that says "inspected by #47." Who ARE these people anyway? Has anyone out there met one of these inspectors? What do they inspect? I mean seriously, if someone bends over and their pants rip, should we say, "Oh no! Who inspected that? Number 63? Whew. That was close. Mine were done by number 34." If there was a problem, what are you supposed to do? Call up the manufacturer and say, "Hello. I hate to be the one to break it to you, but you know number 63? She just isn't going to cut it anymore."

    (Tom Mather, *The Cheeseburger Philosophy*, 1996)

    Purpose: <u>entertain</u>   Clues: <u>humorous—use of overstatement</u>
    <u>and informal speech</u>

    Main idea: <u>We don't know who these inspectors are and what they do.</u>

3. Child labor laws prohibit a 13-year-old from punching a cash register for 40 hours a week, but that same child can labor for 40 hours or more inside a gym or an ice skating rink without drawing the slightest glance from the government. The U.S. government requires the licensing of plumbers. It demands that even the tiniest coffee shop adhere to a fastidious health code. It scrutinizes the advertising claims on packages of low-fat snack food. But it never asks a coach, who holds the lives of his young pupils in his hands, to pass a minimum safety and skills test. Coaches in this country need no license to coach children, even in a high-injury sport like elite gymnastics.

    (Joan Ryan, *Little Girls in Pretty Boxes*, 1995)

    Purpose: <u>persuade</u>   Clues: <u>Even coffee shops have</u>
    <u>to follow codes.</u>

    Main idea: <u>She wants to require coaches to have a license.</u>

4. Alcohol abuse by college students usually takes the form of a drinking pattern called *binge drinking*. Binge drinking is defined as the consumption of five drinks in a row. One large study of more than 17,000 students on 89 campuses found that 49.7 percent of students binged. The strongest predictors for binging were living in a fraternity or sorority, adopting a party-centered lifestyle, and engaging in other risky behavior. The study also suggested that many college students began binge drinking in high school.

(Wayne A. Payne, Dale B. Hahn, and Ellen B. Lucas, *Understanding Your Health,* 10/e, 2009)

Purpose: <u>inform</u>   Clues: <u>objective study</u>

Main idea: <u>Drinking, especially binge drinking by college students, is a major problem.</u>

5. Tina was found dead last week—her neck broken by the jaws of a steel trap. I didn't know Tina. But John and Rachel Williamson knew her, and so did their children, Tyrone and Vanessa. Tina had been a beloved member of their family for 10 years. She was a Samoyed—a handsome, intelligent dog, pure white with soft, dark eyes. When she died she was only 200 yards from her back door. Tina had gone out to play that morning as usual, but this time she found something *un*usual—an odd-shaped box with delicious-smelling food inside. She put her head inside the box to get at the food. When she did, the trap closed and Tina was killed. Unless we crack down on illegal trapping within town property, this tragedy will be repeated. The next time it might be *your* family dog. Or your pet cat. Or your child.

   Purpose: <u>persuade</u>   Clues: <u>vivid description; emotional—</u>

   <u>tragedy; "unless we crack down"</u>

   Main idea: <u>Tina was killed by the illegal use of a steel trap and we must stop this</u>

   <u>from happening again.</u>

6. To keep an adequate supply of pennies in circulation, the U.S. Mint creates approximately 12 billion new pennies each year. The cost of manufacturing these new pennies is .66 of a cent apiece, which adds up to approximately $80 million a year. According to Treasury officials, when you add on storage and handling expenses, it costs the U.S. government more than a penny to transact a penny's worth of business.

   Purpose: <u>inform</u>   Clues: <u>unemotional; "according to</u>

   <u>Treasury officials"</u>

   Main idea: <u>It costs more to make a penny than a penny is worth.</u>

7. As we wait for the plane to climb to the jump altitude of 12,000 feet, my mind races with a frenzied jumble of thoughts: "Okay, this is the moment you've been waiting for. It's going to be great. Am I really going to jump out of an airplane from 12,000 feet? What if something goes wrong? Can I still back out? Come on now, don't worry. It'll be fine." My palms are sweating and my heart is pounding so hard I think it may burst. "Get ready," yells the instructor. As I jump into the blue, I wonder, "What am I doing here?" The blast of air resistance blows me backward like a leaf at the mercy of the autumn wind. In about ten seconds my body levels out and accelerates to a speed of 120 miles an hour. The air supports my body like an invisible flying carpet. Any fears or doubts I had are gone in the exhilaration of free flight. Every nerve in my body is alive with sensation; yet I am overcome by a peaceful feeling and the sense that I am one with the sky.

   (Stephen E. Lucas, *The Art of Public Speaking,* 9/e, 2007)

   Purpose: <u>entertain</u>   Clues: <u>exciting; suspense</u>

   Main idea: <u>"Any fears or doubts I had are gone in the exhilaration of free flight."</u>

The articles presented in the next section all deal, directly or indirectly, with the world of work. Read each article noting the purpose and then answer the questions.

Author's Purpose: To Entertain

The following short story by William Saroyan has entertainment as its purpose.

READING

> *"(My grandmother) said to me: 'You must learn to do some good work, the making of some item useful to man.'"*

TUNING IN TO READING   Have your grandparents ever given you advice about how to conduct your life? Was it advice that you agreed or disagreed with?

BIO-SKETCH   William Saroyan (1908–1981) was an American writer of Armenian descent. Throughout his long and prolific career, he drew upon his heritage to provide him with inspiration for his short stories, novels, and plays. He is best known for the short story collection *The Daring Young Man on the Flying Trapeze;* the play *The Time of Your Life,* which won the Pulitzer Prize; and the novel *The Human Comedy.* In many of his stories, Saroyan invents a family life much different from his own. At the age of 3, he lost his father and was placed in an orphanage by his mother. At the age of 8, he began selling newspapers and working at a variety of odd jobs. He learned to read at the age of 9 and shortly afterward began to write. Eventually, at the age of 15, he left school altogether. Over the years, he has said, it was his writing that kept him sane.

NOTES ON VOCABULARY

humble   to lower in condition, rank, or position. *Humble* is derived from the Latin word *humilis,* which in turn comes from *humus,* meaning "soil." The literal meaning of *humble* is "not far above the ground" or "low."

dungeon   a dark underground cell, vault, or prison.

The Shepherd's Daughter

WILLIAM SAROYAN

I T IS THE OPINION OF MY GRANDMOTHER, God bless her, that all men should labour, and at the table, a moment ago, she said to me: You must learn to do some good work, the making of some item useful to man, something out of clay, or out of wood, or metal, or cloth. It is not proper for a young man to be ignorant of an honourable craft. Is there anything you can make? Can you make a simple table, a chair, a plain dish, a rug, a coffee pot? Is there anything you can do?

And my grandmother looked at me with anger.   2

I know, she said, you are supposed to be a writer, and I suppose you 3 are. You certainly smoke enough cigarettes to be anything, and the whole house is full of the smoke, but you must learn to make solid things, things that can be used, that can be seen and touched.

Ancient Persia was located in the Middle East where Iran is today.

There was a king of the Persians, said my grandmother, and he had a son, and this son fell in love with a shepherd's daughter. He went to his father and he said, My Lord, I love a shepherd's daughter, and I would have her for my wife. And the king said, I am king and you are my son, and when I die you shall be king, how can it be that you would marry the daughter of a shepherd? And the son said, My Lord, I do not know but I know that I love this girl and would have her for my queen. 4

The king saw that his son's love for the girl was from God, and he said, I will send a message to her. And he called a messenger to him and he said, Go to the shepherd's daughter and say that my son loves her and would have her for his wife. And the messenger went to the girl and he said, The king's son loves you and would have you for his wife. And the girl said, What labour does he do? And the messenger said, Why he is the son of the king; he does no labour. And the girl said, He must learn to do some labour. And the messenger returned to the king and spoke the words of the shepherd's daughter. 5

The king said to his son, The shepherd's daughter wishes you to learn some craft. Would you still have her for your wife? And the son said, Yes, I will learn to weave straw rugs. And the boy was taught to weave rugs of straw, in patterns and in colours and with ornamental designs, and at the end of three days he was making very fine straw rugs, and the messenger returned to the shepherd's daughter, and he said, These rugs of straw are the work of the king's son. 6

And the girl went with the messenger to the king's palace, and she became the wife of the king's son. 7

One day, said my grandmother, the king's son was walking through the streets of Baghdad, and he came upon an eating place which was so clean and cool that he entered it and sat at the table. 8

This place, said my grandmother, was a place of thieves and murderers, and they took the king's son and placed him in a large dungeon where many great men of the city were being held, and the thieves and murderers were killing the fattest of the men and feeding them to the leanest of them, and making sport of it. The king's son was of the leanest of the men, and it was not known that he was the son of the king of the Persians, so his life was spared, and he said to the thieves and murderers, I am a weaver of straw rugs and these rugs have great value. And they brought him straw and asked him to weave and in three days he weaved three rugs, and he said, Carry these to the palace of the king of the Persians, and for each rug he will give you a hundred gold pieces of money. And the rugs were carried to the palace of the king, and when the king saw the rugs he saw that they were the work of his son and he took the rugs to the shepherd's daughter and he said, These rugs were brought to the palace and they are the work of my son who is lost. And the shepherd's daughter took each rug and looked at it closely and in the design of each rug she saw in the written language of the Persians a message from her husband, and she related this message to the king. 9

And the king, said my grandmother, sent many soldiers to the place of the thieves and murderers, and the soldiers rescued all the captives and killed 10 all the thieves and murderers, and the king's son was returned safely to the palace of his father, and to the company of his wife, the little shepherd's daughter. And when the boy went into the palace and saw again his wife, he humbled himself before her and he embraced her feet, and he said, My love, it is because of you that I am alive, and the king was greatly pleased with the shepherd's daughter.

Now, said my grandmother, do you see why every man should learn an 11 honourable craft?

I see very clearly, I said, and as soon as I earn enough money to buy a 12 saw and a hammer and a piece of lumber I shall do my best to make a simple chair or a shelf for books.

(William Saroyan, "The Shepherd's Daughter," 1934)

 COMPREHENSION CHECKUP

Multiple Choice

Directions: For each item, write the letter corresponding to the best answer.

b   1. At first the king of the Persians
    a. was pleased by his son's selection of a bride.
    b. was puzzled by his son's selection of a bride.
    c. ignored his son's selection of a bride.
    d. was angered by his son's selection of a bride.

b   2. The messenger was of the opinion that
    a. a king's son must do the bidding of a shepherd's daughter.
    b. a king's son is above doing tasks of manual labor.
    c. the shepherd's daughter should not be made queen.
    d. the king's son should not marry someone of a lowly station.

d   3. The grandson is going to please his grandmother
    a. by giving up his smoking habit.
    b. by learning to weave straw rugs.
    c. by abandoning his desire to be a writer.
    d. by earning enough money by writing to enable him to build something.

a   4. The king's son was initially spared by the thieves and murderers because
    a. he was lean.
    b. it was considered unwise to kill the son of a king.
    c. he was overweight.
    d. he was a well-known weaver.

True or False

Directions: Indicate whether each statement is true or false by writing **T** or **F** in the space provided.

T   5. The grandmother has the most respect for someone who can create something useful.

F   6. The grandmother saved the life of the king's son.

_____T_____ 7. Before the shepherd's daughter agreed to marry the king's son, she required that he learn a craft.

_____F_____ 8. The grandmother approves of her grandson's chosen profession.

_____T_____ 9. The king's son was grateful to the shepherd's daughter for helping rescue him.

Vocabulary in Context

Directions: Look through the given paragraph and find a word that matches the definition.

1. lacking in knowledge or training (1)   ignorant

2. worthy of respect (1)   honorable (honourable)

3. decorative (6)   ornamental

4. without much flesh or fat (9)   leanest

5. not subjected to harm or death (9)   spared

6. hugged (10)   embraced

In Your Own Words

1. What is the main idea of the story?

2. According to the grandmother, what kind of work is admirable? Would the grandmother think that the practice of law is honorable? Include the supporting details from the story that helped you answer this question.

3. What character in the fable has the same attitude toward work as the grandmother?

4. What is the significance of the ending of the fable?

5. What is meant by the last sentence of the story? How will the grandson earn the money for the materials to build a chair or a bookshelf?

6. How much respect is given to the advice of elders in your family?

Written Assignment

Benjamin Franklin said, "He that hath a trade hath an estate." Compare Franklin's view with that of the grandmother and the shepherd's daughter.

Internet Activity

Directions: Complete the following:

The ancient Persian Empire was located in western Asia. At the height of its power, it encompassed much of what today is known as the Middle East, extending east to India and west to the Aegean Sea. Its great cities were Babylon and Persepolis, and its great leaders were Cyrus the Great, Darius the Great, and Xerxes. The Persian Empire lasted for more than 200 years. It was conquered about 330 B.C. by Alexander the Great. Until 1935, Persia was the official name of Iran.

Use the Internet to find additional information about the Persian Empire. Briefly summarize what you learn.

Author's Purpose: To Inform

Read the following article, "From a Melted Candy Bar to Microwaves," by Ira Flatow. Flatow's purpose is to present information about the discovery of the microwave.

READING

"Next time you make a bag of Orville Redenbacher's, you'll be repeating an experiment that heralded the dawning of the age of microwave cooking."

TUNING IN TO READING   Do you own a microwave? If you have one in your home, do you use it for more than reheating coffee or leftovers? By 1997, 90 percent of all American households had a microwave. If you were forced to eliminate one of your appliances, which one could you most easily do without, and why?

Practice your SQ3R techniques with this reading selection. Survey the material by reading the first two paragraphs, the last two paragraphs, and the bio-sketch.

BIO-SKETCH   Ira Flatow, National Public Radio's science correspondent, is the host of *Talk of the Nation's* "Science Friday." In his book *They All Laughed,* "he demonstrates that truth is stranger than fiction." Each of the stories, including this one about the invention of the microwave, is really a story about inquisitive people who won't take no for an answer. While doing research about inventors, Flatow discovered that most of them are hearty souls, unafraid of appearing ridiculous by asking silly questions. He calls this the "quack like a duck" discovery method. If something looks like a duck, walks like a duck, but doesn't quack like a duck, these bold inventors want to know why. In this excerpt, Perry Spencer, noticing the melted candy bar in a lab coat he'd been wearing all day long, should have assumed his own body temperature had been the culprit. Because that answer didn't make "quack noises," Spencer went on to invent the microwave oven.

NOTES ON VOCABULARY

nuke   slang for cooking food in a microwave oven.

cynical   disbelieving; sarcastic, sneering. In ancient Greece, a *Cynic* was a member of a school of philosophers who believed that being virtuous was the highest good. Because *cynics* had contempt for worldly needs and pleasures, they were extremely critical of the rest of society. Today the word refers to anyone who questions the motives or actions of other people.

maven   an expert, a really knowledgeable person. The word *maven* comes from Yiddish.

Microwave oven

FROM A MELTED CANDY BAR TO MICROWAVES
Ira Flatow

Next time you nuke a bag of Orville Redenbacher's, you'll be repeating an experiment that heralded the dawning of the age of microwave cooking.

Almost 50 years ago, 1946 to be exact, one of the great minds in the history of electronics accidentally invented microwave popcorn. 2

Shortly after World War II, Percy L. Spencer, electronic genius and war hero, 3 was touring one of his laboratories at the Raytheon Company. Spencer stopped in front of a magnetron, the power tube that drives a radar set. Suddenly he noticed that a candy bar in his pocket had begun to melt.

Most of us would have written off the gooey mess to body heat. But 4 not Spencer. Spencer never took anything for granted. During his 39 years with Raytheon, he patented 120 inventions. When England was battered by German bombs in the 1940 Battle of Britain, Spencer turned his creative mind toward developing a better version of the British invention radar. His improved magnetron allowed radar tube production to be increased from 17 per week to 2,600 per day. His achievements earned him the Distinguished Service Medal, the U.S. Navy's highest honor for civilians.

So when this inquisitive, self-educated, and highly decorated engineer who 5 never finished grammar school came face to face with a good mystery, he didn't merely wipe the melted chocolate off his hands and shrug off the incident. He took the logical next step. He sent out for popcorn. Holding the bag of unpopped kernels next to the magnetron, Spencer watched as the kernels exploded.

The next morning Spencer brought in a tea kettle. He wanted to see what 6 microwaves would do to raw eggs. After cutting a hole in the side of the kettle, Spencer placed an uncooked egg into the pot. Next he placed a magnetron beside the kettle and turned on the machine.

An unfortunate (cynical?) engineer poked his nose into the pot and was 7 greeted by an explosion of yolk and white. The egg had been blown up by the steam pressure from within. Spencer had created the first documented microwave mess—an experiment to be inadvertently repeated by countless thousands of microwave cooks. He had also shown that microwaves had the ability to cook foods quickly.

Legend has it that this demonstration was reproduced before unsuspect- 8 ing members of Raytheon's board of directors who had trouble visualizing exactly what microwaves could do to food. The ensuing egg shower convinced the board of directors to invest in the "high frequency dielectric heating apparatus" patented in 1953.

That demo and the fact that the military no longer needed 10,000 mag- 9 netron tubes per week for radar sets helped shape the future of microwaves. What better way to recover lost sales than to put in every American home a radar set disguised as a microwave oven?

"Little minds are interested in the extraordinary; great minds in the commonplace."

—Elliot Hubbard

But first the device needed a better name. Raytheon's marketing mavens 10 felt few people would demand a high-frequency dielectric heating apparatus for their kitchens even if they could pronounce it. A contest followed to rename the apparatus. Seeing as how the oven owed its roots to radar, the winning entry suggested "Radar Range." The words were later merged to Radarange. But no words could hide the woeful inadequacies of this first-generation oven.

Weighing 750 pounds and standing five and a half feet [tall], the Radarange 11 required water—and plumbing—to keep its hefty innards cool. Hardly the compact unit that fits under today's kitchen cabinets. The early 1953 design—with its three-thousand-dollar price tag—was strictly for restaurants, railroads (the Japanese railroad system bought 2,500), and ocean liners. These customers would be Raytheon's prime market for two decades.

The microwave oven was no pleasure to cook with, either. Culinary 12 experts noticed that meat refused to brown. French fries stayed white and limp. Who could eat this ugly-looking food? Chefs were driven to distraction. As chronicled in *The Wall Street Journal,* "the Irish cook of Charles Adams, Raytheon's chairman, who turned his kitchen into a proving ground, called the oven 'black magic' and quit."

It would take decades before the consumer oven was perfected. The 13 Tappan Company took an interest in the project and helped Raytheon engineers shrink the size of the magnetron. A smaller power unit meant the hideous plumbing could be done away with and air cooling fans could take over.

Then someone had the brilliant idea that perhaps the magnetron should 14 not be pointed directly at the food but rather out of sight. That's it. Put the food in a box, put the microwave source at the back, and lead the microwaves into the box via a pipe. Now we could truly call it an oven.

And that's what happened. In 1955 Tappan introduced the first consumer 15 microwave oven. Did you have one? Hardly anyone did. It was still too big and costly. Then came 1964 and a breakthrough. From Japan, the country that had a reputation for making "transistorized" (read: small) products out of everything, came an improved electron tube. Smaller than the old magnetron, it put Raytheon on track to placing a microwave oven under everyone's kitchen cabinet.

Needing a consumer-oriented vehicle to sell its new ovens, Raytheon 16 bought up Amana Refrigeration, Inc., in 1965 and put out its first affordable ($495), compact, and practical microwave oven in 1967.

The specter of little microwaves leaking out of the oven scared a lot of 17 people. Their worst fears were realized in 1968 when a test of microwave ovens at Walter Reed Hospital found microwaves did indeed leak out. Federal standards set in 1971 solved that problem.

Today more homes have microwave ovens than dishwashers. And we owe 18 it all to an inquisitive man with a melted candy bar in his pocket and egg on his face.

(Ira Flatow, *They All Laughed . . .*, 1992)

COMPREHENSION CHECKUP

Multiple Choice

Directions: For each item, write the letter corresponding to the best answer.

___d___ 1. The original Radarange achieved little acceptance in which of the following situations?
a. restaurants
b. ocean liners
c. railroads
d. small kitchens

___a___ 2. The original Radarange had all of the following qualities *except* for which?
a. cooked food to perfection
b. had large size and weight
c. required water for cooling
d. was very expensive

___d___ 3. All of the following led to our modern microwave oven *except* for which?
a. Japan reduced the size of the electron tube.
b. Air cooling fans were introduced.
c. The microwave source was placed at the back.
d. Microwave-safe dishes were invented.

___d___ 4. The author's primary purpose is to
a. inform us of hazards involved in the use of microwaves.
b. persuade people to buy microwaves.
c. explain how a microwave oven works.
d. explain the events leading to the creation of the modern microwave.

___a___ 5. What is the main idea of the selection?
a. Spencer, a highly inquisitive man with little formal education, is credited with inventing the microwave oven.
b. Spencer never took anything for granted, including a gooey chocolate bar.
c. In 1946, Spencer invented microwave popcorn.
d. Spencer patented 120 inventions.

___d___ 6. The main idea of paragraph 12 is stated in the first sentence. All the following details support the main idea *except* for which?
a. The meat refused to brown.
b. French fries stayed white and limp.
c. Chefs were driven to distraction.
d. Charles Adams, Raytheon's chairman, turned his kitchen into a proving ground.

True or False

Directions: Indicate whether each statement is true or false by writing **T** or **F** in the space provided.

___T___ 7. The magnetron caused the candy bar in Spencer's pocket to melt.

___T___ 8. Spencer performed additional experiments with the magnetron using unpopped kernels and raw eggs.

_____F_____ 9. The microwave oven was perfected quickly.

_____F_____ 10. Spencer was chosen to select an appropriate name for his new invention.

_____F_____ 11. Chefs were eager to work with the new oven.

_____T_____ 12. Initially, microwaves leaked out of the ovens.

_____F_____ 13. Homes are more likely to have a dishwasher than a microwave oven.

Vocabulary in Context

Directions: Look through the given paragraph and find a word that matches the definition.

1. announced (1)   heralded

2. pessimistic (7)   cynical

3. unintentionally (7)   inadvertently

4. resulting (8)   ensuing

5. experts (10)   mavens

6. pitiful (10)   woeful

7. kitchen (12)   culinary

8. object of fear (17)   specter

In Your Own Words

1. What does the author admire about Spencer?

2. How was the timing of Spencer's discovery beneficial to the military?

3. Although Spencer lacked formal education, he was a highly successful engineer. In the world today, how likely is it that a person without formal education could achieve success in a technical field?

4. What does context tell us about the meaning of the word *inquisitive* in the last sentence of the reading? In paragraph 5?

Internet Activity

To read a biography of Ira Flatow, or to visit "Science Friday," check out the following Web site:

    www.npr.org/programs/scifri/

Author's Purpose: To Persuade

The following article, "Students Who Push Burgers," was first published in *The Christian Science Monitor*. The author, Walter S. Minot, worries that too many students are working too many hours a week while also trying to be full-time students. He would like to see college students give a higher priority to their studies and work fewer hours. Although this article was written in 1988, the information presented is still relevant today. In fact, the actual percentage of working students has increased slightly.

READING

"The world seems to have accepted the part-time job as a normal feature of adolescence. . . . But such employment is a cause of educational decline."

TUNING IN TO READING Do you think students should have jobs? Are there good reasons and bad reasons for students to hold down jobs? Do your fellow students work too much at their jobs and not put enough effort into their studies?

BIO-SKETCH Walter Minot, professor emeritus at Gannon University, taught rhetoric and writing for 36 years before retiring.

NOTES ON VOCABULARY

scapegoat a person, group, or thing made to take the blame for the crime or mistake of others. Under the law of Moses, the high priest of the ancient Jews would bring two goats to the altar on the Day of Atonement. The high priest then cast lots to see which goat would be sacrificed to the Lord and which would be the *scapegoat*. After the priest had confessed the sins of his people over the head of the *scapegoat,* it was taken to the wilderness and allowed to escape, carrying with it all the sins of the people. The other goat was then given in sacrifice. (Definition of *scapegoat* from William Morris and Mary Morris, *Morris Dictionary of Word and Phrase Origins*. Copyright © 1987 by William Morris and Mary Morris. Reprinted by permission of HarperCollins Publishers.)

tripe slang for nonsense, or anything offensive; part of the stomach of cattle, goats, and deer when used for food.

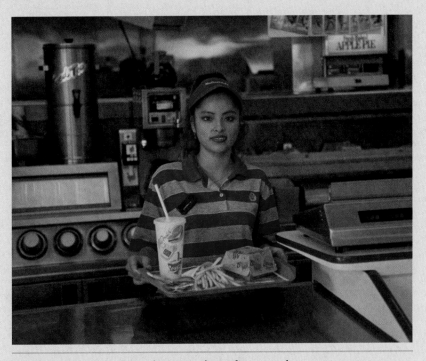

Minot argues that students today often work to support a luxurious lifestyle. Do you agree?

STUDENTS WHO PUSH BURGERS   BY WALTER MINOT

A college freshman squirms anxiously on a chair in my office, his eyes avoiding mine, those of his English professor, as he explains that he hasn't finished his paper, which was due two days ago. "I just haven't had the time," he says.

2   "Are you carrying a heavy course load?"

3   "Fifteen hours," he says—a normal load.

4   "Are you working a lot?"

5   "No, sir, not much. About 30 hours a week."

6   "That's a lot. Do you have to work that much?"

7   "Yeah, I have to pay for my car."

8   "Do you really need a car?"

9   "Yeah, I need it to get to work."

10   This student isn't unusual. Indeed, he probably typifies today's college and high school students. Yet in all the lengthy analyses of what's wrong with American education, I have not heard employment by students being blamed.

11   I have heard drugs blamed and television—that universal scapegoat. I have heard elaborate theories about the decline of the family, of religion, and of authority, as well as other sociological theories. But nobody blames student employment. The world seems to have accepted the part-time job as a normal feature of adolescence. A parochial school in my town even had a day to honor students who held regular jobs, and parents often endorse this employment by claiming that it teaches kids the value of the dollar.

12   But such employment is a major cause of educational decline. To argue my case, I will rely on memories of my own high school days and contrast them with what I see today. Though I do have some statistical evidence, my argument depends on what anyone over 40 can test through memory and direct observation.

13   When I was in high school in the 1950s, students seldom held jobs. Some of us baby-sat, shoveled snow, mowed lawns, and delivered papers, and some of us got jobs in department stores around Christmas. But most of us had no regular source of income other than the generosity of our parents.

14   The only kids who worked regularly were poor. They worked to help their families. If I remember correctly, only about five people in my class of 170 held jobs. That was in a working-class town in New England. As for the rest of us, our parents believed that going to school and helping around the house were our work.

15   In contrast, in 1986 my daughter was one of the few students among juniors and seniors who didn't work. According to Bureau of Labor statistics, more than 40 percent of high school students were working in 1980, but sociologists Ellen Greenberger and Laurence Steinberg in "When Teenagers Work" came up with estimates of more than 70 percent working in 1986, though I suspect that the figure may be even higher now.

16   My daughter, however, did not work; her parents wouldn't let her. Interestingly, some of the students in her class implied that she had an unfair advantage over them in the classroom. They were probably right, for while she was home studying, they were pushing burgers, waiting on tables, or selling dresses 20 hours a week. Working students have little time for homework.

17   I attended a public high school, while she attended a Roman Catholic preparatory school whose students are mainly middle class. By the standards of my day, her classmates did not "have to" work. Yet many of them were working 20 to 30 hours a week. Why?

18   They worked so that they could spend $60 to $100 a week on designer jeans, rock concerts, stereo and video systems, and, of course, cars. They were living lives of luxury, buying items on which their parents refused to throw hard-earned money away. Though the parents would not buy such tripe for their kids, the parents somehow convinced themselves that the kids were learning the value of money. Yet, according to Ms. Greenberger and Mr. Steinberg, only about a quarter of

these students saved money for college or other long-term goals.

19   How students spend their money is their business, not mine. But as a teacher, I have witnessed the effects of their employment. I know that students who work all evening aren't ready for studying when they get home from work. Moreover, because they work so hard and have ready cash, they feel that they deserve to have fun—instead of spending all their free time studying.

20   Thus, by the time they get to college, most students look upon studies as a spare-time activity. A survey at Pennsylvania State University showed that most freshmen believed they could maintain a B average by studying about 20 hours a week. (I can remember when college guidebooks advised two to three hours of studying for every hour in class—30 to 45 hours a week.)

21   Clearly individual students will pay the price for lack of adequate time studying, but the problem goes beyond the individual. It extends to schools and colleges that are finding it difficult to demand quantity or quality of work from students.

22   Perhaps the reason American education has declined so markedly is because America has raised a generation of part-time students. And perhaps our economy will continue to decline as full-time students from Japan and Europe continue to outperform our part-time students.

(Walter S. Minot, "Students Who Push Burgers," 1988)

 COMPREHENSION CHECKUP

Multiple Choice

Directions: For each item, write the letter corresponding to the best answer.

___d___ 1. The college freshman who spoke to Professor Minot
   a. has to work so much so that he can pay for his food and rent.
   b. takes a lighter course load than other college students.
   c. has completed his English paper on time.
   d. is fairly typical of today's college students, according to the author.

___c___ 2. The main idea expressed in this article is that
   a. drugs and television are directly responsible for the decline in American education.
   b. the decline in religious values has led to a corresponding decline in American education.
   c. student employment in the United States is a major cause of educational decline.
   d. parochial schools, unlike public schools, are still able to provide a quality education.

___d___ 3. Which of the following statements is true according to the author?
   a. Students in the 1950s rarely worked.
   b. The majority of students save their wages from part-time jobs for long-term goals.
   c. A parochial school honored students who had regular employment.
   d. Both a and c.

___d___ 4. From Minot's article, we can conclude that many parents
   a. no longer believe that going to school and helping out at home should be a student's only work.
   b. are reluctant to spend their money on frivolous items such as designer jeans.

      c. are convinced that students learn the value of money by working at a part-time job.

      d. All of the above.

b   5. The author's primary purpose is to

      a. describe the educational system of the 1950s.

      b. argue that student employment contributes to educational decline.

      c. describe one student's academic dilemma.

      d. applaud the attitude of today's parents toward part-time student employment.

True or False

Directions: Indicate whether each statement is true or false by writing **T** or **F** in the space provided.

F   6. A Penn State survey indicates that college freshmen believe they can maintain an A average with only 20 hours of studying per week.

T   7. Minot believes that there is a correlation between student employment and a college's ability to maintain high academic standards.

F   8. Although Minot is opposed to student employment, he did allow his daughter to work while she was in high school.

T   9. According to the statistics given in the article, teenage employment has continued to rise over the years.

T   10. Minot has personally observed how student employment harms academic achievement.

Vocabulary in Context

Directions: Indicate whether the word in italics is used correctly or incorrectly by writing **C** or **I** in the space provided.

I   1. It's an act of *generosity* to refuse to help others.

C   2. After the well-known athlete *endorsed* the product, sales immediately rose.

C   3. The student became bored by the lecture and began to *squirm* about in his seat.

I   4. A person who strives for perfection is likely to be satisfied with an *adequate* performance.

C   5. Alejandro was walking down the sidewalk when he *witnessed* a car accident on the nearby street.

C   6. Tenssy made *elaborate* plans for her formal wedding ceremony, which was to have over 500 guests.

I   7. A person in the stage of *adolescence* is very close to retirement age.

C   8. Shawn *typifies* college student-athletes who work long hours at both their studies and their sports.

In Your Own Words

1. Do you think parents today still support the notion that a student's only "job" should be going to school and getting good grades? Why or why not?

2. In grade school, most students are in class until three or four in the afternoon. Most high school students are dismissed much earlier than this. Do you think high schools should require students to spend more time at school?

3. What do parents hope a student will learn from work experience? What do you think students learn from work experience? Would it be better for students with free time to do volunteer work or internships instead of working for a salary?

4. It is well known that students in the United States spend less time in school than do students in any other modern industrial country. What are the global implications of being a nation of part-time students?

5. Many high school and college teachers comment that they no longer require the same amount of work from their students. For example, where once two research papers were required for English 101, now only one is required. What are some possible effects of these reduced standards?

6. Many teachers report that the number of students trying to do their homework in class has increased over the years. The main idea from paragraph 16 supports the observation of these teachers. Write the main idea below.

   Working students have little time for homework.

Written Assignment

Minot's main idea is that student employment is a major cause of educational decline in this country. Do you agree with Minot's viewpoint? Why or why not?

What's Your Opinion?

How much homework do you think is appropriate for children of various ages?

YOU BE THE JUDGE: HOMEWORK SHOULD BE

A Major Part of a Student's Life Because . . .

There is too much material to be mastered only during school time. Given demands on students to learn more and to increase their test scores, much study and learning needs to take place at home. After all, students are in school for just five hours of a 24-hour day.

It brings parents into the learning process. School cannot accomplish its goals alone. Students achieve much more when academics are reinforced at home. By providing guidance and monitoring homework, parents demonstrate their support of learning, becoming true partners with teachers. Closing the school-home gap fosters competent and attentive students.

Many students do not use their time wisely. The average student comes home from school, talks on the phone with friends, "hangs out" at the mall, watches television for hours, and then plays a computer game or two before going to bed. Homework at least gives students something meaningful to do with their time.

Limited and Brief Because . . .

Too much stress is placed on students as it is. Schools have been taken over by this growing obsession with tests. The last thing we need to do is extend this angst to home life. Besides, homework is mostly busywork, unrelated to real learning.

It favors some students and penalizes others. Some children have highly educated parents, home computers, and the resources needed to produce quality homework. Other students have poor and uneducated parents, who may not speak English and who may be working two or more jobs. All too often homework is simply a measure of family resources.

Many students do not have the luxury of extra time. Many students go directly from school to their part-time job. Their families may need the money. Other students must care for younger siblings at home while parents are at work. Increasing homework would place an enormous burden on their families.

(Myra Sadker and David Sadker, *Teachers, Schools, and Society*, 8/e, 2008)

STUDY TECHNIQUE 5: WRITING SUMMARIES

In your reading and English classes, you will be called upon to write summaries. **Summarizing** simply means restating the main ideas of a reading in your own words. Because many supporting details are omitted, a summary is much shorter than the original on which it is based. When you write summaries, you need to present the main ideas in order of importance in an objective fashion. Keep in mind that you are reporting the author's viewpoints and not your own. When writing a summary, you never write something like "I feel" or "I think" or "it seems to me." Instead, you always write only the author's opinions. In a summary, it is always the *author* who feels, thinks, or believes.

It takes practice to learn how to write a good summary. However, since we have now learned how to identify directly stated main ideas and how to state implied ones, we are ready to begin learning how to write a summary of a short article. You just read an article by Walter S. Minot titled "Students Who Push Burgers." This is a relatively easy article to summarize because the author presents his main ideas in a logical sequence. Try to locate the directly stated main ideas. Because not all of the main ideas are stated directly, you will have to come up with several implied main ideas.

In order to identify the key supporting details, try to answer as many of the question words (*who, what, where, when, why,* and *how*) about the topic as possible.

Summarizing an Article

Directions:

1. Provide answers to *who, what, where, when, why,* and *how.* (Not all of these question words will apply to every article.)

Who: _____

What: _____

Where: _____

When: _____

Why: _____

How: _____

2. List four to five main ideas from the article, paraphrasing each main idea. The overall main idea of the article is: Student employment is a major cause of the decline in American education.

1st main idea: _____

_____

2nd main idea: _____

_____

3rd main idea: _____

_____

4th main idea: _____

_____

5th main idea: _____

_____

3. Write at least a half-page summary of the article. Be sure to include the information from numbers 1 and 2 in your summary. Your completed summary should contain no trivia (useless information) and should not be redundant (give information more than once). Remember to present the information in an organized way. After writing your summary, compare your version to the student sample in the Appendices.

Exercise 3: Determining an Author's Purpose

Directions: Label each paragraph according to its general purpose: to inform (**I**), to entertain (**E**), or to persuade (**P**).

_____ 1. Since earliest times the fragrances of certain plants, owing to their essential oils, have been valued as a source of perfumes. It is difficult to pinpoint when people first began using plant fragrances to scent their bodies, but by 5,000 years ago the Egyptians were skilled perfumers, producing fragrant oils that were used by both men and women to anoint their hair and bodies. Fragrances were also used as incense to fumigate homes and temples in the belief that these aromas could ward off evil and disease. In fact, our very word *perfume* comes from the Latin *per* meaning through and *fumus* meaning smoke, possibly referring to an early use of perfumes as incense.

(Estelle Levetin and Karen McMahon, "Alluring Scents," 2008)

_____P_____ 2. The images are vivid and appalling. Emaciated children with haunting eyes and distended stomachs, and too weak to cry, stare at us from news photos and television screens. Throughout the world, the problems of poverty and undernutrition are widespread and growing. The majority of undernourished people live in Asia. However, the largest increases in numbers of chronically hungry people occur in eastern Africa, particularly in Ethiopia, Sudan, Rwanda, Burundi, Sierra Leone, Kenya, Somalia, Eritrea, and Tanzania. Their eyes haunt us. If undernutrition is to be eradicated, the world's nations must examine the problem and assume responsibility. Life is not necessarily fair, but the aim of civilization should be to make it more so. The world has both enough food and the technical expertise to end hunger. What is lacking is the political will and cooperation to do so. It is time for leaders of rich and poor nations alike to come to an agreement on the best possible means to serve all of the world's citizens.

(Gordon Wardlaw, "Undernutrition throughout the World," 2007)

_____E_____ 3. Are you lost in Cyberspace? You went away for three days and returned to find 1,892 messages in your mailbox. You just came out of the computer room and your dog is barking at you as if you were a stranger. You just missed your daughter's soccer game, your son's piano recital, or your best friend's wedding because you were traveling the information superhighway. Your family thinks you moved out a year ago.

(Nancy E. Willard, "Get a Life," 1997)

_____I_____ 4. U.S. society strongly supports marriage, and about nine out of ten people at some point "tie the knot." But many of today's marriages unravel. By 2003, almost four in ten marriages were ending in divorce. Ours is the highest divorce rate in the world. At greatest risk of divorce are young couples—especially those who marry after a brief courtship, have little money, and have yet to mature emotionally. The chance of divorce also rises if a couple marries after an unexpected pregnancy or if one or both partners have substance abuse problems. People whose parents divorced also have a higher divorce rate themselves. Finally, people who are not religious are more likely to divorce than those who have strong religious beliefs.

(John J. Macionis, *Society*, 8/e, 2006)

_____E_____ 5. How would you describe the behavior of Bruce Damon, who held up the Mutual Federal Savings Bank near Brockton, Massachusetts? Using a gun, Damon demanded $40 million. When the teller explained that the bank kept only $40,000 on the premises, he said, "Okay, $40,000." Now get this: He demanded not cash, but a check!

You can imagine the ending. He was arrested a short time later when he tried to deposit the check into his account in another bank. Way to go, Bruce! Not very smart!

(Hamilton Gregory, "Incompetent Criminals," 2005)

P   6. Something must be done about high school dropouts. A student who drops out of high school not only hurts himself or herself, but the decision to leave high school before graduation also has harmful consequences for society. Dropping out of high school does not guarantee poverty, but dropouts do have to scramble harder to start a career—if they ever have one. Society suffers when many young people do not finish school. Dropouts are more likely to end up on welfare, to be unemployed, and to become involved with drugs, crime, and delinquency. In addition, the loss of taxable income burdens the public treasury. Fortunately, with a strong commitment by government, educators, and parents, it is possible to prevent dropping out. We can help millions of young people to have a brighter future. Doing nothing is a national tragedy.

(Diane E. Papalia, et al., "Dropping Out of High School," 2007)

Reading to Determine the Author's Purpose

READING

Olivia

"There've been nights when I've been so tired, I've been ready to quit on papers. But then I look in on Olivia sleeping, and turn right around and go back to my paper. I can't imagine a life without her."

TUNING IN TO READING   The following story is about Wil Smith, a graduate of Bowdoin College in Maine. While attending college, Wil had full custody of his four-year-old daughter Olivia. He juggled his Bowdoin classes with parenting, playing basketball, and serving in the Naval Reserve. Mel Allen, senior editor at *Yankee Magazine,* met Wil Smith last fall and wrote a letter to Olivia about Wil. As you read this story, notice the obstacles that Wil managed to overcome. Are any of you trying to raise a child by yourself? What kinds of difficulties do you experience?

BIO-SKETCH   Mel Allen has been senior features editor for *Yankee Magazine* since 1979. A former Peace Corps volunteer in Colombia, Mel became a fourth-grade teacher in Maine before publishing his first magazine story in 1977. As the father of two sons, he was especially moved by Wil's devotion to his daughter. "Wil's story is one of the most inspirational I have ever covered," Mel says.

NOTES ON VOCABULARY

pickup   a game in which whoever shows up can play. In *pickup* games, there are no established teams.

READING (continued)

conference an athletic *conference* is a group of schools or colleges that compete against each other on a regular basis. The team with the best record wins the *conference* championship. It comes from the Latin words *con*, meaning "together," and *ferre*, meaning "to carry or bring."

anonymous not named or identified. Derived from the Greek words *an*, meaning "without," and *onymos*, meaning "name."

custody the legal right to provide a home for and to care for a child. *Custody* is often established by court ruling.

asthma a condition of the lungs in which many of the air passages are obstructed. *Asthma* is a chronic condition. *Asthma* attacks may be caused by exposure to allergens, a change in weather, or physical exertion. *Asthma* is the Greek word for "panting." A person with *asthma* is literally panting for breath.

reserves units in the armed forces whose members are in civilian life; these units can be called up for active duty when needed.

A LETTER TO OLIVIA BY MEL ALLEN

Dear Olivia,

I am writing this letter to you on November 27, 1999, your father's 31st birthday. I want to tell you the story about your father, Wil Smith, and about your years together at Bowdoin College. One day you will probably ask him about these years, when he was a single dad, with a young daughter, struggling to stay in school, to compete in a tough Division III basketball program, and to provide a home for both of you. Everyone who knows your father says how modest he is, so I suspect he will leave out a lot of the details.

2 You are a bouncy, pretty little four-year-old girl, with braided pigtails and happy brown eyes. During the games you roam through the stands as the free-spirited, and totally trusting child that you are; it must seem as if the whole world knows your name. Wil says that he plays with his head on a swivel, always looking to find you during breaks in the action.

3 You live together in a two-bedroom apartment a few blocks from campus. Both of you eat in the student cafeteria. Most nights you are in bed by nine, and while you sleep Wil studies until 2, then wakes up at 6:30 to get you ready for your day.

4 Assistant basketball coach Charlie Gordon is Maine-born, used to waking at daybreak. He says on road trips he'll be up at 6, only to find Wil dressed and studying in the hotel lobby. "He never complains," says coach Gordon. "He just does what has to be done. We have good kids on the team, but they complain they're tired, or overworked. They have no idea what it means to be Wil Smith."

5 Olivia, when you are older you will remember little of these days, but when you are 12 or 14, or 16, I hope your father gives you this story, so you'll understand why Craig McEwen, the Dean for Student Academic Affairs, calls Wil "the most remarkable and unique student I have known in 20 years at Bowdoin."

6 Wil calls you "my complex joy." He says, "I know people look at it as a disadvantage having Olivia." Wil says, "I see it as an advantage. If it was just me, with the academic background I had coming to Bowdoin, I'd never have made it. There've been nights when I've been so tired, I've been ready to quit on papers. But then I look in on Olivia sleeping, and I turn right around and go back to my paper. To tell you the truth, I can't imagine a life without her."

7 You have always come first, but he is also co-captain of the men's basketball team, a four-year starter on a nationally ranked team at 31—an age when other men are playing weekly pickup games at the YMCA. You will have only a vague

memory of seeing your dad play, and even then he was what we call past his prime. As Wil puts it, "I've lost a few steps." None of his teammates or coaches or opponents has seen him at his prime. When he was younger he was a shooter and a scorer; now he takes pride in stopping the other team's scorers. Last year he led Bowdoin in assists and steals, and he made the conference All-Defensive team. I watched him practice. If a teammate is not playing hard enough he'll hear about it from Wil. Coach Gilbride says, "Next year without Wil, we'll really have to coach again."

8   Over half of the Bowdoin students arrive from lives of privilege and private schools. Your father came from the Navy, a decade after graduating from a public urban high school in Florida. "I remember going to school when a successful day for a teacher was just getting home," he says. "When parents were just concerned with getting food on the table." His first year at college he had to work twice as hard just to keep up with the others. He feels angry about the disparity between his high school preparation and that of his Bowdoin classmates. "All the friends I grew up with," he says, "never had the opportunities that Bowdoin students have had."

9   College administrators say Wil is the first single father to attend Bowdoin. He is a black student and athlete at a college and in a state with few people of color, and he has made it his business to make life better for others who will come after him. "I try to educate people about the people I come from," he says.

10   Wil's story begins in Jacksonville, Florida. When you see your father, when you remember his caring, you are also seeing a woman you never knew, your grandmother Mildred.

11   "My mother was the most incredible person I ever met," Wil says. "I was the last of ten children she raised, pretty much on her own. She worked every day, and still found time to coach boys' and girls' baseball and basketball. When people say it's incredible what I'm doing," Wil says, "I say 'This isn't extraordinary.

This is what I'm supposed to do.' My mother always put us first. A lot of what I do today is because I just want her to be proud of me."

12   Everyone in northwest Jacksonville knew the Smith boys, because they were athletes. At five-foot-ten, Wil was the smallest of all the Smith boys, but he was fast and tough, and nobody worked harder. He wanted to play on his mother's teams, but she said no, she wanted her children exposed to the best competition. She sent her sons to play for coaches who knew the sport better than she did. Wil played sports year-round. Wil was an all-star in football, basketball, and baseball.

13   Mildred never missed a game. She learned how to drive at age 50, just so she could get to the games. When she died of cancer on November 27, 1983, Wil's 15th birthday, she took a lot of Wil's passion for sports with her. "My mother was my biggest fan," Wil says. "When she passed away, it was like, 'Why am I still playing?' A lot of my joy in sports came from my mother's presence."

14   Wil struggled to cope. "I'd never dealt with loss," he says. He still played, and his talent carried him to all-conference honors in three sports. But he was drifting. "I never reached the heights everyone thought I would," Wil says. When colleges sent recruiting letters, he didn't bother to respond.

15   Reluctantly Wil attended Florida A&M in Tallahassee for a year. He played one season of winter baseball, but his heart wasn't in it. He left school. It was now 1987.

16   "I was hanging out at a store with my friends," Wil says, "and I'll never forget this. ESPN came on. It was a baseball highlight. One guy said, 'Wil, man, you don't belong here. You're different. I expected to see you up there, playing ball on TV.' I always remember that. I witnessed pretty heavy stuff. But there's no way to get away from good roots. It's so hard to enjoy being bad if you have good roots."

17   In May 1989, three years after graduating from high school, Wil enlisted in the Navy. He was trained to be an aviation

electronics technician, specializing in land-based anti-submarine aircraft. In June 1991, while stationed in Italy his orders sent him to the Naval Air Station in Brunswick, Maine. "I was happy," he says. "I thought it was Brunswick, Georgia, near my family in Jacksonville. I'd never heard of Brunswick, Maine." In Maine people still glance with curiosity at a black man walking down the street. "Kids at Bowdoin see a police car and think, 'I'm safe,'" says Wil. "When I came to Maine and I'd see a police car, I'd think, 'trouble.'"

18 One night he was driving back to the Navy base with his nephews in the car. He had brought two nephews from Jacksonville to live with him so they could attend Brunswick High School, a school that he knew would give them a better chance to succeed in college. Three squad cars of base policemen pulled him over. "They were looking for a black man driving a blue Thunderbird who had committed a crime," Wil remembers. "It didn't matter that my Thunderbird was white. I showed four different forms of I.D. Still they refused to believe me. They were trying to make me say I was someone else."

19 Each day at the base when Wil finished work he'd head to the gym for pickup basketball, but he wanted to do more with his time. "I'm best as a human being when I have others besides myself to focus on," he says. He saw an ad in the local newspaper for a volunteer football coach at Brunswick Middle School. Wil was the only applicant, and he got the job.

20 "I was 22 years old and I had sixty white kids on my team," Wil says. "Most of these kids had never been in contact with a black man. I had no problem with the kids, but it wasn't an easy adjustment for the parents seeing a young black man coaching their kids. They asked for a meeting with me. They said I was too intense, they didn't think their kids were ready for it. I told them that every day after practice I'd ask the kids, 'Anybody hurt? Anybody not having fun?' The kids always said they were fine. I told the parents, 'I'd like you to be on my side, but as long as your kids are with me, they're mine for three hours a

day.'" By the end of the season, some of those same parents would phone Wil and tell him their kids were slipping in their work, would he come talk with them. Soon Wil became a community fixture, coaching basketball as well as football. His teams played hard, and they won. During the summer of 1995, while coaching at a basketball camp, Wil's ability and character caught the eye of Tim Gilbride, Bowdoin's men's basketball coach. Coach Gilbride asked Wil if he had considered college. Would he like to apply to Bowdoin?

21 Wil was at a professional and personal crossroads. He had served seven years in the Navy. He was due to re-enlist. But the Navy meant six months overseas every year, and by that summer he was your father. You'd been born in May. He had met your mother in Portland after returning from overseas duty. Their relationship broke up. You lived then with your mother, but Wil came for you every Thursday, and kept you until Monday.

22 Wil applied to Bowdoin then left for a six-month overseas assignment to Sicily. It was there that he decided he would go to college and not leave you again for that length of time. His last day of active duty was April 25, 1996, a date that stands out for him because that is also the day your mother gave him full custody of you, then 11 months old.

23 Though Wil had been accepted to Bowdoin, he did not know the questions to ask, questions that so many parents of college students take for granted. He did not know how to apply for student aid or room and board. He started school in September 1996. You were 14 months old, and he had no choice but to bring you to class with him. The professors learned that when you were sick, Wil would not be able to come. The money he had saved from the Navy went faster than he could have imagined. Some days he did not eat for two or three days, just so he had enough food to feed you. "Coach didn't know," Wil says, "but I lost seventeen pounds. I couldn't sleep. I got an F in a course that required you to read about twenty books. I didn't have

money for books, and I didn't know about books being on reserve in the library. I said to myself, 'I can't make it. This is just too hard.'" What he told his advisor was simply, "Things are hard for me right now." The advisor called Betty Trout-Kelly, who oversees Bowdoin's multicultural programs and affirmative action.

24   On a Sunday afternoon late in his first semester Betty Trout-Kelly sat Wil down in her car. "I told him, 'I know you feel you shouldn't need this support system,'" she says, "'but if you don't take the help we can offer, it will be your fault. And if you don't accept it, you won't make it.'"

25   For the first time, Wil told her about his struggles. Later, after meeting with school officials, Trout-Kelly notified Wil that an anonymous donor would give him nearly $25,000 for Olivia's day care and after-school care. Wil would be able to move to campus housing and eat regularly with his daughter at the school. "Thank you," Wil told her. "I'll prove myself worthy."

26   Olivia, in four years your father has become as well-known off-campus as he is on it. He says, "I feel like I have an obligation to every young person I come in contact with." He is a sociology major, and he puts what he learns in the classroom to work. He is the community advisor for civil rights teams at Brunswick and Mount Ararat high schools. He travels around the state of Maine giving talks to educators about the problems and challenges of diversity. During the summer he is a counselor at Seeds of Peace International Camp in Otisfield, Maine, where Israeli and Palestinian kids live together.

27   None of this has come easily. Olivia, you have asthma, and when you're sick, he still has trouble trusting anybody else with your care. Last season you had a fever at the same time the team had a weekend road trip. It took all of Coach Gilbride's skills of persuasion, and his saying that his wife had raised three kids, and would care for you, before Wil agreed to go.

28   During spring semester of his junior year, Wil was called to active duty—he's still a member of the Navy reserves—during the Balkan conflict. Just before he left, he received the Bowdoin Athletic Department's Leadership Award. Before leaving, he scrambled to get you to your aunt in Florida, finished work for two courses, and took incompletes in the rest. He came back before summer, picked you up, finished some papers, and got ready for his final year as a student-athlete.

29   Wil is torn about what to do in the future. Whatever he decides will be in large part because of you, Olivia, because you are more important to him than anything in the world. I talked to Wil on the phone tonight, as I am writing you this letter, and he said he had forgotten to tell me a story about you.

30   "When she was two," he said, "I was walking her to school. It was cold, and I was holding her hand. My mind was in turmoil. I had midterms; my car had broken down; we had no money. Olivia was talking about leaves and trees. I didn't even realize she had let go of my hand. I had taken another ten steps without her when I suddenly turned. She said, 'Dad, talk to me.' She was saying in her own way, 'Look, none of this other stuff matters.' She put life in perspective for me. All she cared about is that we were there. She was glad the car had broken down. That meant we could walk to school together."

Postscript:

31   On May 27, 2000, more than 400 students graduated from Bowdoin College. At the ceremony on the campus quadrangle, when Bowdoin president Robert H. Edwards read off the names "Wil and Olivia Smith," the crowd cheered and gave a standing ovation.

32   Wil, now 33, works as Bowdoin's coordinator of Multicultural Student Programs.

33   Olivia, five years old, is in kindergarten. She accompanies Wil when he does volunteer work. "She is right there along for the ride," Wil says. "I can't imagine a life without her."

(Mel Allen, "A Letter to Olivia," 2000)

"I've learned that simple walks with my father around the block when I was a child did wonders for me as an adult."

—Andy Rooney

Short Answer

Directions: Answer each question briefly, in one or two sentences.

1. Write the main idea: <u>Wil Smith, single father to Olivia, overcame many obstacles</u>
   <u>on the road to success.</u>

2. Write two major details that support the main idea.

   a. <u>Answers will vary.</u>

   b. _____

3. What is the author's purpose? <u>It is to inform Olivia and the reader about Wil's</u>
   <u>character and his drive to succeed</u>

4. Give two reasons to support your choice.

   a. <u>Answers will vary.</u>

   b. _____

Multiple Choice

Directions: For each item, write the letter corresponding to the best answer.

___b___ 1. Olivia was born while Wil was
   a. attending Florida A&M.
   b. in the Navy.
   c. in the Naval Reserves.
   d. attending Bowdoin College.

___b___ 2. This letter was written
   a. to inform readers about Wil's athletic talent.
   b. to inform Olivia and the readers of Wil's exemplary character.
   c. to persuade small schools to welcome cultural diversity.
   d. to persuade students to take their academic studies seriously.

___a___ 3. The example of Mrs. Gilbride babysitting Olivia was used to illustrate
   a. Wil's protectiveness and devotion to Olivia.
   b. Wil's age and declining athletic ability.
   c. the difficulties involved in being co-captain of the football team.
   d. Wil's lack of perspective in academic matters.

___d___ 4. Which of the following statements is true according to the author?
   a. Wil's mother served as a role model for her son.
   b. Wil lost his mother on his 15th birthday.
   c. Much of Wil's love of sports was temporarily lost after his mother's death.
   d. All of the above.

___d___ 5. The writer of this article probably feels that
   a. Wil has been a positive role model for those he has come in contact with.
   b. Wil has succeeded at Bowdoin despite poor academic preparation in his early years.
   c. Wil was wrong to always put the welfare of his daughter Olivia first.
   d. Both a and b.

___d___ 6. The author suggests that
   a. Bowdoin had many minority students.
   b. if Wil had to do it over again, he would not have assumed full custody of Olivia.
   c. the administration at Bowdoin College had little interest in helping Wil succeed.
   d. at times Wil suffered as a result of racial stereotypes.

___c___ 7. The example of the ESPN baseball highlight was used to illustrate
   a. how Wil Smith used his special skills to succeed in professional sports.
   b. that Wil Smith felt his mom had provided him with a poor foundation for life.
   c. that Wil had not fulfilled his potential at that point in his life.
   d. that Wil disliked hanging out with old friends.

___c___ 8. All of the following are accurate according to the story *except* for which?
   a. At times while raising Olivia, Wil had to do without sufficient food and sleep.
   b. Olivia suffered from asthma.
   c. Wil was viewed unfavorably by the dean for Student Academic Affairs.
   d. Wil maintains that he couldn't have been successful without Olivia.

___b___ 9. All of the following are accurate according to the story *except* for which?
   a. On road trips, Wil was often up earlier than the assistant coach of his team.
   b. In his late twenties and early thirties, Wil proved himself to be an offensive star.
   c. At Bowdoin, the majority of students are from well-to-do backgrounds.
   d. Wil's mother learned to drive at age 50 in order to see her son play sports.

___c___ 10. It still makes Wil angry that
   a. he failed to make the conference all-defensive team.
   b. he was unable to motivate his teammates.
   c. there was such disparity between his educational preparation and that of his classmates.
   d. his nephews were unable to attend high school in Brunswick, Maine.

STUDY TECHNIQUE 6: TIME LINE

A time line lists dates in chronological order along a line and then assigns information to the dates.

Directions: An incomplete time line of the reading appears below. Complete the time line with information from the reading.

1983 Wil's mother dies.

1986–1987 Wil attends Florida A & M.

1989 Wil joins the Navy.

1991 Wil goes to the Naval Air station in Brunswick, Maine.

1995 Olivia is born.

1996 Wil gains full custody of Olivia and begins to attend Bowdoin College.

1999 Wil celebrates his 31st birthday.

2000 Wil graduates from college.

Today (the Present) Wil works at Bowdoin.

True or False

Directions: Indicate whether each statement is true or false by writing **T** or **F** in the space provided.

_____T_____ 11. Wil's mother never missed one of his games.

_____F_____ 12. Wil's mother frequently coached her son's teams.

_____T_____ 13. Wil was the first single father at Bowdoin College.

_____F_____ 14. A donor gave $50,000 so that Olivia could attend day care.

_____T_____ 15. At 22, Wil was a community fixture in Brunswick, coaching both basketball and football.

Vocabulary in Context

Directions: In the paragraph indicated in parentheses, find a word that matches the definition given, and write it in the space provided.

1. having a moderate or humble estimate of oneself (1)   _modest_

2. to turn freely around; to revolve (2)   _swivel_

3. indefinite or indistinct (7)   _vague_

4. to face and deal with problems and responsibilities (14)   _cope_

5. pursuing a particular line of study or work (17)   _specializing_

6. having or showing great seriousness (20)   _intense_

7. a point at which a vital decision must be made (21)   _crossroads_

8. loud and long applause by a crowd to show approval (31)   _cheered/ovation_

In Your Own Words

1. According to the article, what roadblocks did Smith encounter in his quest to get an education?

2. Why do you think the author goes into such descriptive detail of Wil Smith and his daily life with Olivia? What stereotypes of single fathers are being discredited by this article? (*Example:* Single fathers put their own needs first.)

3. After Wil asked for help, Bowdoin College provided services to enable him to succeed as both student and parent. What kind of services should school systems provide to meet the needs of students who have family obligations?

4. Racial profiling occurs when police officers make use of racial characteristics to decide whether to stop or arrest a person. Does this article describe an incident involving racial profiling? Should police officers be allowed to engage in racial profiling?

Written Assignment

New research reveals that children who have contact with involved, loving fathers are much less likely to suffer from low self-esteem, do poorly in school, become involved with drugs, or have behavioral disorders. What can be done to encourage single fathers to have more involvement with their children? Write a paragraph giving some concrete suggestions of your own on ways to accomplish this.

Internet Activity

Several Web sites offer useful information on parenting. The first two sites listed below are sponsored by physician groups, while the other sites are commercial. Find an article of interest to you, and describe the author's general and specific purposes.

www.aap.org (American Academy of Pediatrics)

www.kidshealth.org (Nemours Foundation)

parenting.ivillage.com (Scroll down.)

www.parentandchildonline.com (*Scholastic Magazine*)

REVIEW TEST 4: Topics, Main Ideas, Details, and Purpose

Multiple Choice

Directions: Read each passage. Then for each item, write the letter corresponding to the best answer.

A. If our business enterprises are to be as flexible and innovative at all levels as they need to be, our youngsters must be prepared to work with and through other people. While there will always be a need for a certain number of solo practitioners, the more usual requirement will be that combinations of individual skills are greater than their sums. Most of the important work will be done by groups, rather than by individual experts. . . . Young people must be taught how to work constructively together. Instead of emphasizing individual achievement and competition, the emphasis in the classroom should be on group performance. Students need to learn how to seek and accept criticism from their peers, to solicit help, and to give credit to others, where appropriate. They must also learn to negotiate—to articulate their own needs, to discern what others need and see things from others' perspectives, and to discover mutually beneficial outcomes.

(Robert Reich, "Dick and Jane Meet the New Economy," 1989)

____d____ 1. The main idea expressed in this passage is that
   a. most of the work in the future will be done by individuals working alone.
   b. there are advantages and disadvantages to working collectively.
   c. many students are capable of learning to work together productively.
   d. young people need to be taught how to work together productively so that our business enterprises can successfully meet new challenges.

____a____ 2. The author's primary purpose is to
   a. convince us of the necessity of emphasizing group activities in our educational systems.
   b. explain the dynamics of a business enterprise.
   c. entertain us with an interesting anecdote concerning the world of business.
   d. inform us of problems students are likely to face in the near future.

_____ b _____ 3. The examples of seeking and accepting criticism, soliciting help, and giving appropriate credit were used to illustrate
        a. skills students need to develop in order to work individually.
        b. skills students need to develop in order to work cooperatively.
        c. requirements of a top-notch school system.
        d. the complexity of a business organization.

_____ d _____ 4. The best title for the paragraph would be
        a. "Group Dynamics in Action."
        b. "Cooperative Learning."
        c. "The Solo Practitioner."
        d. "Group Learning and Business."

B. In the same way that doctors, janitors, lawyers, and industrial workers develop unique ways of looking at and responding to their work environment, so too do police officers. Police officers are often viewed as suspicious and authoritative. Police work is potentially dangerous, so officers need to be constantly aware of what is happening around them. They are frequently warned about what happens to officers who are too trusting. They learn about the many officers who have died in the line of duty because they did not exercise proper caution. On the street, they need to stay alert for signals that crimes may be in progress: an unfamiliar noise, someone "checking into" an alleyway, a secret exchange of goods. The working environment also demands that officers gain immediate control of potentially dangerous situations. They are routinely called on to demonstrate authority. Uniforms, badges, nightsticks, and guns signify authority—but officers soon learn that this authority is often challenged by a hostile public.

(Freda Adler, Gerhard O. W. Mueller, and William S. Laufer, *Criminal Justice*, 5/e, 2009)

_____ b _____ 5. The best title for this paragraph would be
        a. "Jobs."
        b. "The Outlook of Police Officers."
        c. "The World of Work."
        d. "Becoming a Police Officer."

_____ a _____ 6. All of the following were given as reasons for the effect of police work on an officer's outlook *except* for which?
        a. a belief that courts are too lenient on criminals
        b. a realization of what happens to officers when they are too trusting
        c. the need to constantly monitor a situation
        d. the need to assert authority

Written Assignment

Directions: Choose one of the following:

1. What kind of work gives you the most satisfaction? What kind of work do you find least rewarding? Write a paragraph discussing your answers.

2. Write a paragraph describing your job history. Explain why you liked or disliked your previous jobs. What did each of your previous jobs teach you about what you want to do as a future career?

3. Write a paragraph describing the difference between a "good" boss and a "bad" boss.

4. What kind of work do you want to do? Interview some people already active in the career of your choice. How do these people feel about their work? Write a paragraph discussing your findings.

Chapter Summary and Review

In this chapter, you learned how to determine whether the author's purpose is to entertain, inform, or persuade. You also learned how to summarize. Based on the material in Chapter 3, answer the following questions.

Short Answer

Directions: Answer the questions briefly.

1. What do you do when you summarize?

2. What question words should you keep in mind when writing a summary?

Vocabulary in Context

Directions: Choose one of the following words to complete the sentences below. Use each word only once.

audience	details	entertain
persuasive	purpose	textbooks

3. An author needs to take into account the intended _____audience_____, the people who will be reading the work.

4. An author who is telling a story or making an appeal to your imagination is probably trying to _____entertain_____ you.

5. What you read in your _____textbooks_____ is probably informative writing.

6. Political advertisements that you receive in the mail before elections are good examples of _____persuasive_____ writing.

7. A good summary of an article will include the main ideas and significant supporting _____details_____.

8. To determine an author's _____purpose_____, you should ask yourself why the author wrote the article.

VOCABULARY   Unit 2 Word Parts Dealing with Numbers

Introduction

The Greeks and Romans came up with a system for creating words by putting together smaller word parts. They used three types of word parts: prefixes, suffixes, and roots. *Pre* means "before," and so it makes sense that a prefix comes before the main part of a word. *Suf* means "after," and so a suffix comes at the end of a word.

A root word is the main part of a word and usually comes in the middle. Many English words are composed of at least one root, and many have one or more prefixes and suffixes.

Part of the Greek and Roman system was a set of prefixes that represented numbers. There are many words in English derived from specific numbers. One way to help you remember many of these number prefixes is to think of the months of the year. For example, October has the prefix *oct,* meaning "eight." That might help you remember what *oct* means, except for one big problem—October is not the 8th month, but the 10th. How can this be? The answer is that our calendar evolved from the original Roman calendar, which began in March instead of January and had only 10 months. The months of Januarius and Februarius were added later, around 700 B.C. You can see that making March the first month makes October the eighth month.

Vocabulary Units 2 and 3 will draw on your knowledge of the numbering system. Make sure that you remember that the calendar began in March.

Now we are going to learn some number prefixes.

uni—one	tetra—four	oct—eight
mono—one	quint—five	nov—nine
bi—two	pent—five	dec—ten
duo—two	sex—six	lat—side
di—two	hex—six	ped—foot
tri—three	sept—seven	pod—foot
quad—four	hept—seven	

biped	*Ped* means "foot" as in *pedal* and *pedestrian,* so a *biped* is an animal with two feet, such as a bird.
tripod	Sometimes there are slight variations in the spellings of word parts. *Pod* also means "foot," so a *tripod* has three feet. An example would be a stand for a camera.
quadruped	An animal with four feet, such as a dog or a cat.
hexapod	An organism with six feet, such as an insect. Why aren't spiders *hexapods?* Because they have eight feet.
unicorn	That mythical animal with one horn.
unison	An instance of sounding the same note at the same time.
monopoly	A company that has no competition is called a *monopoly.* The electric and gas companies in your area are probably *monopolies* because they are the only companies allowed to give you service.
monolog(ue)	*Log* means "to speak," so a *monolog* is one person speaking without anyone responding. Jay Leno and David Letterman give *monologs* at the beginning of their shows. Why is the "ue" in parentheses? Words such as *monologue, dialogue,* and *catalogue* are in the process of losing their last two letters. As time passes, there is a tendency to drop unneeded letters from words. A dictionary 50 years from now will probably not list any of these words with the "ue" at the end.
lateral	Toward the side, sideways. The quarterback threw a *lateral* pass.
unilateral	One-sided. The mother made a *unilateral* decision and told her child to go to bed. This was not a decision that was made by discussing it with the child.

hexapod—There are over five million species of insects in the world. The total insect population of the world is at least 1 quintillion (1 followed by 18 zeros).

bilateral	Two-sided. We signed a *bilateral* agreement with Russia.
bicuspids	Your teeth with two points.
dual	Two of a kind, such as *dual* mufflers.
duel	A formal combat with weapons fought between two people in the presence of witnesses.
duet	A musical composition written for two musicians to perform simultaneously.
duo	Two musical performers; a pair.
trio	Three people in a group.
quartet	Four people in a group. A jazz *quartet* has four musicians.
quintuplets	Five children of the same mother born at one time.
sextuplets	Six children of the same mother born at one time.
octuplets	Eight children of the same mother born at one time. In 2009 in California, Nadya Suleman gave birth to octuplets.
monoxide	One oxygen atom, as in carbon *monoxide* (CO).
dioxide	Two oxygen atoms, as in carbon *dioxide* (CO_2).
biplane	A plane with two sets of wings, one over the other, such as the one the Wright brothers flew.
triplane	A plane with three sets of wings, one over the other. The Germans, and specifically the "Red Baron," flew *triplanes* for a short period during World War I, but they were not practical for combat.
tetrahedron	A four-sided, three-dimensional object.
pentagon	A five-sided figure. The Defense Department has its headquarters in this five-sided building located in Virginia just across the Potomac River from Washington, DC.

duel—In 1804, Alexander Hamilton, whose picture you will find on a $10 bill, fought a famous duel with Aaron Burr.

biplane—The first plane flight by Orville Wright lasted 12 seconds, went to a height of 8 to 12 feet, and traveled 120 feet. The name of this plane, flown at Kitty Hawk, North Carolina, was Bird of Prey.

Tetrahedron

A Typical Triplane

*Pentagon—The
Pentagon has 17.5 miles
of corridors, 7,754
windows, and 23,000
people working there.*

The Pentagon

Pentateuch	The first five books of the Old Testament (Genesis, Exodus, Leviticus, Numbers, and Deuteronomy) are called the *Pentateuch*. The Jews consider these books central to their faith and call them the Torah (law).
hexagon	A six-sided figure.
octagon	An eight-sided figure.
octave	Eight notes of the musical scale.
octane	You know it has to do with gas, but *octane* acquired its name because it has eight carbon atoms in its chemical formula (C_8H_{18}).
decade	A 10-year period.
decimal	Our numbering system is called a *decimal* system because it is based on units of 10.
September	Originally the seventh month.
October	Originally the eighth month.
November	Originally the ninth month.
December	Originally the tenth month.
biathlon	Two events, usually sporting.
triathlon	An endurance race combining three consecutive events, usually swimming, bicycling, and running. The Hawaii *Triathlon* requires participants to swim 2 miles, ride a bike 100 miles, and, last but not least, run 26 miles—all of which is done in one day.
heptathlon	An athletic contest for women that requires participants to take part in seven events: 100-meter hurdles, shot put, high jump, 200-meter dash, long jump, javelin throw, and 800-meter run. Jackie Joyner-Kersee won the gold medal in the *heptathlon* at the Olympics in 1988 and 1992.
decathlon	An athletic contest in which each contestant takes part in 10 events: 100-meter dash, 400-meter dash, long jump, 16-pound shot put, high jump, 110-meter hurdles, discus throw, pole vault, javelin

*hexagon—All snow
crystals are hexagonal.*

throw, and 1500-meter run. The decathlon winner is usually pro-claimed "the world's greatest athlete."

sexagenarian   A person in his or her sixties.

septuagenarian A person in his or her seventies.

octogenarian   A person in his or her eighties.

nonagenarian   A person in his or her nineties.

Exercise 1

Directions: Write the definition of each prefix.

1. di   two
2. quad   four
3. oct   eight
4. ped   foot
5. tetra   four
6. duo   two
7. dec   ten
8. lat   side
9. nov   nine
10. pod   foot
11. bi   two

Directions: Read the definition and then write the correct prefix(es).

12. seven—(2)   hept   sept
13. five—(2)   quint   pent
14. one—(2)   mono   uni
15. three—(1)   tri   —
16. six—(2)   hex   sex

Exercise 2: A "Prefixed" Fairy Tale

Directions: Replace the prefix with its definition, and write it in the blank provided.

Once upon a time there was a young (pent, ___5___) -year-old girl named Little Red Riding Hood. She had a grandmother who was (nov × nov, ___81___) years old. Grandmother lived in a house (dec, ___10___) blocks from Little Red's home. (Mono, ___One___) day Little Red set off for Grandma's house. She took a route that was only (di, ___two___) miles long instead of (tri, ___three___) miles. Before she left, she packed a basket filled with (sept, ___seven___) or (oct, ___eight___) goodies. She had gone almost (bi, ___two___) miles, and had been walking about (hept × hept), ___49___) minutes when she came upon a large wolf. He put out his paw and leaned against her (lat, ___side___). After a brief struggle of (quad, __four__) or (quint, __five__) minutes, she noticed Grandma and the woodman. The (duo, __two__) of them quickly came to her rescue. The woodman knocked out the wolf, and soon the wolf slept peacefully for (hex, __6__) hours under a tree. Finally, Little Red was happy after all, but she wouldn't go for a walk on (pod, __foot__) again for at least (tetra, __four__) to (sex, __six__) weeks.

Exercise 3: Vocabulary in Context

Directions: In the blanks below, write the word that best completes the sentence. Use each word only once.

bicuspid	biped	decade	dual	monolog
monopoly	nonagenarian	octagon	pentagon	quartet

1. A stop sign is called an __octagon__ because it has eight sides.
2. Bill Gates, the chair of Microsoft, was accused of creating a(n) __monopoly__ in the software industry.
3. The opening act of the play featured a(n) __monolog__ spoken by one of the actors.
4. The __bicuspid__ teeth arrive when a child is about 10–12 years old.
5. The __Pentagon__ houses the offices of the five U.S. military services: the Air Force, Army, Navy, Marines, and Coast Guard.
6. A kangaroo is considered to be a(n) __biped__ because it has two feet.
7. Together, John, Paul, George, and Ringo formed the Beatles, the famous musical __quartet__ of the 60s.
8. Carlos has __dual__ citizenship; he has legal rights in both Spain and the United States.
9. A(n) __nonagenarian__ is more likely than someone younger to suffer from Alzheimer's disease.
10. The Roaring Twenties was a(n) __decade__ of jalopies, flappers, speakeasies, and jazz.

Exercise 4: Vocabulary in Context

Directions: In the blanks below, write the word that best completes the sentence. Use each word only once.

bilateral	decathlon	duo	hexagonal
lateral	monoxide	octane	octave
quadrupeds	triathlon	triplane	unison

1. Many quartz crystals have a(n) __hexagonal__ shape.
2. At the football game, the crowd yelled in __unison__, "Defense, defense, defense!"
3. After failing to be promoted to assistant principal, the teacher made a(n) __lateral__ move to a teaching position at another school.
4. The __triplane__ was a popular flying machine from about 1905 to 1910.

5. Dogs, cats, and horses are all examples of ___quadrupeds___.

6. Batman and Robin are a dynamic, crime-fighting ___duo___.

7. The Beatles' song "Can't Buy Me Love" (1964) sounds entirely different when sung a(n) ___octave___ lower.

8. The winner of the grueling ___decathlon___ is often featured on the cover of Wheaties, Breakfast of Champions.

9. The old Plymouth needed high- ___octane___ gas to run well.

10. Because of a gas leak and poor ventilation, the family died of carbon ___monoxide___ poisoning.

11. In 1987, a historic ___bilateral___ disarmament agreement was reached between Ronald Reagan of the United States and Mikhail Gorbachev of the Soviet Union.

12. In the ___triathlon___, Frank placed high in swimming and bicycling but made a poor showing in distance running.

Now that you have studied Vocabulary Unit 2, practice your new knowledge by trying the crossword puzzle.

Expanding Your Word Power

The words listed below are not found in this Vocabulary Unit, but they are derived from the vocabulary word parts that you have studied. All of them would be good words for you to learn. See if you can guess the meaning of each word from its word parts.

1. unitard
2. unitarian
3. universal
4. monolingual
5. monosyllabic
6. monotheism
7. monotonous
8. binoculars
9. bipolar
10. deuce
11. triage
12. triceratops
13. tricolor
14. trigonometry
15. trimester
16. quadriplegic
17. impede
18. pedicure
19. podiatrist
20. arthropod

Vocabulary Unit 2 Crossword Puzzle

ACROSS CLUES

1. The abbreviation for what was once the 10th month.
5. A chemical found in gas.
8. The Torah, or first five books of the Old Testament.
9. A word part meaning "side."
10. A word part meaning "one."
15. What the Red Baron flew in World War I.
16. One of five children born at one time.
18. Teeth with two points.
22. All the voices or instruments together.
23. A contest involving seven track events.
25. A business that has no competition.
26. Carbon _____ is one thing that comes out of a car exhaust pipe.
27. The building in Washington, DC, where the military has its headquarters.
29. The abbreviation for what was once the 9th month.
30. What David Letterman delivers at the start of the show.
31. We exhale carbon _____.

DOWN CLUES

1. Two of a kind.
2. The abbreviation for what was once the 8th month.
3. A numbering system that is based on units of 10.
4. An animal with four legs.
6. A person in his or her nineties is a(n) _____.
7. Passing the ball to the side is a(n) _____.
11. An animal with two legs.
12. What Aaron Burr and Alexander Hamilton fought.
13. The eight notes of the musical scale.
14. What the Wright Brothers flew.
17. The mythical animal with one horn.
19. A decision made without consulting the other party is _____.
20. What was originally the 7th month.
21. A musical piece written for two musicians to perform at the same time.
23. A word part meaning "seven."
24. A scientific name for insects.
26. A word part meaning "one."
28. Three in a group.
32. A word part meaning "two."

Transition Words and Patterns of Organization

CHAPTER PREVIEW

In this chapter, you will

• Learn about transition words and phrases.

• Learn about patterns of paragraph organization.

• Learn about relationships within and between sentences.

Introduction to Transition Words and Patterns of Organization

Writers ordinarily try to write so that their thoughts flow smoothly and logically. They try to connect one idea with another in such a way that readers can easily understand what they are saying. They connect their ideas by means of **transition words.** In Latin, the prefix *trans* means "across." Transition words enable the author to carry you from one place in your reading "across" to another.

In your reading it is important to pay close attention to these transition words. These special words help show the relationships between ideas within sentences and ideas within paragraphs. Good drivers learn to closely watch the road ahead, using signposts or markers to make their trips easier and safer. Good readers learn to use the author's transition words, which signal what is ahead.

Look at the sentences below. The addition of a transition word signaling a contrast makes a big difference in our ability to understand Tom's situation.

1. Tom was very eager to leave for college. The thought of leaving familiar surroundings filled him with dread.

2. Tom was very eager to leave for college. **However,** the thought of leaving familiar surroundings filled him with dread.

The first example doesn't really make a lot of sense. If Tom is so eager to leave, why is he filled with dread? The addition of the transition word makes the situation clear in the second example. Although Tom wants to leave for college, he is understandably reluctant to give up his safe and comfortable surroundings.

Now look at these two sentences:

1. Karla did poorly in her English classes. She decided to switch her major to communication.

2. **Because** Karla did poorly in her English classes, she decided to switch her major to communication.

169

The first example makes us guess at the relationship between the two sentences. The addition of the transition word clarifies this relationship.

Following are two more examples. Study the two sentences. Which one is easier to read and understand?

1. Bill did everything he could think of to get a good grade in chemistry. He always attended class, did all of his homework assignments, and studied long hours. He hired a tutor.
2. Bill did everything he could think of to get a good grade in chemistry. He always attended class, did all of his homework assignments, and studied long hours. **In addition,** he hired a tutor.

The transition words *in addition* make the author's meaning easier to understand.
Now look at the next example.

1. Mary did not like to go to the dentist to have her teeth cleaned. She went anyway because she knew that it would be better for her in the long run.
2. **Although** Mary did not like to go to the dentist to have her teeth cleaned, she went anyway because she knew that it would be better for her in the long run.

The transition word *although* helps clarify the relationship between the two thoughts.

Transition Words

Words that can be used to show **classification or division (categories):**

break down	combine	lump
categorize	divide	split
class and subclass	group	type
classify	kind	

Words that can be used to show **cause-and-effect** relationships:

as a consequence	due to	resulting
as a result	for	since
because	for this reason	so
begin	hence	then
bring about	lead to	therefore
consequently	reaction	thus

Words that can be used to show **comparison:**

all	both	like
and	in comparison	likewise
as	just as	similarly

Words that can be used to show **contrast:**

although	in contrast	on the other hand
but	in opposition	rather than
despite	instead	though
even so	nevertheless	unlike
however	on the contrary	yet

continued

Transition Words—*continued*

Words that can be used to show **steps in a process:**

after	finally	process
afterward	first, second, third	step
at this point	next	then
at this stage	now	

Words that can be used to show **examples:**

for example	specifically	to illustrate
for instance	such as	
in particular	to demonstrate	

Words that can be used to **define:**

derives from	is described by	refers to
is called	means	term or concept
is defined as	originates from	

Words that can be used to show **chronological order:**

after	first, second, third	next
at last	finally	seasons
before	following	soon
currently	in a year, month, day	then
during	in the meantime	until

Words and symbols that can be used to show **listing (enumeration):**

follow, following	bullets(•)	functions
first, second, third	asterisks(*)	characteristics
colon (:)	numbers (1, 2, 3)	in addition
also	letters (a, b, c)	next, finally

Words that can be used to show **spatial order:**

above	front	on top
below	left	right
beyond	near	underneath
center	next to	

Words that can be used to show **addition:**

again	further	as well as
also	furthermore	besides
and	in addition	too
another	moreover	

The following transition words are often used in presenting an argument.

Words that can be used to show **summary and conclusion:**

finally	in short	therefore
hence	in summary	thus
in brief	overall	to conclude
in conclusion	so	to sum up

continued

Transition Words—*continued*

Words that can be used to show **reversal:**

granted that	nevertheless	unlike
instead	still	yet

Words that can be used to show **emphasis:**

as indicated	it's important	to repeat
as noted	once again	truly
certainly	to emphasize	unquestionably
here again	to remember	without a doubt

Words that can be used to show **concession:**

although	even though
despite	in spite of

Note: While lists of transition words are helpful, the groupings of the words given in this section are not perfect, and many of these words may be placed in more than one category. The only way to truly determine the function of a transition word is by studying the context of the sentence and the paragraph.

Exercise 1: Transitions

Directions: In the following sentences, provide an appropriate transition word. If you need help, use the transition words chart. Be sure your completed sentence makes sense.

1. (contrast) __Although__ he was failing all of his classes, he still had a positive attitude about school.

2. (cause) __Because__ she worked so many hours at her job, she had no time left for a social life.

3. We can (classification or division) __classify__ parents into two categories: those who are willing to use physical punishment on their children and those who are not.

4. Aggression is (definition) __defined as__ any physical or verbal behavior that is directly intended to hurt someone.

5. (example) __For example__ a slap, a punch, and even a direct insult are all considered forms of aggression.

6. Suppose your boss insults you; (steps in a process) __first__ you go home and yell at your wife, __afterward__ she yells at your son, __then__ he kicks his baby sister, __next__ she pulls the dog's tail, and __finally__ the dog bites the mail carrier.

7. In the winter months of (months of the year in order) __December__, __January__, and __February__, assaults are at an all-time low. In the hotter seasons of __June__, __July__, and __August__, violent crimes are more likely to occur.

Writers organize their supporting sentences and ideas in ways called **patterns of organization.** The most common kinds of patterns of organization are

(1) classification and division, (2) cause and effect, (3) comparison-contrast, (4) steps in a process, (5) examples, (6) definition, (7) chronological order, (8) listing, (9) spatial order, and (10) addition. A writer's chosen pattern of organization will affect the sort of transition words he or she uses. In the sections that follow, we will discuss patterns of organization and the relationships between patterns of organization and transition words.

Classification and Division

Classification is the process of organizing information into categories. We create a category by noting and defining group characteristics. The categories we create make it easier to analyze, discuss, and draw conclusions.

Have you ever scanned the classified ads section of the newspaper? If you have, you are already familiar with classification and division. Ads are not arranged randomly in the newspaper; otherwise, you would never be able to quickly locate the information you need. Instead, ads are grouped into categories, with each category further subdivided as much as needed.

Whenever you do the laundry, you are also probably putting things into categories. Many washers have categories such as: easy care, delicates, casuals, and cottons. Going to the grocery store is made a lot easier because the items are arranged by categories. Fresh fruits and vegetables are together in one location, canned goods in another, and household cleaning supplies in still another.

The following are the main categories of music according to iTunes.

Classical

Rock

Pop

Hip Hop or Rap

Jazz

Alternative

And then there are subgenres such as metal or rock ballads, and love songs.

(iTunes)

The details in many paragraphs are also organized using classification. Look at the three short paragraphs describing unhealthy expressions of anger. The author uses two specific categories to make it easier for us to understand the information being presented.

"Self-control is the quality that distinguishes the fittest to survive."
—George Bernard Shaw

According to University of Arizona psychologist Roger J. Daldrup, there are **two classic ways** of expressing anger in an unhealthy way: misdirecting it, and suppressing it completely.

Misdirected anger, Daldrup says, "is the classic kicking the cat because you're angry at your spouse maneuver. Though people who misdirect their anger seem to be expressing it, they are just burying the real problem and creating more problems along the way."

The other classic response, complete suppression of anger, doesn't work either, because, says Daldrup, it creates what he calls "the keyboard effect." When a person starts repressing one emotion, he begins repressing them all, something he likens to pressing down the soft pedal on the piano: "That pedal will soften all the notes on the piano, just as dulling one emotion will dull them all."

(Brent Q. Hafen, Keith J. Karren, Kathryn J. Frandsen, and N. Lee Smith, *Mind/Body Health,* 1996)

Now look at the following outline to gain a better understanding of major and minor supporting details. Here, MI refers to the main idea, MSD to major supporting details, and msd to minor supporting details.

   I. There are two classic ways of expressing anger in an unhealthy way. (MI)
      A. A person can misdirect anger. (MSD)
         1. It just buries the problem and creates more problems. (msd)
         2. It is the classic kicking the cat because you're angry at a spouse. (msd)
      B. A person can suppress anger. (MSD)
         1. This method doesn't work either. (msd)
         2. It creates a keyboard effect. (msd)

In recent years, many Americans have become fascinated with investigating their ancestral background. They use the information they gather to assemble

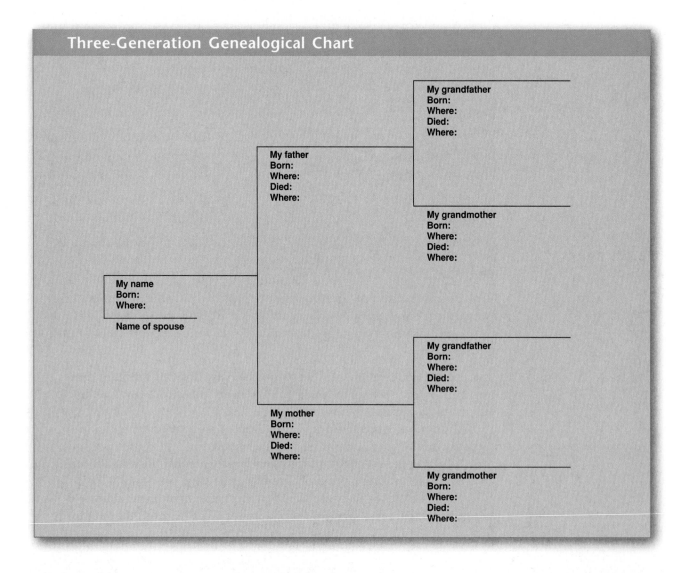

Three-Generation Genealogical Chart

My grandfather
Born:
Where:
Died:
Where:

My father
Born:
Where:
Died:
Where:

My grandmother
Born:
Where:
Died:
Where:

My name
Born:
Where:

Name of spouse

My grandfather
Born:
Where:
Died:
Where:

My mother
Born:
Where:
Died:
Where:

My grandmother
Born:
Where:
Died:
Where:

family trees or genealogy charts showing the names, birth dates, marriages, and deaths of ancestors. In addition to being fun, studying the details of a family's medical past can provide early warning of health problems that might lie ahead for current family members. Many ailments are known to have genetic links, including cancer, diabetes, and alcoholism.

To practice classification, try making a genealogy chart or family tree. Talk with family members to try to gather information about your ancestors. Then record the information on a genealogical chart like the one on the previous page.

Written Assignment

In the process of doing your research, you may discover some interesting stories about your family. Some of these stories are likely true, but others may be part family myth. Write three of these stories in paragraph format, and share them with the class.

Internet Activity

Genealogy Web sites are available on the Internet. The following Web sites are especially helpful in looking up family tree information:

> www.cyndislist.com
>
> www.familysearch.org
>
> www.ancestry.com
>
> www.ellisislandrecords.org

Exercise 2: Classification and Division

Directions: Fill in the blank with an appropriate transition word or phrase from the list below. Some of the transition words will fit in more than one of the sentences, but try to use a different transition word in each sentence. Make sure the sentence makes sense with the transition word you choose.

break down   classify   combine   divide   group

1. We can ___classify___ cohabitating relationships into five types.

2. The first ___group___ is called *temporary casual* and involves two people sharing living space simply because it is convenient and less expensive. Neither party is romantically involved.

3. If we ___combine___ all those who have cohabitated at some point in their lives, we discover that the figure is about 50 percent.

4. We can ___divide___ this category into those who expect to eventually marry their partners and those who do not.

5. We can further ___break down___ those couples into those who intend to have children and those who do not.

Cause and Effect

In a **cause-and-effect** relationship, one thing causes another thing to happen. The second event is the effect or result of the first event.

Try reading the following anecdote to locate cause-and-effect relationships. You will need people to read the narrator's, the farmer's, and the field hand's parts.

> *Narrator:* It happened in the days before mail service and telephones. A wealthy farmer took a long trip. When he arrived home, he asked the first field hand he saw what had happened while he was away. This is how their conversation went:
>
> *Field hand:* Well, the dog died.
>
> *Farmer:* The dog died! How?
>
> *Field hand:* The horses ran over him when they became frightened and ran out of the barn.
>
> *Farmer:* What scared the horses? Why did they run?
>
> *Field hand:* They were running from the flames when the barn caught on fire.
>
> *Farmer:* My God! How did the barn catch on fire?
>
> *Field hand:* Well, sir, flames jumped from the house and caught the barn on fire.
>
> *Farmer:* From the house! Did the house burn down, too?
>
> *Field hand:* Yep. The house is gone, too.
>
> *Farmer:* How on earth did the house burn down?
>
> *Field hand:* You see, one of the candles around your wife's casket fell over and caught the house on fire.

(*Contemporary's Building Basic Skills in Reading, Book I*, 1988)

Now complete the cause-and-effect sentences.

1. Because the candles on the wife's casket fell over, the <u>house burned down.</u>

2. Because flames jumped from the house, the <u>barn caught on fire.</u>

3. Because the horses were scared, they <u>ran over the dog.</u>

You will encounter many cause-and-effect relationships in the textbooks you read for your various classes. The following paragraphs from a health textbook illustrate a cause-and-effect relationship; transition words are set in bold. Read the paragraphs and then study the outline that follows.

"Angers are the sinners of the soul."

—Robert Fuller

Anger has as many different causes as there are situations and people. The most common **cause** is physical or psychological restraint—being held back from something we intensely want or want to do. Others include being forced to do something against our will, being taken advantage of, being frustrated, being insulted, being ridiculed, or having plans defeated. Sometimes other emotions (such as distress, sorrow, or fear) can **lead to** anger.

The most recent research shows that the **effects** of anger are diverse and widespread. Consider the wide range of physiological **reactions** that go with it: changes in muscle tension, scowling, grinding of teeth, glaring, clenching of fists, flushing, goose bumps, chills and shudders, prickly sensations, numbness, choking, twitching, sweating, losing control, or feeling hot or cold. One of the major physiological **effects** of anger is on the release of chemicals and hormones, principally adrenaline and noradrenaline. When the release of adrenaline and noradrenaline is chronic or prolonged, **resulting** in chronic or prolonged anger, some of the most serious **effects** are high blood pressure, headache, heart attack, stroke, and kidney problems. If there's enough anger, almost any part of the body can be harmed. The **effects** can be as serious as cancer and heart disease or as minor (but annoying) as the common cold or skin disorders.

(Brent Q. Hafen, Keith J. Karren, Kathryn J. Frandsen, and N. Lee Smith, *Mind/Body Health*, 1996)

    I. Anger has many different causes. (MI)
        A. One cause is physical or psychological restraint. (MSD)
        B. Other causes include being forced to do something, being taken advantage of, being frustrated, insulted, ridiculed. (MSD)
        C. Other emotions can sometimes cause anger. (MSD)
    II. The effects of anger are diverse and widespread. (MI)
        A. There are a wide range of physiological reactions. (MSD)
            1. Examples are changes in muscle tension, scowling, clenching. (msd)
            2. More examples are flushing, chills, and shudders. (msd)
        B. Anger affects the release of chemicals and hormones. (MSD)
            1. Adrenaline (msd)
            2. Noradrenaline (msd)
        C. Chronic or prolonged anger causes health problems. (MSD)
            1. Effects can be major like cancer and heart disease. (msd)
            2. Effects can be minor like the common cold or skin disorders. (msd)

Exercise 3: Cause and Effect

Directions: Fill in the blank with an appropriate transition word or phrase from the list below. Some of the transition words will fit in more than one of the sentences, but try to use a different transition word in each sentence. Make sure the sentence makes sense with the transition you choose.

    as a result   because   bring about   reaction   therefore

1. ___Because___ working moms with children under the age of five want a familiar face to care for their children, many are turning to grandparents and other relatives for help with child care.

2. Teens who begin drinking before they are old enough to drive have a higher chance of becoming alcoholics at some time in their lives. ___Therefore___, many organizations want to begin early-intervention programs with those teens who begin drinking early.

3. Last year, U.S. residents spent $207 billion on meals prepared by restaurants, with 51 percent of that total for takeout and delivery; ___as a result___, online food order companies are beginning to see the potential for big business.

4. In ___reaction___ to criticism by the Food and Drug Administration, R. J. Reynolds Tobacco Co. discontinued the use of Joe Camel, the cartoon character, in its ads.

5. In order to ___bring about___ positive changes in race relations, more and more open forums discussing problems are being held around the country.

Comparison-Contrast

A **comparison** shows the similarities between two or more things, while a **contrast** shows the differences. Sometimes a writer compares (tells the similarities) and contrasts (tells the differences) at the same time. The following information from the

Internet on Presidents Lincoln and Kennedy illustrates comparison-contrast, with transition words in bold.

There are many curious parallels in the deaths of Presidents Abraham Lincoln and John Fitzgerald Kennedy. President Lincoln was elected in 1860. **And** exactly 100 years later, in 1960, Kennedy was elected president. **Both** were assassinated on a Friday in the presence of their wives. **Both** presidents were deeply involved in civil rights for blacks. **Both** President Lincoln and President Kennedy were succeeded by vice presidents named Johnson who were southern Democrats and former senators. **Both** men were killed by a bullet that entered the head from behind. Lincoln was killed in Ford's Theater. Kennedy met his death while riding in a Lincoln convertible made by the Ford Motor Company. **Both** assassins died before they could be brought to trial. In turn, each assassin's slayer died before he could be punished. Many believe that **both** assassinations were part of a giant conspiracy extending far beyond the one gunman.

On the other hand, there are significant dissimilarities between the two. To name just a few: Lincoln, largely self-educated, was born poor and was raised by his father and a stepmother. **In contrast,** Kennedy was born to a wealthy family and attended elite private schools. Lincoln was president when the country was at war with itself during the Civil War. **In contrast,** Kennedy served during the Cold War when the country was unified against an enemy outside the United States.

To learn more about Ford's Theater and the Lincoln assassination, go to www.nps.gov/foth. To learn more about Kennedy, go to www.jfklibrary.org and take a virtual tour of the John Fitzgerald Kennedy Library and Museum in Boston.

In the two paragraphs that follow, the author explores how different cultures deal with anger. Again, transition words are set in bold. The first paragraph is outlined for you as an example. Try to complete the outline of the second paragraph.

Besides individual **differences** in the way we feel and express anger, there are also some important cultural **differences.** In a number of Latin and Arab cultures the free expression of anger is heartily endorsed; two who are angry at each other may fight because they figure that a strong third party (such as a neighbor or family member) will intervene before things go too far. The Utku Eskimos fall at the **opposite** end of the spectrum: They ostracize anyone who loses his temper, regardless of the reason. Between these two extremes are all kinds of middle ground. The Japanese don't display anger as their traditional Western counterparts do; **instead** of lashing out verbally, the Japanese assume a neutral expression and a polite demeanor when angry. The Mbuti hunter-gatherers of the Democratic Republic of the Congo take it a step further; when angry, they laugh. Some individual disputes have become "full-scale tribal laugh fests."

There are also profoundly **different** "rules" from one culture to another for the way anger is choreographed. Members of Anglo societies follow a fairly predictable course of action: hints, indirect efforts, involvement of a third party, direct confrontation, escalating anger, lawsuits, and, when all else fails, violence. The steps are quite **different, however,** in Iran, Latin America, and some American Indian cultures: There you might observe silent brooding (for five years or even five hundred years) while the tribe decides what to do; or an act of violent revenge, then more resolute measures, such as discussion, direct negotiation, or the involvement of a third party.

(Brent Q. Hafen, Keith J. Karren, Kathryn J. Frandsen, and N. Lee Smith, *Mind/Body Health, 1996*)

I. There are cultural differences in the way anger is expressed. (MI)
   A. In Latin and Arabic cultures expressing anger is heartily endorsed. (MSD)
      1. Two who are angry at each other may fight with each other. (msd)
      2. They expect to be interrupted by a third party. (msd)
   B. The Utku Eskimos ostracize those who lose their tempers. (MSD)
   C. The Japanese assume a neutral expression and polite demeanor when angry. (MSD)
   D. The Mbuti laugh when they are angry.
II. There are different rules for the way anger is choreographed depending on the culture. (MI)
   A. Anglo societies follow a predictable course of action. (MSD)
      1. _hints, indirect efforts_____ (msd)
      2. _involvement of a third party_____ (msd)
      3. _escalating anger, violence_____ (msd)
   B. In Iran, Latin America, and some Indian cultures, the steps are different. (MSD)
      1. _silent brooding_____ (msd)
      2. _act of violent revenge_____ (msd)
      3. _involvement of a third party_____ (msd)

Exercise 4: Comparison-Contrast

Directions: Fill in the blank with an appropriate transition word or phrase from the list below. Some of the transition words will fit in more than one of the sentences, but try to use a different transition word in each sentence. Make sure the sentence makes sense with the transition you choose.

    although   both   however   just as   on the other hand

1. In order to live a healthy lifestyle, people are increasingly being told to _____both_____ eat right and exercise.

2. Joan's advisor gave her some good reasons for going to graduate school, but, _on the other hand_, he also gave her some good reasons for directly starting her career.

3. There are two ways to go to get to the mall, and one way is _____just as_____ good as the other.

4. _____Although_____ linemen on a professional football team need to be large, they also need to be fast.

5. Judging by all the dark clouds in the sky, it looked like it was going to rain. _____However_____, around noontime the sun came out.

Written Assignment

For practice, write a short paragraph comparing and contrasting two ordinary household objects such as a pencil and a pen, or a fork and a spoon. Or you might want to try comparing and contrasting an iPod with CDs and records. Include some of the "compare and contrast" words found in the transition words chart.

Steps in a Process

In the **steps-in-a-process** pattern, something is explained or described in a step-by-step manner. The sequences are clearly identified by specific transition words. A lot of scientific writing uses this particular pattern. In addition, anytime we try to show how to make or do something, we are probably using this pattern of organization. Just for fun, try following these directions explaining how to draw cartoon characters. (You will need a separate piece of paper for your sketches.)

It's easy to draw a cartoon. Just take it step by step. First, start by drawing a shape in pencil, and then lightly sketch in the features. Remember to exaggerate!

Step 1. Draw a basic shape lightly and loosely in pencil.

Step 2. Lightly sketch in the features.

Step 3. Go back over the drawing darkening some of your lines.

Step 4. Erase pencil lines and add details to make your drawing personal.

From *Cartooning* by Loyd Littlepage © 1994. Reprinted by permission. All rights reserved.

In the two paragraphs that follow, the author gives a step-by-step account of the physical changes that accompany anger; transition words are in bold. Try creating your own outline on a separate sheet of paper.

Medical research shows that no matter how many times you work out at the gym or how careful you are to eat correctly, you're putting yourself at risk if you don't manage your anger effectively. The body reacts to anger with immediate physical changes. **First,** blood rushes to the face, the heartbeat speeds up, and the body undergoes a physical reaction much like that of stress. **Next,** respiration speeds up, blood pressure rises, the digestive **process** slows down, and the muscles tense up, all in readiness for action. Our blood "boils," our muscles tense up, our stomach feels like it's tied up in knots, and our cheeks feel like they're burning up. **At this point,** the more angry we become, the stronger and more powerful we feel—and the more pressed to "strike out." Back when people needed the fight-or-flight response to defend themselves against aggressors, they needed anger. It was important to survival. The surge of energy helped early people defend themselves. Anger enabled them to fight with vigor and great strength.

Our culture evolved much more rapidly than our bodies. We are now a society and a civilization who are expected to deal calmly and rationally with each other. We don't need to fight saber-toothed tigers; our battles are waged in boardrooms and bedrooms. **At this stage,** we no longer need the fight-or-flight response, but our bodies still respond that way. We call it stress. We no longer need the physical stimulus of anger either, but we still get angry. Instead of being a benefit, most regard the process of anger as a liability.

(Brent Q. Hafen, Keith J. Karren, Kathryn J. Frandsen, and N. Lee Smith, *Mind/Body Health,* 1996)

Exercise 5: Steps in a Process

Directions: Fill in the blank with an appropriate transition word or phrase from the list below. Some of the transition words will fit in more than one of the sentences, but try to use a different transition word in each sentence. Make sure the sentence makes sense with the transition you choose.

at this point   final   first   process   second   stages

1. The ___process___ of sleeping is complicated, with people progressing through four distinct, 90-minute stages during a night's rest.

2. Each of these sleep ___stages___ is associated with a unique pattern of brain waves.

3. In the ___first___ stage, as people begin to go to sleep, images sometimes appear, as if they were viewing still photos.

4. It is ___at this point___, in stage 1, that rapid eye movement, or REM, sleep occurs. REM sleep is usually accompanied by dreams, which, whether people remember them or not, are experienced by *everyone* during some part of the night.

5. As sleep becomes deeper, people enter the ___second___ stage, which is characterized by a slower, more regular wave pattern.

6. By the time sleepers arrive at the ___final___ stage, they are least responsive to outside stimulation. Stage 4 sleep is most likely to occur during the early part of the night.

(Robert S. Feldman, *Essentials of Understanding Psychology,* 6/e, 2005)

Examples

A paragraph of **examples** usually gives a general statement of the main idea and then presents one or more concrete examples to provide support for this idea. Many writers place the most important or convincing example either first, as an attention-getter, or last, as a dramatic climax. While the terms *example* and *illustration* often are used interchangeably, an illustration is usually longer, and there may be only one in the paragraph.

In this poem, Richard Armour gives a series of short examples about the different ways people relate to money.

MONEY

Workers earn it,
Spendthrifts burn it,
Bankers lend it,
Women spend it,
Forgers fake it,
Taxes take it,
Dying leave it,
Heirs receive it,
Thrifty save it,
Misers crave it,
Robbers seize it,
Rich increase it,
Gamblers lose it,
I could use it.

(Richard Armour, "Money," 1954)

The following paragraphs are on aggression, which is defined as "hostile assault intended to inflict harm." The main ideas in paragraphs 2 and 3 on aggression are underlined. Create your own outline of paragraphs 2 and 3 on a separate sheet of paper.

1. We need look no further than the daily paper or the nightly news to be bombarded with **examples** of aggression, both on a societal level (war, invasion, assassination) and on an individual level (crime, child abuse, and the many petty cruelties that humans are capable of inflicting on one another).

2. <u>Sometimes aggressive behavior is a reaction to frustration.</u> **For example,** suppose you've been working on a paper that is due for a class early the next morning, and your computer printer runs out of ink just before you can print out the paper. You rush to the store to buy more ink, only to find the sales clerk locking the door for the day. Even though the clerk can see you gesturing and begging him to open the door, he refuses, shrugging his shoulders and pointing to a sign that indicates when the store will open the next day. At that moment, the feelings you experience toward the sales clerk probably place you on the verge of real aggression, and you are undoubtedly seething inside. Frustration produces anger, leading to a *readiness* to act aggressively.

(Robert S. Feldman, *Understanding Psychology*, 8/e, 2008)

3. <u>It appears that temporary climate changes can affect human behavior.</u> **For example,** William Griffitt found that compared with students who answered questionnaires in a room with normal temperature, those who did so in an uncomfortably hot room (over 90°F) reported feeling more tired and aggressive and expressed more hostility to strangers. In the real world, drivers without air conditioning in heat-stricken Phoenix, Arizona, are much more likely to honk at a stalled car. And, **in another instance,** during the 1986–1988 major league baseball seasons, the number of batters hit by a pitch was two-thirds greater for games played above 90°F than for games played below 80°F. Pitchers weren't wilder on hot days—they had no more walks and wild pitches. They just clobbered more batters! Across the Northern Hemisphere, not only do hotter days have more violent crimes, so do hotter seasons of the year, hotter summers, hotter years, hotter cities, and hotter regions. If a 4-degree Fahrenheit global warming occurs, scientists project that the United States alone would actually see at least 50,000 more serious assaults.

(David G. Myers, *Social Psychology*, 9/e, 2008)

Exercise 6: Examples

Directions: Fill in the blank with an appropriate transition word or phrase from the list below. Some of the transition words will fit in more than one of the sentences, but try to use a different transition word in each sentence. Make sure the sentence makes sense with the transition you choose.

for example   for instance   in particular   specifically   such as

1. Today's college classrooms include many different kinds of students, ___such as___ Donna, who entered college after working for eight years following high school.

2. One avenue of self-discovery in college is the exploration of new career choices. ___For example___, James was originally interested in a career in teaching, but has since decided to pursue a career in business.

3. ___Specifically___, James has decided to become a marketing major.

4. In the 1970s, high school girls were less likely to go to college. Today, girls ___in particular___ are more likely than boys to go to college.

5. However, even today many women avoid taking academic risks. ___For instance___, they stay away from taking mathematics and science classes.

Definition

A paragraph of **definition** will define, clarify, or explain a key term. Definitions can be developed by providing dictionary meanings or personal meanings. They can also be developed by means of examples or by comparing and contrasting the key word with other words.

In *The Adventures of Tom Sawyer*, Mark Twain **defines** work as "whatever a body is obliged to do while play consists of whatever a body is not obliged to do."

In the following paragraphs, the authors of *Mind/Body Health* attempt to clarify the meaning of anger by providing concrete illustrations, describing its distinguishing characteristics, and comparing and contrasting it with other, similar expressions. After reading the paragraphs, complete the outline that follows.

Everyone experiences it. Just watch two toddlers fighting over a favorite set of blocks, a teenager challenging an unreasonable curfew, an executive whose car gets rear-ended on the way to an important business presentation.

Anger is an emotion. It's temporary. It combines physiological arousal with emotional arousal. It can range in severity all the way from intense rage to "cool" anger that doesn't really involve arousal at all (and might more accurately be **described** as an *attitude,* such as resentment). People express anger in all sorts of ways such as hurling verbal insults, using profanity, slamming doors, or smashing a fist into the nearest available object.

The words we use **to describe** our anger strongly hint at the turmoil that is going on inside our bodies when we're angry. Some of the most common ones were pointed out by social psychologist and anger expert Carol Tavris:

> You make my *blood boil.*
> His pent-up anger *welled up* inside him.
> He was *bursting with anger.*
> I *blew my stack.*
> She *flipped her lid.*
> He *hit the ceiling.*

The **terms** *anger* and *hostility* are often used interchangeably **to describe** a set of negative emotions, but they are not the same. Anger has been **defined** as a temporary emotion that may or may not be accompanied by outward expression (physical or verbal). Hostility, on the other hand, is not a temporary emotion, but rather an attitude. It is anger that is expressed in aggressive behavior motivated by animosity and hatefulness. "Anger is generally considered to be a simpler concept than hostility or aggression," explain researchers Margaret A. Chesney and Ray H. Rosenman.

The **concept** of anger usually refers to an emotional state that consists of feelings that vary in intensity, from mild irritation or annoyance to fury and rage.

(Brent Q. Hafen, Keith J. Karren, Kathryn J. Frandsen, and N. Lee Smith, *Mind/Body Health,* 1996)

I. Anger is an emotion experienced by everyone. (MI)
   A. It has certain characteristics. (MSD)
      1. It is temporary. (msd)
      2. It combines <u>physiological arousal with emotional arousal.</u> (msd)
      3. It can range <u>from intense rage to "cool" anger.</u> (msd)
   B. People express anger in many different ways. (MSD)
      1. Examples of verbal anger are <u>hurling insults, using profanity.</u> (msd)
      2. Examples of physical anger are <u>slamming doors, smashing a fist.</u> (msd)

II. The words used to describe anger show the turmoil it causes. (MI)

III. Anger and hostility are not the same. (MI)

    A. Anger is a temporary emotion that may or may not be expressed outwardly. (MSD)

    B. Hostility is an attitude that is expressed in aggressive behavior. (MSD)

    C. Anger is a simpler concept than hostility. (MSD)

IV. Anger is an emotional state with feelings that vary in intensity. (MI)

    A. It can be expressed as <u>mild irritation</u>. (MSD)

    B. Or it can be expressed as <u>fury and rage</u>. (MSD)

Exercise 7: Definition

Directions: Fill in the blank with an appropriate transition word or phrase from the list below. Some of the transition words will fit in more than one of the sentences, but try to use a different transition word in each sentence. Make sure the sentence makes sense with the transition you choose.

    described as   is called   is defined as   means   term

1. Middle adulthood <u>is defined as</u> the years between 40 and 65.

2. A middle-aged person is sometimes <u>described as</u> someone with grown children and/or elderly parents.

3. Many people age 40 and older need reading glasses for presbyopia, a lessened ability to focus on near objects—a condition associated with aging. (The prefix *presby* <u>means</u> "with age.")

4. The pressures created by a society that believes in looking young, acting young, and being young—added to the real physical losses that people may suffer as they get older—may contribute to what <u>is called</u> the midlife crisis.

5. The <u>term</u> *empty nest* refers to the period when the last child leaves home.

(Diane E. Papalia and Sally Wendkos Olds, *Human Development*, 9/e, 2004)

Chronological Order

The word *chronological* comes from the Greek root *chron*, which means "time." The **chronological** pattern of organization involves arranging events in time in the order that they actually happened. For this reason, historical essays and articles that are date oriented are usually organized by this method. Paragraphs written with this pattern are usually very easy to recognize.

    This short poem illustrates the key elements of the chronological pattern because the events are ordered by time.

Solomon Grundy

Solomon Grundy
Born on a **Monday,**
Christened on **Tuesday,**
Married on **Wednesday,**
Took ill on **Thursday,**
Worse on **Friday,**
Died on **Saturday,**
Buried on **Sunday,**
This is the end
Of Solomon Grundy.
—Anonymous

The following paragraphs from *Anger: The Misunderstood Emotion* are in the chronological order pattern.

Popular opinion has it that time heals all wounds, that human beings are naturally resilient. But some people do not heal from the wounds of divorce. In **1971,** Judith Wallerstein, then working with Joan Kelly, began a study of 131 children and adolescents from sixty families, and their divorcing parents, in Marin County, California. The researchers reinterviewed all family members **eighteen months later,** again **five years after** divorce, and again **ten and fifteen years after** divorce. The parents were upper-middle-class, mostly white, and had been married anywhere from four to twenty-three years. The children were all developmentally normal, doing well in school, and in good psychological health—**until** the divorce hit them.

Wallerstein found that even **after ten years,** half of the women and one-third of the men in her study were still intensely angry at their former spouses, and that the consequences of this anger and conflict for their children were often disastrous.

(Carol Tavris, *Anger: The Misunderstood Emotion,* 1989)

Exercise 8: Chronological Order

Directions: Fill in the blank with an appropriate transition word or phrase from the list below. Some of the transition words will fit in more than one of the sentences, but try to use a different transition word in each sentence. Make sure the sentence makes sense with the transition you choose.

following   frequently   1853   1890   then   until

1. In ___1853___, Vincent van Gogh was born to a Dutch Protestant minister in the town of Groot-Zundert, in Holland.

2. His early life was spent as a lay preacher to the miners of the region and so not ___until___ the age of 27 did he begin to take a serious interest in art.

3. ___Then___ he went to live with his brother Theo, an art dealer in France, where he met the painter Paul Gauguin.

4. The two artists ___frequently___ quarreled, and after one very intense argument, van Gogh cut off a portion of his ear.

5. ___Following___ that bizarre incident, van Gogh committed himself to an asylum where much of the work we now admire, including *Starry Night,* was created.

6. Unfortunately, his despair deepened, and so in July of ____1890____ he shot himself to death.

(Mark Getlein, *Gilbert's Living with Art*, 6/e, 2002)

Listing

When an author simply lists information without regard to order, the pattern of organization is referred to as simple **listing** or enumeration. Sometimes authors use numbers (1, 2, 3), letters (a, b, c), bullets (•), or asterisks (*) to show the individual items in the list. Or they will say *first, second, third*, and so on. Sometimes they use words such as *in addition, next*, or *finally*. Often a colon will be used at the start of a list. A variation of the word *follow* may indicate that a list is about to begin.

Below is a list of laws that were actually enforced at one time in the United States. Many are still "on the books." What do you think the original purpose of these laws might have been?

- It is illegal to buy a bag of peanuts after sunset and before sunrise the next day in Alabama.
- In California, it is illegal to trip horses for entertainment, to possess bear gall bladders, or to peel an orange in your hotel room.
- It is illegal to throw shoes at weddings in Colorado.
- In Connecticut, it is illegal to walk across the street on your hands.
- Women in Florida may be fined for falling asleep under a hair dryer, as can the salon owner.
- It is illegal to take a bath in the wintertime in Indiana.
- Kisses may last for as much as, but no more than, 5 minutes in Iowa.
- In Michigan a woman isn't allowed to cut her own hair without her husband's permission.
- It is illegal to slurp soup in New Jersey.
- Beer and pretzels can't be served at the same time in any bar or restaurant in North Dakota.
- Violators in Oklahoma can be fined, arrested, or jailed for making ugly faces at a dog.
- The state law of Pennsylvania prohibits singing in the bathtub.
- In Tennessee, it is illegal to shoot any game other than whales from a moving automobile.
- In Texas, it is illegal to take more than three sips of beer at a time while standing.
- It is an offense in Washington State to pretend your parents are rich.

(Robert H. Bohm and Keith N. Haley, *Introduction to Criminal Justice*, 6/e, 2010)

Spatial Order

The spatial order pattern is used to describe the location or placement of something. Many of the spatial order transition words are prepositions. The following anecdote illustrates spatial order, with transition words in bold.

A poor man lived **inside** a crowded house, and he was very angry. **Within** his house, he had to contend with his wife, his six children, his mother-in-law, and a boarder. When he lay down to rest at night, there was no room to the **left** of him and no room to the **right.** He complained to a friend who lived **close** by, and the friend gave him one sentence of advice: "Bring your goat **into** the house." A week later the man returned and complained to his friend about the stench and dirt **within** his house from the goat. His friend listened and said: Bring your chickens **into** the house. A week later, the poor man was a nervous wreck with chickens living **above** him in the rafters of his cottage and the goat making his bed **next to** him, keeping him awake all night. **Outside,** he again ran into his friend who listened closely to his complaints and then said: "Put out the goat." The man returned to his friend a few days later and announced that things were better, but he still felt too crowded. The friend said: "Put the chickens **outside**." When the man returned a week later, he said to his friend: "You are a genius! Now I have room all **around** me. My house is as big as a mansion!"

In the paragraph that follows, a description is given of the famous painting the *Third of May* by Goya. Again, transition words are set in bold.

The *Third of May* by Goya

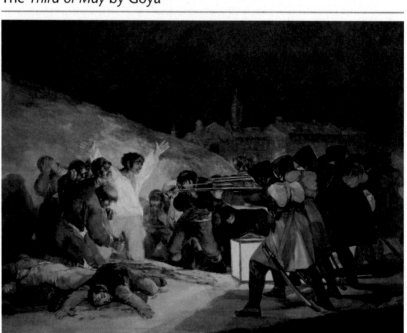

Goya, The *Third of May*, 1808

The *Third of May* by Spanish painter Francisco Goya is a powerful anti-war statement. The painting shows French troops shooting unarmed Spanish civilians. Goya lit the night-time scene with a lamp on the ground **near** the soldiers' feet, casting a harsh light. In the **rear,** the church is dark. In the **left foreground,** a bloody body falls **toward** the viewer. **Behind** is a line of other victims. The victims are the **center** of interest, with a white-shirted man throwing his arms wide in a defiant gesture. With their backs to the viewer, the faceless figures of the firing squad stand locked together directly **opposite** the victims.

Exercise 9: Spatial Order

Directions: Fill in the blank with an appropriate transition word or phrase from the list below. Some of the transition words will fit in more than one of the sentences, but try to use a different transition word in each sentence. Make sure the sentence makes sense with the transition you choose.

across   beneath   next to   north-south   under   west

1. On December 26, 2004, an earthquake measuring 9.0 occurred _____west_____ of the Indonesian island of Sumatra.

2. The focus was about 6 miles _____beneath_____ the ocean floor.

3. The ocean floor was suddenly uplifted, triggering a tsunami that created a path of destruction _____across_____ the 2,800-mile-wide Indian Ocean.

4. If you are ever in an earthquake, stay indoors and seek protection _____under_____ a heavy desk or table. Be sure to protect your head.

5. You can also stand under door frames or _____next to_____ inner walls, as these are the least likely to collapse.

6. The San Andreas fault runs _____north-south_____ for 807 miles through California.

Addition

The addition pattern is often used to discuss a topic in greater depth or to expand or elaborate on it.

In this poem, Shel Silverstein uses the addition pattern in the refrain (the part in parentheses).

JUST ME, JUST ME

Sweet Marie, she loves just me
(She **also** loves Maurice McGhee).
No she don't, she loves just me
(She **also** loves Louise Dupree).
No she don't, she loves just me
(She **also** loves the willow tree).
No she don't, she loves just me!
(Poor, poor fool, why can't you see
She can love others **and** still love thee.)

(Shel Silverstein, *Where the Sidewalk Ends*, 1974)

The following paragraph on jealousy illustrates the addition pattern. The addition transition words are in bold.

How common is jealousy? Very common. Many college students play jealousy games. They flirt openly **and** even manufacture tales to make their partners pay more attention to them. Feelings of jealousy can lead to perceiving anyone as a rival. When women are jealous, they turn to food. **In addition** they turn to friends for consolation. A small group of women **also** turn to vigorous exercise to relieve the stress of jealous feelings. Not only might exercise better reduce stress; **additionally** it will do so without adding pounds, which can lead to self-deprecation **as well as** depression. Women tend to **further** express sexual jealousy through behaviors such as improving their own physical appearance, demanding increased commitment from the partner, **as well as** trying to make the partner jealous himself. Jealousy in women may derive from low self-esteem, feelings of inadequacy **and** a lack of self-confidence.

(David Knox, *Choices in Relationships*, 9/e, 2008)

Exercise 10: Addition

Directions: Fill in the blank with an appropriate transition word or phrase from the list below. Some of the transition words will fit in more than one of the sentences, but try to use a different transition word in each sentence. Make sure the sentence makes sense with the transition you choose.

and   also   another   furthermore   in addition   too

Want to have a happier life? Here are some practical suggestions based on recent research studies.

1. Develop strategies for coping with stress _____and_____ hardship. Just thinking "this ____too____ shall pass" seems to help.

2. Count your blessings. __In addition__, savor life's joys.

3. Practice acts of kindness ____also____.

4. ____Another____ good suggestion is to learn to forgive those who have wronged you in the past.

5. __Furthermore__, it's important to take care of your body by getting enough sleep and exercise.

Internet Activity

There is a great deal of material on the Internet on the topic of anger. Locate two Web sites that discuss anger, and determine the purpose of each site. The following sites might be a good place to start your search:

www.apa.org (then type in "anger")

www.angermgmt.com

The last three letters of any Internet address indicate the type of the site: "org" stands for organization, "net" for networking, and "com" for commercial. Other site types are "edu" for education, "gov" for government, and "mil" for military. This information may help you determine the sort of information found on each site.

Exercise 11: Predicting the Pattern

Directions: The following are headings in actual textbook chapters. Carefully study the given topic and the transition words used by the author in the heading. What type of pattern of organization would you expect the author to use in the chapter? Place the letter of your choice on the line.

a. classification or division (categories)
b. cause and effect
c. comparison and contrast
d. steps in a process
e. examples

f. definition
g. chronological order
h. listing
i. spatial order

_____d_____ 1. The Birth Process

_____g_____ 2. History of Prisons in America

_____c_____ 3. The Prison Experience: Men vs. Women

_____i_____ 4. Space Planning Considerations in Interior Design

_____e_____ 5. Examples of Major Life Changes and Daily Hassles

_____a_____ 6. How Living Things Are Classified

_____b_____ 7. The Causes of the Civil War

_____a_____ 8. What Are the Major Categories of Rock-Forming Minerals?

_____h_____ 9. The Following Are Some Tips on Handling a Stalker

_____f_____ 10. The Definition of Sport

_____c_____ 11. Comparing Cultural Variation within Societies

_____a_____ 12. Types of Crime

_____b_____ 13. Physiological Effects of Caffeine

_____g_____ 14. The History of Plants and Medicine

Exercise 12: Identifying Patterns of Organization and Transition Words

Directions: Identify the dominant pattern of organization for each paragraph. You may look at the transition words chart if necessary.

1. Quick French Onion Soup (serves 4–6)
   In medium fry pan, first saute onion in butter until golden and tender, about 15 minutes. Next, stir in flour. Then add remaining ingredients. Simmer uncovered at least 20 minutes, stirring occasionally. Serve piping hot. For a final touch, if desired, top with melba toast and shredded Gruyere cheese.

   steps in a process
   _____

   Transition Words: first, next, then, final
   _____

2. In ancient Rome, whenever a man wished to be elected to a public office, he canvassed for votes wearing a white robe or toga. The purpose of this was to enable the populace to easily recognize him. The Latin word for white is *candidus,* so the potential official came to be known as a *candidatus,* which means "a person clothed in white." From this derivation comes our English word *candidate.*

   definition
   _____

   Transition Words: word for, which means, derivation
   _____

3. If you were a child growing up in the 50s and you used the f-word, there would probably have been at least a discussion, and more than likely, a bar of soap would have been put to good use. In contrast, today this word is uttered routinely just about everywhere. Kids hear the word riding the bus to

school, in class, in the lyrics of many songs, and on regular network TV. In the 50s, profanity was a shocking rarity. But, in the 2000s, profanity has become part of our language. Some psychologists even say using curse words is healthy because it allows us to express our deepest emotions. Young people of today are so used to hearing the f-word that many linguists predict it will end up meaning as little as the standard curse word of the 50s, "hell."

contrast
_____

Transition Words: contrast, but
_____

4. One hundred years ago, no one "exercised" because their daily life was strenuous enough. As a direct result of the many labor-saving devices we have today, the typical American's weight is rising. Most Americans don't participate in athletics, and many hire others to do their routine home-maintenance chores. Thus, they get almost no vigorous exercise. The most exercise many get is changing the channel on the remote control. The sad consequence of becoming a sedentary, TV-watching nation is that one in three adults is currently overweight.

cause and effect
_____

Transition Words: as a direct result, thus, consequence
_____

5. The Ripley's Museum in Orlando, Florida, is apparently the place to go for those seeking to start a family. In late 1994, two ebony fertility statues were placed in the office lobby. Three employees immediately became pregnant after rubbing the belly of the statue. In another instance, three wives of office personnel all became pregnant despite the fact one was using birth-control pills. In another example, eight women who visited the office became pregnant, including a woman who accidentally bumped into the statue while delivering a package. One Texas woman with five daughters recently came to make the pilgrimage in the hope of having a son. She's convinced the "reproductive magic" will work for her.

example
_____

Transition Words: another instance, another example
_____

6. In a study of workaholics, those people who work too much, Marilyn Machlowitz found that workaholics exhibited the following characteristics:

   1. Tend to be intense and energetic,
   2. Sleep less than most people,
   3. Have difficulty taking vacations,
   4. Spend most of their waking time working,
   5. Frequently eat while they work,
   6. Prefer work to play,
   7. Work hard at making the most of their time,
   8. Tend to blur the distinction between work and play,
   9. Can and do work anywhere and everywhere.

   (Jerrold S. Greenberg, *Comprehensive Stress Management*, 8/e, 2004)

listing
_____

Transition Words: (1, 2, 3, etc.)
_____

7. Consider the gender differences market researchers observe when studying the food preferences of men and women. Women eat more fruit. On the other hand, men are more likely to eat meat. As one food writer put it, "Boy food

doesn't grow. It is hunted or killed." Men are more likely to eat Frosted Flakes or Corn Pops, but women prefer multigrain cereals. Men are big root beer drinkers, but women account for the bulk of sales of bottled water.

(Michael R. Solomon, *Consumer Behavior*, 6/e, 2004)

contrast
_____

Transition Words: on the other hand, but
_____

Exercise 13: Identifying Patterns of Organization and Transition Words

Directions: Choose the correct pattern of organization by noting the transition words.

1. As the "global village" expands and Americans are exposed to an ever-greater variety of cultures and traditions, we find ourselves increasingly joining in the rituals of many ethnic groups and nations. Perhaps the most obvious example is St. Patrick's Day. On every 17th of March, a sea of green engulfs the streets, offices, retail establishments, and bars of all fifty states—and many "wearers o' the green" have not a trace of Irish in their background. Cinco de Mayo ("the fifth of May") is an example of a Mexican-American holiday just now coming into its own. The celebration commemorates Mexico's defeat of the French in the battle of Puebla in 1862. Cinco de Mayo is drawing ever-larger crowds of non-Hispanics who enjoy sharing traditional foods like tamales, roasted corn, and other ethnic specialties, and who love to sway to the beat of mariachi, ranchera, and banda music. Street vendors can't keep up with the demand for spicy Mexican food—and the taps flow freely with Dos Equis, Corona, and other popular Mexican beers.

    (Wayne A. Payne and Dale B. Hahn, *Understanding Your Health,* 6/e, 2000)

    example
    _____

    Transition Words: example
    _____

2. If you want to break the caffeine habit, the following steps may help you to achieve your goal. First, gradually switch from regular to decaffeinated coffee by mixing them before brewing, or substitute decaffeinated instant coffee for some of the caffeinated instant you drink. Then, increase the decaffeinated proportion each day while using more low-fat milk in your coffee to reduce the amount of caffeinated beverage you consume. Next, switch little by little to smaller cups from larger mugs and glasses. If your favorite mug is a comfort to you, don't discard it, but fill it with a caffeine-free beverage. Change your daily routine by taking a walk instead of your usual coffee break. At this stage, if you find your coffee paraphernalia to be a temptation, get rid of those mugs, pots, filters, and grinders. If you get enough sleep, exercise regularly, and follow a healthy diet, you'll be less reliant on the artificial "pep" that caffeine provides.

    (Wayne A. Payne and Dale B. Hahn, *Understanding Your Health,* 6/e, 2000)

    steps in process
    _____

    Transition Words: steps, first, then, next, at this stage
    _____

3. Many of us experience anger and frustration at one time or another, but for some people these feelings represent a pervasive, characteristic set of personality traits defined as the Type A behavior pattern. Type A individuals are

described by experts as being competitive, aggressive, and hostile, both verbally and nonverbally—especially when interrupted while trying to complete a task. They exhibit a driven quality regarding their work and show a constant sense of urgency about time.

(Robert S. Feldman, *Understanding Psychology*, 8/e, 2008)

definition

Transition Words: defined as, described

4. On a more general level, the Internet has brought us both positive and negative consequences. On the one hand, it entertains us, informs us, links us with friends and family, provides us with the world's greatest reference library, and stimulates commerce. On the other hand, it opens up whole new areas of concern: identity theft, fraud, deceptive advertising, pornography, and invasion of privacy.

(Joseph R. Dominick, *The Dynamics of Mass Communication*, 8/e, 2005)

contrast

Transition Words: on the other hand

5. Because you are always the "author" of your dreams, it is not surprising that you often play a leading role. Thus, you have an active role in nearly three-fourths of your dreams, and you are absent from your own dreams only 10 percent of the time. About half of the other characters in your dreams are friends, acquaintances, or family members. The other half are people you do not know or cannot recognize—or are animals.

(Benjamin B. Lahey, *Psychology*, 8/e, 2004)

cause and effect

Transition Words: because, thus

6. How many times have you asked yourself questions such as "Am I as smart as Jill?" "Is Bob better-looking than I am?" or "Is my taste as good as Carmen's?" We gain self-knowledge by comparing ourselves with others. We are more likely to compare ourselves with others who are similar to us. We develop more accurate self-perceptions by comparing ourselves with people in communities similar to where we live, with people who have similar family backgrounds, and with people of the same sex or sexual orientation.

(John W. Santrock, *Psychology*, 7/e, 2003)

comparison

Transition Words: comparing, similar

7. If you're a traditional age student, ask some older students what they ate when they were growing up. You're likely to hear about American favorites that include meatloaf, mashed potatoes and gravy, chicken pot pie, hearty beef stew, and homemade fudge layer cake. Back then big meals served "family style," featuring red meat and lots of side dishes—plus a rich dessert—were considered healthy, as well as essential for growing, active children. Today, in contrast, our food focus is firmly on ethnic dishes, with their novel flavors and textures, their exotic spices, their alluringly foreign names. Unlike the meals of the past, ethnic cuisines feature generous servings of vegetables, with just a bit of fish, meat, or poultry, plus spices for flavor. Dishes are often cooked with heart-healthy olive oil instead of

cholesterol-heavy butter, shortening, or lard. Protein is more likely to come from legumes than from meat, and dessert may be a small wedge of cheese instead of seven-layer fudge cake or rocky road ice cream.

(Wayne A. Payne and Dale B. Hahn, *Understanding Your Health*, 6/e, 2000)

contrast
_____

Transition Words: <u>contrast, unlike, instead</u>
_____

8. One of America's fastest-growing crimes, identity theft, is causing havoc for innocent people across the country. In a recent example, Theresa May, an English professor in Georgia, was victimized by a California woman of the same name who obtained her Social Security number and then applied for loans, defaulted on the payments, and filed for bankruptcy—all in the professor's name. In yet another example, in Ohio, a successful businesswoman's Social Security number was stolen by a thief who escaped to another state, where she used the Ohio woman's identity to obtain a driver's license and several credit cards, on which she ran up a slew of charges.

    (Stephen E. Lucas, *The Art of Public Speaking*, 8/e, 2004)

    example
    _____

    Transition Words: <u>example, another example</u>
    _____

Exercise 14: More Patterns of Organization and Transition Words

Directions: Choose the correct pattern of organization by noting the transition words.

1. At birth, most infants can turn their heads from side to side while lying on their backs. While lying chest down, many can lift their heads enough to turn them. Within the first two to three months, they lift their heads higher and higher, sometimes to the point where they lose their balance and roll over on their backs. After three months, the average infant begins to roll over deliberately—first from front to back and then from back to front. The average baby can sit without support by 6 months of age and can assume a sitting position without help about two and a half months later. Between 6 and 20 months, most babies begin to get around under their own power by means of creeping or crawling. By holding onto a helping hand or a piece of furniture, the average baby can stand at a little past 7 months of age. A little more than four months later, most babies let go and stand alone. The average baby can stand well about two weeks or so before the first birthday. Soon after they can stand alone well, most infants take their first unaided steps. Within a few weeks, soon after the first birthday, the average child is walking well.

    (Diane E. Papalia, Sally Wendkos Olds, and Ruth Duskin Feldman, *Human Development*, 10/e, 2007)

    chronological order
    _____

    Transition Words: <u>at birth, within the first two or three months, after three</u>
    <u>months, etc.</u>
    _____

2. Our daily lives are enriched by other countries and by the diversity of American society. Consider this example of a typical American citizen. Each morning she wakes up in a bed (an invention from the Near East). She puts

on clothes made in Taiwan, Mexico, and Jamaica, shoes from Spain and a wristwatch from Switzerland, jewelry from Kenya and perfume from France. She eats breakfast at a table made in Sweden, using plates from Korea and a tablecloth from India. Her breakfast includes a banana from Honduras and coffee from Colombia. While driving to work in a car made in Japan, she listens to music performed by a band from Cuba. For lunch at a restaurant, she can choose from a wide variety of ethnic cuisines— Thai, Italian, Chinese, Mexican, Korean, Vietnamese, Egyptian, and so on. Throughout the day, she is likely to use or benefit from products invented by immigrants to the United States and their descendants. Her health, for example, is protected by an oral polio vaccine, developed by Albert B. Sabin, a Polish immigrant.

(Hamilton Gregory, *Public Speaking for College and Career*, 7/e, 2005)

example
_____

Transition Words: for example
_____

3. Medical researchers have found that the average human needs about eight hours of sleep each night in order to function well on the job, on the highway, in school, and in the home. But the majority of Americans try to get by on less than eight hours; in fact, 80 percent get six hours of sleep or less each night. Perhaps the most insidious consequence of skimping on sleep is the irritability that increasingly pervades society. Weariness corrodes civility and erases humor, traits that ease the myriad daily frustrations, from standing in supermarket lines to refereeing the kids' squabbles. Because people go without sufficient sleep, tempers flare faster and hotter at the slightest offense.

(Hamilton Gregory, *Public Speaking for College and Career*, 7/e, 2005)

cause and effect
_____

Transition Words: because, consequence
_____

4. One way we simplify our environment is to categorize—to organize the world by clustering objects into groups. A biologist classifies plants and animals. A human classifies people. Ethnicity and sex are, in our current world, powerful ways of categorizing people. Imagine Gina, a 45-year-old, New Orleans real estate agent. Your categories might be "female," "middle-aged," "businessperson," and "southerner."

(David G. Myers, *Social Psychology*, 9/e, 2008)

classification/division
_____

Transition Words: categorize, classifies, categorizing
_____

5. Indian and U.S. cultures have produced different approaches to love and marriage. In India, about 95 percent of marriages are still arranged by the parents. In the U.S., individual mate selection matches the core values of individuality and independence, while arranged marriages match the Indian value of children's deference to parental authority. For Indians, love is a peaceful emotion, based on long-term commitment and devotion to family. Indians think of love as something that can be "created" between two people. For Indians, marriage produces love—however for Americans love produces marriage. Americans see love as having a mysterious element, a passion that suddenly seizes an individual. In contrast, Indians see love as a peaceful

feeling that develops when a man and a woman are united in intimacy and share common interests and goals in life.

(James M. Henslin, *Essentials of Sociology*, 7/e, 2007)

contrast

Transition Words: (different), contrast, however

Exercise 15: Identifying Transition Words and Sentence Relationships

Directions: Read the following paragraphs on the history of underwear and then identify the transition words in each paragraph.

A BRIEF HISTORY OF UNDERWEAR

(1) There is an old saying, "Don't air your dirty linen in public," which means don't spread private, unpleasant details about yourself for everyone to hear. Well, underwear in sixteenth-century England was the original "dirty linen." Shirts and shifts were gray with dirt and smelled of sweat. Underwear was alive with fleas, ticks, and mites because people rarely took baths. Nevertheless, underwear had an important job to do: It protected people's better outer clothes, which were hard to wash, from the dirt and smells of their bodies. It was easier to wash underwear—at least a few times a year.

1. In paragraph 1, what transition word is used to indicate a definition?
   means

2. In paragraph 1, what transition word is used to indicate cause and effect?
   because

3. In paragraph 1, what transition word is used to indicate reversal?
   nevertheless

(2) Elizabeth I (1533–1603), queen of England, loved fine clothes. During her years as queen, women wore the "farthingale," which refers to a petticoat stiffened with hoops of wood or whalebone that held a dress from the body like a dome. Though hooped petticoats changed in size and shape, they continued to be worn in eighteenth-century Europe and America. In the middle of the century, they grew flat in front and back, but they were sometimes as wide as six feet across at the sides. (Imagine holding a yardstick out on either side of you!) Called "panniers," which derives from the French word for "basket," they made a woman look as if she had a basket on each hip. Doorways were difficult, carriages were a problem, and unquestionably sitting in an armchair was impossible.

4. In paragraph 2, which transition words are used to indicate definition?
   refers to

5. In paragraph 2, which transition word indicates emphasis?
   unquestionably

6. In paragraph 2, which transition words indicate spatial order?
   front and back, across, side

(3) Toward the end of the century, young girls began wearing pantalettes underneath their dresses. Each leg was separate from the other and joined at the waist

with drawstrings. Pantalettes would first slowly shrink to become "drawers" in the next century, then "bloomers," and finally women's underpants today.

7. In paragraph 3, which transition words are used to indicate steps in a process?

first, then, finally

8. In paragraph 3, which transition word is used to indicate spatial order?

underneath

(4) Fashions are often not designed for the natural shape of the human body. In nineteenth-century England and France, women learned to live with bodies tightly bound in corsets to have the small, slender waists required by society. However, tightly laced corsets could change a woman's body permanently by altering the position of her internal organs. Since her lungs were compressed, she could take only short, shallow breaths.

___c___ 9. In paragraph 4, the relationship of the second sentence to the third sentence is one of
   a. chronological order.
   b. addition.
   c. contrast.
   d. example.

10. In paragraph 4, what transition word is used to indicate cause and effect?

since

(5) A few women decided they could do very well without corsets. In 1851 in Seneca Falls, New York, a magazine editor, Amelia Bloomer, published a new idea from her friend Elizabeth Smith Miller. The idea was to wear a comfortable tunic over pajama-style pants. Amelia and her friends, who supported women's rights, were free to go on a hike, jump over a fence, even work in the garden! But people were horrified by the sight of women wearing pants. They teased and laughed at the women; children threw snowballs and apple cores at them. However, years later "bloomers" reappeared as part of women's bathing suits and bicycle outfits.

11. In paragraph 5, what transition words are used to indicate contrast?

but, however

(6) Other ideas were also changing the way people dressed in the nineteenth century. In 1864, when Louis Pasteur discovered microbes, or germs, and proved that they cause disease, people became very health-conscious. Many theories for staying healthy circulated, some more scientific than others. In the 1870s Dr. Gustav Jaeger of Germany believed everyone should wear his Sanitary Woolen System for good health. He claimed his knit underwear would hold in the body's warmth, but let the "noxious exhalations of the body" (bad smells) out. Dr. Jaeger convinced so many people to wear his thick, scratchy "woolies" in winter and summer that he made a fortune selling underwear.

12. In paragraph 6, what words are used to indicate chronological order?

1864, 1870s

(7) Woolen "combinations" in England were called "union suits" in the United States. The bottom half of a union suit got the name "long johns" from John L. Sullivan, an American bare-knuckles boxing champion of the

1880s and 1890s. Besides being a prizewinning boxer, he was also known for fighting in his long underwear.

13. In paragraph 7, what transition words were used to indicate definition?
were called

14. In paragraph 7, what transition words were used to indicate addition?
besides, also

(8) As the nineteenth century ended and the twentieth century began, the end of the corset was coming. Women discovered bike riding in 1895 and the joy of getting around on their own. And by 1900 more than four million women in America were working outside the home.

15. In paragraph 8, what transition words indicate chronological order?
nineteenth century, twentieth century, 1895, 1900

_b_ 16. In paragraph 8, the relationship of the second sentence to the third sentence is one of
a. definition.
b. addition.
c. spatial order.
d. comparison.

(9) As hemlines rose in the 1920s and 1930s, silk stockings were very popular. But by the late 1930s, getting silk was a problem. Japan controlled the Chinese silk market, and in the years leading to World War II, relations between the United States and Japan became more strained. Finally, in 1939, the DuPont Company came up with the answer. At the New York World's Fair that year, they introduced a man-made silk called "nylon," the world's first synthetic fiber.

17. In paragraph 9, what transition word indicates contrast?
but

18. In paragraph 9, what transition word was used to indicate a conclusion?
finally

(10) In the 1950s and 1960s, underwear became lighter and more comfortable. By the 1960s parents could also buy disposable diapers. Disposable diapers are popular today not only for babies but for adults—such as astronauts—as well.

19. In paragraph 10, what words indicate chronological order?
1950, 1960s

20. In paragraph 10, what transition words indicate example?
such as

(11) Because it just isn't possible to get to a toilet, astronauts wear long underwear and adult diapers under their space suits. Astronaut R. Mike Mullane once had to wait four hours for his space shuttle to take off. He said he remembers "lying in a very wet diaper, knowing why babies cry when they have wet diapers. It's gross!"

21. In paragraph 11, what word indicates cause and effect?
because

(12) What will happen to underwear in the future? Researchers are working hard to invent new fabrics that will absorb perspiration and take it away

from the body. This process is called "moisture management." In addition T-shirt fabric containing tiny ceramic particles is being tested to see if it will block harmful rays from the sun. Supposedly a person wearing such a shirt will feel five degrees cooler than if he or she were wearing a normal shirt.

(Ruth Freeman Swain, *Underwear*, 2008)

22. In paragraph 12, what words indicate definition?

   <u>is called</u>

_____c_____ 23. In paragraph 12, the relationship of the third sentence to the fourth is one of
   a. contrast.
   b. cause and effect.
   c. addition.
   d. definition and example.

Exercise 16: Patterns of Organization and Sentence Relationships

Directions: Read the paragraphs below and then answer the questions.

(1) You don't have to look very hard to see some high-profile examples of deception. (2) Marion Jones forfeited her Olympic medals after admitting she lied about taking performance-enhancing drugs. (3) Martha Stewart was sentenced to prison for lying to investigators. (4) Further, contestants on reality shows such as *Survivor*, *The Apprentice*, and *Big Brother* often lie to gain an advantage over their competitors. (5) Is deception that common in everyday life, or do these high-profile examples simply make us think it is?

_____c_____ 1. For this paragraph, the author uses an overall pattern of organization that
   a. analyzes the causes of lying.
   b. describes the types of lies people tell.
   c. gives examples of people lying.
   d. compares lies told by men with lies told by women.

_____b_____ 2. The relationship between sentence 3 and sentence 4 is one of
   a. contrast.
   b. addition.
   c. summary.
   d. spatial order.

(1) In a 2004 survey of 3,000 adults, 71% of participants reported they had lied to friends or relatives to spare their feelings; 63% had faked an illness to get out of work; 32% had lied to their spouse about a purchase; and 28% had lied to their spouse about their relationship with someone else.

_____b_____ 3. This paragraph is organized by
   a. identifying the effects of lying.
   b. listing certain lies and their frequency.
   c. analyzing the consequences of lying.
   d. listing suggestions for avoiding lying.

(1) After conducting 3.8 million background checks in April 2005, Automatic Data Processing found that 52 percent of job applicants had lied on their

resumes. (2) However, a different survey by the Gillette Corporation found that, for men, the number was 86 percent.

_____d_____ 4. The relationship between the first sentence and the second sentence is one of
     a. time order.
     b. example.
     c. summary.
     d. contrast.

(1) Researchers at Cornell University wanted to know the frequency of lying behavior, so they asked college students to keep a diary on every social interaction they had for a week involving a lie. (2) As a result of the study, researchers determined that students lied on average in approximately 265 of their interactions, with lying behavior the most common in telephone conversations.

_____a_____ 5. The relationship between the first sentence and the second sentence is one of
     a. cause and effect.
     b. spatial order.
     c. addition.
     d. summary.

(1) Some people may be surprised at how high these figures are. (2) Conversely, others may be surprised at how low they are. (3) In either event, there's no question that we encounter deception regularly in our day-to-day interactions with people.

_____b_____ 6. The relationship between the first sentence and the second sentence is one of
     a. comparison.
     b. contrast.
     c. definition.
     d. spatial order.

(Kory Floyd, *Interpersonal Communication*, 2009)

In Your Own Words

1. Do you think lying is more common today than it used to be? If so, why do you think this is so?

2. Do you believe that lying is sometimes justified? When?

READING

*"Road rage now results in more highway deaths
than drunk driving."*

TUNING IN TO READING Widespread publicity campaigns emphasizing slogans such as "Steer clear of aggressive driving" and "Instead of trying to make good time, try to make time good" have failed to prevent aggressive driving. What kinds of things do you think will help law enforcement rid the streets and highways of the menace of aggressive driving? Do you think it would help if people were encouraged to have and use "I'm Sorry" placards? Or is it simply time for law enforcement to "get tough" on those who willfully endanger the lives of others?

READING (continued)

BIO-SKETCH   Freda Adler and Gerhard O. W. Mueller are both distinguished professors of criminal justice at Rutgers University. William S. Laufer is associate professor of legal studies at the Wharton School of the University of Pennsylvania. All three authors have written books and articles on criminal justice. Drs. Adler and Mueller have also been advisors in criminal justice to the United Nations.

NOTES ON VOCABULARY

boil over   erupt in anger. The phrase alludes to the fact that when something is vigorously boiling, it is apt to spill over unless it is watched carefully or the heat is reduced.

anonymous   with no name either known or acknowledged. *Anonymous* is derived from the Greek words *an* meaning "without" and *onoma* meaning "name." In ancient Greece, *anonymous* was used whenever an author was unknown.

aggressive driving   the operation of a motor vehicle in an unsafe and hostile manner, without regard for others.

Note: For additional practice with transitions, read the following selection and then answer the questions that follow. You may need to refer to the transition words chart on pages 170–171.

ROAD RAGE
Freda Adler, Gerhard O. W. Mueller, and William S. Laufer

It has been known for years as aggressive driving. It is a factor in 28,000 highway deaths per year. It is a disorder that is said to affect over half of all drivers. Symptoms include speeding, tailgating, weaving in and out of busy traffic, passing on the right, making unsafe or improper lane changes, running stop signs and red lights, flashing lights or high beams at other drivers, using obscene gestures, swearing and yelling insults, honking or screaming at other

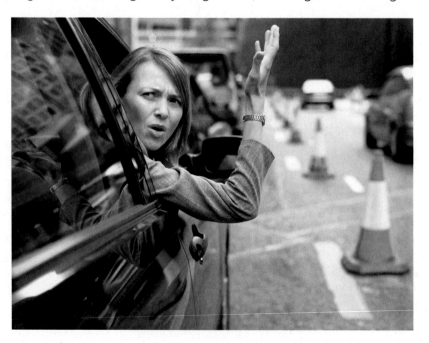

drivers, throwing items at other vehicles, and shooting other drivers or passengers. "The symptoms are incredibly commonplace and sometimes boil over into actual assault and life-threatening situations," explains John Hagerty of the New Jersey State Police.

Road rage now results in more highway deaths than drunk driving. A 2 national study by the AAA Foundation for Traffic Safety found that the majority of aggressive drivers were men aged eighteen to twenty-six, but that dangerous driving behavior is present in women also, and across age levels and economic classes. The same study concluded that from 1990 to 1996, "violent aggressive driving" increased by 7 percent per year. The reasons for this growth depend on whom you ask.

Psychiatrists look to deep-seated personal causes such as stress disorders, 3 which result in impaired judgment. Sociologists see a connection between problems in society and aggressive driving. Others say that the car shields drivers, in effect making them anonymous. This anonymity allows those who become frustrated while driving to ignore society's rules for proper behavior and to behave recklessly. Some claim that drivers see the car as an extension of themselves, and they react angrily when cut off, passed on the highway, or forced to slow down.

As a consequence of young men "dueling" with their cars, two eerily 4 similar accidents happened. The first occurred on the George Washington Memorial Parkway in the nation's capital region. As the two cars raced each other along the parkway, one car crossed the median and hit an oncoming car. Three people were killed. Two of them were drivers not involved in the duel. The second happened as two cars on the New Jersey Turnpike chased each other at speeds of up to 100 miles per hour. The cars wove in and out of lanes of traffic, until the occupant of one of the vehicles allegedly threw an object at the other car. This caused the car to slam into a tree and resulted in the death of two men.

Ricardo Martinez is head of the National Highway Traffic Safety Administra- 5 tion. He blames aggressive driving on a combination of an increase in a "me first" philosophy and reduced levels of traffic enforcement arising from budget cuts, as well as increased congestion and traffic in urban areas. Since 1987, traffic has increased by 35 percent, but new road construction has only increased 1 percent. Pam Fischer, spokeswoman for the New Jersey Automobile Club, also sees congestion on the roadways as a contributing factor. "Any time there is an accident or construction that slows down traffic, people tend to get more aggravated, and normal and rational people do some dumb things because they are running late or just don't want to sit there."

What can be done to prevent this carnage on our highways? In New Jersey, 6 state troopers and municipal police first use plainclothes officers in unmarked cars to cruise dangerous highways during rush hours and spot aggressive drivers. Then, they relay the information to police in marked cars who stop the deviant motorists and give them tickets. In the District of Columbia, Maryland, and Virginia, police have a program called Smooth Operator. In two one-week periods, they issued 28,958 summonses and warnings, including nearly 12,000 for speeding, 3,300 for failing to obey traffic signals, 2,000 for failing to wear a seat belt, and 1,800 for failing to obey a traffic sign.

Another approach calls for making roads bigger. The reasoning is that wider 7 roads reduce traffic congestion and the resulting frustration. But, as noted by Congressman Earl Blumenauer, a Democrat from Oregon, building more roads is "the equivalent of giving a wife beater more room to swing." Instead, he advocates building bicycle lanes and planting trees. These are "features that soften the streets and let drivers know they have to share the road."

It's important to remember that America has faced a deadly threat on its 8 roadways before—drunk driving. Emphasis was placed on changing the laws and making it socially unacceptable to drink and drive. The experts say aggressive driving should be treated the same way. "We have to enforce the law, take bad drivers off the road, and make them pay for their mistakes," urged Colonel Peter J. O'Hagan, director of the New Jersey Division of Highway Safety. The time has come to address aggressive driving through better education, better enforcement, and a get-tough policy. Dr. Martinez warns that "aggressive drivers must get the message that their behavior will not be tolerated, and that they will be prosecuted."

(Freda Adler, Gerhard O. W. Mueller, and William S. Laufer, "Road Rage," 2009)

 COMPREHENSION CHECKUP

Short Answer

Directions: Answer the following questions briefly, using no more than a sentence or two.

1. What is the main idea of the selection? Aggressive driving is an increasing problem, and laws related to it must be enforced.

2. What is the author's overall purpose? to inform

3. What is the cause-and-effect relationship in the last two sentences of paragraph 4?

   Cause: An object was thrown at another car.

   Effect: The car slammed into a tree, killing two men.

4. What is the cause-and-effect relationship in the last sentence of paragraph 5?

   Cause: People are running late or don't want to sit waiting at accidents or construction sites.

   Effect: They get aggravated and do dumb things.

5. Paragraph 7 contains this analogy: Building more roads is "the equivalent of giving a wife beater more room to swing." In your own words, explain what this analogy means. The driver has more room in which to drive aggressively, thus causing more serious problems.

6. Here are some sentences from the selection. Paraphrase them by writing each one in your own words in the space provided.
   a. "This anonymity allows those who become frustrated while driving to ignore society's rules for proper behavior and to behave recklessly."

      Believing they may not be recognized by others, aggressive drivers feel they are not personally responsible for their behavior.

b. "He blames aggressive driving on a combination of an increase in a 'me first' philosophy and reduced levels of traffic enforcement arising from budget cuts, as well as increased congestion and traffic in urban areas."

Aggressive driving can be blamed on a person's self-interest, lack of law

enforcement, and increased traffic and congestion.

Multiple Choice

Directions: For each item, write the letter corresponding to the best answer. You may refer to the transition words chart on pages 170–171.

_____b_____ 1. A key idea expressed in this selection is that
   a. the stress of modern society is solely responsible for road rage.
   b. to get the message across to the public that aggressive driving is unsafe, law enforcement needs to deal with the problem in a manner similar to the way it deals with drunk driving.
   c. making roads bigger is the answer to the problem of road rage.
   d. road rage will be alleviated when there are fewer 16-year-olds and senior citizens on the highways.

_____a_____ 2. The organizational pattern in paragraph 1 could be described as
   a. listing pattern.
   b. spatial order.
   c. chronological order.
   d. compare and contrast.

_____b_____ 3. The transition word *but* in paragraph 2 indicates
   a. conclusion.
   b. contrast.
   c. emphasis.
   d. spatial order.

_____c_____ 4. The transition word *also* in paragraph 2 indicates
   a. reversal.
   b. concession.
   c. addition.
   d. both a and c.

_____d_____ 5. The transition words *such as* in paragraph 3 indicate
   a. addition.
   b. summary.
   c. reversal.
   d. example.

_____a_____ 6. In paragraph 3, all of the following are given as possible reasons for the growth in aggressive driving *except*
   a. intoxication.
   b. anonymity.
   c. problems in society.
   d. stress disorders.

_____c_____ 7. Read the first sentence of paragraph 4. What do the transition words *as a consequence* signal?
   a. summary and conclusion
   b. spatial order
   c. cause and effect
   d. comparison-contrast

____a____ 8. Paragraph 6 uses the transition words *first* and *then*. What pattern of organization do these words signal?
   a. chronological order
   b. examples
   c. cause and effect
   d. comparison-contrast

____c____ 9. The relationship of the second sentence below to the first is one of
   a. addition.
   b. emphasis.
   c. contrast.
   d. summary.

But as noted by Congressman Earl Blumenauer, a Democrat from Oregon, building more roads is "the equivalent of giving a wife beater more room to swing." Instead, he advocates building bicycle lanes and planting trees. (paragraph 7)

True or False

Directions: Indicate whether each statement is true or false by writing **T** or **F** in the space provided.

____F____ 10. Road rage affects men and women in equal numbers.

____F____ 11. Drunk driving is the leading cause of highway deaths.

____T____ 12. Road construction has failed to keep pace with the increase in traffic.

____T____ 13. Experts give various reasons to account for aggressive driving.

____T____ 14. "Dueling" with cars can result in the loss of innocent lives.

Vocabulary in Context

Directions: Use context clues from the article to determine the meaning of the italicized words, and write a definition in the space provided. Then consult your dictionary to see how accurate your definition is.

1. Stress disorders, which result in *impaired* judgment (paragraph 3)
   Definition: diminished, weakened

2. The car *shields* drivers, in effect making them anonymous (paragraph 3)
   Definition: hides, conceals

3. See the car as an *extension* of themselves (paragraph 3)
   Definition: a part, an addition

4. Two *eerily* similar accidents happened (paragraph 4)
   Definition: strangely, mysteriously

5. Drivers not involved in the *duel* (paragraph 4)
   Definition: fight between two people

6. Increased *congestion* and traffic in urban areas (paragraph 5)
   Definition: overcrowding

7. What can be done to prevent this *carnage* (paragraph 6)

   Definition: slaughter (massacre)

8. Stop the *deviant* motorists and give them tickets (paragraph 6)

   Definition: abnormal

9. Their behavior will not be *tolerated* (paragraph 8)

   Definition: allowed to exist, permitted

In Your Own Words

1. Have you ever engaged or been tempted to engage in aggressive driving? Have you ever been affected by someone else's aggressive driving? What do you think led to the behavior? How could it have been prevented?

2. Picture the area around your campus. Are there any problems with aggressive driving in this vicinity? What concrete steps could the college and local police take to address these problems?

3. What is a suitable punishment for someone who speeds? How about someone who screams obscenities at other drivers? Do you think it is possible to reduce or eliminate such misconduct through law enforcement?

Written Assignment

The following are three basic guiding principles from the AAA Foundation for Traffic Safety for avoiding the rage of other motorists. What's your opinion of these suggestions? Are they likely to help deter aggressive driving?

1. **Don't offend.** When surveys ask drivers what angers them most, the results are remarkably consistent. A few specific behaviors seem unusually likely to enrage other drivers:

   a. Cutting off

   b. Driving slowly in the left lane

   c. Tailgating

2. **Watch gestures.** Almost nothing makes another driver angrier than an obscene gesture. Keep your hands on the wheel. Avoid making any gestures that might anger another driver, even "harmless" expressions of irritation like shaking your head.

3. **Don't engage.** One angry driver can't start a fight unless another driver is willing to join in. You can protect yourself against aggressive drivers by refusing to become angry at them.

Internet Activity

Consult the following Web site for tips on not becoming the victim of aggressive driving:

   www.danesheriff.com/roadrage.htm

Do you think these tips are likely to be effective? Can you think of other tips that might be effective?

Are You an Aggressive Driver?

The National Highway Traffic Safety Administration describes an aggressive driver as someone who "commits a combination of moving traffic offenses so as to endanger other persons or property." The NHTSA recommends avoiding the challenges and confrontations of such risk drivers. Do you ever exhibit any of the behaviors of an aggressive driver? To find out, answer yes or no to the following questions:

		Yes	No
1.	Overtake other vehicles only on the left?		
2.	Avoid blocking passing lanes?		
3.	Yield to faster traffic by moving to the right?		
4.	Keep to the right as much as possible on narrow streets and at intersections?		
5.	Maintain appropriate distance when following other motorists, bicyclists, and motorcyclists?		
6.	Leave an appropriate distance between your vehicle and the one you have passed when cutting in after passing?		
7.	Yield to pedestrians?		
8.	Come to a complete stop at stop signs and before making a right turn on red?		
9.	Stop for red traffic lights?		
10.	Approach intersections and pedestrians slowly to show your intention and ability to stop?		
11.	Follow right-of-way rules at four-way stops?		
12.	Drive below posted speed limits when conditions warrant?		
13.	Drive at slower speeds in construction zones?		
14.	Maintain speeds appropriate for conditions?		
15.	Use vehicle turn signals for all turns and lane changes?		
16.	Make eye contact and signal intentions when necessary?		
17.	Acknowledge intentions of others?		

		Yes	No
18.	Use your horn sparingly around pedestrians, at night, and near hospitals?		
19.	Avoid unnecessary use of high-beam headlights?		
20.	Yield and move to the right for emergency vehicles?		
21.	Refrain from flashing headlights to signal a desire to pass?		
22.	Drive trucks at posted speeds and in the correct lanes, changing lanes at proper speeds?		
23.	Make slow U-turns?		
24.	Maintain proper speeds around roadway crashes?		
25.	Avoid returning inappropriate gestures?		
26.	Avoid challenging other drivers?		
27.	Try to get out of the way of aggressive drivers?		
28.	Refrain from using high-occupancy-vehicle or carpool lanes to pass vehicles?		
29.	Focus on driving and avoid distracting activities such as smoking, using a cell phone, reading, or shaving?		
30.	Avoid driving when drowsy?		
31.	Avoid blocking the right-hand turn lane?		
32.	Avoid taking more than one parking space?		
33.	Avoid parking in a disabled space if you are not disabled?		
34.	Avoid letting your door hit the car parked next to you?		
35.	Avoid stopping in the road to talk with a pedestrian or other driver?		
36.	Avoid playing loud music that can be heard in neighboring cars?		

(Michael L. Teague, Sara L. C. Mackenzie, and David M. Rosenthal, *Your Health Today*, 2/e, 2009)

REVIEW TEST 5: Main Idea, Details, Purpose, Transitions, and Patterns of Organization

Directions: Each of the following paragraphs related to aggressive behavior was adapted from commonly used psychology textbooks. Read each passage. Then choose the best answer for each item.

A. Psychologists define *aggression* as physical or verbal behavior intended to hurt someone. Throughout the world, hunting, fighting, and warring are primarily men's activities. In surveys, men admit to more aggression than women do. In laboratory experiments, men exhibit more physical aggression by administering what they believe are hurtful shocks. In Canada, the male-to-female arrest rate is 7 to 1 for murder and 6 to 1 for assault. In the United States, it is 9 to 1 for murder and 4 to 1 for assault. Across the world murder rates vary. Yet in all regions, men are roughly 20 times more likely to murder men than women are to murder women. However, in less violent forms of aggression—say, slapping a family member or verbally attacking someone—women are no less aggressive than men.

(David G. Myers, *Social Psychology*, 7/e, 2002)

_____b_____ 1. In the first sentence of this paragraph, the author uses a(n)
   a. cause-and-effect relationship.
   b. definition.
   c. example.
   d. contrast.

_____a_____ 2. The body of the paragraph is organized to
   a. make a contrast.
   b. show steps in a process.
   c. show events in chronological order.
   d. give a definition.

_____d_____ 3. The last sentence of the paragraph is written to
   a. define what was described above it.
   b. show a cause-and-effect relationship.
   c. show steps in a process.
   d. show a contrast with the body of the paragraph.

B. It is a warm evening. Tired and thirsty after two hours of studying, you borrow some change from a friend and head for the nearest soft-drink machine. As the machine devours the change, you can almost taste the cold, refreshing cola. But when you push the button, nothing happens. You push it again. Then you flip the coin return button. Still nothing. Again, you hit the buttons. You slam them. And finally you shake and whack the machine. You stomp back to your studies empty-handed and shortchanged. Should your roommate beware? Are you now more likely to say or do something hurtful?

(David G. Myers, *Social Psychology*, 9/e, 2008)

_____d_____ 4. The author has written this paragraph using which method?
   a. definition
   b. comparison
   c. classification
   d. chronological order

_b_   5. The example of the student and the vending machine was used to illustrate
   a. the difficulties of a student's life.
   b. the relationship between frustration and aggression.
   c. the problems with vending machines.
   d. the wide variety of things that can go wrong in a day.

C. One of the first psychological theories of aggression, the popular frustration–aggression theory, says that a person who has suffered frustration is more likely to do or say something harmful. "Frustration always leads to some form of aggression," said John Dollard and his colleagues. _Frustration_ is anything (such as the malfunctioning vending machine) that blocks our attaining a goal. Frustration grows when our motivation to achieve a goal is very strong, when we expected satisfaction, and when the blocking is complete.

(David G. Myers, _Social Psychology_, 9/e, 2008)

_b_   6. The main purpose of this paragraph is to
   a. entertain.
   b. inform or explain.
   c. persuade.
   d. criticize.

_a_   7. Which of the following best describes the organizational pattern of this paragraph?
   a. definition and explanation
   b. examples and classification
   c. comparison and contrast
   d. classification and division

D. Our aggressive energy need not explode directly against its source. We learn to inhibit direct retaliation, especially when others might disapprove of us or punish us; instead we displace our hostilities to safer targets. Displacement occurs in the old anecdote about a man who, because he is humiliated by his boss, berates his wife, who yells at their son, who kicks the dog, which bites the mail carrier.

(David G. Myers, _Social Psychology_, 9/e, 2008)

_c_   8. The author in the last sentence of this paragraph uses which of the following?
   a. comparison
   b. classification
   c. cause and effect
   d. definition

E. What kinds of stimuli act as aggressive cues? They can range from the most obvious, such as the presence of weapons, to the subtlest, such as the mere mention of the name of an individual who has behaved violently in the past. For example, in one experiment, angered subjects were more aggressive when in the presence of a rifle and a revolver than in a similar situation in which no guns were present. It appears, then, that frustration does lead to aggression, at least when aggressive cues are present.

(Robert S. Feldman, _Understanding Psychology_, 8/e, 2008)

_____c_____ 9. Which of the following does the author *not* use in this paragraph?
   a. an example
   b. a contrast
   c. a definition
   d. a cause-and-effect statement

_____a_____ 10. The main idea expressed in this passage is that
   a. frustration can more easily lead to aggression when aggressive cues are present.
   b. aggressive cues can be subtle or obvious.
   c. people behave more aggressively when in the presence of weapons.
   d. psychologists don't know what kind of stimuli act as aggressive cues.

Chapter Summary and Review

In this chapter, you learned about the patterns of organization that authors use. You also learned to recognize transition words and phrases. Based on the material in Chapter 4, answer the following.

Short Answer

Directions: List three or four transition words that signal the following patterns of paragraph organization.

1. Comparison _and, both, similarly_____

2. Cause and effect _because since, as a result_____

3. Chronological order _first, finally, after_____

4. Classification _kind, type, divide, combine_____

Vocabulary in Context

Directions: Choose one of the following words to complete the sentences below. Use each word only once.

   chronological   conclusion   contrast   definitions   examples

5. When you write a paper for class, you may want to give specific _examples_ that illustrate your point.

6. On a history test, you might be asked to place the major events leading up to World War II in _chronological_ order.

7. A speaker at a graduation ceremony usually ends the speech with a(n) _conclusion_.

8. When minor league baseball players make it to the Major Leagues for the first time, they are sometimes surprised at the huge _contrast_ between how the game is played in the major and minor leagues.

9. Sometimes authors of textbooks will give _definitions_ for unusual words that they use.

Interpreting What We Read

ELVIS PRESLEY

Legendary Sam Phillips had a recording studio in Memphis, Tennessee, where he primarily recorded black urban blues singers. It was during this time that Phillips became aware of the new interest young whites had in rhythm and blues. He thought that if he could find a young white man with the black sound, he could make a million dollars.

Phillips found his dream in Elvis Presley. Through one of those fateful occurrences, young Presley, a truck driver, came by the studio in 1953 and recorded a couple of songs for his mother's birthday. Phillips called Presley back to the studio, and on the night of July 5, 1954, they recorded "That's Alright Mama," and Rockabilly came of age.

Presley was young and good-looking, with a sexy and defiant look. He wore outrageous clothes, had equally outrageous body movements on stage, and could convincingly sing country, gospel, and blues songs. He quickly became a regional hit.

To get enough money to promote his other artists, Phillips sold Presley's recording contract to RCA Records in Nashville and his managerial contract to Colonel Tom Parker. Presley's first Nashville releases were "Heartbreak Hotel" and "Hound Dog" in 1956. Presley continued with a string of hits throughout the fifties. Then he entered military service, after which he vanished into Hollywood for an extended motion picture contract. Though he remained popular all his life, he never recaptured the spontaneity and natural exuberance of his original recordings. (David Lee Joyner, *American Popular Music*, 3/e, 2009)

TIMED READING If you wish to use "Elvis Presley" as a timed reading, please turn to page A-3 in the Appendices.

213

CHAPTER PREVIEW

In this chapter, you will

- Practice drawing inferences from a variety of sources.

Introduction to Drawing Inferences

Bent Offerings BY
DON ADDIS

Don Addis. *St. Petersburg Times*. Reprinted with permission.

We make **inferences,** or intelligent guesses, every day of our lives. If a teacher sees a student looking at his watch and tapping his foot, the teacher will likely assume the student is anxious to leave class. If someone comes home from work and slams the door, most of us will deduce that the person is upset about something. If Maria's dog doesn't move all day, she's likely to assume her pet is sick and needs to see the vet.

We negotiate through life by means of "cues." We are constantly "reading" situations and adjusting our actions. If we see a car weaving down the road late at night, most of us will become concerned that the driver may be intoxicated, and so we try to stay out of the way.

Study the cartoon *Bent Offerings*. The clerk at the cash register is using observed details about the items the man in the checkout line is purchasing to come to conclusions about him.

The clerk might be wrong about the man in the checkout line, of course. He could be a married man who just happens to like TV dinners. Or he might be buying deodorant for work. In fact, the clerk cannot prove or disprove her observations without the man's help. But her inferences might be considered reasonable deductions based on the available clues and her knowledge and experience with people.

214

Now, look at the picture above and see if you can make some logical inferences. Write them on the lines provided.

1. See explanation below. _____

2. _____

3. _____

4. _____

Explanation

We can infer that the scene is a child's birthday party at a fast-food restaurant, even though no birthday cake is present. We note the tables and chairs, the decor, the age of the children, the paper hats, and especially the balloons, which usually indicate a celebration of some sort. Our inference could be wrong, but we took the available evidence and put it together in a plausible way. We do the exact same thing in our reading.

Now read the First stanza from the poem "Indian Names," by Lydia Sigourney, and record the inferences you can make.

INDIAN NAMES

Ye say they all have pass'd away
  That noble race and brave;
That their light canoes have vanish'd
  From off the crested wave;
That mid the forests where they roam'd,
  There rings no hunter's shout;
But their name is on your waters,
  Ye may not wash it out . . .

(Lydia Huntley Sigourney, "Indian Names," 1834, 1985)

1. See explanation below. _____

2. _____

3. _____

4. _____

Explanation

We can infer that the speaker is not a Native American, or is writing as though she is not one, because she uses the pronoun "their." It also appears as if a conversation is occurring between two or more people because the speaker says, "Ye say." Because of the speaker's use of the word "but," signaling a contrast, it seems likely that an opposing viewpoint is being expressed. The speaker is challenging the ideas of either another person or society in general. We can also infer from the tone of the poem, and the use of the word "noble," that the speaker's attitude toward Native Americans is respectful. At the end, the speaker reminds us that even though particular Native American tribes may have vanished, their influence is present in the names of many places (for example, Lake Huron).

You have probably heard the expression "to read between the lines." This means figuring out an idea that is not directly stated in what you are reading. When you "draw inferences," you make educated guesses using the clues provided by the writer, your own experience, and logic.

To understand the next passage, you must determine the meaning of the word *hora*, which can be accomplished only by reading the last two sentences of the paragraph. After reading the passage, circle the letter of the most logical answer to the questions.

HORA

A corporate president recently made a visit to a nearby reservation as part of his firm's public relations program. "We realize that we have not hired any Native Americans in the five years our company has been located in this area," he told those assembled, "but we are looking into the matter very carefully." "Hora, hora," said some of the audience. "We would like to eventually hire 5 percent of our total workforce from this reservation," he said. "Hora, hora," shouted more of the audience. Encouraged by their enthusiasm, the president closed his short speech by telling them that he hoped his firm would be able to take some hiring action within the next couple of years. "Hora, hora, hora," cried the total group. With a feeling of satisfaction the president left the hall and was taken on a tour of the reservation. Stepping in a field to admire some of the horses grazing there, the president asked if he could walk up closer to the animals. "Certainly," said his driver, "but be careful not to step in the hora."

(John Langan, *Ten Steps to Improving Reading Skills*, 4/e, 2003)

___c___ 1. To get the main point of the passage, we must infer
   a. the location of the reservation.
   b. the kind of company the president headed.
   c. the meaning of the word *hora*.

___b___ 2. From the president's speech, we can infer that
   a. his firm had great interest in hiring Native Americans.
   b. his firm had little interest in hiring Native Americans.

___b___ 3. From the passage, we can infer that
   a. the audience believed the president's speech.
   b. the audience did not believe the president's speech.

___c___ 4. From the passage, we can infer that the president
   a. thought the Native Americans deserved to be hired.
   b. thought his company should not hire the Native Americans.
   c. misinterpreted the Native Americans' reaction to his speech.

___b___ 5. From the passage, we can infer that the main reason the president spoke to the Native Americans about jobs was that
   a. they needed the jobs.
   b. he thought promising jobs to Native Americans would make his company look good.
   c. he thought hiring Native Americans would be good for his company.

Explanation

If we understand the meaning of the word *hora*, we realize that the Native Americans recognized early on that the corporate president was engaging in "empty promises" and had no intention of hiring very many of them. We noted the fact that the firm had been in the area for five years and had not yet hired a single Native American. Moreover, the president was not promising to remedy the situation immediately, but was promising 5 percent employment within "the next couple of years," again indicating no real commitment on his firm's part.

You can see how experience can play a role in our ability to understand inferences. Those of us who know more about how businesses sometimes handle problems with community relations may more easily see the cues indicating the president's lack of sincerity. In this case, the joke was on the corporate president, whose feeling of satisfaction with his speech was completely unjustified.

In the exercises that follow, you will be given an opportunity to practice making inferences.

Exercise 1: Drawing Inferences from Cartoons

Directions: Try to analyze the following cartoons. Remember to read between the lines to discover the attitudes and values that are expressed indirectly.

Thaves

Frank and Ernest

Frank & Ernest used with the permission of the Thaves and The Cartoonist Group. All rights reserved.

1. What does the word *avian* mean? relating to birds

2. What is a tern? a seabird that is like a small gull

3. Is there a homonym for *tern*? turn

THE FAR SIDE® BY GARY LARSON

The real reason dinosaurs became extinct

4. Does the cartoon involve a play on words that involves the word *tern*? yes, right turn, left turn, turn for the worse

5. Why did the tern "take a tern for the worse"? The tern is in very poor shape probably because he smokes.

6. According to the cartoon, why did dinosaurs become extinct? They were smokers.

7. Is the cartoonist making a positive or a negative comment about smoking? negative

---

Exercise 2: More Drawing Inferences from Cartoons

Directions: After reading the dialogue in the cartoon on page 219, try to answer the following questions. Write down the clues that helped you. If there are not enough clues in the cartoon to enable you to answer the question, write "Can't tell."

Answers		Clues
history class	1. What class is the student writing a paper for?	"history paper time"
encyclopedias	2. What is the student using for reference material?	alphabetical order
no, home	3. Is the student working in the library?	couch, pictures, kitchen
yes	4. Is the student guilty of plagiarism?	quotes and printing, bubble; no quotes, pen and cursive

DOONESBURY
BY G. B. TRUDEAU

no   5. Is the student showing his paper to a teacher?   mother in kitchen

no   6. Does the adult believe the paper is the   "our" writing—his and
          student's own work?   encyclopedia's

Exercise 3: Drawing Inferences from Proverbs

A proverb is a traditional saying that offers advice or presents a moral. In order to understand proverbs, you must be able to read between the lines. Proverbs cannot be read in the literal sense. For example, the proverb "Don't put all your eggs in one basket" is not really concerned with collecting eggs. What it implies is that it is not a good idea to rely on just one thing.

Directions: What can you logically infer about the meaning of these proverbs? Working with a partner, see how well you can explain them.

1. The leopard does not change his spots. _A person isn't likely to change._

2. The early bird catches the worm. _An early starter reaps the benefits._

3. The squeaky wheel gets the grease. _Those seeking attention get it._

4. Every cloud has a silver lining. _Something positive comes out of something bad._

5. Don't cross the bridge till you come to it. _Don't worry about something until it happens._

6. A bad workman blames his tools. _An inept person blames everyone but himself or herself._

7. You can lead a horse to water, but you can't make him drink. _You can provide encouragement, but you can't force someone._

Now try to identify these well-known proverbs, which have been rewritten with synonyms for key words. Use your dictionary if necessary.

8. Birds of similar plumage assemble. <u>Birds of a feather flock together.</u>

9. Sanitation is next to piousness. <u>Cleanliness is next to godliness.</u>

10. An examined kettle does not bubble. <u>A watched pot doesn't boil.</u>

11. It is not possible to instruct ancient canines in fresh wiles. <u>You can't teach an old dog new tricks.</u>

12. Where there are fumes, there is blaze. <u>Where there is smoke, there is fire.</u>

13. Inspect before you bound. <u>Look before you leap.</u>

14. Persons who dwell in crystal domiciles should not fling pebbles. <u>People who live in glass houses shouldn't throw stones.</u>

Exercise 4: Drawing Inferences from Popular Literature

Directions: Read each of the following excerpts from popular literature, and use inferential reasoning to answer the questions that follow.

A. I suppose it was inevitable that my brother and I would get into one big fight which also would be the last one. When it came, given our theories about street fighting, it was like the Battle Hymn, terrible and swift. There are parts of it I did not see. I did not see our mother walk between us to try to stop us. She was short and wore glasses and, even with them on, did not have good vision. She had never seen a fight before or had any notion of how bad you can get hurt by becoming mixed up in one. Evidently, she just walked between her sons. The first I saw of her was the gray top of her head, the hair tied in a big knot with a big comb in it; but what was most noticeable was that her head was so close to Paul I couldn't get a good punch at him. Then I didn't see her anymore.

(Norman Maclean, *A River Runs Through It,* 1992)

1. What happened to the boys' mother? <u>She got hit.</u>

B. All he would have to do would be to slip the translation out of his desk, copy it, put it away, and he would pass the examination. All of his worries would be over. His father would be happy that he passed the examination. He wouldn't have to go to summer school. He and Charlie could go out to Colorado together to work on that dude ranch. He would be through with Latin forever. The Latin grade would never pull his average down again. Everything would be all right. Everything would be fine. All he would have to do would be to copy that one paragraph. Everyone cheated. Maybe not at V.P.S. But in other schools they bragged about it. . . . Everyone cheated in one way or another. Why should that one passage ruin everything? Who cared what problems the Romans had!

(C.D.B. Bryan, "So Much Unfairness of Things," 1962, 1964)

1. What subject is the student having difficulty with? <u>Latin</u>

2. How is he rationalizing his decision? <u>"Everyone cheated."</u>

C. "C'mon, mama's boy," Bull whispered. "Bring little mama's boy up to Daddy Bull." Right hand, left hand, right hand, left hand, the ball drummed against the cement as Ben waited for his father to move out against him and Bull held back, fearing the drive to the basket. At the foul line, Ben left his feet for the jump shot, eyed the basket at the top of his leap, let it go softly, the wrist snapping, the fingers pointing at the rim and the ball spinning away from him as Bull lunged forward and drove his shoulder into Ben's stomach, knocking him to the ground. Though he did not see the ball go in, he heard the shouts of his mother and sisters; he saw Matthew leaping up and down on the porch. He felt his father rise off him slowly, coming up beaten by a son for the first time in his life. Screaming with joy, Ben jumped up and was immediately flooded by his family, who hugged, slapped, pummeled, and kissed him.

(Pat Conroy, *The Great Santini*, 1994.)

1. What kind of relationship does Ben have with his father? <u>adversarial</u>

2. Is the family rooting for the father or the son? <u>the son</u>

3. What can we infer about Bull's character from this excerpt? <u>has a conflict with</u> <u>son, dirty player, poor loser—"little Mama's boy," "drove his shoulder into Ben's</u> <u>stomach."</u>

D. A blur outside the car . . . Sherman grabbed the door pull and with a tremendous adrenal burst banged it shut. Out of the corner of his eye, the big one—almost to the door on Maria's side. Sherman hit the lock mechanism. *Rap!* He was yanking on the door handle—CELTICS inches from Maria's head with only the glass in between. Maria shoved the Mercedes into gear and squealed forward. The youth leaped to one side. The car was heading straight for the trash cans. Maria hit the brakes. Sherman was thrown against the dash. A vanity case landed on top of the gear shift. Sherman pulled it off. Now it was on his lap. Maria threw the car into reverse. It shot backward. He glanced to his right. The skinny one. . . . The skinny boy was standing there staring at him . . . pure fear on his delicate face. . . . Maria shoved it into first gear again. . . . She was breathing in huge gulps, as if she were drowning. . .

Sherman yelled, "Look out!"

The big one was coming toward the car. He had the tire up over his head. Maria squealed the car forward, right at him. He lurched out of the way . . . a blur . . . a terrific jolt. The tire hit the windshield and bounced off, without breaking the glass. . . .

Maria cut the wheel to the left, to keep from hitting the cans. . . . The skinny one standing right there. . . . The rear end fishtailed . . . *thok!* . . . The skinny boy was no longer standing. . . . Maria fought the steering wheel . . . a clear shot between the guard rail and the trash cans. . . . She floored it. . . . A furious squeal. . . . The Mercedes shot up the ramp.

(Tom Wolfe, *The Bonfire of the Vanities*, 1987)

1. Which person is wearing something that says "CELTICS"? <u>"the big one"</u>

2. How many people are inside the car? <u>two</u>

3. Who is driving the car? <u>Maria</u>

4. Describe the two people outside the car. Give an identifiable characteristic for each one. <u>"the big one"; "the skinny one"—"delicate face"</u>

5. What happened to the skinny boy? <u>He was knocked down by the car.</u>

6. What is the probable location of this incident? <u>parking garage; freeway off-ramp</u>

7. What is the likely emotion of those in the car? <u>fear</u>

   How do you know? <u>"breathing in huge gulps"</u>

8. What can we infer about the motives of the two outside the car? <u>attempting to</u> <u>steal the car</u>

9. Write a title that is descriptive of the contents of the passage. <u>Answers will vary.</u>

Exercise 5: Drawing Inferences from the Social Sciences

A good reader makes educated guesses based on observable details. We use our intuition and experiences to create a likely interpretation of what is happening in a story, while being careful that our interpretation is logical and realistic.

Directions: Read the following excerpt, answer the questions at the end of the passage, and then write the clue on which your inference is based. To answer the questions, you must read between the lines.

> Even from the glow of the faded red-and-white exit sign, its faint light barely illuminating the upper bunk, I could see that the sheet was filthy. Resigned to another night of fitful sleep, I reluctantly crawled into bed, tucking my clothes securely around my body, like a protective cocoon.
>
> The next morning, I joined the long line of disheveled men leaning against the chain-link fence. Their faces were as downcast as their clothes were dirty. Not a glimmer of hope among them.
>
> No one spoke as the line slowly inched forward. When my turn came, I was handed a Styrofoam cup of coffee, some utensils, and a bowl of semi-liquid that I couldn't identify. It didn't look like any food I had seen before. Nor did it taste like anything I had ever eaten.
>
> My stomach fought the foul taste, every spoonful a battle. But I was determined. "I will experience what they experience," I kept telling myself. My stomach reluctantly gave in and accepted its morning nourishment.
>
> The room was eerily silent. Hundreds of men were eating, each immersed in his own private hell, his head awash with disappointment, remorse, bitterness.
>
> As I stared at the Styrofoam cup of coffee, grateful at least for this small pleasure, I noticed what looked like teeth marks. I shrugged off the thought, . . . concluding, "That must be some sort of crease from handling."
>
> I joined the silent ranks of men turning in their bowls and cups. When I saw the man behind the counter swishing out Styrofoam cups in a washtub of water, I began to feel sick to my stomach. I knew then that the jagged marks on my cup really had come from a previous mouth.
>
> How much longer did this research have to last? I felt a deep longing to return to my family, to a world of clean sheets, healthy food, and "normal" conversations.

(James M. Henslin, *Essentials of Sociology*, 7/e, 2007)

1. What is the likely sex of the writer? <u>man—joins line of other men</u>

2. Where is the writer? What is the writer's location? <u>homeless shelter—hundreds</u> <u>of men at a soup kitchen</u>

3. What is the writer's purpose? <u>research—"'I will experience what they experience.'"</u>

4. What is the likely occupation or profession of the writer? <u>sociologist or reporter</u>
   <u>on assignment—"How much longer did this research have to last?"</u>

5. How do we know the writer is accustomed to a better life? <u>reluctantly crawls</u>
   <u>into bed, tucks clothes, stomach fights food, longing to return to family—clean sheets</u>
   <u>and healthy food</u>

6. Use one word to describe the demeanor of the men in line. <u>downcast;</u>
   <u>depressed; hopeless</u>

<hr>

Exercise 6: Drawing Inferences from Literature

Directions: The following paragraphs are taken from the short story "Flight" by John Steinbeck; intervening paragraphs have been omitted. Answer the questions following each paragraph by using the clues provided by the author.

A. Without warning Pepe's horse screamed and fell on its side. He was almost down before the rifle crash echoed up from the valley. From a hole behind the struggling shoulder, a stream of bright crimson blood pumped and stopped and pumped and stopped. The hooves threshed on the ground. Pepe lay half stunned beside the horse. He looked slowly down the hill. A piece of sage clipped off beside his head and another crash echoed up from side to side of the canyon. Pepe flung himself frantically behind a bush.

   1. What is the probable fate of the horse? <u>dead or dying—"crimson blood,"</u>
      <u>"on its side," "hooves threshed"</u>

   2. Why is Pepe behaving in a frantic manner? <u>being shot at</u>

B. The whole side of the slope grew still. No more movement. And then a white streak cut into the granite of the slit and a bullet whined away and a crash sounded up from below. Pepe felt a sharp pain in his right hand. A sliver of granite was sticking out from between his first and his second knuckles and the point protruded from his palm. Carefully he pulled out the sliver of stone. The wound bled evenly and gently. No vein nor artery was cut.

   3. What is the likely setting of the story? <u>Canyon or ravine in the southwest</u>

   4. How has Pepe been injured? <u>ricochet shot—sliver of granite pierced hand</u>

   5. Is the injury life-threatening? <u>no—"bled evenly," "No vein nor artery was cut"</u>

C. A moment later Pepe heard the sound, the faint far crash of horses' hooves on gravel. And he heard something else, a high whining yelp of a dog.

   6. In what way has Pepe's situation become more desperate? <u>a dog</u>
      <u>now tracking him</u>

D. He sat up and dragged his great arm into his lap and nursed it, rocking his body and moaning in his throat. He threw back his head and looked up into the pale sky. A big black bird circled nearly out of sight, and far to the left another was sailing near.

   7. What can we infer about the status of his injury? <u>more serious now—</u>
      <u>wound infected "great arm," no longer just his hand</u>

8. What is the significance of the circling birds? <u>signifies coming death—birds</u>
<u>are scavengers</u>

E.   Pepe bowed his head quickly. He tried to speak rapid words but only a thick hiss came from his lips. He drew a shaky cross on his breast with his left hand. It was a long struggle to get to his feet. He crawled slowly and mechanically to the top of a big rock on the ridge peak. Once there, he arose slowly, swaying to his feet, and stood erect. Far below he could see the dark brush where he had slept. He braced his feet and stood there, black against the morning sky.

9. What can we infer about how Pepe is feeling physically? <u>dying—thick hiss</u>
<u>indicates thirst, crawls, struggles to feet, sways</u>

10. Is Pepe religious? <u>yes—makes sign of the cross</u>

11. What is Pepe's solution to his dilemma? <u>crawls to top of peak so he is</u>
<u>visible to those pursuing him</u>

F.   There came a ripping sound at his feet. A piece of stone flew up and a bullet droned off into the next gorge. The hollow crash echoed up from below. Pepe looked down for a moment and then pulled himself straight again.

12. Why did Pepe stand erect again? <u>he wasn't hit—they missed</u>

G.   His body jarred back. His left hand fluttered helplessly toward his breast. The second crash sounded from below.

13. What was the end result of Pepe's flight? <u>killed by pursuers</u>

(John Steinbeck, "Flight," 1938, 1966)

READING

"Don't complain."

TUNING IN TO READING   What do you do when life doesn't go your way? Do you get angry? Do you complain? Or do you try to make the best of the situation and even find something positive in it? The following reading describes a specific "life lesson" that was taught by a very special grandmother.

BIO-SKETCH   Maya Angelou is best known as the author of *I Know Why the Caged Bird Sings*, an account of the early years of her life. She has published five collections of poetry, including the inspirational poem "On the Pulse of Morning," which she read at the inauguration of President Bill Clinton. Angelou is currently a professor at Wake Forest University in North Carolina.

NOTES ON VOCABULARY

cut one's eyes at   a rural expression meaning to glance at someone or something.

cooling board   a board used to hold a dead body. In the winter months in rural areas, it might be impossible to bury the dead because the ground is frozen, so a body is wrapped and propped up in a barn until the ground is sufficiently thawed out.

winding sheet   a sheet in which a corpse is wrapped for burial; similar to a shroud.

Complaining

W HEN MY GRANDMOTHER WAS RAISING me in Stamps, Arkansas, she had a particular routine when people who were known to be whiners entered her store. Whenever she saw a known complainer coming, she would call me from whatever I was doing and say conspiratorially, "Sister, come inside. Come." Of course I would obey.

My grandmother would ask the customer, "How are you doing today, 2 Brother Thomas?" And the person would reply, "Not so good." There would be a distinct whine in the voice. "Not so good today, Sister Henderson. You see it's this summer. It's this summer heat. I just hate it. Oh, I hate it so much. It just frazzles me up and frazzles me down. I just hate the heat. It's almost killing me." Then my grandmother would stand stoically, her arms folded, and mumble, "Uh-huh, uh-huh." And she would cut her eyes at me to make certain that I had heard the lamentation.

At another time a whiner would mewl, "I hate plowing. That packed- 3 down dirt ain't got no reasoning, and mules ain't got good sense. . . . Sure ain't. It's killing me. I can't ever seem to get done. My feet and my hands stay sore, and I get dirt in my eyes and up my nose. I just can't stand it." And my grandmother, again stoically with her arms folded, would say, "Uh-huh, uh-huh," and then look at me and nod.

As soon as the complainer was out of the store, my grandmother would 4 call me to stand in front of her. And then she would say the same thing she had said at least a thousand times, it seemed to me. "Sister, did you hear what Brother So-and-So or Sister Much to Do complained about? You heard that?" And I would nod. Mama would continue, "Sister, there are people who went to sleep all over the world last night, poor and rich and white and black, but they will never wake again. Sister, those who expected to rise did not, their beds became their cooling boards, and their blankets became their winding sheets. And those dead folks would give anything, anything at all for just five minutes of this weather or ten minutes of that plowing that person was grumbling about. So you watch yourself about complaining, Sister. What you're supposed to do when you don't like a thing is change it. If you can't change it, change the way you think about it. Don't complain."

It is said that persons have few teachable moments in their lives. Mama 5 seemed to have caught me at each one I had between the age of three and thirteen. Whining is not only graceless, but can be dangerous. It can alert a brute that a victim is in the neighborhood.

(Maya Angelou, *Wouldn't Take Nothing for My Journey Now,* 1933)

✔️ COMPREHENSION CHECKUP

Multiple Choice

Directions: For each item, write the letter corresponding to the best answer.

___b___ 1. Which one of the following character traits most accurately defines Angelou's grandmother in this excerpt?
- a. pessimistic
- b. wise
- c. whiny
- d. self-pitying

___a___ 2. When Angelou says that her grandmother told her the same thing "at least a thousand times," she is
- a. exaggerating.
- b. expressing compassion.
- c. expressing surprise.
- d. being cheerful.

___d___ 3. Angelou most likely feels _____ toward her grandmother.
- a. amusement
- b. resentment
- c. disinterest
- d. gratitude

___b___ 4. We can infer that the words "cooling boards" and "winding sheets" have something to do with
- a. graduation ceremonies.
- b. death and dying.
- c. farming practices.
- d. running a small store.

___c___ 5. A person who is behaving *stoically*
- a. is excitable.
- b. is impatient.
- c. is calm and unaffected.
- d. is distressed.

___c___ 6. A *lamentation* is
- a. an expression of joy and happiness.
- b. a discussion.
- c. an expression of grief.
- d. a eulogy.

___b___ 7. What is Angelou's main purpose in sharing this anecdote?
- a. She wishes to make fun of those individuals inclined to complain about their lot in life.
- b. She wants to share an important lesson she learned from her grandmother.
- c. She wants to honor her grandmother.
- d. She wants to demonstrate that the simple life has more value than a complicated one.

___b___ 8. We can infer that the story takes place in
- a. a large urban city.
- b. a rural area.

_____d_____ 9. We can infer from the story that
        a. Angelou's grandmother did not respect complainers.
        b. Angelou learned not to complain because of her grandmother's teachings.
        c. Angelou had a great deal of respect for her grandmother.
        d. All of the above.

_____c_____ 10. Which of the following best states Angelou's grandmother's philosophy as expressed in this story?
        a. Life is a never-ending series of problems that must be endured until we die.
        b. Strive to always be cheerful.
        c. Try to solve the problem, and if that fails, change your attitude toward it.
        d. A complainer is not likely to have many friends.

True or False

Directions: Indicate whether each statement is ture or false by writing **T** or **F** in the space provided.

_____F_____ 11. Angelou's grandmother took delight in embarrassing the complainers.

_____T_____ 12. Angelou sometimes referred to her grandmother as "mama."

_____F_____ 13. Angelou's grandmother referred to her customers as "brother" or "sister" because they were all close relatives.

_____F_____ 14. Angelou learned that in certain situations whining is a good idea.

_____T_____ 15. When Angelou's grandmother "cut her eyes" at her, she wanted to make sure she had Angelou's complete attention.

_____T_____ 16. Angelou's grandmother taught life lessons by words and example.

_____F_____ 17. A *brute* is likely to be a sensitive person.

_____T_____ 18. If you are *frazzled*, you are likely exhausted both physically and emotionally.

_____T_____ 19. According to Angelou, whining about a problem might lead to further harm.

_____T_____ 20. One of the complainers mentioned in the story disliked the heat and the other disliked plowing.

In Your Own Words

1. What specific lessons did Angelou's grandmother teach her? How did she convey those lessons?

2. How does Angelou's grandmother view life?

Written Assignment

Write a short paragraph discussing the meaning of the following quotation by Dr. Maya Angelou.

    "Complaining is dangerous for your prosperity and it's dangerous to your posterity."

Internet Activity

Have you ever heard of complaint-free bracelets? To find out more about them and to discover how Maya Angelou was the inspiration behind them, search the Internet for "Angelou and the 6 millionth bracelet."

READING

"We are going to take the winning speckled trout out of the freezer tonight."

TUNING IN TO READING   The old sayings "The apple never falls far from the tree" and "Like father like son" are used to illustrate the continuity of family traits. Do you think bad characteristics are passed down from generation to generation? Do you think that it is possible to learn from the mistakes of those who came before us?

BIO-SKETCH   Fannie Flagg is the author of the national best seller *Fried Green Tomatoes at the Whistle Stop Cafe,* which was made into a movie. She is also the author of *Welcome to the World, Baby Girl, A Redbird Christmas,* and *Daisy Fay and the Miracle Man,* from which this excerpt is taken. Writing may not have been a natural career choice for Flagg because, as she says, "I was, *am,* severely dyslexic and couldn't spell, still can't spell, and so I was discouraged from writing and embarrassed." Flagg has been more than just a writer. She has also been an actress, screenwriter, director, and comedienne.

NOTES ON VOCABULARY

caviar   the salted eggs of sturgeon, salmon, or certain other fish, eaten as an appetizer. The word originally came from the Turkish *havyar.* Russian beluga and huso, which are types of sturgeon, are widely thought to be the source of the best *caviar. Caviar* is so expensive that it is often referred to as "black gold."

Excerpt from *Daisy Fay and the Miracle Man*

FANNIE FLAGG

September 6

DADDY AND I ARE EXCITED because the Big Speckled Rodeo Trout Contest is next week and he and I are going to enter and we are going to win. I know that for a fact.

Daddy already bought the winning fish off Harvey Underwood a month 2 ago and put it in the freezer. He told Momma it was a fish he was going to stuff later on this year. It weighs twelve pounds and two ounces. I don't see how anybody could catch a fish bigger than that. The all-time record holder weighed thirteen pounds and that was six years ago. Our chances are excellent!

The person who catches the biggest speckled trout during three days of 3 fishing wins first prize and first prize is an Evinrude outboard motor, valued at \$146.90 and second prize is a Ply-Flex fishing rod valued at \$36. Now all we need is a boat to go with it!

September 15

Tomorrow is the last day of the Speckled Trout rodeo and everything is 4 going just as Daddy and I planned. We went down to the Speckled Trout Rodeo Headquarters the first day and registered early in the morning and headed on up to our spot on the river. Daddy made a big show of how he didn't expect to win, but thought it would be fun for his little girl since he had been so busy all summer and hadn't had a chance to spend any time with her. He made me paddle up and down the river for a while every day so people could see us fishing.

Then every day we went and napped and didn't even fish at all. I took 5 my Red Ryder BB gun and shot at snakes. I ate candy and Daddy drank his beer and told me war stories. At five o'clock we would go back to the Speckled Trout Rodeo Headquarters at the live bait shop. Daddy would say, "Well no luck today. Those fish just aren't biting," and act real disappointed to throw them off the track. . . .

We are going to take the winning speckled trout out of the freezer 6 tonight before we go to bed so it will be good and thawed for tomorrow.

September 18

The trout was still frozen stiff as a board when we took it out of the freezer. 7 So Daddy put it in a pan of boiling water and locked it in the trunk of the car. When we got up to the Speckled Trout Rodeo Headquarters, Daddy carried on some more how he had not caught one fish and how he hoped he caught something today. What kind of fisherman would his little girl think he was? We rowed up and down the river long enough for everyone to see us, just as we always did. Then we went back up to our spot and waited for that trout to thaw out. . . . About two o'clock in the afternoon the trout finally thawed, but putting it in the hot water had turned his eyes all cloudy. It didn't look like a fresh fish to me. Daddy didn't think so either and started cussing. Then he got an idea.

He said, "Don't move from this spot. If anybody comes up here, tell 8 them I have gone to the bathroom." I sat there and waited and I tell you nothing smells worse than a dead trout.

About an hour later he came sneaking through the bushes and nearly 9 scared me half to death. He had me drag the fish up to the bushes where he'd brought his whole taxidermy kit, right down to the artificial eyes, and some airplane glue. It took us forever, but we found some trout eyes. They were a little too big and the wrong color, but he said he didn't think the judges would notice. He cut the real eyes out of that trout and glued those plastic eyes in their place. We sat there and blew on them so they'd dry and at about four o'clock that fish started to look pretty good. The glue had dried funny, but Daddy said it made it appear like the trout had died ter-rifield. I told you my Daddy likes to see the bright side of things.

We were just getting ready to go when some old country man came by 10 in a boat and saw us and yelled out, "I heard Emmet Weaverly caught a thirteen-pounder this morning." Our trout was only twelve pounds and two ounces. I thought Daddy was going to be sick. But he's a quick thinker. He grabbed my box of BBs and stuffed every one of them down that trout's throat. By the time we got to the headquarters, everyone had weighed in but us.

So far the winner was Emmet Weaverly's fish that weighed twelve pounds 11 and eight ounces, not thirteen like that man had said.

When Daddy got in the room, do you know what he did? He handed 12 me that trout and said, "Hey, folks, look what my little girl just caught."

I couldn't believe it. I said, "Oh, no, Daddy. You're the one who really 13 caught it."

He said, "No, honey, you caught it. Run up there and have it weighed." 14

If looks could kill, he'd be deader than that fish with the plastic eyes. I 15 knew what he was doing. He was acting like he really caught it, but he was letting his little girl get all the glory. I tried to hand it back to him, but by then everybody thought the idea was so cute they pushed me up to where the scales were. I put the fish down on the scales very carefully. I didn't want those plastic eyes making a noise if they hit anything.

Our trout weighed twelve pounds and nine ounces. I did some fast fig- 16 uring in my head; that was seven ounces of BBs. Everybody started applauding and saying "Bill Harper's little girl won." I looked around and there was Daddy, smiling, getting patted on the back, taking all the credit. . . .

I never took my eyes off the trout. Just as a judge was about to pick it 17 up, I grabbed it in the nick of time. The offical Speckled Trout Rodeo photographer started posing me for the picture for the paper. They said for me to hold it up by the tail and smile real big. It was hard to smile because if one of those plastic eyes fell out on the floor and they found out that fish had been dead for a month, I would go to jail. . . . The more I thought about it, the worse it got. My heart started pounding and my lips began to tremble. I couldn't smile if my life depended on it. They made me stand there longer and said, "We're not going to let you go until you give us a big smile. So smile big, honey." My hands started to shake and that trout was shaking like crazy, too. I just knew those eyes were going to fall out. One had slipped a little anyway, but I needn't have worried about the eyes because at that moment the BBs started coming out of that trout's mouth one by one all over the floor. I was in a cold sweat, but you never saw anybody smile as big as I did.

I knew they had to get that picture fast! Mrs. Dot said, "Oh look she 18 caught a female fish, it's just full of caviar!" I sure was glad she didn't know the difference between BBs and caviar. Thank goodness Daddy came over and grabbed the fish out of my hand and turned it right side up and said, "I'm taking this trout home and stuffing it to make it into a trophy to donate to the Speckled Trout Rodeo as a gift." Everybody thought that was a fine idea, especially me. He said he had to get it home right away before the trout went bad.

Momma was waiting up for us. Daddy said, "Look what Daisy caught," 19 and didn't even give her time to look at it good before he threw it back in the freezer. He told Momma not to open the freezer until at least twenty-four hours because it would ruin the trout if she did. She believed him. . . .

Daddy won't have a hard time stuffing the fish. He's already got the eyes 20 in. . . . [Now] my daddy has an outboard motor in the shack out by the side of the malt shop. He doesn't have a boat yet, so I don't know what good it is doing him. Momma and I want him to sell it. We need the money for the payment on the malt shop, but Daddy says as soon as he starts stuffing his animals, he will have enough money to pay the note and buy a boat besides.

(Fannie Flagg, *Daisy Fay and the Miracle Man*, © 1981, 2005)

 COMPREHENSION CHECKUP

Multiple Choice

Directions: For each item, write the letter corresponding to the best answer.

___a___ 1. You can infer from the article that
 a. Daisy Fay's daddy didn't see anything wrong with using a frozen trout.
 b. Daisy Fay's daddy was an excellent fisherman.
 c. Daisy Fay's daddy thought "Momma" would readily agree with his scheme to use the frozen fish.
 d. Daisy Fay was initially opposed to her daddy's scheme.

___d___ 2. You can conclude that
 a. Daisy Fay's daddy will be able to use the Evinrude outboard motor right away.
 b. Daisy Fay's daddy was counting on making his old fish look like a fresh fish.
 c. Daisy Fay's daddy may never have a boat to put the motor on.
 d. both b and c.

___c___ 3. Daisy Fay's general attitude toward her daddy is one of
 a. hatred.
 b. fear.
 c. affection.
 d. indifference.

___b___ 4. The words "if looks could kill" suggest that
 a. Daisy Fay was terrified of her father's anger.
 b. Daisy Fay was frustrated and embarrassed.
 c. Daisy Fay was going to kill her father later.
 d. Daisy Fay was happy to have all of the attention focused on her.

___a___ 5. The main idea of paragraph 4 is found in the
 a. first sentence.
 b. second sentence.
 c. third sentence.
 d. last sentence.

_____d_____   6. The article suggests that Daisy Fay's father
        a. is not very honest.
        b. is clever and resourceful.
        c. is not very successful.
        d. all of the above.

True or False

Directions: Indicate whether each statement is true or false by writing **T** or **F** in the space provided.

_____T_____   7. Emmet Weaverly should have won the fishing contest.

_____T_____   8. Daisy Fay was afraid she might go to jail.

_____F_____   9. Daisy Fay laughed when the BBs started falling out of the fish's mouth.

_____F_____   10. Daisy Fay's daddy wanted her to pose with the fish so that she would feel good about catching it.

In Your Own Words

1. What could you infer about Bill Harper's character? List the details from the story that support your conclusions.

2. Would Daisy Fay's mother have approved of the scheme to win the fishing contest? What evidence do you have for your answer?

3. Bill Harper would probably be considered an optimist. What details in the story show that he always looks on the bright side of things?

4. What evidence shows that Bill Harper is resourceful?

5. How do we know that Daisy Fay was not comfortable with the scheme?

Internet Activity

To learn more about Fannie Flagg, including her career as an actress and writer, read an interview of her reported at the following Web site:

    www.randomhouse.com/features/fannieflagg/bookshelf.html

Then write a summary of what you learned about her.

REVIEW TEST 6: Drawing Inferences: "Too Much of a Good Thing"

Directions: This article by Geoffrey Cowley on antibiotics demonstrates that the need to draw inferences is not restricted to literature and the social sciences. Read each paragraph, and then write the letter of the sentence that can be directly inferred from the passage.

A. Like any internist, Dr. Robert Moellering of Boston's Deaconess Hospital has felt the pressure to hand out antibiotics on demand. When he served as director of student health services at Emerson College, he saw a steady stream of students with colds and flus, and many knew just which drug they wanted. Instead of dashing off prescriptions, Moellering would dutifully explain that their ailments were caused by viruses, and that no antibiotic—however new or expensive—can kill a virus. His campaign didn't get very far. As he now recalls, the kids would return days later waving bottles of pills in his face. "They'd tell me, 'My doctor said I almost had pneumonia.'"

_____b_____ 1. We can infer that
    a. students were willing to follow the advice of Dr. Moellering.
    b. students were able to obtain antibiotics from their own personal physicians.
    c. Dr. Moellering acceded to the demands of the college students.

B. If the golden age of antibiotics is ending, the reasons should be no mystery. Bacteria gradually adapt to any antibiotic, and when one is misused, its power to heal is squandered. "If I give my patient too much hypertensive medicine, I might hurt that patient but there's no way I'm going to hurt the next patient," says Dr. Frank Rhame, director of infection control at the University of Minnesota Hospital and Clinic. "If I use an antibiotic too much, I'm making it less useful for everyone." Unfortunately, doctors have been slow to act on that insight. Confronted with a miserable patient, they tend to write a prescription. Antibiotic sales are soaring as a result (sales have already doubled since the mid-1980s), and so are drug-resistant infections.

_____a_____ 2. We can infer that
    a. overuse of antibiotics by one person has repercussions for many others.
    b. overuse of heart medication by one person causes problems for others.
    c. doctors are unlikely to prescribe antibiotics to those with a viral infection.

C. The misuse of antibiotics isn't a new problem. Since the 1970s, various studies have concluded that 50 to 60 percent of all outpatient prescriptions are inappropriate. Other studies have found that 7 in 10 Americans receive antibiotics when they seek treatment for common colds. "Essentially," says Dr. Lee Green, a family practitioner at the University of Michigan, "we have a tradition of prescribing antibiotics to anybody who looks sick."

_____c_____ 3. We can infer that
    a. doctors are unlikely to prescribe antibiotics to relieve the symptoms of the common cold.
    b. the problem of misusing antibiotics is a relatively new phenomenon.
    c. a large percentage of prescriptions for antibiotics are unnecessary.

D. There's plenty of blame to go around. As Moellering has learned in Boston, Americans like quick fixes, and when a doctor doesn't offer one, they look for a doctor who will. Patients aren't the only culprits. When insurance companies fail to cover bacterial tests, they encourage sloppy prescribing. Drug companies, for their part, promote the use of their products by advertising them widely and supplying doctors with free samples.

Experts in health policy agree that the latest patented medications, which can cost 10 times as much as older generics, should be reserved for uniquely stubborn infections. "The more widely you use these newer antibiotics," says Dr. David Kessler, commissioner of the U.S. Food and Drug Administration, "the greater the chances that [bacteria] will develop resistance." But when a manufacturer touts a new product as a high-octane alternative that every patient deserves, doctors can feel duty-bound to prescribe it. "It's another form of defensive medicine," says Dr. Thomas O'Brien of Harvard.

_____b_____ 4. We can infer that
  a. doctors are unlikely to feel pressure to prescribe the newest "wonder drugs."
  b. promotion on the part of drug companies increases the likelihood of abuse of antibiotics.
  c. overusing the new "high-octane" antibiotics increases their effectiveness.

E. Even when doctors dispense antibiotics properly, there is no guarantee they'll be used that way. Studies suggest that a third of all patients fail to use the drugs as prescribed. Many stop taking their medication after just a few days, when it has killed the most susceptible invaders but left hardened survivors to flourish. Besides being harder to treat, those resistant germs can then spread through the community. Besides quitting treatments early, some patients save unused drugs to take later, or pass them around like vitamins. "I've heard of people on trips who take a fellow traveler's antibiotic, thinking it will protect them from illness," says Dr. Stuart Levy of Tufts University. "It just causes widespread resistance."

_____c_____ 5. We can infer that
  a. patients closely follow the directions on their antibiotic prescriptions.
  b. doctors are entirely to blame for the current antibiotic dilemma.
  c. a few days of antibiotic treatment kills off only the least-resistant bacteria.

F. Drug-resistant microbes don't threaten us all equally. A healthy immune system easily repels most bacterial invaders, regardless of their susceptibility to drugs. But when resistant bugs take hold among the weak, the sick or the elderly, they're hellishly hard to control. "I believe resistant infections are present in every hospital and nursing home," says Dr. Thomas Beam of the Buffalo, N.Y., VA Medical Center. "The only question is whether the institution is releasing that information."

_____b_____ 6. We can infer that
  a. it is unlikely that a patient can contract a bacterial infection in a hospital.
  b. the elderly are more susceptible to resistant bacterial infections.
  c. hospitals and nursing homes are likely to inform the patients of any outbreak of drug-resistant infections.

G. Penicillin and tetracycline lost their power over staph back in the 1950s and 60s. Another antibiotic, methicillin, provided a backup for a while, but methicillin-resistant staph is now common in hospitals and nursing homes worldwide. "If it's not in your hospital already," says Dr. David Shlaes of Cleveland's Case Western Reserve University, "the only way to keep it out is to screen patients and keep [carriers] in some kind of holding center until you treat them." In the past, officials at the VA nursing home in Sioux Falls, SD, quarantined half of the facility's 42 residents to control an outbreak of drug-resistant staph.

___c___ 7. We can infer that
   a. staph infections are uncommon in hospitals and nursing homes.
   b. antibiotics never lose their effectiveness against bacteria.
   c. a return to isolating patients is sometimes the only way to control infection.

H. Like staph infections, bugs known as *enterococci* flourish among weak and elderly hospital patients. Shlaes recalls that when a resistant strain of *enterococci* took hold in a Pittsburgh liver-transplant unit, 50 people were infected over the course of two years. The only survivors were patients whose infected tissues could be removed surgically (a trick from the pre-antibiotic era), or whose infections were confined to the urinary tract, where drugs can be used in high concentrations.

___a___ 8. We can infer that
   a. prior to the availability of antibiotics, doctors used to excise the infected body part.
   b. it is unwise to administer high concentrations of antibiotics in the treatment of urinary tract infections to save the life of a patient.
   c. *Staphylococcus* is the only bacterium likely to be a problem for elderly people.

I. Though they're concentrated in hospitals and nursing homes, the superbugs aren't confined to such settings. Out in the community, many bacterial diseases are becoming even harder to treat. Some 20 percent of the nation's gonorrhea is now resistant to one or more antibiotics. A similar proportion of TB now resists the drug isoniazid. As any doctor who has spent a winter throwing one drug after another at a toddler's ear infection can tell you, resistance is common in other bugs as well. But because the government doesn't track drug resistance, clinicians rarely know when to expect it.

___a___ 9. We can infer that
   a. clinicians are not kept well informed of outbreaks of resistant infections.
   b. you are not as likely to encounter a resistant form of bacteria in the community at large.
   c. gonorrhea and TB are no longer serious health threats.

J. To give doctors a better sense of what germs are circulating in their communities, the Centers for Disease Control and Prevention now encourage

"One of the first duties of the physician is to educate the masses not to take medicine."
—William Osler

local health officials to conduct regular surveys for drug resistance. Meanwhile, the World Health Organization is funding a global computer database that doctors can use to report drug-resistant outbreaks. Surveillance alone won't stop the erosion of the wonder drugs. "The classic response has been to develop new and more powerful antibiotics," says Moellering. With luck and perseverance, scientists will discover unimagined new weapons. But the immediate challenge is to get doctors, and patients, to stop abusing the weapons we still have.

____c____ 10. We can infer that
        a. keeping a closer watch on drug-resistant outbreaks is likely to alleviate the problem.
        b. new and powerful antibiotics are readily available.
        c. something must be done to educate both doctors and the populace at large to the danger of using antibiotics inappropriately.

(Geoffrey Cowley, "Too Much of a Good Thing," 1994)

In Your Own Words

1. The use of antibacterial products is widespread. We have antibacterial soaps, sponges, cleaning products, and even toys. Some experts believe that we are killing off the good bacteria as well as the bad, thereby promoting the growth of drug-resistant strains. Do you routinely use antibacterial products in your home? Do you have an opinion about whether the widespread use of antibacterial products is a good idea?

2. Many scientists are concerned about the use of antibiotics in the food supply. For instance, farmers use antibiotics to prevent disease in livestock. In 1998, over 5,000 Americans were made ill by drug-resistant bacteria that had infected chickens. The sick people were immune to the antibiotics that doctors prescribed. Do you think the Food and Drug Administration should consider banning the use of antibiotics to treat poultry and other livestock?

Internet Activity

The following Web sites offer information on the appropriate use of antibiotics:

www.apua.org (Alliance for the Prudent Use of Antibiotics)

www.familydoctor.org/handouts/680.html

Pull up either site and write a list of things the average person can do to help prevent drug-resistant bacterial diseases.

Go to the following Web site to find information about "MRSA." Explain briefly what it is.

www.mayoclinic.com/health/mrsa/DS00735

READING

*"In the Mexican worldview, death is another phase of life,
and those who have passed into it remain accessible."*

TUNING IN TO READING   From pre-Columbian times, the Day of the Dead has been celebrated in Mexico and other Latin American countries. Every November first and second, the living gather to honor and remember their departed loved ones. In the United States, *el Día de los Muertos* is often confused with Halloween, but unlike Halloween, the Mexican holiday is not considered scary. Actually, *el Día de los Muertos* most closely resembles U.S. Memorial Day, because both holidays show honor and respect for the dead.

BIO-SKETCH   Both Paul Insel and Walton T. Roth are professors at Stanford University Medical School.

NOTES ON VOCABULARY
indigenous   originating from a particular country or region
ironic attitude   cool, detached attitude; recognizing the absurdities of life

EL DÍA DE LOS MUERTOS: THE DAY OF THE DEAD
Paul M. Insel and Walton T. Roth

In contrast to the solemn attitude toward death so common in the United States, a familiar and even ironic attitude is more common among Mexicans and Mexican Americans. In the traditional Mexican worldview, death is another phase of life, and those who have passed into it remain accessible. Ancestors are not forever lost, nor is the past dead. This sense of continuity has its roots in the culture of the Aztecs, for whom regeneration was a central theme. When the Spanish came to Mexico in the sixteenth century, their beliefs about death, along with such symbols as skulls and skeletons, were absorbed into the native culture.

Mexican artists and writers confront death with humor and even sarcasm, 2 depicting it as the inevitable fate that all—even the wealthiest—must face. At no time is this attitude toward death livelier than at the beginning of each November on the holiday known as *el Día de los Muertos,* "the Day of the Dead." This holiday coincides with All Souls' Day, the Catholic commemoration of the dead, and represents a unique blending of indigenous ritual and religious doctrine.

Festive and merry, the celebration in honor of the dead typically spans two 3 days—one day devoted to dead children, one to adults. It reflects the belief that the dead return to Earth in spirit once a year to rejoin their families and partake of holiday foods prepared especially for them. The fiesta usually begins at midday on October 31, with flowers and food—candies, cookies, honey, milk—set out on altars in each house for the family's dead. The next day, family groups stream to the graveyards, where they have cleaned and decorated the graves of their loved ones, to celebrate and commune with the dead. They bring games, music, and special food—chicken with mole sauce, enchiladas, tamales, and *pan de los muertos,* the "bread of the dead," sweet rolls in the shape of bones. People sit on the graves, eat, sing, and talk with the departed ones. Tears may be shed as the dead are remembered, but mourning is tempered by the festive mood of the occasion.

During the season of the dead, graveyards and family altars are decorated 4 with yellow candles and yellow marigolds—the "flower of death." In some Mexican villages, yellow flower petals are strewn along the ground, connecting the graveyard with all the houses visited by death during the year.

As families cherish memories of their loved ones on this holiday, the larger 5 society pokes fun at death itself—and political and public figures. The impulse to laugh at death finds expression in what are called *calaveras,* a word meaning "skeletons" or "skulls" but also referring to humorous newsletters that appear during this season. The *calaveras* contain biting, often bawdy, verses making fun of well-known public figures, often with particular reference to their deaths. Comic skeletal figures march or dance across these pages, portraying the wealthy or influential as they will eventually become.

Wherever Mexican Americans have settled in the United States, *el Día de* 6 *los Muertos* celebrations keep the tradition alive, and the cultural processes associated with the Day of the Dead have found their way into the nation's culture. Books and museum exhibitions have brought to the public the "art of the dead," with its striking blend of skeletons and flowers, bones and candles. Even the schools in some areas celebrate the holiday. Students create paintings and sculptures depicting skeletons and skulls with the help of local artists.

Does this more familiar attitude toward death help people accept death 7 and come to terms with it? Keeping death in the forefront of consciousness may provide comfort to the living, reminding them of their loved ones and assuring them that they themselves will not be forgotten when they die. Yearly celebrations and remembrances may help people keep in touch with their past, their ancestry, and their roots. The festive atmosphere may help dispel the fear of death, allowing people to look at it more directly. Although it is possible to deny the reality of death even when surrounded by images of it, such customs as *el Día de los Muertos* may help people face death with more equanimity.

(Paul M. Insel and Walton T. Roth, "El Día de los Muertos," 2002)

 COMPREHENSION CHECKUP

Multiple Choice

Directions: For each item write the letter corresponding to the best answer.

_____b____ 1. Which sentence best expresses the main idea of the selection?
     a. The festival of the Day of the Dead typically begins on October 31.
     b. Mexicans tend to view death as a part of life and have a yearly celebration to remember and honor their loved ones who have died.

> c. Mexican artists treat death with humor and sarcasm.
> d. The souls of deceased children and deceased adults return on separate days.

_____d_____ 2. The authors' primary purpose is to
   a. persuade Americans to interact more with family members.
   b. entertain the reader with personal stories celebrating a unique ritual.
   c. inform the reader of the ways in which death is dealt with around the world.
   d. explain the Day of the Dead celebration.

_____b_____ 3. In paragraph 2, the authors say that Mexican artists and writers depict death as something "that all—even the wealthiest—must face." This means that
   a. "The greatest tragedy in life is not death, but life without a purpose." (Munroe)
   b. "As men we are all equal in the presence of death." (Syrus)
   c. "Death is a distant rumor to the young." (Rooney)
   d. both b and c.

_____c_____ 4. We can infer from the selection that the authors probably feel that
   a. a graveyard is no place for a celebration.
   b. poking fun at death is in poor taste.
   c. yearly celebrations such as the Day of the Dead may help people cope with their own inevitable death.
   d. unlike the lighthearted attitude toward death reflected in U.S. culture, Mexicans exhibit a very serious attitude.

_____a_____ 5. _Indigenous_ ritual, as described in paragraph 2, is likely to be
   a. native.
   b. foreign.
   c. unnatural.
   d. creative.

_____d_____ 6. From this selection, you could conclude that
   a. the Day of the Dead celebrations continue to be popular with many Mexican immigrants to the United States.
   b. the Day of the Dead celebration is popular only with non-Christians.
   c. family and community members participate in the Day of the Dead celebrations.
   d. both a and c.

_____c_____ 7. A synonym for the word _equanimity_ as used in paragraph 7 is
   a. excitability.
   b. indifference.
   c. calmness.
   d. evasion.

_____c_____ 8. The word _tempered_ as used in paragraph 3 means
   a. properly mixed.
   b. tuned.
   c. made less intense.
   d. having a pleasant disposition.

___b___ 9. The Mexican celebration features all the following *except*
a. bread of the dead.
b. a mournful attitude throughout.
c. aromatic flowers.
d. vigils to honor loved ones.

___b___ 10. The authors imply that
a. accepting death as inevitable is a positive thing.
b. the Day of the Dead celebration has much to recommend it.
c. there is much to be gained from having a sense of one's roots.
d. all of the above.

Topics and Supporting Details

Directions: Using the paragraph numbers in the text, match each paragraph with its topic.

1. Uses for the "flower of death" __4__

2. Ridiculing death and political and public figures __5__

3. Psychological and social benefits of the holiday __7__

4. Continuation of aspects of the holiday by Mexican immigrants in the United States __6__

5. Introduction and origin of the holiday __1__

6. Description of food and activities that make up the celebration __3__

7. Lively depiction of death by artists and writers __2__

Below are additional sentences about *el Día de los Muertos*. Using your inference skills, determine the paragraph number in which the sentences are most likely to fit.

8. Mexican marigolds, called *zempascuchitl*, are particularly suited for the Days of the Dead festivities because of the strong, sharp aroma. __4__

9. Concepts of death and afterlife existed in the ancient Maya and Aztec cultures. __1__

10. Mexican poets often write about death, comparing the fragility of life to a dream, a flower, a river, or a passing breeze. __2__

11. These *calaveras* often show individuals dancing with their own skeletons. __5__

12. A teacher at a Phoenix elementary school had her seventh-grade students create papier-mâché skeletons during the Day of the Dead holiday. __6__

Synonyms

Directions: Match each word in column A with its synonym in column B.

Column A		Column B
__b__	1. accessible	a. native
__h__	2. bawdy	b. approachable
__i__	3. depicting	c. rebirth
__j__	4. equanimity	d. face; deal with
__a__	5. indigenous	e. spread

_f_	6. inevitable	f.	unavoidable
_g_	7. partake	g.	participate
_c_	8. regeneration	h.	vulgar
_d_	9. confront	i.	portraying
_e_	10. strewn	j.	calmness

In Your Own Words

1. The goal of the ancient Greeks was to live a full life and then die with glory. What is your definition of a full life?

2. In the United States, many people reach adulthood without having seen any close family member or friend die. This stands in direct contrast to other parts of the world, where death is visible daily. Do you think an early experience with death changes one's attitude toward the dying process? In what way?

3. Many psychologists and other medical professionals feel that the United States as a whole is a nation of "death deniers" and "death avoiders." They point out that we often avoid even saying the word "died" and prefer to use expressions such as "passed on." They also note that many in our culture are in a constant search for the "fountain of youth." These individuals are willing to use whatever cosmetic or surgical means are available to avoid looking their age. How do you feel about this issue?

Written Assignment

Directions: Write a few paragraphs discussing one of the following questions.

1. Are some cultures better than others at providing emotional support to people who have lost a loved one?

2. What are the after-death practices of your specific culture? What are the funeral rites in your culture?

Internet Activity

To learn more about the Day of the Dead celebrations, consult the following Web sites:

www.public.iastate.edu/~rjsalvad/scmfaq/muertos.html

www.dayofthedead.com/html/traditions.htm#skullsandskeletons

READING

*"It was by chance that Allied forces first stumbled
upon the camps, and the GIs . . . were totally
unprepared for what they found."*

TUNING IN TO READING   The horror of war in no way prepared the Allied troops for their liberation of the Nazi concentration camps, which housed the gas chambers. As Allied troops discovered to their dismay, Hitler had authorized the systematic extermination of all European Jews, Gypsies, and homosexuals. The reading selection below describes the discovery of one of these "death" camps.

BIO-SKETCH The lead author of *America Past and Present* is Robert Divine. Before retiring, he taught American diplomatic history for 42 years at the University of Texas at Austin. He is now an emeritus professor at UT and continues to teach in the UT Extension Program and the Organization of American Historians Distinguished Lectureship Program. His latest book, *Perpetual War for Perpetual Peace,* is an analysis of the U.S. involvement in wars during the 20th century.

NOTES ON VOCABULARY

holocaust slaughter and destruction on a very wide scale, especially by fire. When used with a capital *H,* it refers to the Nazi slaughter of Jews in World War II. In pre-Christian times, a *holocaust* was a sacrificial burnt offering to pagan gods. It is derived from the Greek words *holos,* meaning "whole," and *kaustos,* meaning "burnt."

Natzweiler-Struthof Concentration Camp Near Strasbourg

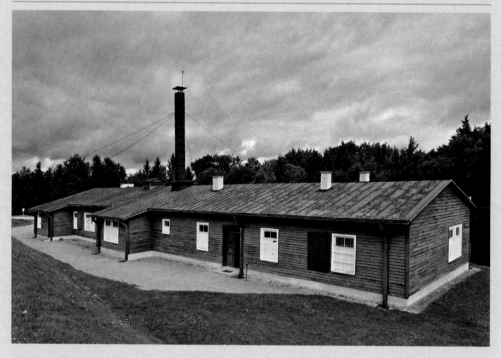

INSIDE THE VICIOUS HEART
Robert Divine

The liberation of the Nazi death camps near the end of World War II was not a priority objective; nor was it a planned operation. Convinced that military victory was the surest way to end Nazi oppression, Allied strategists organized their campaigns without specific reference to the camps; they staged no daring commando raids to rescue the survivors of Nazi genocide. It was by chance that Allied forces first stumbled upon the camps, and the GIs who threw open the gates to that living hell were totally unprepared for what they found.

Not until November 1944 did the U.S. Army discover its first camp, 2
Natzwiller-Struthof, which had been abandoned by the Germans months
before. Viewing Natzwiller from a distance, Milton Bracker of the *New York
Times* noted its deceptive similarity to an American Civilian Conservation Corps
camp: "The sturdy green barracks buildings looked exactly like those that
housed forestry trainees in the U.S. during the early New Deal."

As he toured the grounds, however, he faced a starker reality and slowly 3
came to think the unthinkable. In the crematorium, he reported, "I cranked
the elevator tray a few times and slid the furnace tray a few times, and even
at that moment, I did not believe what I was doing was real."

"There were no prisoners," he wrote, "no screams, no burly guards, no 4
taint of death in the air as on a battlefield." Bracker had to stretch his imagination to its limits to comprehend the camp's silent testimony to the Nazi attempt
to exterminate the Jews of Europe. U.S. military personnel who toured Natzwiller shared this sense of the surreal. In their report to headquarters, they
carefully qualified every observation. They described "what appeared to be a
disinfection unit," a room "allegedly used as a lethal gas chamber," "a cellar
room with a special type elevator," and "an incinerator room with equipment
obviously intended for the burning of human bodies." They saw before them
the evidence of German atrocities, but the truth was so horrible, they could
not quite bring themselves to draw the obvious conclusions.

Inside the Vicious Heart, Robert Abzug's study of the liberation of the con- 5
centration camps, refers to this phenomenon as "double vision." Faced with a
revelation so terrible, witnesses could not fully comprehend the evidence of
systematic murder of more than six million men, women, and children. But as
the Allied armies advanced into Germany, the shocking evidence mounted. On
April 4, 1945, the Fourth Armored Division of the Third Army unexpectedly
discovered Ohrdruf, a relatively small concentration camp. Ohrdruf's liberation
had a tremendous impact on American forces. It was the first camp discovered
intact, with its grisly array of the dead and dying. Inside the compound, corpses
were piled in heaps in the barracks. An infantryman recalled, "I guess the most
vivid recollection of the whole camp is the pyre that was located on the edge
of the camp. It was a big pit, where they stacked bodies—stacked bodies and
wood and burned them."

On April 12, Generals Eisenhower, Bradley, and Patton toured Ohrdruf. The 6
generals, professional soldiers familiar with the devastation of battle, had never
seen its like. Years later, Bradley recalled, "The smell of death overwhelmed us
even before we passed through the stockade. More than 3,200 naked, emaciated bodies had been flung into shallow graves. Others lay in the street where
they had fallen."

Eisenhower ordered every available armed forces unit in the area to visit 7
Ohrdruf. "We are told that the American soldier does not know what he is
fighting for," said Eisenhower. "Now at least he will know what he is fighting
against." He urged government officials and journalists to visit the camps and
tell the world. In an official message Eisenhower summed it up:

We are constantly finding German camps in which they have placed political prison- 8
*ers where unspeakable conditions exist. From my own personal observation, I can
state unequivocally that all written statements up to now do not paint the full horrors.*

On April 11, the Timberwolf Division of the Third Army uncovered Nord- 9
hausen. They found 3,000 dead and only 700 survivors. The scene sickened
battle-hardened veterans.

The odors, well there is no way to describe the odors. . . . Many of the boys I am 10
talking about now—these were tough soldiers, there were combat men who had been
all the way through the invasion—were ill and vomiting, throwing up, just at the
sight of this. . . .

For some, the liberation of Nordhausen changed the meaning of the war. 11

I must also say that my fellow GIs, most thought that any stories they had read 12
in the paper . . . were either not true or at least exaggerated. And it did not sink
in, what this was all about, until we got into Nordhausen.

If the experience at Nordhausen gave many GIs a new sense of mission in 13
battle, it also forced them to distance themselves from the realities of the
camps. Only by closing off their emotions could they go about the grim task
of sorting out the living from the dead and tending to the survivors. Margaret
Bourke-White, whose *Life* magazine photographs brought the horrors of the
death camps to millions on the home front, recalled working "with a veil over
my mind."

People often ask me how it is possible to photograph such atrocities. In photograph- 14
ing the murder camps, the protective veil was so tightly drawn that I hardly knew
what I had taken until I saw prints of my own photographs.

By the end of 1945, most of the liberators had come home and returned to 15
civilian life. Once home, their experiences produced no common moral responses.
No particular pattern emerged in their occupational, political, and religious
behavior, beyond a fear of the rise of postwar totalitarianism shared by most
Americans. Few spoke publicly about their role in the liberation of the camps;
most found that after a short period of grim fascination, their friends and families preferred to forget. Some had nightmares, but most were not tormented by
memories. For the liberators the ordeal was over. For the survivors of the Holocaust, liberation was but the first step in the tortuous process of rebuilding
broken bodies and shattered lives.

(Robert A. Divine et al., *America Past and Present*, 7/e, 2005)

  COMPREHENSION CHECKUP

Multiple Choice

Directions: For each item, write the letter corresponding to the best answer.

_____b_____   1. You could infer from the article that
    a. the United States was fully aware of the existence of concentration
       camps throughout the war.
    b. U.S. soldiers did not know much about concentration camps until
       their discovery.
    c. inmates were still alive in the Natzwiller-Struthof concentration
       camp.
    d. U.S. soldiers who entered the concentration camps were "fresh"
       troops who had not yet experienced the horrors of battle.

_____c_____   2. The primary organizational pattern used in this article is
      a. classification and division.
      b. definition.
      c. chronological order.
      d. steps in a process.

_____a_____   3. The author's primary purpose in writing this article was to
      a. explain what happened when U.S. soldiers discovered the concentration camps.
      b. persuade people to become more interested in the Holocaust.
      c. give a summary of one person's account of what he saw when he entered the camps.
      d. explain the causes of the Holocaust.

_____d_____   4. The best definition of the word *atrocities* as used in paragraph 4 is
      a. good deeds.
      b. mistakes.
      c. plans.
      d. acts of cruelty.

_____b_____   5. The purpose of the first paragraph is to
      a. give an example.
      b. discuss the strategy of the Allies.
      c. draw conclusions.
      d. discuss Nazi oppression.

_____c_____   6. When American GIs entered Natzwiller-Struthof,
      a. they discovered dying prisoners.
      b. they had to fight German guards.
      c. they found a prison that had been completely deserted.
      d. they rejoiced at finally being able to liberate some prisoners.

_____b_____   7. Photographer Margaret Bourke-White stated that she worked with "a veil" over her mind. From this we can conclude that
      a. she wore a veil over her head.
      b. she closed off her emotions.
      c. she tried to find something positive in a depressing situation.
      d. she did not find the concentration camps morally offensive.

_____b_____   8. The author implies that
      a. the people in the surrounding countryside were aware of what was occurring inside the camps.
      b. the green barracks were designed to look innocuous.
      c. every effort was made to provide for the prisoners' comfort and well-being.
      d. at the close of the war the camps served to house German prisoners of war.

_____c_____   9. The author implies that
      a. the World War II veterans liked to talk publicly about the concentration camps.
      b. the prisoners who survived the experience of the concentration camp were able to easily adjust to life after their liberation.
      c. many GIs put the past and the horrors they had witnessed in the concentration camps behind them.
      d. GIs who entered the concentration camps tended to become more religious.

_____ c _____ 10. General Eisenhower

    a. made Ohrdruf off-limits to American soldiers.

    b. prohibited journalists from visiting Ohrdruf.

    c. did not enter Ohrdruf until more than a week after its discovery.

    d. heard about Ohrdruf on news reports but never visited it.

True or False

Directions: Indicate whether each statement is true or false by writing **T** or **F** in the space provided.

_____ T _____ 11. The Allies discovered more than 3,000 dead bodies in the Ohrdruf concentration camp.

_____ F _____ 12. General Eisenhower did not want government officials or journalists to visit the camps.

_____ F _____ 13. Liberating the camps was a high priority for the Allies.

_____ F _____ 14. Allied forces staged a daring raid to rescue prisoners at Natzwiller-Struthof.

_____ T _____ 15. The discovery of Ohrdruf had a tremendous effect on American forces because it was the first concentration camp discovered intact.

Vocabulary in Context

Directions: Use the context clues in the sentences below to determine the meaning of the italicized word, and write the letter corresponding to the best answer.

_____ c _____ 1. "The liberation of the Nazi death camps near the end of World War II was not a *priority* objective. . . ." (paragraph 1)

The student had to decide whether her *priority* concern was going to be studying or watching TV.

Priority means

a. insignificant.

b. believable.

c. more important.

d. historical.

_____ b _____ 2. "Viewing Natzwiller from a distance, Milton Bracker of the *New York Times* noted its *deceptive* similarity to an American Civilian Conservation Corps camp. . . ." (paragraph 2)

The clear sky in the morning was *deceptive* because by noon a bad storm had blown in.

Deceptive means

a. truthful.

b. misleading.

c. dangerous.

d. ornamental.

_____ c _____ 3. "The *sturdy* green barracks buildings . . ." (paragraph 2)

The old woman, despite her recent hospitalization, was still very *sturdy* on her feet.

Sturdy means

a. practical.

b. weak.

     c. strong or stable.

     d. attractive.

_c_   4. "There were no prisoners," he wrote, "no screams, no *burly* guards. . . ." (paragraph 4)

In the football game, the *burly* linebacker was making a lot of tackles.

Burly means

a. weak.

b. relaxed.

c. big and strong.

d. handsome.

_d_   5. "U.S. military personnel who toured Natzwiller shared this sense of the *surreal*." (paragraph 4)

The *surreal* painting *The Persistence of Memory*, by Salvador Dali, which shows one watch hanging limply from a tree, others covered by flies and ants, and the final watch melted over a form representing the artist, illustrates the decay of time.

Surreal means

a. romantic.

b. realistic.

c. funny.

d. unreal; fantastic.

_d_   6. "a room 'allegedly used as a *lethal* gas chamber' . . ." (paragraph 4)

If you are a boxer like Mike Tyson, your fists can be considered *lethal* weapons.

Lethal means

a. useful.

b. simple.

c. mild.

d. deadly.

_b_   7. "It was the first camp discovered intact, with its *grisly* array of the dead and dying." (paragraph 5)

The movie *Silence of the Lambs* and its sequel *Hannibal* portray a *grisly* killer.

Grisly means

a. pleasing.

b. frightful.

c. unusual.

d. well known.

_c_   8. "I can state *unequivocally* that all written statements up to now do not paint the full horrors." (paragraph 8)

He stated *unequivocally* that he was innocent of his wife's murder.

Unequivocally means

a. proudly.

b. humorously.

c. with certainty.

d. doubtfully.

In Your Own Words

1. What do you think are the causes of prejudice?

2. A hate crime is defined as "an offense motivated by hatred against a victim because of his or her race, ethnicity, religion, sexual orientation, handicap, national origin, or tribal membership." (James A. Inciardi, *Criminal Justice*, 9/e, 2010)

    Do you think a crime that is motivated by hate should be punished more severely? Why or why not?

3. How often do you think hate crimes occur in the United States?

4. Do you think the concentration camps were deliberately designed to look like American Civilian Conservation Corps camps? Why might they have been designed that way? Use supporting details from the selection to answer the question.

5. What did Eisenhower mean when he said that even if the Americans did not know what they were fighting for, they at least now knew what they were fighting against? Use supporting details from the selection to answer the question.

Written Assignment

Why did the soldiers who discovered the camps have difficulty believing what they were seeing? In their reports, why did they qualify their observations about the camps? Lee Miller, a former model for *Vogue,* became a war correspondent in 1944. While on assignment, she photographed Dachau, the German concentration camp. She sent her photographs to British *Vogue* and followed with a telegram that said: "I IMPLORE YOU TO BELIEVE THIS IS TRUE." Why would she find it necessary to have a cable like this accompany her photographs? How do comments like this help explain America's initial reluctance to believe in the existence of the camps? Write a couple of paragraphs in response to these questions.

Internet Activity

Find out more about the U.S. Holocaust Museum in Washington, DC, by visiting its Web site at www.ushmm.org. The museum maintains an online exhibit. Write a short paragraph about your reaction to the online exhibit.

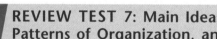

REVIEW TEST 7: Main Ideas, Details, Purpose, Transitions, Patterns of Organization, and Inference

The following paragraphs are taken from college textbooks. The general purpose of each author is to present information about the topic or to explain a specific idea.

Directions: Read each paragraph. Then write the letter corresponding to the best answer for each question on the line provided.

A. Psychologist John Reisman divides enduring friendships into three types: "associative," "receptive," and "reciprocal." An *associative friendship* endures because of circumstances that bring the partners together. Associative friendships include relationships with colleagues at work, at church, at school and members of the same club, athletic team, fraternity, or sorority. The sense of commitment that each partner feels toward the other is due to the situation (belonging to the same club). A *receptive friendship* is based on a difference in status or control. One member is the giver and the other is the taker. Leaders and followers create receptive friendships, as do instructors and students, mentors and trainees, masters and apprentices, or any sets of people whose relationship is based on a relational difference of complementary roles in which one person is the giver and the other is the receiver. A very close relationship is most likely to be a *reciprocal friendship* rather than an associative or receptive one. Partners in a reciprocal friendship feel a commitment specifically to their interpersonal relationship. Moreover, reciprocal friends tend to consider themselves as equals in the relationship. They will switch back and forth between giving and receiving roles and will typically not maintain one role throughout the relationship.

(B. Aubrey Fisher and Katherine L. Adams, *Interpersonal Communication*, 2/e, 1994)

_____b_____ 1. The organizational pattern used in this paragraph is
        a. cause and effect.
        b. classification and division.
        c. comparison-contrast.
        d. chronological order.

_____b_____ 2. Your relationship with a supervisor at work would be an example of which type of friendship?
        a. associative
        b. receptive
        c. reciprocal

_____a_____ 3. You work as a teacher's aide at a local high school and have become friends with a fellow teacher's aide. The two of you often take lunch and recess breaks together. This is an example of a(n) _____ friendship.
        a. associative
        b. receptive
        c. reciprocal

B. The Beatles—the singer-guitarists Paul McCartney, John Lennon, and George Harrison, and the drummer Ringo Starr—have been the most influential performing group in the history of rock. Their music, hairstyle, dress, and lifestyle were imitated all over the world, resulting in a phenomenon known as Beatlemania. All four Beatles were born during the early 1940s in Liverpool, England, and dropped out of school in their teens to devote themselves to rock. Lennon and McCartney, the main songwriters of the group, began working together in 1956 and were joined by Harrison about two years later. In 1962 Ringo Starr became their new drummer. The group gained experience by performing in Hamburg, Germany; and in Liverpool, a port to which sailors brought the latest American rock, rhythm-and-blues, and country-and-western records. In 1961, the Beatles made their first record, and by 1963 they were England's top rock group. In 1964, they triumphed in the United States, breaking attendance records everywhere and dominating the record market. Audiences often became hysterical, and the police had to protect the Beatles from their fans. Beatle dolls, wigs, sweatshirts, and jackets flooded the market. Along with a steady flow of successful records, the Beatles made several hit movies: *A Hard Day's Night, Help!,* and *Yellow Submarine.*

(Roger Kamien, *Music: An Appreciation*, 9/e, 2008)

_____b_____ 1. For this paragraph, the author uses an organizational pattern that
   a. gives examples to support a point.
   b. describes a series of events in chronological order.
   c. compares and contrasts key details.
   d. defines key terms.

_____d_____ 2. You can infer from this paragraph that the Beatles
   a. took college classes in music theory.
   b. had little effect on rock music.
   c. were well-known musicians before joining the group.
   d. changed the course of rock music.

_____c_____ 3. Ringo Starr
   a. was the Beatles' first drummer.
   b. was born in the late 1940s.
   c. joined the group after the Beatles released their first record.
   d. was one of the group's main songwriters.

C. Appearance counts when you are communicating on the Internet. You won't be judged by your physical appearance, your race, your hair color, or your age. But you will be judged by how you appear *in your writings*. You never know who might be lurking or how looking your best could benefit you. People have received job offers, internship and study opportunities, book contracts, and even marriage proposals, all based on their appearance on the Net.

   Here is a list of some guidelines for looking your best when you send a personal e-mail message or post a message to a discussion group:

(1) Be professional about what you say and how you say it. Know what you are talking about and be sure that what you are saying is correct to the best of your knowledge.

(2) Make sure that your message is clear and logical. Focus on one subject per message. Don't be long-winded.

(3) Use informative subject headings and present the most important information in your first several sentences.

(4) Keep your paragraphs short and to the point. Include line breaks between your paragraphs.

(5) Add some color. Using *asterisks* around words and phrases to emphasize a point, or a smiley :-) to indicate an emotion, can make your post more interesting to read. But don't overdo it and PLEASE AVOID SHOUTING.

(6) Be careful when using sarcasm and humor. In the absence of face-to-face communication, your joke could cause offense. It can also be very difficult for people from other cultures to understand "native" humor.

(Nancy E. Willard, *The Cyber Ethics Reader*, 1997)

_____d_____ 1. The organizational pattern used in this paragraph could be described as
   a. description.
   b. comparison-contrast.
   c. cause and effect.
   d. listing.

_____a_____ 2. The main idea expressed in this paragraph is that
   a. although you will not be judged by your physical appearance on the Internet, you will be judged by your written appearance.
   b. humor is cultural and can easily be misunderstood.
   c. brevity counts on the Internet.
   d. presenting a good appearance on the Internet can lead to financial success.

_____b_____ 3. The author's primary purpose is to
   a. warn readers about the dangers of e-mail.
   b. inform readers of proper behavior for communicating on the Internet.
   c. explain the meaning of communication.
   d. entertain readers by comparing the Internet to face-to-face communication.

_____c_____ 4. The author would agree with all of the following *except* for which?
   a. Sloppiness in writing on the Internet does not make a good impression.
   b. We should not use all capital letters.
   c. It's not necessary to include a subject heading.
   d. We should be careful when using jokes or wisecracks as they are easily misunderstood.

D. When you are a *speaker,* you are the source, or originator, of a message that is transmitted to a listener. Whether you are speaking to a dozen people or 500, you bear a great responsibility for the success of the communication. The key question that you must constantly ask yourself is not "Am I giving out good information?" or "Am I performing well?" but rather "Am I getting through to my listeners?" The *listener* is defined as the recipient of the message sent by the speaker. The true test of communication is not whether a message is delivered by the speaker, but whether it is accurately received by the listener. The message is whatever the speaker communicates to the listeners. The message is sent in the form of *symbols*—either *verbal* or *nonverbal.* The *channel* refers to the medium used to communicate the message. A speech can reach an audience by means of a variety of channels: radio, television, the Internet, a public address system, or direct voice communication. *Feedback* means the response that the listeners give the speaker. Sometimes it is *verbal,* as when a listener asks questions or makes comments during a lecture. Listeners also give *nonverbal* feedback. If they are smiling and nodding their heads, they are obviously in agreement with your remarks. If they are frowning and sitting with their arms folded, they more than likely disagree with what you are saying. *Interference* refers to anything that blocks or hinders the accurate communication of a message. When you are a speaker, watch for any signs of interference and if possible take steps to overcome the problem.

(Hamilton Gregory, *Public Speaking for College and Career,* 7/e, 2005)

_____c_____ 1. The organizational pattern used in this paragraph is
   a. sequence/process.
   b. time order.
   c. definition and example.
   d. cause and effect.

_____d_____ 2. The author implies that

      a. successful communication requires a listener to accurately receive a message.

      b. a speaker need be concerned only with presenting a message.

      c. a message can be expressed either verbally or nonverbally.

      d. both a and c.

_____d_____ 3. According to the author, feedback

      a. can be negative as when a listener frowns at something the speaker says.

      b. can be positive as when a listener nods to agree with a speaker.

      c. can be verbal as when a listener asks questions.

      d. all of the above.

E. One of the most striking contrasts between the United States and Brazil, the two most populous nations of the Western Hemisphere, is in the meaning and role of the family. Contemporary North American adults usually define their families as consisting of their husbands or wives and their children. However, when middle-class Brazilians talk about their families, they mean their parents, siblings, aunts, uncles, grandparents, and cousins. Later they add their children, but rarely the husband or wife, who has his or her own family. The children are shared by the two families. Because middle-class Americans lack an extended family support system, marriage assumes more importance. The husband–wife relationship is supposed to take precedence over either spouse's relationship with his or her own parents. This places a significant strain on North American marriages. Living in a less mobile society, Brazilians stay in closer contact with their relatives, including members of the extended family. Residents of Rio de Janeiro and São Paulo, two of South America's largest cities, are reluctant to leave those urban centers to live away from family and friends. Brazilians find it hard to imagine, and unpleasant to live in, social worlds without relatives. Contrast this with a characteristic American theme: learning to live with strangers.

(Conrad Phillip Kottak, *Anthropology: The Exploration of Human Diversity*, 12/e, 2008)

_____b_____ 1. The dominant pattern of organization in this paragraph is

      a. cause and effect.

      b. contrast.

      c. classification.

      d. listing.

_____d_____ 2. The writer of this paragraph probably believes that

      a. spouses in the United States are not as involved with their own extended families as spouses in Brazil.

      b. Brazilians find it more difficult to live away from their relatives than persons in the United States.

      c. the father's side has more involvement with the children in a Brazilian family than the mother's side.

      d. both a and b.

_____a_____ 3. The author's main idea in this paragraph is that

      a. the Brazilian system of marriage stands in contrast to the prevailing system in the United States.

      b. Brazilians don't like to work too far away from their relatives.

    c. an extended family is important to the Brazilians.

    d. the U.S. system of families should become more like the Brazilian system.

F. Among the middle and upper classes of the industrialized nations, some people suffer from a condition called anorexia nervosa. Anorexic individuals suffer from a mistaken perception of their body size. Because they imagine themselves to be heavier than they really are, they desire to be thinner as a result. Anorexia is most common among Caucasian women between the ages of 15 and 30 with an average or above-average level of education. Anorexia is all but unknown among people living in poverty or in undernourished populations anywhere. It never seems to occur where food is scarce, or in times of famine. Anorexia was once extremely rare. Several experts say its marked increase in the United States since World War II is caused by a general standard of beauty that has increasingly glorified thinness, as measured by such criteria as waist and hip measurements of Miss America contestants, *Playboy* centerfolds, and models and ballet dancers generally. In fact, women in professions like modeling and ballet dancing are particularly likely to develop anorexia. Also, female athletes in sports like rowing where competition is organized by weight classes are at high risk for developing anorexia.

(Eli Minkoff and Pamela J. Baker, *Biology Today*, 1996)

___d___ 1. The author suggests that

    a. anorexia is a frequent disease of the poor.

    b. anorexia primarily occurs among well-fed populations.

    c. anorexia rarely occurs in times of famine.

    d. both b and c.

___d___ 2. The writer of this paragraph probably believes that anorexia might be caused by

    a. an inability to accurately "see" one's size.

    b. an identification of thinness with beauty.

    c. the mass media's reliance on role models who are inappropriately thin.

    d. all of the above.

___c___ 3. According to the author, the person most likely to suffer from anorexia is

    a. a Black female age 15–30.

    b. a Caucasian male with an above-average education.

    c. a middle-class Caucasian female age 15–30.

    d. a person who participates in aerobics.

___a___ 4. The dominant pattern of organization in this paragraph is

    a. cause and effect.

    b. time order.

    c. listing.

    d. classification.

G. Innocent victims trigger more compassion if personalized. In a week when a soon-forgotten earthquake in Iran kills 3,000 people, a lone boy dies, trapped in a well shaft in Italy, and the whole world grieves. The projected death statistics of a nuclear war are impersonal to the point of being incomprehensible. So international law professor Roger Fisher proposed a way to personalize the victims:

It so happens that a young man, usually a navy officer, accompanies the President wherever he goes. This young man has a black attaché case which contains the codes that are needed to fire nuclear weapons.

I can see the President at a staff meeting considering nuclear war as an abstract question. He might conclude, "On SIOP Plan One, the decision is affirmative. Communicate the Alpha line XYZ." Such jargon keeps what is involved at a distance.

My suggestion, then, is quite simple. Put that needed code number in a little capsule and implant that capsule right next to the heart of a volunteer. The volunteer will carry with him a big, heavy butcher knife as he accompanies the President. If ever the President wants to fire nuclear weapons, the only way he can do so is by first, with his own hands, killing one human being.

"George," the President would say, "I'm sorry, but tens of millions must die." The President then would have to look at someone and realize what death is—what an *innocent* death is. Blood on the White House carpet: it's reality brought home.

When I suggested this to friends in the Pentagon, they said, "My God, that's terrible. Having to kill someone would distort the President's judgment. He might never push the button."

(David G. Myers, *Social Psychology*, 9/e, 2008)

___a___ 1. The organization pattern used by the author in this paragraph
      a. gives an illustration to support a point.
      b. demonstrates a cause-and-effect relationship.
      c. lists ideas without regard to order.
      d. defines key terms.

___d___ 2. International law professor Roger Fisher probably believes that
      a. in times of war, jargon is used to create distance from one's actions.
      b. it may be easier to bomb an entire village from 40,000 feet than to shoot a single helpless villager face-to-face.
      c. people responsible for killing other people are sometimes emotionally detached from the human reality of their decisions.
      d. all of the above.

___a___ 3. The main idea expressed in this paragraph is that
      a. personalizing the destruction that a nuclear war would cause may help prevent one.
      b. people are sometimes unresponsive to great tragedies.
      c. people are more likely to treat compassionately those they personally relate to.
      d. people are least likely to be compassionate to persons they bomb from the air.

Chapter Summary and Review

In Chapter 5, you learned how to draw inferences from a variety of sources, such as textbook material, literature, and cartoons. Based on the material in Chapter 5, answer the following.

Short Answer

Directions: Answer the following briefly, in a few words or phrases.

1. Explain what an inference is. <u>making educated guesses using the clues provided</u>
   <u>by the author</u>

Vocabulary in Context

Directions: Choose one of the following words to complete the sentences. Use each word only once.

   directly   experiences   inferences   lines

2. In drawing inferences, we make use of our <u>experiences</u> in life.

3. To figure out an idea that is not <u>directly</u> stated, we have to read between the <u>lines</u>.

4. We draw <u>inferences</u> every day of our lives.

VOCABULARY   Unit 3 Word Parts Dealing with Number and Amount

What does the word quadricentennial mean?

_____

When will your state celebrate its quadricentennial?

_____

In this unit, we will continue working with word parts involving number and amount.

centi—100   milli—1,000

century	100 years. In the year 2001, we entered the 21st *century*.
centennial	A 100-year anniversary. *Ann* and *enn* mean "year." Since *centi* means "100" and *enn* means "year," we are simply putting word parts together to make a word meaning 100 years. In 1876, we celebrated the first *centennial* of our independence from England.
bicentennial	A 200-year anniversary.
tricentennial	A 300-year anniversary.
cent	A penny is called a *cent* because it is 1/100 of a dollar.
centipede	*Centi* means "100" and *ped* means "foot," so a *centipede* would be an animal with 100 feet. *Actually,* centipedes don't have 100 feet; they just look like they do.

centipede—The largest centipede in the world, Himantarum gabrielis, has 171 to 177 pairs of legs and is found in southern Europe.

Giant Centipede

centigrade	Divided into 100 parts. On the centigrade, or Celsius, scale, water freezes at 0 degrees and boils at 100 degrees. While most other nations use the *centigrade* scale, the United States uses the Fahrenheit scale. On this scale, water freezes at 32 degrees and boils at 212 degrees.
centimeter	A unit of length in the metric system; 1/100 of a meter, or approximately two-fifths of an inch.
centenarian	A 100-year-old person. There are more women who are *centenarians* than there are men.
millennium	A period of 1,000 years.
millipede	An animal that looks like it has 1,000 feet. The technical difference between a *centipede* and a *millipede* is that a *millipede* has two pairs of legs on each segment, while a *centipede* has only one pair of legs on each segment.
millimeter	1/1000 of a meter. Metric wrenches used for working on bikes and cars made in Europe and Asia are measured in *millimeters.*
million	The word *million* was probably derived by multiplying 1,000 × 1,000. Maybe this will help you remember that *milli* means "1,000."

multi—many   graph—write
poly—many   gam—marriage

multiply	A system of repeating addition many times (3 × 3 = 3 + 3 + 3).
multimedia	A combination of many media. A *multimedia* computer presentation might appeal to more than one of our senses simultaneously, with film, music, and special lighting all in one performance.
multilateral	Many-sided. Remember that *lat* means "side." A treaty signed by more than two nations would be a *multilateral* treaty.
polygon	A many-sided figure. A decagon is a *polygon* that has 10 sides and 10 angles. The simplest *polygon* is the triangle.
polygraph	You probably know that *polygraph* machines are used on someone suspected of lying. *Graph* means "write." The machine works by recording (writing) the many bodily changes (blood pressure, respiration, pulse rate, perspiration) thought to occur when a person lies in answering questions.
polygamy	Being married to more than one person at the same time.
polyglot	Speaking or writing several languages.

semi—half   demi—half   hemi—half

semester	Half an academic year.
semicircle	Half a circle.

semiprofessional	Not fully professional. The baseball player was not good enough to play professionally, so he played in a *semiprofessional* league, or what is commonly called the semipros.
semicentennial	Half of 100 years, or 50 years; a 50th anniversary. Here you are just putting together *semi* meaning "half," *cent* meaning "100," and *enn* meaning "year."
semilunar	Shaped like a half-moon; crescent-shaped.
hemisphere	Half of a sphere or a globe. We live in the Western *Hemisphere.* The word *hemisphere* is also used when referring to the left half or right half of our brain.
demitasse	A small (half) cup. This cup is used for drinking very strong black coffee similar to espresso. A *demitasse* is usually served following dinner.

equi—equal

Don't get *equi* confused with *equus,* which means "horse." *Equestrian* competition involves horse-riding.

equator—The earth is not a perfect sphere because it is slightly flattened at the poles. The greatest circumference of the earth is at the equator and is 24,902 miles.

equal	Evenly proportioned.
equator	The imaginary line around the middle of the earth that splits it into two equal parts.
equidistant	Equally distant.
equinox	*Equi* meaning "equal" and *nox* meaning "night." The *equinox* happens twice a year, once in March and then again in September, when day and night are of exactly *equal* length.
equilibrium	The state of being evenly balanced. Your *equilibrium,* or balance, is controlled by your inner ear.
equilateral	A figure having *equal* sides. A square is an *equilateral.*

omni—all

omnivorous	Eating all sorts of food, especially both animal and vegetable food. Human beings are *omnivorous.*
omnipotent	All-powerful. Many religions consider God to be *omnipotent.*
omniscient	All-knowing. The professor thought he was *omniscient* in his subject area.
omnipresent	Present in all places at the same time. Cartoons are *omnipresent* on TV on Saturday mornings.

ambi, amphi—both; around

These two word parts have the same meaning, one coming from Latin and the other from Greek.

ambidextrous	Able to use both hands equally well.

An Outdoor
Amphitheater in
Greece

ambiguous

Vague; having two or more meanings. Because the teacher's directions were *ambiguous*, many students failed to complete the assignment correctly.

ambivalent

Ambi means "both" and *valens* means "worth," so *ambivalent* means "an inability to decide between two conflicting feelings or thoughts." My parents are *ambivalent* about my getting a job. On the one hand, they would like me to earn money; on the other, they think my grades will suffer.

amphibian

An organism that is able to live or operate on land and in the water. A salamander is an *amphibian*.

amphitheater

A type of theater or stadium that has seats going all around the stage or arena. The Greeks and Romans built outdoor *amphitheaters*, many of which are still in use today. You may have an *amphitheater* in your hometown for summer concerts.

Exercise 1

Directions: In the blanks below, write the word from the list that best completes the sentence. Use each word only once.

ambidextrous	amphitheater	centenarian	century	equal
equilibrium	million	multilateral	polygraph	semester

1. Sarah Delany, the co-author of *Having Our Say—The Delany Sisters' First 100 Years*, is a good example of a ___centenarian___.

2. While many religions consider the wife to be ___equal___ to the husband in the spousal relationship, some religions say a wife "should submit herself graciously" to her husband's leadership.

3. Because of her work for the poor of India, *Time* magazine named Mother Teresa one of the most inspirational people of the 20th ___century___ .

4. The special prosecutor wants those individuals requesting immunity from prosecution to submit to a complete ___polygraph___ examination.

5. If a basketball player can dribble and pass the ball equally well with either hand, we would probably call the player ___ambidextrous___.

6. Marcus was relieved to have the spring ___semester___ of college over so that he could relax over a long summer break.

7. A retired couple just won over a(n) ___million___ dollars in the New Jersey Lottery.

8. The old movie classic *Ben-Hur* has a famous chariot race that takes place in a Roman ___amphitheater___.

9. A(n) ___multilateral___ environmental treaty was signed by six nations.

10. In order to perform well on the balance beam, a gymnast must have a superb sense of ___equilibrium___.

Exercise 2

Directions: In the blanks below, write the word from the list that best completes the sentence. Use each word only once.

ambiguous   centigrade   centimeters   centipede   equator
hemisphere omnipresent   omniscient   omnivorous   polygamy
polyglot   semiprofessional

1. We turned down the wrong street because the directions that the attendant at the gas station gave us were ___ambiguous___.

2. Young children believe their parents to be ___omniscient___ because they expect them to know the answers to any question that they ask.

3. The ___centigrade___ thermometer, devised by Swedish astronomer Anders Celsius, is now used throughout most of the world.

4. The United States and Canada are located in the Western ___Hemisphere___.

5. If ___polygamy___ were allowed in the United States, do you think many men would have more than one wife?

6. Ants seem to be ___omnipresent___ at most picnics.

7. The ___centipede___ is a segmented, nocturnal animal known for its poisonous bite.

8. The ___equator___ is equidistant from the North Pole and the South Pole.

9. My dog Cookie is ___omnivorous___; she'll eat anything.

10. A college teacher who speaks five languages fluently qualifies as a(n) ___polyglot___.

11. The movie *Bull Durham*, starring Kevin Costner, is about a(n) ___semiprofessional___ baseball team.

12. A typical pencil is 19 ___centimeters___ long.

Expanding Your Word Power

The words listed below are not found in this Vocabulary Unit, but they are derived from the vocabulary word parts that you have studied. All of them would be good words for you to learn. See if you can guess the meaning of each word from its word parts.

1. bicoastal
2. semiannual
3. semiautomatic
4. semifinal
5. semisweet
6. equivalent
7. ambient

Vocabulary Unit 3 Crossword Puzzle

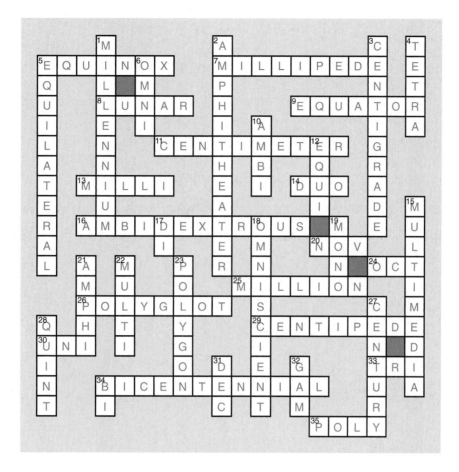

ACROSS CLUES

5. This event happens in September and March.
7. This "critter" has two pairs of legs on each of its segments.
8. A root word meaning "moon."
9. The imaginary line dividing the Northern and Southern Hemispheres.
11. 1/100 of a meter.
13. A word part meaning "1,000."
14. A word part meaning "two."
16. Being able to use both hands equally well.
20. The abbreviation for what was once the ninth month.
24. The abbreviation for what was once the eighth month.
25. 1,000 × 1,000.
26. A person who can speak many languages.
29. A "critter" that appears to have 100 legs.
30. A word part meaning "one."
33. A word part meaning "three."
34. 200-year anniversary.
35. A word part meaning "many."

DOWN CLUES

1. 1,000 years.
2. In ancient Greece, you might have gone to a(n) _____ to watch a play.
3. Water freezes at 0 degrees on this scale.
4. A word part meaning "four."
5. A square is a(n) _____ figure.
6. Word part meaning "all."
10. A word part meaning "both."
12. A word part meaning "equal."
15. Movies are _____ experiences because they combine images and sound.
17. A word part meaning "two."
18. All-knowing.
19. A word part meaning "one."
21. A word part meaning "both."
22. A word part for "many."
23. A figure with many sides.
27. In the year 2001, we entered the 21st _____.
28. A word part meaning "five."
31. An abbreviation for what was once the 10th month.
32. A word part meaning "marriage."
34. A word part meaning "two."

Figurative Language

CHAPTER PREVIEW
In this chapter, you will

_____

- Learn the difference between literal and figurative comparisons.

- Learn about similes, metaphors, and personification.

- Learn about extended metaphors.

- Become familiar with the use of symbolism in writing.

- Become familiar with literary allusions.

- Become familiar with imagery.

Figures of Speech—Similes, Metaphors, and Personification

In order to read well, you must become a *critical* reader. This means understanding not only the author's literal meaning but also the author's implied or inferential meaning. Many authors use figures of speech or figurative language to make their

Figures of Speech Chart

COMPARISONS

Literal	Figurative
(Compares things from the same category)	(Compares things from different categories)
1. Angie is as skinny as her sister.	1. Angie is as skinny as a telephone pole. (Simile: A is like B.) Uses *like*, *as*, or *as if* to make the comparison
	2. Angie is a telephone pole. (Metaphor: A is B.) Uses a state of being verb to make the comparison—*am, is, are, was, were*
	3. The telephone pole reaches its long arms to the sky. (Personification: Something that is not alive takes on human attributes or "person" characteristics.) Note: Personification is a special kind of metaphor.

Shoe-New Business MacNelly. Distributed by King Features Syndicate.

Shoe

writing more colorful and interesting. These **figures of speech** are expressions in which words are used regardless of their true meanings in order to create a special meaning or effect. Often this specialized language enables the author to more clearly convey meaning by making a comparison to something that is more familiar or readily understood.

When words are used conventionally and mean exactly what they say, they are being used *literally*. In figurative language, the words have been stretched to mean something beyond what they say. As an illustration of the difference between literal and figurative, study the *Shoe* cartoon above. In it, Loon takes something literally that is meant to be a figurative expression.

Although writers provide clues to the meaning of their figurative expressions, the critical reader must study the entire context of the expression in order to infer the meaning.

Some frequently used figures of speech are similes, metaphors, and personification. A **simile** is a figure of speech that compares two dissimilar things. Similes usually use the words *like, as,* or *as if* to show the comparison. "Sam is as energetic as Mary" is a comparison, not a simile. "Sam is as energetic as the Energizer bunny" is a simile. Both poems and prose contain similes.

Explain the meaning of each of these similes:

1. She is as confused as a rat in a maze. very confused

2. His muscles are like iron bands. strong

3. The fullback charged as if he were a locomotive. fast and powerful

A **metaphor** connects two unlike things directly without using *like, as,* or *as if.* One thing is spoken of as though it were something else. In "Dreams," the poet Langston Hughes uses a metaphor to show the hopelessness of a life without any dreams:

Hold fast to dreams
For if dreams die
Life is a broken-winged bird
That cannot fly.
Hold fast to dreams
For when dreams go

Life is a barren field
Frozen with snow.

("Dreams," from *The Collected Poems of Langston Hughes* by Langston Hughes, edited by Arnold Rampersad with David Roessel, Associate Editor, copyright © 1994 by the Estate of Langston Hughes. Used by permission of Alfred A. Knopf, a division of Random House, Inc., and by Harold Ober Associates Incorporated.)

An **extended metaphor** sustains the comparison for several lines or for the entire poem or story.

In the following excerpt from *How Good Do We Have to Be?*, Rabbi Harold S. Kushner uses an extended metaphor to express his feelings about life. What comparison is he making?

> Life is not a spelling bee, where no matter how many words you have gotten right, if you make one mistake you are disqualified. Life is more like a baseball season, where even the best team loses one-third of its games and even the worst team has its days of brilliance. Our goal is not to go all year without ever losing a game. Our goal is to win more than we lose, and if we can do that consistently enough, then when the end comes, we will have won it all.

(Rabbi Harold S. Kushner, *How Good Do We Have to Be?* 1996)

Now create your own metaphor for life. Include a short explanation of why you have chosen this metaphor.

Example: Life is a tidal wave; it doesn't stop for anybody or anything.

Student example: Life is an assignment. You have to start it and you have to finish it.

_____

_____

_____

_____

Personification is a type of figurative language that gives human attributes to a nonhuman subject. When Longfellow said, "Time has laid his hand upon my heart, gently," he was personifying the concept of time and his feelings about growing old. In the poem "The Eagle" by Alfred, Lord Tennyson, the first line of each stanza makes use of personification:

He clasps the crag with crooked hands;
Close to the sun in lonely lands,
Ringed with the azure world he stands.

The wrinkled sea beneath him crawls;
He watches from his mountain walls,
And like a thunderbolt he falls.

1. What figure of speech is the last line of the poem? simile _____

2. What does it mean to fall like a thunderbolt? quickly _____

Now choose five inanimate objects, and write a sentence giving each object a human attribute.

Example: My computer sighed, wheezed, and then expired.

1. The car crept through the stop sign. _____

2. My car drank 20 gallons of gas. _____

3. <u>The lamp rests on the table.</u>

4. <u>The clock said 9 A.M.</u>

5. <u>The computer spit out the answer.</u>

Finally, can you find the figures of speech in the cartoon below?

Shoe by Chris Cassatt and Gary Brookins

Shoe-New Business MacNelly. Distributed by King Features Syndicate.

Exercise 1: Literal or Figurative Comparisons

Directions: Indicate whether the comparison is literal or figurative by writing **L** or **F** in the space provided.

Reminder: Not all comparisons are figures of speech. A *figure of speech* makes a comparison between unlike things. A *literal comparison* compares things that are from the same category.

Example:
Lucille is as thin as a bookmark. (F) Different categories
Lucille is as thin as her grandmother. (L) Same category

___F___ 1. Evergreen trees bent *like people leaning out of the window.*

___F___ 2. The baby's breathing was choked and rough, like something pulled through tightly packed gravel.

___L___ 3. She was as strong-willed as her father.

___F___ 4. The animal was as white as cream cheese.

___L___ 5. He was eating as well and sleeping as well as the other students.

___F___ 6. I am a willow swaying gently in the wind.

___F___ 7. The waves beside them danced.

___L___ 8. He complained all day as if no one had anything better to do than listen to him.

___L___ 9. Like her brother before her, she chose to live at home while attending college.

___F___ 10. A gray mist rose on the sea's face.

List the numbers of the sentences containing a personification. _7, 10_

List the number of the sentence containing a metaphor. ___6___

Change the words in italics in sentence 1 to make an original simile.

Reminder: You need something that bends or is bent.

New simile: <u>like a pipe cleaner, McDonald's straw</u>

Exercise 2: Creating Original Comparisons

Comparisons are considered to be **clichés** when they are trite, overused, worn, or hackneyed. To better understand a cliché, read the following riddles. What do these riddles have in common?

1. Why did the judge wear a catcher's mitt?

   The ball was in his court.

2. How come a pickle doesn't sweat?

   It's cool as a cucumber.

3. When does a tea bag tremble?

   When it's in hot water.

Answer: They all have clichés as punch lines.

(Patricia T. O'Conner, *Woe Is I Jr.,* 2007)

Directions: Read the following clichés and try to create a fresh or original comparison.

1. thin as a rail <u>thin as a toothpick, French fry</u>
2. red as a beet <u>red as the tip of a lit cigarette</u>
3. flat as a pancake <u>flat as a tortilla</u>
4. nutty as a fruitcake <u>nutty as crunchy-style peanut butter</u>
5. light as a feather <u>light as a cloud</u>

Now rewrite this paragraph by substituting original comparisons of your own for the italicized trite expressions.

It was late at night, and I was working alone at the office. *Quick as a flash,*
<u>quick as a gunshot</u>

a robber dashed in and pulled a gun on me, demanding that I open the office safe. I managed to stay *cool as a cucumber* despite his gun at my temple
<u>cool as a breeze</u>

and his *grip like a vise* around my chest. Unfortunately, while escorting me
<u>grip like a wrestler</u>

over to the wall safe, he knocked my glasses off my face and stepped on them with a resounding crunch. There I was *blind as a bat,* unable to see
<u>blind as a miner in a coal shaft</u>

the numbers well enough to open the lock. I began to *sweat like a pig,*
<u>sweat like a Popsicle in the sun</u>

realizing I would soon be *dead as a doornail,* when without any warning
<u>dead as shoe leather</u>

the police came to my rescue. To conclude my story, I am now as *happy as a lark.*
<u>happy as a bride-to-be</u>

A special type of comparison is called an **analogy.** A writer uses an analogy to make something understandable or clear by comparing it to something that is different from it but that has something in common with it. Sometimes, however, an attempt to create a fresh and original comparison can go too far. These analogies recently posted on the Internet were labeled "the worst ever written in high-school essays." Try conveying the same information in a meaningful comparison of your own.

1. Her hair glistened in the rain like nose hair after a sneeze.

   glistened like dew at sunrise, stars in the sky

2. He was as tall as a six-foot-three-inch tree.

   tall as an NBA basketball player, Jolly Green Giant

3. The politician was gone but unnoticed, like the period after the Dr. on a Dr. Pepper can.

   unnoticed like a car in a college parking lot

4. His thoughts tumbled in his head, making and breaking alliances like underpants in a dryer without Cling Free.

   tumbled like the balls in the lottery

5. The little boat gently drifted across the pond exactly the way a bowling ball wouldn't.

   drifted like a swan across the pond

Exercise 3: Analyzing Figurative Comparisons

Directions: Each of the following sentences contains a figurative comparison. In the space provided, write down the real subject, what it is compared to, and the meaning of the sentence.

Example

Oliver Wendell Holmes once attended a meeting in which he was the shortest man present. "Doctor Holmes," quipped a friend, "I should think you'd feel rather small among us big fellows."

"I do," retorted Holmes, "I feel like a dime among a lot of pennies."

Subject: Dr. Holmes

Compared to: dime among pennies

Meaning: Dr. Holmes did not let his short stature bother him. Just as a dime, though smaller than a penny, is worth more, Holmes is "worth more" than his friends.

1. Whenever I try to speak to him, his mind wanders everywhere, like a cow following green grass.

   Subject: his wandering mind

   Compared to: the way a cow goes from pasture to pasture

   Meaning: He has trouble focusing on just one subject.

2. Her face looked like it had just come out of a dryer and needed to be pressed.

   Subject: her face

Compared to: <u>wrinkled clothing in need of pressing</u>

Meaning: <u>Her face is badly wrinkled.</u>

3. He bobbed through life's turbulences like driftwood on the sea.

Subject: <u>his way of coping with problems</u>

Compared to: <u>driftwood being jostled in the sea</u>

Meaning: <u>He is not directing his life; he is drifting.</u>

4. His grandparents' home was like a giant security blanket.

Subject: <u>grandparents' home</u>

Compared to: <u>security blanket</u>

Meaning: <u>He feels safe there.</u>

5. He struggled to extricate himself from the powerful undertow like a fly caught in a spider's web.

Subject: <u>his struggle against undertow</u>

Compared to: <u>fly caught in spider's web</u>

Meaning: <u>He's having problems freeing himself from the undertow.</u>

6. The car ran the red light like a bull charging a matador.

Subject: <u>car running red light</u>

Compared to: <u>bull charging a matador</u>

Meaning: <u>He is going very fast through the red light.</u>

Exercise 4: Figurative Comparisons in Fiction

Directions: The figures of speech (set in **boldface**) in the following excerpts were chosen by the authors because they create a fresh effect or demonstrate a new insight. Determine whether the expression is a metaphor, a simile, or a personification, and then decide what image or insight the author is trying to convey.

A. Until I was thirteen and left Arkansas for good, the Store was my favorite place to be. Alone and empty in the mornings, **it looked like an unopened present from a stranger. Opening the front doors was pulling the ribbon off the unexpected gift.** The light would come in softly (we faced north), easing itself over the shelves of mackerel, salmon, tobacco, thread. It fell flat on the big vat of lard and by noontime during the summer the grease had softened to a thick soup. **Whenever I walked into the Store in the afternoon, I sensed that it was tired. I alone could hear the slow pulse of its job half done.** But just before bedtime, after numerous people had walked in and out, had argued over their bills, or joked about their neighbors, or just dropped in "to give Sister Henderson a 'Hi y'all,'" the promise of magic mornings returned to the Store and spread itself over the family in washed life waves.

(Maya Angelou, *I Know Why the Caged Bird Sings,* 1970)

1. What does Angelou mean when she refers to the Store as "an unopened present"? Is this a simile or a metaphor? <u>favorite place—possibilities are</u> <u>endless—simile</u>

2. To what does Angelou compare the opening of the front doors? Does this comparison involve a simile or a metaphor? <u>pulling ribbon off a gift—metaphor</u>

3. What figure of speech does the following phrase use: "I sensed that it [the Store] was tired"? <u>personification</u>

B. Once a week Grandma Mazur went to the beauty parlor and had her hair shampooed and set. Sometimes Dolly would use a rinse and Grandma would have hair the color of an anemic apricot, but mostly Grandma lived with her natural color of steel gray. Grandma kept her hair short and permed with orderly rows of curls marching across her shiny pink scalp. The curls stayed miraculously tidy until the end of the week, when they'd begin to flatten and blend together.

I'd always wondered how Grandma had managed this feat. And now I knew. Grandma rolled her pillow under her neck so barely any skull touched the bed. And Grandma slept like the dead. Arms crossed over her chest, body straight as a board, mouth open. Grandma never moved a muscle, and she snored like a drunken lumberjack.

(Janet Evanovich, *Four to Score*, 1998)

1. To what does Evanovich compare her grandmother's curls? Is this comparison a simile, metaphor, or personification? <u>soldiers—"marching across her shiny</u>
<u>pink scalp"—personification</u>

2. What are three similes in this excerpt?
<u>body straight as a board</u>

<u>slept like the dead</u>

<u>snored like a drunken lumberjack</u>

Exercise 5: Figurative Comparisons in Nonfiction

It is important to realize that not all figures of speech come from fiction. Many writers of nonfiction also use figurative language in their writing. For example, to convey information to readers who are not well versed in scientific procedures, a science writer will often construct an appropriate metaphor. Keeping in mind that the word *metaphor* literally means "to transfer or bring across," Ted Anton and Rick McCourt, editors of *The New Science Journalists,* state that "almost every piece of really good science writing will connect its subject to an unexpected object or larger meaning."

Directions: Each of these figures of speech is taken from a scientific article. Determine what the figurative language suggests in each example, and then indicate whether the statements that follow are true or false by writing **T** or **F** in the space provided.

A.   A DESCRIPTION OF A COMMON ROUNDWORM

Through a microscope, they look like tiny crystal serpents, curving and slithering across the dish with an almost drugged sluggishness, doubling back on themselves as though discovering their tails for the first time, or bumping up against a neighbor clumsily and then slowly recoiling.

(Natalie Angier, "The Very Pulse of the Machine," 1995)

_____F_____   1. The roundworm moves quickly in a purposeful fashion.

_____F_____   2. The roundworm appears well coordinated.

B. A DESCRIPTION OF PROTEINS

The concentration of proteins in the cell is as thick as honey, and young proteins must be sequestered from the surrounding ooze. During the early stages of folding, the polypeptide may form characteristic corkscrew shapes, or linked loops that resemble a Christmas bow, or slender fingerlike projections.

(Natalie Angier, "Chaperoning Proteins," 1995)

____T____ 1. The ooze might jeopardize the development of the young proteins.

____T____ 2. Proteins are highly concentrated in cells.

C. A DESCRIPTION OF A BAT CAVE

The air screams, rustling movements feather against the skin, squeaks and screeches bounce off the stone walls, and a sweet acrid stench rolls across the room. My mouth chews the darkness like a thick paste. . . . The rock walls feel like cloth to the touch. . . . The feces and urine continue to shower down, the mites tickle the surface of my body, the atmosphere tastes like a bad meal and always the air drifting like a thick fog promises the whisper of rabies.

(Charles Bowden, "Bats," 1995)

____F____ 1. Bat caves are quiet, pleasant-smelling environments.

____F____ 2. Visibility is good inside the cave.

____T____ 3. Visitors emerging from a bat cave are likely to be covered in excrement.

D. A DESCRIPTION OF THE BRAIN

Brain is easy to define: It is the wet, oatmeal-colored organ, weighing about three pounds, that resides inside the skull. . . . Mind is not the all-knowing ruler of the brain, but a little circle of firelight in a dark, Australia-sized continent where the unconscious brain processes carry on.

(Timothy Ferris, "The Interpreter," 1995)

____T____ 1. The conscious mind forms a much smaller part of the operations of the brain than the unconscious.

____T____ 2. The mind is not really "running the show."

E. A DESCRIPTION OF CHROMOSOMES

Human chromosomes, shaped like cinch-waisted sausages and sequestered in nearly every cell of the body, are famed as the place where human genes reside.

(Natalie Angier, "A Clue to Longevity," 1995)

____T____ 1. The chromosomes contain human genetic material.

____F____ 2. Chromosomes reside in only a few dominant areas of the human body.

____F____ 3. The chromosome is smallest at the top and at the bottom.

F. A DESCRIPTION OF THE YELLOW JACKET

August is official yellow jacket month, as a number of entomologists have proclaimed on their Internet Web pages, and as anybody within range of a public trash can will attest. This is the season when the wretched little biblical plagues boil forth in force, bobbing and weaving like drunken marionettes, poking in fruit stands, crash-landing on soda cans, and haughtily, viciously, wickedly stinging any human who dares to protest. Actually, it turns out that yellow jackets are not the mean-spirited vermin their victims assume them to be, but instead are family values types that struggle selflessly to support and defend their kin. They just happen to crave the same junk food we do.

(Natalie Angier, "Selfless, Helpful, and Intelligent: The Wasp," 1999)

___T___ 1. August is the month when yellow jackets are out in force.

___F___ 2. Yellow jackets fly in direct routes.

Extended Metaphors

In an extended metaphor, the figurative comparison is developed throughout the entire article. This lengthy comparison helps readers visualize the event much more clearly. As you read the following article, note the extended metaphor and then answer the questions that follow.

READING

"It became a love/hate relationship."

TUNING IN TO READING   What do you know about group support networks such as Weight Watchers and Alcoholics Anonymous? What techniques do these organizations use to help people change their destructive behaviors?

The following letter, by Robert L. Rodgers, made a powerful impression on the readers of the late syndicated advice columnist Ann Landers. It is included in *The Best of Ann Landers.*

BIO-SKETCH   Until her death in 2002, Ann Landers (Eppie Lederer) was the most widely syndicated columnist in the world. During the course of her long career (1955–2002), she dispensed witty advice to help solve the personal problems of millions of people. Her column, which ran seven days a week, ended with her death. Reflecting on her long career, she said that "while it can be a headache, it's never a bore."

NOTES ON VOCABULARY

heart-breaking   causing severe emotional pain or grief. This form of hyperbole (exaggeration) first appeared in the works of Chaucer and Shakespeare. In 1913, George Bernard Shaw wrote a play titled *Heartbreak House.* And of course there is the song recorded by the king himself, Elvis Presley, titled "Heartbreak Hotel."

guts   pluck and perseverance in the face of opposition or adversity. The term dates from the mid-1900s.

been around   been present or active; gained experience or sophistication. The term dates from the first half of the 1900s and over time has acquired a negative meaning.

common-law   a marriage without a civil or religious ceremony based on a couple's living together continuously as husband and wife.

The Love of My Life

Dear Ann Landers: I first met her in high school. She was older than I, and exciting. She'd been around. My parents warned me to have nothing to do with her. They claimed no good could come from our relationship.

But I kept meeting her on the sly. She was so sophisticated and worldly. 2 It made me feel grown up just being with her. It was fun to take her to a party in those days. She was almost always the center of attention.

We began seeing more of each other after I started college. When I got 3 a place of my own, she was a frequent guest. It wasn't long before she moved in with me. It may have been common-law, but it was heartbreaking for my parents. I kept reminding myself I wasn't a kid anymore. Besides, it was legal.

We lived together right through college and into my early days in busi- 4 ness. I seldom went anywhere without her, but I wasn't blind. I knew she was unfaithful to me. What's worse, I didn't care. As long as she was there for me when I needed her (and she always was), it didn't matter.

The longer we lived together, the more attached I became. But it wasn't 5 mutual. She began to delight in making me look foolish in front of my friends. But still I couldn't give her up.

It became a love/hate relationship. I figured out that her glamour was 6 nothing more than a cheap mask to hide her spite and cynicism. I could no longer see her beauty after I came to know her true character.

But old habits are hard to break. We had invested many years in each 7 other. Even though my relationship with her made me lose a little respect for myself, she had become the center of my life. We didn't go anywhere. We didn't do anything. We didn't have friends over. It was just the two of us. I became deeply depressed and knew that she was responsible for my misery. I finally told her I was leaving for good. It took a lot of guts, but I left.

I still see her around. She's as beautiful as when we met. I still miss her 8 now and then. I'm not boasting when I say she'd take me back in a minute. But by the grace of God, I'll never take up with her again.

Forty percent of eighth graders have consumed an alcoholic beverage.

If you see her, give her my regards. I don't hate her. I just loved her 9 too much.

Chances are you know her family. The name is Alcohol. 10

Robert L. Rodgers, Waco, Texas

Dear Robert L. Rodgers: I have never met her personally, but a great 11 many people who have been intimately involved with your old love have written to say she ruined their lives. She has no class and no character and is totally ruthless.

You didn't mention one of the main problems she creates. It's financial. 12 Almost everyone who becomes a victim of her charms ends up with money trouble. She's an expensive "hobby."

Nor did you mention what your companion of the past did to your health. 13 Many of her close friends develop heart trouble, stomach problems, and cirrhosis of the liver.

I'm glad you had the strength to end the relationship. You didn't say 14 whether you had help from Alcoholics Anonymous. Thousands of readers have told me it was the only way they could get out of her clutches.

Incidentally, I heard from a good source that she hated to lose you but 15 she's not lonesome. She's on millions of guest lists around the country. In fact, they wouldn't dream of having a party without her! Funny that some-one so evil and destructive continues to be so popular.

(*The Best of Ann Landers,* 1996)

 COMPREHENSION CHECKUP

Multiple Choice

Directions: For each item, write the letter corresponding to the best answer.

b   1. Rodgers is comparing "Alcohol" to
    a. his parents.
    b. a girlfriend.
    c. a trusted friend.
    d. none of the above.

b   2. Rodgers began drinking in
    a. elementary school.
    b. high school.
    c. college.
    d. his twenties.

d   3. Rodgers rationalized his drinking by saying that
    a. as an adult he was legally able to drink.
    b. alcohol made him feel mature.
    c. alcohol made things exciting.
    d. all of the above.

d   4. Which of the following does Ann Landers wonder about?
    a. Did Rodgers consult a self-help group for assistance in overcoming his addiction?
    b. Did Rodgers's alcoholism cause him health problems?
    c. Did Rodgers get into trouble with the law?
    d. Both a and b.

d   5. Which of the following is not mentioned specifically by either Rodgers or Landers as a possible consequence of misuse of alcohol?
    a. financial difficulties
    b. health complications
    c. looking foolish in front of others
    d. causing accidents

d   6. The idiomatic expression "on the sly" means that
    a. Rodgers was using alcohol secretly.
    b. Rodgers was using alcohol furtively.
    c. Rodgers was using alcohol frequently.
    d. both a and b.

a   7. The phrase that most closely means the opposite of "sophisticated and worldly" is
    a. inexperienced and naive.
    b. smart and powerful.
    c. lazy and ignorant.
    d. cheerful and knowledgeable.

_____c_____ 8. When Rodgers says that "he wasn't blind," he means that
     a. he was in a no-win situation.
     b. he was ignorant of what was going on.
     c. he was aware of what was going on.
     d. he was feeling his way in the relationship.

_____a_____ 9. Ann Landers implies that
     a. she has never used alcohol.
     b. she uses alcohol on an infrequent basis.
     c. she is a frequent user of alcohol.
     d. she fails to understand how someone could become addicted to alcohol.

_____c_____ 10. Why does Ann Landers put the word *hobby* in quotation marks in
     paragraph 12?
     a. She is quoting from someone.
     b. She likes the way the word looks.
     c. She means that alcohol is not really a hobby because it is destructive.
     d. She doesn't approve of hobbies.

In Your Own Words

1. "It is estimated that between 9 and 10 million Americans are either alcoholics or problem drinkers" (*Targeting Wellness,* p. 246). What are some factors mentioned by Rodgers that influence the use of alcohol? How did alcohol help Rodgers relate to people?

2. Although it is often desirable to change patterns of behavior, it is seldom easy. In what ways does the letter from Rodgers illustrate the hidden pressures *not* to change?

3. Neither Rodgers nor Ann Landers mentioned two other destructive effects of alcohol: accidents and violence. Are you aware of any recent situations in which alcohol led to a serious accident? Are you aware of any recent situations in which alcohol was associated with violent or antisocial conduct? What should be the punishment for driving while intoxicated?

4. "A number of psychological traits have been closely associated with alcoholism, including deep-seated feelings of inadequacy, anxiety, and depression." How does Rodgers's letter illustrate these traits?

5. Do you think that Ann Landers's answer is what Rodgers expected? Why or why not?

6. What do you think the expression "love/hate relationship" means?

7. A surprisingly large number of young people are first exposed to either alcohol or drugs by relatives. What is your reaction to such incidents? If the child becomes addicted, should the relatives be held responsible?

Written Assignment

Directions: Complete one of the following:

1. Break into groups of four. Two students will write a paraphrase of Rodgers's letter, and two will write a paraphrase of Ann Landers's response. When you are finished, read your completed paraphrases to the class.

2. Give a short description of the consequences of being addicted to "Alcohol" that Rodgers mentions in his letter. What additional consequences are mentioned by Ann Landers?

3. The Oscar-nominated actor Robert Downey, Jr., was first introduced to marijuana at the age of 6 by his father Robert Downey, Sr. Since then he has waged a very public battle with drug addiction that has included numerous stays in drug rehabilitation facilities and jail. What do you think should be done with individuals such as Robert Downey, Jr., and Lindsay Lohan, who are nonviolent drug offenders? Write a few paragraphs giving your opinion.

4. Write a short letter to someone giving him or her your advice on how to deal with drug or alcohol addiction.

5. Do you personally know anyone who has had a problem with either alcohol or drugs? How did that person first get involved? Did the person seek help? Was he or she able to conquer that addiction? If so, how did he or she succeed?

Internet Activity

1. A major problem on college campuses is binge drinking. Using a search engine, type in "college binge drinking." Locate a Web site that discusses the problems associated with this type of drinking, and then write a paragraph summarizing the information. What is the relevance of this article for you, your friends, or your college?

2. In the past few years, many resource and support groups have become available to help problem drinkers. However, Alcoholics Anonymous still sets the standard for self-help groups. The Web site for this organization is:

   www.alcoholics-anonymous.org

   Go to this Web site to take an alcohol assessment test. For other self-assessment tests related to alcohol, go to a search engine and type in "tests for alcoholism."

The Use of Symbols

A **symbol** is a person, an object, or an event that stands for more than its literal meaning. It is representative of something else. A good symbol captures in a simple form a more complicated reality. For example, a white dove symbolizes peace, a flag symbolizes a country's values and aspirations, a budding flower may symbolize birth and new beginnings, and a logo on a shirt may signify wealth and status. Writers use symbols to create a particular mood or to reinforce a specific theme.

In his poem "The Road Not Taken," Robert Frost uses an extended metaphor to compare life to a journey along a road.

THE ROAD NOT TAKEN

Two roads diverged in a yellow wood,
And sorry I could not travel both
And be one traveler, long I stood
And looked down one as far as I could
To where it bent in the undergrowth;

Then took the other, as just as fair,
And having perhaps the better claim,
Because it was grassy and wanted wear;
Though as for that the passing there
Had worn them really about the same,

And both that morning equally lay
In leaves no step had trodden black.
Oh, I kept the first for another day!
Yet knowing how way leads on to way,
I doubted if I should ever come back.

I shall be telling this with a sigh
Somewhere ages and ages hence:
Two roads diverged in a wood, and I—
I took the road less traveled by,
And that has made all the difference.

The fork in the road is a more specific symbol that represents a major decision in life—a decision that must be made and that likely cannot be taken back. To preserve its symbolic value, the poem does not discuss the particulars of a decision or choice. In this way, the choice made in the poem can stand for any important choice made in life.

The ancient Greeks started the tradition of wearing wedding rings around the third finger of the left hand. They believed that finger contained a vein of love that runs directly to the heart. In actuality, blood flows to the heart through veins in all fingers on both hands.

Exercise 6: Identifying Symbols

Directions: Identify what each of these common symbols represents.

1. wedding ring <u>unity</u>

2. white wedding dress <u>purity</u>

3. rabbit's foot <u>good luck</u>

4. American flag <u>patriotism</u>

5. Lexus or Infiniti <u>status</u>

6. Springtime <u>rebirth; renewal</u>

7. skull and crossbones <u>death or poison</u>

8. gavel <u>justice or rule of law</u>

READING

"The more horrifying the world becomes, the more art becomes abstract."

—Pablo Picasso

"The Germans bombed the town of Guernica. . . . Guernica was devastated and its civilian population massacred."

TUNING IN TO READING   To learn more about one of the greatest achievements of 20th-century art, read the following selection from an art history textbook.

BIO-SKETCH   Although Pablo Picasso (1881–1973) was born in Spain, he spent most of his adult life in France. His early works revealed his strong compassion for those who were poor and suffering. He once said, "Painting is stronger than me, it makes me do what it wants." One of Picasso's finest paintings, *Guernica,* is a passionate expression of social protest, which Picasso painted during the Spanish Civil War (1937). It is hard to view *Guernica* (pictured on the next page) without vicariously experiencing the agony and destruction of war. Picasso was a dominant figure in Western art in the 20th century and is credited with helping to bring back storytelling to art.

NOTES ON VOCABULARY

fury   from Latin *furia* meaning "violent passion, rage, or madness." In classical mythology, the three Furies were winged female monsters with snakes for hair. Their goal was to pursue and punish those who had committed evil deeds.

procrastinate　to put off doing something unpleasant or burdensome until a future time. The word *procrastinate* can be broken down into parts, *pro* meaning "toward" and *cras* meaning "tomorrow." So when you *procrastinate,* you are pushing something toward tomorrow.

Guernica © 2003 Estate of Pablo Picasso/Artists Rights Society (ARS), New York/© Giraudon/Art Resource, NY.

GUERNICA
Rita Gilbert

[*Guernica*] was created by an artist whose sympathies lay with those not in power, an artist who took up his brush with a sense of fury at the "ins" who caused devastation. From his fury came one of the great masterpieces of 20th-century art. The artist was Picasso, and the painting is called *Guernica.*

It is necessary to know the story behind *Guernica* to understand its power. 2 In 1937 Europe was moving toward war, and a trial run, so to speak, occurred in Spain, where the forces of General Francisco Franco waged civil war against the established government. Franco willingly accepted aid from Hitler, and in exchange he allowed the Nazis to test their developing air power. On April 28, 1937, the Germans bombed the town of Guernica, the old Basque capital in northern Spain. There was no real military reason for the raid; it was simply an experiment to see whether aerial bombing could wipe out a whole city. Being totally defenseless, Guernica was devastated and its civilian population massacred.

At the time Picasso, himself a Spaniard, was working in Paris and had been 3 commissioned by his government to paint a mural for the Spanish Pavilion of the Paris World's Fair of 1937. For some time he had procrastinated about fulfilling the commission; then, within days after news of the bombing reached Paris, he started *Guernica* and completed it in little over a month. Despite the speedy execution, however, this was no unreasoning outburst of anger. Picasso controlled his rage, perhaps knowing that it could have better effect in a carefully planned canvas, and he made many preliminary drawings. The finished mural had a shocking effect on those who saw it; it remains today a chillingly dramatic protest against the brutality of war.

At first encounter with *Guernica* the viewer is overwhelmed by its presence. 4 The painting is huge—more than 25 feet long and 12 feet high—and its stark, powerful imagery seems to reach out and engulf the observer. Picasso used no colors; the whole painting is done in white and black and shades of gray, possibly to create a "newsprint" quality in reporting the event. Although the artist's symbolism is very personal (and he declined to explain it in detail), we cannot misunderstand the scenes of extreme pain and anguish throughout the canvas. At far left a shrieking mother holds her dead child, and at far right another woman, in a burning house, screams in agony. The gaping mouths and clenched hands speak of disbelief at such mindless cruelty.

Another victim is the dying horse to the left of center, speared from above 5 and just as stunned by the carnage as any of the human sufferers. Various writers have interpreted the bull at upper left in different ways. Picasso drew much of his imagery from the bullfight, an ingrained part of his Spanish heritage. Perhaps the bull symbolizes the brutal victory of the Nazis; perhaps it, like the horse, is also a victim of carnage. There is even more confusion about the symbols of the lamp and the light bulb at top center. These may be indications that light is being cast on the horrors of war, or they may be signals of hope. Picasso did not tell us, so we are free to make our own associations.

Guernica is like no other painting in the world. Enormous in size, stark in 6 its black-and-white tones, shocking in its images of brutality, vehement in its political protest—Picasso's great work stands alone in the history of art. Although Picasso was prolific as an artist, he never made another picture like *Guernica*. This uniqueness, then, presents a problem: How can the painting be kept from harm? How does one protect a one-of-a-kind masterpiece?

Picasso always intended *Guernica* as a gift to the people of Spain, his home- 7 land, but at the time of its creation in 1937, he did not trust the Spanish government. So, he shipped the picture off to the Museum of Modern Art in New York, where it was to be held "on extended loan" until such time as a "democratic" government was established in Spain.

In New York, *Guernica* was simply hung on a wall—a large wall to be sure. 8 Its impact was staggering when the viewer came around a corner and, suddenly, there it was. If the museum guards decided you were all right, and if you held your breath carefully, you could get quite close to the canvas. Or you could stand far back to take in the whole work at a gulp. So the situation remained for forty years. Only one unpleasant event marred the open relationship between artwork and viewers. In 1974 an Iranian artist splashed the *Guernica* with red paint as a political protest, but no permanent damage was done.

By 1981, eight years after Picasso's death, there was general agreement 9 that Spain's government had become sufficiently "democratic" to satisfy the artist's conditions. Under tight security *Guernica* was sent to Madrid, where it was installed in an annex of the Prado museum. The Prado was taking no chances with its newly acquired masterpiece. *Guernica* was quickly sealed up in what some observers called a "cage"—an immense riot-resistant enclosure under an armor-plated ceiling, with bulletproof glass set some 14 feet in front of the canvas's surface. Obviously, one could no longer move in close to study details. Museum visitors complained that glare on the glass prevented any overall view of the painting. Some grumbled that the protective box dominated the picture, making even a 25-foot-wide painting seem puny. *Guernica* was safe, all right, but at what cost to its expression?

The controversy escalated in 1992, when *Guernica* was moved yet again, 10 this time to the Reina Sofia museum a mile or so from the Prado. This new journey had all the drama of a spy movie. A special steel box, climate-controlled and weighing 3,500 pounds, was built to carry the painting. The transport company practiced its run down the road for weeks in advance, using stand-in paintings. Finally, on the fateful day, an armored truck carried *Guernica* through heavily guarded streets to its new home. The trip took half an hour and cost $200,000. Arriving intact at the Reina Sofia, *Guernica* was once again secured behind bulletproof glass.

One cannot help wondering what Picasso would have thought about all 11 this hullabaloo. His eldest daughter has accused the Spanish art ministry of "murdering" *Guernica.* Perhaps "jailing" it would be a better term. The issue is one of balance. If *Guernica* should be damaged or destroyed, there is no way ever to replace it. But what is the point of keeping this masterpiece so very safe that no one can properly see it? [After many complaints, the glass was removed in 1995.]

(Rita Gilbert, *Living with Art*, 5/e, 1998)

 COMPREHENSION CHECKUP

True or False

Directions: Indicate whether each statement is true or false by writing **T** or **F** in the space provided.

   T   1. Franco's collaboration with Hitler resulted in the bombing of Guernica.

   F   2. Picasso's painting required many months to complete.

   F   3. The colorful painting is generally thought to be very large.

   T   4. Picasso was a Spaniard by birth.

   T   5. The light bulb at the top of the painting may be seen as a sign of hope.

   T   6. Picasso intended *Guernica* to be a gift from him to the people of Spain.

   F   7. Originally *Guernica* was loaned to the Louvre in France.

   T   8. *Guernica* survived an incident in which red paint was splashed on it.

   F   9. Today *Guernica* is secured behind glass.

   T   10. Picasso's oldest daughter feels that the painting has been "murdered."

Vocabulary in Context

Directions: Indicate whether the italicized word is used correctly or incorrectly by writing **C** or **I** in the space provided.

   C   1. The cruel loss of his five children was *devastating.*

   C   2. Because the price of gas in the United States keeps *escalating,* people are no longer going on long car trips.

———I——— 3. When someone has an *outburst,* they are especially calm.

———C——— 4. If you cannot swim and are *engulfed* by a wave, you might need a lifeguard immediately.

———I——— 5. It is considered to be especially polite to *gape* at someone.

———C——— 6. At car speeds of over 100 miles an hour, an *impact* with a wall can cause serious injury.

———C——— 7. Stephen King is a *prolific* writer who has written over 30 best sellers.

———C——— 8. AIDS, a worldwide epidemic, has killed a *staggering* number of human beings.

———I——— 9. His *clenched* fist and scowling face indicated his happiness with his math grade.

———C——— 10. Millions of bats were *massacred* because the townspeople feared rabies.

In Your Own Words

1. How does Rita Gilbert feel about the way the Spanish government chose to exhibit Picasso's *Guernica* prior to 1995? What clues enable you to make this inference?

2. How do you think Picasso might feel about the safe-keeping of his masterpiece?

3. The author suggests that Picasso might have painted *Guernica* in black, white, and shades of gray to create a "newsprint" effect. What other reasons might Picasso have had for using this color scheme?

4. Picasso was fascinated by the ancient sport of bullfighting. The author mentions several things that the bull in the painting might symbolically represent. What do you think the bull in *Guernica* represents?

Internet Activity

View some of Picasso's paintings by visiting

www.abcgallery.com/P/picasso/picasso.html (Olga's Gallery)

or

www.pablopicasso.org

To learn more about Pablo Picasso, visit his official Web site at:

www.picasso.fr

Then choose a favorite painting and write a brief description of it.

READING

"If you can't do the time, don't do the crime"

TUNING IN TO READING Today, many people use yellow ribbons to welcome home soldiers or to serve as a reminder for those who are missing. What does a yellow ribbon symbolize to returning soldiers? Why do families with soldiers who are POWs or MIAs wear or display yellow ribbons?

BIO-SKETCH Pete Hamill (1935–) was born in Brooklyn and attended Catholic schools as a child. He left school at the age of 16 to become a sheet-metal worker and later joined the United States Navy. The G.I. Bill of Rights helped him pay for his education at Mexico City College. In 1960, he began his career in journalism at the *New York Post* and later served as

READING *(continued)*

its editor in chief. He also became editor in chief for the *New York Daily News*. As a journalist, he covered wars in Vietnam, Nicaragua, Lebanon, and Northern Ireland. He has written several fiction and nonfiction books, including *The Drinking Life* and *Downtown: My Manhattan*. "The Yellow Ribbon," originally written for the *Post*, became the inspiration for a TV movie and a song by Tony Orlando titled "Tie a Yellow Ribbon 'Round the Old Oak Tree."

NOTES ON VOCABULARY

solitude   the state of being solitary or alone. It comes from the Latin word *solus*, meaning "sole" or "alone." It is often used to describe the state of being cut off from human contact. The loneliness of such a situation is sometimes stressed.

THE YELLOW RIBBON   BY PETE HAMILL

They were going to Ft. Lauderdale, the girl remembered later. There were six of them, three boys and three girls, and they picked up the bus at the old terminal on 34th Street, carrying sandwiches and wine in paper bags, dreaming of golden beaches and the tides of the sea as the gray cold spring of New York vanished behind them. Vingo was on board from the beginning.

2   As the bus passed through Jersey and into Philly, they began to notice that Vingo never moved. He sat in front of the young people, his dusty face masking his age, dressed in a plain brown ill-fitting suit. His fingers were stained from cigarettes and he chewed the inside of his lip a lot, frozen into some personal cocoon of silence.

3   Somewhere outside of Washington deep into the night, the bus pulled into a Howard Johnson's, and everybody got off except Vingo. He sat rooted in his seat, and the young people began to wonder about him, trying to imagine his life: Perhaps he was a sea captain, maybe he had run away from his wife, he could be an old soldier going home. When they went back to the bus, the girl sat beside him and introduced herself.

4   "We're going to Florida," the girl said brightly. "You going that far?"

5   "I don't know." Vingo said.

6   "I've never been there," she said. "I hear it's beautiful."

7   "It is," he said quietly, as if remembering something he had tried to forget.

"You live there?"   8

"I did some time there in the Navy. 9 Jacksonville."

"Want some wine?" she said. He 10 smiled and took the bottle of Chianti and took a swig. He thanked her and retreated again into his silence. After a while, she went back to the others, as Vingo nodded in sleep.

In the morning they awoke outside 11 another Howard Johnson's, and this time Vingo went in. The girl insisted that he join them. He seemed very shy and ordered black coffee and smoked nervously, as the young people chattered about sleeping on the beaches. When they went back on the bus, the girl sat with Vingo again, and after a while, slowly and painfully and with great hesitation, he began to tell his story. He had been in jail in New York for the last four years, and now he was going home.

"Four years!" the girl said. "What did 12 you do?"

"It doesn't matter," he said with quiet 13 bluntness. "I did it and I went to jail. If you can't do the time, don't do the crime. That's what they say and they're right."

"Are you married?"   14

"I don't know."   15

"You don't know?" she said.   16

"Well, when I was in the can I wrote 17 to my wife," he said. "I told her, I said, Martha, I understand if you can't stay married to me. I told her that. I said I was gonna be away a long time, and that if she couldn't stand it, if the kids kept askin' questions, if it hurt her too much, well, she could just forget me. Get a new guy—she's a wonderful woman, really something—and forget about me. I told her she didn't have to write me or nothing. And she didn't. Not for three-and-a-half years."

18 "And you're going home now, not knowing?"

19 "Yeah," he said shyly. "Well, last week, when I was sure the parole was coming through I wrote her. I told her that if she had a new guy, I understood. But if she didn't, if she would take me back she should let me know. We used to live in this town, Brunswick, just before Jacksonville, and there's a great big oak tree just as you come into town, a very famous tree, huge. I told her if she would take me back, she should put a yellow handkerchief on the tree, and I would get off and come home. If she didn't want me, forget it, no handkerchief, and I'd keep going on through."

20 "Wow," the girl said. "Wow."

21 She told the others, and soon all of them were in it, caught up in the approach of Brunswick, looking at the pictures Vingo showed them of his wife and three children, the woman handsome in a plain way, the children still unformed in a cracked, much-handled snapshot. Now they were 20 miles from Brunswick and the young people took over window seats on the right side, waiting for the approach of the great oak tree. Vingo stopped looking, tightening his face into the ex-con's mask, as if fortifying himself against still another disappointment. Then it was 10 miles, and then 5 and the bus acquired a dark hushed mood, full of silence, of absence, of lost years, of the woman's plain face, of the sudden letter on the breakfast table, of the wonder of children, of the iron bars of solitude.

22 Then suddenly all of the young people were up out of their seats, screaming and shouting and crying, doing small dances, shaking clenched fists in triumph and exaltation. All except Vingo.

23 Vingo sat there stunned, looking at the oak tree. It was covered with yellow handkerchiefs, 20 of them, 30 of them, maybe hundreds, a tree that stood like a banner of welcome blowing and billowing in the wind, turned into a gorgeous yellow blur by the passing bus. As the young people shouted, the old con slowly rose from his seat, holding himself tightly, and made his way to the front of the bus to go home.

(Pete Hamill, "The Yellow Ribbon," 1972)

 COMPREHENSION CHECKUP

Multiple Choice

Directions: For each item, write the letter corresponding to the best answer.

____d____ 1. The main idea expressed in this article is that
a. a prison sentence can easily ruin a marriage.
b. young people on vacation can meet interesting people.
c. love is better the second time around.
d. after serving his time in prison, Vingo returned to Brunswick and discovered that his wife wanted him back after all.

____c____ 2. The author's primary purpose in writing this article is to
a. inform readers about unjust prison sentences.
b. explain to readers how prison disrupts family life.
c. entertain readers with a heartwarming story.
d. persuade readers to show compassion for those returning from prison.

_____c_____ 3. The pattern of organization used in this article is
  a. classification and division.
  b. comparison-contrast.
  c. chronological order.
  d. cause and effect.

_____b_____ 4. You can conclude that Pete Hamill obtained the information needed
  to write this article by
  a. interviewing Vingo.
  b. interviewing a girl who was on the bus with Vingo.
  c. interviewing Vingo's family and friends.
  d. interviewing the boys who were riding on the bus.

_____d_____ 5. We can infer that the young people aboard the bus are going to Florida
  a. to visit relatives.
  b. to get married.
  c. to interview for jobs.
  d. to take a vacation.

_____d_____ 6. We can infer that Vingo's wife was
  a. willing to forgive Vingo.
  b. angry for having to raise their children alone.
  c. a compassionate and caring woman.
  d. both a and c.

_____b_____ 7. We can infer that the young people began their trip in
  a. Washington, DC.
  b. New York.
  c. Florida.
  d. Pennsylvania.

_____a_____ 8. In paragraph 3, the word *rooted* in "He sat rooted in his seat" means
  a. to become established or anchored.
  b. to search about.
  c. to work hard.
  d. to dig.

_____a_____ 9. In paragraph 21, the word *fortifying* in "as if fortifying himself against
  still another disappointment" means
  a. strengthening.
  b. weakening.
  c. praising.
  d. condemning.

True or False

Directions: Indicate whether each statement is true or false by writing **T** or **F** in the space provided.

_____T_____ 10. Vingo was in prison for four years before being paroled.

_____F_____ 11. There were eight young people and two chaperones making the trip.

_____F_____ 12. Vingo had never been to Jacksonville before.

_____T_____ 13. Vingo looked at the pictures of his wife and children a lot.

_____T_____ 14. Vingo felt that you shouldn't commit crimes if you aren't willing to
  do the time.

The Yellow Ribbon: Summary

Following is an incomplete summary of "The Yellow Ribbon." Write the letters of the missing sentences on the lines provided.

(1) Vingo has just been released from a New York prison and is taking a bus home to his wife in Brunswick, Florida. (2) Some young people are on the bus heading to the beaches of Fort Lauderdale. (3) Just outside Washington, everybody gets off the bus except Vingo. (4) __d__ (5) The next morning, the girl again converses with Vingo, and this time he tells his story. (6) __b__ (7) He hasn't heard from his wife in three-and-a-half years. Vingo recently wrote to Martha again when he was certain he would be released from prison. (8) __a__ 9. If there was no handkerchief, he wouldn't get off the bus. (10) The young people become caught up in the excitement and look at the pictures of Vingo's family that he shows them. (11) As they approach Brunswick, the atmosphere inside the bus becomes very tense. (12) Then all of a sudden the young people are celebrating while Vingo stays in his seat stunned. (13) __c__

a. He told Martha to put a yellow handkerchief on a well-known tree on the outskirts of town if she would take him back.

b. Vingo doesn't know whether or not he is married, because he told his wife, Martha, that he would understand if she found another man while he was away.

c. The oak tree is covered with yellow handerchiefs and stands as a banner of welcome as Vingo makes his way home.

d. The young people become curious about Vingo, and when they get back on the bus one of the girls introduces herself and engages him in conversation.

In Your Own Words

1. In the last paragraph, Hamill says that the tree covered with yellow handkerchiefs "stood like a banner of welcome." In Vingo's case, what does the tree symbolically represent?

2. Make a profile sketch of Vingo by listing his key character traits. Some traits are directly stated in the text, and others must be inferred from the evidence presented. Be able to justify each of your traits by citing specific passages.

3. What does it mean to be "frozen into some personal cocoon of silence"?

4. What does Vingo's face look like when he tightens it "into the ex-con's mask"?

5. What inference can you make about why Vingo's wife did not keep in regular contact with him while he was in prison? What kind of woman do you think she is?

Written Assignment

All of us make assumptions about other people just by looking at them. We also judge people by their friends. You can often tell a lot about a person from the people he or she associates with. What do your friends "say" about you? That is, what can someone tell *about you* from knowing or observing your friends? Write a paragraph about yourself from this perspective.

Internet Activity

Many people wear ribbons or bracelets to support various causes. Can you think of some examples? What colors are used? Many people across the United States display yellow ribbons as an expression of solidarity with our troops. Others display these ribbons as a reminder of loved ones in danger and a desire for their safe return home. To learn more about the tradition of wearing yellow ribbons, go to

www.loc.gov/folklife/ribbons

or type "origins of yellow ribbons" into a search engine. Write a paragraph summarizing the information you find.

Literary Allusions

A **literary allusion** is a reference to something that is supposed to be common cultural knowledge. Allusions are a technique writers use to quickly express a complex thought or evoke a certain image or reaction. In this sense, they are much like symbols. To fully understand a literary work, you need to be able to recognize and understand the allusions used by the author. Often, research must be done to discover the meaning of an allusion.

Study the following example from the opening stanza of "Travel" by Robert Louis Stevenson:

I should like to rise and go
Where the golden apples grow;—
Where below another sky
Parrot islands anchored lie,
And, watched by cockatoos and goats,
Lonely Crusoes building boats;—

The word *Crusoe* refers to the main character of Daniel Defoe's 18th-century novel *Robinson Crusoe*. In the novel, Crusoe is shipwrecked and washed ashore on an uninhabited island. Crusoe has come to symbolize a person who can overcome hardships and survive in isolation. The second literary allusion, Parrot islands, refers to the Canary Islands, located in the Atlantic Ocean directly off the northwest coast of Africa. The Canaries, because of their beauty and relative isolation, symbolize serenity. Thus, in the beginning of this poem, the poet is expressing a longing to journey to a remote area.

Cultural Literacy Assignment

Directions: Form groups of four. Each group will then be assigned either Quiz A or Quiz B. You are allowed to help each other.

CULTURAL LITERACY QUIZ A
Mythology and Folklore

1. A weak or sore point in a person's character. A<u>chilles'</u> h<u>eel</u>

2. A magician who acted as King Arthur's primary advisor. M<u>erlin</u>

Proverbs

3. Physical beauty is superficial. B<u>eauty</u> is <u>only</u> <u>skin</u> d<u>eep</u>.

4. If we want to achieve our goal, we must get an early start. The <u>early</u> b<u>ird</u> catches the w<u>orm</u>.

This activity may be done in the library where resource materials to check answers are readily available, or it may be done in class as a contest to see which group can correctly complete the most answers in a given amount of time.

Idioms

5. A disgrace to the family. B<u>lack</u> sh<u>eep</u>

6. If something can go wrong, it will. M<u>urphy's</u> L<u>aw</u>

Literature

7. Author of *Diary of a Young Girl.* A<u>nne</u> F<u>rank</u>

8. "I'll huff and I'll puff, and I'll blow your house down." T<u>hree</u> Little P<u>igs</u>

9. A novel by J. D. Salinger recounting the adventures of the young Holden Caulfield. *The Catcher in the R<u>ye</u>*

Art

10. The creator of the paintings on the ceiling of the Sistine Chapel. M<u>ichelangelo</u>

11. The statue features the words "Give me your tired, your poor, your huddled masses." S<u>tatue</u> of L<u>iberty</u>

History

12. A king of England who beheaded two wives. H<u>enry</u> the <u>VIII</u>

13. The ancient Roman leader who was murdered on March 15. Julius C<u>aesar</u>

14. The inventor of the lightning rod, bifocal glasses, and a stove. B<u>enjamin</u> F<u>ranklin</u>

15. A seamstress who made flags in Philadelphia during the Revolutionary War. B<u>etsy</u> R<u>oss</u>

16. A battle between Custer and Native Americans. L<u>ittle</u> B<u>ighorn</u>

17. The championship game of the NFL held in January. S<u>uper</u> B<u>owl</u>

Bible

18. The principle of justice that requires punishment equal in kind to the offense. An <u>eye</u> for an <u>eye</u>

19. "Do unto others as you would have them do unto you." The G<u>olden</u> R<u>ule</u>

Science

20. Large, white, puffy clouds—some carry rain. C<u>umulus</u>

21. A shuttle that exploded in space. C<u>hallenger</u> / <u>Columbia</u>

CULTURAL LITERACY QUIZ B

Mythology and Folklore

1. The king of the Greek gods. Z<u>eus</u>

2. Small men who resemble elves capable of revealing the whereabouts of a pot of gold at the end of the rainbow. L<u>eprechauns</u>

Proverbs

3. Apples keep us healthy. An <u>apple</u> a day k<u>eeps</u> the d<u>octor</u> a<u>way</u>.

4. Don't assume that you'll get the things you want until you have them. D<u>on't</u> c<u>ount</u> y<u>our</u> ch<u>ickens</u> b<u>efore</u> they h<u>atch</u>.

Idioms

5. Smooth, flattering talk (Irish derivation). B<u>larney</u>

6. To blow an event out of proportion. Don't m<u>ake</u> a m<u>ountain</u> out of a m<u>ole</u> h<u>ill</u>.

Literature

7. Ali Baba and the ___<u>40</u>___ Thieves.

8. "All animals are equal, but some animals are more equal than others." A<u>nimal</u> F<u>arm</u>

9. "Elementary, my dear Watson." Sh<u>erlock</u> H<u>olmes</u>

Art

10. A painting by Leonardo da Vinci of a woman with a mysterious smile. M<u>ona</u> L<u>isa</u>

11. The Spanish painter of *Guernica.* P<u>icasso</u>

History

12. The queen of Egypt famed for her beauty; lover of Marc Antony. C<u>leopatra</u>

13. A female French military leader who claimed God spoke to her in voices. J<u>oan</u> of A<u>rc</u>

14. An English nurse of the 19th century, and a symbol for all nursing. F<u>lorence</u> N<u>ightingale</u>

15. The commander of the Confederate troops. R<u>obert</u> E. L<u>ee</u>

16. His most famous speech is "I Have a Dream." M<u>artin</u> L<u>uther</u> K<u>ing</u>, Jr.

17. The oldest and most famous of the college "bowl games." R<u>ose</u> B<u>owl</u>

Bible

18. The reason people of the earth speak different languages. The T<u>ower</u> of B<u>abel</u>

19. The first children of Adam and Eve. C<u>ain</u> and A<u>bel</u>

Science

20. Lacy or wispy clouds that form at high altitudes. C<u>irrus</u>

21. A very "unlucky" space mission. A<u>pollo 13</u>

Imagery

In addition to the figures of speech mentioned earlier, writers use **imagery** to create word pictures. This means that they describe a person, an object, or a setting by relying on sensory images. The words or phrases that they use may emphasize any one, or all, of our five senses—sight, sound, taste, touch, and smell. Readers must be able not only to recognize these images but also to understand the author's intent in presenting a particular image. For example, in "The Runner," the poet

Walt Whitman uses imagery to convey the sensation of running. The descriptive words in the poem primarily appeal to our visual sense.

> On a flat road runs the well-train'd runner;
> He is lean and sinewy, with muscular legs;
> He is thinly clothed—he leans forward as he runs,
> With lightly closed fists, and arms partially rais'd.

The excerpt below creates a visual picture of a disaster that occurred in 1934.

> On May 9, 1934, a flock of whirlwinds started up in the northern prairie, in the Dakotas and eastern Montana, where people had fled the homesteads two decades earlier. The sun at midmorning turned orange and looked swollen. The sky seemed as if it were matted by a window screen. The next day, a mass of dust-filled clouds marched east, picking up strength as they found the jet stream winds, moving toward the population centers. By the time this black front hit Illinois and Ohio, the formations had merged into what looked to pilots like a solid block of airborne dirt. Planes had to fly fifteen thousand feet to get above it, and when they finally topped out at their ceiling, the pilots described the storm in apocalyptic terms. Carrying three tons of dust for every American alive, the formation moved over the Midwest. It covered Chicago at night, dumping an estimated six thousand tons, the dust slinking down walls as if every home and every office had sprung a leak. By morning, the dust fell like snow over Boston and Scranton, and then New York slipped under partial darkness. Now the storm was measured at 1,800 miles wide, a great rectangle of dust from the Great Plains to the Atlantic, weighing 350 million tons. In Manhattan, the streetlights came on at midday and cars used their headlights to drive. A sunny day, which had dawned cloudless, fell under a haze like that of a partial eclipse. From the observatory at the top of the Empire State Building, people looked into a soup unlike anything ever seen in midtown. They could not see the city below or Central Park just to the North. An off-white film covered the ledge. People coughed, rushed into hospitals and doctors' offices asking for emergency help to clear their eyes. The harbor turned gray, the dust floating on the surface. The grass of the parks and the tulips rising were coated in fine sand. From Governors Island visibility was so bad a person could not see the boats just beyond the shore. Sunlight was measured at 50 percent—that is, only half the ultraviolet rays of a normal sunny spring day made it to the city.

(Timothy Egan, *The Worst Hard Time*, 2006)

READING

"I hunt Black Widow. I have never been bitten."

TUNING IN TO READING   What do you know about spiders? Did you know that they have been on Earth for millions of years and are important to our survival because of the large numbers of insects they consume? While all spiders are poisonous, most species don't cause serious harm to humans. The black widow, though generally shy and retiring, has a very toxic bite. To learn more about the habits of the black widow, read the following selection.

READING *(continued)*

BIO-SKETCH   Gordon Grice is the author of *The Red Hourglass* and *The Deadly Kingdom*. He has written for *The New Yorker*, *Harper's*, and other magazines. His work has been anthologized in *The Best American Essays* and *The Art of the Essay*. His published work includes memoirs, essays, short stories, and poems.

NOTES ON VOCABULARY

gargoyle   a sculpture or decoration depicting grotesque human shapes, beasts, or evil spirits and placed on many buildings in the Middle Ages, especially churches and cathedrals. Some gargoyles acted as spouts that drained rainwater from the roof of the building. The Gothic gargoyle was usually a grotesque bird or animal sitting on the back of a cornice and projecting forward for several feet in order to throw the water far from the building. This form of sculpture declined with the introduction of lead drainpipes in the 16th century. The term originates from the French *gargouille*, meaning "the throat or waterspout."

arthropods   animals with jointed legs and segmented bodies, such as insects, centipedes, scorpions, crustaceans, and spiders.

The Black Widow

GORDON GRICE

I HUNT BLACK WIDOW. When I find one, I capture it. I have found them in discarded wheels and tires and under railroad ties. I have found them in house foundations and cellars, in automotive shops and toolsheds, in water meters and rock gardens, against fences and in cinderblock walls. I have found them in a hospital and in the den of a rattlesnake, and once at the bottom of a chair I was sitting in.

Sometimes I raise a generation or two in captivity. The egg sacs produce 2 a hundred or more pinpoint cannibals, each leaving a trail of gleaming light in the air, the group of them eventually producing a glimmering tangle in which most of them die, eaten by stronger sibs. Finally I separate the three or four survivors and feed them bigger game.

Once I let several egg sacs hatch out in a container about eighteen inches 3 on a side, a tight wooden box with a sliding glass top. As I tried to move the box one day, the lid slid off and I fell, hands first, into the mass of young widows. Most were still translucent newborns, their bodies a swirl of brown and cream. A few of the females had eaten enough to molt; they had the beginnings of their blackness. Their tangle of broken web clung to my forearms. They felt like trickling water in my arm hairs.

The black widow has the ugliest web of any spider. It is a messy-looking 4 tangle in the corners and bends of things and under logs and debris. Often the web is littered with leaves. Beneath it lie the husks of insect prey, their antennae still as gargoyle horns, cut loose and dropped; on them and the surrounding ground are splashes of the spider's white urine, which looks like bird guano and smells of ammonia even at a distance of several feet. This fetid material draws scavengers—ants, sow bugs, crickets, roaches, and so on—which become tangled in vertical strands of silk reaching from the ground up into the web. The widow comes down and, with a bicycling of the hind pair of legs, throws gummy silk onto this new prey.

When the prey is seriously tangled but still struggling, the widow cau- 5 tiously descends and bites the creature, usually on a leg joint. This is a killing bite; it pumps neurotoxin into the victim. The widow will deliver a series of bites as the creature dies, injecting substances that liquefy the organs. Finally it will settle down to suck the liquefied innards out of the prey, changing position two or three times to get it all.

Before the eating begins, and sometimes before the victim dies from the 6 slow venom, the widow usually moves it higher into the web. It attaches some line to the prey with a leg-bicycling toss, moves up the vertical web strand, and here secures the line. It has thus dragged the prey's body up off the ground. The whole operation is like that of a person moving a load with block and tackle.

You can't watch the widow in this activity very long without realizing 7 that the web is not a mess at all but an efficient machine. It allows complicated use of leverage and also, because of its complexity of connections, lets the spider feel a disturbance anywhere in the web—usually with enough accuracy to tell the difference at a distance between a raindrop or leaf and viable prey. The web is also constructed in a certain relationship to movements of air so that flying insects are drawn into it. An insect that is clumsy and flies in random hops, such as a June beetle, is especially vulnerable to this trap.

The architectural complexities of the widow web do not particularly 8 impress the widows. They move around in these webs almost blind, yet they never misstep or get lost. Furthermore, widows never snare themselves, even though every strand of the web is a potential trap. A widow will spend a few minutes every day coating the clawed tips of its legs with the oil that lets it walk the sticky strands. It secretes the oil from its mouth, coating its legs like a cat cleaning its paws.

Widows reportedly eat mice, toads, tarantulas—anything that wanders 9 into that remarkable web. I have seen them eat scarab beetles heavy as pecans; cockroaches more than an inch long; and hundreds of other arthropods of various sizes. Widows begin life by eating their siblings. An adult female will fight any other female; the winner often eats the loser. The widow gets her name by eating her lover, though this does not always happen.

The widow's venom is a soundly pragmatic reason for fear. The venom 10 contains a neurotoxin that can produce sweats, vomiting, swelling, convulsions, and dozens of other symptoms. The variation in symptoms from one person to the next is remarkable. The constant is pain. A useful question for a doctor trying to diagnose an uncertain case: "Is this the worst pain you've ever felt?" A "yes" suggests a diagnosis of black widow bite. Occasionally people die from widow bites. The very young and the very old are especially vulnerable. Some people seem to die not from the venom but from the infection that may follow; because of its habitat, the widow carries dangerous microbes.

I have never been bitten.   11

(Gordon Grice, "The Black Widow," 1995)

 COMPREHENSION CHECKUP

Multiple Choice

Directions: For each item, write the letter corresponding to the best answer.

___b___ 1. The author's purpose in writing this selection was to
  a. describe how black widows are a threat to human beings.
  b. explain how black widows are well suited to survive in their particular environments.
  c. persuade the reader to exercise extreme caution in handling black widows.
  d. entertain the reader with scary stories about the black widow.

___a___ 2. "They felt like trickling water in my arm hairs." This is an example of a
  a. simile.
  b. metaphor.
  c. personification.
  d. symbol.

___a___ 3. "It secretes the oil from its mouth, coating its legs like a cat cleaning its paws." This sentence makes use of
  a. simile.
  b. symbolism.
  c. literary allusion.
  d. metaphor.

___c___ 4. The author suggests all of the following *except* that
  a. the black widow preys on insects.
  b. the female black widow may eat the male.
  c. the black widow has a venomous bite that is always fatal to humans.
  d. the web of a black widow looks messy.

___d___ 5. By describing baby black widow spiders as *pinpoint cannibals,* the author is implying that they
  a. are exceedingly small.
  b. feed on each other.
  c. are warriors.
  d. both a and b.

___a___ 6. From this excerpt you could conclude that the widow's web is all of the following *except*
  a. capable of ensnaring the black widow in a trap.
  b. ugly.
  c. messy but efficient.
  d. architecturally complex.

_____c_____ 7. The black widow does all of the following to its prey *except*
- a. throw gummy silk on its prey.
- b. kill the prey by biting it.
- c. lower the prey to the ground.
- d. suck the liquified innards from the prey.

Vocabulary in Context

Directions: In the paragraphs indicated in parentheses, find a word that correctly matches the definition given, and write it in the space provided. Answers may vary.

1. cast-off (1) — discarded
2. extremely small (2) — pinpoint
3. allowing light to pass through (3) — translucent
4. shed part or all of a coat or outer covering (3) — molt
5. the outer layers or shells (4) — husks
6. upright (4) — vertical
7. foul-smelling (4) — fetid
8. sufficiently developed; living (7) — viable
9. having no specific pattern or purpose (7) — random
10. practical (10) — pragmatic
11. capable of being wounded or hurt (10) — vulnerable
12. an environment providing the food and shelter required for an animal to survive (10) — habitat

In Your Own Words

1. How many cultural references or literary allusions can you think of in regard to the spider? There are good spiders like Charlotte from *Charlotte's Web*. And there is the comic book hero Spider-Man. But there are also giant, nasty spiders, such as Shelob from *The Lord of the Rings* and Aragog from *Harry Potter*. Taken collectively what do these references tell us about spiders?

2. What are your feelings about spiders? Do you think learning about spiders can help us appreciate them better and reduce the fear factor?

Written Assignment

Arachnophobia is an abnormal and persistent fear of spiders. It is among the most common of all phobias. People with arachnophobia feel uneasy in any area they believe could harbor spiders or that has signs of their webs. Their fear of spiders can produce panic attacks. Do you have any specific phobias? How do you think phobias are created? Could there be any advantages to having a specific phobia? Write a few paragraphs giving your opinion.

Internet Activity

1. Check out the following Web site to read an interview with Gordon Grice. Among other things, he discusses what led to his interest in spiders and how he came to marry his wife. You might want to read a fascinating

excerpt from his book *The Red Hourglass,* describing the effects of a black widow bite. Write a paragraph discussing what you found most interesting about his interview:

www.randomhouse.com/boldtype/0598/grice/interview.html

2. Locate information about the black widow by typing "information about black widow spiders" into Google, or use one of the following Web sites:

www.animals.nationalgeographic.com/animals/bugs/black-widow-spider.html

www.desertusa.com/july97/du_bwindow.html

Try to find information that was not covered in the reading selection. Briefly summarize your findings.

3. Do a search of Anansi tales and summarize your favorite. What is the moral or message of the tale that you selected?

READING

"His hideous crumpled wings lay glued and rucked on his back."

TUNING IN TO READING The section of Annie Dillard's book that you will be reading is drawn from her childhood memories. How much of your early childhood can you remember? Do you think that events that happened in your childhood can affect your choice of a vocation?

BIO-SKETCH Annie Dillard was born in 1945 in Pittsburgh, Pennsylvania, and received her BA and MA degrees from Hollins College in Roanoke, Virginia. She has received numerous awards for her writings, which include essays, poetry, memoirs, literary criticism, and even a western novel. Dillard taught for several years as an adjunct professor at Wesleyan University in Middletown, Connecticut, where she is currently professor emeritus.

The following selection is taken from *Pilgrim at Tinker Creek,* for which she won the 1975 Pulitzer Prize for Nonfiction Writing. This book was the result of her stay on Tinker Creek in Virginia's Roanoke Valley, where she observed the natural world while exploring the subjects of theology, philosophy, and science. Many have compared this work to Thoreau's *Walden.*

NOTES ON VOCABULARY

doily a small ornamental mat of lace, or paper made to look like lace, used as decoration.

Polyphemus moth a large yellowish brown American moth having a prominent eyespot on each hind wing.

pupa an insect in the nonfeeding transformation stage between larva and adult.

wracked wrecked; miserable. Derived from the Old English word *wraec,* meaning "misery."

rucked folded; wrinkled; creased. Derived from the Old Norse word *hrukka,* meaning "a wrinkle."

The Fixed

ANNIE DILLARD

ONCE, WHEN I WAS 10 OR 11 YEARS OLD, my friend Judy brought in a Polyphemus moth cocoon. It was January; there were doily snowflakes taped to the schoolroom panes. The teacher kept the cocoon in her desk all morning and brought it out when we were getting

The Polyphemus Moth

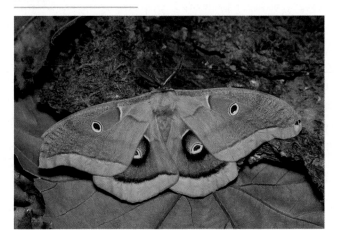

restless before recess. In a book we found what the adult moth would look like; it would be beautiful. With a wingspread of up to six inches, the Polyphemus is one of the few huge American silk moths, much larger than, say, a giant or tiger swallowtail butterfly. The moth's enormous wings are velveted in a rich, warm brown, and edged in bands of blue and pink delicate as a watercolor wash. A startling "eyespot," immense, and deep blue melding to an almost translucent yellow, luxuriates in the center of each hind wing. The effect is one of masculine splendor foreign to the butterflies, a fragility unfurled to strength. The Polyphemus moth in the picture looked like a mighty wraith, a beating essence of the hardwood forest, alien-skinned and brown, with spread, blind eyes. This was the giant moth packed in the faded cocoon. We closed the book and turned to the cocoon. It was an oak leaf sewn into a plump oval bundle; Judy had found it in a pile of frozen leaves.

We passed the cocoon around; it was heavy. As we held it in our hands, 2 the creature within warmed and squirmed. We were delighted, and wrapped it tighter in our fists. The pupa began to jerk violently, in heart-stopping knocks. Who's there? I can still feel those thumps, urgent through a muffling of spun silk and leaf, urgent through the swaddling of many years, against the curve of my palm. We kept passing it around. When it came to me again it was hot as a bun; it jumped half out of my hand. The teacher intervened. She put it, heaving and banging, in the ubiquitous Mason jar.

It was coming. There was no stopping it now. January or not. One end 3 of the cocoon dampened and gradually frayed in a furious battle. The whole cocoon twisted and slapped around in the bottom of the jar. The teacher fades, the classmates fade, I fade: I don't remember anything but that thing's struggle to be a moth or die trying. It emerged at last, a sodden crumple. It was a male; his long antennae were thickly plumed, as wide as his fat abdomen. His body was very thick, over an inch long, and deeply furred. A gray, furlike plush covered his head; a long, tan furlike hair hung from his wide thorax over his brown-furred, segmented abdomen. His multijointed legs, pale and powerful, were shaggy as a bear's. He stood still, but he breathed.

He couldn't spread his wings. There was no room. The chemical that 4 coated his wings like varnish, stiffening them permanently, dried, and hardened his wings as they were. He was a monster in a Mason jar. Those huge wings stuck on his back in a torture of random pleats and folds, wrinkled as a dirty tissue, rigid as leather. They made a single nightmare clump still wracked with useless, frantic convulsions.

The next thing I remember, it was recess. The school was in Shadyside, 5 a busy residential part of Pittsburgh. Everyone was playing dodgeball in the fenced playground or racing around the concrete schoolyard by the swings.

Next to the playground a long delivery drive sloped downhill to the sidewalk and street. Someone—it must have been the teacher—had let the moth out. I was standing in the driveway, alone, stock-still, but shivering. Someone had given the Polyphemus moth his freedom, and he was walking away.

"The greatest joy in nature is the absence of man."

—Bliss Carman

He heaved himself down the asphalt driveway by infinite degrees, unwav- 6 ering. His hideous crumpled wings lay glued and rucked on his back, perfectly still now, like a collapsed tent. The bell rang twice; I had to go. The moth was receding down the driveway, dragging on. I went; I ran inside. The Polyphemus moth is still crawling down the driveway, crawling down the driveway hunched, crawling down the driveway on six furred feet, forever.

(Annie Dillard, *Pilgrim at Tinker Creek*, 1974)

 COMPREHENSION CHECKUP

Identifying Tone

Directions: Answer the questions briefly, with a word, a phrase, or a sentence, as appropriate.

1. Describe the young Annie Dillard's mood (a) at first and (b) by the end of the essay.

   a. delighted

   b. horrified

2. At what point in the essay does Dillard's reaction to what is happening in the classroom change?

   when the moth can't spread its wings

3. How can we tell that the other children were not as concerned as Dillard about the moth's fate?

   Everyone else was playing dodgeball or racing around.

4. To what does Dillard compare the moth in paragraph 4?

   "monster in a Mason jar"

5. What do you suppose caused the moth to start working its way out of the cocoon?

   warmth from all of the children's hands

6. When was the moth supposed to be born?

   spring

7. Why do you think Dillard felt guilty about what happened?

   She was the last child to touch it before the teacher intervened.

8. Does this essay have any symbolic value for humankind's relationship to the environment?

   Sometimes it's best not to interfere because it could backfire.

9. By use of context in paragraph 2, give a definition of the word "intervened."

   come between

10. List the similes and metaphors Dillard uses to describe the body parts of the moth. What part of the moth's body is described most vividly? What overall image is created by Dillard's figures of speech?

"delicate as a watercolor wash," "wrinkled as a dirty tissue," "rigid as leather,"

"like a collapsed tent." Wings are described most vividly. Overall image is great

tragedy.

Vocabulary in Context

Directions: In the paragraphs indicated, find a word that matches the definition given, and write that word in the space provided.

Paragraph 1

1. translucent _____ partially transparent; clear

2. splendor _____ brightness; brilliance; glory

3. fragility _____ delicateness; the state of being easily damaged

4. unfurled _____ open or spread out

5. wraith _____ a ghost; a spectral vision seen before death

6. alien _____ foreign; strange

Paragraph 2

7. urgent _____ calling for haste; insistent

8. ubiquitous _____ present everywhere

Paragraph 3

9. thorax _____ the body segment between the head and abdomen

Paragraph 6

10. infinite _____ endless; very great

11. unwavering _____ showing no doubt or indecision

Written Assignment

In *The Scalpel and the Silver Bear,* Dr. Lori Arviso Alford, who is a Native American, expresses the following viewpoint: "Navajos believe in *hozho* or *hozhoni*—'walking in beauty'—a worldview in which everything in life is connected and influences everything else. A stone thrown into a pond can influence the life of a deer in the forest, a human voice and the spoken word can influence events around the world, and all things possess spirit and power. So Navajos make every effort to live in harmony and balance with everyone and everything else"

(Dr. Lori Arviso Alvord, *The Scalpel and the Silver Bear,* 1999)

Write a few paragraphs discussing how this Navajo philosophy relates to the incident with the moth described by Annie Dillard.

Chapter Summary and Review

In Chapter 6, you learned about the use of figurative language, including similes, metaphors, and personification. You also became familiar with extended metaphors, literary allusions, and imagery.

Short Answer

Directions: Give an example for each of the following.

1. Simile: <u>Answers will vary.</u>

2. Metaphor: _____

3. Personification: _____

Vocabulary in Context

Directions: Choose one of the following words to complete the sentences below. Use each word only once.

> inanimate　language　literally　personification　unlike　visual

4. <u>Personification</u> occurs when human characteristics are assigned to <u>inanimate</u> objects.

5. Both fiction and nonfiction writers use figurative <u>language</u> in their writing.

6. Descriptive poems often appeal to readers' <u>visual</u> sense.

7. Figures of speech should not be taken <u>literally</u>.

8. Similes and metaphors find a similarity in two <u>unlike</u> things.

CHAPTER PREVIEW

In this chapter, you will

- Learn to recognize an author's tone.
- Become familiar with ironic devices.
- Become familiar with satirical devices.

Inferring Tone

The word **tone** refers specifically to the emotional quality of an article. Just as a speaker's voice can convey a wide range of feelings, so can a writer's **voice.** Because tone reveals an author's attitude toward a subject, understanding it is crucial to interpreting what the author has written. Tone is expressed by the words and details an author selects and can often be described by a single adjective.

Following is a list of words that are sometimes used to describe tone. Brief definitions are provided.

Words Used to Describe Tone

1. admiring (thinking of with delight or approval; respecting)
2. alarmed (suddenly afraid or anxious; frightened)
3. amazed (feeling great wonder; astonished)
4. ambivalent (uncertain about a choice; showing mixed feelings)
5. amused (entertained; playful; humorous)
6. angry (feeling strong resentment)
7. appreciative (thankful; grateful)
8. arrogant (feeling superior or self-important)
9. befuddled (confused)
10. bitter (extremely resentful)
11. charming (very pleasing; attractive; delightful)
12. cheerful (full of cheer; glad; joyful)
13. compassionate (full of sympathy)
14. contemptuous (disdainful; scornful; showing little respect)
15. critical (finding fault with; disapproving)
16. cruel (causing great pain; brutal)

continued

Words Used to Describe Tone—*continued*

17. cynical (doubting that people are ever sincere, honest, or good)
18. depressed (sad; gloomy; discouraged)
19. dictatorial (inclined to be domineering; overbearing; tyrannical)
20. disgusted (feeling strong distaste; nausea; loathing)
21. excited (stirred up)
22. formal (not relaxed or familiar; stiff)
23. humorous (funny or amusing; comical)
24. informal (casual; familiar)
25. ironic (meaning the opposite of what is expected or said)
26. irreverent (not showing respect)
27. loving (warmly affectionate)
28. nostalgic (longing for something that happened long ago or is now far away)
29. objective (without bias; neutral)
30. optimistic (looking on the bright side)
31. outraged (great anger aroused by something seen as an injury, insult, or injustice)
32. peevish (cross or irritable)

33. perplexed (filled with doubt; puzzled)
34. pessimistic (expecting the worst)
35. playful (lively; said in fun)
36. remorseful (feeling great guilt or sorrow)
37. sarcastic (mocking, sneering, or cutting speech)
38. scolding (using sharp, angry words to find fault with someone; rebuking)
39. self-pitying (a self-indulgent attitude concerning one's own difficulties)
40. sentimental (having tender, gentle feelings)
41. serious (showing deep thought; not joking or fooling around)
42. solemn (very serious or grave)
43. sorrowful (filled with sadness or grief)
44. surprised (struck by a sudden feeling of wonder by something unexpected)
45. tragic (mournful; dreadful)
46. vindictive (said in revenge; wanting to get even)
47. whiny (complaining or begging in a way that lacks dignity)
48. witty (clever in an amusing way)

Exercise 1: Tone—At the Restaurant

Directions: The following conversations took place at a local restaurant at lunchtime. Choose one of the following words to identify the tone in each numbered passage. Use key words and punctuation as clues, and be able to justify your choices.

amazed	appreciative	cheerful	dictatorial	disgusted
nostalgic	outraged	perplexed	scolding	sorrowful

scolding   1. "Don't you dare talk to me like that! I'm your mother and you owe me a little respect. Sit up straight, stop slouching, and please chew with your mouth closed. Don't you have any manners?"

amazed   2. "Wow! This is really a nice restaurant. From the outside it certainly doesn't look like much."

perplexed   3. Mike looks up at the servers singing Happy Birthday and says, "What is this? What's going on? It's not my birthday."

sorrowful   4. "Mommy, I hate this macaroni," Susie said with a sob. "I don't want to be here anymore," she cried. "Please take me home."

outraged   5. "I'd like to speak to your manager. You've completely ignored me while you've flirted with the young men at the next table. I want you to know I've never been treated like this before. You're going to be sorry your behavior was so rude when you're out of a job."

dictatorial 6. "Gene, clean up the spill at table 6 and then take four glasses of water to table 7."

appreciative 7. "We hope you had a pleasant time and will come back soon. Please tell all your friends about us. We've only been open for two weeks and are grateful for all new customers."

cheerful 8. "Hello, everybody! How are you all today? I'm Susan, your server! The tuna looks terrific today! Can I get you an appetizer to start off?"

disgusted 9. "This food is awful! My lettuce is soggy and it's turning brown. There's a hair in my tomato soup and my sandwich is burnt!"

nostalgic 10. "Oh, honey. Look at that picture on the wall. Remember when we were in Italy? We were so young then and we had such a wonderful time. I wish we could go back to those carefree days."

Exercise 2: Tone—The Lost Dog

Directions: Choose one of the following words to identify the tone in each numbered passage. Use key words and punctuation as clues, and be able to justify your choices.

| arrogant | befuddled | critical | depressed | loving |
| optimistic | pessimistic | remorseful | sentimental | surprised |

remorseful 1. "Oh, my poor little dog Cookie is gone!" shrieked Mrs. Carter. "It's all my fault. I forgot to close the gate this morning! I feel so guilty about this. How could I have been so stupid? I can never forgive myself. What kind of dog mommy am I?"

sentimental 2. "Little sweet Cookie means so much to me. I remember when we got her as a puppy at the pet store. She came right up and gave each one of us a lick. She was the tiniest little thing and so loving. Cookie personally picked us out to be her owners."

depressed 3. "This is so sad. Without her here, I feel like there's a big dark cloud sitting on my head. I can't go in to work today. I'm just going to sit here and wait till I hear something."

optimistic 4. "Maybe somebody will see my posters about the reward for her return. She couldn't have wandered very far. After all, she's only been gone for a short while. Anyway, I'll bet she can find her own way back home. We take her on long walks every evening. I know she's coming back to me. I'm sure she'll be back really soon."

surprised 5. "Oh my goodness, Cookie! Is that really you? What are you doing here?"

befuddled 6. "Have you been here inside the house all this time? How could that happen? I thought you were gone. Did you go away and then come back? What's going on here? Is somebody playing a trick on me?"

loving 7. "Come here, my sweet little doggy. Your mommy is so glad to see you. How's my little precious? Here, sweet Cookie girl. Mommy's got a goodie for you."

critical 8. "Helen, you really need to be a lot more careful," said Mr. Carter. "You need to pay attention to what you're doing. You could've lost Cookie forever just because you didn't take enough time to check the gates."

arrogant 9. "Young man, here's a dollar for you. I'm sure you have nothing better to do today. Go around the neighborhood and remove all of the reward posters. I expect you back here promptly in 10 minutes. Get a move on."

pessimistic 10. "That young boy will probably mess it up. If you want something done right, you have to do it yourself. I'll probably spend the rest of the day receiving phone calls asking about the reward. And people are going to be bringing small dogs to my door and asking me if it's Cookie. What a lousy day this is going to turn out to be."

Exercise 3: Tone—At the Movie Theater

Directions: Choose one of the following words to identify the tone in each numbered passage. Use key words and punctuation as clues, and be able to justify your choices.

admiring	alarmed	angry	appreciative	compassionate
dictatorial	disgusted	ironic	self-pitying	whining

compassionate 1. "I know this has been an especially difficult time for you. This movie will be good for you. You won't have to concentrate on a complex plot. It's just pure light-hearted entertainment. Relax and enjoy yourself and let me take care of everything."

ironic 2. "Is this seat taken? Whoops, I didn't mean to step on your foot. I'm as graceful as a dancing elephant!"

admiring 3. "What a wonderful actress. No matter what role she plays, she always does a beautiful job. It's such a pleasure to attend one of her movies. I don't think she's ever been in a bad one. And she's so lovely, too. Her smile lights up the screen."

alarmed 4. "Oh my goodness. I don't think I remembered to lock the door. I had the key right there in my hand, but I don't think I used it. What am I going to do?"

self-pitying 5. "What is the matter with me? I can't seem to do even the simplest thing right. Things certainly haven't been easy for me lately. Car problems, school problems, health problems, and now this."

dictatorial 6. "Sit there and hold our seats. Don't move. I'll go get the popcorn and drinks."

whining 7. "What's this? I like plain popcorn not buttered. And I don't like Junior Mints at all. I like to eat Raisinettes at the movies. And this drink. You know I don't like diet drinks."

<u>disgusted</u>   8. "Ooh yuck. Somebody must have spilled their drink. There's something sticky all over the floor. And now it's on my shoes. This place is a pit. Doesn't anybody clean up in here. Look, even the seats are a mess."

<u>angry</u>   9. "Are you the manager? Listen here, young man, I want my money back. I demand a refund. This whole evening has been a disaster."

<u>appreciative</u>   10. "Thank you so much for going with me to the movie. This is just what I needed. You are such a good friend to think of me. I don't know what I'd do without you."

Exercise 4: Tone—Do Any of These Sound Familiar?

Directions: For each question, write the letter for the word that best describes the tone of the passage quoted.

<u>c</u>   1. "Hey, it's not my problem. It's your problem. I'm going to do what I'm going to do. You don't like it, that's just tough."
   a. excited
   b. self-pitying
   c. contemptuous

<u>b</u>   2. "I can't decide if I should stay in school or drop out and get a job."
   a. peevish
   b. ambivalent
   c. playful

<u>b</u>   3. "Oh, thank you for the necklace. It's lovely. It's just what I've always wanted."
   a. informal
   b. appreciative
   c. objective

<u>a</u>   4. "Don't feel bad about forgetting my birthday, sweetie. I know you've been busy. It's really not that important."
   a. forgiving
   b. amused
   c. bitter

<u>c</u>   5. "You're late to pick me up again. This is the fifth time this week! Don't give me your excuses. I don't want to hear it."
   a. tragic
   b. surprised
   c. outraged

<u>b</u>   6. "Well, of course you're right and I'm wrong. I keep forgetting that someone as brilliant as you say you are is never wrong."
   a. informal
   b. sarcastic
   c. humorous

<u>a</u>   7. "Of all the nerve. Can you believe some people? Hey, lady! I'm next in line. Wait your turn."
   a. angry
   b. befuddled
   c. sorrowful

_____c_____ 8. "Mike, you're making far too many errors in your papers. I suggest you proofread them more carefully."
   a. surprised
   b. witty
   c. critical

_____a_____ 9. "He's had all kinds of problems and yet he just keeps on trying. I have nothing but respect for the guy."
   a. admiring
   b. solemn
   c. cheerful

_____b_____ 10. "Tina was so sweet. She used to make little flowers and smiley faces for me when she was three. She was such a loving child."
   a. charming
   b. nostalgic
   c. amused

_____c_____ 11. "Mommy, why does Ann always get to sit next to the window? I want to sit next to the window. You never let me sit there. It's not fair! And I'm hungry, too."
   a. optimistic
   b. formal
   c. whining

_____c_____ 12. "I hate to loan you my car. Something bad always happens to it. I know it's not going to be any different this time either. Why should it be?"
   a. ironic
   b. nostalgic
   c. cynical

READING

"During that first summer, I learned to respect the conveyor belt ladies."

TUNING IN TO READING   The excerpt below is taken from Rose Castillo Guilbault's memoir, *Farmworker's Daughter—Growing Up Mexican in America*. In it, Guilbault describes summer vacations during her teenage years working with migrant workers. What kind of jobs have you had? Did any of them profoundly affect you?

BIO-SKETCH   When Rose Castillo Guilbault was 5, she and her mother left Mexico for California's Salinas Valley. Rose, with a great deal of hard work and help from mentors, gradually perfected her English and began writing for her school newspaper. After graduating from college, she became a writer for the *San Francisco Chronicle*. She entered broadcasting and has worked with both CBS and ABC, winning an Emmy for outstanding children's programming. She was appointed to serve on the California Community College Board of Governors.

NOTES ON VOCABULARY

cross to bear   a heavy burden to carry in life or a serious problem to put up with. The phrase alludes to the cross Jesus carried to his crucifixion.

The Conveyor Belt Ladies

ROSE CASTILLO GUILBAULT

THE CONVEYOR BELT LADIES WERE MIGRANT WOMEN, mostly from Texas. I worked with them during the summers of my teenage years. I call them conveyor belt ladies because I got to know them while sorting tomatoes on a conveyor belt.

The women and their families arrived in May for the carrot season, spent the summer in the tomato sheds, and stayed through October for the bean harvest. After that, they emptied from town, some returning to their homes in Texas while others continued on the migrant trail, picking cotton in the San Joaquin Valley or grapefruits and oranges in the Imperial Valley.

Most of these women had started in the fields. The vegetable packing sheds were a step up, easier than the backbreaking jobs in the fields. The work in the sheds was often more tedious than strenuous, paid better, and provided fairly steady hours and clean bathrooms. Best of all, you didn't get rained on.

I had started sorting tomatoes with my mother in high school. I would have preferred working in a dress shop or babysitting like my friends, but I had a dream that would cost a lot of money—college—and the fact was that sorting tomatoes was the highest-paying work in town. The job consisted of picking out the flawed tomatoes on the conveyor belt before they rolled into the shipping boxes at the end of the line. These boxes were immediately loaded onto delivery trucks, so it was important not to let bad tomatoes through.

The work could be slow or intense, depending on the quality of the tomatoes and how many there were. Work increased when the company deliveries got backlogged or after rain delayed picking. During those times, it was not unusual to work from 7:00 A.M. until midnight. I never heard anyone complain about overtime, though. Overtime meant desperately needed extra money.

It would have been difficult not to like the women. They were an entertaining group, easing the long, monotonous hours with bawdy humor and spicy gossip. They poked fun at all the male workers and did hysterical impersonations of the supervisor. Although he didn't speak Spanish (other than "¡*Mujeres, trabajo, trabajo!* Women, work, work!"), he sensed he was being laughed at. He would stamp his foot and forbid us from talking until break time. But it would have been much easier to tie the women's tongues in knots than to keep them quiet. Eventually the ladies had their way and their fun, and the men learned to ignore them.

Pretty Rosa described her romances and her pending wedding to a handsome fieldworker. Berta told me that Rosa's marriage would cause her nothing but headaches because the man was younger and too handsome. Maria, large and placid, described the births of each of her nine children, warning me about the horrors of labor and delivery.

At other moments they could turn melancholic, telling of babies who 8 died because their mothers couldn't afford medical care, the alcoholic husbands who were their "cross to bear," the racism they experienced in Texas, where they were referred to as "dirty Mexicans" or "Mexican dogs" and not allowed in certain restaurants.

I was appalled and deeply moved by these confidences, and the injustices 9 they endured enraged me. I could do little but sympathize. My mother, no stranger to suffering, said I was too impressionable when I emotionally relayed to her the women's stories.

"If they were in Mexico, life would be even harder. At least there are 10 opportunities here; you can work," she'd say.

During that first summer, I learned to respect the conveyor belt ladies. 11

The last summer I worked in the packing shed turned out to be the last I 12 lived at home. I had just finished junior college and was transferring to a university. At this point I was "overeducated" for seasonal work, but if you counted the overtime, it was still the best-paying job. So I went back one last time.

The ladies treated me with warmth and respect. I was a college student 13 and they thought I deserved special treatment.

Aguedita, the crew chief, moved me to softer and better-paying jobs 14 within the plant. I moved from the conveyor belt to shoving boxes down a chute and finally to weighing boxes of tomatoes on a scale—the highest-paying position for a woman.

When the union representative showed up to collect dues, the women 15 hid me in the bathroom. They had determined it was unfair for me to have to pay dues since I worked only during the summer. We played a cat-and-mouse game with him all summer. "You ladies aren't hiding students, are you?" he'd ask suspiciously.

"Why does *la unión* charge our poor students anyway?" The ladies would 16 distract him with questions and complaints until he tired of answering them and had to leave for his next location.

Maria, with the nine children, tried to feed me all summer, bringing extra 17 tortillas, which were delicious. I accepted them with some guilt, wondering if I was taking food away from her children. Others brought rental contracts or other documents for me to explain and translate.

The last day of work was splendidly beautiful, golden and warm. The 18 conveyor belt's loud humming was turned off, silenced for the season. The women sighed as they removed their aprons. Some of them walked off, calling, "*¡Hasta la próxima!* Until next time."

But most of the conveyor belt ladies came over to me, shook my hand, 19 and gave me a blessing or a big hug.

"Don't come back. Make us proud, *hija*."   20

(Rose Castillo Guilbault, *Farmworker's Daughter*, 2005)

COMPREHENSION CHECKUP

Multiple Choice

Directions: For each item, write the letter corresponding to the best answer.

_____c_____ 1. Guilbault met the conveyor belt ladies while
   a. canning tomatoes.
   b. picking carrots.
   c. sorting tomatoes.
   d. harvesting lettuce.

_____c_____ 2. Working in the packing sheds provided all the following *except*
   a. clean restroom facilities.
   b. more money than a field job.
   c. health insurance benefits.
   d. shelter from the elements.

_____d_____ 3. Guilbault liked the conveyor belt ladies for all the following reasons *except* which?
   a. They were entertaining.
   b. They treated her with warmth and respect.
   c. They gave her preferential treatment.
   d. They listened to her gripes and complaints and offered advice.

_____d_____ 4. To entertain themselves at work, the conveyor belt ladies did all the following *except*
   a. impersonate the supervisor.
   b. gossip about their romances.
   c. make fun of their male coworkers.
   d. play tricks on one another.

_____a_____ 5. The conveyor belt ladies described all the following hardships *except*
   a. lack of adequate food and shelter.
   b. experiences with racial discrimination.
   c. problems with husbands who drank too much.
   d. babies dying because of lack of medical care.

_____b_____ 6. Guilbault experienced all the following with the conveyor belt ladies *except* for which?
   a. They hid her from the union representative.
   b. They needed her help in filing complaints over discrimination.
   c. They brought her food.
   d. They asked her help in deciphering documents.

_____b_____ 7. The main idea of the selection is that
   a. migrant workers lead extremely difficult lives.
   b. while working with the conveyor belt ladies, Guilbault came to respect and admire them.
   c. the conveyor belt ladies were grateful for the jobs they held.
   d. supervisors can be very hard to get along with.

_____a_____ 8. The author's purpose in writing the selection is to
   a. describe the experiences she had working in vegetable packing sheds.
   b. persuade the reader to lobby for reforms in the agricultural industry.

___c___   c. inform the reader of the hardships she endured as a child.

d. compare and contrast the lives of field-workers in Mexico with those in the United States.

___d___   9. We can infer all the following *except* for which?

a. The workers Guilbault describes had less formal education than she did.

b. The conveyor belt ladies largely accepted their lot in life.

c. Guilbault's mother had less sympathy for the conveyor belt ladies than did Guilbault.

d. Guilbault's mother wished to return to Mexico.

___d___   10. We can infer all the following *except* for which?

a. The author would have preferred a more traditional teenage job.

b. The conveyor belt women were easily intimidated by authority.

c. The author disliked working with her mother in the packing sheds.

d. Both b and c.

___d___   11. The tone of paragraph 10 is

a. matter-of-fact.

b. unsympathetic.

c. sarcastic.

d. both a and b.

___a___   12. The tone of the last sentence of the selection is

a. encouraging.

b. disgusted.

c. befuddled.

d. ambivalent.

True or False

Directions: Indicate whether each statement is true or false by writing **T** or **F** in the space provided.

___F___   13. The conveyor belt ladies were primarily local women trying to earn extra money.

___F___   14. Guilbault worked year-round at a vegetable packing shed.

___T___   15. A *backbreaking* job is one that demands great effort.

___T___   16. Working in the packing sheds was more boring than exhausting.

___F___   17. Guilbault could make more money by babysitting than by working in the packing sheds.

___T___   18. An antonym of *flawed* is "perfect."

___F___   19. The conveyor belt ladies disliked having to work overtime.

___T___   20. A synonym for *monotonous* is "boring."

___T___   21. A cat-and-mouse game is one in which someone is trying to elude discovery by someone else

Vocabulary Matching

Directions: Match each word in column A with its definition in column B.

Column A	Column B
_f_ 1. appalled	a. postponed
_g_ 2. bawdy	b. boring
_a_ 3. delayed	c. communicated
_i_ 4. impressionable	d. requiring great effort or energy
_h_ 5. melancholic	e. calm; unruffled
_j_ 6. pending	f. dismayed
_e_ 7. placid	g. coarse; vulgar
_c_ 8. relayed	h. characterized by sadness
_d_ 9. strenuous	i. capable of being easily influenced
_b_ 10. tedious	j. about to happen; imminent

In Your Own Words

1. The conveyor belt ladies found a way to make their jobs seem less oppressive. What are some acceptable ways that office and retail workers can make their jobs less oppressive (without getting fired)?

2. At the end of the selection, the conveyor belt ladies told the author, "Don't come back. Make us proud, *hija* [daughter]." What do you think they meant? Why were the ladies so protective of the author?

3. The supervisor in Guilbault's story didn't speak Spanish and sensed that the ladies were making fun of him. Have you ever had a similar experience at work (either as a supervisor or as a worker)? Sometimes customers, employees, and employers complain that when some employees speak another language, they feel excluded and annoyed because they don't know what is being said and worry it might be something negative or personal about them. Do you think this is a problem? Do you think that requiring that only English be spoken in the workplace would be a good solution?

Written Assignment

1. A migrant worker moves from one geographic area to another in search of employment. Migrant workers often harvest crops, and as a result often move around the country following the seasons. What kinds of problems do you think migrant workers face? What kinds of problems do you think their children experience? Write a couple of paragraphs discussing this issue.

2. In a recent series of speeches, Guilbault shared lessons she learned. Her first lesson is to "find your passion." Guilbault says there is always something you can do with your own talent or gift. "It's important to find out what that gift or passion is and to find jobs to sustain it." The next lesson is to "face your fears and believe in yourself." The third lesson is to pay back. Guilbault says, "It's important to remember where you came from and pay back to your community." The fourth lesson is to be true to yourself. "You need to create your own definition of success. Determine what gives you joy, satisfaction, and balance in your life." The final lesson is to celebrate your successes, no matter how small they may be. Guilbault says that success is individualistic. It's what you want it to be. "Your dreams will direct the journey."

    In a few paragraphs, respond to Guilbault's lessons. Do you agree or disagree with them? Try to come up with a few of your own lessons.

Internet Activity

Cesar Chavez founded an organization that advocated for the rights of farmworkers. Use any search engine to find out more about Chavez's life and his organization. Write a few paragraphs summarizing your findings.

Identifying Irony

When there is a contrast between what people say and what they actually mean, they are using **verbal irony.** Since the meaning is usually expressed indirectly, you must use inference to understand this *reversed* meaning, or you will misinterpret the author.

Another form of irony is **situational.** In this form, there is a contrast between what is expected to occur and what actually does happen. Many stories or poems that end with an unexpected twist are based on this type of irony.

Directions: Examine the cartoon below and then answer the following questions.

RUBES. © 1995 by Leigh Rubin. By permission of Leigh Rubin and Creators Syndicate, Inc.

1. Locate the word in the cartoon that best expresses irony. <u>save</u>

2. What can you infer has happened in the cartoon?
   <u>All the trees have been cut down.</u>

3. What key point is being made in the cartoon? What situation is being criticized?
   <u>The organization's actions run counter to its stated aims.</u>

4. Describe the tone or attitude you think is really being expressed in the cartoon.
   <u>irony</u>

The "Forest" cartoon concerns the environment. The sign proclaims the new headquarters of a forest conservation group. This cartoon is ironic because, instead of preserving timberland, the foundation has cleared ground to erect another building. The foundation has destroyed what it was supposed to be protecting. This action has defeated the group's fundamental goal. This is the exact *opposite* of what we would reasonably expect. In the cartoon, the meaning is expressed indirectly, so you must use inference to decipher the reversed meaning.

Look at the sign in the photo below. What inferences can be drawn from the words and the picture? In what way is the sign ironic?

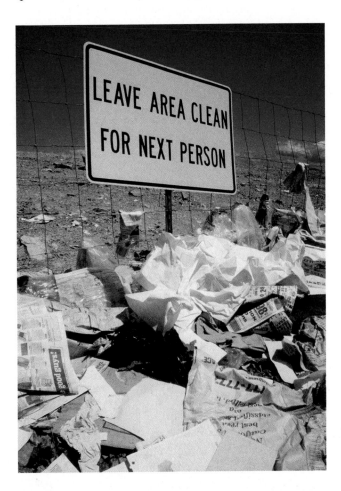

Exercise 5: Detecting Irony

Directions: Read the fable and then answer the questions that follow.

Once, a long time ago, Death came riding into the city of Baghdad looking for Ali Haj, a proud and wealthy merchant. Death was in no hurry to meet Ali Haj, for he had many other old friends whom he wished to honor by a visit. On hearing that Death was in the town and had already called on some of his friends, Ali Haj, who had not gained his riches by stupidity, spoke to his old, blind servant:

"There is a great prince come to town, whom I am eager to see, for I wish to give him a rare jewel to win his friendship. Unfortunately, I cannot hope he would visit the poor home of a humble merchant like myself. Therefore I shall go to seek him. But if he should by chance come here while I am away, welcome him with the choicest of food and drink, and beg him only to wait for me a little while. But see you keep him here."

Then Ali Haj gathered his favorite treasures, his wives and children, and fled on his swiftest horses to Damascus.

When Death knocked at his door the next day, the blind servant appeared. "I seek your master, Ali Haj," Death said.

"He has gone out to seek a great prince to give him a precious jewel," answered the servant. "But if you, my lord, are that prince, then my master begs you to consider this house your own and to stay only a little while till he returns."

"There are many who call me Prince," said Death, "but few so joyful to greet me as Ali Haj. But that is what I expected of him." Then he stared at the ancient man, who was indeed rich in white hairs and wrinkles. "Since you are sure to see him soon, kindly remind him that he need not have gone out today to seek me, for I wished only to ask him to meet me tomorrow in Damascus."

Multiple Choice

Directions: For each item, write the letter corresponding to the best answer.

___c___ 1. Ali Haj succeeds in fooling all of the following *except*
   a. himself.
   b. the old, blind servant.
   c. Death.
   d. his wives and children.

___d___ 2. All of the following are true statements according to the fable *except* for which?
   a. Death had many old friends whom he wished to visit.
   b. The old servant is going to die soon.
   c. Ali Haj is trying to avoid Death.
   d. Ali Haj is going to be able to outsmart Death.

___c___ 3. The main organizational pattern used in this fable is
   a. comparison-contrast.
   b. example.
   c. chronological order.
   d. definition.

___c___ 4. The author's purpose in writing this fable is to
   a. inform.
   b. persuade.
   c. entertain.
   d. convince.

___d___ 5. All of the following are descriptive of Ali Haj *except*
   a. he is clever.
   b. he is rich.
   c. he is proud.
   d. he is brave.

___c___ 6. In context the word *rich* (paragraph 6) means
   a. owning much money and property.
   b. deep and brilliant.
   c. having a lot.
   d. full and mellow.

Written Assignment

Directions: Write a brief response to each question.

1. What is the fable saying about Death?

2. What is ironic about Ali Haj's departure? Why does he ask the servant to keep Death well entertained in Baghdad? What does Death mean when he says he expected this type of welcome from Ali Haj?

3. Is Ali Haj going to succeed in avoiding Death? Explain your answer.

4. What does Death mean when he tells the old servant that he is sure to see his master, Ali Haj, soon?

READING

"God: of the money that I asked for, only seventy pesos reached me. Send me the rest, since I need it very much."

TUNING IN TO READING   Irony is a form of commentary by an author. In this story, pay close attention to the situation described by the author.

BIO-SKETCH   Gregorio Lopez y Fuentes (1897–1966) was a highly acclaimed author who received Mexico's National Prize for Literature in 1935. As the son of a small farmer, he understood the difficulties farmers faced in trying to make a living off the land. This story was translated from Spanish by Donald A. Yates.

NOTES ON VOCABULARY

mortify   the word *mortify* comes from the Latin words *mortis,* meaning "death," and *facere* meaning "to make." Today, *mortify* means "to humiliate or shame."

locusts   migratory grasshoppers that strip vegetation from large areas.

prodigy   something that excites wonder or amazement.

A Letter to God

GREGORIO LOPEZ Y FUENTES

THE HOUSE—THE ONLY ONE IN THE ENTIRE VALLEY— sat on the crest of a low hill. From this height one could see the river and, next to the corral, the field of ripe corn dotted with the kidney-bean flowers that always promised a good harvest.

The only thing the earth needed was a rainfall, or at least a shower. 2 Throughout the morning Lencho—who knew his fields intimately—had done nothing else but scan the sky toward the northeast.

"Now we're really going to get some water, woman."   3

The woman, who was preparing supper, replied: 4

"Yes, God willing."   5

The oldest boys were working in the field, while the smaller ones were 6 playing near the house, until the woman called to them all:

"Come for dinner . . ."   7

It was during the meal that, just as Lencho had predicted, big drops of 8 rain began to fall. In the northeast, huge mountains of clouds could be seen approaching. The air was fresh and sweet.

The man went out to look for something in the corral for no other 9 reason than to allow himself the pleasure of feeling the rain on his body, and when he returned he exclaimed:

"Those aren't raindrops falling from the sky, they're new coins. The big 10 drops are ten-centavo pieces and the little ones are fives. . . ."

With a satisfied expression he regarded the field of ripe corn with its 11 kidney-bean flowers, draped in a curtain of rain. But suddenly a strong wind began to blow and together with the rain very large hailstones began to fall. These truly did resemble new silver coins. The boys, exposing themselves to the rain, ran out to collect the frozen pearls.

"It's really getting bad now," exclaimed the man, mortified. "I hope it 12 passes quickly."

It did not pass quickly. For an hour the hail rained on the house, the 13 garden, the hillside, the cornfield, on the whole valley. The field was white, as if covered with salt. Not a leaf remained on the trees. The corn was totally destroyed. The flowers were gone from the kidney-bean plants. Lencho's soul was filled with sadness. When the storm had passed, he stood in the middle of the field and said to his sons:

"A plague of locusts would have left more than this. . . . The hail has 14 left nothing: this year we will have no corn or beans. . . ."

That night was a sorrowful one: 15

"All our work, for nothing!"   16

"There's no one who can help us!"   17

"We'll all go hungry this year. . . ."   18

But in the hearts of all who lived in that solitary house in the middle of 19 the valley, there was a single hope: help from God.

"Don't be so upset, even though this seems like a total loss. Remember, 20 no one dies of hunger!"

"That's what they say: no one dies of hunger. . . ."   21

All through the night, Lencho thought only of his one hope: the help 22 of God, whose eyes, as he had been instructed, see everything, even what is deep in one's conscience.

Lencho was an ox of a man, working like an animal in the fields, but 23 still he knew how to write. The following Sunday, at daybreak, after having convinced himself that there is a protecting spirit, he began to write a letter which he himself would carry to town and place in the mail.

It was nothing less than a letter to God.   24

"God," he wrote, "if you don't help me, my family and I will go hun- 25 gry this year. I need a hundred pesos in order to resow the field and to live until the crop comes, because the hailstorm . . ."

He wrote "To God" on the envelope, put the letter inside and, still 26 troubled, went to town. At the post office he placed a stamp on the letter and dropped it into the mailbox.

One of the employees, who was a postman and also helped at the post 27 office, went to his boss laughing heartily and showed him the letter to God. Never in his career as a postman had he known that address. The postmaster—a fat amiable fellow—also broke out laughing, but almost immediately he turned serious and, tapping the letter on his desk, commented:

"What faith! I wish I had the faith of the man who wrote this letter. To 28 believe the way he believes. To hope with the confidence that he knows how to hope with. Starting up a correspondence with God!"

So in order not to disillusion that prodigy of faith, revealed by a letter 29 that could not be delivered, the postmaster came up with an idea: answer the letter. But when he opened it, it was evident that to answer it he needed something more than good will, ink and paper. But he stuck to his resolution: he asked for money from his employee, he himself gave part of his salary, and several friends of his were obliged to give something "for an act of charity."

It was impossible for him to gather together the hundred pesos, so he 30 was able to send the farmer only a little more than half. He put the bills in an envelope addressed to Lencho and with them a letter containing only a single word as a signature: GOD.

The following Sunday Lencho came a bit earlier than usual to ask if there 31 was a letter for him. It was the postman himself who handed the letter to him, while the postmaster, experiencing the contentment of a man who has performed a good deed, looked on from the doorway of his office.

Lencho showed not the slightest surprise on seeing the bills—such was 32 his confidence—but he became angry when he counted the money. . . . God could not have made a mistake, nor could he have denied Lencho what he had requested!

Immediately, Lencho went up to the window to ask for paper and ink. 33 On the public writing table, he started in to write, with much wrinkling of his brow, caused by the effort he had to make to express his ideas. When he finished, he went to the window to buy a stamp which he licked and then affixed to the envelope with a blow of his fist.

The moment that the letter fell into the mailbox the postmaster went to 34 open it. It said:

"God: of the money that I asked for, only seventy pesos reached me. 35 Send me the rest, since I need it very much. But don't send it to me through the mail, because the post-office employees are a bunch of crooks. Lencho."

(Gregorio López y Fuentes, "A Letter to God")

"Better to accept whatever happens."

—Horace

 COMPREHENSION CHECKUP

Recognizing Irony

Directions: Answer the questions briefly, in a few words, phrases, or sentences, as appropriate.

1. Record your first impressions about Lencho, his wife, the postman, and the postmaster. Give a brief description of each.

   Lencho—strong, hard-working man; wife—doesn't count on things until they happen;

   postman—sarcastic, incredulous; postmaster—amiable, generous

2. Study the following list of key details and explain what could reasonably be inferred from each.

   a. Lencho knows his fields "intimately."

   He knows every inch of his land.

   b. Lencho's only hope is "the help of God."

   God is his last resort.

   c. The postman goes to his boss "laughing heartily."

   He treats the letter as a joke.

   d. Never had the postman "known that address."

   He has never seen a letter addressed like that.

   e. The postmaster answers the letter "in order not to disillusion that prodigy of faith."

   He answers so that Lencho doesn't lose his faith in God.

   f. The postmaster experiences "the contentment of a man who has performed a good deed."

   The postmaster feels good and righteous for his good deed.

   g. Lencho affixes the stamp "with a blow of his fist."

   He is mad because he thinks they have stolen from him.

3. Why does Lencho react the way he does? Would you react as Lencho does? Explain why or why not.

   He reacts this way because he knows God wouldn't make a mistake like that.

4. Identify and explain a simile and a metaphor in the story.

   "Lencho was an ox of a man, working like an animal in the fields"—he is a strong

   and hard worker. ". . . they're new coins"—the rain is valuable.

5. In what way is the story ironic? Explain your answer.

   Lencho thought God sent him the money, but the postmaster did. The postmaster

   thought Lencho would be grateful, but he wasn't.

Written Assignment

Have you ever tried to help someone, and it turned out that the person resented your efforts? If so, how did you feel about that person? Describe your experience in a short paragraph.

Recognizing Satire

Satire is a kind of writing that uses ridicule to create awareness of flaws and to bring about change. Almost anything can be satirized, including people, institutions, and ideas. Because it relies on exaggeration and distortion, satire often has a humorous effect.

Caricature

Caricature is a form of satire in which certain characteristics, such as physical features, are exaggerated. In the 15th century, when Leonardo da Vinci sketched the faces of clerics and nobles, the "charged portrait" was an important means of political and social criticism. Biting portraits provided a way to tear down a public figure. But the social impact of the political cartoon is not as potent as it used to be. As the 20th century wore on, politicians and other targets of political cartoons began to embrace and benefit from their own caricatures. Most U.S. presidents have become ardent collectors of political cartoons about themselves. President Lyndon Johnson reportedly liked seeing himself in cartoons so much that he didn't care whether they were flattering or not.[1] Look at the following caricature of President George Washington. Which of the features are distorted?

© Don Tywoniw, www.dontywoniw.com

Hyperbole (Overstatement)

Hyperbole is language that exaggerates. It comes from the Greek word *hyperbole*, meaning "excess or extravagance." We are using hyperbole when we say, "He is as strong as a bull." In Mark Twain's classic novel *The Adventures of Huckleberry Finn*, the author uses hyperbole when he gives readers the following warning at the start of the book:

> *NOTICE: Persons attempting to find a motive in this narrative will be prosecuted; persons attempting to find a moral in it will be banished; persons attempting to find a plot in it will be shot.—By Order Of The Author*

Another word for hyperbole is **overstatement.** In overstatement the subject is magnified beyond reality by using adjectives (*big, longer, best*) and sweeping generalizations (*every, always, never*). Look at this example:

> He stood there, tall and proud—taller than Mount Everest and prouder than New England on the day the Patriots won their first Super Bowl.

---

[1]Information from Week in Review, *New York Times*, June 17, 2001, section 4, p. 16.

Much of our humor is comic overstatement. Look at the following example:

> Virginia's young son had been living in the back of his pickup truck for so long she decided to give it an address.

Understatement

The satirist may also use **understatement,** which is saying less about something than is expected. As an example of understatement, consider Mark Twain's comment in the following story. In 1897, Samuel Clemens (Mark Twain) was staying in London at the same time as his cousin, Dr. James Ross Clemens. Dr. Clemens became ill and died, but the press mistakenly reported that it was Mark Twain who had died. To untangle the mix-up, Twain sent a cable from London to the Associated Press that read, "The reports of my death are greatly exaggerated."

Jonathan Swift, well-known satirist of the 18th century and author of *Gulliver's Travels* and *A Modest Proposal*, gave this example:

> Last week I saw a woman flayed alive, and you will hardly believe how it altered her appearance for the worse.

Reprinted from *Bart Simpson's Guide to Life* © 1993 by Matt Groening Productions, Inc. All Rights Reserved. HarperCollins Publishers, Inc. The Simpsons © and ™ Twentieth Century Fox Film Corporation. All Rights Reserved.

The long-running TV show *The Simpsons* received the prestigious George Foster Peabody Award for excellence in television. *The Simpsons* was cited for satire and social commentary. If you have not seen the show, try watching an episode or two. What kinds of things does Matt Groening, creator of *The Simpsons,* satirize? For example, using the "Grandpa" character, what is Groening saying about how elderly people are treated in this country?

The *Calvin and Hobbes* cartoon below uses satire to demonstrate how powerful the popular media are in influencing behavior. Even Calvin, who is portrayed as being very sophisticated about the media, is not immune. Is the cartoonist making a valid point about the media? Do you think young children are easily influenced by messages they receive from television? Why or why not?

When reading satire, pay close attention to the goals of the satirist, the devices used to accomplish his or her goals, and the tone. While a satire can have any tone, the most common are ironic and humorous.

Calvin and Hobbes

CALVIN AND HOBBES © 1995 Watterson. Dist. By Universal Uclick. Reprinted with permission. All rights reserved.

Exercise 6: Detecting Satire

In addition to *The Simpsons*, Matt Groening created *Life in Hell*, a comic book describing life in Los Angeles. This book led to a syndicated comic strip by the same name that appears in about 250 newspapers. He has authored at least seven other *Life in Hell* books.

Directions: Answer the following questions briefly.

1. What is Matt Groening saying about the current school situation? What attitude about learning does the cartoon express?

2. Do you see yourself in this cartoon? Has your school experience been similar? Explain.

3. What attitude about adults does the cartoon express?

READING

"'There are a lot of people in this country who only use a handgun once or twice a year. . . . So we'll rent them a gun for a day or two.'"

TUNING IN TO READING   This article, written in a satirical style, argues for stronger gun-control legislation.

BIO-SKETCH   Art Buchwald was one of the foremost humorists in the United States. His job, as he saw it, was to expose us to our failings as human beings and as members of society. Buchwald wrote numerous books and was a regular contributor to a syndicated newspaper column. He was also a recipient of the Pulitzer Prize.

NOTES ON VOCABULARY

chicken out   lose one's nerve; back out of something because of fear. *Chicken* is a slang term for "cowardly."

Russian roulette   loading a bullet into one chamber of a revolver, spinning the cylinder, and then pulling the trigger while pointing the gun at one's own head.

gutted   destroyed; removed the vital or essential parts from something.

dream come true   wild fancy or hope that is realized.

What is the play on words in Hurts Rent-A-Gun?
It is being compared to Hertz Rent-A-Car.
Hurts—Hertz

Directions: Answer the questions in the margins as you are reading the article.

Hurts Rent-A-Gun

By ART BUCHWALD

Is Buchwald optimistic or pessimistic about the possibility of gun control? (paragraph 1)
pessimistic

1   THE SENATE RECENTLY passed a new gun-control bill, which some observers consider worse than no bill at all. Any serious attempt at handgun registration was gutted, and Senate gun lovers even managed to repeal a 1968 gun law controlling the purchase of .22 rim-fire ammunition.

Why does Buchwald make the last name of his friend "Hurts"? (paragraph 2)
"hurts"—something that will cause pain.

2   After the Senate got finished with its work on the gun-control bill, I received a telephone call from my friend Bromley Hurts, who told me he had a business proposition to discuss with me. I met him for lunch at a pistol range in Maryland.

3   "I think I've got a fantastic idea," he said, "I want to start a new business called Hurts Rent-A-Gun."

Is Buchwald serious about proposing rent-a-gun counters at gas stations? (paragraph 8)
No—he is being facetious.

4   "What on earth for?" I asked.

5   "There are a lot of people in this country who only use a handgun once or twice a year, and they don't want to go to all the expense of buying one. So we'll rent them a gun for a day or two. By leasing a firearm from us, they won't have to tie up all their money."

6   "That makes sense," I admitted.

7   "Say a guy is away from home on a trip, and he doesn't want to carry his own gun with him. He can rent a gun from us and then return it when he's finished with his business."

8   "You could set up rent-a-gun counters at gas stations," I said excitedly.

9   "And we could have stores in town where someone could rent a gun to settle a bet," Hurts said.

10 "A lot of people would want to rent a gun for a domestic quarrel," I said.

11 "Right. Say a jealous husband suspects there is someone at home with his wife. He rents a pistol from us and tries to catch them in the act. If he discovers his wife is alone, he isn't out the eighty dollars it would cost him to buy a gun."

12 "Don't forget the kids who want to play Russian roulette. They could pool their allowances and rent a gun for a couple of hours," I said.

13 "Our market surveys indicate," Hurts said, "that there are also a lot of kids who claim their parents don't listen to them. If they could rent a gun, they feel they could arrive at an understanding with their folks in no time."

14 "There's no end to the business," I said. "How would you charge for Hurts Rent-A-Gun?"

15 "There would be hourly rates, day rates, and weekly rates, plus ten cents for each bullet fired. Our guns would be the latest models, and we would guarantee clean barrels and the latest safety devices. If a gun malfunctions through no fault of the user we will give him another gun absolutely free."

16 "For many Americans it's a dream come true," I said.

17 "We've also made it possible for people to return the gun in another town. For example, if you rent the gun in Chicago and want to use it in Salt Lake City, you can drop it off there at no extra charge."

18 "Why didn't you start this before?"

19 "We wanted to see what happened with the gun-control legislation. We were pretty sure the Senate and the White House would not do anything about strong gun control, especially during an election year. But we didn't want to invest a lot of money until we were certain they would all chicken out."

20 "I'd like the franchise for Washington's National Airport," I said.

21 "You've got it. It's a great location," Hurts said. "You'll make a fortune in hijackings alone."

(Art Buchwald, *I Never Danced at the White House,* 1972, 1973)

What is Buchwald saying in paragraphs 12 and 13?
We often hear about kids who have access to guns using them in this way.

What is Buchwald's concern here? (paragraphs 20–21)
He is concerned that guns will be used in hijackings.

 COMPREHENSION CHECKUP

Multiple Choice

Directions: For each item, write the letter corresponding to the best answer.

___b___ 1. The topic of the article is
    a. car rental agencies.
    b. gun control.
    c. domestic violence.
    d. free enterprise.

___d___ 2. Buchwald chose the name Bromley Hurts because
    a. his wife's cousin has the same name.
    b. it is a "play" on Hertz Rent-A-Car.
    c. it indicates that guns can cause "hurt."
    d. both b and c.

___b___ 3. The author's primary purpose in writing this satire is to
    a. persuade readers to stop buying guns.
    b. condemn the new gun-control bill.
    c. persuade readers to buy handguns.
    d. describe a lucrative business opportunity.

___b___ 4. The tone of this article could best be described as
    a. sentimental and sad.
    b. humorous and ironic.
    c. angry and vindictive.
    d. cautious and logical.

___d___ 5. According to the article, which of the following people would benefit from the fictitious Hurts Rent-A-Gun?
    a. a jealous spouse
    b. a man away from home on a trip
    c. a person wanting to settle a bet
    d. all of the above

___b___ 6. You can infer from the article that Buchwald believes that
    a. people can be trusted to use guns responsibly.
    b. people cannot be trusted to use guns responsibly.
    c. people who use guns should practice at pistol ranges.
    d. disposable guns are the wave of the future.

___c___ 7. The statement "for many Americans it's a dream come true" is an example of
    a. literary allusion.
    b. caricature.
    c. ironic exaggeration.
    d. understatement.

True or False

Directions: Indicate whether each statement is true or false by writing **T** or **F** in the space provided.

___T___ 8. Buchwald likely favors strong gun-control legislation.

___F___ 9. Buchwald is really happy with the new gun-control bill.

___F___ 10. Leasing a gun is the same as owning one.

Short Answer

1. What details indicate Buchwald's desire for a stronger gun-control bill?
Buchwald believes the new bill doesn't have any "teeth" to it and complains that it actually repealed a 1968 gun law. He says it's "worse than no bill at all."

2. Who is Buchwald most critical of in this article? He is criticizing Congress for "chickening out" and passing less-restrictive gun-control legislation.

3. Describe the tone of Buchwald's satire. Angry, bitter, humorous, cynical.

4. Buchwald implies an analogy between renting a gun and renting a car. List the details that show how Hertz Rent-A-Car, or any other car rental agency, is similar to Hurts Rent-A-Gun. (1) both lend a person an item (car or gun) for a day or longer, (2) both allow the person to return the item to a different location, (3) both assume the person won't need the item on a permanent basis, (4) both have hourly, daily, and weekly rates.

5. What are the specific uses for rental guns mentioned in the article? Why are these uses included in the article? <u>Some reasons for renting a gun are: to take on</u> <u>a trip, to threaten to kill one's spouse, to play Russian roulette, to hijack an airplane.</u> <u>Guns are sometimes used in precisely these ways.</u>

6. Does Buchwald believe that the country will be a less or a more dangerous place if handguns are more closely regulated? Give supporting reasons. <u>Buchwald believes that our country would be less dangerous if we regulated</u> <u>hand guns more strictly. His humorous examples (jealous husband) illustrate how the</u> <u>easy availability of guns is likely to lead to more homicides.</u>

Vocabulary in Context

Directions: Underline the word or phrase in the second sentence that helps explain the meaning of the italicized word in the first sentence.

1. I can't imagine that Stephanie would fall for Joshua's *proposition.* After all, she already suffered from his last <u>proposed scheme</u>.

2. Do you think it is likely that they are going to *repeal* that law? They should <u>revoke</u> it because it makes no sense.

3. Doing *domestic* chores is one of my least favorite activities. However, if you don't take care of your <u>home</u>, it will fall apart.

4. Greg's computer *malfunctioned* again causing the loss of valuable data. If it <u>fails to work</u> one more time, I think he should get a new computer.

5. Sutin has the *franchise* for three Baskin-Robbins ice cream stores. As the <u>owner of the right to operate</u> the stores, he is expecting to make a lot of money.

6. Let's *pool* our money and buy some lottery tickets. We'll increase our chances of winning by <u>putting our money together</u>.

In Your Own Words

Do you think the easy availability of guns contributes to the higher rates of violent crime in the United States? Are you in favor of more gun control? Why or why not?

Internet Activity

You can find newspaper columns and articles written by Art Buchwald at www.washingtonpost.com. Type in "Buchwald." Select one of his pieces, print it, and explain what he is satirizing.

Exercise 7: Detecting Satire

Directions: The following cartoon offers an opposing viewpoint to the one expressed by Art Buchwald in the previous article. On the line provided, give the main idea of the cartoon.

Jerry L. Barnett, *The Indianapolis Star*. Reprinted with permission.

The main idea of this cartoon is: The Revolutionary War would not have been won by the colonists without guns.

Internet Activity

1. To obtain additional information about the issue of gun control, visit both of the following Web sites. One site presents the pro position on gun control, and the other site presents the con position. Write a summary paragraph contrasting these two viewpoints on this issue. Which viewpoint do you find more appealing?

    www.bradycampaign.org (The Brady Campaign to Prevent Gun Violence)

    www.nra.org (National Rifle Association)

2. You must be able to draw inferences to understand any cartoon, but political or editorial cartoons require a level of sophistication about current events. Find an editorial cartoon on one of the two Web sites given below, print it, and identify the cartoonist's main idea. What background knowledge on your part was required to interpret the cartoon? What inferences were you able to draw about the cartoonist's viewpoint?

    www.comicspage.com

    www.creators.com

Chapter Summary and Review

In Chapter 7, you learned how to recognize the tone of an article. You also became familiar with irony, satire, hyperbole, caricature, and understatement. Based on the material in Chapter 7, answer the following.

Short Answer

Directions: Give synonyms for each of the following tone words.

1. arrogant ___superior_____

2. whining ___begging_____

3. optimistic <u>positive</u>

4. pessimistic <u>negative</u>

5. vindictive <u>revengeful</u>

6. dictatorial <u>overbearing</u>

Directions: Define the following word.

7. Satire <u>using ridicule to create awareness of flaws and to bring about change</u>

Vocabulary in Context

Directions: Choose one of the following words to complete the sentences below. Use each word only once.

caricatures   emotional   hyperbole   satire

8. The phrase "strong as an ox" is usually an example of <u>hyperbole</u>.

9. Tone refers to the <u>emotional</u> quality of an article.

10. Political cartoonists often like to draw <u>caricatures</u> of our presidents.

11. <u>Satire</u> relies on exaggeration and distortion and often has a humorous effect.

VOCABULARY   Unit 4 Word Parts Dealing with the Senses, Size, and Writing

In Vocabulary Unit 3, you learned that *enn* and *ann* mean "year." In this unit, you will study some more words using these word parts. We will also introduce word parts related to the five senses, size, and writing.

ann—year   enn—year

anniversary	The yearly return of a date or event, as in a wedding *anniversary*.
annual	*Annual* usually means "yearly," but it is also a term used to describe a plant living only one year or season. A sunflower is an example of an *annual* because it completes its life cycle, produces seeds, and dies after growing only one season. *Annual* flowers will not bloom again.
biannual	Happening twice a year. The equinox is a *biannual* event.
biennial	Happening every two years; also a plant that lasts for two years. Congressional elections take place *biennially*.
perennial	Continuing for a long time; year after year; also a plant that has roots that remain alive during the winter and that blooms year after year, such as the iris. The New York Yankees are *perennially* a good baseball team.

Sunflower

anno Domini (A.D.) — *Anno* means "year," and *Domini* means "Lord," so *A.D.* does not mean "after death," but "Year of Our Lord." The Civil War began in *A.D.* 1860.

audio—hear   ology—the study of; the science of   spec(t) —to see

audience — A group of people gathered to hear (and see) a speaker, play, or concert; also a formal interview with someone in a high position. The local parish priest was granted an *audience* with the pope.

audiology — The science of hearing.

auditorium — A room where an audience usually gathers to listen.

audition — A hearing to judge the skills of a musician or actor for a job. When you *audition* for a part in a play, the director will be interested in hearing how you read your lines. There were no microphones in ancient Greece, so actors who were in plays had to be able to say their lines loud enough so that the people in the back row of the amphitheaters could hear them.

auditory — Having to do with the sense of hearing; also your listening skills. In the first part of this textbook, you discovered whether you were an *auditory* learner.

spectator — A person who sees or watches something without being an active participant. You might be a *spectator* at a football game.

spectrum—One beautiful spectrum, the rainbow, occurs when light hits moisture in the air at a certain angle.

speculate — To mentally see something in a serious way. Are you *speculating* about what you are going to do tonight?

spectrum — A *spectrum* is a range of color, as in a rainbow or in light shining through a prism. The word also sometimes refers to a range of ideas. In the college classroom, there was a wide *spectrum* of opinion on the subject of abortion.

vis—see   in—not; into, within

visible — Capable of being seen. The mountains were *visible* from a great distance.

invisible — Not capable of being seen. Here *in* means "not." The Latin prefix *in* appears in many English words. Sometimes it means "not," and other times it means "into." When you come to a word using *in*, you may need to use context clues or your dictionary to determine the correct meaning.

"Vision is the art of seeing things invisible."
—Jonathan Swift

vista — A view or outlook seen from some distance.

visionary — Looking into the future. He had a *visionary* scheme to create human colonies on Mars. *Visionary* also means a prophet or seer. In the Old Testament, prophets were *visionaries* because they looked into the future.

audio-visual — Involving both hearing and seeing. DVD recorders are examples of *audio-visual* equipment.

phono—sound

phonograph	A device for reproducing sound recorded in a turning record. The word literally means "sound written down." We used to listen to records on a *phonograph*. What's the modern-day equivalent of the *phonograph*?
phonics	The study of speech sounds and their written symbols (letters). Your teacher might have taught you *phonics* when you were learning to read.

Thaves

Frank & Ernest used with the permission of the Thaves and The Cartoonist Group. All rights reserved.

macro—large   micro—small, or one-millionth part; enlarging, amplifying   bio—life   scope—an instrument for seeing

microwave	A small electromagnetic wave; also an oven that cooks with *microwaves*. The literal meaning is "small wave."
micrometer	One-millionth of a meter.
microphone	An instrument for amplifying sound. In this word, *micro* means "amplifying what is small or weak."
microscope	An instrument for making very small objects look larger. In this word, *micro* means "enlarging what is small."
microeconomics	An economic analysis of small-scale parts of the economy, such as the growth of a single industry or demand for a single product.
macroeconomics	The part of economic theory that deals with the larger picture, such as national income, total employment, and total consumption.
microbiology	The branch of biology that deals with small life organisms.

magna—large   mega—large; one million   tele—distance

magnify	To make larger.
megaphone	A device for magnifying the voice; literally means "large sound." Police may use *megaphones* to be heard over the noise of the crowd.
megabyte	One million pieces of information; loosely one million bytes.
telescope	An optical device for seeing distant objects; use of a *telescope* makes these distant objects appear to be closer.
telephone	A device for transmitting speech or computerized information over distances; "sound from a distance."

telephone—*The first telephone book was published in 1878 in New Haven, Connecticut. It listed only 50 names.*

telephoto	A camera lens that magnifies a distant object so that it appears to be close. A photographer working for a tabloid magazine was able to get a picture of Prince William by using a camera equipped with a *telephoto* lens.
telepathy	Mind reading; knowledge communicated from one person to another without using any of the five senses; "feeling from a distance."
teleconference	A conference of persons in different locations by means of the telephone or TV.
television	"Seeing from a distance."

television—"All television is educational television. The question is: what is it teaching?"

—Nicholas Johnson

scribe, script—write   biblio—book   pre—before   post—after

scribble	To write carelessly, quickly.
inscription	Something engraved; a short, signed message. (Here *in* means "into.") Because Thomas Jefferson wanted to be remembered for the things he had left to the people, and not for the high offices he had held, the *inscription* on his tomb reads: "Here was buried Thomas Jefferson, author of the Declaration of American Independence, of the Statute of Virginia for religious freedom, and father of the University of Virginia."
prescription	Something advised or ordered; a written direction for the preparation and use of medicine; "written before." Following her attack of the flu, her doctor's *prescription* was lots of fluids and complete bed rest.
postscript	A note written after the signature in a letter (P.S.).
scribe	A writer, author, or secretary. Before the invention of printing, the *scribes* were professional penmen who copied manuscripts and documents.
Scripture	Any sacred writing or book; a Bible passage.
Bible	The sacred book of Christianity; the Old Testament and New Testament.
bibliography	Since *graph* means "write," a *bibliography* literally means "books written down." A *bibliography* is a list of sources of information on a particular subject. When you write a research paper for one of your classes, you will include a *bibliography* at the end of your paper listing the books and articles you used for your research.

Bible—The Bible is the best-selling book in the world. The entire Bible has been translated into at least 337 languages.

Exercise 1: Word Parts

Directions: Write sentences using the following words. Add whatever endings are necessary.

1. audiologist Answers will vary. _____

_____

2. perennial _____

_____

3. speculate _____

_____

4. scribe _____

_____

5. biennial _____

_____

6. visionary _____

_____

7. telepathy _____

_____

8. scribble _____

_____

Exercise 2: Word Parts

Directions: In the blanks below, write the word from the list that best completes the sentence. Use each word only once.

audition   biannual   bibliography   inscription   invisible

magnify   microwave   perennial   phonics   scribbles

1. Marco decided to fill his garden with _____perennial_____ plants that don't have to be replaced year after year.

2. The former employees of the department store hold a(n) _____biannual_____ luncheon in January and July of every year.

3. Educators have not decided whether it is better to teach young children to read by the whole-language approach or to use _____phonics_____ to teach them the sounds the letters make.

4. The mother saved all of her child's drawings, although most were little more than colorful _____scribbles_____.

5. Marla's research paper was excellent, but she received a D because she forgot to include a complete list of her sources in a(n) _____bibliography_____.

6. The _____inscription_____ on the wedding ring read, "To my beloved Luz, the light of my life."

7. Millions of baby boomers need glasses to _____magnify_____ the small print in books.

8. The young actor's _____audition_____ for the play apparently did not go well because he did not get the role.

9. A chameleon can make itself almost _____invisible_____ by changing colors to match its surroundings.

10. The _____microwave_____ is a more popular appliance than the dishwasher.

Exercise 3: Word Parts

Directions: In the blanks below, write the word from the list that best completes the sentence. Use each word only once.

biennial   megaphone   microphones   postscript   spectators

spectrum   teleconference   telepathy   visionary   vista

1. I would think that if anyone could communicate by means of _____telepathy_____ it would be identical twins.

2. The police officer, who was using a _____megaphone_____ to be heard over the crowd, urged the soccer fans to disperse quickly and quietly.

3. Rather than waste time, energy, and money flying to New York to go over the details of the will, all of the parties agreed to hold a _____teleconference_____ instead.

4. Marta's daughter wrote her a wonderful letter for Mother's Day, and as a _____postscript_____ she wrote, "I love you."

5. Although the number of _____spectators_____ actually attending the World Series has not declined, the number of viewers watching on TV certainly has.

6. During the televised debate, both candidates' _____microphones_____ went dead for over 10 minutes.

7. The pansy is a _____biennial_____ plant that produces a flower in the second year.

8. After the arduous climb to the top of Mount Everest, we were rewarded with a sweeping _____vista_____ of Southeast Asia.

9. The polls certainly revealed a wide _____spectrum_____ of opinion about future tax cuts.

10. In his book *The Road Ahead*, Bill Gates clearly demonstrates why he is the leading communications _____visionary_____ of the 21st century.

Expanding Your Word Power

The words listed below are not found in this Vocabulary Unit, but they are derived from the vocabulary word parts that you have studied. All of them would be good words for you to learn. See if you can guess the meaning of each word from its word parts.

1. auditor	11. visitation	21. presume
2. inaudible	12. cacophony	22. prejudge
3. auspicious	13. symphony	23. precocious
4. conspicuous	14. telegenic	24. predispose
5. spectacular	15. manuscript	25. prerequisite
6. introspection	16. describe	26. postdate
7. perspicacious	17. conscription	27. postpartum
8. envision	18. precede	28. posterior
9. visage	19. precook	29. posthumous
10. vis-à-vis	20. prehistoric	30. postmortem

Vocabulary Unit 4 Crossword Puzzle

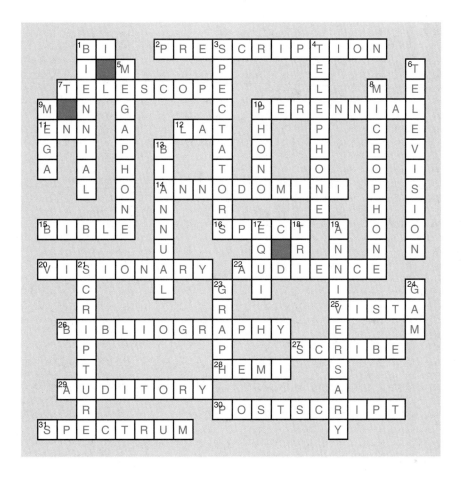

ACROSS CLUES

1. A word part meaning "two."
2. Written before.
7. Instrument to see from a distance.
10. Roses are _____ flowers. They bloom year after year.
11. A word part meaning "year."
12. A word part meaning "side."
14. "Year of Our Lord" (no space between words).
15. The sacred book of Christianity.
16. A word part meaning "to see."
20. A person who looks into the future.
22. The _____ for the Opening Ceremony of the Winter Olympics was one of the largest in history.
25. View seen from a distance.
26. A list of books or references at the end of a paper.
27. A writer.
28. A word part meaning "half."
29. Your listening skills.
30. P.S.
31. A range of light or ideas.

DOWN CLUES

1. Every other year.
3. A group that watches an event.
4. Sound from a distance.
5. Police might use one of these.
6. Seeing from a distance.
8. An instrument for amplifying sound.
9. A word part meaning "1,000,000."
10. A word part meaning "sound."
13. The equinox is a(n) _____ event.
17. A word part meaning "the same amount or size."
18. A word part meaning "three."
19. Happening once a year, such as a wedding _____.
21. Sacred writing.
23. A word part meaning "write."
24. A word part meaning "marriage."

Modes of Writing and of Organization

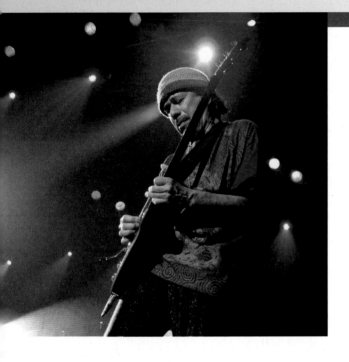

CARLOS SANTANA

The guitarist and songwriter Carlos Santana fuses rock with Latin and African rhythms as well as elements of jazz and the blues. A major figure in Spanish-language rock, and leader of the band Santana, he was inducted into the Rock and Roll Hall of Fame in 1998.

Santana, a fourth-generation musician, was born in 1947 in the town of Autlan de Navarra in Mexico. When he was five his father—a violinist and bandleader—began teaching him the violin, and at eight he switched to the guitar. In 1955, Santana moved with his family to Tijuana, Mexico, where he sang and played guitar on the streets for tourists. At age fourteen, he moved to San Francisco, and five years later he formed the Santana Blues Band. A turning point in Santana's career came in 1969, when his band caused a sensation at the Woodstock rock festival. Its first album, *Santana*, was hailed by *Rolling Stone* magazine as "an explosive fusion of Hispanic-edged rock, Afro-Cuban rhythms, and interstellar improvisation." During the 1970s, Santana's band became one of the most famous in the world.

Besides recording with his band, Santana often records with star performers in other fields like Bob Dylan (folk rock) and Herbie Hancock and Wayne Shorter (jazz). Remarkable for a rock performer, at age fifty-two, Santana created his biggest hit so far, the album *Supernatural* (1999), which was voted Best Rock Album of the Year and has sold over 21 million copies worldwide. (Roger Kamien, *Music*, 2008)

TIMED READING If you wish to use "Carlos Santana" as a timed reading, please turn to page A-3 in the Appendices.

CHAPTER 8

Four Primary Modes of Writing

CHAPTER PREVIEW

In this chapter, you will

- Become familiar with the four modes of writing: narrative, descriptive, expository, and persuasive.

An Introduction to Modes of Writing (Rhetorical Modes)

In longer reading selections, the main idea is often referred to as the **thesis.** The thesis, just like the main idea in paragraphs, expresses the most important point the writer is trying to make. You may also hear the thesis referred to as the *controlling idea* because its primary purpose is to hold the essay or story together.

In the process of creating written work, most writers select a **mode of writing** (sometimes called a *rhetorical mode*) that helps them achieve their purpose. There are four primary modes of writing: narrative, descriptive, expository, and persuasive.

Narrative Mode

Material written in a **narrative mode** tells a story, either true or fictional. In narrative writing, the events of a story are usually ordered by time. The excerpt below is an example of narrative writing. In this excerpt, who is narrating the significant events of the story? What key point is she making?

> The click of the door handle seems entirely too loud as I pull open the door to check the breathing of my three sleeping children. They look so peaceful, sleeping there in the back of my station wagon under the yellow light of a flickering street lamp.
>
> I smooth the curls on Lydia's scarred face and gently close the door. Those scars—they are just one of the reasons I am seeing my children to sleep in my car. Walking through the backdoor of the kitchen, I look back

once and then, all right, just once more. I smile at the cooks as I rush through the kitchen and grab the food for my customers from under the warmers. They'll keep an eye out the door for me.

It's after 1:00 A.M. when my last table leaves. I thought they would never finish. Oh, to have that kind of time to linger over a meal. It's been so long since I've had that kind of freedom. I carefully place the wineglasses in the bus tub next to the dessert plates and haul it all down the stairs. My mother would tell me to take more than one trip, but I'd always rather make one long, painful trip than two or three.

I tip out the bartender and head for the small parking lot behind the restaurant, where, I am told, my children are still blissfully asleep. I realize that I am tiptoeing my way out to the car, which makes no sense at all. I carefully open the car door and sink into the front seat. I let my head fall onto the steering wheel. I am so tired.

I am home.

"Hi, Mom," I hear from behind me. Startled, I whip around to find Matthew, the oldest, who is all of five, blinking his eyes awake.

"How was work?" he asks.

"It was fine," I reply. "Very busy. It's late though—you should go back to sleep. We'll talk in the morning."

"OK," he says, and within seconds he is out again, snuggled up against Alex, who is just fourteen months old. Living in the car doesn't seem to faze any of them in the slightest. Oh sure, they ask why we have to keep sleeping in the car, but the answer seems to suffice, and they don't whine about not having a television. Well, we do have a television, actually. It was a graduation present years before, and it's tucked in front of the passenger seat. I tried to sell it, but it wasn't worth much, so I decided to keep it. A last vestige of middle-class life, if you will. I was a middle-class housewife once upon a time. . . .

Making the leap from given-every-opportunity, spoiled-in-every-way middle-class child to boring middle-class housewife and eventually to homeless single mother should be harder than it is. In reality, it doesn't take much more than a series of bad judgment calls and wrong decisions that, at the time, appear to be perfectly reasonable and in most cases for the better.

My own journey into homelessness did not begin with drug use, alcoholism, or any of the other things we, as a society, so often attribute to such a downward spiral. Instead, I followed my bliss right into the back of a Subaru station wagon.

At eighteen, I was a promising freshman at American University in Washington, D.C. At nineteen, I was married and pregnant with my first child. By the time I was twenty-five, I had three children and within a year, I was separated from my husband and living out of the backseat of my car, my three children all under the age of six.

This is the story of how we were homeless while I simultaneously tried to hide it from my family, my friends, and the rest of the world. By day, I walked the streets of Stone Harbor, Maine, as the completely normal mother of three children, looking in shop windows and going to the library and the Laundromat. By night, however, I was driving around town, looking for a place to sleep and park, bathing at the truck stop, and boiling ramen noodle dinners on public grills.

I had a decent job waiting tables and, although I did my best to hide my situation, I found that revealing myself, even in small amounts, gained me not only a cadre of friends, but an occasional helping hand. In time, I pulled us out of homelessness and returned us to a more normal lifestyle, but the hot days of that summer will never leave me. Neither will what I learned from them.

(Michelle Kennedy, "Prologue," 2005)

Descriptive Mode

With material written in a **descriptive mode,** the emphasis is on providing details that describe a person, place, object, concept, or experience. The writing may employ the use of figurative language and include material that appeals to one or more of the five senses. Descriptive writing most commonly deals with visual perceptions but not always. The excerpt below is an example of descriptive writing. What details does the writer use to give you the sensation of actually experiencing poverty? Name four vivid details the author uses to describe the poverty. After reading the excerpt, what is your overall impression of poverty?

Poverty is getting up every morning from a dirt- and illness-stained mattress. The sheets have long since been used for diapers. Poverty is living in a smell that never leaves. This is a smell of urine, sour milk, and spoiling food sometimes joined with the strong smell of long-cooked onions. Onions are cheap. If you have smelled this smell, you did not know how it came. It is the smell of the outdoor privy. It is the smell of young children who cannot walk the long dark way in the night. It is the smell of the mattresses where years of "accidents" have happened. It is the smell of the milk which has gone sour because the refrigerator long has not worked, and it costs money to get it fixed. It is the smell of rotting garbage. I could bury it, but where is the shovel? Shovels cost money.

(Jo Goodwin Parker, "What Is Poverty?" 1971)

Expository Mode

An author who is trying to explain something will likely use an **expository mode.** Expository writing explains ideas and how things work. It is more likely to be logical and factual. Much of the material that you read in your textbooks follows an expository mode. The excerpt below is an example of expository writing. What is being explained to you? What are some factual details that are intended to inform you?

THE POOR: WHO AND HOW MANY?

The U.S. government defines the poverty line as the annual cost of a thrifty food budget for an urban family of four, multiplied by three to include the cost of housing, clothes, and other necessities. Families whose incomes fall below that line are officially considered poor. In 2007, the poverty line was set at an annual income of roughly $20,000 for a family of four. One in eight Americans—roughly thirty-five million people, including more than ten million children—lives below the poverty line. If they could all join hands, they would form a line stretching from New York to Los Angeles and back again.

America's poor include individuals of all ages, races, religions, and regions, but poverty is concentrated among certain groups. Children are one of the largest groups of poor Americans. One in every five children lives in poverty. Most poor children live in single-parent families, usually with the mother. In fact, a high proportion of Americans residing in families headed by divorced, separated, or unmarried women live below the poverty line. These families are at a disadvantage because most women earn less than men for comparable work, especially in nonprofessional fields. Women without higher education or special skills often cannot find jobs that pay significantly more than the child-care expenses they incur if they work outside the home. Single-parent, female-headed families are roughly five times as likely as two-income families to fall below the poverty line, a situation referred to as "the feminization of poverty."

(Thomas Patterson, *We the People,* 7/e, 2008)

Persuasive Mode

Material written in a **persuasive mode** is meant to convince you of something. Persuasive writing tends to be about controversial topics. It presents an argument and offers evidence. It is writing that is considered to be biased. The excerpt below is an example of persuasive writing. What idea is the author trying to persuade you to accept? What course of action is she recommending?

It is common among the non-poor to think of poverty as a sustainable condition—austere, perhaps, but they get by somehow, don't they? They are "always with us." What is harder for the non-poor to see is poverty as acute distress. The lunch that consists of Doritos or hot dog rolls, leading to faintness before the end of the shift. The "home" that is also a car or a van. The illness or injury that must be "worked through," with gritted teeth because there's no sick pay or health insurance and the loss of one day's pay will mean no groceries for the next.

These experiences are not part of a sustainable lifestyle, even a lifestyle of chronic deprivation and relentlessly low-level punishment. They are, by almost any standard of subsistence, emergency situations. And that is how we should see the poverty of so many millions of low-wage Americans—as a state of emergency.

(Barbara Ehrenreich, "Poverty," 2001)

Readings That Illustrate the Modes of Writing

The reading selections that follow illustrate modes of writing. Though these selections come from a variety of sources, they all, either directly or indirectly, concern the topic of relationships.

Narrative

"The woman said, 'Pick up my pocketbook, boy, and give it here.'"

TUNING IN TO READING   What would you do if someone attempted to steal your purse or wallet? After reading the first paragraph of this short story, what do you think is going to happen next?

As you read this narrative, notice how the action of the story is told in sequence, with a clear beginning, middle, and end. Try to discover the larger message about relationships that the author is illustrating.

BIO-SKETCH   Langston Hughes (1902–1967) is one of the best-known African American writers of the 20th century and the first to live solely from his writings and lectures. Shortly after his birth in Joplin, Missouri, his parents were divorced. As a result, Hughes spent much of his early childhood living in poverty with his maternal grandmother. In the following short story, the character of Mrs. Jones is most probably based on his grandmother. Hughes, a graduate of Lincoln University, was a prolific writer of poems, short stories, and plays. He also wrote two books. Throughout his literary career, he was sharply criticized by other African American writers who believed that he portrayed an unattractive view of African American life.

NOTES ON VOCABULARY

thank you, ma'm   a small bump in the road sometimes put there to force drivers to go slowly. In earlier times, if a young couple went out riding, the male was entitled to a kiss every time he hit one of the bumps. He acknowledged that kiss with a polite *"Thank you, ma'm."*

pocketbook   the original *pocketbook* was a man's purse that resembled an open book with a clasp at the top and that conveniently fit into the owner's pocket.

Thank You, Ma'm

LANGSTON HUGHES

She was a large woman with a large purse that had everything in it but a hammer and nails. It had a long strap, and she carried it slung across her shoulder. It was about eleven o'clock at night, dark, and she was walking alone, when a boy ran up behind her and tried to snatch her purse. The strap broke with the sudden single tug the boy gave it from behind. But the boy's weight and the weight of the purse combined caused him to lose his balance. Instead of taking off full blast as he had hoped, the boy fell on his back on the sidewalk and his legs flew up. The large woman simply turned around and kicked him right square in his blue-jeaned sitter. Then she reached down, picked the boy up by his shirt front, and shook him until his teeth rattled.

After that the woman said, "Pick up my pocketbook, boy, and give it here." 2

She still held him tightly. But she bent down enough to permit him to stoop 3 and pick up her purse. Then she said, "Now ain't you ashamed of yourself?"

Firmly gripped by his shirt front, the boy said, "Yes'm."   4

The woman said, "What did you want to do it for?"   5

The boy said, "I didn't aim to."   6

She said, "You a lie!"   7

By that time two or three people passed, stopped, turned to look, and   8
some stood watching.

"If I turn you loose, will you run?" asked the woman.   9

"Yes'm," said the boy.   10

"Then I won't turn you loose," said the woman. She did not release   11
him.

"Lady, I'm sorry," whispered the boy.   12

"Um-hum! Your face is dirty. I got a great mind to wash your face for   13
you. Ain't you got nobody home to tell you to wash your face?"

"No'm," said the boy.   14

"Then it will get washed this evening," said the large woman, starting   15
up the street, dragging the frightened boy behind her.

He looked as if he were fourteen or fifteen, frail and willow-wild, in   16
tennis shoes and blue jeans.

The woman said, "You ought to be my son. I would teach you right   17
from wrong. Least I can do right now is to wash your face. Are you
hungry?"

"No'm," said the being-dragged boy. "I just want you to turn me   18
loose."

"Was I bothering *you* when I turned that corner?" asked the woman.   19

"No'm."   20

"But you put yourself in contact with *me,*" said the woman. "If you   21
think that that contact is not going to last awhile, you got another thought
coming. When I get through with you, sir, you are going to remember Mrs.
Luella Bates Washington Jones."

Sweat popped out on the boy's face and he began to struggle. Mrs. Jones   22
stopped, jerked him around in front of her, put a half nelson about his neck,
and continued to drag him up the street. When she got to her door, she
dragged the boy inside, down a hall, and into a large kitchenette-furnished
room at the rear of the house. She switched on the light and left the door
open. The boy could hear other roomers laughing and talking in the large
house. Some of their doors were open, too, so he knew he and the woman
were not alone. The woman still had him by the neck in the middle of her
room.

She said, "What is your name?"   23

"Roger," answered the boy.   24

"Then, Roger you go to that sink and wash your face," said the woman,   25
whereupon she turned him loose—at last. Roger looked at the door—looked
at the woman—looked at the door—*and went to the sink.*

"Let the water run until it gets warm," she said. "Here's a clean towel."   26

"You gonna take me to jail?" asked the boy, bending over the sink.   27

"Not with that face, I would not take you nowhere," said the woman. 28
"Here I am trying to get home to cook me a bite to eat, and you snatch my pocketbook! Maybe you ain't been to your supper either, late as it be. Have you?"

"There's nobody home at my house," said the boy. 29

"Then we'll eat," said the woman. "I believe you're hungry—or been 30 hungry—to try to snatch my pocketbook!"

"I want a pair of blue suede shoes," said the boy. 31

"Well, you didn't have to snatch *my* pocketbook to get some suede 32 shoes," said Mrs. Luella Bates Washington Jones. "You could of asked me."
"M'am?" 33

The water dripping from his face, the boy looked at her. There was a 34 long pause. A very long pause. After he had dried his face, and not knowing what else to do, dried it again, the boy turned around, wondering what next. The door was open. He could make a dash for it down the hall. He could run, run, run, *run!*

The woman was sitting on the daybed. After a while she said, "I were 35 young once and I wanted things I could not get."

There was another long pause. The boy's mouth opened. Then he 36 frowned, not knowing he frowned.

The woman said, "Um-hum! You thought I was going to say *but,* didn't 37 you? You thought I was going to say, *but I didn't snatch people's pocketbooks.* Well, I wasn't going to say that." Pause. Silence. "I have done things, too, which I would not tell you, son—neither tell God, if He didn't already know. Everybody's got something in common. So you set down while I fix us something to eat. You might run that comb through your hair so you will look presentable."

An icebox was what people used before electricity. It literally held a block of ice to keep food cold.

In another corner of the room behind a screen was a gas plate and an 38 icebox. Mrs. Jones got up and went behind the screen. The woman did not watch the boy to see if he was going to run now, nor did she watch her purse, which she left behind her on the daybed. But the boy took care to sit on the far side of the room, away from the purse, where he thought she could easily see him out of the corner of her eye if she wanted to. He did not trust the woman *not* to trust him. And he did not want to be mistrusted now.

"Do you need somebody to go to the store," asked the boy, "maybe to 39 get some milk or something?"

"Don't believe I do," said the woman, "unless you just want sweet milk 40 yourself. I was going to make cocoa out of this canned milk I got here."

"That will be fine," said the boy. 41

She heated some lima beans and ham she had in the icebox, made the 42 cocoa, and set the table. The woman did not ask the boy anything about where he lived, or his folks, or anything else that would embarrass him. Instead, as they ate, she told him about her job in a hotel beauty shop that stayed open late, what the work was like, and how all kinds of women came in and out, blonds, red-heads, and Spanish. Then she cut him a half of her ten-cent cake.

"Eat some more, son," she said. 43

When they were finished eating, she got up and said, "Now here. 44 Take this ten dollars and buy yourself some blue suede shoes. And next time, do not make the mistake of latching onto *my pocketbook nor nobody else's*—because shoes got by devilish ways will burn your feet. I got to get my rest now. But from here on in, son, I hope you will behave yourself."

She led him down the hall to the front door and opened it. "Good night! 45 Behave yourself, boy!" she said, looking out into the street as he went down the steps.

The boy wanted to say something else other than, "Thank you, Ma'm," 46 to Mrs. Luella Bates Washington Jones, but he couldn't do so as he turned at the barren stoop and looked back at the large woman in the door. He barely managed to say, "Thank you," before she shut the door. And he never saw her again.

(Langston Hughes, "Thank You, Ma'm," 1996)

 COMPREHENSION CHECKUP

Short Answer

Directions: Answer the question briefly, in no more than a sentence or two.

What is the main idea the author is trying to convey?

Mrs. Jones wants to teach Roger a lesson and maybe change his behavior for the better.

Sequencing

A narrative usually relates a series of events in chronological order. This enables a reader to understand how one event leads directly to another.

Directions: Number the sentences to put the events in the correct chronological (or *time*) sequence.

_____5_____ Roger tells Mrs. Jones that he wants some blue suede shoes.

_____10_____ Roger thanks Mrs. Jones.

_____6_____ Roger combs his hair.

_____7_____ Roger offers to go to the store for Mrs. Jones.

_____2_____ Mrs. Jones kicks Roger and shakes him roughly.

_____8_____ Mrs. Jones serves Roger dinner and tells him about her job.

_____3_____ Mrs. Jones drags Roger behind her.

_____4_____ Roger washes his face.

_____9_____ Mrs. Jones gives Roger ten dollars to buy some blue suede shoes.

_____1_____ Roger tries to steal Mrs. Jones's purse.

In Your Own Words

1. When did Mrs. Jones decide to take Roger home to her house?

2. Why didn't Mrs. Jones call the police? Do you think Roger had tried to steal anything before?

3. Why didn't Roger run when he finally was given the opportunity?

4. When they were finally at her home, why did Mrs. Jones give Roger the chance to steal her purse?

5. Why does Mrs. Jones want Roger to make himself "presentable"? How are her suggestions interpreted by Roger?

6. At the end of their meal together, why did Mrs. Jones give Roger the money to buy his blue suede shoes?

7. What lesson do you think Mrs. Jones was trying to teach Roger?

8. Look at the "Notes on Vocabulary" for an unusual meaning of the phrase "thank you, ma'm." What do you think Hughes means to imply by the title of this story? Do you think he made use of this special meaning?

9. Do you think a similar incident could happen today? Or are people too frightened to get involved in another person's life?

Written Assignment

1. Natural-sounding dialogue can reveal something about the character of the people in the narrative. What does the dialogue in this story reveal about Mrs. Jones and Roger?

2. Trace the character development of Roger. How does his behavior change as the result of Mrs. Jones's actions?

3. Discuss how you helped someone or someone helped you. Give details about what happened and how you felt.

Internet Activity

Discover more about Langston Hughes by going to the following Web site:

www.poets.org/poets/

Type in his name, read a short biography about him, and then read one of his poems. Print the poem and write a short paragraph discussing the tone of the poem and its use of figurative language.

Descriptive

READING

"What I had was a frail and failing old woman who couldn't take a shower on her own."

TUNING IN TO READING   Have you ever helped someone who was very ill for an extended period of time? Do you recall what the experience was like?

READING *(continued)*

While reading this descriptive essay, notice how the key details describe both the author's mother and the author's experience giving her a shower. Because of the emphasis on sensory images, readers can visualize the scene being depicted.

BIO-SKETCH   John Daniel is a poet and essayist living in Oregon. He is the author of two books of poetry, *Common Ground* (1988) and *All Things Touched by Wind* (1994). He is also the author of a work of nonfiction titled *Rogue River Journal: A Winter Alone* (2005). His mother, described in the selection below, died in 1992.

NOTES ON VOCABULARY

Alzheimer's   a progressive, irreversible disease characterized by deterioration or loss of function of brain cells causing severe dementia. Former President Ronald Reagan was an acknowledged sufferer of Alzheimer's, which has been called "the disease of the century." The disease is named after Alois Alzheimer, the German physician who first described the condition.

A Son's Memoir

JOHN DANIEL

> *"The only gift is a portion of thyself."*
>
> —Ralph Waldo Emerson

MY MOTHER WAS TOUGH AS LOBSTER SHELL, solid as New England granite, lively as the wind. . . .

In 1988, when she was 80, my mother agreed to leave her home on the Maine coast and live with my wife and me in Portland, Oregon. She was frail, slowed to a stooped-back shuffle. Her memory was failing. She was frequently disoriented and confused. She lived her last four years with us, and it was to understand those years, their burdens and their blessings, that I wrote *Looking After*. The story that follows is composed of an excerpt from the book.

I never looked forward to helping my mother with her shower. She wasn't the least self-conscious about baring her body in my presence, but something in me shrank from it. To be with her in her nakedness seemed too intimate for a grown son. And some other part of me, the child who wants always to be cared for and never burdened with responsibility, felt put upon and put out. Why was I having to do this? It seemed an indignity, and it touched an open wound. I had no child to bathe, to make faces at, to splash and laugh with. Most likely I never would. What I had was a frail and failing old woman who couldn't take a shower on her own.

Talking her into it was the first challenge. "Oh, I don't need a shower," she would say. "I just had one yesterday, didn't I?"

"You haven't had one for a week."

"But I don't *do* anything. Why do I need a shower?"

It wasn't only bad memory and lapsing judgment that made her resist, of course. It was also that the shower was strenuous for her, and she didn't want to acknowledge, or couldn't, that she needed help with anything so simple. In her own mind, the mind I believe she inhabited most of the time, she was perfectly capable of taking a shower by herself if she wanted to. In this mind, she was still the woman she had been five years ago, a woman who came and went and drove a car, a woman who lived on her own on the coast of Maine and was only temporarily exiled in a distant place. This woman was honestly perplexed when we bought her a cane and asked her, over and over again, to use it. What need had Zilla Daniel for a cane? Somewhere inside her she was not only an able-bodied woman but still a Sea Scout, climbing the rigging in a bright clear wind.

But in her present mind she knew, whenever she leaned far forward in 8 a chair and tried to stiff-arm herself to her feet, whenever she steadied herself with a hand on the wall as she shuffled to the bathroom, just how incapable she had become. She knew, and she hated it. How could she not have hated it? And if she had to bear it, she didn't want me or my wife, Marilyn, or anyone else to have to help her bear it. She wanted to carry herself on her own stooped shoulders. I can still hear her making her way to the toilet with her left hand pulling her nightgown tight behind her, disgustedly whispering "No, no" to her bladder that could not hold back what it should have held back. As if she were castigating an unbroken puppy, but without the tolerance she would have granted an innocent thing. Standing for any length of time was hard for my mother, and so the shower was a kind of siege. She would grip the soap tray with both hands as I got the water temperature right—"Aaant!" she would holler, "too cold!"—and soaped a washcloth to scrub her sway-spined back. Even the soap met resistance.

. . . "It's just one more thing that has to come off."   9

"Well, it does come off," I answered, peeling open a bar of Dial. "It 10 rinses off."

"My dear, it leaves a residue. Plain water is enough."   11

"Mother, for God's sake. . . . You need soap to get clean."   12

"Yes, Father," she said with a scowl.   13

Eventually we worked out a mulish compromise. We used Ivory, which 14 we both agreed was the most natural. I washed her back and buttocks with a soaped washcloth, she held the cloth for a few seconds in the shower spray before washing her front. . . . Then I helped her down to the bath stool, where she rested a while and washed her lower legs and feet. The skin of her shins was dry and papery, perpetually blotched with dark purple—not impact bruises but bruises of age.

As I lathered shampoo into her wet white curls, her head would bow from 15 the pressure of my fingers. I'd ask her to hold it up and she would for a second or two, then it would slowly sink again. It must have taken a major effort just to hold herself as upright as she did in her last years. All the while she was slowly bending, slowly folding, curling toward the fetal comfort of the grave.

She squeezed her eyes shut as I rinsed her hair in the shower stream. She 16 scrunched up her face, stuck her lips out, and sputtered through the soapy runoff. It was in that recurring moment of her life with us, her hair flattened to her head, darkened a little with that soaking spray, that I could almost see my mother as a girl—swimming the cold swells off Hancock Park, splashing and laughing, shouting something toward shore, laying into the water with strong, even strokes that would take her where she wanted to go.

She would let me stop rinsing only when she could rub a bit of her hair 17 between finger and thumb and make it squeak. Then I would steady her out of the shower stall, her two hands in mine. It felt at moments like a kind of dance, a dance that maybe I knew how to do and needed to do. Who was that, doing the dance? Who was it who allowed himself those moments of pleasure helping his mother from the shower? When I look back at that scene in the bathroom, I see a boy in my place. A solemn boy with a bit of a smile, a boy attending his mother out of love and duty blended as one. The boy was there, and he was there now and then at other times in those years my mother was with us. He was there when I'd let him be there.

I helped my mother down into a straight-backed chair and left her in 18 the bathroom with towels, clean underwear, and a little space heater to keep her warm. She took her time, as with everything. Often it was half an hour or longer before she emerged in her dressing gown, her hair beginning to fluff, her face smiling. No matter how hard she might have resisted the idea, a bath or shower always seemed to renew her. Soap, or no soap, the old woman came forth cleaner of spirit.

"She was pure as the driven snow," she usually quoted, gaily, then a 19 pause: "But she drifted."

I guess I came out of the bathroom cleaner of spirit myself. Soap or no 20 soap, whatever the tenor of our conversation, I appreciate now what a privilege it was to help my mother with her shower. I wish I'd seen it more clearly at the time. We don't get to choose our privileges, and the ones that come to us aren't always the ones we would choose, and each of them is as much burden as joy. But they do come, and it's important to know them for what they are.

One morning as my mother came out of her shower she paused at the 21 bottom of the stairs. I was reading the paper in the living room.

"Do you feel them sprouting?" she said, smiling in her white gown.   22

"Do I feel what sprouting?"   23

"Your wings," she said. She stood there, barefooted and bright, smiling 24 right at me and through me, smiling as though she weren't feeble of body and failing of mind but filled with an uncanny power that saw things I could only glimpse.

"Mother, I don't have wings," I said.   25

But she was still smiling as she headed up the stairs, gripping the banister 26 hand over hand, hauling herself up 15 carpeted steps to her room and her bed made of sea-weathered posts and boards, where she would read for a while, gaze out her window at sky and treetops, then drift into sleep.

(John Daniel, *Looking After*, 1997)

COMPREHENSION CHECKUP

Short Answer

Directions: Answer the questions briefly.

1. How did the author describe his mother when she was younger? <u>tough as</u>
   <u>lobster shell, solid as New England granite, lively as the wind</u>

2. How did he describe his mother in her old age when he was taking care of her?
   <u>frail, slow, disoriented, confused—feeble of body and failing of mind</u>

3. Looking at how the author treated his mother, how would you describe the
   sort of person he is? <u>selfish and resentful at first, but also caring,</u>
   <u>compassionate, and appreciative of his opportunity to care for his mother</u>

Multiple Choice

Directions: For each item, write the letter corresponding to the best answer.

___d___ 4. The author implies that in the past his mother
  a. was strong in mind and body.
  b. was highly independent.
  c. was often depressed.
  d. both a and b.

___b___ 5. The author's purpose in writing this selection was to
  a. entertain readers with amusing anecdotes about his mother.
  b. describe and share an important experience in his life.
  c. persuade readers that we need more funding for preventing and
     treating Alzheimer's.
  d. convince readers that Alzheimer's patients should be cared for
     in the home by family members rather than in health care
     facilities.

___c___ 6. We can conclude from the selection that
  a. the relationship of the son and mother has not changed since the
     author was a young boy.
  b. the son is comfortable with viewing his mother's naked body.
  c. the son was somewhat resentful of having to care for his mother.
  d. the things we are forced to do by circumstances rarely turn out to
     be worthwhile experiences.

___a___ 7. How is paragraph 8 related to paragraph 7?
  a. It provides a contrast to the events described in paragraph 7.
  b. It provides an explanation for the son's dislike of his mother.
  c. It clarifies Daniel's relationship with his mother.
  d. It provides a list of activities to assist caregivers in entertaining
     their charges.

___d___ 8. In paragraph 3 the author's tone could be described as
  a. self-pitying.
  b. vindictive.
  c. bitter.
  d. both a and c.

Vocabulary in Context

Directions: Use the context clues from the sentences below to determine the meaning of the italicized words, and write a definition in the space provided. Then consult your dictionary to check how closely you came to the correct definition.

1. "It was also that the shower was *strenuous* for her, and she didn't want to acknowledge, or couldn't, that she needed help with anything so simple."

   After engaging in a *strenuous* workout at the Y, he would come home and take a long nap.

   strenuous: _____ Your guess
   requiring great effort _____ Dictionary meaning

2. "As if she were *castigating* an unbroken puppy, but without the tolerance she would have granted an innocent thing."

   After the teacher finished *castigating* the student for his sloppy classwork, she made him stay after class for an hour.

   castigating: _____ Your guess
   punishing or rebuking severely _____ Dictionary meaning

3. "The skin of her shins was dry and papery, *perpetually* blotched with dark purple—not impact bruises but bruises of age."

   He was *perpetually* late to class even though he got up early enough each morning.

   perpetually: _____ Your guess
   constantly _____ Dictionary meaning

4. "A *solemn* boy with a bit of a smile, a boy attending his mother out of love and duty blended as one."

   When she was naturalized as a new citizen of the United States, she *solemnly* swore her allegiance to her new country.

   solemn: _____ Your guess
   serious, grave _____ Dictionary meaning

5. "Soap or no soap, whatever the *tenor* of our conversation, I appreciate now what a privilege it was to help my mother with her shower."

   If you persist in taking that *tenor* with me, I'll have to ask you to leave my house.

   tenor: _____ Your guess
   drift, tone _____ Dictionary meaning

6. "In this mind, she was still the woman she had been five years ago, a woman who came and went and drove a car, a woman who lived on her own on the coast of Maine and was only temporarily *exiled* in a distant place."

   When Juan Peron lost political power in Argentina he lived in *exile* in Spain.

   exile: _____ Your guess
   banished (banishment) _____ Dictionary meaning

In Your Own Words

1. What is the main idea of this selection?

2. Why does Daniel feel resentful about having to help his mother with her shower?

3. Why does his mother initially resist taking a shower? What is the larger issue in their battle over the soap? What is the implication of his mother saying "Yes, Father" to him?

4. When does Daniel catch a glimpse of his mother as she might have been as a young girl?

5. What is the son implying when he describes attending to his mother as a kind of "dance"?

6. What image does the author use to describe his mother's impending death?

7. How do both mother and son feel at the conclusion of the shower?

8. What is the mother implying by her comment about "wings sprouting"?

Written Assignment

How do you think elderly people are treated in the United States? How much respect is shown to them here? What about in other countries? Write a few paragraphs giving your opinion.

Internet Activity

Further information about Alzheimer's may be obtained from the Web sites given below:

www.alz.org (Alzheimer's Association)

www.alzheimers.org (Alzheimer's Disease Education and Referral Center)

The first site provides general information about Alzheimer's, and the second more technical information. Print a page that gives good information about Alzheimer's, and summarize the information.

Expository

<hr/>

READING

"In some instances, siblings may be stronger socializing influences on the child than parents are."

TUNING IN TO READING   It appears that siblings as well as parents have a profound effect on people's lives, shaping their personalities and affecting their views of the world. In a recent Gallup poll of incoming first-year college students, many felt they had either been physically abused (kicked, punched, or bitten) or mentally abused (criticized, berated, and put down) by their siblings. Between the two types of abuse, most felt that mental abuse had caused more lasting "scars." What was the situation in your family? Did your siblings set the stage for your later relationships with others? Do you think having siblings helps you learn how to deal with others? More than 80 percent of American children have one or more siblings (brothers or sisters).

In the textbook selection that follows, the author relates the information in a direct, unemotional manner. The material, written in an expository mode, presents many facts and statistics to explain the topic of sibling relationships.

BIO-SKETCH   John Santrock, a professor at the University of Texas, is the author of textbooks in the areas of psychology, child development, and life-span development.

READING *(continued)*

NOTES ON VOCABULARY

sibling   one of two or more persons born of the same parents, or sometimes having only one parent in common. The word can refer to either a brother or a sister. *Sibling* comes from the Old English *sibb*, meaning "kinship," and can be traced back to the heroic poem *Beowulf* (approximately A.D. 725), the earliest long work of literature in English.

sibling rivalry   competition between children in a family.

SIBLING RELATIONSHIPS AND BIRTH ORDER
John Santrock

A mother's anecdote captures some of the many possibilities of sibling relationships:

> Jamie and Andy were fighting over wooden building blocks and began throwing them at each other. The stress was depleting my strength and ability to cope. I didn't know what to do so I sent them to their bedrooms while I took time to think.
>
> Then a curious thing happened. While still in their rooms, the kids began talking to each other. Jamie thought of a way they could solve the problem. Andy vetoed it. They continued talking back and forth until a settlement was reached, all without my saying a word!

Of course, many sibling interactions involve less civilized endings. Sandra describes to her mother what happened in a conflict with her sister:

> We had just come home from the ball game. I sat down on the sofa next to the light so I could read. Sally [the sister] said, "Get up. I was sitting there first. I just got up for a second to get a drink." I told her I was not going to get up and that I didn't see her name on the chair. I got mad and started pushing her. Her drink spilled all over her. Then she got really mad. She shoved me against the wall, hitting and clawing at me. I managed to grab a handful of hair. At this point, Sally comes into the room and begins to tell her side of the story. Sandra interrupts, "Mother, you always take her side."

Does this sound familiar? Any of you who have grown up with siblings probably have a rich memory of aggressive, hostile interchanges. But sibling relationships . . . have many pleasant, caring moments as well. Children's sibling relationships include helping, sharing, teaching, fighting, and playing. Children can act as emotional supports, rivals, and communication partners.

Is sibling interaction different from parent–child interaction? There is some evidence that it is. Observations indicate that children interact more positively and in more varied ways with their parents than with their siblings. Children also follow their parents' dictates more than those of their siblings, and they behave more negatively and punitively with their siblings than with their parents.

In some instances, siblings may be stronger socializing influences on the child than parents are. Someone close in age to the child—such as a sibling— may be able to understand the child's problems and be able to communicate more effectively than parents can. In dealing with peers, coping with difficult teachers, and discussing taboo subjects such as sex, siblings may be more influential to the socialization process than parents.

Is sibling interaction the same around the world? In industrialized societies, 7 such as the United States, parents tend to delegate responsibility for younger siblings to older siblings primarily to give the parents freedom to pursue other activities. However, in non-industrialized countries, such as Kenya, the older sibling's role as caregiver to younger siblings has much more importance. In industrialized countries, the older sibling's caregiving role is often discretionary; in non-industrialized countries, it is more obligatory.

Because there are so many possible sibling combinations, it is difficult to 8 generalize about sibling influences. Among the factors to consider are the number of siblings, the ages of siblings, birth order, age spacing, and the sex of siblings. There is something unique about same-sex sibling relationships. Aggression, dominance, and rivalry occur more in same-sex sibling relationships than opposite-sex sibling relationships.

Temperamental traits ("easy" and "difficult," for example), as well as dif- 9 ferent treatment of siblings by parents, influence how siblings get along. Siblings with "easy" temperaments who are treated in relatively equal ways by parents tend to get along with each other the best. By contrast, siblings with "difficult" temperaments, or whose parents have given one of them preferential treatment, get along the worst. Variations in sibling relationships are also linked to birth order.

Birth order is a special interest of sibling researchers. The oldest sibling is 10 expected to exercise self-control and show responsibility in interacting with younger siblings. When the oldest sibling is jealous or hostile, parents often protect the younger siblings. The oldest sibling is more dominant, competent, and powerful than the younger siblings. The oldest sibling is also expected to assist and teach younger siblings. Indeed, researchers have shown that older siblings are both more antagonistic—hitting, kicking, and biting—*and* more nurturant toward their younger siblings than [younger sibling are toward older].

The influence of birth order goes well beyond its link with sibling relation- 11 ships. Indeed, many people are fascinated by links between birth order and personality. For example, firstborn children are more adult oriented, helpful, conforming, anxious, and self-controlled than their siblings. Firstborns excel in academic and professional endeavors. Firstborns are overrepresented in *Who's Who* and Rhodes scholars, for example. They also have more guilt, anxiety, difficulty in coping with stressful situations, as well as higher admission to child guidance clinics, than other children.

What accounts for such differences related to birth order? Proposed expla- 12 nations usually point to variations in interactions with parents and siblings associated with being in a particular position in the family. This is especially true in the case of the firstborn child. The oldest child is the only one who does not have to share parental love and affection with other siblings—until another sibling comes along. An infant requires more attention than an older child; this means that the firstborn sibling now gets less attention than before the newborn arrived. Does this result in conflict between parents and the firstborn? In one research study, mothers became more negative, coercive, and restraining and played less with the firstborn following the birth of a second child.

Even though a new infant requires more attention from parents than does 13 an older child, parents and firstborns often maintain an especially intense relationship throughout the life span. Parents have higher expectations for firstborn children than for later-born children. They put more pressure on them for achievement and responsibility. They also interfere more with their activities. The extra attention that firstborns receive has been linked to firstborns' nurturant behavior. Parental demands and high standards established for firstborns have been associated with both their achievements and their difficulties, such as anxiety and guilt. Given the differences in family dynamics involved in birth order, it is not surprising that firstborns and later-borns have different characteristics.

What is the only child like? The popular conception is that the only child 14 is a "spoiled brat" with such undesirable characteristics as dependency, lack of self-control, and self-centered behavior. But researchers present a more positive portrayal of the only child. Only children often are achievement-oriented and display a desirable personality, especially in comparison with later-borns and children from large families.

So far our consideration of birth-order effects suggests that birth order 15 might be a strong predictor of behavior. However, an increasing number of family researchers believe that birth order has been overdramatized and overemphasized. The critics argue that, when all of the factors that influence behavior are considered, birth order itself shows limited ability to predict behavior. Consider just sibling relationships alone. They vary not only in birth order, but also in number of siblings, age of siblings, age spacing of siblings, and sex of siblings.

Think about some of the other important factors in children's lives that 16 influence their behavior beyond birth order. They include heredity, models of competency or incompetency that parents present to children on a daily basis, peer influences, school influences, socioeconomic factors, socio-historical factors, and cultural variations. When someone says firstborns are always like this, but last-borns are always like that, you know that the person is making overly simplistic statements that do not adequately take into account the complexity of influences on a child's behavior. Keep in mind, though, that, although birth order itself may not be a good predictor of children's behavior, sibling relationships and interaction are important dimensions of family processes.

(John Santrock; *Child Development,* 11/e, 2007)

 COMPREHENSION CHECKUP

Multiple Choice

Directions: For each item, write the letter corresponding to the best answer.

_____a_____ 1. Which of the following would be the best subtitle for this selection?
   a. "The Roles Siblings Play"
   b. "The Lonely Only"
   c. "Firstborns and Success"
   d. "The Forgotten Sibling"

_____c_____ 2. The author's purpose is to
a. entertain.
b. persuade.
c. explain.
d. show steps in a process.

_____a_____ 3. The tone of the selection is
a. objective.
b. excited.
c. argumentative.
d. both a and b.

_____c_____ 4. All of the following would probably be considered positive sibling interactions *except*
a. helping.
b. sharing.
c. bickering.
d. teaching.

_____d_____ 5. All of the following statements *except* one are true about parent–child interactions. Which is *not* true?
a. Siblings may be a stronger socialization influence on a child than the parents in the area of dealing with peers.
b. Children are likely to interact more positively with their parents than their siblings.
c. Children are likely to follow the dictates of their parents over those of their siblings.
d. Children interact in more varied ways with their siblings than with their parents.

_____a_____ 6. All of the following are likely to be considered industrialized countries *except*
a. Kenya.
b. the United States.
c. Japan.
d. Germany.

_____d_____ 7. Sibling relationships are influenced by
a. birth order.
b. different treatment of siblings by parents.
c. temperamental traits of siblings.
d. all of the above.

_____d_____ 8. Researchers have concluded that only children are often
a. achievement oriented.
b. lacking in self-control.
c. possessors of a desirable personality.
d. both a and c.

_____c_____ 9. The selection mentions all of the following variables affecting sibling relationships *except*
a. number and age of siblings.
b. sex of siblings.
c. degree of material possessions.
d. spacing between siblings.

_____d_____ 10. Children's behavior can be influenced by
   a. birth order and heredity.
   b. parental incompetency or competency.
   c. peer and school influences.
   d. all of the above.

Identifying Key Characteristics

Directions: Put a check beside the descriptions that are most likely to apply to a firstborn child.

____✓____ 1. He or she is likely to tell the other siblings what they need to do and when they need to do it.

_____ 2. He or she has difficulty abiding by the rules.

_____ 3. He or she acts helpless and is always on the lookout for potential saviors.

_____ 4. He or she is likely to say, "I've always felt invisible."

____✓____ 5. He or she is likely to say, "Competition is everything! Being number one is who I am."

____✓____ 6. He or she is likely to get good grades.

True or False

Directions: Indicate whether each statement is true or false by writing **T** or **F** in the space provided.

____T____ 1. Sibling interaction is different from parent–child interaction.

____F____ 2. Sibling interaction is the same around the world.

____F____ 3. Aggression and dominance are more likely to occur in opposite-sex sibling relationships.

____F____ 4. Parents expect the oldest sibling to be irresponsible and exhibit little self-control.

____T____ 5. Older siblings are more likely to be both nurturant and antagonistic toward younger siblings.

____F____ 6. Younger siblings are more likely to exhibit guilt and anxiety than firstborns.

____T____ 7. In general, parents have higher expectations for firstborn children than for later-born children.

____F____ 8. Research has determined that only children tend to be "spoiled brats."

____T____ 9. Only children tend to be achievement oriented.

____T____ 10. Many researchers feel that birth order is overemphasized.

Vocabulary in Context

Directions: Choose one of the following words to complete each of the sentences below. Use each word only once.

anecdote	antagonistic	depleting	discretionary
hostile	nurturant	obligatory	preferential
simplistic	vetoed		

1. The students' assignment in the speech class was to share a personal ___anecdote___ about their first day on a college campus.

2. Marla's budget was so strict that she had no money left over for ___discretionary___ spending.

3. The Arctic, with its frigid temperatures, is considered by most to be a ___hostile___ environment.

4. Despite being urged by his advisors to sign the bill, the president followed his conscience and ___vetoed___ it.

5. Environmental groups are especially concerned that we are ___depleting___ our natural resources.

6. In most states, attending high school is ___obligatory___ until age 16.

7. Mike was chosen so often by the teacher to be line leader that the other children complained about his obvious ___preferential___ treatment.

8. The problem was far too complicated for any ___simplistic___ solution.

9. Bill and Todd were always getting into schoolyard fights and had a competitive, ___antagonistic___ relationship.

10. The kindergarten teacher was popular with her young charges because of her kind and ___nurturant___ behavior.

In Your Own Words

1. Do you think position in the family (first, middle, last child) influences certain personality traits? Do you think birth order can affect a person's future lifestyle?

2. The following is a summary of what some researchers have to say about birth order. Do you agree with the information presented? Or do you think that the information in birth-order books sounds a lot like that provided in horoscopes?

Firstborn Children

There have been more firstborn U.S. presidents and Nobel Prize winners than any other birth ranking. They are overrepresented in professions requiring higher education such as medicine, engineering, and law. In terms of personality, they tend to be conscientious, ambitious, aggressive, good at problem solving, strong-willed, determined, controlling, jealous, and moralistic.

Middle Children

Middle children are easygoing and peer oriented. Because they mediate between siblings they tend to have excellent people skills. They are flexible and giving. They have lots of friends, but they can also be manipulative. Many feel forced to assume roles that their older siblings for one reason or another are unable to fulfill, and this may leave them with a chip on their shoulder.

Youngest Children

Later-born children always have someone ahead of them to compete against. Parents are more relaxed and less strict with later-born children, who can be rebellious but are also pleasant, agreeable, and easygoing. They tend to be creative, unconventional, and often feel like the "baby," even when they are adults.

3. Dr. Toni Falbo, professor of educational psychology at the University of Texas, has focused her research on only children and one-child families. She has determined that "onlies" are as normal as their peers in larger family units. In fact, she has discovered that instead of being at a disadvantage, they actually have advantages in certain areas. For instance, their educational attainment is somewhat higher than that of other children, and they tend to have close relationships with their parents. What characteristics of an only child's environment would likely account for this?

4. Frank Sulloway, a professor at the University of California, Berkeley, developed a theory about birth-order effects, which he calls "de-identification." Siblings who want to stand out in their families do so by observing what the eldest child does and then doing the exact opposite. For instance, if the eldest child gets good grades, the second child may become a "slacker." What do you think about this theory? Can you think of any examples from your personal experience?

5. What kinds of lessons do you think are learned from living with siblings? Do you think understanding the role that your siblings played in your life will help you lead a more productive and happy life?

6. If you grew up with a sibling, you likely showed some jealousy of your sibling and vice versa. What can parents do to help children reduce their jealousy toward a sibling?

Written Assignment

Directions: Write a short paragraph explaining one of the following quotations.

1. "In general parents serve the same big-picture role as doctors on grand rounds. Siblings are like the nurses on the ward. They're there every day." (Daniel Shaw, psychologist at the University of Pittsburgh)

2. "Overall, 65% of mothers and 70% of fathers have a favorite child." (Katherine Conger, sociologist at the University of California, Davis)

3. "After the shooting stops, even the fiercest sibling wars leave little lasting damage. Indeed, siblings who battled a lot as kids may become closer as adults." (Thomas O'Connor, professor of psychiatry at the University of Rochester Medical Center)

Internet Activity

Two good Web sites on the topic of sibling rivalry are:

www.kidshealth.org/parent/emotions/feelings/sibling_rivalry.html

www.med.umich.edu/1libr/yourchild/sibriv.htm

Consult one of them to learn more about what causes sibling rivalry and how to control it. Write a few paragraphs discussing your favorite tips on helping kids get along better.

Persuasion/Argumentation

READING

*"On television things that are not visually interesting,
such as thinking, reading and talking, are ignored."*

TUNING IN TO READING   How has TV affected you positively? Negatively? How much TV do you watch in a typical day? In the following excerpt, written in a persuasive mode, the author compares and contrasts the community of the past with the new MTV community. She offers personal and other evidence in an effort to change how we think about the media.

According to the A. C. Nielsen Company, the average American watches 3 hours and 46 minutes of television each day (more than 52 days of nonstop television watching per year). By age 65, the average American will have spent nearly 9 years glued to the tube.

BIO-SKETCH   Dr. Mary Pipher is a clinical psychologist, part-time instructor at the University of Nebraska, nationwide lecturer, and best-selling author. Her book *Reviving Ophelia,* published in 1994, explored the stresses placed on teenage girls by modern society. In 1999, Pipher published *Another Country,* a book about elderly people in America. She observes that "to grow old in the U.S. is to inhabit a foreign country, isolated, disconnected, and misunderstood." In her 1996 book *The Shelter of Each Other,* from which this excerpt is taken, Pipher turns her attention to the stresses placed on the family as a whole. In Pipher's view, the family is so burdened with problems that it can no longer protect family members from the "enemy within," which she defines as inappropriate stimulation from a variety of sources, with TV being at the top of her list.

NOTES ON VOCABULARY

Romeo and Juliet   a tragedy by William Shakespeare about two ill-fated lovers whose romance ends in death because of the feud between their two families.

persona   a character in a fictional work; the public role or personality a person assumes. In Latin, the word for "mask" was *persona.* In ancient Rome, actors wore masks that covered the entire face. Each Roman god was represented by a particular mask so that the audience always knew what god an actor was portraying.

nuance   a slight difference or distinction. The term was borrowed from French and originally referred to a slightly different shade of color.

decry   to denounce or disparage openly.

rule of thumb   a practical method or principle that is based on the wisdom of experience. The expression dates from the 1600s and originally referred to making rough estimates of measurements by using one's thumb.

Tonga Islands   a group of islands in the southwest Pacific Ocean slightly east of Fiji. They are also known as the Friendly Islands.

TV

MARY PIPHER

I N A COLLEGE CLASS I ASKED, "What would it be like to grow up in a world without media?" A student from the Tonga Islands answered, "I never saw television or heard rock and roll until I came to the United States in high school." She paused and looked around the room. "I had a happy childhood. I felt safe all the time. I didn't know I was poor. Or that parents hurt their children or that children hated their parents. I thought I was pretty."

Television has probably been the most powerful medium in shaping the new community. The electronic community gives us our mutual friends, our significant events and our daily chats. The "produced" relationships of television families become our models for intimacy. We know media stars better than we know our neighbors. Most of us can discuss their lives better than we can discuss those of our relatives. We confuse personas and persons. That is, we think a man who plays a doctor on TV actually knows something about medicine. We think a chatty talk show host is truly good-natured. This confusion is especially common with young children, who are developmentally incapable of distinguishing between reality and fantasy. But even adults get mixed up about this.

Most real life is rather quiet and routine. Most pleasures are small pleasures—a hot shower, a sunset, a bowl of good soup or a good book. Television suggests that life is high drama, love and sex. TV families are radically different from real families. Things happen much faster to them. On television things that are not visually interesting, such as thinking, reading and talking, are ignored. Activities such as housework, fund raising and teaching children to read are vastly underreported. Instead of ennobling our ordinary experiences, television suggests that they are not of sufficient interest to document.

These generalizations even fit the way TV portrays the animal kingdom. Specials on animals feature sex, births and killing. Dangerous and cuddly-looking animals are favored. But in reality, most animals are neither dangerous nor cute. Sharks and panda bears are not the main species on the planet. Most animals, like most people, spend most of their time in rather simple ways. They forage and sleep.

TV isolates people in their leisure time. People spend more time watching music videos but less time making music with each other. People in small towns now watch international cable networks instead of driving to their neighbor's house for cards. Women watch soaps instead of attending church circles or book clubs. When company comes, the kids are sent to the TV room with videos. Television is on during meals and kids study to television or radio.

Parents are not the main influences in the lives of their children. Some of the first voices children hear are from the television; the first street they know is Sesame Street. A child playing Nintendo is learning different lessons than a child playing along a creek or playing dominoes with a grandfather. Many children have been conditioned via the media into having highly dysfunctional attention spans.

Adults too have diminished concentration. Neil Postman in *Amusing Ourselves to Death* writes of the 1858 Lincoln/Douglas debates. The average citizen sat for up to seven hours in the heat and listened to these two men discuss issues. People grasped the legal and constitutional issues, moral nuances and political implications. In addition, they could listen to and appreciate intricate and complex sentences. In the 1990s President Clinton's speeches

"Television has proved that people will look at anything rather than each other."

—Ann Landers

Forty percent of 2-year-olds watch three or more hours of TV every day.

were decried by the press and the public when they lasted more than an hour. To an audience socialized to information via sound bite, an hour seems like a long time.

The time devoted to violence on TV in no way reflects its importance 8 in real life. In real life, most of us exercise, work, visit our friends, read, cook and eat and shop. Few of us spend any significant amount of our time solving murders or fleeing psychotic killers. On television there are many more detectives and murderers than exist in the real world. A rule of thumb about violence is "If it bleeds, it leads." Violence captures viewer attention. Our movies have become increasingly violent, and as James Wolcott wrote in *The New Yorker,* "Violence is the real sex now."

Some might argue that there is nothing new under the sun. Of course, 9 in a narrow sense, they are correct. There have always been murderers and rapists, and stories about violence have been themes of literature and song. But things are different now. Children, including toddlers, are exposed to hundreds of examples of violence every day. The frequency and intensity of these images is unprecedented in the history of humanity. We have ample documentation that this exposure desensitizes children, makes it more likely they will be violent and increases their fear levels about potential violence.

Another difference is in the attitudes about violence. *Romeo and Juliet,* 10 for example, was a tragedy. The deaths in the play were presented as a cause of enormous suffering to friends and families and as a terrible waste. When Juliet and Romeo died, something momentous happened in the universe. The very gods were upset. Often today, death is a minor event, of no more consequence than, say the kicking of a flat tire. It's even presented as a joke.

It is one thing to read Shakespeare, which at least requires that the per- 11 son can read. It's another to, day after day, see blood splattered across a screen by "action heroes." It is one thing to show, as Shakespeare did, that violence can be the tragic consequence of misunderstandings, and another to show violence as a thrill, as a solution to human problems or merely as something that happens when people are slightly frustrated or men need to prove they are men.

Of course, one could argue that parents can keep televisions out of 12 their homes. This is extremely hard for the average parent to do. Even if they succeed, their children go from these "protected environments" to play with children who have watched lots of TV and who behave accordingly.

I don't often go to violent movies, but I do have a stake in them. I don't 13 like living in a world where thousands of teenage boys, some of whom own guns, have been reared on them. Walking city streets, I may be accosted by a youth who has spent most of his life watching violent media. Unfortunately, needy children are the ones most affected. Children with the least available parents watch the most TV. Violent television is like secondhand smoke; it affects all of us.

Heavy viewers develop the "mean world syndrome." This leads to a 14 vicious-cycle phenomenon. Because children are afraid and the streets are not safe, they come home right after school and stay indoors. They watch more TV, which makes them more afraid and thus more likely to stay indoors. With everyone indoors the streets are less safe. Families watch more TV and are more fearful and so on.

Television and electronic media have created a new community with 15 entirely different rules and structures than the kinds of communities that have existed for millions of years. Families gather around the glow of the TV as the Lakota once gathered around the glow of a fire on the Great Plains or as the Vikings once huddled around fires in the caves of Scandinavia. They gather as New England families gathered in the 1800s around a fireplace that kept them warm and safe. But our TVs do not keep us warm, safe and together. Rapidly our technology is creating a new kind of human being, one who is plugged into machines instead of relationships, one who lives in a virtual reality rather than a family.

(Mary Pipher, "TV," 1996)

 COMPREHENSION CHECKUP

Short Answer

Directions: Answer the following questions briefly, in no more than a sentence or two.

1. Write the main idea in paragraph 1.

   A life without TV can be a positive, rewarding experience.

2. Write the main idea that is directly stated in paragraph 2. Explain what Pipher means when she says we have trouble distinguishing between "personas and persons." Are children the only ones who have trouble with this?

   The first sentence in paragraph 2 is the main idea. Children and adults both have

   trouble recognizing that the way people behave on TV is different from the way

   they are in real life, that David Letterman isn't necessarily "funny."

3. Summarize the key points that Pipher makes in paragraph 3. How does what you see on the evening local or national news reinforce Pipher's argument?

   We see only extremes on TV, not everyday, ordinary occurrences. News highlights

   the extreme, bizarre, and violent.

4. In paragraph 4, Pipher says that TV distorts our impression of animals. How does TV do this?

   It highlights cute and cuddly animals and the ones that frighten us.

5. What does Pipher say in paragraph 5 about what is happening to our sense of belonging to a community? Is the Internet likely to create strong community ties or weaken them?

   People don't interact face-to-face in their free time. The Internet may cause people to retreat even more.

6. Do you agree with Pipher's assertion that parents are not the primary influences in their children's lives? Why or why not? How do the media contribute to children's short attention spans?

   Parents may no longer be the primary influences. TV is used as an electronic babysitter. TV's short segments in order to fit in a commercial contribute to short attention spans.

7. Paragraphs 8–13 are devoted to a discussion of violence on TV. Why does television portray so much violence? What are some of the effects of violent TV programs on the young?

   Violence raises the ratings. Exposure to violence can cause the young to be less sensitive to real tragedy.

8. Pipher compares and contrasts the modern media's attitude to violence and death with that portrayed in *Romeo and Juliet*. What is the difference she perceives?

   The other characters reacted to their deaths as if it was a great tragedy. Today, we might regard death as no big deal.

9. Many people would suggest that parents are responsible for their own children and so should restrict the amount of time their kids spend watching TV. What is Pipher's response to these critics?

   Even if parents monitor their own children carefully, they are still exposed to other children who watch a lot of TV.

10. Explain the cause-and-effect relationships in paragraph 14.

    Cause: Because children are afraid

    Effect: they stay indoors

    Cause: Because everybody is inside

    Effect: the streets are less safe

11. This article is written in the persuasive mode. What are the key points that Pipher is trying to persuade readers to accept?

    She is trying to persuade us to spend more time interacting with each other and less time interacting with machines.

12. Paragraph 15 compares and contrasts two communities. List the similarities and differences between the two. Then fill in the Venn diagram on the next page with your details.

    Today—gather around TV, separates us, plugged into machines. Then—gather around fire, kept us safe and together, plugged into family.

STUDY TECHNIQUE 7: VENN DIAGRAM

Directions: Making a Venn diagram is a good way to compare and contrast two things. Create a Venn diagram to compare and contrast pre-TV and post-TV communities. First, list everything about the pre-TV community in area A. Next, do the same with the post-TV community in area C. Then, list everything that A and C have in common in area B. When you are finished, the outer areas will show how the two communities are different, and the overlapping area in the middle will show the similarities between the two communities. Use the information in your Venn diagram to write a paragraph comparing and contrasting the two communities.

A   B   C

1. gather around glow of fire
2. keeps us safe, warm, together
3. plugged into relationships
4. lives in family

Family of the past

1. gathering around something
2. relating to something
3. creation of a "community"

1. gather around glow of TV
2. isolates us, produces fear
3. plugged into machines
4. lives in virtual reality

Family of today

Multiple Choice

Directions: For each item, write the letter corresponding to the best answer.

_____a_____ 1. The organizational pattern used in paragraph 2 is
   a. main idea, details.
   b. details, main idea, details.
   c. details, main idea.
   d. no directly stated main idea.

_____d_____ 2. What does Pipher mean by the term "protected environments" in paragraph 12?
   a. She is referring to homes that are middle class.
   b. She is referring to homes in gated communities.
   c. She is referring to homes that have only one television.
   d. She is referring to homes that do not have a television.

_____b_____ 3. From this selection you could conclude that
   a. no one should watch TV.
   b. people should limit the amount of television they and their families watch.
   c. people should spend more time on the Internet.
   d. the government should regulate the content of TV programs.

_d___   4. A likely title for this selection would be
   a. "TV—The Cause of Violence."
   b. "TV versus Shakespeare."
   c. "TV in the Tonga Islands."
   d. "TV and Its Effects on Relationships."

_c___   5. If the author was reading this selection orally, her tone of voice would probably be
   a. admiring.
   b. optimistic.
   c. critical.
   d. amused.

_b___   6. What does Pipher mean when she says that "Violent television is like secondhand smoke" (paragraph 13)?
   a. She means that the effects of violence on television quickly disappear like cigarette smoke.
   b. She means that people who don't watch violence on television are affected by people who do.
   c. She means that there's too much violence on television.
   d. She means that the networks should curb violence on television.

True or False

Directions: Indicate whether each statement is true or false by writing **T** or **F** in the space provided.

_T___   7. Pipher suggests that children whose parents are most available watch the least TV.

_F___   8. Watching television is likely to significantly increase a person's ability to concentrate.

_F___   9. According to Pipher, things happen much more quickly in real life.

_T___ 10. Pipher believes that violence on television causes children to view the world as mean and unsafe.

Vocabulary in Context

Directions: Use the context clues to determine the meaning of the italicized word, and then write a definition for the word in the space provided.

1. Roxana is living a _fantasy_ life, buying clothes, cars, and jewelry she cannot afford.
   unrealistic; product of the imagination

2. Gladys is such a _chatty_ person that Yoko feels a deep need for solitude after spending only a short while with her.
   talkative

3. Wild animals sometimes enter towns to _forage_ for food.
   hunt for; search

4. Children like to sleep with their cute and _cuddly_ teddy bears.
   comfortable; soft and huggable; lovable

5. The _implication_ of running a red light could be a car accident or a ticket.
   result; consequence

6. She was trying to pretend that she was not angry, but *nuances* in her behavior told you that she was.

subtle or slight changes

7. Something *momentous* happened to Tamotsu yesterday—he won the lottery!

of great importance

8. Sandy decided to give up jogging late at night after she was *accosted* by a stranger for the second time in a week.

confronted boldly

Drawing Inferences

Directions: Study the following cartoon carefully, then consider the statements below. If the statement appears to be a valid inference based on the details found in the cartoon, mark it **Y** for yes. If it seems to be an unlikely conclusion, mark it **N** for no.

____Y____ 1. The people standing in line are purchasing tickets to a violent movie.

____N____ 2. They are expecting the film to foster decent values.

____Y____ 3. The cartoonist feels the general public is responsible for the decline in high moral standards in the entertainment industry.

Non Sequitur

NON SEQUITUR © 1995 Wiley Ink, Inc. Dist. By Universal Uclick. Reprinted with permission. All rights reserved.

Written Assignment

Directions: Write a paragraph or two in response to one of the following.

1. Summarize the information presented in a local news show. Identify the subject of each story (murder, robbery, fire, accident, etc.) and the approximate amount of time given to coverage of the story.

2. Watch a TV drama, detective show, soap opera, or movie, and keep track of how many specific acts of violence the show portrays.

3. Find a cartoon in a magazine or newspaper, and write down all that you can logically infer from it. Share the cartoon with a classmate and see if your inferences "match."

4. How does the cartoon support Mary Pipher's argument?

Internet Activity

If you have children at home, you may want to limit the amount of time they spend watching TV. The site below, sponsored by the Kansas National Education Association, has some information that may help you. Print out a page and highlight the tips that you think might work.

http://ks.nea.org/parents/tvviewing.html

Chapter Summary and Review

In Chapter 8, you became familiar with the four modes of writing: narrative, descriptive, expository, and persuasive. Based on the material in Chapter 8, answer the following.

Short Answer

Directions: Find an example for each of the modes of writing from previous selections in this book. Explain your choices.

1. Narrative: Answers will vary.

   Reasons for choice: _____

2. Descriptive: _____

   Reasons for choice: _____

3. Expository: _____

   Reasons for choice: _____

4. Persuasive: _____

   Reasons for choice: _____

Vocabulary in Context

Directions: Choose one of the following words to complete the sentences below. Use each word only once.

      arguments   controversial   expository   mode   time-order   visual

5. Textbook material is usually written in a(n) __expository__ mode.

6. Persuasive writing often presents __arguments__ about __controversial__ topics.

7. An article written in the descriptive mode usually draws on __visual__ perceptions.

8. Stories written in the narrative mode often follow a(n) __time-order__ sequence.

9. Sometimes an author will use more than one __mode__ of writing.

Vocabulary   Unit 5 Word Parts Dealing with Direction and Position

All the word parts in this unit are related to either direction or position.

super—above or over
sub—under, below, beneath

supersonic   *Super* means "above," and *sonus* means "sound," so *supersonic* means moving at a speed greater than that of sound.

supersonic—Chuck Yaeger made the first supersonic flight October 14, 1947, over Edwards Air Force Base in California.

supervisor	A person who oversees or directs work or workers. The original meaning of the word was "to see from above."
superscript	A figure, letter, or symbol written above the line. In math, 10 squared would be written 10^2, with the 2 being a *superscript.*
subscript	A figure, letter, or symbol written below the line. The chemical formula for water, H_2O, has a *subscript.*
subscribe	To agree to pay for a service or periodical. Originally, when you *subscribed* to a magazine, you signed your name at the bottom of the contract on the dotted line.
subliminal	*Limen* means "threshold." If something is *subliminal,* it is below the threshold of consciousness. The sale of audiocassette tapes with *subliminal* self-help messages is a big business in the United States. While you are sleeping, you could listen to a weight-loss tape with a *subliminal* message saying "eat less."

retro—backward, back, behind

retroactive	Having an effect on things that are past; going back in time. If you received *retroactive* pay, you would be paid for work that was done in the past.
retrorocket	A small rocket that produces a backward thrust in order to reduce speed.
retrogress	To move backward toward an earlier or worse condition; to decline. After learning new study techniques, the student *retrogressed* to her old methods of studying and just read the chapter the night before the quiz.
retrospect	To see back in time; hindsight. In *retrospect,* the cook should have added more garlic to her soup.

ante(i)—before, in front of, prior to
ad—toward

Sometimes spellings of word parts change over the years. In the word part *anti,* sometimes the "e" changes to "i." This causes confusion with the word part *anti* meaning "opposite of." What do you think was the original meaning of the word *antifreeze?* Sometimes you have to use the context of a sentence to determine the meaning of a word part. When in doubt, consult a dictionary.

anticipate	To look forward to something before it happens. She was *anticipating* a pleasant two-week vacation in Hawaii.
ante	In poker, each player must *ante* up (place a bet) before receiving cards.
anteroom	A small room before a larger or more important room. *Anterooms* can be lobbies, vestibules, or waiting rooms.
antecedent	Coming before in time, order, or logic. In English grammar, the *antecedent* of a pronoun is the noun to which the pronoun refers. In the sentence "The team will win the game if it plays well," the *antecedent* of the pronoun "it" is the word "team."
antebellum	*Bellum* means "war," so *antebellum* means "before the war." The word is often used in relation to the American Civil War. The *antebellum* days of the South were approximately 1820–1860.

advance	*"Ance"* originally came from *ante,* and so the word *advance* literally translates as "toward before." The hurricane rapidly *advanced* on the helpless town.
adolescent	A person moving toward adulthood or maturity.
advent	*Ven* means "come," so *advent* means "to come toward." To Christians, the season of *Advent* includes the four Sundays before Christmas.
advertise	*Vert* means "to turn," so *advertise* means "to turn toward." *Advertising* praises a service or product so that people will want to turn toward it, or buy it.

circ—ring; around   cycle—circle; wheel

circulate—In one year, the human heart circulates 770,000 to 1.6 million gallons of blood. This is enough to fill 200 tank cars, each with a capacity of 8,000 gallons.

circumference—The circumference of a quarter has 119 grooves; a dime has one fewer.

circle	A *circle* is a plane figure, but the word also means "to surround" or "move around."
circulate	To move in a circle and return to the same point; to move around freely. Blood *circulates* through the body.
circumference	The measure of the distance around a circle.
circumnavigate	To sail or fly around, as in *circumnavigating* the earth. The first American to *circumnavigate* the earth in a space vehicle was John Glenn.
circumscribe	To draw a line around. The student *circumscribed* the correct answer on the quiz by drawing a circle around it.
circumspect	To look all around or to consider all circumstances before deciding.
circadian	Relating to a person's daily biological cycle.
circa	*Circa* means "around" or "approximately," in reference to a period of time or the date of an event, especially when the exact dates are not known. Jazz began in the United States *circa* 1920.
bicycle	To ride or travel on a two-wheeled vehicle.
cyclorama	No, not a track for bicycles. A *cyclorama* is a series of large pictures put on the wall of a circular room so that a spectator standing in the middle can see all around (360 degrees). If you have been to Disneyland, you might have seen a movie in a *cyclorama.*
cyclical	Moving or occurring in a circular pattern. Fashions in clothing tend to be *cyclical.* Men's ties gradually become wider, and then gradually become narrower, and then start the cycle over.

pan—all; every; around   peri—around; about

Panavision®	See all around. The movie was in *Panavision.* Movies in *Panavision* are not really all around you, but are simply on a large screen.
Panasonic®	Sound all around. Do you think you really get sound all around you from a *Panasonic* transistor radio?
panorama	A wide view. A synonym for *panorama* is *vista.* From the top of the mountain, the sunset produced a beautiful *panorama.*

Pan-American—The Pan-Am Highway is the longest driveable road in the world. It is 15,000 miles long. It goes from northwest Alaska, down through Santiago, Chile, east through Argentina, and ends in Brasilia, Brazil.

panacea   A cure-all; or the act of going around the problem. Owners of sports teams often resort to firing the coach as a *panacea* for the team's failure to win enough games. Some people view building more prisons as a *panacea* to the crime problem.

Pan-American   Common to North, South, and Central America together. The diplomats negotiated a *Pan-American* treaty to deal with poaching of endangered species.

perimeter   The outer boundary or measurement around a figure or area. The soldiers guarding the camp walked along its *perimeter*.

peripheral   Lying at the outside. Because he has so much money already, it is of only *peripheral* importance to him whether he gets a job. You might have your driver's license revoked if you have poor *peripheral* vision.

periscope   An optical instrument used on submarines that goes up to the surface and allows a person to "look around."

Exercise 1

Directions: In the blanks below, write the word from the list that best completes the sentence. Use each word only once.

adolescent	anteroom	anticipating	circulate	circumspect
panacea	perimeter	retrospect	subscribe	supervisor

1. Ginny can't seem to get along with her ___supervisor___ at work, so she's going to have to start looking for another job.

2. Oscar was ___anticipating___ his 21st birthday because his friends were taking him to Las Vegas to celebrate.

3. There is no easy ___panacea___ for the problem of poverty in the United States because every possible solution creates a host of unforeseen complications.

4. In trying to win a sweepstakes award, many people ___subscribe___ to a large number of magazines they don't really want.

5. In ___retrospect___, Herminia should have known that the free, all-expenses-paid vacation to the Bahamas was too good to be true.

6. The legislator waited in the ___anteroom___ for about 30 minutes talking to the president's secretary before being admitted to the president's private study.

7. At a wedding reception, it's considered good manners for the bride and groom to ___circulate___ among all of their guests.

8. Many parents find it difficult to understand and cope with a(n) ___adolescent___ and are glad when the teenage years finally end.

9. Since his last brush with the law, Mark has behaved in a very ___circumspect___ manner, going out of his way to stay out of trouble.

10. Bandit patrols the ___perimeter___ of his yard to make sure no other dog has dared trespass.

Exercise 2

Directions: Write the word from the list that best completes the sentence. Use each word only once.

advent	antebellum	antecedent	circa	circumference
circumscribe	cyclical	panorama	peripheral	retroactive

1. The most famous and probably most photographed ____antebellum____ mansion in Louisiana is Oak Alley, where parts of *Interview with a Vampire* and *Primary Colors* were filmed.

2. Does the ____circumference____ of a person's head have anything to do with how smart the person is? Some studies suggest there may be a correlation.

3. Only one item has been in the White House since the very beginning—the Gilbert Stuart painting of George Washington ____circa____ 1800.

4. The cab crashed because of a number of ____antecedent____ events, including the cab company's failure to replace faulty brakes and its hiring of a careless driver.

5. With the ____advent____ of winter, Victor knew he would soon have to put snow tires on his car.

6. After a six-month training period at Bank of America, Diarra received a salary of $9 an hour. She also got some back pay, because her new salary was ____retroactive____ to when she first started her training.

7. Watching her young daughter go out the door in a tank top and bell bottoms reminded Charlene of clothes she had worn as an adolescent. She realized just how ____cyclical____ fashion is.

8. Edwin stood on the edge of the Grand Canyon and looked at the ____panorama____ spread before him. The breathtaking view filled him with awe.

9. My father, who is in his eighties, is no longer allowed to drive because of an impairment of his ____peripheral____ vision.

10. The teacher told the student to look on the map of California and ____circumscribe____ Santa Clara County in red ink.

Expanding Your Word Power

The words listed below are not found in this Vocabulary Unit, but they are derived from the vocabulary word parts that you have studied. All of them would be good words for you to learn. See if you can guess the meaning of each word from its word parts.

1. superimpose	9. retrofit	17. circumvent
2. superstar	10. antechamber	18. pandemic
3. supernatural	11. anterior	19. pandemonium
4. substandard	12. antacid	20. panopoly
5. subconscious	13. antipathy	21. peistalsis
6. subway	14. antithesis	22. periodontal
7. subjugate	15. antisocial	23. peripatetic
8. subversion	16. circuitous	

Vocabulary Unit 5 Crossword Puzzle

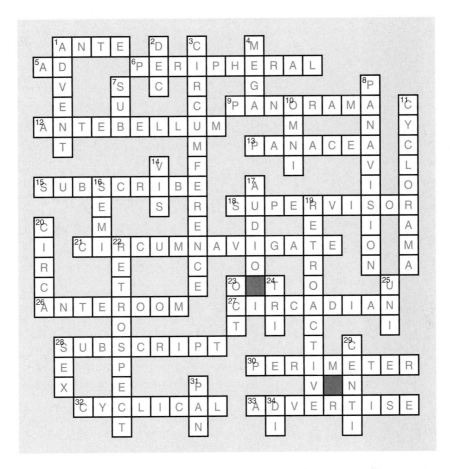

ACROSS CLUES

1. What you might do at the beginning of a poker game before receiving your cards.
5. A word part meaning "toward."
6. _____ vision is to the side.
9. You might see a beautiful _____ (synonym for *vista*) from the top of a mountain.
12. The _____ days of the South were those preceding the Civil War.
13. A cure-all.
15. To sign your name at the bottom of a contract.
18. A person who oversees.
21. John Glenn was able to _____ the earth.
26. A lobby or vestibule.
27. Your daily biological rhythm is your _____ cycle.

28. The formula for carbon dioxide has a(n) _____ in it.
30. An outer boundary is called a(n) _____.
32. Occurring in cycles.
33. The literal meaning is "to turn toward."

DOWN CLUES

1. The period of time before Christmas.
2. The abbreviation for what was once the 10th month.
3. The distance around a circle.
4. A word part meaning "large."
7. A word part meaning "under."
8. The movie was in _____.
10. A word part meaning "all."
11. Large pictures all around you in a circular room.

14. A word part meaning "see."
16. A word part meaning "half."
17. A word part meaning "hear."
19. Back pay is _____.
20. The antique was _____ 1900.
22. In hindsight or _____.
23. The abbreviation for what was once the 8th month.
24. A word part meaning "three."
25. A word part meaning "one."
28. A word part meaning "six."
29. A word part meaning "100."
31. A word part meaning "around."
34. A word part meaning "two."

CHAPTER 9

Modes of Organization

CHAPTER PREVIEW

In this chapter, you will

- Become familiar with the following modes, or patterns, of organization: classification or division (categories); listing; comparison-contrast; examples; chronological order; steps in a process; and cause and effect.

- Practice writing summaries of longer selections.

- Practice study techniques.

Introduction to Modes of Organization

Once a writer has selected a mode of writing, he or she needs to select one or more **modes of organization.** The modes of organization are (1) classification or division (categories); (2) listing; (3) comparison-contrast; (4) examples; (5) chronological order; (6) steps in a process; and (7) cause and effect. These categories should be familiar to you, because they previously appeared in this book as patterns of organization for paragraphs.

A writer who wishes to write in a persuasive mode might choose as modes of organization comparison-contrast, definition, and examples. A writer who wishes to write in a descriptive mode might select examples and chronological order. Sometimes an author may organize an entire selection using only one mode of organization.

Writers select the modes of writing and organization that will best enable them to communicate with their audience. Being able to recognize the different modes of writing and organization will help you become a better reader.

Readings about Happiness That Illustrate the Modes of Organization

What makes for a happy life is an age-old question, and this section of the book seeks to shed some light on the issue.

There is an ancient fable about happiness that is common in many cultures. Once upon a time there was an old king who was greatly worried about his son. The young prince was terribly unhappy, and although the king tried everything in his power, he could not convince his son to enjoy life. In despair, the king called his advisors to him. They counseled him by saying that the only cure for unhappiness was to obtain the shirt of a happy man and present it to the young prince. The king, thinking this to be a simple task, was greatly relieved. He eagerly sent his messengers out to search. For two years, they roved far and wide throughout the kingdom, visiting every town and village. At last, they rejoiced in locating one supremely happy man. Unfortunately, for the king and the young prince, the poor farmer, though gloriously happy, possessed no shirt.

The moral of this fable is that happiness does not depend upon material possessions, can't be given to another, and, above all, is elusive. The writer Nathaniel Hawthorne once said, "Happiness is a butterfly, which when pursued, is always just beyond your grasp, but which, if you will sit down quietly, may alight upon you."

This book has already introduced a variety of study techniques, and you have practiced many of them. In this chapter, we will review some of the techniques you are already familiar with and present some new ones. You will have a chance to practice your skills with a variety of reading selections that illustrate the different modes of organization. All focus on the theme of happiness. By the time you finish, perhaps you will have reached some sort of conclusion about what happiness means to you.

STUDY TECHNIQUE 8: MORE PRACTICE WITH SQ3R

SQ3R (**S**urvey, **Q**uestion, **R**ead, **R**ecite, and **R**eview) is a classic system for reading and studying textbook material. You are going to be practicing the SQ3R study skills techniques on the next reading selection "The Roots of Happiness: An Empirical Analysis." We have marked the first nine paragraphs of the reading selection. You are going to mark the remaining paragraphs when you get to Step 3 of SQ3R. (If you need to refresh your memory about SQ3R, refer to the information presented in Chapter 1.)

STEP 1: SURVEY

Directions: Survey the pre-reading sections of "The Roots of Happiness: An Empirical Analysis" (Tuning in to Reading, Bio-Sketch, and Notes on Vocabulary), the title of the selection, the headings and subheadings, and the scale. Then answer the following questions.

1. Think about what you already know about the subject of happiness. Do you personally know anyone who is happy? Can you say why that person is happy? Write a sentence below about happiness.
   <u>Answers will vary.</u>

2. Judging from the information about the author in the bio-sketch and the title of the selection, do you think the author's purpose is to inform, to entertain, or to persuade?
   <u>Inform</u>

3. What factors aren't very important in promoting happiness?
   <u>money, age, gender, parenthood, intelligence, physical attractiveness</u>

4. What factors are somewhat important in promoting happiness?
   <u>health, social activity, and religion</u>

5. What factors are very important in promoting happiness?
   <u>love and marriage, work, and personality</u>

continued

STUDY TECHNIQUE *continued*

6. Judging from the information in the faces scale, did the majority of respondents in the United States choose a happy face or an unhappy face to express their feelings about their "life as a whole"?

happy face

STEP 2: QUESTION

Directions: Compose at least one question that you'd like to have answered by the reading, and then turn a subheading into a question that you can answer.

1. After surveying the selection, you should have at least one question about the material. Write your question below.

Answers will vary.

2. Now turn a subheading into a question. For instance, for subheading 1, you might ask, "Why isn't money very important to happiness?" Or "Don't you need money to be happy?" Write a question for subheading 2 below.

Answers will vary.

STEP 3: READ

Directions: While you are looking for answers to your questions, underline or highlight the key words, the key phrases, and the main ideas in the selection. Make notes in the margins to explain the key points in your own words. The three introductory paragraphs, along with the first heading—"What Isn't Very Important?"—and the six subheadings—money, age, gender, parenthood, intelligence, and physical attractiveness—have been annotated for you as an example. Examine what we've done and then go ahead and annotate the following headings and subheadings.

Try to answer the following questions. If you have difficulty, read the material again.

1. On the average, are wealthier people happier than those in the middle class?

Yes, but they are only slightly happier.

2. Is job satisfaction strongly related to happiness?

Yes, it is.

STEP 4: RECITE

Directions: Organize the material you have learned and put it into your own words. Then say it out loud.

Recite the answers to the following questions.

1. What exactly makes a person happy?

love and marriage, work, and personality

2. What is the best predictor of an individual's future happiness?

past happiness

STEP 5: REVIEW

Directions: Continual review leads to success. Test yourself on the material over and over again. Go back to your original questions. Can you still answer them? Quiz yourself on the material you underlined. Make sure you can sum up the author's main ideas.

Can you fill in the missing details below?

1. Happiness depends more on ____internal____ factors than on ____external____ factors.

2. Job ____satisfaction____ is strongly related to general happiness.

3. ____Married____ people are happier than people who are single or divorced.

Now read "The Roots of Happiness: An Empirical Analysis" carefully and answer the Comprehension Checkup questions.

Categories, Listing, and Comparison-Contrast

This reading is divided into three categories: factors that do not predict happiness ("What Isn't Very Important?"), moderately good predictors of happiness ("What Is Somewhat Important?"), and strong predictors of happiness ("What Is Very Important?"). It looks at a list of factors, such as money, age, and gender, and then seeks to evaluate how important each factor is for achieving happiness. For instance, the reading takes gender and then considers whether males or females have a better chance of happiness (comparison-contrast). So you can see that this reading involves the following patterns of organization: categories, listing, and comparison-contrast.

READING

"Not surprisingly, people who like themselves tend to be happier than those who do not."

TUNING IN TO READING   While the Declaration of Independence says that everyone has the right to "life, liberty, and the pursuit of happiness," only recently have psychologists begun to explore what makes people happy. A 2002 study conducted at the University of Illinois by Edward Diener and Martin Seligman found that students reporting the highest levels of happiness had strong ties to friends and family. The researchers concluded that close relationships with others are important in order to be happy. They also discovered that some people are more likely to be happy than others. In general, those who have an optimistic personality are more likely to label themselves as happy. Read the following selection to find out what else correlates with happiness. As you read, note the primary mode of organization: comparison-contrast.

BIO-SKETCH   Wayne Weiten, a professor of psychology at the University of Nevada, Las Vegas, is a trained social psychologist with a research interest in stress and health psychology. He has received many awards for excellence in teaching and research, and is the author and coauthor of several best-selling psychology textbooks.

Margaret A. Lloyd retired from teaching in 2004. She is currently professor emerita and chair of psychology at Georgia Southern University and has been a recipient of that institution's Award for Excellence for Contributions to Instruction. She was also very active in the establishment and development of the Women's and Gender Studies program at Georgia Southern.

NOTES ON VOCABULARY

commonsense   exhibiting sound practical judgment. Coming in out of the rain is considered a *commonsense* action.

heartfelt   deeply or sincerely felt. An Academy Award winner might give *heartfelt* thanks to the movie's producer and director.

voracious   insatiable; greedy. From the Latin *vorare,* meaning "to devour." Many dogs have *voracious* appetites.

THE ROOTS OF HAPPINESS: AN EMPIRICAL ANALYSIS
Wayne Weiten and Margaret A. Lloyd

MI
EX **W**hat exactly makes a person happy? This question has been the subject of much speculation. Commonsense theories about the roots of happiness abound. For example, you have no doubt heard that money cannot buy happiness. But do you believe it? A television commercial says, "If you've got your health, you've got just about everything." Is health indeed the key? What if you're healthy but poor, unemployed, and lonely? We often hear about the joys of parenthood, the joys of youth, and the joys of the simple, rural life. Are these the factors that promote happiness?

In recent years, social scientists have begun putting these and other theo- 2 ries to empirical test. Quite a number of survey studies have been conducted

Summary
MI

to explore the determinants of happiness. The findings of these studies are quite interesting. <u>As you will see, many commonsense notions about happiness appear to be inaccurate.</u>

Contrast

MI

The first of these is the apparently widespread assumption that most peo- 3 ple are relatively unhappy. Writers, social scientists, and the general public seem to believe that people around the world are predominantly dissatisfied, <u>yet</u> surveys consistently find that the vast majority of respondents characterize themselves as fairly happy. When people are asked to rate their happiness, only a small minority place themselves below the neutral point on the various scales used. <u>The overall picture seems rosier than anticipated.</u>

What Isn't Very Important?

Money

There is a positive correlation between income and feelings of happiness, but 4 the association is surprisingly weak. Admittedly, <u>being very poor can make people unhappy,</u> but once people ascend above the poverty level, there is little relation between income and happiness. On the average, even <u>wealthy people are only slightly happier</u> than those in the middle classes. The problem with money is that in this era of voracious consumption, most people find a way to spend all their money and come out short, no matter how much they make. <u>Complaints about not having enough money are routine</u> even among affluent people who earn six-figure incomes.

Age

Age and happiness are consistently found to be unrelated. <u>Age accounts for 5 less than 1 percent</u> of the variation in people's happiness. The key factors influencing people's thoughts about their own well-being may shift some as people grow older—work becomes less important, health more so—but <u>people's average level of happiness tends to remain remarkably stable over the life span.</u>

Gender

Women are treated for depressive disorders about twice as often as men, so 6 one might expect that women are less happy on the average. However, <u>like age, gender accounts for less than 1 percent of the variation</u> in people's happiness.

Parenthood

Children can be a tremendous source of joy and fulfillment, but they also can 7 be a tremendous source of headaches and hassles. Compared to childless couples, parents worry more and experience more marital problems. Apparently <u>the good and bad aspects of parenthood balance each other out,</u> because the evidence indicates that people who have children are neither more nor less happy than people without children.

Intelligence

Intelligence is a highly valued trait in modern society, but researchers have <u>not 8 found an association between IQ scores and happiness. Educational attainment</u> also appears to be unrelated to life satisfaction.

Physical Attractiveness

Good-looking people enjoy a variety of advantages in comparison to unattract- 9 ive people. Given that physical attractiveness is an important resource in West- ern society, we might expect attractive people to be happier than others, but the available data indicate that the <u>correlation between attractiveness and hap- piness is negligible</u>.

What Is Somewhat Important?

Research has identified three facets of life that appear to have a moderate 10 impact on subjective well-being: health, social activity, and religious belief.

Health

Good physical health would seem to be an essential requirement for happi- 11 ness, but people adapt to health problems. Research reveals that individuals who develop serious, disabling health conditions aren't as unhappy as one might guess. Furthermore, good health does not, by itself, produce happi- ness, because people tend to take good health for granted. Researchers found only a moderate positive correlation between health status and subjective well-being.

Social Activity

Humans are social beings, and people's interpersonal relations do appear to 12 contribute to their happiness. People who are satisfied with their friendship networks and who are socially active report above-average levels of happiness. At the other end of the spectrum, people troubled by loneliness tend to be very unhappy.

Religion

A number of large-scale surveys suggest that people with heartfelt religious 13 convictions are more likely to be happy than people who characterize them- selves as nonreligious.

What Is Very Important?

The list of factors that turn out to be very important ingredients of happi- 14 ness is surprisingly short. Only a few variables are strongly related to overall happiness.

Love and Marriage

Romantic relationships can be stressful, but people consistently rate being in 15 love as one of the most critical ingredients of happiness. Furthermore, although people complain a lot about their marriages, the evidence indicates that mar- ital status is a key correlate of happiness. Among both men and women, mar- ried people are happier than people who are single or divorced.

Work

Given the way people often complain about their jobs, we might not expect 16 work to be a key source of happiness, but it is. Although less critical than love and marriage, job satisfaction is strongly related to general happiness. Studies also show that unemployment has devastating effects on subjective well-being.

Personality

The best predictor of individuals' future happiness is their past happiness. [17] Some people seem destined to be happy and others unhappy, regardless of their triumphs or setbacks. Several studies suggest that happiness does not depend on external circumstances—having a nice house, good friends, and an enjoyable job—as much as internal factors, such as one's outlook on life. With this reality in mind, researchers have begun to look for links between personality and subjective well-being, and they have found some relatively strong connections. For example, self-esteem is one of the best predictors of happiness. Not surprisingly, people who like themselves tend to be happier than those who do not. Other personality correlates of happiness include extraversion, optimism, and a sense of personal control over one's life.

(Wayne Weiten and Margaret A. Lloyd, *Psychology Applied to Modern Life*, 7/e, 2003)

Most People in the United States Rate Themselves as Happy, While Only a Small Minority Indicate They Are "Not too Happy."

Faces Scale

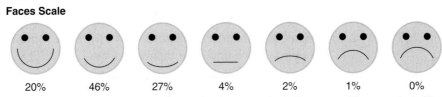

| 20% | 46% | 27% | 4% | 2% | 1% | 0% |

"Which face comes closest to expressing how you feel about your life as a whole?"

Source: Myers, 2000, p. 57, drawn from Social Indicators of Well-Being: Americans' Perceptions of Life Quality (pp. 207 and 306), by F. M. Andrews and S. B. Withey, 1976. New York, Plenum. Copyright 1976 by Plenum.

✔ COMPREHENSION CHECKUP

True or False

Directions: Indicate whether each statement is true or false by writing **T** or **F** in the space provided.

___T___ 1. Happy people like themselves.

___T___ 2. Happy people feel in control of the events in their lives.

___F___ 3. Happy people are pessimistic.

___F___ 4. Single people are happier than married people.

___F___ 5. Most people are moderately unhappy most of the time.

___T___ 6. Being very poor can make people unhappy.

___T___ 7. Men and women are about equally happy.

___T___ 8. Job satisfaction correlates favorably with happiness.

___T___ 9. An extravert is more likely to be happy than an introvert.

___T___ 10. People tend to take good health for granted.

Vocabulary in Context

Directions: In the blanks below, write the word from the list that best completes the sentence. Use each word only once.

above-average	adapt	childless	correlation	depressive
essential	ingredient	internal	loneliness	marital
negligible	nonreligious	satisfaction	weak	

1. There is a positive association between income and feelings of happiness, but the association is surprisingly __weak__.

2. Women are treated for __depressive__ disorders about twice as often as men.

3. Compared with __childless__ couples, parents worry more and experience more __marital__ problems.

4. We might expect attractive people to be happier than others, but the available data indicate that the __correlation__ between attractiveness and happiness is __negligible__.

5. Good physical health would seem to be a(n) __essential__ requirement for happiness, but people __adapt__ to health problems.

6. People satisfied with their friendship networks report __above-average__ levels of happiness, but people troubled by __loneliness__ tend to be very unhappy.

7. People with heartfelt religious convictions are more likely to be happy than people who characterize themselves as __nonreligious__.

8. While romantic relationships can be stressful, people rate being in love as a critical __ingredient__ of happiness.

9. Although less critical than love and marriage, job __satisfaction__ is strongly related to general happiness.

10. Studies suggest that happiness does not depend on external circumstances as much as on __internal__ factors.

Vocabulary Matching

Directions: Match the vocabulary words in Column A with their antonyms in Column B. Place the correct letter in the space provided.

	Column A	Column B
_f_	1. rosier	a. objective
_i_	2. affluent	b. incidental
_d_	3. routine	c. unsocial
_g_	4. negligible	d. unusual
_a_	5. subjective	e. pessimism
_b_	6. essential	f. gloomier
_j_	7. moderate	g. significant
_c_	8. interpersonal	h. disaster
_e_	9. optimism	i. impoverished
_h_	10. triumph	j. extreme

Completion

Directions: In the chart below, rank the following traits for their importance to your happiness: wealth, parenthood, health, social activity, religious commitment, marriage, and work. Explain your ranking.

1. _____

2. _____

3. _____

4. _____

5. _____

6. _____

7. _____

_____

_____

_____

In Your Own Words

1. Why do you think the loss of a job can be so devastating to a person's sense of well-being? Does it help that a person is able to turn life's lemons into lemonade?

2. Are you surprised that parenthood is in the category "What Isn't Very Important"? What kinds of stresses do parents face today? Do you think raising children today is harder or easier than it was a generation ago?

3. Are you surprised that "wealthy people are only slightly happier than those in the middle classes"? Does it surprise you that people who win the lottery soon revert to their level of happiness before their big win? How do you account for this?

4. Does acting happy or putting on a happy face actually help you feel happy?

Written Assignment

Professor Martin Seligman believes that "interpersonal virtues like kindness and gratitude are strongly tied to happiness." According to research, he says, "giving puts meaning into your life." This premise is illustrated in the success of *Extreme Makeover Home Edition,* a popular reality show in which a lucky individual receives a completely remodeled house. In some cases, hundreds of volunteers have participated in the makeovers. Dubbed "Good Samaritan" TV, the program is just the first in a list of similar programs. Does practicing "random acts of kindness" really lead to happiness? Write a short essay giving your opinion.

Internet Activity

Ed Diener, a psychology professor at the University of Illinois, has developed "The Satisfaction with Life" scale. To take the quiz, go to:

www.psych.uiuc.edu/~ediener/hottopic/hottopic.html

Explain what you learned about yourself. Did the quiz confirm what you already knew about yourself? Did it give you new insight into your personality?

Examples

The following selection from a sociology textbook gives examples of individuals who won a great deal of money in the lottery, but then didn't exactly live "happily ever after."

READING

"In other words, sudden wealth poses a threat that has to be guarded against."

TUNING IN TO READING   What would you do if you won a million dollars? Do you think it would make you happy? Or do you think suddenly acquiring considerable wealth might cause problems in your life?

BIO-SKETCH   James M. Henslin is a professor emeritus in the department of sociology at Southern Illinois University. He has written textbooks and published extensively in sociology journals. His two favorite activities are writing and traveling.

NOTES ON VOCABULARY

lottery   a way of raising money by selling numbered tickets and giving prizes to the holders of the numbers drawn at random.

scratch-off ticket   With this particular type of ticket, you don't have to wait for a specific date and time to find out if you're a winner. You buy a ticket and scratch a special coating off. If it's a winning ticket you'll know right away.

anomie   a personal state of isolation and anxiety that comes from a lack of purpose or ideals.

status inconsistency   According to sociologists, there are three dimensions of social class: property, prestige, and power. If people have a mixture of high and low ranks, the condition is called status inconsistency. Instant wealth can often cause status inconsistency.

THE BIG WIN: LIFE AFTER THE LOTTERY
James M. Henslin

"If I just win the lottery, life will be good. These problems I've got, they'll be gone. I can just see myself now."

So goes the dream. And many Americans shell out megabucks every week, 2 with the glimmering hope that "Maybe this week, I'll hit it big."

Most are lucky to hit for $10, or maybe just another scratch-off ticket.   3

But there are the big hits. What happens to these winners? Are their lives 4 all roses and chocolate afterwards?

Unfortunately, we don't have any systematic studies of the big winners, so 5 I can't tell you what life is like for the average winner. But several themes are apparent from reporters' interviews.

The most common consequence of hitting it big is that life becomes topsy- 6 turvy. All of us are rooted somewhere. We have connections with others that provide the basis for our orientations to life and how we feel about the world. Sudden wealth can rip these moorings apart, and the resulting *status inconsistency* can lead to a condition sociologists call *anomie*.

First, comes the shock. As Mary Sanderson, a telephone operator in Dover, 7
New Hampshire, who won $66 million, said, "I was afraid to believe it was real,
and afraid to believe it wasn't." Mary says she never slept worse than her first
night as a multimillionaire. "I spent the whole time crying—and throwing up."

Reporters and TV cameras appear on your doorstep. "What are you going 8
to do with all that money?" they demand. You haven't the slightest idea, but
in a daze you mumble something.

Then come the calls. Some are welcome. Your mom and dad call to con- 9
gratulate you. But long-forgotten friends and distant relatives suddenly remember how close they really are to you—and strangely enough, they all have
emergencies that your money can solve. You even get calls from strangers who
have sick mothers, sick kids, sick dogs . . .

You have to unplug the phone and get an unlisted number.   10

Some lottery winners are flooded with marriage proposals. These individu- 11
als certainly didn't become more attractive or sexy overnight—or did they?
Maybe money makes people sexy.

You can no longer trust people. You don't know what their real motives 12
are. Before, no one could be after your money because you didn't have any.
You may even fear kidnappers. Before, this wasn't a problem—unless some
kidnapper wanted the ransom of a seven-year-old car.

The normal becomes abnormal. Even picking out a wedding gift is a prob- 13
lem. If you give the usual toaster, everyone will think you're stingy. But should
you write a check for $25,000? If you do, you'll be invited to every wedding
in town—and everyone will expect the same.

Here is what happened to some lottery winners: 14

As a tip, a customer gave a lottery ticket to Tonda Dickerson, a waitress at 15
the Waffle House in Grand Bay, Alabama. She won $10 million. Her co-workers
sued her, saying they had always agreed to split such winnings.

Then there is Michael Klingebiel of Rahway, New Jersey. When he won 16
$2 million, his mother, Phyllis, said they had pooled $20 a month for years to
play the lottery. He said that was true, but his winning ticket wasn't from their
pool. He bought this one on his own. Phyllis sued her son.

Frank Capaci, a retired electrician in Streamwood, Illinois, who won 17
$195 million, is no longer welcome at his neighborhood bar, where he had
hung out for years. Two bartenders had collected $5 from customers and
driven an hour to Wisconsin to buy tickets. When Frank won, he gave $10,000
to each of them. They said he promised them more. Also, his former friends
say that Capaci started to act "like a big shot," buying rounds of drinks but
saying, "Except him," while pointing to someone he didn't like.

Those who avoid *anomie* seem to be people who don't make sudden 18
changes in their lifestyles or their behavior. They hold on to their old friends,
routines, and other moorings in life that give them identity. Some even keep
their old jobs—not for the money, of course, but because it anchors them to
an identity with which they are familiar and comfortable.

In other words, sudden wealth poses a threat that has to be guarded 19
against.

And I can just hear you say, "I'll take the risk!"   20

(James M. Henslin, *Essentials of Sociology*, 7/e, 2007)

COMPREHENSION CHECKUP

Multiple Choice

Directions: For each item, write the letter corresponding to the best answer.

_____c_____ 1. A *systematic* study is one that is
    a. methodical.
    b. orderly.
    c. both a and b.
    d. none of the above.

_____c_____ 2. What is the meaning of "average winner" as used in paragraph 5?
    a. equitable
    b. intermediate
    c. usual or typical
    d. mediocre

_____a_____ 3. What is the meaning of "all roses and chocolate" as used in paragraph 4?
    a. happiness and prosperity
    b. petals and thorns
    c. hard work and trouble
    d. gardens and candy stores

_____a_____ 4. In paragraph 4, the transition word *but* implies a
    a. contrast.
    b. definition.
    c. conclusion.
    d. comparison.

_____d_____ 5. What is the relationship between the sentence beginning in paragraph 7 ("First, comes the shock") and the sentence beginning in paragraph 9 ("Then come the calls")?
    a. cause and effect
    b. comparison-contrast
    c. definition and example
    d. steps in a process

_____c_____ 6. The author describes all of the following events happening to lottery winners *except*
    a. being besieged by requests from various people.
    b. being sued by coworkers who claimed to be cowinners.
    c. being forced to file for bankruptcy within a few years.
    d. being inundated by marriage proposals.

_____c_____ 7. Identify the statement that most accurately states the main idea.
    a. Money makes people sexy.
    b. Winning the lottery makes life good.
    c. Sudden wealth creates problems that have to be managed.
    d. For a lottery winner, wise financial investments are essential.

_____d_____ 8. From the selection, we can conclude all of the following about winning a lottery *except* that
    a. it can cause stress.
    b. it can cause the loss of friendships.

c. it can cause a lack of trust.

d. it can cause a desire to give vast amounts of money to charity.

_____b_____ 9. The examples of Tonda Dickerson, Michael Klingebiel, and Frank Capaci were used to illustrate

a. that good things continue to happen to good people.

b. the difficulty in maintaining relationships after a big financial windfall.

c. the generosity of strangers.

d. that money can solve all problems.

_____b_____ 10. The author of this selection suggests that

a. lottery winners will be besieged by investment companies who want to handle their money.

b. winning the lottery may not be all good.

c. lottery winners will have to move and begin new lives.

d. lottery winners will spend all of their winnings in a few years.

_____b_____ 11. The selection suggests that people who cope best with sudden wealth may do any of the following *except*

a. keep their old friends and routines.

b. splurge on big-ticket items like a house and then save their money thereafter.

c. avoid making sudden changes in their behavior.

d. keep their old jobs.

_____a_____ 12. As used in paragraph 15, the word *tip* means

a. an amount of money given to someone in return for service.

b. a helpful hint or warning.

c. a piece of inside information.

d. a narrow or pointed end of something.

Vocabulary Matching

Directions: Match the vocabulary words in Column A with their definitions in Column B. Place the correct letter in the space provided.

	Column A	Column B
_o_	1. ransom	a. an indeterminately large sum of money
_d_	2. apparent	b. faint
_j_	3. big shot	c. in utter confusion or disorder
_k_	4. consequence	d. clear
_f_	5. daze	e. stabilizing influences
_g_	6. flooded	f. stunned state
_b_	7. glimmering	g inundated
_a_	8. megabucks	h. put into a common fund
_e_	9. moorings	i. to utter words in a low, indistinct manner
_i_	10. mumble	j. a person of consequence or promise
_h_	11. pooled	k. result
_c_	12. topsy-turvy	o. money paid or demanded for the release of someone or something from captivity

In Your Own Words

1. Do you agree or disagree with the old adage "Be careful what you wish for because you just might get it"? Do you think more money causes more problems?

2. Many psychologists say that if you were unhappy before wining a huge amount of money, then you will probably still be unhappy afterward. Apparently, money will only temporarily cover up the problems you face. How is this theory supported by the lottery winners cited in the selection? Do you think money can solve all problems?

3. Fully one-third of multimillion-dollar lottery winners become bankrupt in just a few years after their big win. Many winners immediately buy a big mansion but don't take into account the upkeep of such a home such as higher utilities, a security system, insurance, and taxes. The one thing most fail to do is learn anything about investing. How would you handle your big win? What would you do first? To whom would you turn for advice?

4. Americans spend more than $25 million a year on lottery tickets. Does that amount surprise you? Do you buy lottery tickets? If so, how much do you spend on tickets per week?

5. Experts have compiled a list of tips to help lottery winners adjust to their new wealth. Here are a few of their suggestions:
   a. Give yourself a modest initial spending spree and then invest the rest of the money wisely so that you can live on the interest.
   b. Don't quit your job. Even working part-time is better than quitting altogether. You need something to do all day besides running around spending money.

   What do you think of these suggestions? Can you think of any others?

Written Assignment

Some experts believe there is a real risk with acquiring sudden wealth. One expert says that "often lottery-winners can keep the money and lose family and friends, or lose the money and keep family and friends." Write a few paragraphs giving your opinion on this issue.

Internet Activity

1. To calculate your odds of winning the lottery, check out the following Web site:

   www.webmath.com/lottery.html

   Did you know that you have a better chance of getting into a car accident, suffering a plane accident, or being struck by lightning than of winning the lottery?

2. For information about the history of the lottery, go to:

   www.naspl.org/05/history.html

   Write a few paragraphs about what you find interesting.

STUDY TECHNIQUE 9: MAPPING

Recall our discussion of left-brain and right-brain orientations in Chapter 1. If you have trouble making a formal outline, or you find it an unpleasant task, it may be that you have a right-brain orientation. What you may find more useful is an organizing technique that is more visual and free-form. Mapping is just such a technique.

You will see that you have topics, main ideas, details, and so on, just as you have in a formal outline. And like a formal outline, mapping seeks to organize topics to show the relationships among them. But it organizes in a way that is less restricted by rules and has more visual significance.

To begin mapping, write down a short description of the main idea or thesis, and put a circle around it. Next find the material that directly supports the main idea. Organize this material into categories, write down a short description for each category, and put circles around your descriptions. Now use lines to connect your categories to the circle for the main idea or thesis. If you want, you may create subcategories for your categories, write brief descriptions, circle them, and use lines to connect these circles to your category circles. Of course, you can use boxes instead of circles. What you end up with is a logical, graphical summary of the material.

We have provided you with a sample map of "The Big Win: Life after the Lottery." Notice that the main idea of the reading appears at the top and the related ideas branch off from it. Do you think this map would help you study for a test on this material?

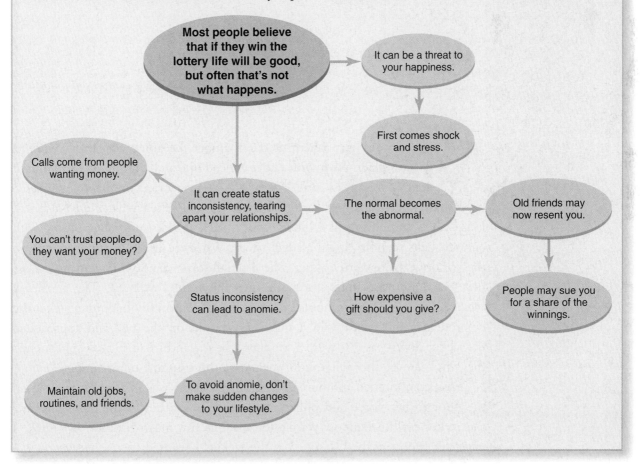

Chronological Order

The information in this descriptive narrative is presented chronologically, making it easy to construct a time line. After you complete the Comprehension Checkup, you will practice that study technique, which was first introduced in Chapter 3.

"My clothes have failed me."

TUNING IN TO READING   Growing up poor in South Fresno, California, Gary Soto often felt as if he didn't fit in. He explores that feeling of self-consciousness in the following selection. Have you ever felt as though your clothes (or something else) set you apart from others? How did you deal with the situation? How did that experience make you feel about yourself?

BIO-SKETCH   Gary Soto, a Mexican American writer, has won numerous awards with his autobiographical writings and poetry. He has written over 35 books, which have sold nearly four million copies. His life as a writer is featured in the Gary Soto Literary Museum at Fresno City College, where he began his writing life in 1972 as a student.

NOTES ON VOCABULARY
Braille   a system of writing for the blind consisting of raised dots interpreted by touch.
camouflage   fabric dyed with patches of green, brown, black, or tan (earth tones) intended to make the wearer hard to distinguish from a natural, outdoor background.

The Jacket

GARY SOTO

My clothes have failed me. I remember the green coat that I wore in sixth grade when you either danced like a champ or pressed yourself against a greasy wall, bitter as a penny toward the happy couples.

When I needed a new jacket and my mother asked what kind I wanted, 2 I described something like bikers wear: black leather and silver studs, with enough belts to hold down a small town. We were in the kitchen, steam on the windows from her cooking. She listened for so long while stirring dinner that I thought she understood for sure the kind I wanted. The next day when I got home from school, I discovered draped on my bedpost a jacket the color of day-old guacamole. I threw my books on the bed and approached the jacket slowly, as if it were a stranger whose hand I had to shake. I touched the vinyl sleeve, the collar, and peeked at the mustard-color lining.

From the kitchen mother yelled that my jacket was in the closet. I closed 3 the door to her voice and pulled at the rack of clothes in the closet, hoping the jacket on the bedpost wasn't for me but my mean brother. No luck. I gave up. From my bed, I stared at the jacket. I wanted to cry because it was so ugly and so big that I knew I'd have to wear it a long time. I was a small kid, thin as a young tree, and it would be years before I'd have a new one. I stared at the jacket, like an enemy, thinking bad things before I took off my old jacket, whose sleeves climbed halfway to my elbow.

I put the big jacket on. I zipped it up and down several times and rolled 4 the cuffs up so they didn't cover my hands. I put my hands in the pockets and flapped the jacket like a bird's wings. I stood in front of the mirror, full face, then profile, and then looked over my shoulder as if someone had called me. I sat on the bed, stood against the bed, and combed my hair to see what I would look like doing something natural. I looked ugly. I threw it on my brother's bed and looked at it for a long time before I slipped it on and went out to the backyard, smiling a "thank you" to my mom as I passed her in the kitchen. With my hands in my pockets, I kicked a ball against the fence, and then climbed it to sit looking into the alley. I hurled orange peels at the mouth of an open garbage can, and when the peels were gone I watched the white puffs of my breath thin to nothing.

I jumped down, hands in my pockets, and in the backyard, on my knees, 5 I teased my dog, Brownie, by swooping my arms while making bird calls. He jumped at me and missed. He jumped again and again, until a tooth sunk deep, ripping an L-shaped tear on my left sleeve. I pushed Brownie away to study the tear as I would a cut on my arm. There was no blood, only a few loose pieces of fuzz. Damn dog, I thought, and pushed him away hard when he tried to bite again. I got up from my knees and went to my bedroom to sit with my jacket on my lap, with the lights out.

That was the first afternoon with my new jacket. The next day I wore 6 it to sixth grade and got a D on a math quiz. During the morning recess, Frankie T., the playground terrorist, pushed me to the ground and told me to stay there until recess was over. My best friend, Steve Negrete, ate an apple while looking at me, and the girls turned away to whisper on the monkey bars. The teachers were no help: they looked my way and talked about how foolish I looked in my new jacket. I saw their heads bob with laughter, their hands half covering their mouths.

Even though it was cold, I took off the jacket during lunch and played 7 kickball in a thin shirt, my arms feeling like Braille from goose bumps. But when I returned to class I slipped the jacket on and shivered until I was warm. I sat on my hands, heating them up, while my teeth chattered like a cup of crooked dice. Finally warm, I slid out of my jacket but put it back on a few minutes later when the fire bell rang. We paraded out into the yard where we, the sixth graders, walked past all the other grades to stand against the back fence. Everybody saw me. Although they didn't say out loud, "Man, that's ugly," I heard the buzz-buzz of gossip and even laughter that I knew was meant for me.

And so I went, in my guacamole-colored jacket. So embarrassed, so hurt, 8 I couldn't even do my homework. I received C's on quizzes and forgot the state capitals and the rivers of South America, our friendly neighbor. Even the girls who had been friendly blew away like loose flowers to follow the boys in neat jackets.

I wore that thing for three years until the sleeves grew short and my 9 forearms stuck out like the necks of turtles. All during that time no love came to me—no little girl in a Sunday dress she wore on Monday. At lunchtime I stayed with the ugly boys who leaned against the chainlike fence and looked around with propellers of grass spinning in our mouths. We saw girls walk by alone, saw couples, hand in hand, their heads like bookends pressing air together. We saw them and spun our propellers so fast our faces were blurs.

I blame that jacket for those bad years. I blame my mother for her bad 10 taste and her cheap ways. It was a sad time for the heart. With a friend I spent my sixth-grade year in a tree in the alley, waiting for something good to happen to me in that jacket, which had become the ugly brother who tagged along wherever I went. And it was about that time that I began to grow. My chest puffed up with muscle and, strangely, a few more ribs. Even my hands, those fleshy hammers, showed bravely through the cuffs, the fingers already hardening for the coming fights. But that L-shaped rip on the left sleeve got bigger, bits of stuffing coughed out from its wound after a hard day of play. I finally Scotch-taped it closed, but in rain or cold weather the tape peeled off like a scab and more stuffing fell out until the sleeve shriveled into a palsied arm. That winter the elbows began to crack and whole chunks of green began to fall off. I showed the cracks to my mother, who always seemed to be at the stove with steamed-up glasses, and she said that there were children in Mexico who would love that jacket. I told her that this was America and yelled that Debbie, my sister, didn't have a jacket like mine. I ran outside, ready to cry, and climbed the tree by the alley to think bad thoughts and watch my breath puff white and disappear.

But whole pieces still casually flew off my jacket when I played hard, 11 read quietly, or took vicious spelling tests at school. When it became so spotted that my brother began to call me "camouflage," I flung it over the fence into the alley. Later, however, I swiped the jacket off the ground and went inside to drape it across my lap and mope.

I was called to dinner: steam silvered my mother's glasses as she said grace; 12 my brother and sister with their heads bowed made ugly faces at their glasses of powdered milk. I gagged too, but eagerly ate big rips of buttered tortilla that held scooped-up beans. Finished, I went outside with my jacket across my arm. It was a cold sky. The faces of clouds were piled up, hurting. I climbed the fence, jumping down with a grunt. I started up the alley and soon slipped into my jacket, that green ugly brother who breathed over my shoulder that day and ever since.

(Gary Soto, *Coming of Age in America*, 1994)

 COMPREHENSION CHECKUP

Multiple Choice

Directions: For each item, write the letter corresponding to the best answer.

b   1. When the narrator states that his chest "puffed up with muscle and, strangely, a few more ribs," he is providing an image that primarily appeals to our sense of

     a. smell.

     b. sight.

     c. taste.

     d. hearing.

_____d_____ 2. Which one of the following sentences lends a tone of sadness to the selection?
   a. "That winter the elbows began to crack and whole chunks of green began to fall off."
   b. "And so I went, in my guacamole-colored jacket."
   c. "There was no blood, only a few loose pieces of fuzz."
   d. "It was a cold sky. The faces of clouds were piled up hurting."

_____c_____ 3. "Bits of stuffing coughed out from its wound" is an example of
   a. simile.
   b. metaphor.
   c. personification.
   d. symbol.

_____b_____ 4. All the following are similes *except*
   a. "bitter as a penny."
   b. "white puffs of my breath thin to nothing."
   c. "flapped the jacket like a bird's wings."
   d. "my forearms stuck out like the necks of turtles."

_____b_____ 5. "Tape peeled off like a scab" is an example of
   a. personification.
   b. simile.
   c. synonym.
   d. antonym.

_____d_____ 6. When the narrator said that he wanted a jacket "with enough belts to hold down a small town," he was using
   a. exaggeration.
   b. understatement.
   c. hyperbole.
   d. both a and c.

True or False

Directions: Indicate whether each statement is true or false by writing **T** or **F** in the space provided.

_____F_____ 7. The narrator wore the jacket for five years.

_____T_____ 8. The narrator suggests that fighting is in his future.

_____T_____ 9. The narrator's brother calls him "camouflage" because of the jacket's appearance.

_____F_____ 10. The narrator has numerous girlfriends during the period he describes.

_____T_____ 11. The narrator's mother reminds her son that there are others who would feel fortunate to have his jacket.

_____T_____ 12. In sixth grade, the narrator is small and thin.

Short Answer

Directions: Answer the following questions briefly, in a few words, phrases, or sentences, as appropriate.

1. What is the main idea? A young boy, struggling to fit in, is made to feel very different when he must wear a hated jacket.

2. What is the author's purpose? <u>It is to show how something that many people</u>
<u>could see as unimportant can have a major effect.</u>

3. What words demonstrate that the jacket had a profound effect on the narrator's life even after he no longer had to wear it? <u>He refers to the jacket as</u>
<u>"that green ugly brother who breathed over my shoulder that day and ever since."</u>

4. The narrator blames his jacket for many of his misfortunes. What are four things that go wrong in the narrator's life after receiving the jacket? <u>He got</u>
<u>a D on a math quiz and got pushed to the ground. His best friend ate an apple</u>
<u>while staring at him and girls whispered. He couldn't do his homework, he got Cs</u>
<u>on quizzes, he forgot key information, and no love came his way.</u>

5. What details in the story indicate that the narrator comes from a background where money is not plentiful? <u>The jacket was big and he knew he'd have to</u>
<u>wear it for a long time before he could get a new one. His old jacket was not</u>
<u>replaced until the sleeves were at his elbows. They are drinking powdered milk</u>
<u>even though the children dislike it, probably because it is less expensive than milk</u>
<u>in a carton or bottle.</u>

6. What is the narrator's relationship with his mother during the period described in the story? <u>He thinks that she is unfair in her treatment of him. He</u>
<u>also feels that she doesn't understand him and that she is cheap and lacking in taste.</u>

7. In what ways does the narrator demonstrate his insecurity while wearing the jacket? <u>He thinks that the teachers and his fellow pupils are talking about him and</u>
<u>laughing at his ugly jacket.</u>

8. What does the narrator mean when he describes the jacket as an ugly brother breathing over his shoulder? <u>He can't get rid of it. It tags along wherever he goes.</u>

Vocabulary in Context

Directions: Choose the correct definition of each word according to how it is used in the sentence.

<u>c</u>   1. An artist drawing your *profile* will show a view from the
   a. front.
   b. back.
   c. side.

<u>c</u>   2. If something is *bobbing*, it is
   a. dangling.
   b. stationary.
   c. moving up and down.

<u>a</u>   3. If something *shrivels*, it
   a. shrinks
   b. expands
   c. festers

<u>b</u>   4. A *forearm* is located
   a. between the elbow and the shoulder.
   b. between the wrist and the elbow.
   c. between the wrist and the knuckles of the hand.

_____c_____ 5. If your friend is *moping*, she is
a. dejected.
b. in low spirits.
c. both a and b.

_____b_____ 6. A *vicious* spelling test is one that is
a. easy.
b. brutal.
c. dangerous.

In Your Own Words

1. The narrator feels that his clothes have failed him. Do you think clothes that are not of your own choosing, but instead are forced upon you, can have an adverse effect on self-confidence? On happiness?

2. What is your opinion about the saying "Clothes make the man"?

3. In your opinion, how important are possessions to overall happiness?

Written Assignment

Directions: Choose one of the following quotations and write a few short paragraphs giving your opinion.

> "If most of us are ashamed of shabby clothes and shoddy furniture, let us be more ashamed of shabby ideas and shoddy philosophies. . . . It would be a sad situation if the wrapper were better than the meat wrapped inside it. —Albert Einstein

> "People seldom notice old clothes if you wear a big smile." —Lee Mildon

> "What a strange power there is in clothing. —Isaac Bashevis Singer

> "There is much to support the view that it is clothes that wear us and not we them." —Virginia Woolf

Internet Activity

Check out Gary Soto's Web site at www.garysoto.com.

What new information about Soto did you learn? Write a short paragraph summarizing Soto's personal and literary accomplishments.

STUDY TECHNIQUE 10: MORE PRACTICE WITH TIME LINES

A time line is a specialized way of organizing information. Time lines are useful when material needs to be organized chronologically. When you are working with historical articles, or other kinds of articles that describe a sequence of events, it sometimes helps to prepare a time line.

All that a time line does is place events in chronological order along a line and then assign information to the dates. You can make a time line vertically (up and down) or horizontally (across). How specific you want to make a time line in terms of the number of dates and the amount of information you assign to each date depends on the reading material and your needs.

The following time line shows important events in Gary Soto's life.

continued

STUDY TECHNIQUE *continued*

1952	date of birth
1956	father is killed in an accident
1972	took his first poetry-writing class
1974	graduated from college with a bachelor's degree in English
1975	married Carolyn Oda
1977	began teaching at the University of California at Berkeley
1978	collection of poetry is nominated for a Pulitzer Prize
1985	publishes first book of prose
1995	is a finalist for the National Book Award
2010	Gary Soto Literary Museum established at Fresno City College

a. The boy Scotch-tapes the L-shaped rip closed.

b. Brownie rips a hole in the jacket.

c. The boy discovers the jacket draped on his bedpost.

d. The boy's brother calls him "camouflage" because the jacket is so spotted.

e. The boy gets a D on a math test and gets pushed to the ground at recess.

f. The boy's mother asks what kind of jacket he wants.

COMPLETION

Directions: Reorder the following events so that they follow the same sequence as in the story. Write the events in the correct order in the following box. We have done the first event for you.

1. The boy's mother asks what kind of jacket he wants.
2. c
3. b
4. e
5. a
6. d

Categories and Steps in a Process

The authors divide intimate relationships into two categories: the growth of relationships (coming together) and the decline of relationships (coming apart). They then describe the stages of communication that relationships pass through. At the end of the Comprehension Checkup, we introduce you to outlining, a formal way to organize the material presented in the reading.

READING

"The integrating stage is a time when individuals give up some characteristics of their old selves and develop shared identities."

TUNING IN TO READING   The following excerpt on the stages in a relationship comes from *Looking Out/Looking In,* a textbook on interpersonal communications written by Ronald Adler, Russell Proctor, and Neil Towne. The purpose of this textbook is to aid students in communicating more effectively with the important people in their lives.

BIO-SKETCH   Ronald B. Adler is a professor of communications at Santa Barbara City College. In addition to writing and teaching, Adler works with professionals to improve on-the-job communication. Russell F. Proctor II is a communications professor at Northern Kentucky

READING *(continued)*

University and serves as advisor to the Speech Communications Club. Neil Towne is now retired after four decades of teaching. He currently conducts communication workshops on conflict resolution.

NOTES ON VOCABULARY

goosebumps   a bristling of the hair on the skin causing small raised bumps. The term compares the skin of a human who is cold or afraid to the skin of a plucked goose.

starstruck   dazzled or enraptured, especially with romance; also, especially idealistic or optimistic. The term compares the shining of stars to eyes aglow with love or enthusiasm.

token of affection   a sign or symbol of one's devotion. A *token* originally was a badge worn to indicate allegiance to a particular person.

handwriting is on the wall   a warning of impending doom. The expression comes from the Old Testament. King Belshazzar sees a disembodied hand writing four words on his palace wall. He summons the prophet Daniel to interpret the meaning of the message and is told that the words foretell his eventual overthrow. Shortly thereafter, the king is slain.

CATHY © 1985 Cathy Guisewite. Reprinted with permission of Universal Uclick. All rights reserved.

Cathy

DEVELOPMENTAL STAGES IN INTIMATE RELATIONSHIPS

Ronald B. Adler, Russell F. Proctor II, and Neil Towne

The process of interpersonal attraction is only the beginning of a relationship. As attraction motivates us to seek intimacy with some people we encounter, communication passes through several stages that characterize different levels of intimacy.

The following stages are especially descriptive of intimate, romantic rela- 2 tionships and close friendships. The pattern for other intimate relationships, such as families, would follow different paths.

Initiating The goals in the first stage of a relationship are to show that you 3 are interested in making contact and to show that you are the kind of person worth talking to. Communication during this **initiating** stage is usually brief, and it generally follows conventional formulas: handshakes, remarks about innocuous subjects like the weather, and friendly expressions. These kinds of behavior may seem superficial and meaningless, but they are a way of signaling that we're interested in building some kind of relationship with the other person. They allow us to say without saying, "I'm a friendly person, and I'd like to get to know you."

Experimenting After we have made contact with a new person, the next 4 stage is to decide whether we are interested in pursuing the relationship further. This involves **uncertainty reduction**—the process of getting to know others by gaining more information about them. A usual part of uncertainty reduction is the search for common ground, and it involves the conversational basics such as "Where are you from?" or "What's your major?" From there we look for other similarities: "You're a runner, too? How many miles do you do a week?"

The hallmark of the **experimenting** stage is small talk. As Mark Knapp says, 5 this small talk is like Listerine: "We hate it, but we take large quantities every day." Small talk serves several functions. First, it is a useful way to find out what interests we share with the other person. It also provides a way to "audition" the other person—to help us decide whether a relationship is worth pursuing. In addition, small talk is a safe way to ease into a relationship. You haven't risked much as you decide whether to proceed further.

Intensifying Several changes in communication patterns occur during 6 intensifying. The expression of feelings toward the other becomes more common. Dating couples use a wide range of communication strategies to describe their feelings of attraction. About one-quarter of the time they express their feelings directly. More often they use less direct methods of communication: spending an increasing amount of time together, asking for support from one another, doing favors for the partner, giving tokens of affection, hinting and flirting, expressing feelings nonverbally, getting to know the partner's friends and family, and trying to look more physically attractive.

The **intensifying** stage is usually a time of relational excitement and even 7 euphoria. For romantic partners, it's often filled with starstruck gazes, goosebumps, and daydreaming. As a result it's a stage that's regularly depicted in movies and romance novels—after all, we love to watch lovers in love. The problem, of course, is that the stage doesn't last forever. Sometimes romantic partners who stop feeling goosebumps begin to question whether they're still in love. Although it's possible that they're not, it's also possible that they've simply moved on to a different stage in their relationship—integrating.

Integrating As a relationship strengthens, the parties begin to take on an 8 identity as a social unit. In romantic relationships, invitations begin to come addressed to the couple. Social circles merge. The partners begin to take on each other's commitments: "Sure, we'll spend Thanksgiving with your family." Common property may begin to be designated—our apartment, our car, our song. Partners may even begin to speak alike, using personal idioms and sentence patterns. In this sense, the **integrating** stage is a time when individuals give up some characteristics of their old selves and develop shared identities.

As we become more integrated with others, our sense of obligation to them 9 grows. We feel obliged to provide a variety of resources such as class notes and

Cathy

money, whether or not the other person asks for them. Surprisingly, partners make fewer straightforward requests than they did in earlier relationship stages. This isn't as surprising as it might at first seem: As partners become better acquainted, their knowledge of each other makes overt requests less necessary.

Bonding During the **bonding** stage, the parties make symbolic public ges- 10 tures to show the world that their relationship exists. The most common form of bonding in romantic relationships is a wedding ceremony and the legal ties that come with it. Bonding generates social support for the relationship. Custom and law both impose certain obligations on partners who have officially bonded.

Bonding marks a turning point in a relationship. Up to now the relation- 11 ship may have developed at a steady pace: experimenting gradually moved into intensifying and then into integrating. Now, however, there is a spurt of commitment. The public display and declaration of exclusivity make this a distinct stage in the relationship.

Differentiating Bonding is the peak of the "coming together" phase of 12 relational development. But people in even the most committed relationships need to assert their individual identities. This **differentiating** stage is the point where the "we" orientation that has developed shifts, and more "me" messages begin to occur. Partners use a variety of strategies to gain privacy from each other. Sometimes they confront the other party directly, explaining that they don't want to continue a discussion. At other times they are less direct, offering nonverbal cues, changing the topic, or leaving the room.

Differentiation is likely to occur when a relationship begins to experience 13 the first, inevitable feelings of stress. This need for autonomy needn't be a negative experience, however. People need to be individuals as well as parts of a relationship, and differentiation is a necessary step toward autonomy. The key to successful differentiation is maintaining a commitment to the relationship while creating the space for being an individual as well.

Circumscribing So far we have been looking at the growth of relationships. 14 Although some reach a plateau of development, going on successfully for as long as a lifetime, others pass through several stages of decline and dissolution.

Cathy

In the **circumscribing** stage, communication between members decreases 15 in quantity and quality. Restrictions and restraints characterize this stage. Rather than discuss a disagreement (which requires energy on both sides), members opt for withdrawal—either mental (silence or daydreaming and fantasizing) or physical (where people spend less time together). Circumscribing doesn't involve total avoidance, which may come later. Rather, it involves a shrinking of interest and commitment—the opposite of what occurred in the integrating stage.

Stagnating If circumscribing continues, the relationship enters the **stagnat-** 16 **ing** stage. The excitement of the intensifying stage is long gone, and the partners behave toward each other in old, familiar ways without much feeling. No growth occurs. The relationship is a hollow shell of its former self. We see stagnation in many workers who have lost enthusiasm for their job yet continue to go through the motions for years. The same sad event occurs for some couples who unenthusiastically have the same conversations, see the same people, and follow the same routines without any sense of joy or novelty.

Avoiding When stagnation becomes too unpleasant, parties in a relation- 17 ship begin to create physical distance between each other. This is the **avoiding** stage. Sometimes they do it indirectly under the guise of excuses ("I've been sick lately and can't see you"); sometimes they do it directly ("Please don't call me; I don't want to see you now"). In either case, by this point the handwriting is on the wall about the relationship's future.

The deterioration of a relationship from bonding through circumscribing, 18 stagnating, and avoiding isn't inevitable. One of the key differences between marriages that end in separation and those that are restored to their former intimacy is the communication that occurs when the partners are unsatisfied. Unsuccessful couples deal with their problems by avoidance, indirectness, and less involvement with each other. By contrast, couples who "repair" their relationship communicate much more directly. They confront each other with their concerns (sometimes with the assistance of a counselor) and spend time and effort negotiating solutions to their problems.

Terminating Characteristics of the final stage, **terminating,** include sum- 19 mary dialogues of where the relationship has gone and the desire to dissociate.

The relationship may end with a cordial dinner, a note left on the kitchen table, a phone call, or a legal document. Depending on each person's feelings, this stage can be quite short, or it may be drawn out over time, with bitter jabs at each other.

Relationships don't always move toward termination in a straight line. [20] Rather they take a back-and-forth pattern, where the trend is toward dissolution. Regardless of how long it takes, termination doesn't have to be totally negative. Understanding each other's investments in the relationship and needs for personal growth may dilute the hard feelings. In fact, many relationships aren't so much terminated as redefined. A divorced couple, for example, may find new, less intimate ways to relate to each other.

In romantic relationships, the best predictor of whether the parties will [21] become friends is whether they were friends before their emotional involvement. The way the couple splits up also makes a difference. It's no surprise to find that friendships are most possible when communication during the breakup is positive: expressions that there are no regrets for time spent together and other attempts to minimize hard feelings. When communication during termination is negative (manipulative, complaining to third parties), friendships are less likely.

(Ronald B. Adler, Russell F. Proctor II, and Neil Towne, *Looking Out, Looking In,* 11/e, 2005)

 COMPREHENSION CHECKUP

Multiple Choice

Directions: For each item, write the letter corresponding to the best answer.

____a____ 1. All of the following are examples of the initiating stage *except*
   a. soulful kisses.
   b. handshakes.
   c. discussions about the weather.
   d. discussions about sports.

____d____ 2. All of the following are typical of the experimenting stage *except*
   a. gaining more information about others.
   b. reducing uncertainty.
   c. practicing small talk.
   d. spending large amounts of time with each other.

____c____ 3. All of the following were given as reasons for the use of small talk *except* for which?
   a. It is a way to discover interests in common.
   b. It is a way to interact with others.
   c. It is a way to test the commitment of a partner.
   d. It is a way to decide whether the relationship is worthwhile.

____a____ 4. Which stage is marked by spending increasing amounts of time together, exchanging gifts, and making introductions to close friends and family members?
   a. intensifying
   b. initiating
   c. experimenting
   d. circumscribing

_b_   5. Paragraph 11 contains the following sentence: "Now, however, there is a spurt of commitment." What is this sentence's relationship to the preceding sentence in the paragraph?
   a. comparison
   b. contrast
   c. cause and effect
   d. definition

_d_   6. You could infer from paragraphs 12 and 13 that
   a. the need to differentiate is not necessarily a negative experience.
   b. some stress in relationships is inevitable.
   c. couples use verbal and nonverbal strategies to communicate a need for autonomy.
   d. all of the above.

_b_   7. The stagnation stage can best be described as
   a. shrinking interest and commitment.
   b. going through the motions with little enthusiasm.
   c. confronting each other over problems and negotiating solutions.
   d. continuing to grow in small, significant ways.

_d_   8. It is possible to remain friends after the final breakup if
   a. communication during the breakup was positive.
   b. the partners were friends prior to their romantic involvement.
   c. attempts were made to minimize hard feelings.
   d. all of the above.

_b_   9. The authors' tone for this selection can best be described as
   a. optimistic.
   b. objective.
   c. sarcastic.
   d. perplexed.

_d_   10. The authors' primary purpose in writing this selection is to
   a. inform readers of the difficulties in maintaining successful relationships.
   b. persuade readers to delay marriage until they have reached a mature age.
   c. tell a story about relationships.
   d. explain the communication stages in a typical relationship.

True or False

Directions: Indicate whether each statement is true or false by writing **T** or **F** in the space provided.

_F_   11. Something told in a _straightforward_ fashion can be expected to be ambiguous.

_T_   12. When you _confront_ someone, you directly challenge him.

_T_   13. Honesty is the _hallmark_ of a good judge.

_F_   14. If you _impose_ on someone, you can count on her being grateful.

_F_   15. If something is _inevitable,_ you should be able to avoid it.

_F_   16. After the two countries _merged,_ they remained two separate entities.

_____T_____ 17. Once the tired climber reached the *plateau,* she could begin to walk on level ground.

_____T_____ 18. Two students who don't like each other might try to avoid having an accidental *encounter* on campus.

_____T_____ 19. A driver with a speeding ticket might *opt* to go to traffic school and get the ticket dismissed rather than pay a fine.

_____F_____ 20. A boxer whose *jabs* keep missing will likely win the fight.

Completion

Directions: Complete the following steps-in-a-process diagram.

Step 5: Bonding   Differentiating: Step 1
Step 4: Integrating   Circumscribing: Step 2
Step 3: Intensifying   _stagnating_: Step 3
Step 2: Experimenting   _avoiding_: Step 4
Step 1: Initiating   _terminating_: Step 5

Vocabulary Matching

Directions: Match the vocabulary words in Column A with their antonyms in Column B. Place the correct letter in the space provided.

	Column A	Column B
_f_	1. superficial	a. secret
_j_	2. conventional	b. inclusivity
_a_	3. overt	c. unfriendly
_h_	4. innocuous	d. strengthen
_b_	5. exclusivity	e. avoidable
_c_	6. cordial	f. profound
_i_	7. euphoria	g. unification
_d_	8. dilute	h. harmful
_e_	9. inevitable	i. depression
_g_	10. dissolution	j. unusual

In Your Own Words

1. Considering the information provided in this selection, do you think it's possible to live "happily ever after"? Explain your answer.

2. In your opinion, based on your own personal observations, do "opposites attract"? Or is it more likely that "birds of a feather flock together"? Explain.

3. Is living together more likely or less likely to lead to marriage? Which proverb do you think is more accurate: "Out of sight out of mind" or "Absence makes the heart grow fonder"? Give reasons for your answers.

4. What kind of personality traits lead to success in marriage? What factors are associated with increased likelihood of divorce? Why do you think there is more divorce today?

5. What do you think of the practice of arranged marriages? Do you see any advantages to an arranged marriage?

Written Assignment

1. Look at each of the *Cathy* cartoons in the reading, and write the main idea from the selection that each cartoon illustrates.

2. Write a one- or two-sentence summary of each of the stages in a relationship.

3. In the initiating stage, two people are probably attracted to each other on the basis of characteristics such as physical appearance, social standing, reputation, dress, race, age, education, and religion. Which of these characteristics do you feel is most important to the typical male? To the typical female? Which are most important to you?

Internet Activity

Robert Sternberg of Yale University developed the widely used three-dimensional theory of love based on the components of intimacy, commitment, and passion. Recently, his research has sought to determine why so many relationships fail. Consult his Web site at:

> www.psy.pdx.edu/PsiCafe/KeyTheorists/Sternberg.htm

From that site, you can link to Sternberg's homepage to read about his research projects. There is also a "Measure Your Love" questionnaire that you might wish to take.

You might also take an Internet relationships test. Go to a search engine and type in "relationships tests." Take a test that suits your needs (and make sure it's free!). Write a paragraph about what you found out about your relationships. Does the test correlate with the stages of relationships you read about in the reading selection?

STUDY TECHNIQUE 11: OUTLINING

Outlining is a formal way of organizing material. An outline should reflect an orderly arrangement of ideas going from the most general to the most specific. If you create a good outline of what you have read, you will have a very useful study aid. Often you can use the headings in a textbook selection as the main topics in an outline, and the subheadings as main ideas. A good outline shows the topics covered, the relationships between the topics, and the importance of the ideas in the order in which they were covered in the original material. The reason outlining is called a *formal* way of organizing information is that it follows certain rules. These rules are described below.

OUTLINING RULES

Each division in an outline is more specific than the division that precedes it. Main headings (topics) are represented by roman numerals (I, II, III, IV, V, etc.). The next level of headings (main ideas) is represented by capital letters (A, B, C, etc.), the next level (major supporting details) by arabic numbers (1, 2, 3, 4, etc.), and the next level (minor supporting details) by lowercase letters (a, b, c, d, etc.).

continued

In an outline, you cannot have just one subtopic; there must always be two or more. For example, if there is a main idea A, there must be a main idea B. If there is major supporting detail 1, there must be major supporting detail 2. The reason for this is that if a topic is divided, there must be at least two parts, although there could be three or four or more parts depending on how many times the topic is divided.

Below is a partial outline of "Developmental Stages in Intimate Relationships."

I. The Growth of Relationships (Coming Together)

A. Initiating

1. The goal is to show you're interested and interesting.

2. Communication is brief with conventional formulas.
   a. Handshakes
   b. Remarks about the weather
   c. Friendly expressions

B. Experimenting

1. The goal is to decide whether to pursue the relationship further.
   a. Uses uncertainty reduction—gain more information
   b. Need to find common ground—similarities

2. The hallmark is small talk.
   a. It's useful to find shared interests.
   b. It provides a way to "audition" the person.
   c. It's a safe way to ease into the relationship.

C. Intensifying

1. Expression of feelings is more common.
   a. Feelings can be expressed directly by telling person.

b. Feelings can be expressed indirectly by spending time together, doing favors, giving gifts, getting to know friends and family.

2. This stage is characterized by excitement and euphoria.
   a. Regularly depicted in movies and romance novels—as lovers in love.
   b. Doesn't last forever.

D. Integrating

1. The couple becomes a social unit.
   a. Invitations are addressed to the couple.
   b. Social circles merge.
   c. Take on each other's commitments.
   d. Common property is designated.

2. The sense of obligation grows between the couple.
   a. Couples feel obliged to provide resources, such as money.
   b. Overt requests are now less necessary.

E. Bonding

1. Parties make symbolic public gestures—wedding.

2. There's a spurt of commitment with declaration of exclusivity.

II. The Decline of Relationships (Coming Apart)

A. Differentiating

B. circumscribing

C. stagnating

D. avoiding

E. terminating

Now it's your turn. Starting with "Differentiating," represented by capital letter A, complete the outline.

Cause and Effect

This short story demonstrates a cause-and-effect relationship. Alan wishes to change his beloved Diana forever by making her more responsive to him. He pursues his dream without ever realizing the unintended, or ironic, effects. After you have completed the Comprehension Checkup, you will be writing a summary of the material.

READING

> *"'Is it true,' asked Alan, 'that you have a certain mixture that has—er—quite extraordinary effects?'"*

TUNING IN TO READING   Try to determine the personalities of Alan and the old man after reading the first three paragraphs of the story. Do you think Alan is being "suckered" into doing something against his will?

   The dialogue in this short story reads very much like a play. Have two people in your class play the parts of Alan and the old man by reading the dialogue in quotation marks for each character.

BIO-SKETCH   John Collier was born in London in 1901 and died in California in 1980. In his lengthy career, he was a successful novelist, playwright, and screenwriter, but he is primarily remembered today for his sinister short stories. Many of these stories, though focused on evil, were written with great wit and irony. Each word in a Collier short story was carefully chosen to heighten a particular effect. Most critics consider Collier's particular strength his use of dialogue.

NOTES ON VOCABULARY

sinister   ominous; threatening harm or evil. The original Latin meaning was simply "left" or "on the left." The origins of this word have to do with an ancient prejudice favoring what is to the right over what is to the left. So, the more important guests at a banquet would be seated to the right of the host or hostess.

au revoir   a French interjection meaning "until we see each other again; good-bye for the present."

chaser   a milder beverage taken after a drink of liquor.

draught   a current of air in any enclosed space; the British spelling of *draft*.

phial   a small glass bottle or vial.

siren   a beautiful or tempting woman. In classical mythology, *sirens* were evil creatures who sang in beautiful voices, luring sailors to shipwreck and death. The word's origin is Greek.

The Chaser

JOHN COLLIER

ALAN AUSTEN, AS NERVOUS AS A KITTEN, went up certain dark and creaky stairs in the neighborhood of Pell Street, and peered about for a long time on the dim landing before he found the name he wanted written obscurely on one of the doors.

   He pushed open this door, as he had been told to do, and found himself in a tiny room, which contained no furniture but a plain kitchen table, 2 a rocking-chair, and an ordinary chair. On one of the dirty buff-coloured walls were a couple of shelves, containing in all perhaps a dozen bottles and jars.

An old man sat in the rocking-chair, reading a newspaper. Alan, without 3 a word, handed him the card he had been given. "Sit down, Mr. Austen," said the old man very politely. "I am glad to make your acquaintance."

"Is it true," asked Alan, "that you have a certain mixture that has—er— 4 quite extraordinary effects?"

"My dear sir," replied the old man, "my stock in trade is not very 5 large—I don't deal in laxatives and teething mixtures—but such as it is, it is varied. I think nothing I sell has effects which could be precisely described as ordinary."

"Well, the fact is . . ." began Alan. 6

"Here, for example," interrupted the old man, reaching for a bottle from 7 the shelf. "Here is a liquid as colourless as water, almost tasteless, quite imperceptible in coffee, wine, or any other beverage. It is also quite imperceptible to any known method of autopsy."

"Do you mean it is a poison?" cried Alan, very much horrified. 8

"Call it a glove-cleaner if you like," said the old man indifferently. 9 "Maybe it will clean gloves. I have never tried. One might call it a life-cleaner. Lives need cleaning sometimes."

"I want nothing of that sort," said Alan. 10

"Probably it is just as well," said the old man. "Do you know the price 11 of this? For one teaspoonful, which is sufficient, I ask five thousand dollars. Never less. Not a penny less."

"I hope all your mixtures are not as expensive," said Alan apprehensively. 12

"Oh dear, no," said the old man. "It would be no good charging that 13 sort of price for a love potion, for example. Young people who need a love potion very seldom have five thousand dollars. Otherwise they would not need a love potion."

"I am glad to hear that," said Alan. 14

"I look at it like this," said the old man. "Please a customer with one 15 article, and he will come back when he needs another. Even if it is more costly. He will save up for it, if necessary."

"So," said Alan, "you really do sell love potions?" 16

"If I did not sell love potions," said the old man, reaching for another 17 bottle, "I should not have mentioned the other matter to you. It is only when one is in a position to oblige that one can afford to be so confidential."

"And these potions," said Alan. "They are not just—just—er—" 18

"Oh, no," said the old man. "Their effects are permanent, and extend 19 far beyond the mere casual impulse. But they include it. Oh, yes, they include it. Bountifully, insistently. Everlastingly."

"Dear me!" said Alan, attempting a look of scientific detachment. "How 20 very interesting!"

"But consider the spiritual side," said the old man. 21

"I do, indeed," said Alan.   22

"For indifference," said the old man, "they substitute devotion. For 23 scorn, adoration. Give one tiny measure of this to the young lady—its flavour is imperceptible in orange juice, soup, or cocktails—and however gay and giddy she is, she will change altogether. She will want nothing but solitude and you."

"I can hardly believe it," said Alan. "She is so fond of parties."   24

"She will not like them anymore," said the old man. "She will be afraid 25 of the pretty girls you may meet."

"She will actually be jealous?" cried Alan in a rapture. "Of me?"   26

"Yes, she will want to be everything to you."   27

"She *is,* already. Only she doesn't care about it."   28

"She will, when she has taken this. She will care intensely. You will be 29 her sole interest in life."

"Wonderful!" cried Alan.   30

"She will want to know all you do," said the old man. "All that has 31 happened to you during the day. Every word of it. She will want to know what you are thinking about, why you smile suddenly, why you are looking sad."

"That *is* love!" cried Alan.   32

"Yes," said the old man. "How carefully she will look after you! She 33 will never allow you to be tired, to sit in a draught, to neglect your food. If you are an hour late, she will be terrified. She will think you are killed, or that some siren has caught you."

"I can hardly imagine Diana like that!" cried Alan, overwhelmed with joy. 34

"You will not have to use your imagination," said the old man. "And, 35 by the way, since there are always sirens, if by any chance you *should,* later on, slip a little, you need not worry. She will forgive you, in the end. She will be terribly hurt, of course, but she will forgive you—in the end."

"That will not happen," said Alan fervently.   36

"Of course not," said the old man. "But if it did, you need not worry. 37 She would never divorce you. Oh, no! And, of course, she will never give you the least, the very least grounds for—uneasiness."

"And how much," said Alan, "is this wonderful mixture?"   38

"It is not as dear," said the old man, "as the glove-cleaner, or life-cleaner, 39 as I sometimes call it. No. That is five thousand dollars, never a penny less. One has to be older than you are, to indulge in that sort of thing. One has to save up for it."

"But the love potion?" said Alan.   40

"Oh, that," said the old man, opening the drawer in the kitchen table, 41 and taking out a tiny, rather dirty-looking phial. "That is just a dollar."

"I can't tell you how grateful I am," said Alan, watching him fill it.   42

"I like to oblige," said the old man. "Then customers come back, later 43 in life, when they are better off, and want more expensive things. Here you are. You will find it very effective."

"Thank you again," said Alan. "Good-bye." 44

"*Au Revoir*," said the old man. [Good-bye. Until we meet again.] 45

(John Collier, "The Chaser," 1940, 1951, 1979)

 COMPREHENSION CHECKUP

Multiple Choice

Directions: For each item, write the letter corresponding to the best answer.

___c___ 1. A chaser is a drink that takes away the taste of another drink. What is Diana's likely chaser?
   a. orange juice
   b. milk
   c. poison
   d. beer

___d___ 2. The old man describes the glove-cleaner as having all of the following qualities *except* for which?
   a. It is colorless as water.
   b. It is almost tasteless.
   c. It is imperceptible in most beverages.
   d. It is ordinary.

___c___ 3. In the story, the word *siren* refers to
   a. a device that gives out a loud wailing sound as a warning.
   b. a sea nymph who is part woman and part bird.
   c. a woman who is seductive and beautiful.
   d. a member of the salamander family.

___d___ 4. When the old man says that later on Alan might "slip a little," he means that Alan might
   a. lose his footing.
   b. move stealthily.
   c. make a verbal error.
   d. cheat on Diana.

___a___ 5. Before taking the love potion, Diana is described as being
   a. fond of parties.
   b. deeply in love with Alan.
   c. jealous of other women Alan meets.
   d. all of the above.

___b___ 6. After taking the love potion, Diana will
   a. want to share Alan's company with others.
   b. want to be alone with Alan.
   c. continue to be lighthearted and exuberant.
   d. be neglectful of Alan's well-being.

___a___ 7. The old man's profession is most similar to that of
   a. a pharmacist or a chemist.
   b. a psychologist.
   c. a therapist.
   d. a lawyer.

_d_   8. A synonym for *oblige* is
a. bother.
b. to do a favor or service for.
c. satisfy.
d. both b and c.

_a_   9. At the beginning of the story, Alan feels all the following *except*
a. exhausted.
b. horrified.
c. nervous.
d. apprehensive.

_c_   10. At the conclusion of the story, Alan feels all the following *except*
a. joyful.
b. grateful.
c. fearful.
d. relieved.

_c_   11. The story is told by
a. Alan.
b. Diana.
c. a narrator.
d. the old man.

_d_   12. The main idea of the story is that
a. young people never know what will make them happy.
b. love potions don't work.
c. Alan will get over his crush on Diana and find a new love interest.
d. Alan thinks he's going to be happy with an all-consuming love, but he's going to find it suffocating.

True or False

Directions: Indicate whether each statement is true or false by writing **T** or **F** in the space provided.

_F_   13. The old man says that if Alan becomes tempted by another woman, Diana will never forgive him.

_T_   14. The old man implies that at some point in Alan's life he will grow tired of Diana.

_T_   15. Someone referred Alan to the old man.

_F_   16. The old man sells many items that could be considered ordinary.

_F_   17. The old man's shop is in an affluent area.

_T_   18. The mixture referred to as a "glove-cleaner" is actually poison.

_T_   19. In contrast to the "glove-cleaner," the love potion is inexpensive.

_T_   20. The old man makes his money on customers returning for more-expensive items.

_T_   21. The love potion will cause Diana to be incapable of anything but permanent devotion to Alan.

_T_   22. The old man indicates that he likes to please his customers.

Completion

Directions: Complete the following cause-and-effect diagram.

Cause (Why?)	Effect (What result?)
Alan purchases a love potion to make Diana "love" him.	1. Diana will fall "head over heels" in love with Alan.
	2. Alan will eventually feel suffocated by Diana's devotion.
	3. Alan will <u>poison Diana.</u>

Vocabulary in Context

Directions: In the blanks below, write the word from the list that best completes each sentence. Use each word only once.

autopsy	confidential	creaky	detachment	imperceptible	indulge
obscure	peered	scorn	sole	solitude	

1. Although I try to stay away from rich foods, every once in a while I ____<u>indulge</u>____ myself by having a hot fudge sundae with nuts, whipped cream, and a cherry.

2. A tiny baby was the ____<u>sole</u>____ survivor of American Airlines Flight 209.

3. Sue wanted to surprise her husband on his birthday with a special present, and so she looked everywhere for a(n) ____<u>obscure</u>____ hood ornament for his 1965 Corvette.

4. Unable to see a thing without his glasses, the old man ____<u>peered</u>____ closely at the bus schedule in his hand.

5. Although Raymond tried to be a fair and open-minded person, he felt only revulsion and ____<u>scorn</u>____ for the man who had cut off the young girl's arms.

6. The ____<u>autopsy</u>____ revealed that the young child had died of a fractured skull.

7. Investigative reporters who work for *The National Enquirer* claim that they frequently search people's garbage in order to obtain private, <u>confidential</u> information.

8. Although she had her heart set on a sleek, modern home with up-to-date conveniences, her husband was resolved to own the Victorian mansion with the ____<u>creaky</u>____ stairs.

9. There was so much chaos at the rock concert, that Tom found himself longing for the peace and ____<u>solitude</u>____ of his home.

10. Because our dog Bandit didn't like to swallow pills, they had to be hidden in the middle of a hot dog where they became <u>imperceptible</u> to his taste and sight.

11. The judge tried not to be biased in favor of one side or the other, and so maintained a level of professional <u>detachment</u>.

In Your Own Words

1. In the very first sentence of this story, what descriptive words give the setting a sinister aspect?

2. What word or words are used to describe Alan?

3. What effects does Alan think the potion will have? Why does Alan want to purchase it? How will the potion actually affect Diana?

4. Does the old man think that Alan will return later in life? Refer to specific details in the story to support your answer. At the end of the story, what does the old man mean by "more expensive things"?

5. What does the old man mean when he says: "Young people who need a love potion very seldom have five thousand dollars. Otherwise they would not need a love potion"? What viewpoint about love is he expressing?

6. What point is Collier making about love? How can something that we want very badly end up causing us grief?

7. Why is one bottle referred to by words such as a "glove-cleaner," or a "life-cleaner"?

8. What is ironic about this story? What does Alan expect to happen? What is really going to happen?

Written Assignment

Breaking up is always hard to do, and doing it in person is almost always better than using a phone call, an instant message, or an e-mail. However, for those who just can't cope with the in-person ordeal, the authors of the popular *Dating and Sex Handbook* provide an example of a rejection letter. The trick, according to them, is to be kind, but firm.

Dear _____, [their name]

I won't be able to make it this Saturday, or any Saturday, in fact. The truth is, I just can't be in a committed relationship right now. It's not you, it's me. I'm just not able to appreciate all that you have to give.

I feel like we've been spinning our wheels these last few years/ months/ weeks/days. I can't believe how wonderful you've been to me and how much you've put up with. You deserve better. I can't put you through this anymore and I can't give you what you need/want/deserve right now. I need more space, and I need time to figure out who the real [your name here] is.

It may take some time, but I hope we can still be friends.

Sincerely,

_____ [your name here]

Just for fun, try writing your own rejection letter. Use concrete examples, but don't be too nasty!

STUDY TECHNIQUE 12: SUMMARIZING LONGER ARTICLES

Your ability to summarize will help you in college because in the process of summarizing, you will be organizing and mastering the material. Summarizing may also help you at work. For instance, a nurse might summarize a patient's condition, a sportswriter might summarize the action in a basketball game, and a police officer might summarize the events leading up to an accident.

You summarize a reading selection by stating the main idea and key supporting details in your own words. A summary condenses the original

continued

STUDY TECHNIQUE *continued*

material, and good summaries are about one-fourth the length of the original. If a summary is written well, you may not have to go back and read the selection again.

You just read "The Chaser." Now, let's summarize it. First, answer the following questions about the topic. Your answers will provide you with important details about the story.

Who is the story about? Alan Austen, Diana, and the old man

What is the story about? unrequited love on Diana's part

Where does the story take place? a tiny room on Pell Street

When does the story take place? after Alan has been rejected by Diana

Why is Alan visiting the old man? Alan wants Diana to fall in love with him.

How is Alan going to make Diana love him? Alan wishes to purchase a love potion.

In your own words, write five main points from the selection, along with a supporting detail for each main point.

Point 1: Alan Austen is in love with Diana and wants her to be in love with him.

Detail: Diana is completely indifferent to Alan.

Point 2: Alan visits the old man to purchase a love potion.

Detail: Someone has recommended the old man's potions to Alan.

Point 3: The old man describes another potion, which is actually poison for use later on after Alan tires of Diana's excessive devotion.

Detail: The poison is undetectable in an autopsy, but it's expensive.

Point 4: Alan purchases the love potion even after hearing about its permanent effects.

Detail: The love potion will change Diana into a person unlike her current self.

Point 5: Alan thinks he's going to be happy with Diana, but the old man thinks he'll be coming back to purchase the poison.

Detail: The old man says good-bye until we meet again.

Now try to write your summary. Focus on the main points and include just enough details to support your main points. You may have to add a few details so that the summary makes sense. Use transition words to smoothly connect everything. After completing your summary, compare your version with the one found in the Appendices.

Chapter Summary and Review

In Chapter 9, you became familiar with several modes of organization. You also practiced summarizing longer reading passages. Based on the material in Chapter 9, answer the following questions.

Short Answer

Directions: Answer the following questions briefly, in a few words or sentences as appropriate.

1. What questions should you ask yourself in writing a summary? __Who?__ __What?__ __Where?__ __When?__ __Why?__ and __How?__

2. How many steps does SQ3R require? __Five__

Vocabulary in Context

Directions: Choose one of the following words to complete the sentences below. Use each word only once.

   categories   cause   chronological   condenses   effect   mapping   modes
   outlining   survey   time line

1. When you fail to study for a test and do poorly, your lack of preparation is a(n) __cause__ and your poor performance is a(n) __effect__.

2. People usually tell stories in __chronological__ order.

3. Chronological order and cause and effect are __categories__ that describe __modes__ of organization.

4. A less formal and more visual way of outlining information is called __mapping__.

5. __Outlining__ is a formal way of organizing written material.

6. The first step of SQ3R is __survey__.

7. When written material needs to be organized chronologically, a __time line__ might be useful.

8. A summary __condenses__ the original material.

Reading Critically

AMERICAN IDOL

In the imagination of the public, nothing is more compelling than the "star is born" scenario, where a hopeful unknown gets a big break, and becomes a celebrity. For decades this drama has been played out in television shows featuring amateur competition. Some contestants become sensations while mediocre performers are, at best, rejected and, at worst, subjected to ridicule and insults.

Premiering in the summer of 2002 on the FOX network, *American Idol* tapped into the current craze for "reality" television. It granted viewers a window into the lives of real people—in this case, someone trying to become a star, from start to finish. In the case of *American Idol*, the finish could come sooner rather than later. One of the show's more effective features was a harsh judge, successful British entertainment producer Simon Cowell, who not only accepted or rejected the hopeful, but mercilessly belittled the poor contestant who didn't meet his approval. The very first winner of *American Idol*, female vocalist Kelly Clarkson, went on to record two multi-platinum albums and was nominated for a Grammy Award. Winning second place wasn't bad either. In the second season, runner-up Clay Aiken became the sentimental favorite and his career eclipsed that of the winner, Ruben Studdard. Carrie Underwood was the first major country star to have been a product of *American Idol*. She won the top spot on the show in 2005 and soon recorded her first album, *Some Hearts*, which featured the hit single "Jesus, Take the Wheel." (252 words) **(David Lee Joyner, *American Popular Music*, 3/e 2009)**

TIMED READING If you wish to use "American Idol" as a timed reading, please turn to page A-4 in the Appendices.

Fact and Opinion

CHAPTER PREVIEW
In this chapter, you will

• Develop strategies to help you tell the difference between fact and opinion.

Introduction to Fact and Opinion

Fact

A **fact** is a statement that can be proved to be true or false in some objective way. You can prove it yourself, or you can turn to some objective authority such as records, tests, or historical or scientific documents. Statements of fact often rely on concrete data or measurements. Here are some examples of facts and how they can be proved.

"So many men, so many opinions."

—Terence

Statements of Fact	Sources of Proof
1. Abraham Lincoln was the 16th president of the United States.	History book
2. Sara is taller than Kate.	Measurement
3. My favorite candidate won the election.	Counting votes
4. The movie is playing at 6:15.	Looking at movie listings

It is important to realize that statements of fact can sometimes be false. At one time in the past, it was considered to be a "fact" that the earth was at the center of the universe. Of course, we now know this is not true. Until recently, the following statement was considered to be a fact.

Star Wars is the top domestic money-earner of all time.

This is no longer a true "fact" because in 1997, the movie *Titanic* surpassed *Star Wars* in box office receipts. Now *Avatar* has surpassed *Titanic*.

Some ""statements of fact" are false because they are based on erroneous information. Comedians like to joke that if you ask most women over 40 their age, you're going to get a false answer. Other "facts" that are based on numbers and statistics may be false because data of this sort can be easily manipulated. In evaluating such information, it is best to keep in mind what Mark Twain famously said: "There are lies, damn lies, and statistics."

Opinion

Opinions are statements of belief or judgment that cannot be proved by any objective means. Any statement that deals with probabilities or future events is an opinion because it cannot be proved. For example, if I said that the United States will do better in the next World Cup tournament, I would be expressing an opinion. Opinions often rely on words that express a value judgment. Below are some examples of opinions. While some people may agree with these statements, others will disagree. The words that express value judgments are in italics.

Statements of Opinion

1. Abraham Lincoln was a *great* president. (value judgment)
2. It's *better* to be tall than to be short. (value judgment)
3. My candidate was the *most interesting*. (value judgment)
4. The movie is a *good* one. (value judgment)
5. He is going to get the most votes in the next election. (future event)
6. She is the nicest person in the world. (exaggeration)

The following are some examples of words that signal an opinion.

Words and Phrases That Signal an Opinion

I believe	Perhaps	This suggests
Apparently	In my view	Presumably
It seems likely	Many experts agree	In my opinion
One interpretation is	One possibility is	

Following are some examples of words that can signal value judgments.

Words That Signal Value Judgment

necessary	interesting	effective
beautiful, attractive, *etc.*	highest *or* lowest	most *or* least
best *or* worst	bad	nice
greatest	successful	wonderful

Some opinions have more validity than others. Opinions that are backed up by facts belong to this category. To make a case for Abraham Lincoln being a great president, I could talk about his many achievements. My statement would still be an opinion, only now it would be well supported. Opinions given by experts are more reliable than opinions given by someone lacking specialized knowledge. For instance, Michael Jordan's opinion on basketball would carry more weight than that of someone who has never played the game.

Much of what we read and hear is a combination of fact and opinion. To evaluate such information, we need to be able to distinguish between the two.

Exercise 1: Thinking about Facts and Opinions

Directions: Using complete sentences, write six facts about yourself. Then think about some opinions you have, and write down six of them.

Facts about You

1. Answers will vary. _____
2. _____
3. _____
4. _____
5. _____
6. _____

Your Opinions

1. _____
2. _____
3. _____
4. _____
5. _____
6. _____

Exercise 2: Recognizing Facts and Opinions

Directions: Place an **F** in the blank for those statements that are mostly factual and an **O** in the blank for those statements that are mostly opinion. Circle the abstract or value judgment words in the statements of opinion.

___O___ 1. The community college is a (better) place to attend school for the first two years than a university or a four-year school.

___F___ 2. *U.S. News & World Report* found that 100 percent of the students at Harvard University were in the top quarter of their high school graduating class.

___O___ 3. David McCullough's *John Adams* is a (convincing) portrait of one of the (dominant) men of the Revolutionary War.

___F___ 4. According to Sharon Thompson's 2011 research study, teenagers' rates of drug use, eating disorders, depression, and suicide are rising.

___F___ 5. The book I'm reading now is number one after its second week on the *New York Times* fiction best-seller list.

___O___ 6. At $13.95 a copy, the book is a (real bargain.)

___F___ 7. In a 2011 study, the American Medical Association reported that drinking is heaviest among singles and the newly divorced.

___F___ 8. A 2011 study by A. C. Nielsen Company showed that home use of the Internet has cut TV viewing, with wired homes watching an average of 13 percent less television.

    F   9. According to data reported in *Retirement Places Rated*, Las Vegas, with a grade of 84.5, is America's number-one retirement destination.

    F   10. Researchers from the University of Arizona recently tested 500 used kitchen dishcloths and found that two-thirds contain bacteria that can make people sick.

    O   11. Toothpaste containing peroxide and baking soda is (far better) at producing clean and (attractive) teeth.

    F   12. Researchers at Ohio State University found that women experience anxiety and depression about 30 percent more often than men.

    O   13. Women have (greater burdens) and (limitations) placed on them in both the workplace and the family.

Exercise 3: More Recognizing Facts and Opinions

Directions: Read the following sentences and put an **O** in the blank if the statement is an opinion or an **F** if the statement is a fact. Circle the opinion words that indicate probabilities or future events.

    F   1. The Victoria's Secret catalog offers 45 items in satin.

    O   2. You (will learn) more from reading books than you (will from watching) television.

    O   3. By the year 2020, we (will be unable) to function as a society without computers.

    F   4. A recent Ohio State study showed that playing the violin or the cello burns 40 percent more calories than watching TV.

    F   5. In 1923, F. Scott Fitzgerald called a collection of his short stories *Tales of the Jazz Age*.

    F   6. The National Highway Department, in its 2010 study, concluded that elderly drivers (those over the age of 70) are responsible for the majority of driving fatalities in the United States.

    O   7. The United States is (certain) to do better in the (next) Olympic competition.

    F   8. The United Nations Human Development Program reports that the divorce rate in the United States is now the highest of any major industrialized nation.

    F   9. An Education Department survey showed that 70 percent of 5,500 secondary school principals approve of requiring school uniforms.

    O   10. Schools that maintain a dress code (will tend) to have fewer instances of assault, robbery, and vandalism, and at the same time (will tend) to report improved academic performance.

Exercise 4: Rewriting Opinion Statements

Directions: Working in a group, determine whether the given statement is a fact (**F**) or an opinion (**O**), and write your answer on the line provided. Then on a separate piece of paper rewrite all statements of opinion as statements of fact. Be sure to eliminate all abstract and value judgment words. Your fact sentence should use concrete words and be verifiable.

Example:

Opinion: My current house is **too small** for my family.

Fact: I have a one-bedroom house and 10 people in my family.

or

Fact: I have a 900-square foot home and 10 people in my family.

____F____ 1. My husband and I took a three-mile hike on Sunday.

____O____ 2. My spring break was much too short.

____O____ 3. My Honda Accord gets excellent gas mileage.

____F____ 4. The yearly salary for the principal of John F. Kennedy School is $75,000.

____O____ 5. He is a reckless and irresponsible driver.

____O____ 6. The iMac computer was very reasonably priced.

____F____ 7. The temperature in the oven is 375 degrees.

____O____ 8. My English teacher graded my last essay unfairly.

____O____ 9. Of all my college classes, my computer class has been the most helpful.

____O____ 10. Tiger Woods is the best golfer in Professional Golf Association (PGA) history.

Exercise 5: Distinguishing Fact from Opinion

Many writers try to convince readers of the wisdom of their arguments by combining facts and opinions, often within the same sentence. The following sentences contain both fact and opinion. The facts have been italicized.

1. *With half of all American marriages failing,* it appears that "till death do us part" simply means until the going gets rough.

2. *A USA Today poll showed that 65 percent of Americans were unable to identify* the Bill of Rights, thus demonstrating the widespread ignorance of the population at large.

Directions: After reading each sentence, underline only the facts.

1. With the <u>National Institute on Drug Abuse estimating that at least 500,000 high school students use or have used steroids</u>, it is obvious that something needs to be done about the growing drug threat among teens.

2. <u>Immediately after divorce, the income of households with kids declines by 21 percent</u>, thereby creating an unfortunate new class of people in poverty—divorced women with children.

3. Male adults who enjoy light or moderate drinking should keep right on enjoying imbibing, since <u>research by Serge Renaud of the National Institutes of Health on 36,000 middle-age men demonstrated that those who drank two to four glasses of wine a day had a 30–40 percent reduction in mortality from all causes.</u>

4. In the state of Illinois, the delicate balance between a boss's right to know what's going on in the office and an employee's right to privacy has been upset by a 1995 state law that permits bosses to eavesdrop on employees' work telephones.

5. California, the state where 1.8 million civil lawsuits were filed in 2007, perhaps should have a new motto emblazoned on all license plates—Home of Litigators.

6. In 1981, the product NutraSweet was introduced to the public as a boon to the overweight, yet the Centers for Disease Control and Prevention recently reported that U.S. obesity rates have actually increased since that time.

7. Despite the fact that many physicians, scientists, and consumer advocates regard homeopathic medicines as ineffective at best and dangerous at worst, the National Center for Homeopathy reports that Americans are spending more than $165 million annually on homeopathic preparations.

READING

"People like to think that their opinions are supported by the 'facts.' However, they sometimes form their opinions first and then devise 'facts' that support those opinions."

TUNING IN TO READING   Can you think of a recent issue that has attracted a lot of attention? Today when public officials want to gauge the public's feelings about an issue, they commission a public opinion poll. It may surprise you to know that pollsters arrive at their results after polling only a small group of people. They assume that the opinions of this small group will reflect the opinions of the public at large. Most of the time, polling leads to fairly accurate results. But this is not always true. Can you think of any recent instances when what pollsters were saying about public opinion turned out to be misleading or wrong?

BIO-SKETCH   Thomas Patterson is Bradlee Professor of Government and the Press in the John F. Kennedy School of Government at Harvard University. Previously he was a Distinguished Professor of Political Science at Syracuse University. He has received many awards for his books and articles.

NOTES ON VOCABULARY
entails   makes necessary; requires; involves.

THE NATURE OF PUBLIC OPINION
Thomas Patterson

Public opinion can be defined as the politically relevant opinions held by ordinary citizens that they express openly. This expression need not be verbal. It could also take the form, for example, of a protest demonstration or a vote for one candidate rather than another. The crucial point is that a person's private thoughts on an issue become public opinion when they are expressed openly.

How Informed Is Public Opinion?

A practical obstacle to government by public opinion is that people have dif- 2
fering opinions; in responding to one side of an issue, government is compelled
to reject other preferences. Public opinion can also be contradictory. Polls indicate, for example, that most Americans would like better schools, health care,
and other public services, while also favoring a reduction in taxes. Which opinion of the people should govern—their desire for more services, or their desire
for lower taxes?

Another limitation is that people's opinions, even on issues of great impor- 3
tance, are often misinformed. In the buildup to the U.S. invasion of Iraq in
2003, for example, polls revealed that more than half of the American public
wrongly believed that Iraqis were among the nineteen terrorists who had flown
airplanes into the World Trade Center and Pentagon on September 11, 2001.
Moreover, despite opposition to the war on the part of most Europeans, Asians,
South Americans, and Africans, one-fourth of Americans wrongly believed that
world opinion favored the war. Americans who held such views were more
supportive of the Iraq war than were other Americans.

The public's relatively low level of accurate information is due partly to 4
what is called "the will to believe." People like to think that their opinions are
supported by the "facts." However, they sometimes form their opinions first
and then devise "facts" that support those opinions.

Moreover, most Americans are not closely attentive to politics and therefore 5
do not possess a lot of factual information. Americans are not unique in this
respect, but in some areas they are less informed than citizens of most other
Western democracies. In a seven-country survey, Americans ranked next to last
in their ability to respond correctly to five factual questions about prominent
world leaders and developments. Despite America's leading role in the world,
most Americans are less informed about global affairs than are most Europeans.
Analysts suggest that America's "ocean isolation" is a reason why its citizens
are insular. Unlike Europeans, Americans are not surrounded by a host of other
countries. But ocean isolation is not a complete explanation. Americans share
a border with Canadians and Mexicans, for example, but know much less about
Canada and Mexico than Canadians and Mexicans know about the United
States.

Even many college-educated Americans lack basic information about pub- 6
lic affairs. A survey of Ivy League students found that one-third could not
identify the British prime minister, half could not name both U.S. senators
from their state, and three-fourths could not identify Abraham Lincoln as the
author of the phrase "a government of the people, by the people, and for
the people."

Of course, citizens do not always have to be well informed about an issue 7
to have a reasonable opinion about it. Opinions derive largely from people's
values and interests. People can have sound opinions on the abortion issue, for
example, without precise knowledge of what courts and lawmakers have done
on the issue. Nevertheless, the public's lack of information limits the role that
public opinion can play in policy formation. The choice among policy options
in some cases requires an understanding of the consequences of the different
opinions. Citizens usually lack this type of information.

Citizenship entails responsibilities, one of which is to stay informed about 8 problems and developments that affect the community, the state, and the nation. As an informed citizen, you will be better able to make judgments about policy issues, to choose wisely when voting during elections, and to recognize situations that call for greater personal involvement. Fortunately, you have access to one of the most substantial news systems in the world. News about public affairs is virtually at your fingertips—through your computer, on television, and in the newspaper. Spending only a small amount of time each day following the news will enable you to be a more effective and involved citizen.

(Thomas Patterson, *The American Democracy*, 8/e, 2008)

 COMPREHENSION CHECKUP

Fact and Opinion

Directions: Indicate whether each statement is a fact or an opinion by writing **F** or **O** in the blank provided.

____O____ 1. Another limitation is that people's opinions, even on issues of great importance, often are misinformed.

____O____ 2. People like to think that their opinions are supported by the "facts."

____O____ 3. Moreover, most Americans are not closely attentive to politics and therefore do not possess a lot of factual information.

____F____ 4. Polls indicate, for example, that most Americans would like better schools, health care, and other public services, while also favoring a reduction in taxes.

____F____ 5. In a seven-country survey, Americans ranked next to last in their ability to respond correctly to five factual questions about prominent world leaders and developments.

____F____ 6. A survey of Ivy League students found that one-third could not identify the British prime minister, half could not name both U.S. senators from their state, and three-fourths could not identify Abraham Lincoln as the author of the phrase "a government of the people, by the people, and for the people."

____O____ 7. Spending only a small amount of time each day following the news will enable you to be a more effective and involved citizen.

____O____ 8. Of course, citizens do not always have to be well informed about an issue to have a reasonable opinion about it.

____O____ 9. People can have sound opinions on the abortion issue, for example, without precise knowledge of what courts and lawmakers have done on the issue.

____O____ 10. Citizens usually lack this type of information.

Directions: Determine whether the paragraph indicated is primarily one of fact (**F**) or opinion (**O**).

____F____ 11. Paragraph 3

____O____ 12. Paragraph 4

_____O_____ 13. Paragraph 7

_____O_____ 14. Paragraph 8

Vocabulary in Context

Directions: Cross out the incorrect word in each sentence, and replace it with its antonym from the box below.

attentive	global	informed	limitation	opposition
precise	prominent	reduction	relevant	unique

_____prominent_____ 1. Only ~~insignificant~~ dignitaries were selected to accompany the president to the pope's funeral in Rome.

_____global_____ 2. The world today is so interconnected that many problems, such as air pollution, are of ~~local~~ concern.

_____precise_____ 3. Her directions, which were ~~vague~~ and to the point, enabled me to find the party easily.

_____attentive_____ 4. As a performer, he was especially grateful whenever he had ~~distracted~~ audiences.

_____unique_____ 5. There is only one Mark Twain. He is ~~ordinary~~, an American original.

_____opposition_____ 6. The political party in power will usually encounter ~~support~~ from the party out of power.

_____relevant_____ 7. Generally considered to be an authority in his field, all of his comments on the subject were ~~immaterial~~.

_____informed_____ 8. The library was going to be closed on the Fourth of July. The librarian repeatedly ~~misinformed~~ the students of this fact so that they could plan their studying accordingly.

_____reduction_____ 9. Many people credit gastric-bypass surgery for a big ~~increase~~ in their weight.

_____limitation_____ 10. His chief ~~strength~~ as a sales representative is his shyness.

In Your Own Words

In Your Own Words

1. Is government sufficiently responsive to public opinion? Can you cite examples when the government has responded by aligning itself with public opinion? What about times when the government has ignored public opinion?

2. Do you think it is important that people base their opinions on facts? Or should people pay more attention to their values and feelings when forming opinions?

3. Analyze the following quotations: Do you agree with either one? Why or why not?

   "I have learned to hold popular opinion of no value." —Alexander Hamilton

   "Public opinion in this country is everything." —Abraham Lincoln

   "We are concerned in public affairs, but immersed in our private ones." —Walter Lippmann

4. Many countries around the world have higher rates of voter turnout at elections than the United States. Why do you suppose the United States has a lower rate? What do you think could be done to improve voter participation?

Written Assignment

Directions: Write a few paragraphs discussing one of the following questions.

1. Do you think there is a significant difference between the genders on political issues? In your opinion, which gender is more likely to favor the death penalty, want stricter gun control laws, think the government should provide health insurance, and think the government should do more for the homeless? Ask 10 friends (5 male and 5 female) and compile a list of their responses. Did you find a gender gap on these issues?

2. What is your opinion of online surveys? Do you think it's possible to get a truly representative sample online?

3. Do you think people have more political sophistication today than they did in the past? Do you think citizens are better informed?

4. Why do you think people don't participate more in the political process?

Internet Activity

The Pew Research Center is a nonprofit organization that researches public opinion on current subjects. Go to its Web site at:

http://people-press.org/

Click on "About the Center." Can you find a listing of current issues the center is studying? Write a summary of what you found out about the center.

Fact and Opinion Quiz 1

Directions: Indicate whether the statement is a fact or an opinion by writing **F** or **O** in the blank provided.

__F__ 1. According to a study of kids age 12–17 conducted by the Pew Internet & American Life Project, 73 percent of kids in the United States are online.

__F__ 2. Using fire department and medical examiner reports, the *New England Journal of Medicine* found that risk of harm from house fires was 2.8 times higher for elderly people.

__O__ 3. The simplest way to have psychologically healthy children is to avoid divorce.

__O__ 4. Rudeness is the worst problem in the U.S. workplace because it damages the mental health and productivity of employees.

__F__ 5. The National Fatherhood Initiative reports that about 4 out of 10 first marriages end in divorce.

__O__ 6. Workers who bring their lunches from home and eat them at their desks make a big mistake because they end up working longer hours without a break.

__F__ 7. Over half of criminal behavior nationally is committed by individuals under the influence of drugs, according to studies by the National Institute of Justice.

__O__ 8. Astrology is a good method for predicting future events and identifying individual characteristics.

_____F_____ 9. In a government survey of 5,001 youngsters, one in five adolescents who regularly socialize on the Internet encountered a stranger who wanted "cybersex."

_____O_____ 10. Women who date strangers should hire a private detective to run a background check on potential suitors.

_____O_____ 11. Capital punishment is immoral.

_____O_____ 12. The Internet is not likely to become as essential as the telephone and the television are today.

_____F_____ 13. The research of California State University psychologist Diane Halpern demonstrates that men are likely to be better than women at finding their destinations in unfamiliar settings.

_____O_____ 14. Oprah Winfrey is a positive role model for television watchers.

_____F_____ 15. According to the Bureau of Justice Statistics, the number of local, state, and federal prisoners has risen by 676,000 since 1990.

Fact and Opinion Quiz 2

Directions: Indicate whether the statement is a fact or an opinion by writing **F** or **O** in the blank provided.

_____O_____ 1. Sixteen-year-olds shouldn't be allowed to drive because they are involved in too many accidents.

_____F_____ 2. The Insurance Institute for Highway Safety reported that the death rate for 16-year-old drivers has nearly doubled.

_____F_____ 3. According to a recent study by Dr. Bruce Pomeranz, bad reactions to prescription and over-the-counter medicines kill more than 100,000 Americans and seriously injure 2.5 million more each year.

_____O_____ 4. Middle-class families with children have a lot less money to spend.

_____O_____ 5. If young children know the difference between right and wrong, they won't be bothered by violence on TV.

_____F_____ 6. The U.S. Justice Department survey showed that 78 percent of all jail inmates reported using marijuana at some point in their lives.

_____O_____ 7. The most difficult job for the working parent is balancing the demands of work with those of family.

_____O_____ 8. Many people make the mistake of not becoming vegetarians until they have experienced a major health crisis.

_____F_____ 9. In 1997 Diana, Princess of Wales, was killed in a car crash.

_____O_____ 10. Today's workers have to work harder and faster, and they never seem to have enough time to get everything done.

_____O_____ 11. Compact cars are a lot more practical than full-size cars.

_____O_____ 12. Recent proposals by elementary school districts across the country to eliminate recess are part of an alarming trend in education.

_____F_____ 13. According to the Census Bureau, nearly a third of young children under the age of 5 are cared for in day care centers.

_____O_____ 14. Parents should search a teenager's bedroom only if they suspect the teen has been abusing drugs.

_____F_____ 15. Researchers in Scotland cloned an adult mammal, a lamb named Dolly, who is a genetic copy of her mother.

READING

"Now the son became the father, and the father the son."

TUNING IN TO READING   Tim McGraw is considered to be country music royalty. He is at the pinnacle of his career, receiving many accolades from his peers and from the public at large. However, his life wasn't always so rosy, and in fact he endured many hardships as a youth before he achieved such great professional success. In the following selection, Alanna Nash describes the long road he had to travel and the obstacles he had to overcome before he distinguished himself as a musician.

BIO-SKETCH   Alanna Nash writes for The *New York Times* and *Entertainment Weekly*. She has produced numerous books, including *Golden Girl* about Jessica Savitch, which was made into the movie *Up Close and Personal,* starring Michelle Pfeiffer and Robert Redford. She has written several books on Elvis, including *Baby, Let's Play House* (2010).

NOTES ON VOCABULARY

do-rag   a scarf or kerchief used to cover the head and often tied at the nape of the neck. The term derives from *do*, as in *hairdo*.

honky-tonk   was originally the name of a type of bar found throughout the United States. The first music known as honky-tonk was a style of piano playing related to ragtime. Later, honky-tonk came to refer to a style of country music called "hillbilly." The song lyrics focused on rural life with themes of lost love, loneliness, and alcoholism.

TIES THAT BIND   BY ALANNA NASH

Chance

Wearing a faded blue do-rag instead of his usual black Resistol cowboy hat, Tim Mc-Graw can sit nearly unrecognized in the corner of a noisy Nashville catering hall. The bandanna is only the latest in a long line of gear that McGraw uses to cover his head—and therein lies a mystery, since there really is hair under there.

2   "Not much!" says the personable country music star, flashing a winning grin. "I'm just trying to stay young."

3   And doing a fine job of it, from the looks of things. McGraw has the trim, hard body of a man a decade younger. He's married to the stunning Faith Hill, the country-pop chanteuse with whom he has three daughters. He tours constantly, ministering to a stalwart band of fans who have purchased more than 30 million of his CDs. So what if his hair is thinning?

4   "Tim McGraw occupies the Tom Cruise slot in the current country pantheon," says venerable music journalist Chet Flippo, editorial director of the country website cmt.com. "Men admire him and women desire him. No one in the country audience or the country industry, for that matter, does not like him and respect his work."

5   Work is exactly what it took for Mc-Graw to get where he is today. He grew up in rural Start, Louisiana, and can recall always having a fierce drive "to do something. I didn't know what it was going to be, but I knew that I was going to take advantage of it when I got the chance."

6   For starters, McGraw wanted to make life better for his family. "My stepfather [truck driver Horace Smith] was a wild man, a great, big-hearted guy, but he could be meaner than anybody you've ever met," says McGraw, who tried to shield his mother, Betty, and two younger sisters from the "really scary" abuse that went on in their house on a nightly basis. After his mother and Smith split in 1977, Betty sometimes held three jobs at once. When she wasn't working, the family got by on welfare. At one point, they lived in a barn with hay on the floor. Timmy Smith, as he was called then, dreamed of becoming a pro athlete and taped the baseball card of his favorite player, Tug McGraw, to his bedroom wall. In a now famous story, at age 11 he ran across his birth certificate while looking for pictures for a school project. He was astonished to read that his baseball hero and biological father were one and the same.

7   Tug—a standout relief pitcher for the Phillies and Mets—agreed to a meeting later that year. Though Tug, who now had a family of his own, remembered a tryst with the boy's mother in Jacksonville in 1966, he convinced himself that Timmy Smith could not possibly be his son. For a time, he refused to answer the boy's letters and calls—a period Tim now refers to as "the stormy years."

8   When Tim turned 18, a straight-A student graduating second in his class and heading to Northeast Louisiana University to study music and pre-law, Tug agreed to pay his tuition. But he said he wanted nothing else to do with him, and had legal documents drawn up to that effect. Tim wanted one last face-to-face meeting with Tug before he would sign the papers, so the two met in a Houston hotel.

9   "Once I turned around and saw Tim, I knew that he was my boy," Tug wrote in his autobiography, *Ya Gotta Believe!* "It was as if I was looking at a picture of myself 20 years earlier."

10   And so a relationship began, although it was rocky at first. Tug still kept Tim at arm's length, but in 1991 he helped his son get an initial record deal through a baseball pal. Years later, Tim says that reuniting with Tug inspired him to aim for the top in his career. "It made me think, If he can do that, I can do that."

Voice of the Underdog

11   With his first big single, 1994's "Indian Outlaw," Tim McGraw established himself as the voice of the underdog who insisted on standing up and being heard. He eventually moved away from a more honky-tonk sound and infused his music with the rhythms of '70s rock.

12   "There are certainly better singers in country music," explains Michael McCall, staff writer at *Country Weekly* magazine, "but there aren't better communicators."

13   His son's success amazed Tug, whose own celebrity was by then beginning to fade. Their father-son bond strengthened after Tim married and started his own family.

14   Faith and Tim say they felt instantly comfortable with each other when they first toured together in early 1996. Tim—who wears his wife's name as a tattoo on his right arm, a red heart dotting the "i"—says Faith changed his freewheeling ways. "Of course, all through your life, your wife is going to jerk you back in line about once or twice a week," he says with a laugh. "But when you get married and have a family, you get very focused on what that means and how easily it can get away from you. There's no way that I would ever dishonor my wife. Your career can come and go at any time, and you can survive losing that. But I could not stand losing my family."

15   Married later that same year, Tim and Faith have three daughters, Gracie, Maggie, and Audrey. McGraw and Hill say they work hard at instilling solid values in their children. They want to spoil them, but they also want the girls to realize what opportunities they enjoy. "I think the key thing that you have to do is teach them a sense of humility," says Tim. "We always tell them that there will be girls who are prettier and smarter, but who will never

have the chances that they do. And we say, 'Even if you don't think you deserve those chances, go out and do the best you can.'"

16   The McGraws demonstrate that philosophy themselves through their charity work. Tim supports Gridiron Heroes, a group that helps high school football players with spinal cord injuries, and he launched Swampstock, his own nonprofit organization, which funds sports associations and scholarships for kids in his Louisiana hometown. And Faith gives her time to a literacy campaign, in honor of her adoptive father, a factory worker who didn't learn to read until he reached adulthood.

"It's a Love Story"

17   McGraw says one of his chief goals is to be a devoted father, in contrast to his own role models. But Tim—who could never bring himself to call his biological father "Dad," only Tug—also wanted to be a better son.

18   The heartbreaking story of a boy who grew up without his father, then found him, and finally gained his acceptance and love, seemed to have a happy ending. But the most painful part was yet to come. The senior McGraw, who'd long seen the world as his private oyster, found himself penniless and homeless at age 58. Not long after, he learned he had brain cancer. Tim saw to it that Tug received the best medical care imaginable. Now the son became the father, and the father the son.

19   "It wasn't even a thought process," says the younger McGraw. "He got sick, and I was the one in the position to deal with it in the best possible way. I think he felt comfortable with me doing it."

20   For a while, the treatment—a combination of surgery and medical cocktails—worked, and Tug hoped he was getting better. But just after Christmas 2003, his doctor looked at him and said, "We've run out of weapons, Tugger."

21   Friends asked him where he wanted to go. Tug said Tim and Faith's cabin in Tennessee. "They had a wonderful relationship at the end, and Tug was so in awe of Tim," remembers Jennifer Brusstar, who helped care for Tug during the final phase of his illness. "It's a love story."

22   For five days, Tim sat by Tug's side and held his hand for 12 hours at a time, even though Tug was often unconscious. "It would be two or three in the morning, and Tim still wouldn't leave him," says Brusstar. "I'd walk by the bedroom and glance in, and Tim would be in a curled up position next to Tug, just like a five-year-old boy crawling up into Daddy's lap and not wanting to let go." At 4:40 in the afternoon, January 5, 2004, Tug's daughter, Cari, at Faith's suggestion, placed a cross in her father's hand. Tug awoke, opened his eyes, and then was gone. Tim, as Brusstar remembers, broke down. "I think I will miss him as though I had him all along," Tim later wrote in the introduction to Tug's book.

23   After two weeks at home, Tim went into the studio to record "Live Like You Were Dying," the title song of his CD. Tug's older brother was in the studio that night. "We all looked at each other and said, 'Let's try it,'" says Tim. "And everybody in the room [felt it]. There was magic on every note." "Live Like You Were Dying" has garnered nominations for best single and best song at the Country Music Association awards, sitting pretty with McGraw's nomination for Entertainer of the Year.

24   While McGraw has plans to keep making music—he packs even the hard-to-sell-out arenas—he's also taken a shot at acting. In 2009, he co-starred with Sandra Bullock in *The Blind Side,* which was nominated for the best picture award.

25   Despite such accomplishments, when he looks in the mirror, McGraw sees not a confident, soaring superstar, but the young, determined boy he used to be. "I'm just the same kid," he says, "still trying to prove something to somebody."

(Alanna Nash, "Ties That Bind," 2004)

✔ **COMPREHENSION CHECKUP**

Multiple Choice

Directions: For each item, write the letter corresponding to the best answer.

___c___ 1. Which statement below best states the main idea of the selection?
 a. What doesn't kill us is likely to make us stronger.
 b. Tim McGraw communicates his feelings in his songs.
 c. Tim McGraw has overcome many difficulties in life to achieve happiness and success.
 d. Tim McGraw is a very good father to his three daughters.

___b___ 2. The purpose of the selection is to
 a. entertain the reader with funny anecdotes about Tim McGraw.
 b. share the personal history of a country star.
 c. inform the reader of an incident in the life of a famous baseball player.
 d. discuss the importance of the parental bond.

___d___ 3. The author's primary pattern of organization is
 a. spatial order.
 b. definition and example.
 c. compare and contrast.
 d. chronological order.

___d___ 4. From this selection, you could infer that
 a. when Tug McGraw first met Tim, he was eager to claim Tim as his son.
 b. DNA was not used to determine whether Tug was Tim's father.
 c. Tug McGraw had not managed his money well.
 d. both b and c.

___c___ 5. This selection indicates that
 a. Tim McGraw is the type of person to hold a grudge.
 b. Tim's wife, Faith Hill, didn't encourage Tim to have a relationship with his father.
 c. Tim forgave Tug for his years of neglect and rejection.
 d. Tug was not instrumental in helping to jump-start Tim's career.

True or False

Directions: Indicate whether each statement is true or false by writing **T** or **F** in the space provided.

___T___ 6. Tim McGraw is noted for wearing a black cowboy hat.

___T___ 7. In addition to a music career, Tim McGraw is trying his hand at acting.

___F___ 8. Tug McGraw was survived by his younger brother and a daughter.

___F___ 9. Tug McGraw was immediately accepting of the news that he was Tim's father.

___T___ 10. Young Tim Smith was a fan of Tug McGraw long before he knew him as a father.

___F___ 11. Tim McGraw always wanted a music career.

___T___ 12. Horace Smith was often abusive to his wife and two daughters.

___T___ 13. As a divorced mother, Betty Smith sometimes ended up on welfare.

_T_____ 14. Tim's birth certificate identified Tug McGraw as his father.

_T_____ 15. Tim McGraw was never able to call Tug McGraw "Dad."

Fact and Opinion

Directions: Indicate whether each sentence is a statement of fact or expresses an opinion by writing **F** or **O** in the blank provided.

_O_____ 1. And he's doing a fine job of [staying young], from the looks of things.

_O_____ 2. McGraw has the trim, hard body of a man a decade younger.

_F_____ 3. After his mother and Smith split in 1977, Betty sometimes held three jobs at once.

_F_____ 4. When Tim turned 18, a straight-A student graduating second in his class and heading to Northeast Louisiana University to study music and pre-law, Tug agreed to pay his tuition.

_F_____ 5. Tim supports Gridiron Heroes, a group that helps high school football players with spinal cord injuries, and he launched Swampstock, his own nonprofit organization, which funds sports associations and scholarships for kids in his Louisiana hometown.

_O_____ 6. But the most painful part was yet to come.

_F_____ 7. After two weeks at home, Tim went into the studio to record "Live Like You Were Dying," the title song of his CD.

_F_____ 8. Tug's older brother was in the studio that night.

_O_____ 9. There was magic on every note.

_F_____ 10. In 2009, he co-starred with Sandra Bullock in *The Blind Side*, which was nominated for the best picture award.

Vocabulary in Context

Directions: Look through the given paragraph, and find a word that matches the definition.

1. pleasant or amiable (2)   personable
2. a female singer (3)   chanteuse
3. loyal; dependable (3)   stalwart
4. spot; place; position (4)   slot
5. famous people connected with an activity (4) pantheon
6. area in the countryside (5)   rural
7. a secret rendezvous (7)   tryst
8. in the beginning (10)   initial
9. rough; difficult (10)   rocky
10. filled; injected; laced (11)   infused
11. implanting (15)   instilling
12. the lack of false pride (15)   humility
13. full of admiration (21)   awe
14. gathered; acquired (23)   garnered

Vocabulary in Context Continued

Directions: Write a definition in the blank provided for each of the following words or phrases.

15. arm's length (10)   a distance sufficient to exclude intimacy

16. underdog (11)   one that is at a disadvantage; expected to lose

17. freewheeling (14)   carefree

18. seen the world as his private oyster (18)   seen the world as a place where he could do whatever he wanted

In Your Own Words

1. After reading the selection, what can you infer about Tim McGraw's character? What are his key character traits? Do you think these traits contributed to his success? In what ways?

2. Why do you think Tim McGraw kept trying to establish a connection with his father despite his father's overt rejection of him?

3. What do you think of the character traits that Tim and Faith are trying to instill in their own family? What do those traits have to say about their value system?

4. What does the title of the selection—"The Ties That Bind"—mean to you?

5. Is the author's opinion of Tim McGraw favorable or unfavorable? How can you tell?

Written Assignment

Directions: In a short essay, explain the meaning of one of the following quotes.

"Forgiveness is the attribute of the strong." —Mahatma Gandhi

"Through forgiveness the wrong is released from its emotional stranglehold on us, so that we can learn from it." —David McArthur

"Resentment is like a glass of poison that a man drinks; then he sits down and waits for his enemy to die." —Unknown

"Forgiveness does not change the past, but it does enlarge the future." —Paul Boese

"If we really want to love, we must learn how to forgive." —Mother Teresa

Internet Activity

Directions: Choose one of the following.

1. To learn more about Tug McGraw, consult the following Web sites:

   www.tugmcgraw.org (Tug McGraw Foundation)

   www.baseball-almanac.com/quotes/guomcg.shtml (Tug McGraw Quotes)

   Make a list of 10 facts that you discover about McGraw. Then state a few of his opinions.

2. Read the lyrics to "Live Like You Were Dying" (or listen to them). What opinions about life in general are being expressed in the song? Do you agree with them? Write a paragraph summarizing your reaction to the lyrics.

Exercise 6: Identifying Fact and Opinion in a Movie Review

THE BLIND SIDE MOVIE REVIEW

An Overview

Named one of the top 10 sports movies of all time by film critics, *The Blind Side* is perfect family fare for all but the very youngest. The movie depicts the inspirational story of Michael Oher, currently an offensive lineman for the Baltimore Ravens. Oher, born to a mother addicted to crack, is one of 13 children. He spent his early years being placed in, and running away from, various foster homes. As a result of the trauma of his early upbringing, Oher struggled with reading and writing and with an inability to trust others to help him. "Big Mike's" story began to change when he encountered the Tuohy family (Sean, Leigh Anne, Collins, and S.J.). The Tuohys, a well-to-do evangelical Christian family, put their faith to the test when they set out to help the 16-year-old Michael succeed in academics and life.

The Acting in *The Blind Side*

The heart of the movie is the very talented Sandra Bullock. She has starred in a number of romantic comedies, such as *Miss Congeniality* and *While You Were Sleeping*, and also the dramas *Crash, Speed,* and *A Time to Kill.* Bullock won the 2010 Best Actress Academy Award for her portrayal of the strong-willed Leigh Anne Tuohy. Bullock was initially hesitant to accept the role, claiming she didn't think she could accurately portray Leigh Anne. Thankfully, she put her misgivings aside because her performance is powerful. Her Leigh Anne Tuohy is a person of great compassion, relentless drive, and fierce loyalty. Bullock's forthright portrayal is both refreshing and quite funny. She was well-deserving of an Oscar.

A pleasant surprise is well-known country singer Tim McGraw in the role of Sean Tuohy. He makes Sean come across as well-meaning, likable, and supportive. Academy Award-winning actress Kathy Bates has a small but pivotal role as Miss Sue, Michael's tutor. With Miss Sue's patient guidance and unconventional teaching methods, Michael is able to raise his GPA to 2.52, making him eligible to play college football.

Children are sure to enjoy the performance of Jae Head as S.J. (Sean Tuohy Jr.). The scenes where S.J. helps get Michael into top physical condition, asks for numerous "small favors" from the college coaches recruiting Michael, and survives a horrific car accident thanks to Michael's protective instincts and quick reflexes are some of the most memorable in the movie.

The movie also stars Quinton Aaron as the troubled African-American homeless teen Michael Oher, who eventually becomes a college All-American and first-round NFL draft pick. Although Aaron has relatively few lines, he manages to convey a lot of emotional depth, particularly in the scenes when he begins to doubt his adopted parents' selfless love for him. The Tuohys and Miss Sue are all graduates of The University of Mississippi (Ole' Miss). As an impressively gifted athlete, Michael Oher is heavily recruited by college coaches across the country, including by Notre Dame's Lou Holtz playing himself. When Oher makes a decision to attend his adoptive parents' alma mater, an NCAA investigation is launched to determine the motives of the Tuohy family. Was their decision to adopt him really as selfless as it had originally appeared? Or were the Tuohys motivated by a desire to help their beloved university produce a championship season? Here is where Quinton Aaron shines as an actor. He manages to convey all of the scarred, reclusive teen's emotional agony over the possible betrayal of a family he has come to love and trust.

Although *The Blind Side* was nominated for a best picture Academy Award, it did not win. Still, it has become a classic feel-good movie. When it was originally screened, moviegoers routinely clapped at the end. To date more than 3 million

DVD copies have been sold. Sales of the book by Michael Lewis, upon which the movie is based, have also been impressive.

The Present

Leigh Anne Tuohy, Sean Tuohy, and Michael Oher have published books about the experiences depicted in the movie. In 2010, the Tuohys published *In a Heartbeat: Sharing the Power of Cheerful Giving*. Michael Oher's memoir, published in 2011, is titled *I Beat the Odds: From Homelessness to The Blind Side and Beyond*. Both books aim to inspire others to charitable giving.

Oher continues to thrive as a left tackle for the Baltimore Ravens, protecting the blind side of quarterback Joe Flacco. The Tuohys continue to see as many of his games as possible. Now they'll all have a renewed interest in being in Maryland. Sean Tuohy Jr. has decided to play college basketball at Loyola University in Maryland. While breaking with tradition was wrenching (his father was a guard at Ole' Miss), both S.J. and Michael see a positive in his decision to attend Loyola. He and Michael will be living only fifteen minutes away from each other. Now S.J. can easily attend Michael's games, and Miichael can easily attend S.J.'s. The two siblings are looking forward to seeing more of each other!

The Blind Side

Color/128 minutes, rated PG-13
One scene involves brief violence, drugs, and sexual references.

Fact and Opinion

Directions: The following sentences contain both fact and opinion. After reading each sentence, underline only the facts.

1. <u>Named one of the top 10 sports movies of all time by film critics</u>, *The Blind Side* is perfect family fare for all but the very youngest.

2. <u>The movie depicts</u> the inspirational story of <u>Michael Oher, currently an offensive lineman for the Baltimore Ravens.</u>

3. A pleasant surprise is well-known <u>country singer Tim McGraw in the role of Sean Tuohy.</u>

4. With Miss Sue's patient guidance and unconventional teaching methods, <u>Michael is able to raise his GPA to 2.52, making him eligible to play college football.</u>

Directions: Indicate whether each statement is a fact or an opinion by writing **F** or **O** in the blank provided.

___F___   5. Oher, born to a mother addicted to crack, is one of 13 children.

___F___   6. He spent his early years being placed in, and running away from, various foster homes.

___F___   7. The Tuohys and Miss Sue are all graduates of The University of Mississippi (Ole' Miss).

___O___   8. He makes Sean come across as well-meaning, likable, and supportive.

___O___   9. Children are sure to enjoy the performance of Jae Head as S.J. (Sean Tuohy Jr.).

___F___ 10. When Oher makes a decision to attend his adoptive parents' alma mater, an NCAA investigation is launched to determine the motives of the Tuohy family.

_____O_____ 11. Here is where Quinton Aaron shines as an actor.

_____O_____ 12. He manages to convey all of the scarred, reclusive teen's emotional agony over the possible betrayal of a family he has come to love and trust.

_____F_____ 13. Although *The Blind Side* was nominated for a best picture Academy Award, it did not win.

_____F_____ 14. To date more than 3 million DVD copies have been sold.

_____F_____ 15. Leigh Anne Tuohy, Sean Tuohy, and Michael Oher have published books about the experiences depicted in the movie.

Directions: Label each numbered sentence in the following paragraph as (F) for fact, (O) for opinion, or (B) for both.

(1) The heart of the movie is the very talented Sandra Bullock. (2) She has starred in a number of romantic comedies, such as *Miss Congeniality* and *While You Were Sleeping*, and also the dramas *Crash*, *Speed*, and *A Time to Kill*. (3) Bullock won the 2010 Best Actress Academy Award for her portrayal of the strong-willed Leigh Anne Tuohy. (4) Bullock was initially hesitant to accept the role, claiming she didn't think she could accurately portray Leigh Anne. (5) Thankfully, she put her misgivings aside because her performance is powerful. (6) Her Leigh Anne Tuohy is a person of great compassion, relentless drive, and fierce loyalty. (7) Bullock's forthright portrayal is both refreshing and quite funny. (8) She was well-deserving of an Oscar.

Sentence 1 _O_____

Sentence 2 _F_____

Sentence 3 _B_____

Sentence 4 _F_____

Sentence 5 _O_____

Sentence 6 _O_____

Sentence 7 _O_____

Sentence 8 _O_____

READING

"Toothpaste manufacture is a very lucrative occupation."

TUNING IN TO READING   Most of us attempt to maintain healthy teeth and good oral hygiene by brushing at least once a day. But have you ever stopped to consider what's actually in the toothpaste we're using? Are those ingredients that we can't pronounce good for us, or at least not causing us harm?

In June 2007, the U.S. Food and Drug Administration (FDA) advised consumers to avoid certain brands of toothpaste manufactured in China after batches of Chinese-made toothpaste were found to contain the poisonous chemicals diethylene glycol (also called diglycol or DEG). The chemical is used in antifreeze as a solvent, and ingesting it is potentially fatal. As stated on most tubes, toothpaste is not intended to be swallowed. In fact, it can be harmful especially to children.

When you examine the ingredients on the label of your own tube of toothpaste, you may see the following: hydrated silica (sand), which is the abrasive found in most gel toothpastes; common detergents such as sodium lauryl sulfates and lauryl sarcosinate; sodium carbonate peroxide or titanium dioxide for whitening; and triclosan, a controversial chemical, which is found in some brands.

READING (continued)

BIO-SKETCH David Bodanis earned a degree in mathematics from the University of Chicago. Bodanis has a talent for explaining complex topics in simple, easy-to-understand language. Some of the books he has written are $E = MC^2$, *The Secret Family, The Secret Garden, The Body Book,* and *The Secret House,* from which this excerpt is taken.

NOTES ON VOCABULARY

hunker down   to settle in a location for an extended period; hide out; hold firm. The phrase is from the Old Norse word *hokra,* meaning "to crouch."

errant   straying; wayward. From Old French *erer,* meaning "to travel about."

dollop   a small portion or amount. From the Norwegian word *dolp,* meaning "lump."

gustatory   of or relating to the sense of taste. From the Latin *gustare,* meaning "to taste."

What's in Your Toothpaste?

DAVID BODANIS

INTO THE BATHROOM GOES OUR MALE RESIDENT, and after the most pressing need is satisfied, it's time to brush the teeth. The tube of toothpaste is squeezed, its pinched metal seams are splayed, pressure waves are generated inside, and the paste begins to flow. But what's in this toothpaste, so carefully being extruded . . .?

Water mostly, 30 to 45 percent in most brands: ordinary, everyday simple tap water. It's there because people like to have a big glob of toothpaste to spread on the brush, and water is the cheapest stuff there is when it comes to making big globs. Dripping a bit from the tap onto your brush would cost virtually nothing. Whipped in with the rest of the toothpaste, the manufacturers can sell it at a neat and accountant-pleasing $4 per pound equivalent. Toothpaste manufacture is a very lucrative occupation.

Second to water in quantity is chalk: exactly the same material children use to draw on sidewalks. It is collected from the crushed remains of long-dead ocean creatures. In the Cretaceous seas, chalk particles served as part of the wickedly sharp outer skeletons that these creatures had to wrap around themselves to keep from getting chomped by all the slightly larger ocean creatures they met. Their massed graves are our present chalk deposits.

The individual chalk particles—the size of the smallest mud particles in your garden—have kept their toughness over the eons, and now on the toothbrush they'll need it. The enamel outer coating of the tooth they'll have to face is the hardest substance in the body—tougher than skull, or bone, or nail. Only the chalk particles in toothpaste can successfully grind into the teeth during brushing, ripping off the surface layers like an abrading wheel grinding down a boulder in a quarry.

The craters, slashes, and channels that the chalk tears into the teeth will 5 also remove a certain amount of built-up yellow in carnage, and it is for that polishing function that it's there. A certain amount of unduly enlarged extra-abrasive chalk fragments tear such cavernous pits into the teeth that future decay bacteria will be able to hunker down there and thrive; the quality control people find it almost impossible to screen out these errant super-chalk pieces, and government regulations allow them to stay in.

In case even the gouging doesn't get all the yellow off, another substance 6 is worked into the toothpaste cream. This is titanium dioxide. It comes in tiny spheres, and it's the stuff bobbing around in white wall paint to make it come out white. Splashed around onto your teeth during the brushing, it coats much of the yellow that remains. Being water soluble, it leaks off in the next few hours and is swallowed, but at least for the quick glance up in the mirror after finishing, it will make the user think his teeth are truly white. Some manufacturers add optical whitening dyes—the stuff more commonly found in washing machine bleach—to make extra sure that the glance in the mirror shows reassuring white.

These ingredients alone would not make a very attractive concoction. 7 They would stick in the tube like a sloppy white plastic lump, hard to squeeze out as well as revolting to the touch. Few consumers would savor rubbing in a mixture of water, ground-up blackboard chalk, and the whitener from latex paint first thing in the morning. To get around that finicky distaste the manufacturers have mixed in a host of other goodies.

To keep the glop from drying out, a mixture including glycerine glycol— 8 related to the most common anti-freeze ingredient—is whipped in with the chalk and water, and to give *that* concoction a bit of substance (all we really have so far is wet colored chalk), a large helping is added of gummy molecules from the seaweed *Chondrus crispus*. This seaweed ooze spreads in among the chalk, paint, and anti-freeze, then stretches itself in all directions to hold the whole mass together. A bit of paraffin oil (like fuel that flickers in camping lamps) is pumped in with it to help the moss ooze keep the whole substance smooth.

With the glycol, ooze, and paraffin we're almost there. Only two major 9 chemicals are left to make the refreshing, cleansing substance we know as toothpaste. The ingredients so far are fine for cleaning, but they wouldn't make much of the satisfying foam we have come to expect in the morning brushing.

To remedy that, every toothpaste on the market has a big dollop of 10 detergent added too. You've seen the suds detergent will make in the washing machine. The same substance added here will duplicate that inside the mouth. It's not particularly necessary, but it sells.

The only problem is that by itself this ingredient tastes, well, too like 11 detergent. It's horribly bitter and harsh. The chalk put in toothpaste is pretty foul-tasting too for that matter. It's to get around that gustatory discomfort that the manufacturers put in the ingredient they tout perhaps the most of all. This is the flavoring, and it has to be strong. Double rectified peppermint oil is used—a flavor so powerful that chemists know better than to sniff it in the raw state in the laboratory. Menthol crystals and saccharine or other sugar simulators are added to complete the camouflage operation.

Is that it? Chalk, water, paint, seaweed, anti-freeze, paraffin oil, detergent, 12 and peppermint? Not quite. A mix like that would be irresistible to the hundreds of thousands of individual bacteria lying on the surface of even an immaculately cleaned bathroom sink. They would get in, float in the water bubbles, ingest the ooze and paraffin, maybe even spray out enzymes to break down the chalk. The result would be an uninviting mess. The way manu-facturers avoid that final obstacle is by putting something in it to kill the bacteria. Something good and strong is needed, something that will zap any accidentally intrudant bacteria into oblivion. And that something is formaldehyde—the disinfectant used in anatomy labs.

So it's chalk, water, paint, seaweed, anti-freeze, paraffin oil, detergent, 13 peppermint, formaldehyde, and fluoride (which can go some ways towards preserving children's teeth)—that's the usual mixture raised to the mouth on the toothbrush for a fresh morning's clean. If it sounds too unfortunate, take heart. Studies show that thorough brushing with just plain water will often do as good a job.

(David Bodanis, *The Secret House,* 2003)

 COMPREHENSION CHECKUP

Short Answer

Directions: Answer the questions briefly.

1. What is the topic of the selection? toothpaste ingredients

2. What is the selection's main idea? Toothpaste has many unappetizing ingredients, some of which may actually be harmful to our health.

3. List three details supporting the author's main idea. Toothpaste contains chalk particles, titanium dioxide (the whitener from latex paint), glycerine glycol (similar to antifreeze), seaweed, paraffin oil, detergent, peppermint, and formaldehyde.

Fact and Opinion

Directions: Determine whether the paragraph indicated is primarily one of fact (**F**) or opinion (**O**).

____F____ 4. Paragraph 3

____O____ 5. Paragraph 7

Directions: Identify each numbered sentence in the following paragraphs as either a fact (**F**) or an opinion (**O**).

(1) "With the glycol, ooze, and paraffin we're almost there." (2) "Only two major chemicals are left to make the refreshing, cleansing substance we know as

toothpaste." (3) "The ingredients so far are fine for cleaning, but they wouldn't make much of the satisfying foam we have come to expect in the morning brushing."

___F___ 6. Sentence 1

___O___ 7. Sentence 2

___O___ 8. Sentence 3

(1) "So it's chalk, water, paint, seaweed, anti-freeze, paraffin oil, detergent, peppermint, formaldehyde, and fluoride (which can go some ways towards preserving children's teeth)—that's the usual mixture raised to the mouth on the toothbrush for a fresh morning's clean." (2) "If it sounds too unfortunate, take heart. (3) Studies show that thorough brushing with just plain water will often do as good a job."

___F___ 9. Sentence 1

___O___ 10. Sentence 2

___F___ 11. Sentence 3

Directions: In each of the following sentences, underline the words that indicate an opinion.

12. "Only two major chemicals are left to make the refreshing, cleansing substance we know as toothpaste."

13. "Whipped in with the rest of the toothpaste, the manufacturers can sell it at a neat and accountant-pleasing $4 per pound equivalent."

14. "Toothpaste manufacture is a very lucrative occupation."

Multiple Choice

Directions: For each item, write the letter corresponding to the best answer.

___a___ 1. The main ingredient in toothpaste is
   a. water.
   b. chalk.
   c. formaldehyde.
   d. none of the above.

___a___ 2. Which of the following is true, according to the selection?
   a. The chalk in toothpaste comes from long-dead ocean creatures.
   b. Toothpaste gels are healthier than regular paste.
   c. It's a good idea to brush after each meal.
   d. Children should be encouraged to chew gum to clean their teeth.

___c___ 3. From the selection, you could conclude that
   a. toothpaste contains only harmful ingredients.
   b. toothpaste contains only healthful ingredients.
   c. toothpaste contains many unappetizing ingredients.
   d. toothpaste contains lead and other metals.

___c___ 4. According to the selection, the enamel in teeth
   a. is very prone to yellowish stains.
   b. is water soluble.
   c. is the hardest substance in the body.
   d. should be scraped clean on a regular basis.

_____d_____ 5. According to information presented in the selection
    a. seaweed is added to toothpaste to create a refreshing taste.
    b. the chalk in toothpaste is unlike the kind children play with.
    c. titanium dioxide is found in Windex.
    d. detergent is added to toothpaste to create foam.

True or False

Directions: Indicate whether each statement is true or false by writing **T** or **F** in the space provided.

_____T_____ 6. Formaldehyde is added to toothpaste to kill bacteria.

_____T_____ 7. Peppermint oil is added to toothpaste to counter the taste of detergent and chalk.

_____T_____ 8. Chalk particles may be responsible for creating holes in teeth.

_____F_____ 9. Whitening agents added to toothpaste make teeth permanently white.

_____T_____ 10. Toothpaste manufacturers add some ingredients to camouflage the taste of other ingredients.

Vocabulary in Context 1

Directions: Use the context clues from the paragraph indicated to determine the meaning of the italicized words. (Remember, no looking in the dictionary.)

1. Paragraph 1: *pressing*

   Definition: urgent

2. Paragraph 2: *extruded*

   Definition: squeezed or forced out; pushed out

3. Paragraph 2: *lucrative*

   Definition: profitable; money-making

4. Paragraph 5: *unduly*

   Definition: excessively

5. Paragraph 5: *cavernous*

   Definition: vast

6. Paragraph 6: *bobbing*

   Definition: moving up and down; floating

7. Paragraph 6: *soluble*

   Definition: easily dissolved

8. Paragraph 6: *reassuring*

   Definition: renewing confidence

9. Paragraph 7: *revolting*

   Definition: horrible and disgusting

10. Paragraph 10: *remedy*

    Definition: correct

11. Paragraph 10: *duplicate*

    Definition: <u>copy; repeat; reproduce</u>

12. Paragraph 12: *immaculately*

    Definition: <u>spotlessly</u>

Vocabulary in Context 2

Directions: Choose one of the following words to complete each of the sentences below. Use each word only once. Be sure to pay close attention to the context clues provided.

camouflage	carnage	concoction	eons
finicky	gouging	ingests	oblivion
savor	screen out	thrive	tout

1. No longer heard on the radio, many songs from the 1930s and 1940s have passed into <u>oblivion</u>.

2. If a child <u>ingests</u> poison, it may be necessary to induce vomiting.

3. Dinosaurs roamed the earth <u>eons</u> ago.

4. Most house plants will <u>thrive</u> if they receive enough water and proper light.

5. The goal of the company was to <u>screen out</u> half of the applicants after the initial interview.

6 Using only the ingredients she had on hand, Stella created a savory <u>concoction</u> for dinner.

7. After winning the primary, the politician took time to <u>savor</u> his success.

8. She was so <u>finicky</u> about her food that she ended up eating very little.

9. Many studies <u>tout</u> the benefits of adding fluoride to toothpaste.

10. The army wanted to <u>camouflage</u> the tanks with green and brown paint to help them blend into their surroundings.

11. The battle at Gettysburg resulted in dreadful <u>carnage</u> with thousands of soldiers killed or wounded.

12. The little children were <u>gouging</u> out enough sand on the beach to make a castle.

In Your Own Words

1. If you couldn't brush your teeth with toothpaste, how else would you do it?

2. Do you think the FDA should be more zealous in evaluating toothpaste and other products manufactured in foreign countries?

3. Would you be willing to brush your teeth with a foul-tasting substance if it had all-natural ingredients and would not harm your health?

4. What do you think the author's attitude toward toothpaste is? Do you think he uses toothpaste himself?

Written Assignment

Do you think it's a good idea to know more about the ingredients of everyday products? Write a paragraph giving your opinion.

Internet Activity

1. Try to find out who invented toothpaste or who first marketed it successfully. Use your favorite search engine to discover the facts, and write a brief paragraph summarizing your findings.

2. Toothpaste has a history that stretches back thousands of years. Do some research to determine what the ancient Egyptians and Chinese used to clean their teeth. Write a paragraph presenting a brief history.

3. Bodanis suggests in the final paragraph that toothpaste is an unnecessary product. Many of the products we buy and use routinely are, strictly speaking, unnecessary. What are some other examples of unnecessary products? Why do we use them?

4. Personal care products such as toothpaste are not the only products containing chemical additives. Most food products do as well. Read the labels on several kinds of packaged food. List the most frequently occurring additives, and then look those additives up to learn what purpose they serve. Visit the Web site of the U.S. Food and Drug Administration (www.fda.gov/).

     Triclosan is considered by many to be a worrisome chemical in toothpaste. Do some research to identify toothpastes that contain this chemical and to see whether scientists consider it safe for daily use.

Chapter Summary and Review

In Chapter 10, you learned how to tell the difference between fact and opinion. Based on the material in Chapter 10, answer the following.

Short Answer

Directions: Answer the following briefly.

1. Write three factual statements.

     a. Answers will vary. _____

     b. _____

     c. _____

2. Write three opinion statements.

     a. Answers will vary. _____

     b. _____

     c. _____

Vocabulary in Context

Directions: Choose one of the following words to complete the sentences below. Use each word only once.

     fact   opinion   signal   value

3. *Perhaps, presumably,* and *apparently* are words that ___signal___ a(n) ___opinion___.

4. It is a(n) ___fact___ that the title of this book is *Reading and All That Jazz.*

5. If you said that *Titanic* was the best movie of all time, you would be making a(n) ___value___ judgment.

VOCABULARY   Unit 6 Word Parts Dealing with Opposing Meanings

This unit begins with the word part *auto,* found in many English words. It then looks at word parts having opposing meanings, such as "over" and "under," and "same" and "different." The last section covers some words that are commonly confused.

auto—self or same

automobile	*Auto* means "self," so an *automobile* is a self-moving vehicle.
autograph	*Graph* means "write," and *auto* means "self," so an *autograph* is a person's own signature. The literal meaning is self-written.
automaton	Acting unthinkingly or automatically, like a robot. After the police officer had informed the Millers of their daughter's murder, the couple acted like *automatons* in making arrangements for her funeral.
autonomous	*Auto* means "self" and *nomos* means "law," so the literal meaning of *autonomous* is "self law." The word refers to self-government or being independent. The United States is an *autonomous* country. Individual states in the United States are not totally *autonomous* because they are part of the United States. Are individual citizens in the United States *autonomous*?

co, com, con—with, together

contra—against; opposite

cooperate	To act or work together with another or others.
committee	A group of people chosen to work together on a particular matter.
consensus	Comes from *con* meaning "with" and *sentire* meaning "to think or feel." It refers to a thinking together or a general agreement.
compare	*Par* means "make equal," so if you *compare* two things, you are technically showing their similarities. But people, including college instructors, often use this word when they really mean to show similarities and differences. If one of your instructors asks you to do a *comparison,* find out whether the instructor wants you to show similarities only, or really wants you to show similarities and differences.
contrast	*Contra* means "against," so *contrast* means "to point out differences," or how one thing goes against another.
contradict	Comes from *contra* meaning "against" and *dict* meaning "say," as in *diction* and *predict.* The literal meaning of *contradict* is

"say against." To *contradict* means "to deny the statement" of another person.

contraband   *Ban* originally meant "to officially forbid," so *contraband* means "to forbid against." Today it refers to something that is illegal to import or export. Cocaine would be considered *contraband*.

> extra—over; more than; beyond
>
> ultra—over; more; beyond
>
> infra—under, below, beneath

extramarital   Relating to a sexual relationship with someone other than one's spouse.

extraterrestrial *Terra* means "earth," so an *extraterrestrial* is a being from outside the earth's limits. The title character from the movie *E.T.* was an *extraterrestrial*. Scientists are actively searching for signs of *extraterrestrial* intelligence.

extrasensory   Some people believe that they have a power of perception beyond the normal senses. They credit this *extrasensory* perception, or ESP, for their ability to predict the future, read someone else's thoughts, or visualize an unknown event. For example, have you ever felt that something tragic has happened to a close friend, and it turned out you were right? That might be ESP. Scientists, though, are very skeptical about the validity of ESP.

ultraviolet   *Ultraviolet* light is above violet on the color spectrum. It is invisible because its wavelengths are too short. The ozone layer blocks most, but not all, of the harmful *ultraviolet* radiation, which is what causes sunburns.

ultramicroscope An instrument that allows a person to see things too small to be seen by an ordinary microscope.

infrared   *Infrared* light is below red on the color spectrum. It is invisible because its wavelengths are too long for the human eye. The army uses *infrared* light to see at night. TV remote controls use *infrared* light.

infrastructure The basic structure or underlying foundation of something. The *infrastructure* of a house is its foundation and framing. The *infrastructure* of a community is its roads, schools, power plants, and transportation and communication systems.

> trans—across

transportation *Port,* as in portable, port-a-potties, and import, means "to carry." So, *transportation* refers to the act of carrying something from one place to another.

transmission   *Mis,* as in missile and missionary, means "to send," so *transmission* means "the act of sending across." The *transmission* of a car sends energy from the engine across the drive shaft to the wheels. You can also *transmit* a message to another person by writing a letter, using e-mail, voice mail, or text messaging.

transsexual	A person who undergoes surgery and hormone treatments to change his or her sex. So, it could be said that a *transsexual* goes across sexual boundaries.
transvestite	A *transvestite* dresses in the clothing of the opposite sex. So, a *transvestite* dresses across sexual boundaries. If you can't remember the difference between this word and the one above, keep in mind that a vest is a piece of clothing. It comes from *vestire,* which means "to dress."

homo—same; equal; like

hetero—different

homosexual	Having sexual desire for the same sex.
heterosexual	Having sexual desire for the opposite sex.
homogeneous	The same in structure or quality; having similar parts. Your class is fairly *homogeneous* in terms of age if you are all of a comparable age.
heterogeneous	Dissimilar; composed of unlike parts. Your class may be *heterogeneous* because you come from different backgrounds, cultures, and countries.
homogenization	The *homogenization* process of milk mixes the fat particles of the cream evenly throughout so that the cream doesn't separate. In milk taken straight from the cow, the lighter cream rises to the top. This is different from the process of pasteurization, named after inventor Louis Pasteur, which uses heat to kill bacteria.

Here are some words that are often confused with one another. Though some may appear to use the word parts mentioned in this unit, they really do not.

compliment	Something said in praise; to make a nice remark about someone.
complement	That which completes or makes whole or perfect; to balance. The team plays well because the players *complement* each other; they fit together well. Steve needs to get his date a corsage that will *complement* the color of her dress.
supplement	Comes from *sub* meaning "under" and *plere* meaning "to fill," and refers to something added to make up for a lack. Physicians often prescribe vitamin *supplements* to pregnant women.
council	A group of people called together to make decisions, such as a city council.
counsel	A mutual exchange of ideas; to give or take advice.
consul	A government official appointed to live in a foreign country and look after his or her country's citizens who are in the foreign country. If you were in a foreign country and having passport problems, you might go to the U.S. *consulate* for help. If you are from another country, you may wish to visit your country's *consulate*.

continuous   Going on without any interruption; unbroken. Think of "ous" to help you remember the meaning of this word, as in "one uninterrupted sequence." The cars backed up in a *continuous* line on the freeway.

continual   Repeated often; over and over again but with interruptions. The weather forecaster predicted *continual* showers over the Labor Day weekend.

Exercise 1: Writing Sentences

Make up your own sentences using each of the following words:

complement Answers will vary.

_____

homogeneous _____

_____

autonomous _____

_____

infrastructure _____

_____

continuous _____

_____

extrasensory _____

_____

automaton _____

_____

Exercise 2 Word Parts: Opposing Meanings

Directions: In the blanks below, write the word from the list that best completes the sentence. Use each word only once.

autograph	automaton	committee	compare	complement
consul	contraband	extramarital	heterogeneous	homogeneous

1. After Duy's daughter was killed in a drive-by shooting, he performed his job like a(n) ____automaton____, just going through the motions.

2. To address morale problems in the school district, a(n) ____committee____ was formed composed of teachers, parents, administrators, and students.

3. Many educators believe that a national test in reading and math is needed so that people can ____compare____ student performance in their state with what is happening in other states.

4. Many major league baseball stars will only sign a(n) ____autograph____ for a child.

5. Drug traffickers often use "mules" to transport ____contraband____ into the United States.

6. People who form successful partnerships often have individual traits that ____complement____ each other.

7. Stranded in Brazil with no money and no passport, Kathleen sought help from the U.S. ____consul____.

8. In the workplace today, diversity is widespread, creating a(n) ____heterogeneous____ mix of people and ideas.

9. In the past few years, the media has often exposed the ____extramarital____ affairs of leading political candidates.

10. A high school composed solely of Catholic boys age 14–18 would have a(n) ____homogeneous____ student body.

Exercise 3 Word Parts: More Opposing Meanings

Directions: In the blanks below, write the word from the list that best completes the sentence. Use each word only once.

autonomous   complimented   consensus   continual   continuously
contradict   council   counsel   extraterrestrials   supplement

1. We all ____complimented____ my daughter-in-law, Bonnie, and her friend, Kathleen, on the outstanding meal they had prepared.

2. The teacher was not going to be able to attend class on Monday. She told her students that if they could achieve a(n) ____consensus____ about doing an extra assignment, she would agree to cancel class. Otherwise, she would have to get a substitute.

3. Betsy, a battered wife, sought ____counsel____ on how to get a restraining order against her husband.

4. The city ____council____ passed an ordinance requiring those under the age of 18 to be home by 10:00 P.M. on weekdays and by midnight on weekends.

5. While working at the preschool with the two- and three-year olds, Elvira had a(n) ____continual____ headache.

6. The Colorado River flows ____continuously____.

7. If Bart wanted to be completely ____autonomous____ and his own man, why did he call his parents every Sunday asking for money?

8. A president needs to have advisors willing to ____contradict____ him. It is not a good idea for him to be surrounded by a bunch of "yes men."

9. Many police officers ____supplement____ their incomes by working in department stores as security guards on their days off.

10. He won an award for his science fiction story about ____extraterrestrials____ on Mars.

Expanding Your Word Power

The words listed below are not found in this Vocabulary Unit, but they are derived from the vocabulary word parts that you have studied. All of them would be good words for you to learn. See if you can guess the meaning of each word from its word parts.

1. autoimmune
2. autism
3. extraneous
4. extrapolate
5. extraordinary
6. extravagant
7. transcendent
8. transient
9. translation
10. transfuse
11. transfiguration
12. coauthor
13. cohabitate
14. contraceptive

Vocabulary Unit 6 Crossword Puzzle

ACROSS CLUES

3. A person who has had a sex change operation.
8. A word part meaning "same."
9. A word part meaning "across."
10. To point out differences.
13. A word part meaning "around."
14. A word part meaning "below."
17. E.T.
21. An abbreviation for what was once the 10th month.
23. A word part meaning "toward."
25. Your state is not _____ because it is part of the United States.
26. A word part meaning "two."
27. _____ milk has been heated to kill bacteria.
28. A word part meaning "back."
30. An abbreviation for what was once the 8th month.
32. A word part meaning "year."
33. A group called together for discussion.
35. A word part meaning "see."
36. A word part meaning "three."
37. _____ light has wavelengths longer than ordinary light.
39. A word part meaning "over, more, beyond."

DOWN CLUES

1. A word part meaning "self."
2. A person who wears the clothing of the opposite sex.
4. Self-written.
5. A word part meaning "side."
6. To give advice.
7. To deny the statement of someone.
11. A word part meaning "distance."
12. A person who directs work or workers.
15. Light that causes sunburn.
16. The chemical formula for water has a(n) _____ in it.
18. The foundation and frame of a building.
19. That which completes; to balance.
20. In a(n) _____ group, the members are alike.
22. A word part meaning "large."
24. To sign your name at the bottom of a document.
29. A word part meaning "before."
31. A word part meaning "more or over."
33. A word part meaning "around."
34. A word part meaning "with."
38. A word part meaning "two."

CHAPTER PREVIEW

In this chapter, you will

- Learn to distinguish between denotative and connotative meanings.

- Learn to identify positive and negative connotations.

- Learn to recognize euphemisms.

- Learn to recognize an author's personal bias.

- Develop familiarity with writing that has a biased viewpoint.

Introduction to Bias

In the previous chapter, we learned how important it is to be able to distinguish between fact and opinion. To be critical readers, we also need to be aware of our biases and the biases of others. A **bias** is defined as a strong leaning in either a positive or a negative direction.

Authors have biases, and it is the critical reader's job to discover what they are. A careful reader will study the author's line of reasoning, notice whether opinions have been supported by facts and reasons, and then decide if the author's bias has prevented the making of a good argument.

In the drawing "The Investigation" on the next page, the suspect in the investigation is in the center. Each of the individuals (and the Martian life-form?) briefly describes the suspect's appearance and gives his or her point of view. **Point of view** is defined as an opinion, an attitude, or a judgment on the part of an individual.

Notice how the descriptions they give the interviewer reflect their personal biases. Can you list some of these biases? Now read the essay "The Defendant's Characteristics" while noting the effect bias can have on legal judgments.

john jonik. Reprinted with permission.

READING

"There is a physical attractiveness stereotype:
Beautiful people seem like good people."

TUNING IN TO READING   Have you ever served on a jury? Did you enjoy the experience? Can you think of any instances when a jury verdict was not popular with the public? Was the defendant found guilty or not guilty? Can you explain the difference between popular perception and the verdict?

BIO-SKETCH   David G. Myers is an active writer with many articles and books to his credit, including the textbook *Social Psychology,* from which this excerpt is taken. He is the John Dirk Werkman Professor of Psychology at Hope University in Michigan.

NOTES ON VOCABULARY

Clarence Darrow   a lawyer known for his legal writings and for his defense of unpopular causes in the late 19th and early 20th centuries. Darrow was the defense attorney in the famous *Scopes* trial of 1925. John Scopes, a high school biology teacher, was arrested for teaching the theory of evolution to his students. Although Scopes was eventually found guilty and had to pay a $100 fine, Darrow was considered to be the winner in the trial.

Cicero   a famous orator and statesman who lived in Rome from 106 B.C. to 43 B.C. He is known as one of ancient Rome's finest writers of prose. Many of his essays on philosophy are based on the works of Aristotle and Plato.

THE DEFENDANT'S CHARACTERISTICS
David G. Myers

According to the famed trial attorney Clarence Darrow, jurors seldom convict a person they like or acquit one they dislike. He argued that the main job of the trial attorney is to make the jury like the defendant. Was he right? And is it true, as Darrow also said, that "facts regarding the crime are relatively unimportant"?

Darrow overstated the case. One study of more than 3,500 criminal cases 2 and some 4,000 civil cases found that 4 times in 5 the judge agreed with the jury's decision. Although both may have been wrong, the evidence usually is clear enough that jurors can set aside their biases, focus on the facts, and agree on a verdict. Darrow was too cynical; facts do matter.

Nevertheless, when jurors are asked to make social judgments—would *this* 3 defendant commit *this* offense? intentionally?—facts are not all that matter. Communicators are more persuasive if they seem credible and attractive. Jurors cannot help forming impressions of the defendant. Can they put these impressions aside and decide the case based on the facts alone? To judge from the more lenient treatment often received by high-status defendants it seems that some cultural bias lingers. But actual cases vary in so many ways—in the type of crime, in the status, age, gender, and race of the defendant—that it's hard to isolate the factors that influence jurors. So experimenters have controlled such factors by giving mock jurors the same basic facts of a case while varying, say, the defendant's attractiveness or similarity to the jurors.

There is a physical attractiveness stereotype: Beautiful people seem like 4 good people. Michael Efran wondered whether this stereotype would bias students' judgments of someone accused of cheating. He asked some of his University of Toronto students whether attractiveness should affect presumption of guilt. They answered: "No, it shouldn't." But did it? Yes. When Efran gave other students a description of the case with a photograph of either an attractive or an unattractive defendant, they judged the most attractive as least guilty and recommended that person for the least punishment.

To see if these findings extend to the real world, Chris Downs and Phillip 5 Lyons asked police escorts to rate the physical attractiveness of 1,742 defendants appearing before 40 Texas judges in misdemeanor cases. Whether the misdemeanor was serious (such as forgery), moderate (such as harassment), or minor (such as public intoxication), the judges set higher bails and fines for less-attractive defendants. What explains this dramatic effect? Are unattractive people also lower in status? Are they indeed more likely to flee or to commit crime, as the judges perhaps suppose? Or do judges simply ignore the Roman statesman Cicero's advice: "The final good and the supreme duty of the wise man is to resist appearance."

If Clarence Darrow was even partly right in his declaration that liking or 6 disliking a defendant colors judgments, then other factors that influence liking should also matter. Among such influences is the principle that likeness (similarity) leads to liking. When people pretend they are jurors, they are indeed more sympathetic to a defendant who shares their attitudes, religion, race, or (in cases of sexual assault) gender. For example, when Cookie Stephan and Walter Stephan had English-speaking people judge someone accused of assault, they were more likely to think the person not guilty if the defendant's testimony was in English, rather than translated from Spanish or Thai.

So it seems we are more sympathetic toward a defendant with whom we 7 can identify. If we think *we* wouldn't have committed that criminal act, we may assume that someone like us is also unlikely to have done it.

Ideally, jurors would leave their biases outside the courtroom and begin a 8 trial with open minds. So implies the Sixth Amendment to the U.S. Constitution: "The accused shall enjoy the right to a speedy and public trial by impartial jury." In its concern for objectivity, the judicial system is similar to science: Both scientists and jurors are supposed to sift and weigh the evidence. Both the courts and science have rules about what evidence is relevant. Both keep careful records and assume that others given the same evidence would decide similarly.

When the evidence is clear and jurors focus on it, their biases are indeed 9 minimal. The quality of the evidence matters more than the prejudices of the individual jurors.

(David G. Myers, *Social Psychology*, 9/e, 2008)

 COMPREHENSION CHECKUP

Multiple Choice

Directions: For each item, write the letter corresponding to the best answer.

a   1. The main idea expressed in this selection is that
    a. jurors can be influenced by the physical appearance and actions of a defendant.
    b. jurors are unlikely to pay attention to the physical characteristics of a defendant.
    c. in Texas, judges were affected by the attractiveness of the defendants.
    d. jurors are unlikely to be sympathetic to those who are like them.

b   2. Paragraph 2 contains the following statement: "Darrow overstated the case." This is a statement of
    a. fact.
    b. opinion.

b   3. As used in paragraph 3, the word *credible* means
    a. easily deceived.
    b. believable.
    c. childish.
    d. doubtful.

c   4. In paragraph 4, the example of Efran's University of Toronto students was used to illustrate that
    a. attractive people receive more lenient sentences in court.
    b. the way we treat attractive and unattractive people shapes the way they think about themselves.
    c. attractive people are thought to be less likely to have committed a crime.

_____b_____ 5. In paragraph 5, the author helps readers understand the different types of misdemeanors by providing
   a. definitions.
   b. examples.
   c. cause-and-effect relationships.
   d. chronological order.

_____b_____ 6. Based on Cicero's statement, readers can conclude that he would advise jurors to
   a. carefully consider the appearance of the defendant during jury deliberations.
   b. disregard the appearance of the defendant during jury deliberations.

_____b_____ 7. Paragraph 8 contains the following statement: "Ideally, jurors would leave their biases outside the courtroom and begin a trial with open minds." This is a statement of
   a. fact.
   b. opinion.

_____c_____ 8. The mode of writing used in this selection is
   a. narrative.
   b. descriptive.
   c. expository.
   d. persuasive.

Short Answer

Directions: Answer the following questions briefly.

1. According to the selection, what are some biases that can affect a jury's ability to reach a fair decision? the defendant's likability; his or her appearance, similarity, attitudes, religion, race, gender .

2. What key point made by famed trial attorney Clarence Darrow is illustrated by the cartoon on page 452? "jurors seldom convict a person they like" .

3. According to the context clues in paragraph 2, what does the word *cynical* mean? "Darrow was too *cynical*; facts do matter."

   Cynical means distrustful; pessimistic; negative .

4. In paragraph 3, what does the transition word *nevertheless* signal?

   Nevertheless signals reversal–contrast .

5. According to the context clues in paragraph 6, what does the word *colors* mean? "If Clarence Darrow was even partly right in his declaration that liking or disliking a defendant *colors* judgments . . ."

   Colors means to alter or influence to some degree .

6. What two things are being compared in paragraph 8?
   judicial system (court) and science .

7. According to the context clues in paragraph 8, what does the word *objectivity* mean?
   "In its concern for *objectivity* . . ."

   Objectivity means unbiased, without prejudice, detached .

"And so I ask the jury—is that the face of a mass murderer?"

In Your Own Words

1. Do you think jurors are capable of setting aside their biases and deciding cases on the facts and law alone? What leads you to your conclusion?

2. Do you think jurors are less likely to convict someone who seems similar to them?

Written Assignment

The reading selection mentions a physical attractiveness stereotype. Do you think an attractive appearance gives someone a big advantage in life? Or do you think people are unlikely to be influenced by superficial qualities because they believe that "beauty is only skin deep" and "you can't judge a book by its cover"? Write a short essay giving your opinion.

Internet Activity

Consult the Web site titled "Teaching Tolerance" developed by the Southern Poverty Law Center. It explores the topic of stereotypes and prejudices and provides a test you can take to discover if you have any unconscious or hidden biases.

www.tolerance.org/hiddenbias

Denotation and Connotation

When you look up a word in your dictionary, you are determining its **denotation,** or dictionary meaning. However, words also have **connotations,** or meanings beyond simple dictionary definitions. These words carry an extra emotional "charge." We can think of these words as being positive, negative, or neutral.

For example, even though the words *thin, slender,* and *skinny* all have similar dictionary definitions, they have different connotative meanings. Most of us think *slender* has a positive connotation and *skinny* a negative one. *Thin* has a more neutral meaning. In using words that have connotative meanings, we reveal our personal biases.

Authors can do exactly the same thing as speakers by choosing one particular word over another. If an author begins a novel by referring to the title character as someone who is *thrifty,* what picture of that person comes to your mind? How about if the author refers to the title character as *cheap* or *stingy*?

In the following cartoon, the word *problems* and the word *challenges* have very similar denotative meanings. However, as the son points out to his dad, they have very different connotative meanings.

© 1998 Creators Syndicate, Inc. By permission of Rick Detorie and Creators Syndicate, Inc.

One Big Happy

Exercise 1: Spotting Biased Words

Directions: Read the following comments from a parent–teacher conference and, for each word pair, circle the word with the more positive connotation.

I am very proud of Tommy and his *diligent*/*plodding* effort to improve his arithmetic grade. He does seem to have a(n) *self-confident*/*arrogant* approach toward the work at this grade level. However, he is not placing enough emphasis on producing quality homework. It is done in a(n) *sloppy*/*untidy* way. In general, he is a very *able*/*gifted* child. He does, however, need to improve his social and emotional conduct. His contributions to the class are made in a(n) *enthusiastic*/*hyperactive* way, and he is sometimes *rude*/*insensitive* in his comments to others. He does seem *eager*/*willing* to participate in most activities in the classroom, but he needs to learn to do so in a less *assertive*/*aggressive* manner. On the playground and in his relations with his peers, he is often *shy*/*reserved,* but he is beginning to be asked to enter into new activities. I enjoy having Tommy in my room and I hope we can make the rest of the year a pleasant one.

Exercise 2: Positive and Negative Connotation

Directions: Below are two versions of the same speech. One uses positive words to favor Senator X and the other uses words slanted against him. Read both speeches and circle all of the biased words or phrases. Then rewrite the speech as a neutral observer reporting only facts rather than giving opinions or making value judgments. As a guideline answer *who, what, where, when, why,* and *how* questions. Be careful not to substitute your own biased words for the ones you eliminate.

Answers will vary somewhat.

In Favor of Senator X

In a (well-reasoned) statement to an (admiring) audience, the (dignified) and (courtly) Senator X today (forcefully argued) for his proposal to limit violence in the media. The auditorium filled with laughter as the (esteemed) senator showed his trademark (dry wit.) By (disarming) the opposition, it looks like the senator will emerge (triumphant) and his (insightful) proposal will (carry) (the day.)

Against Senator X

In his (usual dour style,) the (aging) Senator X today (sought to persuade) the crowd in the auditorium to accept his proposal to limit violence in the media. The audience, (clearly repulsed) by his crude, (cynical attempts) at humor, appeared to be (laughing more at the senator) than with him. (Frightened) by his (threats,) the opposition will probably be (goaded) into backing his program.

Neutral Version

Answers will vary.

_____

_____

_____

_____

_____

Euphemisms

When we substitute inoffensive words or phrases for ones that are likely to offend someone, we are using **euphemisms.** Generally, we use euphemisms to be polite or to avoid controversy. For example, a euphemism such as "passed away" might be substituted for the word "died."

The use of euphemisms to purposely mislead others and obscure the truth is called **doublespeak.** In the working world, layoffs have become commonplace, but because the word "layoff" has a negative connotation, many new euphemisms have been created both to appease the person being fired and to mislead the general public. Thus, when a company fires a large group of workers and announces a "force reduction program," they are guilty of doublespeak. Read the following information on doublespeak and inflated language from Hamilton Gregory's *Public Speaking for College and Career.*

BEWARE OF DOUBLESPEAK

When some federal and state legislators raise taxes, they don't refer to their action as "raising taxes." To do so might anger taxpayers. No, timidly and sneakily, they say they voted for "revenue enhancement."

"Revenue enhancement" is an example of **doublespeak.** Here are some additional examples:

- After one of its planes crashed, National Airlines described the event—in its annual report to stockholders—as an "involuntary conversion of a 727," a legal term designed to conceal the truth.
- When politicians in Washington, DC, slashed funding for national parks in 2004, they asked park superintendents to call the budget cuts "service level adjustments."

Euphemisms become harmful when they mask a problem that should be dealt with. When homeless people are called "urban nomads," does this romantic euphemism cause the public to turn its eyes from a problem that needs attention?

The best advice is this: Use euphemisms if tact and kindness require them, and avoid them if they serve to deceive or confuse.

In his book *The New Doublespeak,* William Lutz discusses another type of doublespeak called **inflated language.** Lutz says, "inflated language is designed to make the ordinary seem extraordinary; to make everyday things seem impressive; to give an air of importance to people, situations, or things that would not normally be considered important." For example:

- A used car is advertised as a *preowned car* or *pre-enjoyed automobile.*
- A clothing store calls its salespeople *wardrobe consultants.*
- A national pizza delivery chain announces that its drivers will henceforth be known as *delivery ambassadors.*

Some inflated language seems harmless. If garbage collectors prefer to be called *sanitation engineers,* most people will not criticize too strenuously. If they believe that the term dignifies their valuable but unglamorous work, most won't object to the use of the term. But the problem is that inflated language is spreading rapidly into all areas of life, causing misunderstanding and confusion. If you saw an advertisement for a *grief therapist,* wouldn't you envision a counselor for a mourning individual whose loved one has just died? If so, you'd be wrong, because *grief therapist* is an inflated term for an undertaker. How are we to know that an *excavation technician* is a ditch digger? That a *communications monitor* is a switchboard operator? That a *customer engineer* is a salesperson? That a *corrosion control specialist* is the person who sends your car through a car wash?

An inflated term may begin in kindness, but it often ends in confusion. Avoid its use unless you know that it is clearly understood.

(Hamilton Gregory, *Public Speaking for College and Career,* 9/e, 2008)

Note: William Lutz suggests that people fight doublespeak by becoming "first-rate crap detectors." One way to accomplish this is to start collecting and trading examples of doublespeak. Try to bring in examples to your class on a topic such as the economy, unemployment, or foreign aid.

The *Far Side* cartoon on the following page shows a "swamp thing" that would rather be referred to as a "wetlands-challenged mutant" because it has a more positive connotation. Is this an example of doublespeak or inflated language?

THE FAR SIDE®   By GARY LARSON

© 1994 FarWorks, Inc. All Rights Reserved/Dist. by Creators Syndicate

"Well, actually, Doreen, I rather resent being called a 'swamp thing.' ... I prefer the term 'wetlands-challenged-mutant.'"

Exercise 3: Euphemisms

Directions: Give euphemisms for each of the following words or phrases.

1. older person   retiree, senior citizen
2. toilet   bathroom, restroom, powder room
3. drunk   inebriated, tipsy, intoxicated
4. pregnant   having a baby, with child
5. lazy   underachiever
6. pornography   adult entertainment

Directions: Turn these euphemistic words or phrases into regular words.

1. to be temporarily without funds   broke
2. lingerie   underwear
3. cemetery   graveyard
4. mixed-breed dog   mutt
5. preowned vehicle   used car
6. chemically dependent   addicted
7. to misappropriate the company's funds   steal
8. night club   bar
9. telemarketing   phone sales

10. to score below average on a test <u>fail</u>
11. vertically challenged <u>too short or too tall</u>
12. to stretch the truth somewhat <u>lie</u>
13. learning resources center <u>library</u>
14. to depart from this life <u>die</u>

Exercise 4: Detecting Bias in Magazines and Newspapers

Directions: For each passage, write the letter corresponding to words that suggest the writer's bias on the line provided.

<u>c</u> 1. Citizenship today is in a precarious state. Citizen involvement in community and government has been declining. Government responsiveness to citizens may also be on the wane. Some scholars believe the reciprocal bonds of citizenship are fraying. Although we believe that the low level of citizen involvement in government today gives us cause for concern about the health of our democracy, we are not overly pessimistic. Once we understand the reasons for low levels of participation and open a dialogue about how we might change this relationship for the better, we can do something about it.

(Joseph Losco, *AM GOV*, 2002)

a. health, overly, understand, citizen
b. reciprocal, involvement, state, responsiveness
c. precarious, wane, fraying, declining

<u>a</u> 2. Who ever would have thought that good old PB&J could be a health hazard? Sad but true: the peanut-butter-and-jelly sandwich is under assault, along with its cousin the fluffer nutter, the peanut-butter cracker, the Reese's Piece, the peanut M&M and all the other delectable forms the humble peanut comes in. At the Breck School in Minneapolis, PB&J sandwiches must now be eaten at separate tables. The Bradstreet Early Childhood Center in North Andover, Massachusetts, is one of many kindergartens to have created peanut-free classrooms this fall, and the Trinity School in New York City has expelled all forms of the peanut from the premises. Why the frenzy over goobers? Because 1 percent of American children are now estimated to have a peanut allergy.

(John Sedgwick, "Goodbye to the Goobers," 1996)

a. hazard, sad, expelled, frenzy, assault
b. goobers, separate, peanut-free, premises
c. cracker, estimated, allergy, health

<u>a</u> 3. Any work is potentially censorable by someone, someplace, sometime, for some reason. Nothing is permanently safe from censorship, not even most books most teachers and librarians would regard as far removed from censorial eyes—not *Hamlet*, *Julius Caesar*, *Treasure Island*, or anything else. If one book is removed from a classroom or library, no book is safe any longer. If a censor succeeds in getting one book out, every other person in the community who objects to another book should, in courtesy, be granted the same privilege. When everyone has walked out of the library carrying all those objectionable books,

nothing of any consequence will be left no matter how many books remain. Some books are certain to offend some people and be ardently defended by others. Indeed, every library has books offensive to someone, maybe everyone. After all, ideas do offend many people.

(Alleen Pace Nilsen and Kenneth L. Donelson. *Literature for Today's Young Adults,* 8/e, 2009)

a. offend, offensive, objectionable, censorship
b. courtesy, granted, someplace, potentially
c. classroom, library, removed, reason

_____a_____ 4. There was blood, sweat, and a puddle of tears on kitchen tables across America this morning, the detritus of a long afternoon, stretching into evening, of yesterday's homework. Sure, some students probably whipped out their perfectly organized assignment pad, did each task cheerfully and finished with time to spare for reading, television, or play. We just don't know any. Something that infuriates parents, sabotages family time, and crowds out so much else in a child's life might be tolerable if it also helped kids learn and if it imbued them with good study habits and a lifelong love of learning. Unfortunately, "for elementary-school students the effect of homework on achievement is trivial, if it exists at all," concludes psychologist Harris Cooper of the University of Missouri, whose analysis of more than 100 studies has stood up for 10 years.

(Sharon Begley, "Homework Doesn't Help," 1998)

a. infuriates, sabotages, crowds out, trivial
b. puddle, learning, imbued, exists
c. analysis, sweat, task, family

_____a_____ 5. Querulous, funny, serious, playful, fearless, caring, and curious—the roadrunner sports a jaunty outlook wrapped in a bundle of tan, white, black, and metallic bronze. The roadrunner earned its name when settlers traveling westward first discovered that this odd, vivacious bird liked to race their wagons. But Mexicans were calling the bird *corre camino* ("it runs the road") long before Europeans settled the lands in the southwestern United States. It measures just 22 to 24 inches in length—half of which is tail—but has earned quite a reputation and many names from many cultures. In Texas, it goes by the name "chaparral cock," in New Mexico it's known as "snake eater," and in Mexico it's dubbed *paisano* ("compatriot" or "countryman"). Confident and crowned with a feather crest, the roadrunner earns king-of-the-road bragging rights. So swift of foot that it rarely takes flight, this clever member of the cuckoo family snatches airborne insects and smaller birds with leaps up to 6 feet in the air.

(Carrie M. Miner, "Roadrunner Facts & Fantasy," 2001)

a. jaunty, vivacious, confident, clever
b. wrapped, reputation, names, dubbed
c. outlook, metallic, crest, rights

_____b_____ 6. White-coated experts at the Faster Living Institute, alarmed by a nationwide study that showed the average American constantly running behind schedule, have just announced the results of their drive to isolate the cause and find a solution. Where does all the time go? It's stolen, is the institute's shocking answer, by our own medicine chests and the obsolete nineteenth-century medication-taking process. "Don't let that innocent-looking little bathroom cabinet fool you," says one college-trained researcher. "It's a diabolical time trap. You can finally stop torturing yourself about always running late when you realize that two minutes per day, fourteen minutes per week, fifty-six minutes per month, or twelve hours per year, are wasted in finding, selecting, uncapping, and ingesting medication."

(Bruce McCall, "Hurry-Up Experts Say Medicine Chest Doomed," 2001)

a. white-coated, constantly, isolate
b. stolen, shocking, diabolical
c. nationwide, average, ingesting

_____b_____ 7. The taunts from the parents and the coaches always got to him. They rained like showers of sparks from the sidelines: Get your fat body down the field. You're blind. You're just doing this for the money. Last summer, Mr. Lazarevic, who has worked for 18 years as a referee in basketball, soccer, and baseball in suburban Chicago, hung up his whistle. "When people started saying personal things about me, about what I was as a person, I decided it was time to get out," he said. Mr. Lazarevic, a 32-year-old middle school science teacher, is among thousands of referees who have left high school and youth sports in recent years because of poor sportsmanship on the part of spectators, said Bob Still, a spokesman for the National Association of Sports Officials. But that is only one of the many results of what players, coaches, scholars, and sports psychologists say is a rising tide of misbehavior at high school and youth sports especially among adult spectators. Some call it "sideline rage." From hockey arenas in Maine to soccer fields in New Mexico, parents and amateur coaches are yelling and jeering— even spitting and brawling—as never before, experts say.

(Edward Wong, "New Rules for Soccer Parents," 2001)

a. sparks, personal, thousands, sportsmanship
b. taunts, misbehavior, rage, jeering
c. spectators, tide, amateur, experts

Exercise 5: Detecting Bias: "Who Gets In?"

The college can admit only 5 more students. As a member of the board, it is your responsibility to rank the 10 students listed on the following page according to who most deserves to be accepted. Descriptions of their precollege situation and performance are given.

In your group, keep in mind the following factors as you select the **5** you consider the most deserving:

1. The person's potential, abilities, or capabilities
2. The person's motivation to perform
3. The probability of successful completion of a college education

Your group must be in complete agreement about your choices. After selecting your 5, write a brief sentence or two explaining the rationale for your choices. When everyone has completed the assignment, the group leader should write the selections on the board. Be prepared to defend your selections to the rest of the class.

L'Tisha

Very intelligent; senior class valedictorian; has won awards in the National Science Fair for exhibits; has definite plans to major in chemistry; high school counselor says she has difficulty relating to others; she was involved in several disputes with high school classmates over chemistry experiments.

Julio

An all-state center in high school; plans to play college basketball and would help the team; scored poorly on the college admittance test although his high school grades were average; plans to become a physical therapist.

Jill

Ranked in the middle of her graduating class; did well in high school math; has good study habits; high school counselor says she has interfering, confrontational parents.

Carolyn

A divorced mother with two children; 24 years old, trying to return to college to continue her education after dropping out six years ago; works and raises her family; no financial support from her former husband; will need financial aid; wishes to become an elementary schoolteacher.

Dominique

An applicant from Venezuela; has already earned a degree in her own country; did very well academically; she wants to enroll to experience our lifestyle and perfect her English; not interested in any specific subject; plans to return home.

Juan Carlos

High school counselor says he is outgoing and well-liked among his peers; poor grades; studied little in high school and has poor study skills; test results reveal a very high IQ.

Howard

Ranked in the top 5 percent of his graduating class; high school counselor says he is a loner who lacks social skills; had no extracurricular activities in high school; has a great deal of academic potential; wants to be a doctor like his father.

Jiao

Had attendance problems in high school; grades were mediocre; worked in excess of 40 hours a week; IQ in gifted range; will need financial aid.

Evelyn

She is 58 years old; worked in a day care center for the past 15 years; prior to that she was a housewife and mother; wants to earn a degree in child psychology; high test scores.

Dakin

Average grades; works 28 hours a week to pay for his education; is aiming for a degree in engineering; high potential in math; a very hard worker.

(David B. Ellis, *Becoming a Master Student*, 7/e, 1994)

Exercise 6: Point of View

This story by Katherine Brush is told from the point of view of an observer seated in a restaurant watching the action unfold.

A BIRTHDAY PARTY

They were a couple in their late thirties, and they looked unmistakably married. They sat on the banquette opposite us in a little narrow restaurant, having dinner. The man had a round, self-satisfied face, with glasses on it; the woman was fadingly pretty, in a big hat. There was nothing conspicuous about them, nothing particularly noticeable, until the end of their meal, when it suddenly became obvious that this was an Occasion—in fact, the husband's birthday, and the wife had planned a little surprise for him.

It arrived, in the form of a small but glossy birthday cake, with one pink candle burning in the center. The headwaiter brought it in and placed it before the husband, and meanwhile the violin-and-piano orchestra played "Happy Birthday to You" and the wife beamed with shy pride over her little surprise, and such few people as there were in the restaurant tried to help out with a pattering of applause. It became clear at once that help was needed, because the husband was not pleased. Instead he was hotly embarrassed, and indignant at his wife for embarrassing him.

You looked at him and you saw this and you thought, "Oh now don't *be* like that!" But he was like that, and as soon as the little cake had been deposited on the table, and the orchestra had finished the birthday piece, and the general attention had shifted from the man and the woman, I saw him say something to her under his breath—some punishing thing, quick and curt and unkind. I couldn't bear to look at the woman then, so I stared at my plate and waited for quite a long time. Not long enough, though. She was still crying when I finally glanced over there again. Crying quietly and heartbrokenly and hopelessly, all to herself, under the gay big brim of her best hat.

(Katherine Brush, "A Birthday Party," 1946)

After reading the story, most people feel that the narrator is clearly sympathetic to the wife's feelings and is solely representing the wife's point of view. But is this true? Try reading the story again looking at the situation from the husband's perspective. The narrator indirectly tells the reader a great deal about these particular characters and their relationship to each other. Look specifically at the details of physical description that are given.

Directions: Answer the following questions briefly.

1. Why is the wife who is "fadingly pretty" wearing a "big hat" in a "little, narrow restaurant"? She wants to call attention to herself.

2. Why does the narrator note that they "looked unmistakably married"? Should the wife have been aware of the type of surprise her husband would have enjoyed? The narrator makes note of this because they have probably been married for quite a while, and the wife should have been aware of the sort of birthday celebration that her husband would have enjoyed.

3. What does it say about the husband that he waits until the "general attention had shifted" before he says "some punishing thing" to her "under his breath"? He doesn't like to call attention to himself. He is either shy or reserved.

4. The narrator states that (he/she) waited "quite a long time," and yet the woman continued "crying quietly and heartbrokenly and hopelessly." Is there another more appropriate action that the wife could have taken? What is her crying in a public place likely to do? <u>She could have excused herself and gone to the</u>
<u>restroom. By staying, she continues to call attention to herself.</u>

5. Do you think the "one pink candle" suggests for whom the wife really planned the surprise? Which of the two is more likely to enjoy this type of attention?
<u>She planned it for herself. It was something she was likely to enjoy. Pink is a color</u>
<u>usually associated with girls.</u>

6. The author reveals her point of view by the words she chose to use to tell the story. What is the author's point of view about the birthday party? Is she sympathetic toward the husband or the wife? Or both? <u>The story is meant to be</u>
<u>read on two levels. On the first reading, most are likely to side with the wife. A</u>
<u>closer examination causes the reader to understand the husband's point of view.</u>
<u>The author is probably sympathetic to both husband and wife.</u>

Exercise 7: Detecting Bias—Sex-Based Words

A. Each word or phrase below is usually associated with only one sex. Using your knowledge of cultural history, determine why these phrases are associated with one sex but not with the other.

Feminine Based

1. mother nature <u>birth; renewal</u>

2. black widow spider <u>devours mate</u>

3. lazy Susan serving tray <u>in kitchen</u>

4. *The Clarissa* (clipper ship) <u>graceful</u>

5. the statue of justice <u>impartial</u>

6. a ladybug <u>cute; harmless</u>

Masculine Based

1. old man winter <u>harsh</u>

2. daddy longlegs spider <u>protector</u>

3. LA-Z-BOY lounging chair <u>relax w/TV</u>

4. man-of-war (battleship) <u>aggressive</u>

5. a father of modern science <u>inventor</u>

THE FAMILY CIRCUS.   **By Bil Keane**

©2001 Bil Keane, Inc.
Dist. by King Features Synd.
www.familycircus.com

"How come we don't hear anything about FATHER Nature?"

Family Circus © Bil Keane, Inc. King Features Syndicate.

Write a general statement about your findings.

Answers will vary.

B. The (animal) words listed below are nearly always associated with one sex or the other. Mark **M** for the terms you would most likely use with males and **F** for terms you would most likely use with females. See if you can come to any conclusions as to how the two lists differ and what they show about cultural expectations for males and females.

M 1. a beast   F 1. to be mousy

F 2. a bird   M 2. a rat

M 3. to be bullheaded M 3. a loan shark

F 4. a social butterfly M 4. a fox

F 5. to be catty   M 5. a tiger

F 6. a chick   F 6. a tigress

M 7. a donkey   F 7. a vixen

F 8. to be kittenish M 8. a vulture

M 9. a hog   M 9. a wolf

F 10. a lamb   F 10. doe eyes

Conclusions: Answers will vary.

C. Change the following "man words" to "gender-inclusive" alternatives.

Example: congressman—congressional representative

1. workman worker

2. anchorman anchor

Herman

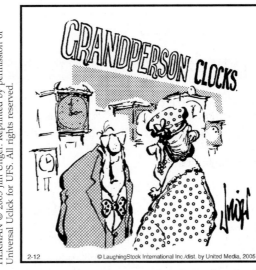

"We're living in very strange times, Martha."

　　3. the best man for the job _the most qualified_

　　4. weatherman _meteorologist, weathercaster_

　　5. foreman _supervisor_

　　6. businessman _executive_

　　7. salesman _sales representative_

　　8. mailman _mail carrier_

　　9. insurance man _insurance agent_

　10. fireman _firefighter_

　11. cameraman _photographer_

　12. freshman _first-year student_

　13. spokesman _representative_

　14. man-sized job _large job_

　15. sportsmanship _fair play_

D.　Change the following "female words" to "gender-inclusive" alternatives.

　　1. cleaning lady _housekeeper_

　　2. housewife _homemaker_

　　3. ladylike _polite, well-mannered_

E.　Change the following titles, used to distinguish female workers from males, to neutral terms for both men and women.

　　1. lady doctor _physician_

　　2. stewardess _flight attendant_

　　3. policewoman _police officer_

　　4. waitress _server_

F.　What is the problem with using language that is sexist or biased?
　　Answers will vary.

_____

_____

(Alleen Pace Nilsen, *Changing Words in a Changing World,* 1980)

Exercise 8: Bias in Publications

Directions: Study the list of publications and the given topic. Would you expect the publication to be biased or objective (neutral) on this particular topic? Write an **O** for objective or a **B** for biased in the space provided.

Publication	Topic	
1. *Los Angeles Times* editorial	marijuana	B
2. *The New England Journal of Medicine*	marijuana	O
3. *The Catholic Star Church Newsletter*	marijuana	B
4. *American Medical Association Complete Medical Encyclopedia*	marijuana	O

5. *The Partnership for a Drug-Free America Newsletter*   marijuana   ___B___

6. *The Scourge of Drugs* by Wendell Collins   marijuana   ___B___

7. *Sociology* by James N. Henslin   marijuana   ___O___

8. *Understanding Psychology* by Charles G. Morris   marijuana   ___O___

READING

"The public image of policing is heavily influenced by stereotypes about police officers: about who they are, what they believe, and how they act."

TUNING IN TO READING   Almost all of us have a point of view about the police that is dependent on our own personal experiences or the experiences of people we know. What image of the police springs to your mind? Is it of the officer pulling someone over to write a ticket for speeding? Is it of the cop breaking up a party of underage drinkers? Is it of a police officer hitting someone with a nightstick? Is it of a detective tracking down a killer or robber or rapist? Are your feelings about the police in the United States largely negative, positive, or neutral?

BIO-SKETCH   Dr. Samuel Walker is Isaacson Professor of Criminal Justice at the University of Nebraska at Omaha. He is the author of numerous books and journal articles on policing, criminal justice, and civil liberties. He is currently engaged in research on police accountability systems. Dr. Charles Katz is an associate professor in the Department of Criminal Justice and Criminology at Arizona State University West. He is currently engaged in research on the police response to gangs and police organizational theory.

NOTES ON VOCABULARY

Rorschach   The Rorschach inkblot test was developed by the Swiss psychiatrist Hermann Rorschach. A series of inkblots are presented to the individual being tested. He or she then suggests what the inkblots represent. The therapist analyzes the results and makes an assessment about the patient's personality traits.

BEYOND STEREOTYPES OF COPS
Samuel Walker and Charles Katz

How many times have you heard someone make a statement such as "All cops are _____"? How many jokes have you heard about police officers spending all their time at donut shops? How often have you heard someone say that people became cops because they like to use force? Statements and jokes of this sort reflect negative stereotypes about police officers.

At the same time, how many times have you heard someone say that police 2 officers do no wrong or, more likely, that they have such dangerous and stressful jobs that we should never criticize them for maybe using a little too much force in some situation? This point of view reflects a positive stereotype about police officers.

The public image of policing is heavily influenced by stereotypes about 3 police officers: about who they are, what they believe, and how they act. These stereotypes fall into two categories. On the one side, a negative stereotype views

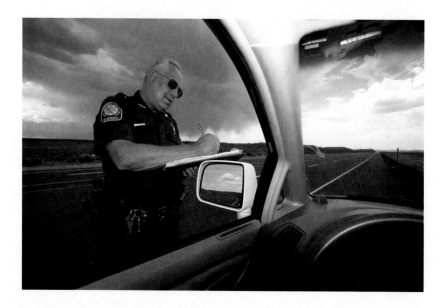

officers as uneducated, untrained, prejudiced, brutal, and corrupt. On the other side, a positive stereotype views them as heroic saints, risking their lives in the face of hostility from the public, the media, and the courts. Arthur Niederhoffer characterizes the police officer as a "Rorschach in uniform." "To people in trouble the police officer is a 'savior,' but to others he is a 'fierce ogre.'"

Neither stereotype is accurate. As Bayley and Mendelsohn conclude in their 4 study of police-community relations in Denver, the average police officer is a rather average person in terms of values and political beliefs, although a little more conservative than the population as a whole. The special nature of police work does, however, encourage certain attitudes and behavior, and there is a distinct police subculture among officers. No studies, however, have concluded that police officers are fundamentally different from other people in any important respect.

Inaccurate stereotypes about policing affect the recruitment of new officers. 5 The National Center on Women and Policing argues that stereotypes emphasizing officer use of force and the need for physical size and strength discourage women from considering careers in policing. In reality, most police work is uneventful, and police-citizen encounters primarily require communication skills.

Reality Shock: Beginning Police Work

Police officer attitudes toward the public change significantly during the first 6 weeks and months on the job. McNamara found that the percentage of officers agreeing with the statement "Patrolmen almost never receive the cooperation from the public that is needed to handle police work properly" rose from 35 percent at the beginning of academy training to 50 percent after two years on the job. Meanwhile, at the start of academy training, 31 percent agreed that it was necessary to use force to gain respect in "tough" neighborhoods, while two years later 55 percent agreed.

Changes in officers' attitudes are the result of several different aspects of 7 police work. Officers encounter some hostility from citizens. This is a shock because officers tend to choose law enforcement as a career because they want to work with people and help the community. Officers also experience being stereotyped, with citizens reacting to the uniform, the badge, and the gun. As is the case with racial stereotyping, it is an unpleasant experience to have people react to you as a category rather than as an individual. In still other instances, citizens feel discomfort at being around a person with arrest powers. To avoid the discomfort of these incidents, police officers tend to socialize primarily with other officers, thereby increasing their isolation from the public.

Police officers' attitudes also change because they perform society's "dirty work," handling unpleasant tasks that no one else wants to perform or is able to handle. The police see humanity at its worst. They are the first people to find the murder victim, for example. Officers encounter the victims of serious domestic abuse, child abuse, and rape firsthand. These kinds of situations accumulate over time, affecting their attitudes about people in general. In one study, for example, officers ranked dealing with an abused child as the most stressful kind of situation they encounter.

Police–Community Relations

Conflict between the police and racial and ethnic minority communities is one of the most serious problems in American policing. The focus of the problem in recent years has been the controversy over "driving while black" or "driving while brown" (DWB)—the allegation that the police single out African-American or Hispanic drivers for traffic stops on the basis of their race or ethnicity rather than suspected criminal conduct.

In a survey of Cincinnati residents, 46.6 percent of African-Americans indicated they had been personally hassled by the police, compared with only 9.6 percent of whites. Hassled was defined as being "stopped or watched closely by a police officer, even when you had done nothing wrong." Among many African-American families there is much fear of the police. A *New York Times* article in 1997 described how some African-American and Hispanic parents made a special effort to teach their children to be very respectful of police officers, primarily because they were afraid their children might be arrested, beaten, or even shot if they displayed any disrespect to an officer.

The use of deadly force has been the source of major conflict between minorities and the police. James Fyfe concluded that "blacks and Hispanics are everywhere overrepresented among those on the other side of police guns." One of the most controversial incidents in recent years was the fatal shooting of Amadou Diallo by New York City police officers in 1999 (and the subsequent acquittal of officers on criminal charges). Diallo was unarmed and apparently reaching for his wallet when he was shot. This shooting, together with other incidents of police misconduct, created a strong feeling among many minorities in the city that they are the target of systematic police abuse.

Allegations of police brutality, defined as the use of excessive physical force, represent the most common complaint voiced by minorities about the police. The videotaped beating of Rodney King in 1991 by Los Angeles police officers provided dramatic visual evidence of this problem.

The issue of excessive physical force is particularly complex. Police officers are authorized by law to use force in certain situations: to protect themselves, to effect an arrest, to overcome resistance, and to bring a dangerous situation under control. The relevant question is, "when is the use of force excessive?" Officers are supposed to "use only the force necessary to accomplish lawful objectives."

Whether or not a certain level of force is necessary in a particular situation is 14 frequently a matter of opinion. It often involves conflicting perceptions of whether a person was resisting arrest, or whether he or she posed a threat to the safety of the officer. The Bureau of Justice Statistics found that police officers used some kind of force in less than 1 percent of all encounters with citizens. About two-thirds of all uses of force are justified, given the circumstances, and about one-third are unjustified, or excessive. Thus, police use excessive force in an estimated one-third of 1 percent (0.3 percent) of all encounters with citizens.

The 1 percent figure acquires a different meaning when examined more 15 closely. The Bureau of Justice Statistics estimate of 421,000 force incidents per year translates into 1,100 per day. Thus, there are about 360 excessive force incidents every day of the year. The result is that a sizable number of racial and ethnic minorities experience police misconduct at one time or another.

Summary

Conflict between the police and racial and ethnic communities remains a seri- 16 ous problem in American policing. This problem persists despite general improvements in policing. Many of these problems are the responsibility of the police themselves. At the same time, conflict between police and minorities is a product of the larger structure of racial discrimination in American society.

(Samuel Walker and Charles M. Katz, *The Police in America*, 6/e, 2008)

 COMPREHENSION CHECKUP

Multiple Choice

Directions: For each item, write the letter corresponding to the best answer.

___d___ 1. In paragraph 3, the authors
   a. discuss positive and negative stereotypes of police officers.
   b. mention that the public's view of the police is influenced by stereotypes.
   c. use antonyms to describe officers as either savior or ogre.
   d. all of the above.

___b___ 2. The authors present information that supports all of the following *except* for which?
   a. The police are only slightly more conservative than the populace as a whole.
   b. The majority of police work is high-risk and exciting.
   c. A distinct police subculture does exist.
   d. Women are discouraged from applying for positions as police officers because of the emphasis on brute strength.

___b___ 3. Police attitudes toward the public at large
   a. change little over the course of their careers.
   b. change about the need for the use of force.
   c. become more positive.
   d. none of the above.

_c_ 4. All of the following are true about police officers _except_ for which?
   a. Officers frequently encounter hostility from the citizenry they are hired to protect.
   b. Officers tend to choose police work for altruistic reasons.
   c. Officers are treated as individuals.
   d. Officers frequently socialize with other officers.

_d_ 5. The police are called upon
   a. to do society's unpleasant tasks.
   b. to deal with victims of domestic abuse.
   c. to deal with murder victims.
   d. all of the above.

_d_ 6. Minorities frequently say that they are
   a. stopped or watched closely by a police officer even when they have committed no crime.
   b. the victims of excessive force on the part of the police.
   c. treated fairly by the police.
   d. both a and b.

_d_ 7. Officers are authorized by law to use force
   a. to protect themselves from danger.
   b. to bring control to a possibly dangerous situation.
   c. to overcome resistance on the part of a suspect.
   d. all of the above.

_b_ 8. The authors mention Amadou Diallo and Rodney King to illustrate
   a. videotaped beatings.
   b. excessive physical force.
   c. problems with New York City police officers.
   d. problems with the Los Angeles Police Department.

True or False

Directions: Indicate whether each statement is true or false by writing **T** or **F** in the space provided.

_T_ 9. The job of policing tends to isolate the police from the public at large.

_T_ 10. Among officers there is a distinct police subculture.

_T_ 11. African Americans are more likely to be hassled by the police than Whites.

_F_ 11. An officer may properly use as much force as the officer wants regardless of the circumstances.

Fact and Opinion

Directions: Indicate whether each sentence is a statement of fact or expresses an opinion by writing **F** or **O** in the blank provided.

_O_ 1. Neither stereotype [about police officers] is accurate.

_F_ 2. As Bayley and Mendelsohn conclude in their study of police-community relations in Denver, the average police officer is a rather average person in terms of values and political beliefs.

_F_ 3. No studies, however, have concluded that police officers are fundamentally different from other people in any important respect.

_____F_____ 4. At the start of academy training, 31 percent agreed that it was necessary to use force to gain respect in "tough" neighborhoods, while two years later 55 percent agreed.

_____O_____ 5. As is the case with racial stereotyping, it is an unpleasant experience to have people react to you as a category rather than as an individual.

_____F_____ 6. In one study, for example, officers ranked dealing with an abused child as the most stressful kind of situation they encounter.

_____F_____ 7. In a survey of Cincinnati residents, 46.6 percent of African Americans indicated they had been personally hassled by the police, compared with only 9.6 percent of whites.

_____O_____ 8. The issue of excessive physical force is particularly complex.

_____F_____ 9. The Bureau of Justice Statistics found that police officers used some kind of force in less than 1 percent of all encounters with citizens.

_____O_____ 10. At the same time, conflict between police and minorities is a product of the larger structure of racial discrimination in American society.

Vocabulary in Context

Directions: Match each word to its definition. Use each word only once.

acquittal   controversy   corrupt   excessive   hassled

heroic   incidents   isolation   ogre   relevant

1. in fairy tales, a flesh-eating monster or giant _____ogre_____

2. found not guilty in a court of law _____acquittal_____

3. too much or too great _____excessive_____

4. by itself; separated _____isolation_____

5. pertinent; to the point _____relevant_____

6. dispute or disagreement _____controversy_____

7. larger than life; brave _____heroic_____

8. dishonest; debased _____corrupt_____

9. annoyed, harassed, disturbed _____hassled_____

10. occurrences _____incidents_____

In Your Own Words

1. Many people express anger at the way they feel the police have treated them. In general, do you think the police treat people respectfully or rudely?

2. Although the United States already has the highest percentage of its population in prison of any country in the world, many people say we need to get tougher on crime. What is your opinion?

3. In Youngstown, Ohio, seven principles were established to guide police forces in both established and emerging democracies around the world. Principle 7 is: "The police are expected to discharge their duties in a nondiscriminatory manner." Do you think American police forces are successful in respecting this principle? Why or why not?

4. What is your opinion of reality-based police television shows? Do these shows help the public understand the nature of police work? Or do they offer a one-sided view of police work?

5. How important do you think it is to have a police department that mirrors America? Should police departments strive to actively recruit more women and minorities? How important is it to have bilingual officers?

Written Assignment

Do you think the police are more likely to discriminate against minorities, males, the poor, and the young? Or do you think these groups are more likely to be the ones involved in situations that attract the attention of the police? Write a short essay giving your opinion.

Internet Activity

Consult the following Web site that serves police officers:

www.officer.com

Pull up material of interest to you and write a few paragraphs about it. Does the Web site reflect a general bias? Can you find a more specific bias in each of the topics discussed?

READING

"We all had a drink together, native and European alike, quite amicably. The dead man was a hundred yards away."

TUNING IN TO READING   All of us have strong opinions on a variety of subjects. Our particular backgrounds and experiences influence our points of view.

Authors also have a point of view that may be directly expressed in their work or simply implied. As you read "A Hanging" by George Orwell, keep in mind that he is presenting a classic argument against capital punishment. Look at the following questions before you read the essay to begin familiarizing yourself with the issue of capital punishment. Put a check mark next to the statements you agree with.

_____ 1. Society has a right to execute its "mad dogs."

_____ 2. Not using the death penalty signals a lessened regard for the victim's life.

_____ 3. The death penalty is nothing more than state-sponsored murder.

_____ 4. The death penalty is a fair and just punishment for reprehensible crimes.

_____ 5. Two wrongs do not make a right.

_____ 6. It is more humane to sentence murderers to life imprisonment without parole.

_____ 7. Although the death penalty is not flawless, it is a necessary evil.

_____ 8. The death penalty is necessary to prevent individuals from taking the law into their own hands to avenge the murder of a loved one.

_____ 9. The death penalty is applied in a way that discriminates against minorities and the poor.

_____ 10. Only the death penalty can prevent a murderer from being pardoned and possibly murdering others.

READING (continued)

BIO-SKETCH   George Orwell (1903–1950) is best known as the author of the novels *1984* and *Animal Farm. 1984* is Orwell's version of the future and was meant to serve as a warning to humankind. It was completed just before his death at the age of 46. *Animal Farm,* a clever satire of dictatorships, was published in 1945 just after the end of World War II. During his lifetime, Orwell published 10 books and two collections of essays. The essay "A Hanging," originally published in 1931, is considered to be a classic. It is the only surviving example of his early years as a writer, and the only work originally published under his real name of Eric Blair.

Blair was born in Bengal, a province of British India, to a father who was a minor official in the Indian customs office. From 1917 to 1921, he attended Eton, a preparatory school in England, and then, instead of going on to a university, he served with the British Imperial Police in Burma, the setting of "A Hanging." It is obvious from the details carefully described in the essay that the incident of the hanging made a deep impression on him.

"A Hanging" takes place at Insein, where the second-largest prison in Burma was located. At the time of the essay, the prison held approximately 2,000 inmates. It was while he was serving as a police officer that Orwell's lifelong hatred of imperialism began. His experiences in Burma allowed him to see "the dirty work of the Empire at close quarters." What was especially painful to him was the power of life and death that the British officials held over their subjects. He agonized when he saw human beings being treated as though they were "things." Blair felt that in order to hang a man for a crime, one had to see him as less than human. Otherwise, one would be forced to admit the "unspeakable wrongness" of taking his life.

When "A Hanging" was published in the *Adelphi,* it received such good critical reviews that Orwell's career as a writer was launched. In the essay, the now-mature Blair is reflecting on an event that took place five years before. The story is deceptively simple. A condemned man, a Hindu, is taken out of his cell and escorted across the jail yard where the gallows are located. During his walk, two things of importance occur. First, he is greeted by a large, friendly dog, and second, he steps aside to avoid a puddle in his path. Years later, Blair, now using the pen name of George Orwell, wrote: "I watched a man hanged once; it seemed to me worse than a thousand murders. I never went into a jail without feeling that my place was on the other side of the bars."

READING (continued)

NOTES ON VOCABULARY

Burma formerly, the name of a country in Southeast Asia on the Bay of Bengal. Burma was colonized by the British in 1824. In 1948, Burma overthrew its colonial government and became an independent nation. Today, the official name for Burma is Union of Myanmar.

pariah Today, the word *pariah* means any person (or animal) who is a social outcast. However, originally, *Pariahs* were members of one of the lowest castes in India, who served as slaves to the higher castes. The word is derived from a Tamil word meaning "drummer." Members of the *Pariah* caste frequently beat the drum (*parai*) at various festivals. At the time of Orwell's essay, the *Pariahs* served as household servants to the British, and the term *pariah* was used to designate anyone of low caste.

warder a person who guards something. *Warder* is the British term for a prison guard or officer.

rupee the basic monetary unit of India, Pakistan, Nepal, and Burma (Myanmar).

A Hanging

GEORGE ORWELL

It was in Burma, a sodden morning of the rains. A sickly light, like yellow tinfoil, was slanting over the high walls into the jail yard. We were waiting outside the condemned cells, a row of sheds fronted with double bars, like small animal cages. Each cell measured about ten feet by ten and was quite bare within except for a plank bed and a pot for drinking water. In some of them brown silent men were squatting at the inner bars, with their blankets draped round them. These were the condemned men, due to be hanged within the next week or two.

One prisoner had been brought out of his cell. He was a Hindu, a puny 2 wisp of a man, with a shaven head and vague liquid eyes. He had a thick, sprouting moustache, absurdly too big for his body, rather like the moustache of a comic man in films. Six tall Indian warders were guarding him and getting him ready for the gallows. Two of them stood by with rifles and fixed bayonets, while the others handcuffed him, passed a chain through his handcuffs and fixed it to their belts, and lashed his arms tightly to his sides. They crowded very close about him, with their hands always on him in a careful, caressing grip, as though all the while feeling him to make sure he was there. It was like men handling a fish which is still alive and may jump back into the water. But he stood quite unresisting, yielding his arms limply to the ropes, as though he hardly noticed what was happening.

Eight o'clock struck and a bugle call, desolately thin in the wet air, floated 3 from the distant barracks. The superintendent of the jail, who was standing apart from the rest of us, moodily prodding the gravel with his stick, raised his head at the sound. He was an army doctor, with a gray toothbrush moustache and a gruff voice. "For God's sake hurry up, Francis," he said irritably. "The man ought to have been dead by this time. Aren't you ready yet?"

Francis, the head jailer, a fat Dravidian in a white drill suit and gold 4 spectacles, waved his black hand. "Yes sir, yes sir," he bubbled. "All iss satisfactorily prepared. The hangman iss waiting. We shall proceed."

"Well, quick march, then. The prisoners can't get their breakfast till this 5 job's over."

We set out for the gallows. Two warders marched on either side of the 6 prisoner, with their rifles at the slope; two others marched close against him, gripping him by arm and shoulder, as though at once pushing him and supporting him. The rest of us, magistrates and the like, followed behind. Suddenly, when we had gone 10 yards, the procession stopped short without any order or warning. A dreadful thing had happened—a dog, come goodness knows whence, had appeared in the yard. It came bounding among us with a loud volley of barks and leapt round us wagging its whole body, wild with glee at finding so many human beings together. It was a large woolly dog, half Airedale, half pariah. For a moment it pranced round us, and then, before anyone could stop it, made a dash for the prisoner and, jumping up, tried to lick his face. Everyone stood aghast, too taken aback even to grab at the dog.

"Who let the bloody brute in here?" said the superintendent angrily. 7 "Catch it, someone!"

A warder, detached from the escort, charged clumsily after the dog, but 8 it danced and gamboled just out of his reach, taking everything as part of the game. A young Eurasian jailer picked up a handful of gravel and tried to stone the dog away, but it dodged the stones and came after us again. Its yaps echoed from the jail walls. The prisoner, in the grasp of the two warders, looked on incuriously, as though this was another formality of the hanging. It was several minutes before someone managed to catch the dog. Then we put my handkerchief through its collar and moved off once more, with the dog still straining and whimpering.

It was about 40 yards to the gallows. I watched the bare brown back of 9 the prisoner marching in front of me. He walked clumsily with his bound arms, but quite steadily, with that bobbing gait of the Indian who never straightens his knees. At each step his muscles slid neatly into place, the lock of hair on his scalp danced up and down, his feet printed themselves on the wet gravel. And once, in spite of the men who gripped him by each shoulder, he stepped lightly aside to avoid a puddle on the path.

It is curious, but till that moment I had never realized what it means to 10 destroy a healthy, conscious man. When I saw the prisoner step aside to avoid the puddle I saw the mystery, the unspeakable wrongness, of cutting a life short when it is in full tide. This man was not dying, he was alive just as we were alive. All the organs of his body were working—bowels digesting food, skin renewing itself, nails growing, tissues forming—all toiling away in solemn foolery. His nails would still be growing when he stood on the drop, when he was falling through the air with a tenth of a second to live. His eyes saw the yellow gravel and the gray walls, and his brain still remembered, foresaw, reasoned—reasoned even about puddles. He and we were a party of men walking together, seeing, hearing, feeling, understanding the same world; and in two minutes, with a sudden snap, one of us would be gone—one mind less, one world less.

The gallows stood in a small yard, separate from the main grounds of 11 the prison, and overgrown with tall prickly weeds. It was a brick erection like three sides of a shed, with planking on top, and above the two beams and a crossbar with the rope dangling. The hangman, a gray-haired convict in the white uniform of the prison, was waiting beside his machine. He greeted us with a servile crouch as we entered. At a word from Francis the two warders, gripping the prisoner more closely than ever, half led half pushed him to the gallows and helped him clumsily up the ladder. Then the hangman climbed up and fixed the rope around the prisoner's neck.

We stood waiting, five yards away. The warders had formed in a rough 12 circle round the gallows. And then, when the noose was fixed, the prisoner began crying out to his god. It was a high, reiterated cry of "Ram! Ram! Ram! Ram!" not urgent and fearful like a prayer or a cry for help, but steady, rhythmical, almost like the tolling of a bell. The dog answered the sound with a whine. The hangman, still standing on the gallows, produced a small cotton bag like a flour bag and drew it down and over the prisoner's face. But the sound, muffled by the cloth, still persisted, over and over again: "Ram! Ram! Ram! Ram!"

The hangman climbed down and stood ready, holding the lever. Minutes 13 seemed to pass. The steady, muffled crying from the prisoner went on and on, "Ram! Ram! Ram!" never faltering for an instant. The superintendent, his head on his chest, was slowly poking the ground with his stick; perhaps he was counting the cries, allowing the prisoner a fixed number—fifty, perhaps, or a hundred. Everyone had changed color. The Indians had gone gray like bad coffee, and one or two of the bayonets were wavering. We looked at the lashed, hooded man on the drop, and listened to his cries—each cry another second of life; the same thought was in all our minds; oh, kill him quickly, get it over, stop that abominable noise!

Suddenly the superintendent made up his mind. Throwing up his head 14 he made a swift motion with his stick. "Chalo!" he shouted almost fiercely.

There was a clanking noise, and then dead silence. The prisoner had 15 vanished, and the rope was twisting on itself. I let go of the dog, and it galloped immediately to the back of the gallows; but when it got there it stopped short, barked, and then retreated into a corner of the yard, where it stood among the weeds, looking timorously out at us. We went round the gallows to inspect the prisoner's body. He was dangling with his toes pointed straight downward, very slowly revolving, as dead as a stone.

The superintendent reached out with his stick and poked the bare 16
brown body; it oscillated slightly. "*He's* all right," said the superintendent.
He backed out from under the gallows, and blew out a deep breath. The
moody look had gone out of his face quite suddenly. He glanced at his
wristwatch. "Eight minutes past eight. Well, that's all for this morning,
thank God."

The warders unfixed bayonets and marched away. The dog, sobered and 17
conscious of having misbehaved itself, slipped after them. We walked out of
the gallows yard, past the condemned cells with their waiting prisoners, into
the big central yard of the prison. The convicts, under the command of
warders armed with lathis, were already receiving their breakfast. They squat-
ted in long rows, each man holding a tin pannikin, while two warders with
buckets marched round ladling out rice; it seemed quite a homely, jolly
scene, after the hanging. An enormous relief had come upon us now that
the job was done. One felt an impulse to sing, to break into a run, to snig-
ger. All at once everyone began chattering gaily.

The Eurasian boy walking beside me nodded toward the way we had 18
come, with a knowing smile: "Do you know sir, our friend [he meant the
dead man] when he heard his appeal had been dismissed, he pissed on the
floor of his cell. From fright. Kindly take one of my cigarettes, sir. Do you
not admire my new silver case, sir? From the boxwalah, two rupees, eight
annas. Classy European style."

Several people laughed—at what, nobody seemed certain.   19

Francis was walking by the superintendent, talking garrulously. "Well, 20
sir, all hass passed off with the utmost satisfactoriness. It was all finished—
flick! like that. It iss not always so—oah no! I have known cases where the
doctor wass obliged to go beneath the gallows and pull the prisoner's legs to
ensure decease. Most disagreeable!"

"Wriggling about, eh? That's bad," said the superintendent.   21

"Ach, sir, it iss worse when they become refractory! One man, I recall, 22
clung to the bars of hiss cage when we went to take him out. You will
scarcely credit, sir, that it took six warders to dislodge him, three pulling at
each leg. We reasoned with him. 'My dear fellow,' we said, 'think of all the
pain and trouble you are causing to us!' But no, he would not listen! Ach,
he wass very troublesome!"

I found that I was laughing quite loudly. Everyone was laughing. Even 23
the superintendent grinned in a tolerant way. "You'd better all come and
have a drink," he said quite genially. "I've got a bottle of whiskey in the
car. We could do with it."

We went through the big double gates of the prison into the road. "Pull- 24
ing at his legs!" exclaimed a Burmese magistrate suddenly, and burst into a
loud chuckling. We all began laughing again. At that moment Francis' anecdote seemed extraordinarily funny. We all had a drink together, native and
European alike, quite amicably. The dead man was a hundred yards away.

(George Orwell, "A Hanging," 1950)

COMPREHENSION CHECKUP

Multiple Choice

Directions: For each item, write the letter corresponding to the best answer.

__c__ 1. The first paragraph of the narrative serves to
  a. express Orwell's feelings about capital punishment.
  b. introduce the reader to the person being executed.
  c. introduce the reader to the setting of the story.
  d. describe the hanging process in detail.

__b__ 2. From the story, you could infer that Orwell
  a. would support the continued use of capital punishment.
  b. viewed the death penalty process as ironic.
  c. saw no problems in executing a man.
  d. had been opposed to the death penalty before he went to Burma.

__d__ 3. Orwell serves as the narrator of the story. Which role does the narrator play?
  a. the person responsible for hanging the prisoner
  b. a fellow prisoner due to be executed later
  c. the superintendent of the prison
  d. an observer to the hanging process

__c__ 4. The organizational pattern used in paragraph 17 is
  a. cause and effect.
  b. comparison-contrast.
  c. chronological order.
  d. definition and example.

True or False

Directions: Indicate whether each statement is true or false by writing **T** or **F** in the space provided.

__F__ 5. The prisoner was accused of committing murder in a fit of rage.

__F__ 6. A British official was responsible for serving as the executioner.

__T__ 7. On the way to the gallows, they were interrupted by a large, friendly dog.

__F__ 8. After the hanging, everyone felt a great deal of grief and began to wail and cry.

__T__ 9. The men, both British and local, later drank together quite amicably.

__F__ 10. It was possible to see the prisoner's face when he was executed.

Vocabulary in Context

Directions: Use the context clues to determine the meaning of the italicized words, and then write a definition for that word in the space provided.

1. a *sodden* morning of the rains (1)   wet, soaked

2. a *puny* wisp of a man (2)   weak

3. a bugle call, *desolately* thin in the wet air (3)   lonely, forlorn

  4. Everyone stood *aghast* (6)   shocked

  5. it danced and *gamboled* (8)   frolicked

  6. All *toiling* away (10)   working hard

  7. It was a high, *reiterated* cry (12)   repeated

  8. never *faltering* for an instant (13)   hesitating, wavering

  9. looking *timorously* out at us (15)   fearfully

 10. it *oscillated* slightly (16)   vibrated

 11. Francis was . . . talking *garrulously* (20)   chattering

 12. when they become *refractory* (22)   stubbornly disobedient

 13. he said quite *genially* (23)   cheerfully

 14. Francis' *anecdote* seemed extraordinarily   short account
     funny (24)

 15. native and European alike, quite *amicably* (24)   friendly

Short Answer

Directions: Answer the questions briefly, in a few words or sentences as appropriate.

  1. What is the overall main idea of the essay?

     The author, while serving as a British police officer, became convinced that

     executing a healthy human being was wrong.

  2. What was the author's purpose in writing the essay?

     convince readers that capital punishment is wrong

  3. Orwell is noted for his use of figurative language. List a few examples from
     the first paragraph.

     "sickly light like yellow tin foil," "row of sheds—like small animal cages"

  4. As a writer, Orwell was often preoccupied with detail. At the beginning of the
     essay, he is concerned with using concrete details to set the scene for the reader.
     Give an example of this type of detail. What is the tone of paragraph 1?

     "each cell measured about ten feet by ten," gloomy

  5. Give some descriptive details about the prisoner's appearance at the start of
     the essay.

     "puny wisp of a man," "shaven head," "vague liquid eyes," "thick, sprouting

     moustache"

  6. Considering Orwell's emphasis on details, why doesn't he tell us more
     about the prisoner, such as his name and the reason he was being
     hanged? How does this selective omission of key details reveal Orwell's
     point of view?

     Orwell feels capital punishment is morally wrong. If we knew the prisoner had

     committed a horrible act, we might be less sympathetic to him.

  7. What is ironic about the dog's reaction to the prisoner? How does the
     dog's behavior serve as a contrast to the behavior of the human beings in

the story? How does the inclusion of this incident reveal Orwell's point of view?

The dog is behaving in an affectionate way toward the prisoner. The men are

treating the prisoner like an object. The dog is displaying qualities that Orwell

associates with humans. The humans are acting like animals.

8. Analyze the simile Orwell uses to describe the way the guards handle the prisoner: "It was like men handling a fish which is still alive and may jump back into the water."

   Subject: guards handling the prisoner

   Compared to: men handling a fish

   Meaning: They are behaving as though the prisoner is dangerous and may try

   to escape.

9. In paragraph 10, the author discovers that he is opposed to capital punishment. What are his reasons for opposing it? What trivial incident on the part of the prisoner brought him to this realization?

   When the prisoner walks around the puddle, Orwell realizes that he is still a

   functioning part of society.

10. After the author realizes he is opposed to capital punishment, how does the way he describes the prisoner change? What words does he use to describe our common bond with the prisoner? How does his choice of words reveal his point of view?

    The words "one mind less, one world less" emphasize our shared humanity. He

    feels that we are all interconnected. Originally Orwell emphasizes the prisoner's

    puny size; later he emphasizes the prisoner's dignity.

11. Identify the similes in paragraphs 13 and 15.

    "The Indians had gone gray like bad coffee," "as dead as a stone"

12. What is ironic about the superintendent's statement in paragraph 16?

    The prisoner can't be "all right" because he is dead.

13. What is ironic about the description of the scene in paragraph 17?

    It is described as being a "homely, jolly scene." But there has just been a hanging.

14. After the hanging, what clues does the author give us indicating that those who participated in the execution were uncomfortable with their role?

    They felt relief—they are laughing and chattering about things that aren't very funny.

15. What is the irony in paragraph 22?

    They are criticizing the prisoner for not cooperating in his own hanging.

Written Assignment

Have you heard about a murder in the news media that shocked you? Write an essay telling as much as you know about what happened—the circumstances of the murder, the police investigation, the trial, the sentence imposed. What is your personal reaction to those events?

Internet Activity

Visit one of the Web sites below. Find information either in favor of or opposed to the use of the death penalty, print the information, and highlight any words that demonstrate a clear bias.

    www.prodeathpenalty.com

    www.ncadp.org

REVIEW TEST 8: Identifying Author Bias

Directions: Use what you learned about connotation and denotation, euphemism, point of view, and fact versus opinion to identify the author's bias. Then state this bias briefly in your own words.

1. Tropical forests (home for 66% of the plant species, 90% of nonhuman primates, 40% of birds of prey, and 90% of insects), used to cover 6–7% of the total land surface of the Earth—an area roughly equivalent to our contiguous 48 states. Every year, humans destroy an area of forest equivalent to the size of Oklahoma.

    At this rate, these forests and the species they contain will disappear completely in just a few more decades. The destruction of tropical rain forests gives only short-term benefits but is expected to cause long-term problems. If tropical rain forests are preserved, the rich diversity of plants and animals will continue to exist for scientific and pharmacological study. One fourth of the medicines we currently use come from tropical rain forests. It is hoped that many of the still unknown plants will provide medicines for other human ills. Worldwide, without tropical rain forests, there could be changes in climate that would affect the entire human race. Preserving these forests is a wise investment. Such action promotes the survival of most of the world's species—indeed, the human species, too.

    (Sylvia S. Mader, *Human Biology,* 8/e, 2004)

    Bias: We are destroying not only the rain forest but also the wildlife that
    _____

    lives there.
    _____

2. I can think of some pretty good reasons why vouchers for private schools are a bad idea. First of all, and probably most important, these schemes deprive public schools of the support they deserve. Parents who choose to send their kids to private school still have a responsibility to support public education, not the other way around. Pat Robertson, one of the biggest endorsers of voucher schemes, has said: "They say vouchers would spell the end of public schools in America. To which we say, so what?" What in the world is he thinking? Look, 42 million of our kids go to public school each day. Their future is America's future. No matter what we choose for our own kids, we all have a stake in the success of public education.

    There's something else I want you to understand. Just because vouchers are public money doesn't mean that the participating private schools will be accountable to the public. Wondering about the curriculum at the David Koresh Academy? How about the expulsion policy at the Louis Farrakhan School? Well, stop wondering. It ain't any of your business now, and it will never get to be your business, even if they used your tax dollars to send somebody to these schools.

(James Carville, *We're Right, They're Wrong,* 1996)

Bias: <u>He feels that private school vouchers are inherently bad and might ruin</u>

<u>public schools.</u>

3. Girls today are much more oppressed. They are coming of age in a more dangerous, sexualized and media-saturated culture. They face incredible pressures to be beautiful and sophisticated, which in junior high means using chemicals and being sexual. As they navigate a more dangerous world, girls are less protected.

   As I looked at the culture that girls enter as they come of age, I was struck by what a girl-poisoning culture it was. The more I looked around, the more I listened to today's music, watched television and movies and looked at sexist advertising, the more convinced I became that we are on the wrong path with our daughters. America today limits girls' development, truncates their wholeness, and leaves many of them traumatized.

   (Mary Pipher, *Reviving Ophelia,* 1994)

   Bias: <u>Girls today face many more outside pressures.</u>

4. The information age has brought us many wonders, but it has also made possible an unprecedented level of record keeping and high-tech snooping into the lives of others. While we dazzle ourselves in virtual worlds and strange new digital communities that stretch around the globe, it's easy to forget that the same technology that connects us can keep track of us as never before.

   Employers have more freedom to infringe on the privacy of employees than do the police, who still need court approval to tap most telephone or data lines, notes Andre Bacard, author of the *Computer Privacy Handbook.* Supervisors, he says, "can tap an employee's phones, monitor her e-mail, watch her on closed-circuit TV, and search her computer files, without giving her notice."

   (Reed Karaim, "The Invasion of Privacy," 1996)

   Bias: <u>Employers are more able than ever to investigate employees.</u>

5. As college students you are exposed to loud music and other noise all the time. You go to parties, clubs, and concerts where the volume is so loud you have to shout so the person next to you can hear what you are saying. You turn your personal CD players so high they can be heard halfway across the room. And you seldom give it a second thought. But you should, because excessive noise can have a serious impact on your health and well-being. Noise-induced hearing loss can begin as early as 10 years of age. There are now 21-year-olds walking around with hearing-loss patterns of people 40 years their senior. The problem with hearing loss is that it creeps up on you. Today's hard-rock fans won't notice the effect of their hearing loss for another 15 years. And then it will be too late. Unlike some physical conditions, hearing loss is irreversible. Loud noise damages the microscopic hairs in the inner ear that transmit sound to the auditory nerve. Once damaged, those hairs can never recover and can never be repaired. Now are you convinced? At least think about the possible

consequences the next time you are set to pump up the volume on your personal CD player.

(Stephen E. Lucas, *The Art of Public Speaking*, 8/e, 2004)

Bias: <u>College students should be concerned about hearing loss from excessive noise.</u>

6. Super Bowl beer ads, and beer ads in general, have for many years seemed to be directed toward juveniles. Whether or not advertisers do this intentionally, children pick up on them. This kind of advertising impact is especially troublesome because young people see nearly 2,000 commercials for beer and wine each year. For every public service announcement with a message like "Just say no," teens will view 25 to 50 beer and wine commercials that say essentially "Drinking is cool." Meanwhile, underage drinking remains a widespread problem. Many young people are beginning to consume alcohol around the age of 13, and a large majority will do their heaviest drinking before their 21st birthday. Beer advertisements in particular often glamorize drinking and provide no information about the potential negative effects alcohol has on the body, including nausea, blackouts, and liver problems.

(George Rodman, *Mass Media in a Changing World*, 2006)

Bias: <u>Drinking by the young is a big problem, so directing beer ads at them is very troublesome.</u>

7. For more than 200 years, America has been known as the "Land of Opportunity" where anyone who works hard can enjoy both material success and the freedom of living in a democracy. Indeed, millions of immigrants from all around the globe have poured into the United States eager to work, learn, and build a better future for themselves and their families. However, for many immigrants and refugees who come to America, the hard work they hope will be the path to the good life often puts them at risk for workplace-related illness and injury. Immigrants who have little education and lack work and language skills often are forced to take jobs that are low-paying, hazardous, or both. They sew for long hours in garment sweatshops, work with hazardous materials like asbestos or toxic chemicals without adequate protection, or labor in settings where they are targets of violent crime. Clearly, all workplaces should be safe and healthy environments for their workers. Just as clearly, immigrants with low levels of skill and education must be protected from a host of workplace hazards that can cause illness, injury, and even death.

(Wayne A. Payne and Dale B. Hahn, *Understanding Your Health*, 6/e, 2000)

Bias: <u>Workplaces should be safe and healthy environments for everyone.</u>

8. National attention has recently been focused on a serious and growing problem on our highways—people who talk on the phone while they drive. Police, state legislators, and local activists say that something must be done. A handful of counties and municipalities have already enacted ordinances limiting the use of cell phones for drivers and at least 40 states are considering similar bills. But the powerful cell phone lobby is battling back, stressing public education over a new generation of anti–cell phone laws. Although 80 percent of cell-phone users say they talk while driving, good numbers on how many car accidents are caused by cell phones are

hard to come by. In most states, accidents filed by the police don't reflect whether cell phones played a role. The medical community has provided the most sound, and most damning, statistics. A 1997 study published in *The New England Journal of Medicine* found that the collision rate for drivers using handheld cell phones were roughly the same as for drivers who were legally drunk.

(Peg Tyre and Julie Scelfo, "A Car, a Call and a Terrible Crash," 2001)

Bias: Cell-phone use while driving is a growing problem and is implicated by doctors in causing accidents.

Chapter Summary and Review

In Chapter 11, you learned to identify writing that has a biased viewpoint and to recognize an author's personal bias. You also learned about the difference between denotative and connotative meanings and between positive and negative connotations. Based on the material in Chapter 11, answer the following.

Short Answer

Directions: List three organizations you think may have a biased point of view, and indicate their bias.

Name of Organization   Bias of Organization

1. Answers will vary. _____   _____

2. _____   _____

3. _____   _____

Vocabulary in Context

Directions: Choose one of the following words to complete the sentences below. Use each word only once.

    bias   euphemism   positive

4. Some cities do not admit that they have potholes. Instead, they use a __euphemism__ and call their potholes "pavement deficiencies."

5. Three driver-training teachers became part of a jury pool in a drunk-driving case. The judge dismissed them from serving as jurors because of their presumed __bias__ against drunk drivers.

6. The term *administrator* has a more __positive__ connotation than the term *bureaucrat.*

Propaganda Techniques, Logical Fallacies, and Argument

CHAPTER PREVIEW

In this chapter, you will

- Become familiar with common propaganda techniques and logical fallacies.

- Learn to apply knowledge of propaganda techniques and logical fallacies to reading selections.

- Become familiar with the structure of an argument.

- Recognize valid and invalid arguments.

What Are Propaganda Techniques and Logical Fallacies and How Are They Used?

We have learned the difference between fact and opinion, and we have also discussed bias. Now we are going to look at the related topic of propaganda.

The word *propaganda* was first used by Pope Urban VIII (1623–1644), who created a "congregation for propagating the faith." Thus, **propaganda** originally meant spreading the Christian faith with missionary activity throughout the world. Today *propaganda* refers to the spreading of ideas to further a cause. Political parties often use *propaganda* to persuade people to vote for their candidates or support their programs. Advertising is a form of propaganda designed to persuade consumers that certain products or brands are superior.

Because modern propaganda often makes use of distortion and deception, the word *propaganda* now has a negative sound to it. But propaganda is sometimes destructive and sometimes beneficial. Tobacco companies use propaganda to persuade people to smoke, and more specifically to persuade people to smoke particular brands of cigarettes. Many people would characterize this use of propaganda as destructive because smoking is damaging to health. But in recent years, propaganda has been used in antismoking campaigns to inform people of the dangers of smoking and to try to persuade them to stop smoking. These antismoking campaigns use propaganda for a positive, beneficial purpose, as illustrated by the advertisement from an antismoking ad campaign on the next page.

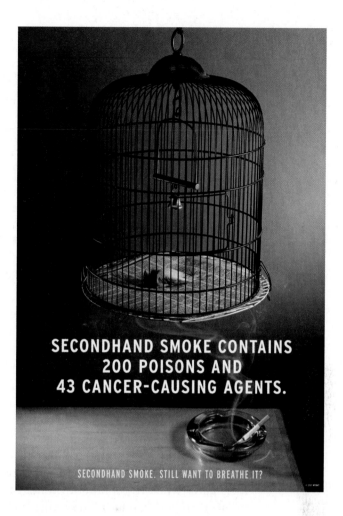

SECONDHAND SMOKE CONTAINS 200 POISONS AND 43 CANCER-CAUSING AGENTS.

SECONDHAND SMOKE. STILL WANT TO BREATHE IT?

Propaganda works by using certain techniques to manipulate reason and emotion. Because propaganda is manipulative, it is important for you to be familiar with these techniques so that you will know when propaganda is being directed at you. Once you are aware that propaganda techniques are being used, your knowledge of these techniques will also help you evaluate the accuracy and fairness of the message. Does the message really make sense? Is the cause being promoted by the propaganda something that you want to support? Our special focus is on the use of propaganda techniques in written material. You want to know when a writer is using propaganda techniques so that you can more accurately and fairly evaluate what is being said.

The Institute for Propaganda Analysis was formed in 1937 to study propaganda and educate the American public about it. The institute identified seven propaganda techniques. Other techniques have since been added to the list, including logical fallacies (errors in reasoning). We will discuss the main propaganda techniques and logical fallacies in this chapter and give you some practice in identifying them.

Original Seven Propaganda Techniques

1. **Name-calling (personal attack, ad hominem).** This technique consists of attaching a negative label to a person or thing. Politicians routinely attack one another for changing a position on an issue by calling the offender a

"flip-flop." When politicians engage in name-calling, they are usually trying to avoid supporting their own position with facts. Rather than explain what they believe in, they try to tear their opponent down. Many of us engage in the same type of technique when someone disagrees with us. We might call someone we disagree with "radical," "reactionary," "foolish," or "stupid."

2. **Glittering generalities.** This technique involves important-sounding "glad words" that have little or no real meaning. When glad words are used, it is hard to prove or disprove a statement. The words "good," "honest," "fair," and "best" are examples of glad words. When an automobile manufacturer says in an advertisement that its cars are the "best," what does the manufacturer really mean? Does one particular model have the "best" safety record? Have the "best" warranty? Get the "best" mileage?

3. **Transfer.** In this technique, an attempt is made to transfer the prestige of a positive symbol to a person or an idea. At both the Republican and the Democrat national conventions, the backdrop is always the American flag. Politicians want us to think that they are patriotic and will do what is right for the country. Advertising also makes use of transfer. Both the U.S. Postal Service Express Mail and a nationwide legal firm specializing in injury and wrongful death use an eagle in their advertisements.

4. **Testimonial.** This technique is easy to understand. Often big-name models and athletes, as well as movie and TV stars, are paid huge amounts of money to endorse a product. Whenever you see someone famous endorsing a product, ask yourself how much that person knows about the product, and what he or she stands to gain by promoting it. In the area of politics, national political leaders often give ringing endorsements of members of their party who are running for office at the state or local level. They hope to use their prestige to influence the voting.

5. **Plain folks.** This technique uses a folksy approach to persuade us to support someone or something. At election time, politicians appear at local diners, coffee shops, or malls to prove they are just like us. A man or a woman running for president will be photographed making breakfast, taking out the garbage, or grocery shopping. To sell products such as headache remedies, cereal, or toilet bowl cleaners, advertisers will depict ordinary-looking people doing ordinary activities.

6. **Card stacking.** This term comes from the act of stacking a deck of cards in your favor. Propagandists effectively use card stacking to slant the message. Key words or unfavorable statistics may be omitted in an ad or commercial, leading to a series of half-truths. An advertisement stating that "four out of five dentists surveyed recommend Zest toothpaste" may be true, but it may also fail to disclose that only five dentists were actually contacted, and of those five, four accepted money to provide an endorsement. Keep in mind that an advertiser is under no obligation "to tell the truth, the whole truth, and nothing but the truth." If you go into a car dealership to purchase a new car, the salesperson is not likely to inform you that the model you are interested in has a problem with paint discoloration. The telemarketer trying to solicit funds to feed hungry children in Asia is unlikely to reveal how much of your donation goes to pay his salary and other administrative costs.

7. **Bandwagon (ad populum).** The bandwagon approach encourages you to think that because everyone else is doing something, you should do it, too, or you'll be left out. When soft drink or beer ads show many attractive people having fun on a beach, they are using bandwagon propaganda. Ads urging you to live it up because it's "Miller time" are using a bandwagon appeal. The technique embodies a "keeping up with the Joneses" philosophy. If a commercial says, "No wonder six million people bought our product last year," they're using the bandwagon technique to exploit the fear of missing out on something.

Exercise 1: Identifying Propaganda Techniques

Directions: The following statements make use of the propaganda techniques we've just studied. For each statement, identify the propaganda technique used. Some techniques will be used more than once.

1. Vote for Jack Hazelhurst. Governor Brown is voting for him.
testimonial

2. E-Z LIVING recliners are the best that money can buy. glittering generality

3. Before giving his speech, Senator Jones had the band play "The Star-Spangled Banner." transfer

4. Basketball star Michael James says, "You should buy QuickLift tennis shoes. They'll help you lift off for a great day." testimonial

5. Congressional candidate Fred Goodwin says that people should vote for him because he is fair, honest, and kind. glittering generality

6. In a recent interview, Governor Herman said that those who oppose his reform measures are "misguided, arrogant fools." name-calling

7. Hurry down to our car dealership before we sell our last sale car.
bandwagon

8. Governor Swellguy put on a hard hat and took a tour of the new mining operations at National Mining Company. plain folks

9. All the guys down at Barney's Bar drink Blitz beer. bandwagon

10. Brightwhite toothpaste makes your smile bright again. It gets rid of ugly discoloration caused by coffee and tea. It makes that special person in your life eager to get close. card stacking

11. Mayor Walker is for the little guy. You don't see him driving an expensive car or sending his daughter to a private school. plain folks

12. My opponent has been stingy in helping the nation's unemployed. And he ignorantly voted against all the bills to build a rapid transit system.
name-calling

More Propaganda Techniques and Logical Fallacies

The following were not part of the original seven techniques identified by the Institute for Propaganda Analysis in 1937. They were added at a later date and are known as both propaganda techniques and *logical fallacies or errors in reasoning.*

8. **False analogy (false comparison).** In this fallacy, two things that may or may not really be similar are portrayed as being similar. The store brand can of peas may look like the name brand, but is it exactly the same? We have to ask ourselves several questions to determine the answer. For instance, are the peas of the same quality? Are they the same size? Are there as many peas in the can? In most false analogies, there is simply not enough evidence available to support the comparison.

9. **Either/or fallacy.** This fallacy is also called "black-and-white thinking" because only two choices are given. You are either for something or against it; there is no middle ground or shades of gray. People who exhibit this type of thinking have a "bumper sticker" mentality. They say things like "America—love it or leave it" and "Put up or shut up." According to this line of reasoning, you are either in favor of gun control or against it, or in favor of abortion or opposed to it. When we attempt to polarize an issue, we negate all attempts to find a common ground.

10. **Circular reasoning (begging the question).** In this fallacy, the conclusion simply restates the information presented as evidence. Here's an example: "She lost the election because she didn't get enough votes." Here's another example: "The team is in first place because they've won more games than the other teams."

11. **Red herring.** This fallacy involves directing attention away from a debatable point to one that is irrelevant (the red herring). By changing the topic, the discussion goes in a new, unhelpful direction. Here's an example: "I know I forgot to buy groceries, but nothing I do ever pleases you." This is similar to what students do when they try to distract the teacher with lots of questions in order to postpone a scheduled test.

12. **Hasty generalization (stereotyping).** In this fallacy, assumptions are made about a whole group based on an inadequate sample. Stereotypes fall into this category. Here are some examples of hasty generalizations. Mark hears that both Tracy and Melanie were in accidents, so he says that "women drivers are worse than men." Or Roberta sees that all her female friends are struggling with math but her male friends are doing well, so she says that "men are better than women in math." In both of these examples, the sample population is just too small to support the broad conclusion.

13. **Faulty cause and effect.** This fallacy suggests that because B follows A, A must *cause* B. When we hear people say, "I know it's going to rain today because I just washed my car," they are guilty of faulty cause and effect. Remember, just because two events or two sets of data are related does not necessarily mean that one caused the other to happen. It is important to evaluate the data carefully and not jump to the wrong conclusion. Is the man in the cartoon guilty of faulty cause and effect?

" WILL YOU SHUT THAT THING OFF ?
THE MAN IS PUTTING ! "

Bob Zahn. www.cartoonfile.net. Reprinted with permission.

Exercise 2: Identifying Propaganda Techniques and Logical Fallacies

Directions: The following statements make use of propaganda techniques and logical fallacies 8–13. For each statement, identify the technique used. Some techniques will be used more than once.

1. You are either part of the solution or part of the problem. _either/or_

2. Jeremy saw Mike hanging out with Tim, who has just gotten out of jail. "Now Mike will end up in jail, too," he said. _false analogy_

3. Having a pit bull or a Rottweiler in the home around small children is dangerous because it's unsafe. _circular reasoning_

4. Yang Chow Chinese dinners are just as good and appetizing as what is served in expensive Hong Kong restaurants. _false analogy_

5. All college students have a lot of credit card debt. _hasty generalization_

6. I feel lucky today, so my favorite basketball team is going to win. _faulty cause and effect_

7. We can communicate effectively with people all the way around the world, so it should be easy for parents to communicate with their own kids in their own house. _false analogy_

8. People shouldn't get upset when drivers who are texting cause traffic accidents. After all, drivers cause accidents when they eat in the car, too. _red herring_

9. College students today are lazy and irresponsible. _hasty generalization_

10. Either he is a genius or he is a fraud. _either/or_

Exercise 3: Analyzing a Propaganda Technique

What propaganda technique does the "got milk?" ad illustrate? To whom do you think the ad is likely to appeal? Write your answers on the lines below the ad.

The taste of fame. Center stage, silver screen, joyful new mom. How do I keep this show on the road? Milk. Its wholesome goodness helps make my family strong at every stage. Talk about a powerful performance.

got milk?

whymilk.com/jenniferhudson

Answers will vary. _____

_____

_____

REVIEW TEST 9: Propaganda Techniques and Logical Fallacies

Directions: For each passage, identify the propaganda technique being used.

bandwagon _____ 1. "Get behind the wheel of the most popular car on the road today!"

card stacking _____ 2. "You need a toothpaste that does it All. All toothpaste fights cavities, plaque, bad breath, and gingivitis. Plus it brightens your smile. Face your day the All-prepared way!"

either/or _____ 3. "Either this community votes to fund mass transit or all of us will be personally affected by gridlock on our streets."

testimonial _____ 4. Sports star: "I've tried every brand of pain relief medication on the market, and, believe me, nothing out there works better than Pain-away."

plain folks _____ 5. Politician running for election: "When I was very young, my father died, leaving my mother with debt and no way to support our family. Unlike my opponent, I know what it's like to struggle to put food on the table and pay the bills. Give me your vote on election day."

faulty cause and effect _____ 6. Broncos fan watching the Super Bowl on TV: "I better go away. Every time I come in to watch the game, the Packers score a touchdown."

name-calling _____ 7. "My opponent for the school board has the morals of an alley cat. Maybe his wife can tolerate his 'affairs' but the rest of us should not allow him to become a role model to our children."

glittering generality _____ 8. "A lot of us want only the best—the best house, in the best neighborhood, with the best car in our garage. Don't you think it's about time to be thinking about the best phone service. Call 1-800-BEST for a free consultation."

false analogy _____ 9. "Your sister has always gotten good grades and worked part-time to pay for her expenses. Don't you think you should be doing the same?"

transfer _____ 10. "This is Chuck Jones standing in front of 'Old Faithful' in Yellowstone National Park. Remember to use Old Faithful laxative if you have problems with irregularity."

red herring _____ 11. "How dare my opponent accuse me of fraud when I'm working hard for the American people!"

hasty generalization _____ 12. Mark's girlfriend left him for somebody else, so he said to his friend Mike, "You just can't trust women."

circular reasoning _____ 13. Marijuana should not be legalized because it's against the law to legalize drugs.

READING

"The rush to smoke was also fueled by the fight for suffrage; women wanted equality."

TUNING IN TO READING   More than 172,000 Americans were diagnosed as having lung cancer in 2005. Lung cancer kills more people than the combined death toll from alcohol, cocaine, heroin, homicide, suicide, automobile accidents, and AIDS. Although smoking in the United States has declined markedly, millions of Americans—particularly the young—still smoke. Smoking is also more common among people who are highly stressed, divorced or separated, unemployed, or in the military.

BIO-SKETCH   Dr. Stanley J. Baran has had a long and distinguished academic career. He currently teaches at Bryant College in Rhode Island, where he is chair of the Communications Department. In addition to earning numerous awards for both research and teaching excellence, Dr. Baran has published over 10 books.

NOTES ON VOCABULARY

suffrage   the right to vote in political elections. The U.S. Constitution states, "No state shall be deprived of its equal *suffrage* in the Senate."

crusade   a vigorous movement or enterprise on behalf of a cause. Originally, the word referred to the Crusades, which were European military expeditions in the 11th–13th centuries to "recover" the Holy Lands from the Muslims.

coup   a highly successful act. *Coup* came from the French word meaning "blow" or "stroke," as in *coup d'état.* Among the Plains Indian tribes, *coup* referred to a daring deed performed by a warrior in battle against an enemy.

taboo   something prohibited or forbidden. In Fijian, a Polynesian language, the word originally meant "marked as holy." The first *taboos* were prohibitions against the use or mention of certain things. Violating a *taboo* was believed to make the gods angry.

BOOSTING SMOKING AMONG WOMEN AND CHILDREN
Stanley J. Baran

Before the early 1900s, smoking was seen as an unsavory habit, permissible for men, never for women. But with the turn of the century, women too wanted to light up. Advertising campaigners first began targeting female smokers in 1919. The American Tobacco Company slogan "Reach for a Lucky instead of a sweet," along with ads designed to help women understand that they could use cigarettes to keep their figures, was aimed at this new market. The rush to smoke was also fueled by the fight for suffrage; women wanted equality. The right to vote was an important goal, but if men could smoke without a fight, why couldn't women?

As more women began to smoke, antismoking crusades attempted to deter 2 them. The protection of women's morality, not their health, inspired the crusaders. Many cities forbade the use of tobacco by women in public places. Yet the number of women who started smoking continued to grow. George Washington Hill, head of American Tobacco, wanted this lucrative market to continue to expand, and he wanted to own as large a part of it as possible. He turned to public relations and Edward Bernays.

Lucky Strike used advertising and an effective public relations campaign to break the taboo on women smokers.

A nephew of Sigmund Freud, Bernays was 3 employed to conduct psychological research aimed at understanding the relationship between women and cigarettes. He learned that women saw cigarettes as symbols of freedom, as the representation of their unfair treatment in a man's world, and as a sign of their determination to be accepted as an equal.

Bernays had several objectives: (1) to let 4 the public know that it was quite all right for women to smoke; (2) to undercut the bans on public smoking by women that existed in many places; and (3) to position Lucky Strike cigarettes as a progressive brand.

In meeting these goals, Bernays perpetrated 5 a publicity stunt that is still heralded as a triumphant coup among public relations practitioners. New York City had a ban on public smoking by females. Because of, rather than despite this, Bernays arranged for 10 socially prominent young women to enter the 1929 annual Easter Parade down Fifth Avenue as "The Torches of Liberty Contingent." As they marched, the debutantes lit their Lucky "torches of freedom" and smilingly proceeded to puff and walk. For reporters on the scene, this made for much better news and photos than the usual little kids in their spring finery. The blow for female emancipation was front-page news, not only in New York, but nationally. The taboo was dead.

Later in his life, Bernays would argue that had he known of the link between 6 cigarette smoking and cancer and other diseases, he would never have taken on American Tobacco as a client.

In the 1980s as U.S. levels of smoking continued to decline, R. J. Reynolds 7 introduced a new campaign for its Camel brand cigarettes. The campaign featured a sun-bleached, cool, and casual camel who possessed human qualities. Joe Camel, as he was called, was debonair, in control, and the center of attention, whether in a pool hall, on a dance floor, leaning against his convertible, or lounging on the beach. He wore the hippest clothes. He sported the best sunglasses. R. J. Reynolds said it was trying a new campaign to boost brand awareness and corner a larger portion of a dwindling market. But antismoking groups saw in Joe Camel the echo of Edward Bernays' strategy to open smoking to an untapped market. They accused the company of attempting to attract young smokers—often adding that these were the lifelong customers the tobacco company needed to replace those it was killing.

The battle heated up in 1991, and an entire issue of the *Journal of the* 8 *American Medical Association* was devoted to the impact of smoking on the culture. One of the articles reported on a study of Joe Camel's appeal to youngsters.

Researcher Dr. Joseph DiFranza had discovered that Joe Camel was the single most recognizable logo in the country. Children as young as 3 years old could recognize Joe, and more kids could identify him than could identify Mickey Mouse.

R. J. Reynolds attempted to discredit the study and its author and claimed 9 that it had a First Amendment right to advertise its legal product any way it wanted. Nonetheless, soon after the publication of the *JAMA* issue, antismoking activist Janet Mangini filed a lawsuit in San Francisco against the tobacco company. Several California counties and cities joined the suit, alleging that the Joe Camel campaign violated state consumer protection laws designed to protect minors from false or misleading tobacco advertising.

Just before it was to go to trial in 1997, the country's second largest 10 tobacco company, while admitting no wrongdoing, agreed to settle out of court with a payment of $10 million. It also agreed to a court order to suspend the Joe Camel campaign, the first time in history that a tobacco company had been forced to abandon an advertising campaign. What may have encouraged the cigarette company to cooperate were internal memos in the hands of the court that would later be made public. An R. J. Reynolds Tobacco memo from 1975 said: "To ensure increased and long-term growth for Camel Filter, the brand must increase its share penetration among the 14–24 age group." Other memos identified target smokers as young as 12 years old!

(Stanley J. Baran, *Introduction to Mass Communication*, 5/e, 2008)

 COMPREHENSION CHECKUP

Multiple Choice

Directions: For each item, write the letter corresponding to the best answer on the line provided.

_____a_____ 1. All of the following are true according to the selection *except* for which?
  a. Women wanted men to quit smoking.
  b. Women wanted to enjoy the same privileges as men.
  c. Women viewed smoking as a liberating activity.
  d. Women worried about their weight.

_____d_____ 2. We can conclude that Edward Bernays
  a. always took pride in his association with American Tobacco.
  b. helped change public attitudes about women and smoking.
  c. masterminded a public relations success.
  d. both b and c.

_____b_____ 3. By using "10 socially prominent young women" to smoke their "torches of freedom" in the Easter Parade, Bernays employed all of the following propaganda techniques *except*
  a. testimonial.
  b. name-calling.
  c. bandwagon.
  d. transfer.

_d_ 4. For women in the early 1900s, Lucky Strike cigarettes were associated
with all of the following *except*
a. emancipation.
b. slimness.
c. glamour.
d. disease.

_b_ 5. In paragraph 5, "the taboo is dead" suggests that
a. women were now permitted to vote.
b. women were now free to smoke in public places.
c. women no longer received less pay for the same work.
d. women were free to work outside the home.

_a_ 6. In paragraph 7, the word *debonair* means
a. suave.
b. careless.
c. crotchety.
d. none of the above.

_d_ 7. In paragraph 7, the word *But* signals
a. classification and division.
b. definition.
c. example.
d. contrast.

_d_ 8. As used in paragraph 7, "corner a larger portion" means to
a. relinquish a part of.
b. engender awareness of.
c. push to the side.
d. gain control of.

_d_ 9. R. J. Reynolds Tobacco
a. felt that it should be allowed to advertise cigarettes any way that it
desired.
b. tried to discredit DiFranza's study.
c. agreed to discontinue using Joe Camel in its advertisements.
d. all of the above.

_b_ 10. The mode of writing for this selection is primarily
a. descriptive.
b. narrative.
c. expository.
d. persuasive.

True or False

Directions: Indicate whether each statement is true or false by writing **T** or **F** in the
space provided.

_T_ 11. Smoking was once seen as a man's activity.

_T_ 12. "Cool" Joe Camel was designed to appeal to the young.

_F_ 13. DiFranza discovered that Mickey Mouse was the most recognized
logo in the United States.

_F_ 14. Just one California city sued R. J. Reynolds.

_F_ 15. R. J. Reynolds admitted to targeting children with its Joe Camel campaign.

Vocabulary in Context

Directions: Use context clues to determine the meaning of the italicized word, and then write a definition for that word in the space provided.

1. smoking was seen as an *unsavory* habit (paragraph 1)

   Definition: offensive; distasteful; unappealing

2. the rush to smoke was also *fueled* by the fight (paragraph 1)

   Definition: encouraged; stimulated

3. antismoking crusades attempted to *deter* them (paragraph 2)

   Definition: discourage, hinder

4. wanted this *lucrative* market to continue to expand (paragraph 2)

   Definition: profitable; money making

5. a publicity stunt that is still *heralded* as a triumphant coup (paragraph 5)

   Definition: proclaimed

6. the *echo* of Edward Bernays's strategy (paragraph 7)

   Definition: repetition

7. corner a larger portion of a *dwindling* market (paragraph 7)

   Definition: decreasing; shrinking; diminishing

8. most recognizable *logo* in the country (paragraph 8)

   Definition: symbol

In Your Own Words

1. Whose responsibility is it to educate young people about the dangers of smoking? Parents? The public school system? The federal government? Cigarette manufacturers?

2. The ad on page 493 features the 1930s movie star Jean Harlow. Under her picture, it says the following: "She's mischievous, restless and 20, weighs 112 pounds. Miss Harlow has smoked Luckies for two years." What propaganda techniques are being used here to promote the Lucky Strike brand?

3. In 2009, more than half of PG-13 films featured tobacco imagery, a disturbing trend given that the National Cancer Institute concluded that adolescents imitate the smoking they see in the movies. What propaganda technique is being used by the tobacco industry? Do you think that movies rated for young people should be smoke-free?

4. Although smoking has declined in the United States, it has actually increased in the rest of the world, partly because of aggressive marketing campaigns by U.S. tobacco companies. Because many of the poorest countries do not warn their citizens about the dangers of smoking, children as young as 7 and 8 smoke in these countries. Should tobacco companies be required to inform the citizens of all countries about the health risks of smoking?

Written Assignment

The Virginia Slims brand of cigarettes was introduced by Philip Morris in 1968. Throughout the 1970s and 1980s, Philip Morris promoted this product with the slogan "You've come a long way, baby." One panel of the ad would depict women stacking wood for stoves or washing the laundry by hand and then hanging it out on clotheslines to dry. The other panel would depict a stylish, sexy woman doing modern activities. Do some research on the original ad campaign. Why do you think the word "slim" was included in the brand name of the cigarette? Can you identify other brands that are designed to appeal to specific segments of society? Should tobacco companies be allowed to target particular groups?

Internet Activity

The character of Joe Chemo, a camel who wished he'd never smoked, was developed by Scott Pious, a psychology professor at Wesleyan University. Check out the Joe Chemo Web site at:

> www.joechemo.org

Then test your tobacco IQ in the 10-item test to get your "smoke-o-scope." Do you think the tips on quitting are likely to help long-term smokers?

READING

*"Does observing violent and antisocial acts in the media
lead viewers to behave in similar ways?"*

TUNING IN TO READING   The following excerpt is from *Understanding Psychology* by Robert S. Feldman. This author sees a correlation between violence in the media and aggressive behavior in children, but he hesitates to state that there is a direct cause-and-effect relationship between the two.

If a definite link between watching violent television shows or playing violent video games and subsequent aggressive acts were established, would you support a ban on such media? Why or why not? While reading the selection, be thinking of other ways to limit aggression among children who frequently watch TV or play video games.

BIO-SKETCH   Robert S. Feldman is a professor of psychology at the University of Massachusetts. Dr. Feldman has written numerous books and articles. He is also noted for his research on honesty and deception.

NOTES ON VOCABULARY

mobster   a member of a criminal gang.

henchman   originally meant "trusted attendant or follower." In the 19th century, Scottish novelist Sir Walter Scott got the word confused with "haunchman," which meant "an obedient or unscrupulous follower." Thus, *henchman* today refers to a ruthless subordinate, often a gang member.

dismember   to divide into parts; to cut up.

copycat   to imitate or mimic. The origins of this word are uncertain. *Copycat* may simply be derived from the actions of a kitten mimicking its mother.

VIOLENCE IN TELEVISION AND VIDEO GAMES: DOES THE MEDIA'S MESSAGE MATTER?

Robert S. Feldman

In an episode of "The Sopranos," fictional mobster Tony Soprano murdered one of his associates. To make identification of the victim's body difficult, Soprano, along with one of his henchmen, dismembered the body and dumped the body parts.

A few months later, two real-life half brothers in Riverside, California, stran- 2 gled their mother and then cut her head and hands from her body. Victor Bautista, 20, and Matthew Montejo, 15, who were caught by police after a security guard noticed that the bundle they were attempting to throw in a dumpster had a foot sticking out of it, told police that the plan to dismember their mother was inspired by the "Sopranos" episode.

Like other "media copycat" killings, the brothers' cold-blooded brutality 3 raises a critical issue: Does observing violent and antisocial acts in the media lead viewers to behave in similar ways? Because research on modeling shows that people frequently learn and imitate the aggression that they observe, this question is among the most important being addressed by psychologists.

Certainly, the amount of violence in the mass media is enormous. By the 4 time of elementary school graduation, the average child in the United States will have viewed more than 8,000 murders and more than 800,000 violent acts on network television. Adult television shows also contain significant violence, with cable television leading the way with such shows as "When Animals Attack" and "World's Scariest Police Shootouts."

Most experts agree that watching high levels of media violence makes 5 viewers more susceptible to acting aggressively, and recent research supports this claim. For example, a recent survey of serious and violent young male offenders incarcerated in Florida showed that one-fourth of them had attempted to commit a media-inspired copycat crime. A significant proportion of those teenage offenders noted that they paid close attention to the media.

Violent video games have also been linked with actual aggression. In one 6 of a series of studies by psychologist Craig Anderson and his colleagues, for example, college students who frequently played violent video games were more likely to have been involved in delinquent behavior and aggression. Frequent players also had lower academic achievement.

Several aspects of media violence may contribute to real-life aggressive 7 behavior. For one thing, experiencing violent media content seems to lower inhibitions against carrying out aggression—watching television portrayals of violence or using violence to win a video game makes aggression seem a legitimate response to particular situations. Exposure to media violence also may distort our understanding of the meaning of others' behavior, predisposing us to view even non-aggressive acts by others as aggressive. Finally, a continuous diet of aggression may leave us desensitized to violence, and what previously would have repelled us now produces little emotional response. Our sense of the pain and suffering brought about by aggression may be diminished.

(Robert S. Feldman, *Understanding Psychology,* 9/e, 2009)

 COMPREHENSION CHECKUP

Multiple Choice

Directions: For each item, write the letter corresponding to the best answer on the line provided.

_____d_____   1. The author's main idea is that
      a. displays of violence in the media are quite common.
      b. *The Sopranos* is a violent television program.

      c. parents should watch violent television programs with their young children rather than let them view such programs by themselves.

      d. there is a significant association between observing violent acts in the media and behaving in an aggressive manner.

_____a_____ 2. The word *modeling* as used in paragraph 3 means

      a. imitating.

      b. observing.

      c. extending.

      d. preserving.

_____d_____ 3. The transition word *finally* in paragraph 7 indicates a

      a. comparison.

      b. contrast.

      c. addition.

      d. conclusion.

_____c_____ 4. An *insensitive* person is one who

      a. shows consideration for others.

      b. lacks creativity.

      c. is not affected by the suffering of others.

      d. feels a great deal of pain.

_____c_____ 5. The author would agree with all of the following *except* for which?

      a. Observing aggression in the media increases the likelihood that viewers will act aggressively.

      b. Viewing programs such as *Sesame Street* is unlikely to lead to aggressive behavior in young children.

      c. There is little actual violent material on television.

      d. Exposure to media violence desensitizes viewers to acts of aggression.

_____d_____ 6. After watching a violent program, a person might

      a. mistake a nonthreatening act for a threatening one.

      b. become overly sensitive to the suffering of others.

      c. respond in a threatening way to a slight by another person.

      d. both a and c.

_____a_____ 7. The author's purpose in writing this selection is to

      a. explain.

      b. persuade.

      c. entertain.

      d. define.

_____c_____ 8. According to recent research, all of the following are associated with playing violent video games *except*

      a. lower academic achievement.

      b. delinquent behavior.

      c. personal generosity.

      d. acts of aggression.

Vocabulary in Context

Directions: Choose one of the following words to complete the sentences on the following page. Use each word only once.

antisocial	desensitized	diminished	distorts	incarcerated
inhibitions	linked	proportion	repelled	susceptible

1. Margaret has missed a great deal of school because she is especially ___susceptible___ to colds and flu.

2. Because the coach frequently berated him, Nick had a(n) ___diminished___ interest in continuing with the team.

3. To be able to participate in karaoke, people need to overcome their ___inhibitions___ about performing in public.

4. After having been ___incarcerated___ for over 20 years, Carlos was set free when DNA evidence conclusively proved he could not have committed the murder.

5. His ___antisocial___ behavior was responsible for his lack of close friends.

6. What ___proportion___ of the population favors tax reform?

7. After years of hearing his crude jokes, Blanca had become ___desensitized___ to their impact.

8. Scientists at the University of California have ___linked___ infant exposure to pesticides to the development of autism.

9. Duc was so ___repelled___ by the foul odor in the air that he had to leave the building immediately.

10. Presidential candidates frequently complain that the press ___distorts___ what they say.

In Your Own Words

1. Assuming that there is a cause-and-effect relationship between watching violent programs in the media and engaging in violent behavior, can you think of ways to help solve this problem? Is there anything the media could do? What about parents?

2. Can you think of some desirable traits in children that are fostered by television? By playing video games?

3. Look at the cartoon below by Bill Watterson, creator of *Calvin and Hobbes*. What position does he seem to be taking on the issue of TV and violence?

Calvin and Hobbes

CALVIN AND HOBBES © 1995 Watterson. Dist. By Universal Press Syndicate. Reprinted with permission. All rights reserved.

4. TV wrestling shows are very popular with males aged 12–34. However, Court TV produced a recent film, *Wrestling with Death*, that documented kids imitating the aggressive acts they saw performed on the TV shows in their own

backyards. In these backyard wrestling matches, kids routinely hit each other with objects such as chairs. Do you think World Wrestling Entertainment bears some responsibility for these incidents? Do you think the wrestling programs on TV glamorize violence? Are you in favor of censoring these kinds of programs?

Written Assignment

James P. Steyer is a Stanford University professor and author of *The Other Parent: The Inside Story of the Media's Effect on Our Children*. In that book, he presents the following 10 steps that parents can take to help create a safer media environment for their kids.

TOP 10 STEPS FOR PARENTS

1. Establish good media habits early.

2. Location, location, location: no TV or computer in your child's room.

3. Set a media diet and stick to it.

4. Teach your child to ask permission to use media.

5. Watch and listen with your kids—then tell them what you like and don't like, and why.

6. Set clear rules regarding your child's media use in other homes.

7. Have pediatricians review your kids' media use as part of their annual checkup.

8. Teach media literacy in school and at home.

9. Read to your child and share positive media experiences.

10. Switch the dial to "off."

What do you think of Steyer's suggestions? Are they likely to work? Write a short essay discussing his suggestions. Try to include a few suggestions of your own.

(James P. Steyer, *The Other Parent*, 2002)

Internet Activity

LimiTV is a nonprofit North Carolina corporation formed in 1995 to educate parents, teachers, and children about the effects of excessive television viewing, including the relationship between TV violence and aggressive behavior. Go to its Web site at:

www.limitv.org

Find an article on the site of interest to you, and try to identify any propaganda techniques used in the presentation. List any examples you find.

The Structure of an Argument

An argument takes one side of an issue that people disagree about. For instance, the question "Do many athletes use performance-enhancing drugs?" is not a debatable issue. We can answer it with research and statistical evidence. However, if we change the question to "Should performance-enhancing drugs be allowed in sports?" we have a debatable issue. That is because drug use in sports is a controversial topic. Some people will support allowing performance-enhancing drugs in sports and others will oppose it.

The Parts of an Argument

An argument has four parts or characteristics: the issue, the claim, the evidence, and the assumptions.

Issue: a controversial or debatable subject. It must be something about which people have differing opinions, such as illegal immigration or the death penalty.

Claim: the key point. This is what the author is trying to prove. All the following are claims: Convicted felons should be allowed to vote. The space shuttle program should be continued. Illegal immigrants should be allowed a path to citizenship.

Evidence: support given by the author for the claim. It can be almost anything that could be persuasive, such as facts, statistics, expert opinion, research, personal experience, or experiences of others.

Assumptions: things that the author believes to be true but may or may not be true. If someone is always checking books out of the library, we assume they like to read. If someone exercises three times a week, we assume that this person values fitness. Authors sometimes do not state their assumptions.

Exercise 4: Writing Opposing Claims

Directions: For each of the following claims, write an opposing claim.

EXAMPLE

Claim: Schools should have programs that help students stay physically fit.

Opposing Claim: Schools should keep their focus exclusively on academic goals.

1. **Claim:** Texting while driving should be made illegal.

   Opposing Claim: The law should not restrict texting while driving.

2. **Claim:** The death penalty should be abolished in the United States.

   Opposing Claim: The death penalty should remain available in the United States.

3. **Claim:** The use of marijuana for medical purposes should be prohibited.

   Opposing Claim: People should be allowed to use marijuana for medical purposes.

4. **Claim:** The selling of beef from cattle that were given growth hormones should be banned.

   Opposing Claim: Beef from cattle that were given growth hormones should be available for purchase.

5. **Claim:** State lotteries should be abolished.

   Opposing Claim: States should be free to hold lotteries.

Exercise 5: Identifying the Evidence That Supports the Claim

Directions: Each group of sentences below begins with a claim. Some of the sentences directly support the claim and some don't. Put an **S** (for support) on the line next to a sentence that directly supports the claim. Leave the other sentences blank.

EXAMPLE

Claim: High schools should use iPads instead of textbooks as learning tools.

_____ The iPad is just a cool new toy that students will play with for a while before becoming bored by it.

__S__ In contrast to textbooks, iPads allow students to correspond with their teachers, file papers and homework assignments, and keep a digital record of their work.

_____ The educational value of iPads has yet to be demonstrated.

__S__ iPads extend the learning experience beyond what can be found between the covers of a textbook.

_____ The money spent on iPads would be better spent trying to recruit, train, and retain teachers, says Larry Cuban, professor of education at Stanford University.

__S__ iPads are lightweight and offer students relief from hauling around heavy textbooks that weigh down their backpacks.

1. **Claim:** Colleges should make more of an effort to reduce excessive drinking by students.

   _____ When school administrations try to further regulate drinking, they simply make students more secretive about it.

   __S__ The National Institute on Alcohol Abuse and Alcoholism estimates that 1,700 college students between ages 18 and 24 die of alcohol-related causes each year, while about 600,000 suffer from alcohol-related injuries.

   __S__ Nearly 25 percent of all college students report academic consequences of excessive drinking, including missing class, falling behind, doing poorly on exams or papers, and receiving lower grades overall.

   _____ Most college drinking takes place off campus.

   __S__ There are practical steps that colleges can take to reduce excessive drinking by students, such as requiring incoming freshmen to attend an orientation session on alcohol abuse.

2. **Claim:** College students should be taught to be cautious in their use of online social network sites such as Facebook.

   __S__ Students can easily be drawn into spending too much time on such sites, causing their studies to suffer.

   _____ These sites give students an easy, convenient way to keep in touch with friends and relatives.

   __S__ Students are well aware of the advantages of these sites, but they have little understanding of their dangers.

_____S_____ Activities on these sites that students view as harmless fun may be held against them years later by a potential employer doing a background check.

_____ These sites can provide students with a way to relieve the stress of college life.

3. **Claim:** States should legalize all forms of gambling.

_____S_____ Legalizing gambling would boost a state's economy by creating jobs and generating tax revenue.

_____ Gambling is an evil that has a corrupting influence on society.

_____S_____ People should be free to do what they want with their money so long as it does not directly harm others.

_____ Too many people whose money would best be spent on basic necessities waste it on gambling.

_____S_____ Gambling is simply another form of entertainment.

_____ Gambling can be as destructive and addictive as alcohol.

4. **Claim:** Animal testing of drugs should be prohibited.

_____ Animal testing aids researchers in developing drugs and treatments that improve health and save lives.

_____S_____ According to the Humane Society of the United States, 92 percent of drugs that pass animal testing fail human safety trials.

_____ Treatments for cancer, HIV drugs, antibiotics, and vaccines have been made possible by animal testing.

_____S_____ The reaction of a drug in an animal's body is often quite different from what happens in a human body.

_____S_____ Humans can consent to testing; animals cannot.

_____ Animal testing of drugs is important in ensuring the safety of drugs on the market.

_____S_____ Animal testing of drugs too often subjects animals to horrible cruelty and even death.

_____ The benefits of animal testing of drugs outweighs its drawbacks.

5. **Claim:** It should be more difficult for people to obtain credit cards.

_____ Credit cards are handy for dealing with life's emergencies.

_____S_____ It can take five years to pay off $1,000 of credit card debt if you make only the minimum payment.

_____ Using a credit card wisely helps people build a good credit rating so that they can later obtain loans for such important purchases as a home or a car.

_____S_____ The easy convenience of credit cards too often causes some people to sink deeply into debt.

_____S_____ Credit cards make it too easy for people to make impulse purchases of things they don't really need.

_____ People need credit cards to be able to make purchases online.

_____ Credit cards are much more convenient than carrying cash or writing checks.

_____S_____ Banks take advantage of credit card holders by charging excessive fees and high interest rates.

Exercise 6: Identifying the Assumptions

Now let's look at an additional argument. Notice that in this example the assumption the author is making is included.

> **Claim:** The driving age should be raised to age 18.
>
> **Evidence:** Statistics show 16-year-olds are more likely to cause accidents than those 18 or older.
>
> **Assumption:** There would be fewer accidents if the driving age were raised to age 18.

Directions: Identify the assumptions for the following claims from Exercise 5. Write your answers below.

1. **Claim:** Colleges should make more of an effort to reduce excessive drinking by students.

   Assumption: The author assumes that colleges have the ability to limit alcohol abuse by students.

2. **Claim:** College students should be taught to be cautious in their use of online social network sites such as Facebook.

   Assumption: The author assumes that social network sites such as Facebook can be hazardous.

3. **Claim:** Animal testing of drugs should be prohibited.

   Assumption: The author assumes that simply regulating animal testing of drugs would not be enough.

4. **Claim:** It should be more difficult for people to obtain credit cards.

   Assumption: The author assumes that there are problems with how people use credit cards.

Valid or Invalid Arguments

Many authors support their arguments with a combination of facts and opinions. The trick is to determine which reasons cited by the author are strong and support the argument and which are weak or irrelevant and fail to support the argument. Propaganda techniques and errors in reasoning are commonly used in arguments that are intended to convince the reader by any means necessary. An argument that relies too much on such devices is a poor or invalid argument.

Exercise 7: Recognizing Valid or Invalid Arguments

Directions: Read the passages and answer the questions that follow.

A. (1) Drowsy drivers should be held criminally liable for the crashes they cause. (2) An estimated 60 million Americans are operating vehicles each day without adequate sleep. (3) The National Highway Traffic Safety Administration estimates that 100,000 police-reported crashes are the direct result of driver-fatigue each year, resulting in 1,550 deaths and 71,000 injuries. (4) AAA reports that driving while sleep-deprived can have some of the same hazardous effects on the driver as being drunk. (5) Its studies concluded that coordination, reaction-time, and judgment are all impaired by lack of sufficient sleep. (6) The next time you're tempted to get in a car and drive when you're sleepy, just remember you're putting yourself and others at risk.

_a_ 1. The author's claim is given in which sentence?
a. Sentence 1
b. Sentence 4
c. Sentence 5
d. Sentence 6

_a_ 2. What type of support is offered for the author's claim?
a. primarily facts
b. primarily opinions

_d_ 3. What is the author not taking into account with this argument?
a. Drowsy driving is difficult to detect by police officers.
b. Too many people wouldn't be honest about how little sleep they've had.
c. How would the prosecution be able to prove that a person was too sleepy to drive?
d. All of the above.

_a_ 4. AAA's conclusion stated in sentence 4 is an example of
a. a fact.
b. an opinion.
c. a propaganda device.
d. an assumption.

B. (1) More than 5,000 teens die each year in car crashes. (2) The rate of crashes per mile driven for 16-year-old drivers is almost 10 times the rate for drivers ages 30 to 59, according to the National Highway Traffic Safety Administration. (3) Statistics show 16-year-olds are more likely to cause accidents than those 18 or older. (4) Many countries in Europe and elsewhere have a driving age of 17 or 18. (5) Americans increasingly favor raising the driving age, according to Gallup polls. (6) If we prohibit 16-year-olds from purchasing a handgun, we also need to prohibit them from being in control of a car, which has the potential to become a deadly weapon. (7) This issue is not really debatable any longer. (8) We should raise the driving age to 18.

_d_ 1. The author's claim is given in which sentence?
a. Sentence 1
b. Sentence 4
c. Sentence 5
d. Sentence 8

_a_ 2. Sentence 3 is an example of
a. a fact.
b. an opinion.

_b_ 3. Sentence 6 is an example of
a. a fact.
b. an opinion.

_b_ 4. Sentence 7 is an example of
a. a fact.
b. an opinion.

_____ b _____ 5. Sentence 5 is an example of which propaganda technique?
   a. name-calling
   b. bandwagon
   c. transfer
   d. card stacking

_____ d _____ 6. Which of the following are important issues that the author fails to fully take into account?
   a. All teenagers do not mature at the same time.
   b. Perhaps the problem is the lack of driver's training and practice for teenagers.
   c. If teenagers aren't able to drive at 16, how will they get to jobs and school and social activities.
   d. All of the above.

_____ a _____ 7. The author notes that 5,000 teens die each year in car crashes. How well does this statement support the author's argument?
   a. Not much, because the author doesn't tell us in how many of these accidents teens were the drivers.
   b. A lot, because the reader should assume that a teen was the driver in all these accidents.

C. (1) The start time for high school should not be changed to accommodate the needs of high school students who have trouble getting up early in the morning. (2) Changing the school start time so that self-indulgent, lazy high school students can sleep later does nothing but reinforce the notion among spoiled teenagers that the world revolves around them. (3) A more vigorous approach to parental discipline would yield a much better result in the long run than changing school hours. (4) Children are responsible for their actions, such as staying up too late. (5) They can learn the hard way that there are negative consequences for the poor choices they make. (6) Changing the start of the school day to allow kids to stay up late isn't teaching children the right life lesson.

_____ a _____ 1. The author's claim is given in which sentence?
   a. Sentence 1
   b. Sentence 3
   c. Sentence 4
   d. Sentence 6

_____ b _____ 2. Sentence 2 is an example of
   a. a fact.
   b. an opinion.

_____ c _____ 3. Sentence 2 is an example of which propaganda device?
   a. bandwagon
   b. transfer
   c. name-calling
   d. testimonial

_____ b _____ 4. The author's claim is
   a. adequately supported with factual evidence.
   b. inadequately supported because it depends primarily on personal opinion.

D. (1) Almost half of all U.S. marriages end in divorce. (2) McGeorge and Carlson (2006) compared 1,000 couples exposed to an 8-week course of marriage preparation with those who did not take such a course and found a greater readiness for marriage among the first group. (3) Kirby (2006) upon testing over 1,000 married couples found that those who had taken a course in marriage preparation scored higher in marital satisfaction. (4) Everybody knows that couples who attend premarital courses communicate with each other better than those who do not. (5) To reduce the divorce rate, high school students should attend classes where they are taught about the responsibilities of marriage. (6) Sure, teachers complain about being overworked, but this would be time and money well spent.

_____d_____ 1. The author's claim is given in which sentence?
   a. Sentence 1
   b. Sentence 2
   c. Sentence 4
   d. Sentence 5

_____a_____ 2. Sentence 2 is an example of
   a. a fact.
   b. an opinion.

_____b_____ 3. Sentence 4 is an example of
   a. a fact.
   b. an opinion.

_____d_____ 4. Which of the following is the author of this argument not likely to agree with?
   a. This is an area of education best left to churches.
   b. This is an area of education best left to community groups.
   c. Schools should be responsible for teaching students only reading, writing, and mathematics.
   d. All of the above.

_____b_____ 5. The author fails to take into account all the following *except* for which?
   a. Many high schools lack a teacher qualified to teach marriage preparation courses.
   b. Giving couples planning to get married a marriage course increases marital satisfaction.
   c. It could be years before the high school students who take the course get married, if they get married at all.
   d. The research was conducted on couples and not on individual high school students who may or may not be in a relationship.

_____a_____ 6. Is the author leaping to a conclusion in arguing that courses in marriage preparation given in high school will reduce divorce rates?
   a. yes
   b. no

_____a_____ 7. If someone says, "Why bother to teach students about relationships when a lot of them don't even know who Abraham Lincoln is?" that person is
   a. giving an opinion.
   b. expressing a fact.

Chapter Summary and Review

In Chapter 12, you became familiar with different types of propaganda techniques and learned how to apply your knowledge of these techniques to reading selections. You also learned about faulty cause and effect. Based on the material in this chapter, answer the following.

Short Answer

Directions: From advertising or your own experience, give an example of the following propaganda techniques. Explain how your example illustrates the technique. Answers will vary.

Propaganda Technique	Example	Explanation
1. Name-calling	_____	_____
2. Transfer	_____	_____
3. Glittering generalities	_____	_____
4. False analogy	_____	_____
5. Either/or fallacy	_____	_____

Vocabulary Review

Directions: Fill in the blank with an indicated propaganda technique. Use each word only once.

bandwagon   card stacking   plain folks   testimonial

6. A famous model in a commercial promoting a particular line of cosmetics.   <u>testimonial</u>

7. A cell phone provider telling you all of the favorable features of the product, but failing to mention that the rate goes up in three months.   <u>card stacking</u>

8. A politician putting on a hard hat and going into a coal mine.   <u>plain folks</u>

9. A commercial featuring a bar filled with people who are drinking one particular brand of beer.   <u>bandwagon</u>

VOCABULARY   Unit 7 Word Parts Dealing with More Opposing Meanings

This vocabulary unit will continue with word parts having opposite or nearly opposite meanings. Some of these, such as *hyper* and *hypo,* and *inter* and *intra,* are commonly confused. The middle section discusses word parts having to do with phobias. The last section discusses a word part meaning "false."

synonym—There are 2,660 synonyms for being intoxicated, more than for any other condition or object.

syn—same; together   pro—for

anti—opposite, against   nym—name

synonym   Same name. *Synonyms* are words that have the same or similar meanings. For example, *vista* and *panorama* are synonyms.

symphony—Beethoven was totally deaf when he wrote his Ninth Symphony.

antonym	Different name. *Antonyms* are words having opposite meanings. *Homogeneous* and *heterogeneous* are words with opposite meanings.
symphony	*Sym* means "together" and *phono* means "sound," so a *symphony* orchestra produces music by blending sounds together.
antiphony	Opposition of sounds. An *antiphony* is a musical piece that has half of a choral group singing in front of the audience and half in back. Such singing was popular in the Middle Ages.
analyze	To separate into its parts. *Ana* means "up" and *lyze* means "to loosen," so the literal meaning of the word is "to loosen something up." When you *analyze* why you did not do very well on your psychology test, you try to take apart what happened to see what went wrong.
synthesize	*Syn* means "together," and so *synthesize* means to form a whole by bringing together the separate parts. What does a *synthesizer* do in music? It combines different sounds to produce a new sound.
antithesis	*Anti* means "opposite," so an *antithesis* is something that is in opposition. The *antithesis* of segregation is integration.
pro-choice	*Pro* means "in favor of," so a person who is *pro-choice* is supportive of a woman's right to *choose* legal abortion.
anti-abortion	If you are *anti-abortion*, you are opposed to legal *abortion*.
antidote	*Dote* comes from the root word meaning "to give," so an *antidote* is something given to counteract something else. If your child drinks a toxic liquid that is acidic, the container may give instructions recommending bicarbonate of soda as an *antidote*. (Remember that you should still call a doctor.)
syndicated	*Syn* means "same" and *dic* means "to say," so *syndicated* means "saying the same thing." If something is *syndicated*, it appears in many newspapers, magazines, or radio or TV stations. *Garfield* is a *syndicated* cartoon that appears in newspapers around the country.

hypo—under, below   hyper—above, over, excessive

hypothermia—A person may die of hypothermia when the body temperature is 95 degrees or less.

hyperactive	A *hyperactive* child is excessively active. If you were *hyperactive* as a child, there's a good chance you still are.
hypoactive	Meaning "underactive." Depressed people are often *hypoactive*.
hyperthermia	The state of being overheated or too hot; very high temperature. Long-distance runners in hot weather need to be careful to drink enough water to avoid *hyperthermia*.
hypothermia	The state of being too cold or of having a below-normal body temperature. A person lost in a snowstorm might die of *hypothermia*.
hypodermic	Many of you know that *derm* means "skin," so a *hypodermic* needle is one that goes under the skin.
hyperbole	A *hyperbole* is an exaggeration, such as "strong as an ox." In the cartoon on the following page, Calvin says that his bad day makes

him feel as though he has been run over by a train. This is an example of *hyperbole*. *Hyperbole* is discussed in the section on satire.

Calvin and Hobbes

mania—craving

phobia—irrational fear of something

claustrophobia	Irrational fear of small, tightly enclosed places.
acrophobia	Fear of high places. Acrobats obviously do not have this *phobia*.
monophobia	Fear of being alone.
homophobia	Fear of homosexuals (gay men and lesbians) or homosexuality.
pyromania	A compulsion to start fires.
monomania	An excessive interest in one thing. A *monomaniac* has a mental disorder characterized by preoccupation with one subject.

intra—within or inside   inter—between or among

intercollegiate	Between or among colleges or universities. Your college's *intercollegiate* baseball team plays other colleges.
intramurals	Literally, this word means "within the walls," so an *intramural* sports program would be one that takes place within the walls of your college. In *intramural* athletics, student teams play against each other.
interstate	Between or among states. The *interstate* highway system connects 48 states.
intrastate	Within a state. Your telephone bill may have a list of your *intrastate* calls.
international	Between or among nations.
intravenous	Within or directly into a vein, such as an *intravenous* injection or IV bottle.

para—alongside, beside, side; partial; similar

parallel	*Parallel* lines run side by side. *Parallel* ideas are similar thoughts.

paraphrase	Literally, a similar phrase. When you *paraphrase* something, you put it into your own words.
paraprofessional	Alongside a professional. This word refers to a person who is not a member of a given profession but who assists those who are. *Paramedics* and *paralegals* are *paraprofessionals*.
paramedic	A person with limited medical duties such as a nurse's aide; a person trained to rescue others.
paralegal	Persons trained to aid lawyers but not licensed to practice law.
paranoid	*Para* means "beside" and *noid* refers to the mind. *Paranoia* is characterized by extreme suspiciousness or delusions of persecution.
paraplegic	A *paraplegic* has a paralysis of the lower half of the body, or is partially paralyzed.
quadriplegic	Total paralysis of the body from the neck down; having all four limbs paralyzed.

pseudo—false

pseudoscience	A false science; a system of theories that presumes without warrant to have a scientific basis. Astrology, which studies the placement of the moon, sun, and stars to predict the future, is considered by many to be a *pseudoscience*. Astronomy is the real scientific study of the universe.
pseudonym	A false name; a fictitious name, such as a pen name used by a writer to preserve anonymity. The book *Primary Colors,* describing an insider's look at the American political system, was written by Joe Klein using the *pseudonym* of Anonymous. Who is the most famous American author to write under a *pseudonym?* Hint: His two most well-known books are *The Adventures of Tom Sawyer* and *The Adventures of Huckleberry Finn.*
alias	Also a false name, but usually used by criminals to disguise their identity.
misnomer	To attach the wrong name to a person or a thing. What do you call that cuddly, tree-dwelling little animal from Australia? If you called this animal a Koala bear, you have just used a *misnomer,* because Koalas aren't bears at all. They are marsupials and carry their young in pouches like a kangaroo.

Exercise 1: Using Word Parts to Understand Meaning

Directions: Choose one of the following words to complete the sentences below. Use each word only once.

anti-abortion   claustrophobia   pseudoscience   hyperactive   hyperthermia
hypodermic   hypothermia   paraplegics   synonym   ultraviolet

1. A(n) _____synonym_____ for *irritate* is *annoy.*
2. Too much exposure to _____ultraviolet_____ radiation can cause skin cancer.

3. The goal of the ___anti-abortion___ group Operation Rescue was to shut down abortion clinics.

4. ___Paraplegics___ and other persons with disabilities who are in wheelchairs sometimes encounter physical barriers such as the lack of ramps.

5. Most of the victims of ___hypothermia___ are elderly people who have poorly heated homes.

6. A(n) ___hyperactive___ child is impulsive, is full of energy, and sleeps less than other children.

7. Many people consider palm reading and fortune telling to be a form of ___pseudoscience___.

8. When he was 3 years old, Jeremy was locked in a closet. Now he suffers from ___claustrophobia___ and has trouble riding in an elevator.

9. After spending three days in the Arizona-Sonora desert without water, Brandon was suffering from ___hyperthermia___ and was transported to the Tucson Medical Center.

10. AIDS can be spread when drug users inject themselves with unsterile ___hypodermic___ needles.

Exercise 2: Using Word Parts to Understand Meaning

Directions: Choose one of the following words to complete the sentences below. Use each word only once.

acrophobia	antidote	antonym	hyperbole	hypoactive
misnomer	parallel	paraphrase	pseudonyms	syndicated

1. *Peanuts* is a nationally ___syndicated___ cartoon that appears in hundreds of newspapers across the country.

2. The men who clean the windows on the Empire State Building most likely do not suffer from ___acrophobia___.

3. The chair of the Federal Reserve Board cut interest rates as a(n) ___antidote___ for a slowing economy.

4. Because a whale is a mammal, to call it a fish would be a(n) ___misnomer___.

5. "Be true to yourself" is a(n) ___paraphrase___ of "To thine own self be true."

6. The young child diagnosed as ___hypoactive___ appeared to lack energy and rarely ran around and played with other children.

7. It is a(n) ___hyperbole___ to say that Dave is as tall as a tree.

8. *Introvert* is a(n) ___antonym___ of *extrovert*.

9. Many famous authors, such as O Henry, whose real name is William Sydney Porter, used ___pseudonyms___ to keep their identities secret.

10. You can choose to travel on the coastal route or the interstate; the two run ___parallel___ to each other.

Exercise 3: Using Word Parts to Make Words

Directions: Make a word using each of the following word parts. Then in your own words, define or explain the meaning of your word. Do not create any nonsense words. Answers will vary.

Word Part	Your Word	Meaning
1. syn	_____	_____
2. sym	_____	_____
3. anti	_____	_____
4. phobia	_____	_____
5. mania	_____	_____
6. inter	_____	_____
7. intra	_____	_____
8. pro	_____	_____

Expanding Your Word Power

The words listed below are not found in this Vocabulary Unit, but they are derived from the vocabulary word parts that you have studied. All of them would be good words for you to learn. See if you can guess the meaning of each word from its word parts.

1. hypocrisy
2. hypochondriac
3. hypothetical
4. hypercritical
5. hypersensitive
6. hyperextend
7. hypertension
8. paranormal
9. paramilitary
10. paradigm
11. paradox
12. paragon
13. parameter

Vocabulary Unit 7 Crossword Puzzle

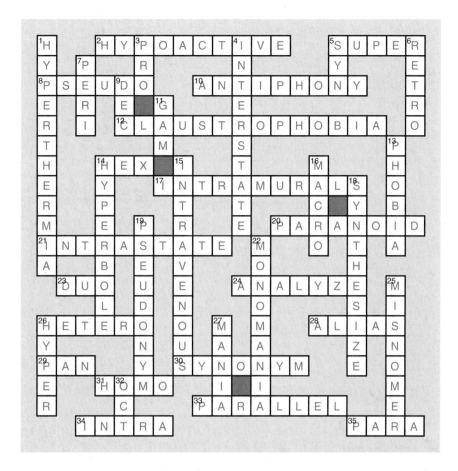

ACROSS CLUES

2. Underactive.
5. A word part meaning "above."
8. A word part meaning "false."
10. An opposition of sounds.
12. The fear of enclosed spaces.
14. A word part meaning "six."
17. Team sports on campus.
20. A person with delusions of persecution.
21. Within a state.
23. A word part meaning "two."
24. To separate into parts.
26. A word part meaning "different."
28. Used by a criminal to disguise identity.
29. A word part meaning "all around."
30. A(n) _____ for *vista* might be a *panorama*.
31. A word part meaning "same."
33. Lines running side by side.
34. A word part meaning "within" or "inside."
35. A word part meaning "alongside."

DOWN CLUES

1. Overheated.
3. A word part meaning "in favor of."
4. Between or among states.
5. A word part meaning "same."
6. A word part meaning "back."
7. A word part meaning "around" or "about."
9. An abbreviation for what was once the 10th month.
11. A word part meaning "marriage."
13. A word meaning "irrational fear."
14. An exaggeration.
15. IV.
16. A word part meaning "large."
18. To bring elements together.
19. Mark Twain is the _____ of Samuel Clemens.
22. An excessive interest in one thing.
25. The wrong name for an object.
26. A word part meaning "above" or "over."
27. A word part meaning "craving."
32. An abbreviation for what was once the 8th month.

CHAPTER PREVIEW

In this chapter, you will

- Learn about persuasive writing techniques.
- Become familiar with inductive and deductive reasoning.
- Evaluate persuasive writing selections.

Introduction to Persuasive Techniques

Instead of using neutral, objective language, authors sometimes use language designed to arouse readers emotionally. This is often a sign of bias on the author's part and serves as a signal to you that the author is trying to influence you. Authors may use any or all of the following persuasive techniques.

1. **Emotionally loaded language** designed to appeal directly to your feelings rather than your reasoning abilities

   In the example below, the boldfaced words have strong emotional power:

   > The **promise** of America **sparkles** in the eyes of every child. Their dreams are the **glittering dreams** of America. When those dreams are **dashed**, when **innocent hopes** are **betrayed**, so are the **dreams and hopes** of the entire nation. It is our **duty**—to me, it is a **sacred duty**—to give all children the chance to **learn and grow**, to share **equally** in the **American dream** of **freedom**, **justice**, and **opportunity**.

   (Stephen E. Lucas, *The Art of Public Speaking*, 10/e, 2009)

2. **Tear-jerking stories** or references to people and causes that you empathize with

   > Nathan was only five years old when the fever struck him. At first, no one knew what was wrong. No one knew that parasites inside his body had infected his red blood cells. No one knew those cells were clumping together, choking the flow of blood through his body and damaging his vital organs. No one knew his kidneys would soon fail and seizures would begin. No one knew he would end up in a coma.

The parasites in Nathan's body came from a mosquito bite, a bite that gave him malaria. And Nathan is not alone. The World Health Organization tells us the horrible truth: In Africa, a child dies from malaria every 30 seconds.

(Stephen E. Lucas, *The Art of Public Speaking*, 10/e, 2009)

3. **Manipulation of tone**

The author uses irony in the following description of an execution:

It didn't quite go as planned in Florida recently. The humming of the electricity was joined by a more ominous crackling sound like cellophane crinkling. Then great waves of gray smoke poured out and flames leaped from the prisoner's head. The smell of cooked human flesh and burning hair became pronounced. Despite the evidence to the contrary, proponents of capital punishment hasten to insist that the execution was not "cruel and unusual."

4. **Propaganda techniques** such as name-calling and testimonial, and logical fallacies such as circular reasoning can be used to manipulate the reader

Animal rights activists are frequently at odds with medical researchers. The activists may refer to those conducting research as "cruel" or "sadistic." Researchers, on the other hand, may call the activists names like "fanatic" or "kook."

Those in support of animal research may use a testimonial such as this one from Dr. Michael E. DeBakey, chair of surgery, and director of the DeBakey Heart Center at Baylor College of Medicine in Houston, Texas:

Even with today's technology, I could not have developed on a computer the roller pump that made open-heart surgery possible or the artificial artery that restored to health previously doomed patients with aneurysms. Nor could we have attempted the first successful coronary artery bypass or implanted the first temporary mechanical heart with which we saved a patient's life two decades ago.

(Michael E. DeBakey, "Holding Human Health Hostage," 1988, 1991)

When an author uses a testimonial, ask yourself the following questions:

Is the writer an authority in that particular field?

Is this the writer's specific area of competence?

Is the writer biased?

Is the writer likely to gain some advantage from the testimonial?

5. **Psychological appeals**

This technique is used frequently by the media to create ads that appeal directly to our desire for power, prestige, sex, or popularity.

For example, People for the Ethical Treatment of Animals (PETA) used "sex appeal" when it had a series of well-known models and actresses, such as Pamela Anderson, Eva Mendes, Audrina Partridge, and Khloe Kardashian, pose naked to protest the buying of fur coats.

6. **Moral appeals**

Authors may seek to appeal to your sense of morality or fair play.

C. S. Lewis was a professor of English literature at Oxford and Cambridge Universities. He is known for his writings on Christianity and morality. His tales for children include the popular *The Lion, the Witch, and the Wardrobe* in

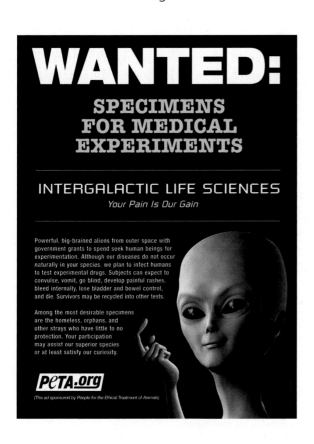

the Chronicles of Narnia series. Lewis, in arguing against experimental surgery on animals, said:

> If we cut up beasts simply because they cannot prevent us and because we are backing our own side in the struggle for existence, it is only logical to cut up imbeciles, criminals, enemies, or capitalists for the same reason.

(C. S. Lewis, "Vivisection," 1947, 1991)

On this same issue, PETA has publicized an ad showing a bulbous-headed alien looking for humans for scientific experiments. The caption in this ad says:

> Powerful, big-brained aliens from outer space with government grants to spend seek human beings for experimentation. Although our diseases do not occur naturally in your species, we plan to infect humans to test experimental drugs. Subjects can expect to convulse, vomit, go blind, develop painful rashes, bleed internally, lose bladder and bowel control, and die. Survivors may be recycled into other tests. Among the most desirable specimens are the homeless, orphans, and other strays who have little or no protection. Your participation may help our superior species or at least satisfy our curiosity.

PETA officials say they began the campaign because laboratories that use animals for research often justify their action by assigning a superior status to human beings. PETA spokesperson Joey Penello said, "We are trying to address the issue of vivisection (surgery on living animals) in a new way. How would we feel if they did to us what we've been doing to animals for years?"

(Michael E. DeBakey, "Holding Human Health Hostage," 1988, 1991)

7. **Appeal to authority**

Authors may call attention to their integrity, intelligence, and knowledge to persuade you to trust their judgment and believe them.

Judge Alex Kozinski wrote an article for *The New Yorker* magazine supporting the death penalty. Near the beginning of the article, he established his authority on this topic by saying:

> As a judge on the United States Court of Appeals for the Ninth Circuit, I hear cases from nine states and two territories spread over the western United States and Oceania.

In addition to the above techniques, be sure to note the author's

Affiliations. Look for information in the introduction that tells you what types of people or organizations the author associates with.

Assumptions. Be sure to note the author's principal beliefs. What ideas does the author hold that enable him or her to present this particular argument?

Organization. Authors are more likely to be trying to persuade you of something when they withhold the purpose or the main idea until the end.

Source. What is the author's source? Is the source reliable?

In summary, authors who are trying to persuade do not usually write material that is entirely objective and meant solely to inform. Instead, such authors tend to use factual material to bolster their opinions on a particular subject. By recognizing persuasive techniques and understanding the author's motives, you can avoid being manipulated and become better able to evaluate the issue on its own merits.

Drawing Conclusions: Inductive and Deductive Reasoning

In the final step of analyzing a selection, readers must evaluate the soundness of the author's reasoning.

All of us draw conclusions based on what we think is reasonable and acceptable. Often these conclusions are based on inductive or deductive reasoning.

Inductive Reasoning

The word parts for "inductive" are *in* meaning "into" and *duc* meaning "to lead." In **inductive reasoning,** specific examples, evidence, or propositions lead to a more general conclusion. We reason inductively all the time.

An example of inductive reasoning is the following:

> It's time for me to plan my vacation. The last time Steve flew on Snoozy Airlines, they lost his luggage. My friend Greg says Skyloft is never on time. Tony says RightAir is always too crowded. Ryan and Bonnie have flown many miles on SureFlight and have never had any problems. Therefore, I think I'll fly on SureFlight too.

As this example implies, a conclusion reached by inductive reasoning is only as valid as the specific information on which it is based. Maybe if I had talked to more people, I would have heard some critical comments about SureFlight or some flattering comments about Snoozy or SkyLoft.

So you can see that inductive reasoning leads to a conclusion that is only probably correct. A conclusion becomes more likely to be correct when the specific information on which it is based improves.

Deductive Reasoning

Deductive reasoning goes in the opposite direction from inductive reasoning. *De* means "away from," and **deductive reasoning** moves away from the general to the specific. A conclusion reached through deductive reasoning is seen as following logically from more general propositions or statements. Just as we often reason inductively, we also often reason deductively.

A **syllogism** is a common kind of deductive reasoning. The following is an example of a syllogism:

> All men are mortal.
>
> Brad Pitt is a man.
>
> Brad Pitt is mortal.

Here is another example of a syllogism:

"All of the comedies starring Ben Stiller are really enjoyable. He's starring in the movie *Night at the Museum 3*. This movie is going to be really enjoyable."

You can see that whether the conclusion drawn by deductive reasoning is valid depends on whether the general statements on which it is based are correct. If not all Ben Stiller comedies really are enjoyable—maybe some were boring—then it does not follow that his movie *Night at the Museum 3* has to be enjoyable. Or maybe all Ben Stiller comedies are enjoyable, but he is not really starring in *Night at the Museum 3* and instead is just playing a supporting role, Again, the conclusion would not follow.

Does the *Zits* cartoon shown here make use of a syllogism? Is the conclusion a valid one?

Zits

© ZITS Partnership. King Features Syndicate.

Evaluating the Evidence in Persuasive Writing

The next section of this chapter focuses on the current U.S. policy toward marijuana. You will be reading and evaluating persuasive writings in the form of editorials, letters to the editor, an advertisement, and a political cartoon. First, however, we will provide you with some background information from a popular health textbook and a news article on the topic of marijuana. We will also provide some guidelines in evaluating editorials.

Marijuana—Background Information

Even authors of textbook material have biases. Their biases influence the way they present the material. Although textbooks deal primarily with factual material, authors must decide what facts to include, omit, and emphasize. Pay attention to the author's tone and choice of words to determine whether he or she is biased. Such caution is especially important when the materials deal with a controversial issue, such as marijuana.

CANNABINOIDS

The most widely used illicit drug in the United States is marijuana. In 2006, there were an estimated 14.8 million users among Americans aged 12 or older, and over 15 percent of young people aged 12 to 17 had used marijuana at least once.

Marijuana is derived from the hemp plant, *Cannabis sativa*, thus the name *cannabinoids*. The leaves of the plant are usually dried and smoked, but they can also be mixed in tea or food. Hashish is a resin that seeps from the leaves; it is usually smoked. The active ingredient in marijuana is delta-9-tetrahydrocannabinol (THC). The potency of the drug is determined by the amount of THC in the plant, which in turn is affected by the growing conditions. Since the 1960s, the amount of THC in marijuana sold on the street has increased from 1–5 percent to as much as 10–15 percent.

Marijuana use produces mild euphoria, sedation, lethargy, short-term memory impairment, distorted sensory perceptions, a distorted sense of time, impaired motor coordination, and an increase in heart rate. Effects typically begin within a few minutes and last from 3 to 4 hours. Sometimes the drug causes anxiety or a negative mood. At high doses marijuana can have hallucinogenic effects accompanied by acute anxiety and paranoid thinking. Chronic, heavy users of marijuana may develop tolerance to its effects and experience some withdrawal symptoms if they stop using it, but most dependence seems to be psychological.

Researchers have found that THC has a variety of effects on the brain. One effect is the suppression of activity in the information processing system of the hippocampus, perhaps accounting for some impairments in problem solving and decision making associated with being high on marijuana. Marijuana smoke has negative effects on the respiratory system; it contains more carcinogens than tobacco smoke and is highly irritating to the lining of the bronchioles and lungs. In addition to coughs and chest colds, users may experience more frequent episodes of acute bronchitis and may be more likely to develop chronic bronchitis.

Like alcohol, marijuana affects the skills required to drive a car safely, including concentration, attention, coordination, reaction time, and the ability to judge distance. Because it also impairs judgment, people who are high may not realize their driving skills are impaired.

Many people claim that marijuana does have medical uses, especially as a treatment for glaucoma, for the pain and nausea associated with cancer and chemotherapy, and for the weight loss associated with AIDS. Research suggests that smoking marijuana is no more effective than taking THC in pill form for these purposes, but the use of marijuana for medical reasons has become a matter of political debate. Proponents of its use assert that it makes life livable for many people with painful and debilitating medical conditions and that there is no reason not to legalize it. Opponents argue that legalizing marijuana would imply approval of its use for recreational purposes and open the floodgates to abuse of all drugs.

(Michael L. Teague et al., *Your Health Today Brief*, 2009)

MEDICAL MARIJUANA RULING   ASSOCIATED PRESS

In June of 2005, the United States Supreme Court ruled that federal authorities may prosecute sick people whose doctors prescribe marijuana to ease pain, concluding that state laws don't protect users from a federal ban on the drug. The court said the prosecution of marijuana users under the federal Controlled Substances Act was constitutional. Justice John Paul Stevens, writing the 6–3 decision, said the court was not passing judgment on the potential medical benefits of marijuana. In the court's main decision, Stevens raised concerns about abuse of marijuana laws. "Our cases have taught us that there are some unscrupulous physicians who over-prescribe when it is sufficiently profitable to do so," he said.

(Associated Press, "Medical Marijuana Ruling," 2005)

Questions

1. Do you think the material on cannabinoids is objective or biased? Give reasons for your choice.

   _____

   _____

2. Do you think medical marijuana should be legalized? Why or why not?

   _____

   _____

3. What is your opinion of the United States Supreme Court medical marijuana ruling?

   _____

   _____

Evaluating the Evidence: Editorials

In contrast to news stories, which try to be objective, an **editorial** is a statement of personal opinion. As such, editorials are much more subjective than textbook selections or newspaper and magazine articles. The purpose of an editorial is to persuade readers to believe one thing rather than another. Editorials are found in magazines, in newspapers, and also on radio, television, and the Internet. Editorials tend to be short and direct, and so they are particularly appealing to those who dislike lengthy articles and complex analyses.

Tips for Evaluating Editorials

While most editorials provide a quick update of a topic, it is generally advisable to have some knowledge of the topic being discussed in advance so that you are in a better position to evaluate the material. When you are reading or listening to an editorial, it is sometimes helpful to engage in a mental dialogue with the author. When you are having a discussion (or an argument) with a friend, you might ask such questions as "Is that so?" "Where did you get that information?" and "But, what about this?" You might try to ask similar questions when you are evaluating an editorial. Here are some additional tips for reading editorials.

1. Think about the author. How authoritative is he or she? Is this topic within the author's area of expertise? Editorials, being personal in nature, reveal a lot about the author. Is he or she someone you respect?

2. Read the title of the editorial first. The title may reveal the author's position at the outset.

3. While a good editorial is passionate, it is your job as reader to identify the author's biases and determine whether or not you agree with the positions presented. Try to determine the author's predispositions or biases as you read.

4. Consider how the author of the editorial handles opposing positions. Does he or she acknowledge other positions? Does he or she attempt to rebut the opposing arguments?

5. Consider whether the editorial writer differentiates between important and trivial arguments. Make a list to see whether you can determine which arguments are important to making the case and which are not.

6. Consider whether the author recommends a solution to the problem. If so, is the solution reasonable or practical? Can it be implemented? If the problem cannot be solved, does the author provide constructive suggestions for improving the situation?

ARGUMENTS FOR AND AGAINST LEGALIZING THE USE OF
MARIJUANA FOR MEDICINAL PURPOSES

The following two editorials from *The American Legion Magazine* discuss the issue of medical marijuana.

The first editorial was written by Ethan Nadelmann, founder and executive director of the Drug Policy Alliance, an organization that promotes alternatives to the war on drugs.

"FOR" ARGUMENT BY ETHAN NADELMANN

Marijuana may be an unconventional medicine, but it works. Montel Williams, decorated former naval intelligence officer and talk-show host, uses medical marijuana to help him control the symptoms of multiple sclerosis. So does Keith Vines, an assistant district attorney, retired Air Force Captain and former federal narcotics prosecutor living with AIDS.

2   These men are just two of hundreds of thousands of Americans who use marijuana to treat pain from accidents or debilitating conditions such as MS; to help restore appetite during chemotherapy; to treat the symptoms of AIDS, glaucoma, and epilepsy; and for a host of other medical reasons.

3   The vast majority are law-abiding citizens who suffer from chronic pain and illness. They use marijuana as medicine because it works better than anything else, with fewer negative side effects. Many never smoked marijuana until they became sick. Dozens of scientific studies demonstrate marijuana's safety and therapeutic value.

More than two thirds of Americans say 4 marijuana should be legal for medical purposes—and that's the law now in 15 states.

Only one big problem: the federal 5 government. The Clinton administration was callous, and the Bush administration was downright cruel, arresting and prosecuting patients and providers. Federal drug enforcement agents, acting at the behest of the Justice Department, even raided a hospice and handcuffed frail and elderly patients who use marijuana as medicine.

The crackdown represented a shame- 6 ful abuse of power: punishing sick people for using the medicine that works best for them, threatening doctors who exercise responsible medical judgment, and prohibiting state governments from acting in the interests of their own citizens.

It's time to tell the feds to get out of 7 the doctors' offices and medicine cabinets, and out of the way of citizens who simply want to do what's right.

(Ethan Nadelmann, "Legalize Medicinal Marijuana," 2004)

The second editorial was written by John P. Walters, the federal drug czar under President George W. Bush and past deputy director for supply reduction in the Office of National Drug Control Policy.

"AGAINST" ARGUMENT BY JOHN P. WALTERS

In America today, well-financed organizations and individuals are exploiting the pain of sick people, and the compassion of those who care about them, to legalize marijuana. Advocating for the use of a smoked weed under the guise of medicine is dishonest, scientifically irresponsible and contradictory to the high standards of quality effectiveness guaranteed by the U.S. Food and Drug Administration.

Our medical system relies on proven 2 scientific research to protect U.S. citizens from unsafe and ineffective products. Research has not demonstrated that smoked marijuana is helpful as medicine. The FDA has also stated that while marijuana use has no proven benefits, it does have long-term risks associated with it. Furthermore, the British Lung Foundation says that smoking three to four marijuana cigarettes a day is as harmful for your lungs as smoking 20 tobacco cigarettes.

3 Some claim smoking marijuana helps ease symptoms associated with certain illnesses. The fact that smoking a joint may make them feel better is not in dispute. But simply feeling better is not the standard of modern medicine. If it were, snake oils and miracle potions would still line our medicine cabinets today.

4 The reality is that modern science has afforded us safe alternatives to smoking a crude plant. The FDA-approved drug Marinol makes the component in marijuana known as THC available in pill form. A product that delivers marijuana's THC through an inhaler is currently in development. The difference between these medicines and smoking a joint: the user does not get high.

5 Our veterans have sacrificed much to secure the blessings we enjoy today, including a safe and reliable medical system grounded in research and unparalleled in the world. We owe it to them to protect the integrity of that system and to prevent those seeking to legalize marijuana from riding on the coattails of our compassion.

(John P. Walters, "Legalize Medicinal Marijuana," 2004)

Exercise 1: Evaluating the Editorials for Propaganda Techniques and Logical Fallacies

Editorials frequently use propaganda techniques and logical fallacies in an effort to make their case. Try to identify the technique or the fallacy used in these editorials. If you need to, refer back to the discussion of propaganda techniques and logical fallacies in Chapter 12.

Directions: Below is a chart for you to fill in. First, take the argument in favor of legalizing the use of marijuana for medicinal purposes and see how many propaganda techniques or logical fallacies you can identify. When you find a technique or a fallacy being used, record it in the appropriate box. Some boxes have already been filled in for you. Then look at the arguments against legalizing the use of marijuana for medicinal purposes and see how many propaganda techniques or logical fallacies you can identify. Record these, too. When you finish filling in the chart, answer the question that follows.

Propaganda Technique	"For" Argument	"Against" Argument
Name-calling	Clinton administration—callous; Bush administration—cruel	Advocating use of marijuana under guise of medicine is dishonsest, scientifically irresponsible, and contradictory.
Glittering generalities	It works.	Safe and reliable medical system
Transfer		*Veterans sacrificed much*
False analogy		*Comparing the effects of marijuana to the effects of snake oils and miracle potions*
Testimonial	*Montel Williams and Keith Vines*	*FDA; British Lung Foundation*
Plain folks	*Law-abiding citizens*	*Veterans*
Card stacking	*No discussion of possible side effects of marijuana*	*No discussion of possible beneficial effects of marijuana to patients*
Bandwagon	*Hundreds of thousands of Americans who use marijuana for medical reasons*	
Either/or fallacy	*Either allow use of marijuana for medical purposes or people suffer.*	*Either use Marinol or get high on marijuana.*

What conclusions can you make about the use of propaganda techniques or logical fallacies in these two editorials?

Answers will vary.

_____

_____

_____

_____

_____

Exercise 2: Evaluating the Use of Persuasive Techniques in an Editorial

Directions: Now that you have read the two editorials, choose one of them and use it to answer the following questions. Answers will vary.

1. **Author's purpose.** Is it the author's primary purpose to inform or to persuade? Why do you think so?

   _____

   _____

   _____

   _____

2. **Emotional appeals.** Where does the author use language that is meant to appeal to your emotions? Give an example of material that is included in the editorial for its emotional appeal.

   _____

   _____

   _____

   _____

3. **Ethical appeals.** Does the editorial cite any experts? What do the experts have to say about the topic of the editorial? How much trust should you put in what the experts say? Might other experts have different opinions?

   _____

   _____

   _____

   _____

4. **Logical appeals.** What logical or reasonable arguments are included in the editorial? Does the editorial make use of inductive or deductive reasoning?

   _____

   _____

   _____

   _____

5. **Psychological appeals.** Does the editorial say anything that is intended to manipulate you psychologically by appealing to your need for acceptance, power, prestige, and so forth?

_____

_____

_____

_____

6. **Tone.** What is the author's tone? Is the tone meant to influence or manipulate you? Give specific examples of how the author uses tone to affect you.

_____

_____

_____

_____

7. **Bias.** What is the author's specific bias? Where does this bias appear in the editorial—at the beginning, the middle, or the end?

_____

_____

_____

_____

Exercise 3: War on Drugs—Opposing Viewpoints

The following two editorials are from _USA Today_. The first was written by the editorial staff and represents the viewpoint of the newspaper itself. The opposing viewpoint is by John Walters, who also wrote the opposing viewpoint presented previously.

Directions: Read each of the editorials and then answer the questions that follow.

WAR ON DRUGS GONE TO POT BY _USA TODAY_ EDITORIAL STAFF

Our View: Massive Arrests Just Smoke Screen Hiding Impotency of Crackdown

Marijuana is the most widely used illegal substance. About 15 million Americans smoke it, and police make nearly 7,000,000 pot related arrests each year, accounting for nearly half of all drug arrests.

2   The $35-billion-a-year war on drugs has turned largely into a war on marijuana and a losing war at that. Pot isn't harmless, but shouldn't law enforcement focus more of its resources on hard drugs—cocaine, heroin, and methamphetamines—that are associated with violence and devastated lives.

According to a new study by The Sen- 3 tencing Project, a liberal research group that favors alternatives to incarceration:

- Marijuana arrests increased 113 percent from 1990 through 2002, while arrests for all other drugs rose just 10 percent.
- Four of five marijuana arrests are for possession, not dealing.

4   The theory behind the war on drugs is that enough arrests will curtail both supply and demand. But the impact of increased marijuana arrests appears negligible. According to private and government studies, overall marijuana use is the same as it was in 1990, while daily use by high school seniors has nearly tripled, from 2.2 percent to 6 percent. Since 1992, the inflation-adjusted price of pot has fallen about 16 percent while potency has doubled, the studies show.

5   So the intensified crackdown has coincided with cheaper, stronger pot that's readily available. Law enforcement's efforts to arrest marijuana smokers are diverting resources from combating other crimes and those who traffic in hard drugs.

6   Few people arrested for possessing marijuana serve jail time, but the consequences they face are severe. They may not qualify for federal student loans or entry to public housing, may lose the right to vote, and face a job market with criminal records they must report to potential employers.

The drug war against low-level users 7 also sparks resentment against police, particularly in the minority community. African-Americans represent 14 percent of marijuana users but account for 30 percent of arrests, The Sentencing Project study found.

The get-tough approach is showing 8 cracks both at home and abroad. Twelve states have some form of decriminalization or reduced sentences. Great Britain, Canada and Russia have decriminalized possession of small amounts of the drug.

Today's more potent marijuana carries 9 substantial health and social risks. It can lead to depression, thoughts of suicide and schizophrenia, especially among teens, according to government research. Its use should be discouraged. But it's a smoke screen to suggest that rising arrest numbers show the war on drugs is working. It's time for a serious debate on whether massive arrests of low-level users are worth the cost or having any benefit.

(*USA Today,* 2005)

Questions

Directions: For each item, write the letter corresponding to the best answer on the line provided.

_____c_____ 1. Which of the following best expresses the main idea?
   a. Marijuana is a harmful drug.
   b. Marijuana does less damage to individuals and society as a whole than hard drugs do.
   c. The current war on drugs is not working.
   d. Marijuana use by teens should be discouraged.

_____c_____ 2. Which of the following statements directly supports the author's main idea?
   a. African-Americans represent 14 percent of marijuana users but account for 30 percent of arrests.
   b. [Marijuana] can lead to depression, thoughts of suicide, and schizophrenia, especially among teens, according to government research.
   c. According to private and government studies, daily use by high school seniors has nearly tripled from 2.2 percent to 6 percent.
   d. None of the above.

_____b_____ 3. "It's time for a serious debate on whether massive arrests of low-level users are worth the cost or having any benefit." This sentence makes a statement of
   a. fact.
   b. opinion.

_____a_____ 4. An antonym for the word *potent* is
   a. weak.
   b. powerful.
   c. strong.
   d. none of the above.

_____b_____ 5. The main purpose of the editorial is to
   a. explain.
   b. persuade.
   c. entertain.
   d. define.

_____d_____ 6. The author chose the title "War on Drugs Gone to Pot" because
   a. it is a "play" on the word *pot.*
   b. it indicates that the war on drugs is not going well.
   c. it indicates that the focus of the war on drugs is "pot" rather than hard drugs such as cocaine and heroin.
   d. all of the above.

_____b_____ 7. The phrase "smoke screen" indicates
   a. an openness toward new information.
   b. a concealing of the truth with misleading information.
   c. the placement of a device similar to a smoke detector.
   d. none of the above.

_____c_____ 8. The phrase "impotency of crackdown" implies that the U.S. government is
   a. winning the war on drugs.
   b. holding its own in the war on drugs.
   c. ineffective in the war on drugs.
   d. none of the above.

_____c_____ 9. According to the editorial, all of the following statements are true about the war on drugs *except* for which?
   a. The U.S. government's position is that if enough people are arrested, both the supply of drugs and the demand for drugs will decrease.
   b. During the period of "cracking down" on drugs, marijuana has gotten cheaper and more potent, and become more readily available.
   c. Most people arrested for possessing small amounts of marijuana serve lengthy sentences.
   d. Those arrested for possession of marijuana may be ineligible for a host of government-related benefits.

_____c_____ 10. According to the editorial, marijuana use is linked to all of the following *except*
   a. depression.
   b. suicidal thoughts.
   c. cancer.
   d. schizophrenia.

_____b_____ 11. An antonym for the word *negligible* is
   a. irrelevant.
   b. significant.
   c. minor.
   d. infinitesimal.

Directions: Indicate whether each statement is true or false by writing **T** or **F** in the space provided.

____T____ 12. Nearly half of all drug arrests are pot-related.

____T____ 13. The majority of marijuana arrests are for possession, not dealing.

____F____ 14. Daily use of pot by high school seniors is currently lower than in the 1990s.

____F____ 15. The majority of states have decriminalized possession of marijuana.

____F____ 16. Marijuana use is associated with few, if any, health risks.

MARIJUANA POLICY JUST RIGHT   BY JOHN WALTERS

Opposing View: Focus Is Response to New Research on Drug's Potency, Use, and Risks

Assertions that our nation's drug policy minimizes cocaine and heroin while focusing on marijuana are misleading. The fallacy involves interpreting drug arrests as signals of changed drug policy, rather than as indicators of drug use. As drug use went down in the 1980s, arrests fell accordingly. When drug use climbed between 1992 and 1997, arrests followed suit. And when the cocaine epidemic struck, cocaine arrests rose steeply, only to drop as the epidemic waned.

2   The commonsense conclusion is that drug use rates and criminal justice responses are linked. Thus the key to reducing drug arrests is reducing drug use. Important progress has already occurred—youth drug use has declined 17 percent since 2001.

3   Our drug policy balances prevention, treatment and interdiction. Criminal justice sanctions are sometimes necessary, but we are not locking up low-level marijuana offenders. Rather, drug courts, which use supervised treatment to help users (rather than prison) are a critical component of our approach.

4   We are more concerned about marijuana today. Studies long ago established marijuana as a risky substance. For youth, it is the single largest source of abuse and dependency. But compelling new research shows an increased public health threat.

5   First, marijuana potency has more than doubled within the past 10 years. Second, kids are using marijuana at younger ages, during crucial periods in their development, and thereby increasing risks that extend into adult life. And third, research from many nations now implicates marijuana's role in mental illness.

6   Youth marijuana use elevates risks of depression, psychosis, even schizophrenia. For those with predispositions to mental disorders, the risk is compounded. Some studies show marijuana can trigger the onset or increase the severity of mental illness.

7   Coming to grips with new facts, we are focusing on marijuana. As we do so, we respond to a fundamental public health problem in a balanced and responsible manner.

(*USA Today,* 2005)

Questions

Directions: Answer the following questions briefly, in a few words or sentences as appropriate.

1. Explain the cause-and-effect relationships in paragraph 1.

    Cause: Because drug use went down during the 1980s,

    Effect: arrests fell.

    Cause: Because drug use climbed between 1992 and 1997,

    Effect: arrests climbed.

2. Because the author sees a cause-and-effect relationship between drug use and arrest rates, he believes that the key to reducing drug arrests is to
   reduce drug use.

3. What does the author mean by the expression "coming to grips with new facts"?
   confronting squarely; dealing decisively with

Directions: For each item, write the letter corresponding to the best answer on the line provided.

_____d_____ 4. The "epidemic waned" means that it
   a. increased.
   b. abated.
   c. declined.
   d. both b and c.

_____c_____ 5. The author believes that marijuana is a public health threat for all of the following reasons *except* for which?
   a. Marijuana today is more powerful than it used to be.
   b. Children begin using marijuana at critical points in their development.
   c. Marijuana is a gateway drug that leads to harder drugs.
   d. Marijuana has been correlated to mental illness.

_____c_____ 6. The author would agree with all of the following *except* for which?
   a. Because of the new research, the focus of the U.S. drug program should be on marijuana.
   b. The nation's current drug policy is both balanced and responsible.
   c. Little or no progress has been made in reducing youth drug abuse.
   d. Drug courts, which treat rather than imprison, are a key part of the current approach to controlling drug abuse.

_____d_____ 7. Which of the following statements is an opinion?
   a. The commonsense conclusion is that drug use rates and criminal justice responses are linked.
   b. We are more concerned about marijuana today.
   c. When drug use climbed between 1992 and 1997, arrests followed suit.
   d. Both a and b.

_____c_____ 8. If you have a *predisposition* to something, you are
   a. ignorant of it.
   b. angry about it.
   c. more susceptible to it.
   d. more resistant to it.

Directions: Indicate whether each statement is true or false by writing **T** or **F** in the space provided.

_____T_____ 9. *Interdiction* means an official prohibition or restraint.

_____F_____ 10. Youth drug use has increased since 2001.

_____T_____ 11. More young people are dependent on marijuana than on any other drug.

_____F_____ 12. Low-level marijuana offenders are increasingly being incarcerated.

_____T_____ 13. Long-term studies show that marijuana is a risky substance.

_____F_____ 14. The U.S. government favors locking up low-level marijuana offenders.

___T___ 15. There is a correlation between drug-use rates and criminal justice responses.

___T___ 16. Money has been requested to expand the drug court program.

Evaluating the Evidence: Letters to the Editor

People sometimes respond to controversial issues by writing a letter to the editor stating their opinion. Read the following letters to the editor and consider their claims.

Exercise 4: Evaluating Letter 1

FOR LEGALIZING THE USE OF MARIJUANA FOR MEDICINAL PURPOSES

It is sad that something so critical to many Americans' health and well-being is being withheld by politics. Elderly patients are more likely to encounter adverse reactions from conventional medications because of slowed metabolisms and other consequences of aging. The Food and Drug Administration's litany of recalls and drug warnings point up the need for nontoxic alternatives like marijuana.

2   Washington politicians not only claim we have the best health care in the world but tout this nation's commitment to democracy, liberty and freedom. These will remain just claims until our lawmakers restore the freedom to use cannabis as medicine that they revoked with the passage of the Controlled Substances Act in 1970.

Gary Storck, cofounder,
Is My Medicine Legal YET?,
Madison, Wisconsin

(Gary Stork, Letter to the Editor, 2005)

Questions

Directions: For each item, write the letter corresponding to the best answer on the line provided.

___b___ 1. The principal point the writer makes is that
   a. marijuana has always been illegal.
   b. marijuana should be made available as a medicine to those who could benefit from it.
   c. marijuana alleviates the side effects of chemotherapy.
   d. none of the above.

___b___ 2. The writer would probably agree with which of the following statements?
   a. Marijuana can be toxic in moderate doses.
   b. Elderly people could benefit from the availability of marijuana as a medicine.
   c. Conventional drugs are always just as effective as marijuana.
   d. Marijuana is as dangerous as cocaine.

___d___ 3. The writer implies that
   a. the dangers of marijuana are greatly exaggerated.
   b. conventional drugs are not free of risk and drawbacks.
   c. withholding marijuana from the public should not happen in a country that honors liberty and freedom.
   d. all of the above.

_____d_____ 4. An assumption the writer makes is that
   a. elderly patients should refrain from taking conventional medications.
   b. the Controlled Substances Act allows the distribution of marijuana as a legal medication.
   c. marijuana is more likely to cause problems for elderly people than conventional medications.
   d. none of the above.

Exercise 5: Evaluating Letter 2

AGAINST LEGALIZING THE USE OF MARIJUANA FOR MEDICINAL PURPOSES

On March 28, 2005, the television show The O'Reilly Factor aired a segment on medical fraud in which a FOX News producer strolled into one of California's cannabis buyers' clubs and bought an eighth ounce of marijuana with no questions asked. The club required the producer to obtain the recommendation of a doctor. With no serious health problems, he obtained the recommendation within fifteen minutes for $250. He then walked into the buyers' club and bought the marijuana for $65. The recommendation from the doctor never expires, so this producer is free to go back as often as he wishes for more pot.

2 Our Executive Director, Calvina Fay, was a guest on the follow-up show. "This incident clearly shows the loopholes in the legislation allowing marijuana to be distributed for so-called medical purposes. It is accessible to everybody, which is the ultimate goal of the pro-legalization movement."

Clearly this is an example of how peo- 3 ple are toking up under the guise of treating "serious maladies" such as premenstrual syndrome, athlete's foot, and even ingrown toenails. The reality is that people with fatal diseases are not smoking pot to treat them—they are already under the care and supervision of legitimate doctors and are receiving valid medicines to treat their ailments.

Letter to the Editor, Unsigned,
Drug Free America Foundation.

(Unsigned, Letter to the Editor)

Questions

Directions: For each item, write the letter corresponding to the best answer on the line provided.

_____d_____ 1. Which of the following statements is an opinion?
   a. The producer was required to obtain the recommendation of a doctor.
   b. He then walked into the buyers' club and bought an eighth ounce of marijuana for $65.
   c. Our Executive Director, Calvina Fay, was a guest on the follow-up show.
   d. This incident clearly shows the loopholes in the legislation allowing marijuana to be distributed for so-called medical purposes.

_____d_____ 2. Which of the following is a generalization the writer makes?
   a. Nearly anyone can obtain marijuana at a cannabis buyers' club in California.
   b. Smoking marijuana can prevent athlete's foot.
   c. People with fatal diseases aren't obtaining marijuana for treatment purposes.
   d. Both a and c.

___b___   3. Which of the following best describes the writer's main purpose?
  a. He wants to encourage people to avail themselves of inexpensive drugs.
  b. He wants people to understand that medical marijuana is a ruse to achieve the legalization of marijuana.
  c. He wants people with serious ailments to frequent cannabis buyers' clubs.
  d. He wants people who purchase pot illegally to serve lengthy prison sentences.

___b___   4. A reasonable inference that can be made from the writer's letter is that
  a. people with serious medical problems will stop going to doctors and start going to cannabis buyers' clubs.
  b. medical marijuana is currently being dispensed to treat trivial problems.
  c. an ingrown toenail is a serious malady.
  d. none of the above.

Exercise 6: Evaluating Letter 3

AGAINST THE CURRENT WAR ON DRUGS

Americans will be disappointed to learn that the war on drugs is not what they thought it was. Many of us grew up supporting this war, thinking it would imprison high-level traffickers in hard drugs and keep cocaine and heroin off the streets. Instead, law enforcement officers devote precious hours on hundreds of thousands of arrests for possession of a little marijuana, only to have prosecutors deem the infractions too minor to take to court.

This tremendous waste of time and re- 2 sources must stop.

Mitch Earleywine, Author,
Understanding Marijuana,
Associate Professor, Psychology,
University of Southern
California, Los Angeles

(Mitch Earleywine, Letter to the Editor, 2005)

Questions

Directions: For each item, write the letter corresponding to the best answer on the line provided.

___a___   1. The tone of the writer toward the war on drugs is
  a. outraged.
  b. sympathetic.
  c. indifferent.
  d. optimistic.

___c___   2. A reasonable inference that can be drawn is that
  a. the writer believes that the war on drugs has been worth the time and money allocated to it.
  b. the writer believes that the war on drugs has greatly reduced the availability of hard drugs.
  c. the writer wants the government to change its priorities in the war on drugs.
  d. the writer is pleased that small-time drug traffickers have often been imprisoned.

_____d_____ 3. In paragraph 1, the word *deem* means
 a. consider.
 b. think.
 c. judge.
 d. all of the above.

Exercise 7: Evaluating Letter 4

AGAINST THE CURRENT WAR ON DRUGS

If U.S. drug czar John Walters thinks marijuana is so harmful, why does he want it to remain completely unregulated, untaxed, and controlled by criminal gangs.

2 Only legal products of any kind can be regulated, taxed, and controlled by any government.

3 Regarding the so-called high potency of today's marijuana, in my view, if we smoked the world's most potent marijuana all day long, the worst effect would be a severe case of the munchies. On the other hand, drinking more than 80 cups of caffeinated coffee could result in a lethal dose of caffeine.

4 Perhaps we should criminalize coffee instead of marijuana.

Kirk Muse, Mesa, Arizona

(Letter to the Editor, 2005)

Questions

Directions: For each item, write the letter corresponding to the best answer on the line provided.

_____d_____ 1. The author's use of the phrase "so-called" in reference to the potency of today's marijuana implies that
 a. the author feels that marijuana is far more potent today than in the past.
 b. the author has doubts about how potent today's marijuana really is.
 c. the author doesn't agree with authorities who call today's marijuana high-potency.
 d. both b and c.

_____c_____ 2. The author makes use of the following persuasive technique when he equates drinking coffee with smoking marijuana:
 a. testimonial.
 b. plain folks.
 c. false analogy.
 d. bandwagon.

_____b_____ 3. The author suggests criminalizing coffee instead of marijuana because
 a. he really wants to see coffee criminalized.
 b. he is being ironic.
 c. he believes that smoking marijuana is more harmful than ingesting large amounts of coffee.
 d. none of the above.

Evaluating the Evidence: Advertisements

There is an old saying that "a picture is worth a thousand words." In an advertisement, the purpose of the visual image is to persuade you to buy something, or do something, or think about something in a particular way.

Advertisements often make an argument, which may be stated directly or implied. When studying an advertisement, ask yourself what its argument is. What is the advertisement's purpose? What does it want you to do or think or buy? What reasons is it giving you to act? Who sponsors or pays for the advertisement?

Exercise 8: Evaluating an Advertisement

Directions: The advertisement below was sponsored by the White House Office of National Drug Control Policy through its national youth antidrug campaign. Study the ad carefully and then answer the following questions.

1. What is the topic of the ad? Answers will vary. _____

2. What is the main idea of the ad? _____

_____

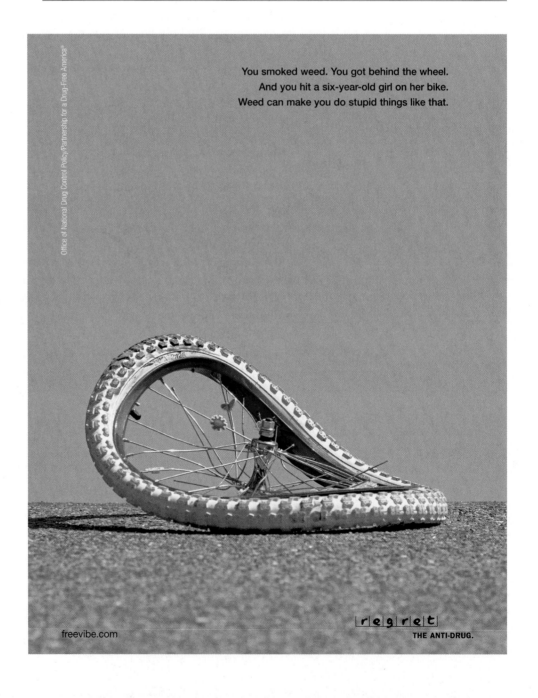

3. What is the ad's purpose? _____

4. What is the overall tone of the ad? _____

5. What is the point of view of the ad? _____

6. What support is given for the argument presented? Give specific examples.

_____

7. Can you tell who sponsored the ad from reading the ad alone, or would you need to do further research? How might you find this information on the Internet? (Hint: Many Web sites include information about the organization; go to the Web site listed in the ad. You might want to consult the following Web sites: www.drugfree.org, www.campaigns.drugfreeamerica.org/)

Evaluating the Evidence: Political Cartoons

A political (or editorial) cartoon is a drawing that has a political or social message. Most political cartoons employ satire or humor to communicate a specific point of view about a current event or issue. Many political cartoons feature caricatures of prominent public figures. They also often make use of common symbols. For instance, the Democratic Party is represented by a donkey, and the Republican Party by an elephant. A drawing of Uncle Sam stands for the United States as a whole.

Political cartoons can be difficult to decipher. Understanding them often requires a knowledge of current events. It also helps to be familiar with social and political issues.

Exercise 9: Evaluating a Political Cartoon

Directions: Study the cartoon below to determine what the cartoonist, Scott Stantis, has to say about the war on drugs. What is his point of view on the topic? Is he for the current policy or against it?

© 1998 by Scott Stantis. By permission of Scott Stantis and Creators Syndicate, Inc.

The cartoonist doesn't think the war on drugs has been successful.

Chapter Summary and Review

In Chapter 13, you learned about persuasive writing techniques, evaluated persuasive writing selections, and became familiar with inductive and deductive reasoning. Based on the material in Chapter 13, answer the following questions.

Short Answer

Directions: Answer the following questions briefly, using no more than a few words or sentences as appropriate.

1. Give an example of inductive reasoning. <u>Answers will vary.</u>
   _____

2. Give an example of deductive reasoning. <u>Answers will vary.</u>
   _____

3. Do you think that harsher penalties will deter people from using marijuana?
   <u>Answers will vary.</u>

4. Should marijuana be legalized and regulated like cigarettes and alcohol?
   <u>Answers will vary.</u>

5. What resources are available in your area to help people who abuse drugs?
   <u>Answers will vary.</u>

Vocabulary in Context

Directions: Choose one of the following words to complete the sentences below. Use each word only once.

   authority   deductive   inductive   subjective

6. When a person who is giving an opinion on cloning states that she is a professor of bioethics, she is making an appeal to <u>authority</u>.

7. When people relate their personal feelings and opinions, they are being <u>subjective</u>.

8. Trying to draw conclusions from a hypothesis or a general principle is <u>deductive</u> reasoning.

9. <u>Inductive</u> reasoning begins with gathering evidence and then draws a conclusion from that evidence.

In Conclusion

Using a search engine such as Google, Yahoo!, or MSN, find an article of interest related to the medical use of marijuana. Print out and evaluate that article in relation to the seven types of persuasive writing techniques discussed at the beginning of this chapter.

Becoming Ready for Content-Area Classes

ESPERANZA SPALDING

Esperanza Spalding won the 2011 Grammy for Best New Artist, but some have reveled in her talent for years. A 26-year-old, classically trained musician and singer of jazz/chamber fusion music, Spalding has been making headlines in the jazz world even before her 2006 debut solo album, "Junjo." And for good reason: she's a multifaceted performer. When she's not wowing audiences with a heavenly-sounding soprano or scatting like the veterans of old, she's impressing them with her bass playing (she also plays other instruments). She is so gifted musically that after finishing the renowned Berklee College of Music in Boston at an accelerated pace, she became an instructor there when she was 20, making her the college's youngest faculty member. Her outstanding musicianship has won her praise from the likes of Stevie Wonder and Herbie Hancock, and other critical acclaim. President Barack Obama selected Spalding to perform at the Oslo City Hall in Sweden when he accepted his 2009 Nobel Prize, as well as at a White House poetry jam.

"I feel really lucky that I got to be acknowledged on this stage in front of so many people who hopefully will get to experience my music, and I got there by doing what's really dear to my heart," she told the AP after her win. "The music that I make is pretty sincere; it's from my heart and I love it, and what just happened is more people have started to connect with my heart." (*The Huffington Post*, 2011)

TIMED READING If you wish to use "Esperanza Spalding" as a timed reading, please turn to page A-4 in the Appendices.

Rehearsing Study Techniques and Visual Aids

CHAPTER PREVIEW

In this chapter, you will

- Practice scanning.
- Practice skimming.
- Practice additional study techniques.
- Become familiar with visual aids.

Scanning

Scanning is the process of quickly searching reading material to locate specific bits of information. When you scan, you don't start at the beginning and read through to the end. Instead, you jump around in the text, trying to find the information you need. You probably already scan when you search the dictionary for the definition of a word, or a book index for a topic, or a Web site online. Scanning, which was discussed in the Introduction, is especially helpful when you are doing research.

The purpose of this section is to provide you with additional material with which to practice your scanning skills. We will first practice scanning material you are probably already familiar with. Then we will practice scanning some more difficult textbook reading material.

Exercise 1: Scanning a Nutritional Content Chart

Directions: The purpose of this exercise is to increase your scanning speed. Complete the exercise as quickly as you can by moving your eyes rapidly across the nutritional content chart on the next page to find the answers to the questions that follow.

1. How many calories does a bean burrito have? <u>370</u>

2. How much sodium is in a Nachos BellGrande? <u>1050 mg</u>

3. Which of the listed items has the least sodium? <u>Mexican rice</u>

4. How much protein is in a steak quesadilla? <u>25 g</u>

5. Which of the listed items has the most protein? <u>XXL Grilled Stuft Burrito, beef</u>

6. How much sugar is in Pintos 'n cheese? <u>1 g</u>

7. How much cholesterol is in Nachos Supreme? <u>30 mg</u>

8. How many carbohydrates are in a bean burrito? <u>56 g</u>

Nutritional Content of Popular Items from a Fast-Food Restaurant

Taco Bell	Serving size (g)	Calories	Calories from fat	Saturated fat (g)	Total fat (g)	Trans fat (g)	Cholesterol (mg)	Sodium (mg)	Carbohydrates (g)	Dietary fiber (g)	Sugar (g)	Protein (g)	Fresco style meets 25% reduction in fat
Crunchy Taco	78	170	90	3.5	10	0	30	330	12	3	1	8	-
Crunchy Taco Supreme®	113	200	100	5	12	0	35	350	15	3	2	9	√
Soft taco, beef	99	210	80	4	9	0	30	560	21	3	2	10	-
Gordita Supreme®, steak	153	270	90	4	11	0	30	550	29	2	6	14	√
Grilled steak soft taco	124	250	130	4	14	0	30	550	19	2	2	11	√
Gordita Baja®, chicken	153	310	130	3.5	15	0	35	600	28	3	6	17	√
Chalupa Supreme, beef	153	370	190	5	21	0.5	35	600	31	4	4	13	-
Chalupa Supreme, chicken	153	350	160	4	18	0	35	520	29	3	4	17	√
1/2 lb.* combo burrito	241	460	160	7	18	0.5	50	1400	53	10	3	21	-
Bean burrito	198	370	90	3.5	10	0	5	980	56	10	3	13	-
Burrito Supreme®, chicken	248	400	110	5	12	0	40	1060	51	7	5	21	√
XXL Grilled Stuft Burrito, beef	445	880	370	14	41	1	75	2130	95	14	7	32	√
Tostada	170	250	90	3.5	10	0	15	550	30	9	2	10	√
Express taco salad w/chips	432	580	260	10	28	1	60	1350	59	9	7	23	√
Steak quesadilla	184	520	250	12	28	1	65	1250	41	4	3	25	N/A
Nachos Supreme	191	440	220	5	24	0	30	680	42	8	3	12	-
Nachos BellGrande®	305	770	380	7	42	0.5	30	1050	79	14	5	19	√
Pintos 'n cheese	128	170	50	3	6	0	10	580	20	8	1	9	√
Mexican rice	85	120	35	0	3.5	0	0	200	20	1	0	2	√

http://www.tacobell.com/nutrition/information

(Thomas D. Fahey et al., *Fit & Well*, 8/e, 2009)

Exercise 2: Scanning a Food Label

Directions: Scan the food label on page 542 as quickly as you can to find the answers to the following questions.

1. What is a serving size? <u>1 muffin</u>

2. What are the main ingredients of honey wheat muffin mix?
   <u>enriched wheat flour, sugar, hydrogenated vegetable oil</u>

3. How many servings are there per container? <u>6</u>

4. How many calories are in the muffin mix? <u>123</u>

5. How much sodium is in the muffin mix? <u>210 mg</u>

6. How much protein is in the muffin mix? <u>1 g</u>

7. How many eggs are needed to prepare the muffin mix? <u>1 egg</u>

8. How long do the muffins need to bake? <u>15 minutes</u>

Food Labels

Honey Wheat Muffin Mix

Directions
Combine mix with:
1/3 c. whole milk
1 T. oil
1 egg
Stir and pour into prepared muffin tin. Bake 15 minutes at 400°.

Nutrition Facts

Serving Size 1 muffin (from 31g mix)
Servings Per Container 6

Amount Per Serving	Mix	Prepared
Calories	123	162
Calories from Fat	27	54

	% Daily Value**	
Total Fat 3g*	4%	10%
Saturated Fat 0.5g	3%	7%
Trans Fat 0.5g		
Cholesterol 0mg	0%	12%
Sodium 210mg	9%	9%
Potassium 15mg	<1%	1%
Total Carbohydrate 23g	8%	8%
Dietary Fiber <1g	2%	2%
Sugars 12g		
Other Carbohydrate 11g		
Protein 1g		
Calcium	0%	2%
Iron	2%	2%

Not a significant source of vitamin A and vitamin C.
*Amount in mix. As prepared, one serving provides 6g fat (1.5g saturated fat; 1.0g trans fat), 35mg cholesterol, 220mg sodium, 45mg potassium, 24g total carbohydrate (12g sugars) and 3g protein.
**Percent Daily Values are based on a 2,000 calorie diet. Your daily values may be higher or lower depending on your calorie needs:

		Calories:	2,000	2,500
Total Fat	Less than		65g	80g
Sat Fat	Less than		20g	25g
Cholesterol	Less than		300mg	300mg
Sodium	Less than		2,400mg	2,400mg
Potassium			3,500mg	3,500mg
Total Carbohydrate			300g	375g
Dietary Fiber			25g	30g

Calories per gram:
Fat 9   •   Carbohydrate 4   •   Protein 4

Ingredients: Enriched Wheat Flour, Sugar, Hydrogenated Vegetable Oil (Coconut and/or Palm Kernel), Corn Syrup, Salt, Cellulose Gum, Dextrose, Rice Flour, Artificial Flavor.

Gwen Robbins, Debbie Powers, and Sharon Burgess, *A Fit and Well Way of Life*. New York: McGraw-Hill, 2008, p. 401.

Exercise 3: Scanning an Essay

Directions: The following exercise makes use of a reading selection titled "The American Environment: 'Silent Spring'" (pages 543–545). Scan the essay to locate the date that corresponds to each of the following statements. Write the date on the line.

TIME LINE FOR "THE AMERICAN ENVIRONMENT: 'SILENT SPRING'"

<u>1868</u>   Gypsy moths are accidentally introduced to the Boston area.

<u>1939</u>   Paul Muller discovers DDT's toxicity to insects.

<u>1942</u>   American scientists become aware of Muller's discovery.

<u>1942–44</u>   DDT is used on a typhus outbreak in Italy.

<u>1945</u>   DDT enters the marketplace.

<u>1948</u>   Muller is awarded the Nobel Prize in Medicine; DDT-resistant housefly appears.

<u>1949</u>_____   A DDT-resistant mosquito appears.

<u>1951</u>_____   Rachel Carson publishes *The Sea Around Us.*

<u>1957</u>_____   The nature sanctuary behind Olga Huckins's house is sprayed with
                  DDT; a letter is sent to the newspaper and Rachel Carson.

<u>1962</u>_____   Rachel Carson publishes *Silent Spring.*

<u>1964</u>_____   Rachel Carson dies of cancer.

<u>1972</u>_____   The United States bans the sale of DDT.

Now carefully read the essay and answer the questions that follow.

READING

*"Silent Spring became one of the most controversial
books of the 1960s."*

TUNING IN TO READING   Rachel Carson in her landmark book, *Silent Spring,* presented
a simple message: Artificial pesticides, particularly DDT, are harmful to the health of people,
wildlife, and ecosystems. At the time of her book's publication, pesticides were being
indiscriminately sprayed over residential neighborhoods, parks, and beaches in the belief that
they would cause no harm. Her book is credited with awakening the public to the possible
negative effects of both pesticides and industrial chemicals.

BIO-SKETCH   Alan Brinkley is the Alan Nevins Professor of History at Columbia University
and the author of many books on American history, including *Voices of Protest* (1982), *The End
of Reform* (1995), and *Eyes of a Nation* (1998).

NOTES ON VOCABULARY
sanctuary   a refuge for wildlife
voracious   having a huge appetite; ravenous
wreaking havoc   causing great devastation or destruction

THE AMERICAN ENVIRONMENT: "SILENT SPRING"
Alan Brinkley

One summer day in 1957, a small plane flew over the nature sanctuary
behind Olga Huckins's house in Duxbury, Massachusetts. It sprayed the
land below with an oily mist and then vanished. The next day, Huckins found
seven dead songbirds, their beaks gaping in apparent agony. She was so furious that she wrote an angry letter to a local newspaper; as an afterthought,
she sent a copy to her friend Rachel Carson. It was one of those small events
that alters the course of history.

Carson was a biologist and a gifted writer. Educated at Johns Hopkins Uni- 2
versity at a time when few women became scientists, she had gone to work
for the government as an aquatic biologist, where—despite her painful shyness—
she distinguished herself as a writer able to explain scientific issues to a wider
public. In the meantime, she began to write popular essays about her special
love, the ocean. In 1951 she published *The Sea Around Us.* It became an international best seller, bringing Carson a fame she never imagined and enough

income to retire from government. By 1957, when she received Huckins's letter, she was one of the most popular nature writers of her generation.

The mist that the plane had sprayed behind Huckins's house was a mixture 3 of ordinary fuel oil and a chemical called dicholoro-diphenyl-trichloroethane: DDT. In 1939, a Swiss chemist named Paul Muller had discovered that although DDT seemed harmless to human beings and other mammals, it was extremely toxic to insects. American scientists learned of Muller's discovery in 1942, just as the army was grappling with the insect-borne tropical diseases—especially malaria and typhus—that threatened American soldiers.

Under these circumstances DDT seemed like a godsend. It was first used 4 on a large scale in Italy in 1942–1944 during a typhus outbreak, which it quickly helped end. Soon it was being sprayed in mosquito-infested areas of Pacific islands where American troops were fighting the Japanese. No soldiers suffered any apparent ill effects from the spraying, and the incidence of malaria dropped precipitously. DDT quickly gained a reputation as a miraculous tool for controlling insects, and it undoubtedly saved thousands of lives. For its discovery, Paul Muller was awarded the Nobel Prize in medicine in 1948. With so many benefits and no obvious drawbacks, the new chemical was first released for public use in 1945. DDT entered the marketplace billed as an extraordinarily safe and effective poison, the ultimate weapon against destructive insects.

For the next decade, the new chemical continued to live up to its early 5 billing. It helped farmers eliminate chronic pests and was widely used to control mosquitoes. One of its most impressive successes was in virtually eliminating the gypsy moth, a voracious insect that had been stripping the leaves from northeastern forests ever since being accidentally introduced to the Boston area in 1868.

By the time Rachel Carson received Olga Huckins's letter, however, signs 6 of trouble were beginning to appear in areas that had been sprayed with the chemical. For one, its effectiveness against certain insects declined as they developed resistance to its effects, so that higher doses were needed to produce the same lethal effect. A resistant housefly had appeared as early as 1948, and a resistant mosquito in 1949.

More worrisome were the chemical's effects on larger animals. Some were 7 killed outright, like the birds in Olga Huckins's back yard. But DDT also seemed to inhibit some animals' ability to reproduce. It would later be learned that the eggshells of certain birds were so thinned by the chemical that young birds were crushed in their nests even before they hatched. The extraordinary persistence of DDT in the environment, and its tendency to accumulate in fatty tissues, meant that animals could concentrate surprising quantities in their flesh. This was especially true of those at the top of food chains—eagles, trout, and, not least, people. Many bird lovers were noting a general reduction in bird populations, and people who fished were catching fewer fish. As the woods became emptier and more silent, DDT seemed the most likely culprit. Rachel Carson had worried about pesticides for years, but it was not until reading Olga Huckins's letter that she decided to do something about them. Meticulously gathering the best available data, she wrote a book that was published in 1962, *Silent Spring*. In it, she warned that the indiscriminate use of pesticides was wreaking havoc with the web of life, destroying wildlife populations, and threatening human health. She wrote of a landscape in which sickness and death threatened animals and people alike, in which "a strange stillness" had replaced the familiar songs of birds. Her eloquence was made all the more urgent by her private knowledge as she finished the book that she herself was dying of cancer.

Silent Spring became one of the most controversial books of the 1960s. It 8 sold nearly half a million copies within six months of its publication and was discussed everywhere. The chemical industry was outraged. After first trying to suppress the book's publication altogether and threatening lawsuits against its author and publisher, pesticide manufacturers began a long campaign to discredit Carson and repair the damage her book had done. In the end, though, Carson won at least a partial victory: the U.S. finally banned the sale of DDT in 1972. More important, her book raised public awareness about the threats human activities pose to the natural environment. Although she died in 1964, no single person would be more important in shaping environmental policies over the next thirty years.

(Alan Brinkley, *American History*, 11/e, 2003)

 COMPREHENSION CHECKUP

True or False

Directions: Indicate whether the statement is true or false by writing **T** or **F** in the space provided.

_T___ 1. Rachel Carson had a special fondness for the ocean.

_T___ 2. DDT was responsible for saving thousands of lives.

_T___ 3. DDT was initially thought to be both safe and effective.

_F___ 4. Rachel Carson wrote *Silent Spring* to make the public aware of the helpful effects of pesticide use.

_T___ 5. DDT is toxic to both beneficial and harmful species.

_F___ 6. As a result of her exposure to pesticides, Rachel Carson contracted cancer.

_F___ 7. DDT was first used to eradicate typhus in Germany.

_T___ 8. Some mosquitoes became resistant to DDT.

_F___ 9. Rachel Carson was praised by the chemical industry.

_T___ 10. Rachel Carson was a nature writer.

Outlining

An outline is a type of graphic organizer. It is often a useful study tool. Its goal is to summarize and to show the relationship between the author's key points. An outline is most effective for studying if you write the material in your own words rather than copying sentences from the reading. While you can write in complete sentences, it is also acceptable to use a few words, abbreviations, or short phrases to express your thoughts. We previously discussed outlining as a study technique in Chapter 9.

The following is an outline of the reading selection titled "The American Environment: 'Silent Spring.'"

Directions: Study the outline carefully and then complete Roman numeral VI.

I. An event near Olga Huckins's house
   A. In 1957, a plane sprayed a nearby nature sanctuary with DDT
   B. Huckins found dead songbirds the next day
   C. She wrote to her friend Rachel Carson about what happened
II. Rachel Carson's background
   A. She was a biologist and a writer
   B. She first worked as an aquatic biologist for the federal government
   C. She had a talent for explaining scientific issues to the general public
   D. In 1957, she published *The Sea Around Us*, which became a best seller
III. Early History of DDT
   A. In 1939, Paul Muller, a Swiss chemist, discovered DDT
      1. It seemed harmless to humans and mammals
      2. But very toxic to insects
   B. The American armed services made much use of it during World War II
      1. Tropical diseases such as typhoid and malaria were killing troops
      2. DDT was very successful in controlling these diseases
      3. The troops seemed to suffer no ill effects
   C. Later, DDT was released to the public as a safe and effective insecticide
      1. At first all went well
      2. DDT almost eliminated the gypsy moth that was damaging forests in the northeast
IV. Later History of DDT
   A. Insects began developing a resistance to DDT, which meant that higher doses needed to be used
   B. More importantly, DDT was harming larger animals, including humans
      1. The birds behind Huckins's house were killed
      2. Some birds could not reproduce because their eggshells were too thin
      3. DDT accumulated at high levels in fatty tissue
      4. Bird and fish populations were decreasing
V. Why Carson wrote *Silent Spring*
   A. Carson had been worried about pesticides before receiving Huckins's letter
   B. Huckins's letter made her decide to do something about it
   C. She researched pesticides and DDT and wrote *Silent Spring*
VI. What *Silent Spring*, written in 1963, accomplished
   A. It warned about the widespread use of insecticides
      1. Threats to wildlife and human health
      2. A "strange stillness" was replacing bird songs
   B. It became one of the most controversial books of the 1960s
   C. The pesticide industry tried to suppress it and discredit Carson
   D. It led to the U. S. banning the sale of DDT in 1972
   E. It raised consciousness about human-created threats to the environment

Skimming

The purpose of **skimming** (first discussed in the Introduction) is to gain a quick overview in order to identify the main points. When skimming, you will often skip words, sentences, and paragraphs. When you are satisfied that you have a general understanding of the author's key points, you put aside the reading material. Skimming, then, serves as a substitute for careful reading.

When you are skimming, be sure to move rapidly through the material, skipping the information you are already familiar with. You may wish to read the first and last sentences of each paragraph because that is often where main ideas are located. Read the introduction and the summary if one is provided. When examples are given, you may want to read a few of them until you understand the concepts they are meant to illustrate. When skimming a textbook chapter, glance quickly at the title, subheadings, italicized words, boldface print, and illustrations.

The selection you are about to skim (see pp. 548–549) is from the textbook *Human Biology* by Sylvia Mader.

Exercise 5: Skimming a Textbook Selection

1. First, read the title and the introductory paragraph, and answer the following questions based on them.

   a. What is a pesticide?

   any one of 55,000 chemical products used to kill insects

   b. Based on the title, what point of view do you think the author is going to be taking?

   balanced

   c. What effects do pesticides have on the immune system?

   allergic responses, suppression of immune system

   d. According to the EPA, what are the effects of pesticide residues on food?

   suppression of immune system, disorders of nervous system, birth defects, cancer

2. Now read the last paragraph. What can citizens do to promote the biological control of pests?

   a. Urge elected officials to support eco-friendly legislation.

   b. Use native plants.

   c. Cut down on pesticides, herbicides, and fertilizers.

   d. Use alternative methods for household pest control.

   e. Dispose of pesticides safely.

3. Now read just the first and second sentences of each paragraph and answer the following questions.

   a. Are there any alternatives to the use of pesticides?

   yes—integrated pest management

   b. Are enough natural enemies available to be used instead of pesticides?

   yes, they abound

   c. Which method of pest control is the most sophisticated?

   biological control

READING

"The argument for using pesticides at first seems attractive."

TUNING IN TO READING   In integrated pest management (IPM), numerous techniques are integrated to achieve a long-term solution to pests. Chemicals are used only when absolutely necessary. Many scientists have concluded that pesticides actually make the problem of pests worse because they kill off the natural enemies of the pest, as well as adding to the problem of pollution. IPM programs are already in use in the United States on a variety of crops. IPM is also being used to try to eliminate the current bedbug infestation.

BIO-SKETCH   Dr. Sylvia Mader is the author of several college textbooks in biology, including *Inquiry into Life, Introduction to Biology, Understanding Human Anatomy and Physiology,* and *Human Biology,* from which this excerpt is taken.

NOTES ON VOCABULARY

rodent   any of the small mammals that have large incisors useful for gnawing, such as the rat, mouse, squirrel, or beaver

eradicate   to get rid of; exterminate

PESTICIDES: AN ASSET AND A LIABILITY
Sylvia Mader

A pesticide is any one of 55,000 chemical products used to kill insects, plants, fungi, or rodents that interfere with human activities. Increasingly, we have discovered that pesticides are harmful to the environment and humans. The effect of pesticides on the immune system is a new area of concern; no testing except for skin sensitization has thus far been required before pesticide products are put on the market. Contact or respiratory allergic responses are among the most immediately obvious toxic effects of pesticides. But pesticides can also cause suppression of the immune system, leading to increased susceptibility to infection or tumor development. Lymphocyte impairment was found following the worst industrial accident in the world, which took place in India in 1984. Nerve gas used to produce an insecticide was released into the air; 3,700 people were killed, and 30,000 were injured. Vietnam veterans claim a variety of health effects due to contact with a herbicide called Agent Orange that was used as a defoliant during the Vietnam War. The Environmental Protective Agency (EPA) says that pesticide residues on food possibly cause suppression of the immune system, disorders of the nervous system, birth defects, and cancer.

The argument for using pesticides at first seems attractive. Pesticides are 2 meant to kill off disease-causing agents, increase crop yield, and work quickly with minimal risk. But over time, it has been found that pesticides don't meet these claims. Instead, pests become resistant to pesticides, which kill off natural enemies in addition to the pest. Then the pest population explodes.

There are alternatives to the use of pesticides. Integrated pest manage- 3 ment uses a diversified environment, mechanical and physical means, natural enemies, disruption of reproduction, and resistant plants to control rather than eradicate pest populations. Chemicals are used only as a last resort. Maintaining hedgerows, weedy patches, and certain trees can provide diverse habitats and food for predators and parasites that help control pests. The use of strip farming and crop rotation by farmers denies pests a continuous food source.

Natural enemies abound in the environment. When lacewings were released 4 in cotton fields, they reduced the boll weevil population by 96% and increased cotton yield threefold. A predatory moth was used to reclaim 60 million acres in Australia overrun by the prickly pear cactus, and another type of moth is now used to control alligator weed in the southern United States. Also in the United States the *Chrysolina* beetle controls Klamath weed, except in shady places where a root-boring beetle is more effective.

Sex attractants and sterile insects are used in other types of biological 5 control. In Sweden and Norway, scientists synthesized the sex pheromone of the *Ips* bark beetle, which attacks spruce trees. Almost 100,000 baited traps collected females normally attracted to males emitting this pheromone. Sterile males have also been used to reduce pest populations. The screwworm fly parasitizes cattle in the United States. Flies raised in a laboratory were made sterile by exposure to radiation. The entire Southeast was freed from this parasite when female flies mated with sterile males and then laid eggs that did not hatch.

In general, biological control is a more sophisticated method of controlling 6 pests than the use of pesticides. It requires an in-depth knowledge of pests and/or their life cycles. Because it does not have an immediate effect on the pest population, the effects of biological control may not be apparent to the farmer or gardener who eventually benefits from it.

Citizens can promote biological control of pests by: 7

- Urging elected officials to support legislation to protect humans and the environment against the use of pesticides.
- Allowing native plants to grow on all or most of the land to give natural predators a place to live.
- Cutting down on the use of pesticides, herbicides, and fertilizers for the lawn, garden, and house.
- Using alternative methods such as cleanliness and good sanitation to keep household pests under control.
- Disposing of pesticides in a safe manner.

(Sylvia S. Mader, *Human Biology*, 9/e, 2006)

Mapping

The following is a map (a type of graphic organizer) of "Pesticides: An Asset and a Liability." Making a map helps you learn material by forcing you to think about it and organize it. To make a map, you need to find the main ideas and the details that support them. In the process, you make clear to yourself the structure of the material. We previously discussed mapping as a study technique in Chapter 9.

A partial map is shown on page 550 with the main idea of the reading selection at the top. The supporting details branch off from the main idea. Complete the map with additional supporting details from the reading.

Growing Awareness that Pesticides Aren't a Good Idea

They Don't Work in the Long Run.
- Kills natural enemies and pests.
- Pests become resistant.
- Pest population explodes.

They Can Be Harmful.
- Cancer
- Birth defects
- Disorders of the nervous system
- Suppression of immune system
- Allergic response

An Alternative Exists Called I.P.M.
- Drawbacks
  - Requires knowledge of pests
  - Takes time to work
- Promotes diverse habitats
- Release of natural enemies
- Uses strip farming and crop rotation

What Citizens Can Do
- Encourage spread of native plants
- Dispose of pesticides in a safe way
- Cut down on use of pesticides
- Cleanliness and good sanitation help control household pests.
- Support legislation to limit pesticides

Organizing Text Comparisons and Contrasts

You will find below "A Fable for Tomorrow" by Rachel Carson. Read the essay, noting the comparisons and contrasts, and then complete the chart that follows.

READING

"There once was a town in the heart of America where all life seemed to live in harmony with its surroundings. . . . Then a strange blight crept over the area and everything began to change."

TUNING IN TO READING   In 1963, Rachel Carson published *Silent Spring,* a book devoted to protecting the natural environment from pesticides. Carson, who died of breast cancer one year after the book's publication, wrote, "The beauty of the living world I was trying to save has always been uppermost in my mind—that, and anger at the senseless, brutish things that were being done."

BIO-SKETCH   Rachel Carson (1907–1964) was a biologist and best-selling author. Many consider Carson to be one of our best nature writers because of her ability to translate scientific fact into lyrical prose. The publication of *Silent Spring* was meant to serve as a wake-up call to conserve natural resources and to protect both human health and the environment. While critics objected to the book, calling it exaggerated and emotional, Carson is credited with sowing the seeds of the environmental movement. Carson is also the author of *The Sea Around Us.* The following selection is from *Silent Spring.*

NOTES ON VOCABULARY

maladies   disorders or diseases of the body. In Latin, the word *malus* means "bad." The word *maladies* is derived from an Old French word meaning "sickness."

scores   a great many. The word is derived from the Old Norse *skor,* meaning "notch." *Score* can also more specifically refer to a quantity of 20.

brooded   sat on, hatched. The word is derived from the Old English *brod,* meaning "heat or warmth."

counterpart   one person or thing that closely resembles another. From the Old French *countrepartie. Counter* means "opposite to" and *partie* means "a copy of a person or thing."

specter   an object or source of terror or dread. From the Latin word *spectrum,* meaning "appearance, vision, apparition."

A Fable for Tomorrow

RACHEL CARSON

THERE WAS ONCE A TOWN IN THE HEART OF AMERICA where all life seemed to live in harmony with its surroundings. The town lay in the midst of a checkerboard of prosperous farms, with fields of grain and hillsides of orchards where, in spring, white clouds of bloom drifted above the green fields. In autumn, oak and maple and birch set up a blaze of color that flamed and flickered across a backdrop of pines. Then foxes barked in the hills and deer silently crossed the fields, half hidden in the mists of the fall mornings.

Along the roads, laurel, viburnum and alder, great ferns and wildflowers 2 delighted the traveler's eye through much of the year. Even in winter the roadsides were places of beauty, where countless birds came to feed on the berries and on the seed heads of the dried weeds rising above the snow. The countryside was, in fact, famous for the abundance and variety of its bird life, and when the flood of migrant birds was pouring through in spring and fall people traveled from great distances to observe them. Others came to fish the streams, which flowed clear and cold out of the hills and contained shady pools where trout lay. So it had been from the days many years ago when the first settlers raised their houses, sank their wells, and built their barns.

Then a strange blight crept over the area and everything began to change. 3 Some evil spell had settled on the community: mysterious maladies swept the flocks of chickens; the cattle and sheep sickened and died. Everywhere was a shadow of death. The farmers spoke of much illness among their families. In the town the doctors had become more and more puzzled by new kinds of sickness appearing among their patients. There had been several sudden and unexplained deaths, not only among adults but even among children, who would be stricken suddenly while at play and die within a few hours.

There was a strange stillness. The birds, for example—where had they 4 gone? Many people spoke of them, puzzled and disturbed. The feeding stations in the backyards were deserted. The few birds seen anywhere were moribund; they trembled violently and could not fly. It was a spring without voices. On the mornings that had once throbbed with the dawn chorus of robins, catbirds, doves, jays, wrens, and scores of other bird voices there was now no sound; only silence lay over the fields and woods and marsh.

On the farms the hens brooded, but no chicks hatched. The farmers 5 complained that they were unable to raise any pigs—the litters were small and the young survived only a few days. The apple trees were coming into bloom but no bees droned among the blossoms, so there was no pollination and there would be no fruit.

The roadsides, once so attractive, were now lined with browned and 6 withered vegetation as though swept by fire. These, too, were silent, deserted by all living things. Even the streams were now lifeless. Anglers no longer visited them, for all the fish had died.

In the gutters under the eaves and between the shingles of the roofs, a 7 white granular powder still showed a few patches; some weeks before it had fallen like snow upon the roofs and the lawns, the fields and streams.

No witchcraft, no enemy action had silenced the rebirth of new life in 8 this stricken world. The people had done it themselves.

This town does not actually exist, but it might easily have a thousand coun- 9 terparts in America or elsewhere in the world. I know of no community that has experienced all the misfortunes I describe. Yet every one of these disasters has actually happened somewhere, and many real communities have already suffered a substantial number of them. A grim specter has crept upon us almost unnoticed, and this imagined tragedy may easily become a stark reality.

(Rachel Carson, "A Fable for Tomorrow," 1962, 1990)

STUDY TECHNIQUE 13: COMPLETING A COMPARISON-CONTRAST CHART

One technique for organizing information pertaining to similarities and differences is to create a comparison-contrast chart. Some material, such as that in "A Fable for Tomorrow," lends itself nicely to this type of graphic organizer.

Following is a comparison-contrast chart to complete. It will help you identify the differences in the environment described by Rachel Carson "before the blight" and "after the blight." The first column (columns go up and down) lists the categories to be compared and contrasted. The second column is for the information before the blight, and the third column for the information after the blight. We have filled in the first two rows (rows go across) for you. Your assignment is to fill in the remaining rows by scanning the reading selection. After you complete the chart, read the material more carefully and then answer the Comprehension Checkup questions below.

Answers will vary.

Category	Before Blight	After Blight
Birds	Abundance and variety, especially with flood of migrant birds in spring and fall	Gone or moribund; no voices or sound—silence
Farms	Prosperous	Cattle and sheep died, no chicks hatched, unable to raise pigs
Wildlife	Foxes and deer	Probably little or no wildlife
Trees	Blaze of color with oak, maple, and birch trees in autumn	Apple trees bloomed, but no fruit because no pollination from bees
Fishing	Clear streams and shady pools with trout	All the fish dead
People and families	Life in harmony; tourists in spring and fall	Illness among families of farmers, sudden and unexplained deaths
Roadsides	Laurel, viburnum, alder, ferns, berries, wildflowers	Browned and withered vegetation

 COMPREHENSION CHECKUP

Multiple Choice

Directions: For each item, write the letter corresponding to the best answer on the line provided.

_____b_____ 1. The author has created a feeling that could best be described as
   a. loving.
   b. sorrowful.
   c. optimistic.
   d. admiring.

_____d_____ 2. The author's primary purpose in writing this article is to
   a. tell a story about a particular town in a farming community.
   b. inform readers of the difficulties of living in a small town.
   c. entertain readers with a personal story.
   d. persuade readers of a serious environmental problem.

_c_   3. The blight described in the article was probably the result of
   a. a fire.
   b. a nuclear explosion.
   c. chemical pesticides.
   d. the population explosion.

_a_   4. From this article you could conclude that the author is
   a. a conservationist.
   b. CEO of a large corporation.
   c. a research assistant.
   d. a politician.

_c_   5. What is the relationship between paragraphs 1 and 2, taken together, and paragraph 3?
   a. cause/effect
   b. classification/division
   c. compare/contrast
   d. definition/example

_c_   6. "Then a strange blight crept over the area and everything began to change" is an example of a
   a. simile.
   b. metaphor.
   c. personification.
   d. symbol.

_a_   7. What is the meaning of the word _moribund_ as used in paragraph 4?
   a. dying
   b. distressed
   c. confused
   d. frightened

_b_   8. Paragraph 7 contains a
   a. metaphor.
   b. simile.
   c. symbol.
   d. personification.

_b_   9. Paragraph 8 contains the following statement: "The people had done it themselves." This is a statement of
   a. fact.
   b. opinion.

_c_   10. In the context of paragraph 9, the word _stark_ means
   a. stiff or rigid.
   b. outlined or prominent.
   c. bleak or harsh.
   d. emptied or stripped.

True or False

Directions: Indicate whether each statement is true or false by writing **T** or **F** in the space provided.

_F_   11. All of the people in the town died within 10 years of the incident described.

_F_   12. The community described is urban.

_____F_____ 13. After the blight, there were still plenty of apples available.

_____T_____ 14. Before the blight, people came from long distances to view the birds.

_____F_____ 15. The story probably takes place in the West.

In Your Own Words

1. Many developing nations continue to apply DDT to control crop pests and to kill mosquitoes, which transmit malaria. Do you think the United Nations should try to end the use of DDT throughout the world?

2. Environmentalists refer to it as the "circle of poison." Although the United States banned the use of DDT, U.S. companies still manufacture and export the compound to developing nations. Thus, pesticide-laden food may find its way back into the United States. How do you feel about this?

3. Some scientists are working to increase crop yields by means of genetic engineering, which can make plants resistant to pest species and so reduce the need for insecticide spraying. Do you think such genetic engineering is a good idea? Can you think of any risks that could result from it?

4. List four words from the selection that show a positive bias and four words that show a negative bias.

5. Why does Carson call her selection "A Fable for Tomorrow"? In the fable what do the silent birds symbolize?

Written Assignment

Michael Pollan—a professor at the University of California at Berkeley, a best-selling author, and an avid gardener—decided to plant a potato called "NewLeaf" that has been genetically engineered to produce its own insecticide. The enemy of every potato is the potato beetle, a voracious insect. However, a potato beetle eating only a tiny part of the NewLeaf plant is doomed by the toxin the potato plant manufactures. Do you think genetically modified potatoes are a good idea? Should growers or sellers of the new potato be required to warn the consumer? Currently, under existing regulations, warnings or labels are not required. In fact, Pollan speculates that most of us have already consumed NewLeaf potatoes in either French fries or potato chips.

If everything in nature affects everything else, what are the possible consequences of genetically altered foods? How do you feel about eating genetically modified food?

Internet Activity

To find out more about Rachel Carson, visit the following Web site:

www.rachelcarson.org

For a more critical analysis, consult Rachel Carson in _Time_ 100:

www.time.com/time/time100/scientist/profile/carson03.html

The author presents a mixed review of Carson's legacy.

Organizations such as Greenpeace are opposed to modifying food genetically. To find out why, key in "genetic engineering" at the following Web site:

www.greenpeace.org

Visual Aids: How to Use and Interpret Tables, Diagrams, Charts, and Graphs

Visual aids are useful tools that help us understand written material. Visual aids can be as simple as a street map or as complex as a statistical table. Because textbook authors frequently use visual aids to explain complicated information, it is very important to look closely at all graphic illustrations and understand what they represent. Those of you who are strong in visual-spatial intelligence may find this section easier than those of you who have strengths in other areas. In this section, we will help you learn how to read and interpret the graphs and tables found in various books, magazines, and newspapers.

Here are some steps to follow when looking at a visual aid:

1. **Read the title and subtitle.** These will tell you what the table, chart, graph, or map is about.
2. **Read the key or legend.** These will explain how to interpret the visual aid.
3. **Determine the purpose of the visual aid.** Why did the author include it? Is it there to provide objective information? Or to support the author's bias?
4. **Determine the source of the information provided.** A table, chart, graph, or map published by a government agency may be more objective than one published by a special-interest group.
5. **Look at how the graph or chart is set up.** If there are horizontal or vertical scales, determine what they measure. If there is no scale, read the caption or look closely at the item to determine the scale. What is the unit of measurement? Thousands? Millions?
6. **Look for highs, lows, trends, and relationships.** What conclusions can you reach?

Exercise 6: Tables

Tables display information in rows (across) and columns (up and down). The table titled "The Twelve Most Contaminated Foods" ranks fruits and vegetables most commonly contaminated with pesticide.

THE TWELVE MOST CONTAMINATED FOODS AT THE GROCERY STORE

Rank	Food
1.	Apples
2.	Celery
3.	Strawberries
4.	Peaches
5.	Spinach
6.	Nectarines (imported)
7.	Grapes (imported)
8.	Sweet Bell Peppers
9.	Potatoes
10.	Blueberries (domestic)
11.	Lettuce
12.	Kale/collard greens

Source: Environmental Working Group, Washington, DC, 2010.

1. What is the most contaminated vegetable? <u>celery</u>
2. What is the most contaminated fruit? <u>apples</u>
3. What group assembled this data? <u>Environmental Working Group</u>
4. When was this data collected? <u>2010</u>
5. Why do you suppose celery has such a high pesticide residue?
   <u>It has no protective skin.</u>

Exercise 7: Diagrams

A **diagram** is a drawing or picture that is meant to illustrate how something works or how different processes or ideas relate to one another. It is a special type of graphic organizer. The diagram titled "Routes of Exposure to Toxic and Hazardous Environmental Factors" illustrates various routes by which dangerous substances may enter our bodies.

Routes of exposure to toxic and hazardous environmental factors.

William P. Cunningham, *Principles of Environmental Science*, 6th Edition, New York: McGraw-Hill, 2011, p. 193.

1. What two environmental toxins are shown under the category of air in the diagram? <u>industrial pollution</u> and <u>cigarettes</u>
2. What does dermal exposure refer to? <u>contact with the skin</u>
3. What does occupational exposure refer to? <u>exposure to toxins in the workplace</u>
4. What substances are depicted as possible incidental toxins? <u>cosmetics</u>

Exercise 8: Flow Chart

A **flow chart** is a type of graphic organizer often used in textbooks to show cause-and-effect relationships and a sequence of events. The action moves, or flows, in the direction of arrows or numbers, or sometimes just from left to right, or up to down. The flow chart below, which appears in an introductory environmental science textbook, illustrates how pests develop resistance to pesticides.

1 Pests attack crops

2 Pesticide is applied

3 Most pests are killed. A few with innate resistance survive.

4 Survivors breed and produce a pesticide-resistant population.

5 Pesticide is applied again

6 Pesticide has little effect. New, more toxic, pesticides are developed

Jay Withgott, *Environment,* 3rd Edition. San Francisco: Pearson, 2008, p. 269.

1. The flow chart demonstrates that effectiveness of pesticides tends to <u>decline</u> with time.

2. While initially many pests are killed by a particular pesticide, other pests survive because of <u>innate resistance</u>.

3. When a pesticide ceases to be effective, a more <u>toxic</u> replacement pesticide is developed.

Exercise 9: Pie Graph

Pie graphs are types of graphic organizers that show percentages or proportions as pie-shaped sections of a circle. The whole interior of the circle represents 100 percent, and each pie slice is a percentage of that whole. The pie graphs on the next page illustrate percentages of genetically modified crops by type and by nation. Many genetically modified crops are engineered to resist insects. Others are engineered to resist herbicides so that farmers may apply herbicides without harming the crops. Refer to the pie charts to answer the following questions. (Genetically modified crops is abbreviated to GM crops.)

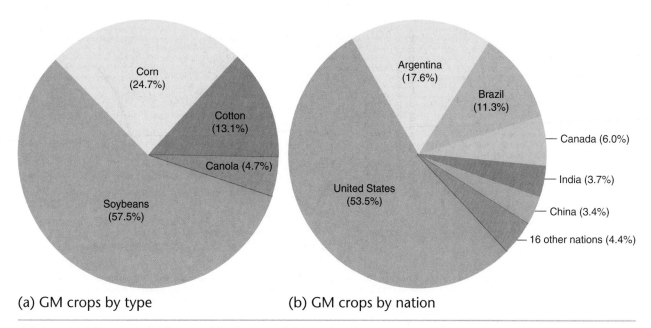

(a) GM crops by type   (b) GM crops by nation

Of the world's genetically modified crops **(a)**, soybeans constitute the majority so far. Of the world's nations **(b)**, the United States devotes the most land area to GM Crops.

International Service for the Acquisition of Agri-Biotech Applications (ISAAA), 2007.

1. What is the most common GM crop? soybeans _____ What is the percentage? 57.5% _____

2. Which country grows the most genetically modified crops? United States _____ What is the percentage? 53.5% _____

3. Which country has the next highest total of GM crops? Argentina _____ What is the percentage? 17.6% _____

4. What is the least common GM crop according to the graphs? canola _____

Exercise 10: Line Graph

A line graph is a way to summarize how two pieces of information are related and how they vary depending on one another. A typical line graph has two scales—a horizontal one (left to right) and a vertical one (top to bottom). Line graphs are commonly used to show changes over time. On the next page is just such a graph, relating changes in pesticide levels in food (vertical scale) to changes in time (horizontal scale). Refer to the graph to answer the following questions.

1. The horizontal scale measures time in years _____.

2. What was the percent of food samples with pesticide levels exceeding EPA tolerance levels in 1994? 0.05 _____

3. What was the percent for 2007? 0.40 _____

4. From 1994 to 2004, did the percent increase or decrease? increase _____

5. What was the approximate total increase in percent of food samples with pesticide levels exceeding EPA tolerance levels from 1996 to 2003? 0.15 _____

Percent of Food Samples with Pesticide Levels Exceeding EPA Tolerance Levels, 1994–2008

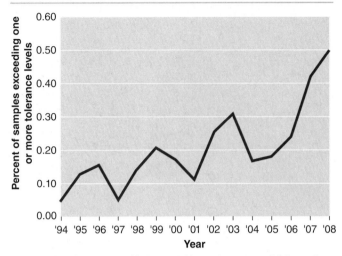

Coverage: Based on a survey of fruits, vegetables, grains, meat, and dairy products across the U.S., with different combinations of commodities sampled in different years. Samples were analyzed for more than 290 pesticides and their metabolites.

SOURCE: "Exhibit 4–22. Pesticides Exceeding EPA Tolerance Levels in Food in the U.S., 1994–2007," in *Pesticide Residues in Food*, U.S. Environmental Protection Agency, June 1, 2009, http://cfpub.epa.gov/eroe/index.cfm?fuseaction=detail.viewMidImg&lShowInd=0&subtop=312&lv=list.listByNewest&r=201566#10504 (accessed July 1, 2009).

Environmental Protection Agency, June 1, 2009.

Exercise 11: Bar Graph

Bar graphs use either vertical (top to bottom) or horizontal (left to right) bars to illustrate comparisons. In 2007, Gallup pollsters asked Americans about whether they had participated in certain environmentally friendly activities. The U.S. results were then compared with those obtained from China, Russia, Japan, and India. The bar graph below depicts the findings.

Public Participation in Environmentally Friendly Activities, by Country, 2007

Which of these, if any, have you done in the past year?
Percentage of respondents who say "yes, have done"

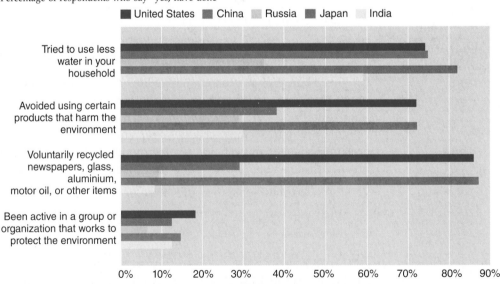

SOURCE: Magali Rheault, "Which of these, if any, have you done in the past year?" in *In Top Polluting Nations, Efforts to Live "Green" Vary*, The Gallup Organization, April 22, 2008, http://www.gallup.com/poll/106648/Top-Polluting-Nations-Efforts-Live-Green-Vary.aspx (accessed June 22, 2009). Copyright © 2008 by The Gallup Organization. Reproduced by permission of The Gallup Organization.

The Gallup Organization, April 22, 2008.

1. What percentage of Americans said they had been active in an environmental group or organization? _nearly 20%_

2. Which country had the largest percentage of respondents saying that they had tried to use less water in their households? _Japan_

3. Which country had the lowest percentage of respondents saying that they voluntarily recycled particular items? _India_

4. Which two countries had the highest percentage of respondents saying that they avoid products that harm the environment? _United States and Japan_

5. According to the poll data, which country of the five compared appears to have the highest overall concern for environmental issues? _United States_

Chapter Summary and Review

In Chapter 14, you practiced scanning material to locate specific pieces of information. You also practiced skimming a textbook selection to gain an overview of the main points. In addition, you learned how to interpret visual aids.

Based on the material in Chapter 14, answer the following.

Short Answer

Directions: List some examples of written materials you might scan and the information you would be looking for. The first one is done for you as an example.

Written Material	Information You Might Look For
1. *Frommer's Guide to California*	attractions in San Diego
2. _____	_____
3. _____	_____
4. _____	_____

Vocabulary in Context

Directions: Choose one of the following words to complete the sentences below. Use each word only once.

headings   horizontal   percent   scan   skimming   substitute   vertical

5. If you had a limited amount of time to answer five specific questions on a chapter in a U.S. history textbook, you could _____scan_____ through the chapter to find the answers.

6. When _____skimming_____ an article, you want to read the introduction and summary and the first and last sentence of each paragraph.

7. Noticing _____headings_____ and subheadings is a good idea when you are scanning.

8. Skimming is not a _____substitute_____ for careful reading.

9. A _____vertical_____ bar goes from top to bottom.

10. A _____horizontal_____ bar goes from side to side.

Vocabulary Word Parts

Following is a list of the word parts we have studied.

	Word Parts	Meaning	Examples
365	ad	toward	advance
257	ambi	both	ambiguous, ambidextrous
257	amphi	both	amphibian
325	ann, enn	year	annual, biennial
365	ante(i)	before	anteroom, anticipate
509	anti	against	antiperspirant
326	audio	hear	audience, auditory
439	auto	self	automobile, autograph
161	bi	two	bicycle, biathlon
328	biblio	book	Bible, bibliography
255	centi	hundred, 1/100	century, centimeter
366	circ	around, ring	circle, circumference
439	co, com, con	with	coordinate, compare, connect
439	contra	against	contradict, contrast
366	cycle	circle, wheel	bicycle
161	dec	ten	December, decade
256	demi	half	demitasse
161	di	two	dioxide
161	duo	two	duet, duel
257	equi	half	equator, equinox
440	extra	over, above	extraordinary, extraterrestrials
256	gam	marriage	polygamy
256	graph	write	polygraph
256	hemi	half	hemisphere
441	hetero	different	heterosexual, heterogeneous
441	homo	same	homogenized
510	hyper	over, above	hyperactive, hyperventilate
510	hypo	under, below	hypoactive, hypothermia
326	in	in, not	inside, invisible
440	infra	under	infrared, infrastructure
511	inter	between, among	intercollegiate, interstate
511	intra	within	intravenous, intrastate

	Word Parts	Meaning	Examples
161	lat	side	lateral
327	macro	large	macroeconomics
327	magna	large	magnify, magnificent
511	mania	craving	pyromania
327	mega	large, 1,000,000	megabucks, megabyte
327	micro	small, 1/1,000,000	microwave, micrometer
256	milli	thousand, 1/1000	millennium, millimeter
161	mono	one	monologue, monoxide
256	multi	many	multicultural
161	nov, non	nine	November, nonagenarian
161	oct	eight	October, octopus
326	ology	study of	sociology, psychology
257	omni	all	omnipotent, omnivorous
366	pan	around	panorama, Panasonic
511	para	beside, partial, similar	parallel, paralegal, paraphrase
161	ped, pod	foot	pedal, pedestrian
161	pent	five	Pentagon, pentathlon
366	peri	around	periscope, perimeter
511	phobia	fear	claustrophobia, acrophobia
327	phono	sound	phonograph, phonics
256	poly	many	polygon
328	post	after	postscript, postnatal
328	pre	before	pre-test, prenatal
509	pro	for	pro-democracy
512	pseudo	false	pseudoscience, pseudonym
161	quad, quar	four	quartet, quadrangle
161	quint	five	quintuplets, quintet
365	retro	backward	retroactive
327	scope	instrument for seeing	microscope, telescope
328	scrib, script	write	inscribe, scripture
256	semi	half	semicircle
161	sept, hept	seven	September, septuplet, heptathlon
161	sex, hex	six	sextuplet
326	spect	see	spectator, spectrum
364	sub	under, below	subtract, subscript
364	super	above, over	supersonic, superscript

	Word Parts	Meaning	Examples
509	syn	same	synonym, symphony
327	tele	distance	television
161	tetra	four	tetrahedron
440	trans	across	transportation
161	tri	three	tricycle, triangle
440	ultra	over, more, beyond	ultraconservative, ultrasonic
161	uni	one	unicycle, unison
326	vis	see	vision, visionary

Vocabulary Review Exercise

Directions: Complete the following sentences with words from the vocabulary list on the preceding pages.

1. Your telephone bill may list _____intrastate_____ calls that you have made to other cities within your state.

2. If you eat a salad with your hamburger, you are eating both meat and plants, and so you are _____omnivorous_____.

3. A jazz _____quintet_____ would have five members.

4. The _____equinox_____ occurs twice a year, once in March and once in September.

5. You now know that if you went to a nursery and bought some _____annual_____ flowers, they would not bloom again next year.

6. Most whole milk that you purchase at the store is called _____homogenized_____ because the milk and the cream are mixed together.

7. In Chapter 1, you learned about _____auditory_____, visual, and kinesthetic learning styles.

8. *Panorama* is a(n) _____synonym_____ for *vista*.

9. The chemical formula for water has a(n) _____subscript_____ in it.

10. People who believe in unidentified flying objects are likely also to believe that _____extraterrestrials_____ have visited us.

11. Many of us are _____ambidextrous_____ to some extent because we use both our hands.

12. The _____Pentagon_____ in Washington, DC, houses the Defense Department.

13. Present-day jazz music is recorded on compact discs. Jazz used to be recorded on 78 rpm _____phonograph_____ records that could hold only three minutes on a side.

Vocabulary Review Puzzle

Directions: Complete the puzzle on the following page with words from vocabulary Units 1–7.

Vocabulary Unit 8 Crossword Puzzle

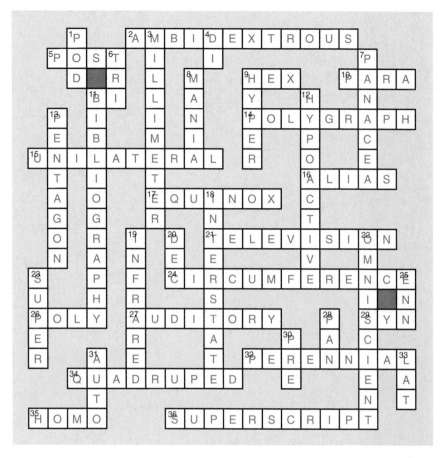

ACROSS CLUES

2. The ability to use both hands equally well.
5. A note written after the signature in a letter is a(n) _____script.
9. A word part meaning "six."
10. A(n) _____legal is a person trained to aid lawyers but not licensed to practice law.
11. A word part meaning "two."
14. A machine used on someone suspected of lying.
15. A one-sided decision.
16. A false name used by criminals to disguise their identity.
17. The time when day and night are of approximately equal length all over the earth.
21. "Seeing from a distance."
24. The measure of the distance around a circle.
26. A word part meaning "many."
27. Your listening skills; having to do with the sense of hearing.
29. A word part meaning "same; together."
32. A plant lasting more than two years.
34. An animal with four feet.
35. A word part meaning "same; equal; like."
36. A figure, letter, or symbol written above the line.

DOWN CLUES

1. Word part meaning "foot."
3. 1/1000 of a meter.
4. A word part meaning "two."
6. A word part meaning "three."
7. A cure-all; the act of going around the problem.
8. Pyro_____ is a compulsion to start fires.
9. The state of being overheated or too hot is _____thermia.
11. Literally means "books written down."
12. A child with an energy level below normal could be called _____.
13. A five-sided building containing the U.S. military establishment.
18. Between or among states.
19. Light that is below red on the color spectrum.
20. Abbreviation for what was originally the 10th month.
22. "All-knowing."
23. A word part meaning "above or over."
25. A word part meaning "year."
28. A word part meaning "all; every; around."
30. A word part meaning "before."
31. A(n) _____maton acts unthinkingly or automatically, like a robot.
33. A word part meaning "side."

Appendices

We have chosen to include "Timed Reading Information," "Using the Dictionary," and "Test-Taking Techniques" in the Appendices. For these three sections, we include an explanation of the topic, as well as practice exercises. At the end of the Appendices, you will find summaries and sample copies of some of the forms that appear in the text.

Timed Reading Rate Information, Questions, and Answers

The average adult reading rate on material of moderate difficulty is about 250 words per minute with 70 percent comprehension. For each of its six parts, this book has an opener reading that features a music-related topic. All these readings are from college textbooks, and all are of about the same level of difficulty. Each reading has approximately the same number of words:

Part 1 Opener reading: Louis Armstrong (258 words)

Part 2 Opener reading: Johnny Cash (248 words)

Part 3 Opener reading: Elvis Presley (245 words)

Part 4 Opener reading: Carlos Santana (246 words)

Part 5 Opener reading: American Idol (252 words)

Part 6 Opener reading: Esperanza Spalding (248 words)

To practice increasing your reading speed, you may wish to time yourself on each of the opener readings. Or you could do this in groups or as a whole class. Stop reading after one minute has elapsed. Questions for each opener reading appear below. Try to get three to four questions correct for each reading.

For the first opener reading, read at your normal reading pace and then answer the questions without looking back at the material.

For the readings of Parts 2–6, experiment with the following techniques to see if any of them help you.

- Read the material as rapidly as you can.
- Try not to reread any material.
- Keep your mind focused on the subject matter. Don't give in to distractions.
- Try to read silently without moving your lips.
- Don't read word by word, but instead try to read in phrases or thought units.
- Use your pen or pencil as a pacer by sweeping it underneath the words.

Questions for Part 1 Opener Reading: Louis Armstrong

Directions: Without looking back at the selection, indicate whether each statement is true or false by writing **T** or **F** on the line provided.

_____ 1. Louis Armstrong learned to play the bugle and the cornet at the Colored Waifs' Home.

_____ 2. Armstrong is famous for his recordings of "Hello Dolly" and "What a Wonderful World."

_____ 3. Armstrong was born in San Francisco and grew up in California.

_____ 4. Armstrong gained a reputation as the "Johnny Appleseed" of jazz.

_____ 5. Armstrong's pistol-shooting incident occurred during a Mardi Gras celebration.

Questions for Part 2 Opener Reading: Johnny Cash

Directions: Without looking back at the selection, indicate whether each statement is true or false by writing **T** or **F** on the line provided.

_____ 1. Johnny Cash once recorded a humorous song titled "A Boy Named John."

_____ 2. At one time, Cash became addicted to prescription drugs.

_____ 3. Cash was known as "the man in blue" because of the striking color of his eyes.

_____ 4. Cash was inducted into both the Country Music Hall of Fame and the Rock and Roll Hall of Fame.

_____ 5. Cash had a reputation as a dark loner who came from humble beginnings.

Questions for Part 3 Opener Reading: Elvis Presley

Directions: Without looking back at the selection, indicate whether each statement is true or false by writing **T** or **F** on the line provided.

_____ 1. Elvis Presley was discovered by Sam Phillips.

_____ 2. Presley was discovered when he went to a sound studio to record a few songs for his wife's birthday.

_____ 3. Presley's distinctive sound was called "country-western."

_____ 4. After serving in the military, Presley went to Hollywood.

_____ 5. Presley had a number of hits throughout the fifties.

Questions for Part 4 Opener Reading: Carlos Santana

Directions: Without looking back at the selection, indicate whether each statement is true or false by writing **T** or **F** on the line provided.

_____ 1. As a young boy, Carlos Santana played and sang on the streets in Tijuana, Mexico.

_____ 2. The album _Supernatural_ was recorded when Santana was in his fifties.

_____ 3. Santana was extremely skilled on the drums.

_____ 4. Santana's band performed at the Woodstock rock festival.

_____ 5. Santana never performs with artists from other fields.

Questions for Part 5 Opener Reading: American Idol

Directions: Without looking back at the selection, indicate whether each statement is true or false by writing **T** or **F** on the line provided.

_____ 1. *American Idol* can rightly be called reality television.

_____ 2. The British judge Simon Cowell was considered to be harsh on some contestants.

_____ 3. Clay Aiken and Aretha Franklin are two successful past winners of *American Idol*.

_____ 4. Kelly Clarkson was the very first *American Idol* winner.

_____ 5. Carrie Underwood, a past *American Idol* winner, has gone on to success in country music.

Questions for Part 6 Opener Reading: Esperanza Spalding

Directions: Without looking back at the selection, indicate whether each statement is true or false by writing **T** or **F** on the line provided.

_____ 1. Esperanza Spalding is a classically trained musician.

_____ 2. Spalding won the 2011 Grammy Award for song of the year.

_____ 3. Despite her youth, Spalding has taught music at the college level.

_____ 4. Spalding is noted for her ability at the piano keyboard.

_____ 5. Spalding has performed at the White House.

Answers to the Questions for the Part Opener Readings

Louis Armstrong	Johnny Cash	Elvis Presley
1. T	1. F	1. T
2. T	2. T	2. F
3. F	3. F	3. F
4. T	4. T	4. T
5. F	5. T	5. T

Carlos Santana	American Idol	Esperanza Spalding
1. T	1. T	1. T
2. T	2. T	2. F
3. F	3. F	3. T
4. T	4. T	4. F
5. F	5. T	5. T

Using the Dictionary

Introduction

It is essential that you have access to a good college dictionary, whether it is printed or online. A dictionary is an invaluable tool, provided you have one that suits your purposes and you know the basics of how to use it.

Many students use online dictionaries, which often have an audio feature that lets you hear a word's correct pronunciation. Following are some good online dictionaries.

http://www.merriam-webster.com

www.onelook.com

www.yourdictionary.com

www.encarta.com

The exercises in the next section are designed to give you practice mastering the fundamentals of dictionaries, both print and online.

Organization

The discussion and examples below will often refer to the sample dictionary page found on page A-6. We have taken an excerpt from the *Random House Webster's College Dictionary*, 2nd ed., 2001, enlarged the print, and adapted the pages for your use.

1. Entry words
Dictionaries are organized like telephone books, in alphabetical order. Each entry word is usually in **boldface** type. Often dictionaries will also give common two- or three-word phrases as entry words.

What boldface entry comes after "sawbones"? _sawbuck_____

2. Guide words
As in a telephone book, there are guide words at the top of each page that indicate the first and last entries on that page.

What are the guide words for this page? _savvy to sayyid_____

3. Entry word division versus pronunciation—syllabication division
For each entry, the word division and the pronunciation and syllabication division are usually the same.

How many syllables are there in the word "saxophone"? _3_____

savvy to sayyid

sav•vy (sav′ē), *n., adj.,* **-vi•er, -vi•est,** *.v.,* **-vied, -vy•ing.** —*n.* **1.** Also, **sav′vi•ness.** practical understanding; shrewdness or intelligence; common sense: *political savvy.* —*adj.* **2.** shrewdly informed; experienced and well-informed; canny. —*v.t., v.i.* **3.** to know; understand. [1775–85; prob. orig. < *sábi* "know" in E creoles (< Pg *sabe,* pres. 3rd sing. of *saber* to know < L *sapere* to be wise; see SAPIENT)] —**sav′vi•ly,** *adv.*

saw[1] (sô), *n., v.,* **sawed, sawed** or **sawn, saw•ing.** —*n.* **1.** a tool or device for cutting, typically a thin blade of metal with a series of sharp teeth. **2.** any similar tool or device, as a rotating disk, in which a sharp continuous edge replaces the teeth. —*v.t.* **3.** to cut or divide with a saw. **4.** to form by cutting with a saw. **5.** to make cutting motions as if using a saw: *to saw the air with one's hands.* **6.** to work (something) from side to side like a saw. —*v.i.* **7.** to use a saw. **8.** to cut with or as if with a saw. —*Idiom.* **9. saw wood,** to snore loudly while sleeping. [bef. 1000; ME *sawe,* OE *saga,* c. MLG, MD *sage* (D *zaag*), OHG *saga,* ON *sog;*] —**saw′er,** *n.*

circular saw   hacksaw   butcher's saw

handsaw   lumberman's saw

saws (def. 1)

saw[2] (sô), *v.* pt. of SEE[1].

saw[3] (sô), *n.* a maxim; proverb; saying; *an old saw.* [bef. 950; ME; OE *sagu;* c. OFris *sege,* OHG, G *sage,* ON *saga* (cf. SAGA); akin to SAY]

Sa•watch (sə′wäch′), *n.* a mountain range in central Colorado: part of the Rocky Mountains. Highest peak, Mt. Elbert, 14,431 ft. (4400 m).

saw•bones (sô′bōnz′), *n., pl.* **-bones, -bones•es.** (*used with a sing. v.*) *Slang.* a surgeon or physician. [1830–40]

saw•buck (sô′buk′), *n.* **1.** a sawhorse. **2.** *Slang.* a ten-dollar bill. [1860–65, *Amer.;* cf. D *zaagbok;* (def. 2) so called from the resemblance of the Roman numeral X to the crossbars of a sawhorse]

saw•dust (sô′dust′), *n.* fine particles of wood produced in sawing.

sawed′-off′, *adj.* **1.** cut off at the end, as a shotgun. **2.** *Slang.* smallish; of less than average size or stature. [1865–70, *Amer.*]

saw•fish (sô′fish′), *n., pl.* (*esp. collectively*) **-fish,** (*esp. for kinds or species*) **-fish•es.** any large, sharklike ray of the genus *Pristis,* living along tropical coasts and lowland rivers, with a bladelike snout edged with strong teeth. [1655–65]

saw•fly (sô′flī′), *n., pl.* **-flies.** any of numerous insects of the family Tenthredinidae, the female of which has a sawlike ovipositor for inserting the eggs in the tissues of a host plant. [1765–75]

saw•horse (sô′hôrs′), *n.* a movable frame or trestle for supporting wood while it is being sawed. [1770–80]

saw•mill (sô′mil′), *n.* a place or building in which timber is sawed into planks, boards, etc., by machinery. [1545–55]

sawn (sôn), *v.* a pp. of SAW[1].

saw-off (sô′ôf′, -of′), *n. Canadian.* **1.** an arrangement between political rivals by which each agrees not to run for the same office as another. **2.** any arrangement that involves concessions. [1905–10]

saw′palmet′to, *n.* a shrublike palmetto, *Serenoa repens,* native to the southern U.S., having green or blue leafstalks set with spiny teeth.

saw•tooth (sô′tooth′), *n., pl.* **-teeth** (-tēth′), *adj.* —*n.* **1.** one of the cutting teeth of a saw. —*adj.* **2.** having a zigzag profile, like that of the cutting edge of a saw; serrate. [1595–1605]

saw′-toothed′, *adj.* having sawlike teeth; serrate. [1580–90]

saw′-whet′owl′, *n.* a small North American owl, *Aegolius acadicus,* with a persistently repeated, mechanical sounding note. [1825–35, *Amer.;* from its cry being likened to a saw being whetted]

saw•yer (sô′yr, soi′ər), *n.* **1.** a person who saws wood, esp. as an occupation. **2.** any of several long-horned beetles, esp. one of the genus *Monochamus,* the larvae of which bore in the wood of coniferous trees. [1300–50; ME *sawier = sawe* saw[1] + *-ier* -IER[1]]

sax (saks), *n.* a saxophone. [by shortening]

Sax., **1.** Saxon. **2.** Saxony.

sax•a•tile (sak′sə til), *adj.* living or growing on or among rocks; saxicoline. [1645–55; < L *saxātilis* frequenting rocks, der. of *sax*(um) rock]

Saxe (SAKS), *n.* French name of SAXONY.

Saxe-Co•burg-Go•tha (saks′kō′bûrg gō′thə), *n.* **1.** a member of the present British royal family, from the establishment of the house in 1901 until 1917 when the family name was changed to Windsor. **2. Albert Francis Charles Augustus Emanuel, Prince of,** ALBERT, Prince.

sax•horn (saks′hôrn′), *n.* any of a family of brass instruments close to the cornets and tubas. [1835–45; after A. *Sax* (1814–94), a Belgian who invented such instruments]

sax•ic•o•line (sak sik′ə lin, -līn′) also **sax•ic•o•lous** (-ləs), *adj.* living or growing among rocks. [1895–1900; < NL *saxicol*(a) (L *saxi-,* comb. form of *saxum* rock + *-cola* dweller; see -COLOUS) + -INE[1]]

sax•i•frage (sak′sə frij), *n.* any of numerous plants of the genus *Saxifraga,* certain species of which grow wild in the clefts of rocks, other species of which are cultivated for their flowers. [1400–50; late ME < L *saxifraga* (*herba*) stone-breaking (herb) = *saxi-,* comb. form of *saxum* stone + *-fraga,* fem. of *-fragus* breaking; see FRAGILE]

sax•i•tox•in (sak′si tok′sin), *n.* a neurotoxin produced by the dinoflagellate *Gonyaulax catenella,* the causative agent of red tide. [1960–65; < NL *Saxi*(domus), a clam genus infected by the dinoflagellates (L *sax*(um) stone + *-i- -i-* + *domus* house) + TOXIN]

Sax•o Gram•mat•i•cus (sak′sō grəmat′i kəs), *n.* c1150–1206?, Danish historian and poet.

Sax•on (sak′sən), *n.* **1.** a member of a Germanic people or confederation of peoples, occupying parts of the North Sea littoral and adjacent hinterlands in the 3rd–4th centuries A.D.: later notorious as sea raiders, groups of whom invaded and settled in S Britain in the 5th–6th centuries. **2.** a native or inhabitant of Saxony. **3.** a native of England, or person of English descent, esp. as opposed to an inhabitant of the British Isles of Celtic descent. —*adj.* **4.** of or pertaining to the early Saxons. **5.** of or pertaining to Saxony or its inhabitants. [1250–1300; ME, prob. < LL *Saxō, Saxonēs* (pl.) < Gmc; r. OE *Seaxan* (pl.)]

sax•o•ny (sak′sə nē), *n.* **1.** a fine, three-ply woolen yarn. **2.** a soft-finish, compact fabric for coats. [1825–35; from SAXONY]

Sax•o•ny (sak′sə nē), *n.* **1.** a state in E central Germany, 4,900,000; 6561 sq. mi. (16,990 sq. km). *Cap.:* Dresden. **2.** a former state of the Weimar Republic in E central Germany. 5788 sq. mi. (14,990 sq. km). *Cap.:* Dresden. **3.** a medieval division of N Germany with varying boundaries: extended at its height from the Rhine to E of the Elbe. German, **Sachsen;** French, **Saxe.** —**Sax•o′ni•an** (-sō′nēən), *n., adj.*

Sax′ony-An′halt, *n.* a state in central Germany. 3,000,000; 9515 sq. mi. (24,644 sq. km). *Cap.:* Magdeburg. German, **Sachsen-Anhalt.**

sax•o•phone (sak′sə fōn′), *n.* a musical wind instrument consisting of a conical, usu. brass tube with keys or valves and a mouthpiece with one reed. [1850–55; *Sax* (see SAXHORN) + -o- + -PHONE]—**sax′o•phon′ic** (-fon′ik), *adj.* —**sax′o•phon′ist,** *n.*

saxophone

say (sā), *v.,* **said, say•ing,** *adv., n., interj.* —*v.t.* **1.** to utter or pronounce; speak: *to say a word.* **2.** to express in words; state; declare: *Say what you think.* **3.** to state as an opinion or judgment: *I say we should wait here.* **4.** to recite or repeat. **5.** to report or allege; maintain. **6.** to express (a message, viewpoint, etc.), as through a literary or other artistic medium. **7.** to indicate or show: *What does your watch say?* —*v.i.* **8.** to speak; declare; express an opinion, idea, etc. —*adv.* **9.** approximately; about: *It's, say, 14 feet long.* **10.** for example. —*n.* **11.** what a person says or has to say. **12.** the right or opportunity to state an opinion or exercise influence: *to have one's say in a decision.* **13.** a turn to say something. —*interj.* **14.** (used to express surprise, get attention, etc.) —*Idiom.* **15. go without saying,** to be completely self-evident. [bef. 900; ME *seyen, seggen,* OE *secgan;* c. D *zeggen,* G *sagen,* ON *segja;* akin to SAW[3]] —**say′er,** *n.*

say•a•ble (sā′ə bəl), *adj.* **1.** of the sort that can be said or spoken. **2.** capable of being said or stated clearly, effectively, etc. [1855–60]

Sa•yan′Moun′tains (sä yän′), *n.pl.* a mountain range in the S Russian Federation in central Asia. Highest peak, 11,447 ft. (3490 m).

Say•ers (sā′ərz, sârz), *n.* **Dorothy L(eigh),** 1893–1957, English detective-story writer, dramatist, essayist, and translator.

say•est (sā′ist) also **sayst** (sāst), *v. Archaic.* 2nd pers. sing. of SAY.

say•ing (sā′ing), *n.* something said, esp. a proverb or maxim.

sa•yo•na•ra (sī′ə när′ə), *interj., n.* farewell. [1870–75; < Japn]

says (sez), *v.* 3rd pers. sing. pres. indic. of SAY.

say′-so′, *n., pl.* **say-sos. 1.** one's personal statement or assertion. **2.** right of final authority. **3.** an authoritative statement. [1630–40]

say•yid or **say•ed** or **say•id** (sä′yid, sā′id), *n.* **1.** a supposed descendant of Muhammad through his grandson Hussein. **2.** an Islamic title of respect, esp. for royal personages. [1780–90; < Ar: lord]

You should realize that some dictionaries divide their entry words as you would for printers and typesetting, so the entry word and pronunciation divisions may not be exactly the same. Take a look at the word "curious." Notice that the entry word is divided differently than its pronunciation.

cu•ri•ous (kyo͞or′ē əs), *adj.*   **1.** eager to learn or know. **2.** taking an undue interest in others' affairs; prying. **3.** arousing attention or interest through being unusual or hard to explain; odd; strange; novel. **4.** *Archaic.* **a.** made or done skillfully or painstakingly. **b.** careful; fastidious. **c.** marked by intricacy or subtlety. [1275–1325; ME < L *cūriōsus* careful, inquisitive, prob. back formation from *incūriōsus* careless, der. of *incūria* carelessness]—**cu′ri•ous•ly,** *adv.* —**cu′ri•ous•ness,** *n.*

(*Random House Webster's College Dictionary,* 2/e, 2000)

4. Pronunciation

Notice how most entries are followed by their pronunciations but the words are written quite differently. Dictionaries will use letters and symbols that represent sounds. Usually you will find a complete key to these sounds in the front part of the dictionary. On page A-8 is the Random House pronunciation key. Sometimes variant pronunciations will also be given. For example, the word "sawyer" has two pronunciations (see page A-6).

What words show how "oi" is pronounced? <u>oil, joint, joy</u>

Write out the pronunciations for the following words:

sayable <u>sā′ ə bəl</u>

sawyer (both pronunciations) <u>sô′ yr, soi′ ər</u>

sawtooth <u>sô′ tooth′</u>

5. Parts of speech

Each word will also have its part or parts of speech listed: "n." is for a noun, "v." is for a verb, and so forth. Note that "v.t." is for a transitive verb and "v.i." is for an intransitive verb. A transitive verb takes a direct object while an intransitive does not.

Find the parts of speech for the words below. Write out the whole word, such as "adjective" for "adj."

Saxe <u>noun</u>

sayable <u>adjective</u>

sayyid <u>noun</u>

6. Etymology

We have been studying word etymologies, or word histories, in the vocabulary units throughout this book. We will not list all the abbreviations used for different languages, but "L" is the abbreviation for Latin and "Gk" stands for Greek.

Find out the Latin meaning for

savvy <u>Latin sapere (to be wise)</u>

saxicoline <u>Latin saxi, comb. form of saxum (rock) and cola (dweller)</u>

Many words in English come from other languages. From what language does the word "sayonara" come? <u>Japanese</u>

ENGLISH SOUNDS

a	act, bat, marry	**l**	low, mellow, bottle (bot'l)	**th**	that, either, smooth
ā	age, paid, say	**m**	my, summer, him	**u**	up, sun
âr	air, Mary, dare	**n**	now, sinner, button (but'n)	**ûr**	urge, burn, cur
ä	ah, balm, star	**ng**	sing, Washington	**v**	voice, river, live
b	back, cabin, cab	**o**	ox, bomb, wasp	**w**	witch, away
ch	child, pitcher, beach	**ō**	over, boat, no	**y**	yes, onion
d	do, madder, bed	**ô**	order, ball, raw	**z**	zoo, lazy, those
e	edge, set, merry	**oi**	oil, joint, joy	**zh**	treasure, mirage
ē	equal, bee, pretty	**o͝o**	oomph, book, tour	**ə**	used in unaccented
ēr	earring, cheerful, appear	**o͞o**	ooze, fool, too		syllables to indicate the sound of the re-
f	fit, differ, puff	**ou**	out, loud, cow		duced vowel in alone,
g	give, trigger, beg	**p**	pot, supper, stop		system, easily,
h	hit, behave	**r**	read, hurry, near		gallop, circus
hw	which, nowhere	**s**	see, passing, miss	**ᵊ**	used between i and r
i	if, big, mirror	**sh**	shoe, fashion, push		and between ou and r
ī	ice, bite, deny	**t**	ten, matter, bit		to show triphthongal
j	just, tragic, fudge	**th**	thin, ether, path		quality, as in fire (iᵊr),
k	keep, token, make				hour (ouᵊr)

NON-ENGLISH SOUNDS

A	as in French **ami** (A mē′)	**R**	[a symbol for any non-English r sound,		pronounced with voice]
KH	as in Scottish **loch** (lôKH)		including a trill or flap in Italian and Spanish	**Y**	as in French **tu** (tY)
N	as in French **bon** (bôN) [used to indicate that the preceding vowel is nasalized]		and a sound in French and German similar to KH but	**ᵊ**	as in French **bastogne** (ba stôn′yᵊ)
Œ	as in French **feu** (fŒ)				

7. Words in phrases

Some dictionaries, such as the *Random House Webster's College Dictionary*, give some words in sample phrases. Take a look at the definitions for "say" and see how this word is used in sample phrases.

What are some of the phrases used for this word? <u>"to say a word," "say what you think," "What does your watch say?" "It's, say, 14 feet long." "to have one's say in a decision"</u>

8. Geographical and biographical information

Most dictionaries place this information in with the regular entries. Other dictionaries, such as the Merriam Webster dictionaries, give this information at the end of the dictionary.

Where is Saxony and what is its capital city? <u>a state in east central Germany; Dresden</u>

Exercise 1: Dictionary Usage

Directions: Use the dictionary page provided to answer the following questions.

1. How many syllables does each of the following entry words have?

   sawyer <u>2</u>

   saxicoline <u>4</u>

   sayable <u>3</u>

2. Write the part(s) of speech for each of the following entry words:

   saw <u>noun and verb</u>

   Saxon <u>noun and adjective</u>

3. Write the plural forms for the following words:

   sawbones <u>sawbones, sawboneses</u>

   sawfly <u>sawflies</u>

   sayso <u>saysos</u>

   sawtooth <u>sawteeth</u>

4. Find an entry word that is an example of each of the following:

   a place <u>Sawatch, sawmill, Saxony, Saxony-Anhalt, Sayan Mountains</u>

   a person <u>sawbones, sawyer, Sax, Saxe-Coburg-Gotha, Saxo Grammaticus,</u>
   <u>Saxon, sayyid</u>

   an animal <u>sawfish, sawfly, sawwhet owl</u>

5. Name two entries that have pictures as aids to understand their meanings.

   <u>saw</u>

   <u>saxophone</u>

6. How many meanings are given for each of the following entry words?

   saw^1 <u>8, 9 with idiom</u>

   sawyer <u>2</u>

   Saxon <u>5</u>

7. What suffixes are used to change "savvy" to different parts of speech?
   <u>vier, viest, vied, vying, savviness, savvily</u>

8. What is the origin of the word "saxatile"? <u>from Latin saxatilis frequenting</u>
   <u>rocks from sax(um) rock</u>

9. Pronounce the following words. Then write each word using correct spelling.

   sak si tok sin <u>saxitoxin</u>

   sā ing <u>saying</u>

   sez <u>says</u>

   saks <u>sax</u>

Directions: Indicate whether the following statements are true or false by writing **T** or **F** in the space provided.

_T_ 10. **Sawbones** is slang for a surgeon or physician.

_F_ 11. To **saw wood** means to sing loudly.

_F_ 12. A **savvy** person is dull-witted.

_T_ 13. The British royal family no longer uses the name **Saxe-Coburg-Gotha.**

Exercise 2: Abbreviations

Directions: Most dictionaries use many abbreviations. Using any available dictionary, write what the following abbreviations and symbols mean.

1. ME _Middle English_
2. pl. _plural_
3. n. _noun; nominal_
4. v.t. _transitive verb_
5. v.i. _intransitive verb_
6. adj. _adjective, adjectival_
7. adv. _adverb, adverbial_
8. prep. _preposition_
9. conj. _conjunction_
10. pron. _pronoun, pronounced_
11. fem. _feminine_
12. masc. _masculine_
13. OE _Old English_
14. < _descended from; borrowed from_
15. E. _English_
16. etym. _etymology, etymological_
17. Fr. _French_
18. Ger. _German_
19. It. _Italian_
20. L _Latin_

21. Gk. _Greek_
22. sing. _singular_
23. obs. _obsolete_
24. orig. _origin, originally_
25. poss. _possessive_
26. pres. _present, present tense_
27. Russ _Russian_
28. Sp. _Spanish_
29. Syn. _synonym_
30. Heb. _Hebrew_

Test-Taking Techniques

How to Improve Your Performance

The Multiple-Choice Test

As a college student, you are going to have to take many multiple-choice and true/false tests and quizzes. While nothing substitutes for thoroughly knowing the material and preparing well, the following are some basic test-taking tips that you should be familiar with:

1. Read directions carefully.
2. Pay attention to oral instructions.
3. Look through the entire test, and plan your time accordingly.
4. Do not dwell on any question too long. If you can't answer the question, move on and come back to the question if you have time at the end.
5. If in doubt between two answers, go with your first gut-level reaction. Don't change an answer unless you are positive you are making the correct choice. You may be changing a right answer to a wrong answer. Your time can probably be better spent elsewhere on the test.
6. Even if you think you have more knowledge about the material than the author of the material or you think the author is wrong, go with what the author says, not what you think.
7. Read through all the answers before picking one.
8. If one of your choices is a combination of two or more answers (such as "A and B"), remember that all parts of the answer must be correct. (A must be a correct answer and B must also be a correct answer.)
9. When in doubt, and one answer includes language from the question, go with that answer. Also look for clues in the question that may help give away the answer.
10. Look at long answers first, especially if one answer is much longer than the others. A longer answer is more likely to be correct than a shorter answer. Why? It usually takes more words to write a correct answer because it needs to be phrased carefully. Also, right answers may need qualifying phrases to make them correct. Wrong answers are wrong anyway, so it doesn't matter how they are written.
11. When the question asks you to pick a missing word, use grammar clues such as *a* and *an*. An *a* goes with words beginning with consonants, and an *an* goes with words beginning with vowels.
12. Eliminate answers with all-inclusive words such as *all, everyone, none, always,* and *nobody.* Answers that include such words are quite likely wrong. Usually, the only time answers with such words are correct is when that is exactly what the author said. If there is one exception, the answer will be wrong.

13. When a question asks for the main idea of the selection or the best possible title, make sure your answer is broad enough to cover all parts of the selection.

14. Sometimes the last answer will be "All of the above." If you are fairly sure that two of the three answers are correct but are unsure about the third answer, go with "All of the above."

15. Two questions on the test may be similar. Use the correct answer for one question to help you find the correct answer for the other.

16. Allow at least a minute or two to check over your answer sheet. Is your name on it? Do you need to date it? Have you skipped any questions?

17. If you are putting your answers on a Scantron, make sure that you have completely erased any earlier answers. Scantrons will pick up incomplete erasures.

The True-or-False Test

Of course, you have a 50 percent chance of getting a true-or-false statement correct. However, you can increase your odds of getting the right answer if you realize that if any part of the statement is false, the entire statement must be false. Double-check the numbers, facts, and dates in true-or-false statements. Sometimes this information may be altered slightly, making the statement false.

Be careful when statements contain absolutes such as *all*, *always*, *everyone*, *never*, and *no one*. Statements are more likely to be false if they contain such words. For example, consider the following statement: "It is always a bad idea to change your answer to a question." The statement is false.

On the other hand, statements that include qualifiers such as *sometimes*, *perhaps*, and *maybe* are more likely to be true. For example, consider this statement: "It is sometimes a bad idea to change your answer to a question." This time the statement is true.

Unfortunately, none of these rules leads you to the correct answer all of the time.

The Matching Test

Read through all the choices before you actually begin matching. Then do the matches that you are absolutely sure of first. Put a check mark by the items that you have used rather than crossing them out completely. If new information occurs to you, you might have to go back and reassess your original answers. A completely crossed-out answer might be difficult to read.

The Short-Answer Test

The emphasis here is on expressing yourself briefly and concisely. Try jotting down a brief outline so that you can organize your answer before you begin writing. Remember to cover the main points.

The Essay Test

Before the Test

There is no substitute for simply knowing all of the course material well. But that can be a big task, and realistically, some parts of the material are probably more important, and more likely to appear on an essay test, than other parts.

One way to give your preparation some focus is to try to think of questions that might appear on the test. Because your teacher will likely be the one who writes the test, ask yourself what questions you think your teacher might ask. Review your class notes and any handouts to determine what the teacher emphasized in the course. What topics did the teacher spend the most time on? What topics did the teacher seem to care the most about?

Keep in mind that an essay question may ask for information on a specific topic or it may be directed at a general understanding of the course material. You need to prepare yourself for both kinds of questions.

General or "big picture" essay questions often deal with relationships among topics or concepts. A good way to prepare for these questions is to make an outline or map of the course material. Look at your class notes, any handouts, and your textbook, and organize this material into an outline. If your teacher has closely followed a textbook, the book's table of contents should give you a good start on making your outline.

Once you have come up with a list of possible questions, use some of your study time preparing answers to these questions. You may even want to practice writing out answers.

During the Test

Carefully read the question; you can't expect to write a good answer to a question you don't understand. In fact, you might write a wonderful essay, but if it doesn't answer the question, it will not do you much good. What is the question asking you to do? Does the question use any of the keywords discussed on pages A-15–A-16? If so, think about what that keyword means.

Once you understand the question, begin thinking about how best to answer it. It's probably not a good idea to start writing immediately. Give yourself some time to think first. What material from the course will the answer involve? What do you remember about this material? At this point, you might want to start jotting some notes. If you prepared well for the test, the more you think about this material, the more of it you will remember.

Organizing Your Answer

Once you have recalled the material you need in order to answer the questions, you need to begin thinking about how to organize your answer. Knowing the information goes a long way toward writing a good essay, but how you organize the information also counts. This is especially true for a "big picture" essay question. Your organization will show the teacher how well you understand what is important and what the relationships are among ideas and concepts.

A traditional essay has an introduction, a conclusion, and three paragraphs of development. This does not mean that a good essay cannot have more or less than three paragraphs of development, but ordinarily an essay that is three paragraphs long will say what needs to be said without saying too much. Usually the three paragraphs of the traditional essay are developed in the same order in which their main ideas are mentioned in the introductory statement.

Here is an example of an introductory statement:

> An increase in state financial aid for public education will raise student scores on standardized tests because (1) teacher salaries can be increased, which will attract more-talented people into teaching; (2) more teachers can be hired, which will reduce class size; and (3) school districts will have more money available for learning resources and activities.

So, the first paragraph of this essay would discuss the need for more-talented teachers and why the hiring of more-talented teachers should lead to an increase in the test scores. The second paragraph would discuss the need for smaller classes and how smaller classes should lead to increased scores. The third paragraph would discuss the need for more learning resources and activities and how improved resources and activities should boost test scores.

Often the secret to writing a good essay is constructing a good introductory statement, because once you have a good introductory statement, the rest of the essay follows from it. This is one reason it makes sense to do some thinking and organizing before you start to write.

To write a good introductory statement, it sometimes helps to take the question and rearrange it into an introductory statement. For example, assume that the question says the following:

> Discuss whether an increase in state financial aid for public education will raise student scores on standardized tests.

Then you might use the following introductory statement:

> An increase in state financial aid for public education will/will not raise student scores on standardized tests because . . .

Some Practical Pointers

1. Research shows that neatness counts, so write carefully and legibly. Try to avoid messy erasures, crossed-out words, and words written between lines and in the margins. You might want to consider using pens with erasable ink.
2. When a question has more than one part, make sure you answer all parts.
3. Remember that each paragraph should develop only one main idea.
4. Give specific examples to illustrate your points.
5. Answer in complete sentences.
6. Check to see if what you have written answers the questions *who, what, where, when, why,* and *how.*
7. Save some time to proofread your essay for spelling and other errors that are likely to produce a bad impression.
8. If you find you have no time to answer questions at the end of the test, write some notes in summary form. These will often earn you at least partial credit.
9. Make use of your returned test papers. You can learn a lot by reading the instructor's comments and correcting the answers.

Keywords That Often Appear in Essay Questions

Following is a list of keywords that often appear in essay questions. If you are going to write a good answer to an essay question that uses one of these terms, you need to know what the term means.

analyze	to break down the subject into parts and discuss each part. You will want to discuss how the parts relate to each other.
comment on	to discuss or explain.
compare	to show differences and similarities, but with the emphasis on similarities.
contrast	to show differences and similarities, but with the emphasis on differences.
criticize	The narrow meaning of *criticize* is to examine something for its weaknesses, limitations, or failings. Does the theory, article, or opinion make sense? If not, why not? In a more general sense, *criticize* means to find both strengths and weaknesses. In this sense, the meaning of *criticize* is similar to that of *evaluate*.
define	to state the meaning of a term, theory, or concept. You will want to place the subject in a category and explain what makes it different from other subjects in the category.
describe	to explain what something is or how it appears. What you need to do is draw a picture with words.
diagram	to make a chart, drawing, or graph. You also will want to label the categories or elements, and maybe give a brief explanation.
discuss	to fully go over something. You will want to cover the main points, give different perspectives, and relate strengths and weaknesses.
enumerate	to make a list of main ideas by numbering them.
evaluate	to examine for strengths and weaknesses. You will need to give specific evidence and may wish to cite authorities to support your position.
explain	to make clear; to give reasons. An explanation often involves showing cause-and-effect relationships or steps.
illustrate	to use a diagram, chart, figure, or specific examples to further explain something.
interpret	to indicate what something means. A question that asks for an *interpretation* usually wants you to state what something means to you. What are your beliefs or feelings about the meaning of the material? Be sure to back up your position with specific examples and details.
justify	to give reasons in support of a conclusion, theory, or opinion.
list	to put down your points one by one. You may want to number each of the points in your list.
outline	to organize information into an outline, using headings and sub-headings. Your outline should reflect the main ideas and supporting details.

prove	to demonstrate that something is true by means of factual evidence or logical reasoning.
relate	to discuss how two or more conclusions, theories, or opinions affect each other. Explain how one causes, limits, or develops the other.
review	usually, to summarize. A narrower meaning is to analyze critically.
summarize	to put down the main points; to state briefly the key principles, facts, or ideas while avoiding details and personal comments.
trace	to follow the course of development of something in a chronological or logical sequence. You will want to discuss each stage of development from the beginning to the end.

Exercise: Essay Exam Skills

Read the explanations below. In the blank, write a term that the instructor might use when posing the question to the students in the class.

1. In class, the instructor has discussed the contributions of Auguste Comte, Herbert Spencer, and Max Weber to the field of sociology. On the essay exam, he wants the students to briefly go over the contribution of each of these persons while avoiding their own personal comments. What term will he use for this question?

   summarize

2. In a child development class, the instructor has discussed the development of language from birth to 36 months. She now wants the students to present the process of language acquisition in chronological sequence. What term should she use?

   trace

3. In an art history class, the instructor wants the students to show the difference between engraving, drypoint, and etching. Which term will she use in the question?

   contrast

4. In an American history class, the professor has discussed the Manhattan Project, which developed the atomic bomb during World War II. He now wants the students to examine the project for its weaknesses. What term will he use in the question?

   criticize

5. In a biology class, the professor has explained the term "cloning." On a quiz, she wants to make sure her students understand the meaning of the concept. What term will she use in her question?

   define

6. In an economics class, the professor wants the students to graph the 2000–2001 recession, showing the rise and fall of the unemployment rate and consumer spending. What term should she use on her exam?

   diagram

7. In a geography class, the teacher wants the students to make clear how pollution caused harm to the Costa Rican rain forest. What term will he use?

   explain

8. In a psychology class, the instructor wants the students to describe the ways in which long-term memory and short-term memory are alike and the ways in which they are different. What term will she use?

   compare (contrast)

9. In a reading class, the teacher wants the students to write down the steps of SQ3R one by one, numbering each. What term will she use in her question?

   list

Sample Summaries

Who: high school and college students

What: are spending too little time studying and too much time working

Where: in the United States

When: the author compares attitudes in the '50s to attitudes in the late '80s

Why: students work to buy luxury items parents won't pay for

How: because of increased acceptance on the part of parents and teachers

Overall Main Idea

Student employment is a major cause of the decline in American education.

Other Main Ideas

1. Today student employment is widely accepted as normal for teens, but in the past going to school was a student's "job." (implied)
2. Working students have little time for homework. (directly stated)
3. Students work to buy luxury items and then feel they need to go out and have fun. (implied)
4. Thus, by the time they get to college, most students look upon studies as a spare-time activity. (directly stated)
5. The problem doesn't just affect the individual student, but the quality of education as a whole. (implied)

Student Summary

Walter S. Minot in his article "Students Who Push Burgers" feels that U.S. education has declined because students hold part-time jobs. Minot compares the educational system of the 1950s to that of the 1980s. In the past, kids only worked to help out their families financially. Today's students work to buy luxury items, fooling their parents into thinking that they are learning the value of a dollar. Because these students work so hard at their jobs, they feel they deserve to have a good time after work, and they don't have enough time or energy to do their homework. As a result, schools are finding it difficult to get quality work from their students, and have had to reduce their standards. Minot feels this problem doesn't just affect individual students or schools, but the quality of education as a whole.

Student Sample: Summary of "The Chaser" (page 402)

Alan Austen is in love with a young woman named Diana, who is indifferent to him. Someone recommends the shop of an old man who deals in extraordinary potions. Alan has been told that the old man can provide him with a potion that will make Diana fall in love with him. The old man shows very little interest in the love potion, and instead describes an undetectable poison that he calls a "glove" or "life cleaner." The cost of this potion is exactly $5,000. Alan wants nothing to do with it, and worries that all of the potions will be that expensive. He is overjoyed to learn that the old man really does carry love potions and the cost is only $1.00. The old man describes in detail the effects the love potion will have on Diana, but Alan is undeterred and happily purchases it. The old man bids him good-bye and indicates that he will be seeing Alan again.

ASSIGNMENTS

MONDAY

TUESDAY

WEDNESDAY

THURSDAY

FRIDAY

OTHER ASSIGNMENTS, TESTS, ETC.

MONTH _____						
SUNDAY	MONDAY	TUESDAY	WEDNESDAY	THURSDAY	FRIDAY	SATURDAY

ASSIGNMENT SHEET

SUBJECT(S) _____

Date	Assignments	Due	Finished

STUDY SCHEDULES

	MONDAY	TUESDAY	WEDNESDAY	THURSDAY	FRIDAY	SATURDAY	SUNDAY
6:00–7:00 am							
7:00–8:00 am							
8:00–9:00 am							
9:00–10:00 am							
10:00–11:00 am							
11:00–12:00 pm							
12:00–1:00 pm							
1:00–2:00 pm							
2:00–3:00 pm							
3:00–4:00 pm							
4:00–5:00 pm							
5:00–6:00 pm							
6:00–7:00 pm							
7:00–8:00 pm							
8:00–9:00 pm							
9:00–10:00 pm							
10:00–11:00 pm							
11:00–12:00 am							
12:00–1:00 am							

Credits

Text/Line Credits

Part 1: p. 1, From David Lee Joyner, *American Popular Music* 3rd edition, pp. 81–84. © 2009. Copyright © 2009 by The McGraw-Hill Companies, Inc. Reprinted with permission.

Introduction: pp. 5–6, From R. Feldman, *Power Learning* 4th Ed., pp. 12, 14. Copyright © 2009 McGraw-Hill Companies, Inc. Reprinted with permission; **pp. 9–12,** From Byron Pitts, *Step Out on Nothing*, 2009, pp. 37–47. St. Martin's Press. Used by permission; **pp. 15–16,** From Pablo Neruda, "Oda al presente," from the work *Nuevas odas Elementales* © Fundación Pablo Neruda, 2011. English translation ("Ode to the Present") from *Neruda's Garden: An Anthology of Odes*, transl. Maria Jacketti. Pittsburgh, PA: The Latin American Review Press, 1995, p. 105. Reprinted by permission of Agencia Literaria Carmen Balcells, and by permission of the publisher, Latin American Literary Review Press.

Chapter 1: pp. 24–25, From Kory Floyd, "Naming Defines and Differentiates Us" in *Interpersonal Communication: The Whole Story* 1st edition, pp. 175–177. Copyright © 2009 by The McGraw-Hill Companies, Inc. Reprinted with permission; **pp. 32–33,** From David G. Myers, *Social Psychology*, 8th Edition, p. 59. Copyright © 2005 by The McGraw-Hill Companies, Inc. Reprinted with permission; **pp. 33–34,** From Gary Funk and Jan Bradley, *Thrills, Spills, and Study Skills*. Dubuque, IA: Kendall/Hunt, 1992, pp. 65–66; **pp. 35–37,** "The Two Most Dangerous Hours of Your Day" by Lowell Ponte, *Reader's Digest*, March 1992. Reprinted with permission from Reader's Digest. Copyright © 1992 by The Reader's Digest Association, Inc.; **pp. 44–45,** From Isaac Asimov, "What Is Intelligence, Anyway?" Copyright © by Isaac Asimov. Reprinted by permission of the Estate of Isaac Asimov; **pp. 48–49,** Adapted from Thomas H. Holmes & Richard H. Rahe, "Social Readjustment Rating Scale," *Journal of Psychosomatic Research* 11(2) August 1967 p. 214. Copyright 1967, with permission from Elsevier, http://www.elsevier.com; **p. 49,** From Dennis Coon, *Introduction to Psychology (with InfoTrac)*, 8th Edition, p 465. © 1998 Wadsworth, a part of Cengage Learning, Inc. Reproduced by permission. www.cengage.com/permissions; **pp. 50–52,** "Strive to be the Best You Can Be" from *First Things First* by Kurt and Brenda Warner. Copyright © 2009 by Kurt and Brenda Warner. Used by permission of Tyndale House Publishers, Inc. All rights reserved; **pp. 60–65,** From Fred T. Hofstetter, *Internet Literacy*, 4th Edition, pp. 84–91. Copyright © 2006 by The McGraw-Hill Companies, Inc. Reprinted with permission; **p. 61,** Copyright © 1991 Computer Ethics Institute. Author: Dr. Ramon C. Barquin, 1707 L. Street, NW, Suite 1030, Washington, DC 20036, Ramon C. Barquin, President, Computer Ethics Institute. Used with permission; **p. 69,** From Timothy J. O'Leary and Linda I. O'Leary, *Computing Essentials 2008*, Complete Edition, 19th Edition, p. 35. Copyright © 2008 by The McGraw-Hill Companies, Inc. Reprinted with permission.

Part 2: p. 77, From David Lee Joyner, *American Popular Music* 3rd edition, pp. 81–84. © 2009. Copyright © 2009 by The McGraw-Hill Companies, Inc. Reprinted with permission.

Chapter 2: p. 79, From Ronald B. Adler, Russell F. Proctor II, and Neil Towne, *Looking Out, Looking In (with CD-ROM and InfoTrac)*, 11th Edition, p. 229. © 2005 Wadsworth, a part of Cengage Learning, Inc. Reproduced by permission. www.cengage.com/permissions; **p. 80,** From Michael Hughes and Carolyn J. Kroehler, *Sociology: The Core*, 7th Edition, p. 79. Copyright © 2005 by The McGraw-Hill Companies, Inc. Reprinted with permission; **p. 82,** From Joseph R. Dominick, *The Dynamics of Mass Communication*, 8th Edition, p. 379. Copyright © 2005 by The McGraw-Hill Companies, Inc. Reprinted with permission; **pp. 82–83,** From Diane E. Papalia, Sally Wendkos Olds, and Ruth Duskin Feldman, *Human Development*, 10th Edition, pp. 482–83. Copyright © 2007 by The McGraw-Hill Companies, Inc. Reprinted with permission; **p. 83,** From Estelle Levetin and Karen McMahon, *Plants and Society*, 5th Edition, p. 6. Copyright © 2008 by The McGraw-Hill Companies, Inc. Reprinted with permission; **pp. 83–84,** From Stephen E. Lucas, *The Art of Public Speaking*, 9th Edition, p. 25. Copyright © 2007 by The McGraw-Hill Companies, Inc. Reprinted with permission; **p. 84,** From Ronald B. Adler, Russell F. Proctor II, and Neil Towne, *Looking Out, Looking In (with CD-ROM and InfoTrac)*, 11th Edition, p. 229. © 2005 Wadsworth, a part of Cengage Learning, Inc. Reproduced by permission. www.cengage.com/permissions; **p. 84,** From Kitty O. Locker and Donna S. Kienzler, *Business and Administrative Communication*, 8th Edition, p. 443. Copyright © 2008 by The McGraw-Hill Companies, Inc. Reprinted with permission; **pp. 84–85,** From Bethami A. Dobkin and Roger C. Pace, *Communication in a Changing World*, 2006 Edition, p. 169. Copyright © 2006 by The McGraw-Hill Companies, Inc. Reprinted with permission; **p. 85,** From Bethami A. Dobkin and Roger C. Pace, *Communication in a Changing World*, 2006 Edition, p. 171. Copyright © 2006 by The McGraw-Hill Companies, Inc. Reprinted with permission; **p. 85,** From Bethami A. Dobkin and Roger C. Pace, *Communication in a Changing World*, 2006 Edition, p. 164. Copyright © 2006 by The McGraw-Hill Companies, Inc. Reprinted with permission; **pp. 85–86,** From Terry Kwal Gamble and Michael Gamble, *Communication Works*, 9th Edition, p. 137. Copyright © 2008 by The McGraw-Hill Companies, Inc. Reprinted with

Brunvand. Used by permission of W. W. Norton & Company, Inc.; **p. 112,** From *The Vanishing Hitchhiker: American Urban Legends and Their Meanings* by Jan Harold Brunvand, p. 126. Copyright © 1981 by Jan Harold Brunvand. Used by permission of W. W. Norton & Company, Inc.; **pp. 112–113,** Adapted from Brunvand, "The Baby on the Roof" from *The Choking Doberman*. From *The Choking Doberman and Other "New" Urban Legends* by Jan Harold Brunvand, pp. 93–94. Copyright © 1984 by Jan Harold Brunvand. Used by permission of W. W. Norton & Company, Inc.; **p. 113,** From *The Choking Doberman and Other "New" Urban Legends* by Jan Harold Brunvand, pp. 93–94. Copyright © 1984 by Jan Harold Brunvand. Used by permission of W. W. Norton & Company, Inc; **p. 113,** From Joseph R. Dominick, *The Dynamics of Mass Communication*, 6th Edition. New York: McGraw-Hill, 1999, p. 324. Copyright © 1999 The McGraw-Hill Companies, Inc. Reprinted with permission; **pp. 114–115,** From Curtis O. Byer, et al., *Dimensions of Human Sexuality*, 6th Edition, pp. 27–28. Copyright © 2002 by The McGraw-Hill Companies, Inc. Reprinted with permission; **p. 115,** From "How Wide Is Your Communication Gender Gap?" by Hazel Rozema, Associate Professor, Communication Department, University of Illinois at Springfield, and John Gray, Emeritus Professor, University of Arkansas at Little Rock. Reprinted with permission of Hazel Rozema, Ph.D.; **pp. 117–118,** Dave Barry, "Neither Man Nor Rat Can Properly Fold Laundry," *The Miami Herald*, July 2, 2000. Copyright © 2000 by Dave Barry. Reprinted with permission; **pp. 121–123,** From Dennis Coon, *Psychology*, 10e, pp. 652–54. © 2006 Wadsworth, a part of Cengage Learning, Inc. Reproduced by permission. www.cengage.com/permissions

Chapter 3: **p. 129,** From Joseph R. Dominick, *The Dynamics of Mass Communication*, 8th Edition, p. 309. Copyright © 2005 by The McGraw-Hill Companies, Inc. Reprinted with permission; **p. 130,** From Jerrold S. Greenberg, *Comprehensive Stress Management*, 8th Edition, pp. 275–76. Copyright © 2004 by The McGraw-Hill Companies, Inc. Reprinted with permission; **p. 131,** From Richard T. Schaefer, *Sociology*, 10th Edition, p. 306. Copyright © 2007 by The McGraw-Hill Companies, Inc. Reprinted with permission; **pp. 132–133,** From Wayne A. Payne, Dale B. Hahn, and Ellen B. Lucas, *Understanding Your Health*, 10th Edition, p. 242. Copyright © 2009 by The McGraw-Hill Companies, Inc. Reprinted with permission; **p. 133,** From Stephen E. Lucas, *The Art of Public Speaking*, 9th Edition, pp. 389, 458. Copyright © 2007 by The McGraw-Hill Companies, Inc. Reprinted with permission; **pp. 134–136,** William Saroyan, "The Shepherd's Daughter," from *The Daring Young Man on the Flying Trapeze*. © 1934 by William Saroyan. Reprinted by permission of the Trustees of Leland Stanford Junior University; **pp. 139–141,** "From a Melted Candy Bar to Microwaves" [pp. 57–60] from *They All Laughed…* by Ira Flatow. Copyright © 1992 by Ira Flatow. Reprinted by permission of HarperCollins Publishers; **pp. 144–145,** "Students Who Push Burgers," by Walter S. Minot as appeared in *The Christian Science Monitor*, November 22, 1988. © 1988 by Walter S. Minot. Reprinted by permis-

sion of the author; **p. 147,** From Myra Sadker and David Sadker, *Teachers, Schools, and Society*, 8th Edition, p. 204. Copyright © 2008 by The McGraw-Hill Companies, Inc. Reprinted with permission; **p. 149,** From Estelle Levetin and Karen McMahon, "Alluring Scents," *Plants and Society*, 5th Edition, p. 84. Copyright © 2008 by The McGraw-Hill Companies, Inc. Reprinted with permission; **p. 149,** From Nancy E. Willard, "Get a Life," *The Cyber Ethics Reader*, p. 65. Copyright © 1997 by The McGraw-Hill Companies, Inc. Reprinted with permission; **pp. 149–150,** From Hamilton Gregory, "Incompetent Criminals," *Public Speaking for College and Career*, 7th Edition, p. 427. Copyright © 2005 by The McGraw-Hill Companies, Inc. Reprinted with permission; **p. 150,** From Diane E. Papalia, Sally Wendkos Olds, and Ruth Duskin Feldman, "Dropping Out of High School," *Human Development*, 10th Edition, p. 429. Copyright © 2007 by The McGraw-Hill Companies, Inc. Reprinted with permission; **pp. 151–154,** "A Letter to Olivia" by Mel Allen. Copyright © 2000 *Bowdoin Magazine*. Reprinted by permission; **p. 159,** From Freda Adler, Gerhard O. W. Mueller, and William S. Laufer, *Criminal Justice*, 5th Edition, p. 192. Copyright © 2009 by The McGraw-Hill Companies, Inc. Reprinted with permission.

Chapter 4: **pp. 173–174,** From Brent Q. Hafen, Keith J. Karren, Kathryn J. Frandsen, N. Lee Smith, *Mind/Body Health: The Effects of Attitudes, Emotions, and Relationships*, 1st Edition, © 1996, 172. Reprinted by permission of Pearson Education, Inc., Upper Saddle River, New Jersey; **p. 176,** Adapted from *Contemporary's Building Basic Skills in Reading, Book I*, pp. 93–94. Copyright © 1988 by The McGraw-Hill Companies, Inc. Reprinted with permission; **pp. 176–177,** From Brent Q. Hafen, Keith J. Karren, Kathryn J. Frandsen, N. Lee Smith, *Mind/Body Health: The Effects of Attitudes, Emotions, and Relationships*, 1st Edition, © 1996, pp. 174–175. Reprinted by permission of Pearson Education, Inc., Upper Saddle River, New Jersey; **pp. 178–179,** From Brent Q. Hafen, Keith J. Karren, Kathryn J. Frandsen, N. Lee Smith, *Mind/Body Health: The Effects of Attitudes, Emotions, and Relationships*, 1st Edition, © 1996, p. 171. Reprinted by permission of Pearson Education, Inc., Upper Saddle River, New Jersey; **p. 181,** From Brent Q. Hafen, Keith J. Karren, Kathryn J. Frandsen, N. Lee Smith, *Mind/Body Health: The Effects of Attitudes, Emotions, and Relationships*, 1st Edition, © 1996, pp. 174, 170–171. Reprinted by permission of Pearson Education, Inc., Upper Saddle River, New Jersey; **p. 181,** Adapted from Robert S. Feldman, *Essentials of Understanding Psychology*, 6th Edition, pp. 141–42. Copyright © 2005 by The McGraw-Hill Companies, Inc. Reprinted with permission; **p. 182,** Richard Armour, "Money" from *Light Armour: Playful Poems on Practically Everything*. New York: McGraw-Hill, 1954. Reprinted by permission of Geoffrey Armour; **p. 182,** From Robert S. Feldman, *Understanding Psychology*, 8th Edition, pp. 612, 614. Copyright © 2008 by The McGraw-Hill Companies, Inc. Reprinted with permission; **p. 183,** From David G. Myers, *Social Psychology*, 9th Edition, pp. 355–56. Copyright © 2008 by The McGraw-Hill Companies, Inc. Reprinted with permission; **p. 184,** From Brent Q. Hafen, Keith J. Karren,

Kathryn J. Frandsen, N. Lee Smith, *Mind/Body Health: The Effects of Attitudes, Emotions, and Relationships*, 1st Edition, © 1996, pp. 169–170. Reprinted by permission of Pearson Education, Inc., Upper Saddle River, New Jersey; **p. 185,** From Diane E. Papalia and Sally Wendkos Olds, *Human Development*, 9th Edition, pp. 528–30. Copyright © 2004 by The McGraw-Hill Companies, Inc. Reprinted with permission; **p. 186,** From Mark Getlein, *Gilbert's Living with Art*, 6th Edition, p. 11. Copyright © 2002 by The McGraw-Hill Companies, Inc. Reprinted with permission; **p. 187,** From Robert H. Bohm and Keith N. Haley, *Introduction to Criminal Justice* 6e, NY: McGraw-Hill, 2010, pp. 29–30. Copyright © 2010 by The McGraw-Hill Companies, Inc. Reprinted with permission; **p. 189,** From Shel Silverstein, *Where the Sidewalk Ends.* Copyright © 1974, renewed 2002 Evil Eye Music, LLC. Reprinted with permission from the Estate of Shel Silverstein and HarperCollins Children's Books; **p. 193 #1,** From Wayne A. Payne and Dale B. Hahn, *Understanding Your Health*, 6th Edition, p. 36. Copyright © 2000 by The McGraw-Hill Companies, Inc. Reprinted with permission; **p. 193 #2,** From Wayne A. Payne and Dale B. Hahn, *Understanding Your Health*, 6th Edition, pp. 230–31. Copyright © 2000 by The McGraw-Hill Companies, Inc. Reprinted with permission; **pp. 193–194,** From Robert S. Feldman, *Understanding Psychology*, 8th Edition, p. 500. Copyright © 2008 by The McGraw-Hill Companies, Inc. Reprinted with permission; **p. 194,** From Joseph R. Dominick, *The Dynamics of Mass Communication*, 8th Edition, pp. 294–95. Copyright © 2005 by The McGraw-Hill Companies, Inc. Reprinted with permission; **p. 194,** From John W. Santrock, *Psychology*, 7th Edition, pp. 650–51. Copyright © 2003 by The McGraw-Hill Companies, Inc. Reprinted with permission; **pp. 194–195,** From Wayne A. Payne and Dale B. Hahn, *Understanding Your Health*, 6th Edition, p. 139. Copyright © 2000 by The McGraw-Hill Companies, Inc. Reprinted with permission; **p. 195,** From Stephen E. Lucas, *The Art of Public Speaking*, 8th Edition, p. 440. Copyright © 2004 by The McGraw-Hill Companies, Inc. Reprinted with permission; **p. 195,** From Diane E. Papalia, Sally Wendkos Olds, and Ruth Duskin Feldman, *Human Development*, 10th Edition, pp. 142–43. Copyright © 2007 by The McGraw-Hill Companies, Inc. Reprinted with permission; **pp. 195–196 #2,** From Hamilton Gregory, *Public Speaking for College and Career*, 7th Edition, pp. 75–76. Copyright © 2005 by The McGraw-Hill Companies, Inc. Reprinted with permission; **p. 196 #3,** From Hamilton Gregory, *Public Speaking for College and Career*, 7th Edition, p. 32. Copyright © 2005 by The McGraw-Hill Companies, Inc. Reprinted with permission; **p. 196,** From David G. Myers, *Social Psychology*, 9th Edition, p. 324. Copyright © 2008 by The McGraw-Hill Companies, Inc. Reprinted with permission; **pp. 196–197,** Adapted from James M. Henslin, *Essentials of Sociology: A Down-to-Earth Approach*, 7th Edition, p. 320. © 2007. Reprinted by permission of Pearson Education, Inc., Upper Saddle River, New Jersey; **pp. 203–205,** From Freda Adler, Gerhard O. W. Mueller, and William S. Laufer, "Road Rage," *Criminal Justice*, 5th Edition, pp. 184–85. Copyright © 2009 by The McGraw-Hill Companies, Inc. Reprinted with permission; **p. 209 A,** From David G. Myers, *Social Psychology*, 7th Edition, p. 184. Copyright © 2002 by The McGraw-Hill Companies, Inc. Reprinted with permission; **p. 209 B,** From David G. Myers, *Social Psychology*, 9th Edition, p. 349. Copyright © 2008 by The McGraw-Hill Companies, Inc. Reprinted with permission; **p. 210 C,** From David G. Myers, *Social Psychology*, 9th Edition, p. 349. Copyright © 2008 by The McGraw-Hill Companies, Inc. Reprinted with permission; **p. 210 D,** From David G. Myers, *Social Psychology*, 9th Edition, p. 349. Copyright © 2008 by The McGraw-Hill Companies, Inc. Reprinted with permission; **p. 210,** From Robert S. Feldman, *Understanding Psychology*, 8th Edition, p. 614. Copyright © 2008 by The McGraw-Hill Companies, Inc. Reprinted with permission.

Part 3: p. 213, From David Lee Joyner, *American Popular Music* 3rd edition, pp. 81–84. © 2009. Copyright © 2009 by The McGraw-Hill Companies, Inc. Reprinted with permission.

Chapter 5: p. 215, From Lydia Huntley Sigourney, "Indian Names" (1834), in Donald Hall, ed., *The Oxford Book of Children's Verse in America.* New York: Oxford University Press, 1985, p. 24; **p. 216,** From John Langan, *Ten Steps to Improving Reading Skills*, 4e. Marlton, NJ: Townsend Press, 2003, p. 301; **p. 222,** Adapted from James M. Henslin, *Essentials of Sociology: A Down-to-Earth Approach*, 7th Edition, p. 3. © 2007. Reprinted by permission of Pearson Education, Inc., Upper Saddle River, New Jersey; **pp. 223–224,** "Flight," from *The Long Valley* by John Steinbeck, pp. 62, 63–64, 67, 69, copyright 1938, renewed © 1966 by John Steinbeck. Used by permission of Viking Penguin, a division of Penguin Group (USA) Inc. and Penguin Books Ltd; **p. 225,** From Maya Angelou, "Complaining," in *Wouldn't Take Nothing for My Journey Now* by Maya Angelou. © 1993 by Maya Angelou. Used by permission of Random House, Inc. and Virago, an imprint of Little, Brown Book Group. For on-line information about other Random House , Inc. books and authors, see the Internet web site at http://www.randomhouse.com; **pp. 228–231,** From Fannie Flagg, *Daisy Fay and the Miracle Man.* Reprinted by permission of The Wendy Weil Agency, Inc. First published by William Morrow & Co. as *Coming Attractions*; reissued by Warner Books and Ballantine Books as *Daisy Fay and the Miracle Man.* © 1981, 2005 by Fannie Flagg; **pp. 232–236,** From Geoffrey Cowley, "Too Much of a Good Thing." From *Newsweek*, March 28, 1994. © 1994 The Newsweek/Daily Beast Company LLC. All rights reserved. Used by permission and protected by the Copyright Laws of the United States. The printing, copying, redistribution, or retransmission of the Material without express written permission is prohibited. http://www.thedailybeast.com/newsweek.html; **pp. 237–238,** From Paul Insel & Walton Roth, "El Dia de los Muertos: the Day of the Dead," from *Core Concepts in Health* 9e NY: McGraw-Hill, 2002, p. 579. Copyright © 2002 by The McGraw-Hill Companies, Inc. Reprinted with permission; **pp. 242–244,** From Divine, Robert A.; Breen, T. H. H.; Fredrickson, George M.; Williams, R. Hal; Gross, Ariela J.; and Brands, H. W.; *America Past and Present, Single Volume Edition*, 7th Edition, pp. 800–801. Copyright © 2006. Reprinted by permission of Pearson Education, Inc., Upper Saddle River, New Jersey.

Chapter 6: p. 270, From "The Very Pulse of the Machine" from *The Beauty of the Beastly* by Natalie Angier, p. 53. Copyright © 1995 by Natalie Angier. Reprinted by permission of Houghton Mifflin Harcourt Publishing Company. All rights reserved; **p. 271,** From "Chaperoning Proteins" from *The Beauty of the Beastly* by Natalie Angier, p. 70. Copyright © 1995 by Natalie Angier. Reprinted by permission of Houghton Mifflin Harcourt Publishing Company. All rights reserved; **p. 271,** From "A Clue to Longevity" from *The Beauty of the Beastly* by Natalie Angier, p. 72. Copyright © 1995 by Natalie Angier. Reprinted by permission of Houghton Mifflin Harcourt Publishing Company. All rights reserved; **pp. 271–272,** From Natalie Angier, "Selfless, Helpful and Intelligent: The Wasp." From *The New York Times*, August 17, 1999. © 1999 The New York Times. All rights reserved. Used by permission and protected by the Copyright Laws of the United States. The printing, copying, redistribution, or retransmission of the Material without express written permission is prohibited. www.nytimes.com; **pp. 272–274,** "The Love of My Life," letter from Robert L. Rodgers to Ann Landers From *The Best of Ann Landers.* New York: Bantam Books, 1996, pp. 269–70; **pp. 278–280,** From Rita Gilbert, *Living with Art*, 5th Edition, pp. 56–58. Copyright © 1998 by The McGraw-Hill Companies, Inc. Reprinted with permission; **pp. 282–283,** "The Yellow Ribbon" Pete Hamill. Reprinted by permission of International Creative Management, Inc. Copyright © 1972 by Pete Hamill; **p. 289,** From *The Worst Hard Time: The Untold Story of Those Who Survived the Great American Dust Bowl* by Timothy Egan. Copyright © 2005 by Timothy Egan. Reprinted by permission of Houghton Mifflin Harcourt Publishing Company. All rights reserved; **pp. 290–292,** From Gordon Grice, "The Black Widow." First published in *High Plains Literary Review*. Copyright © 1995 by Gordon Grice. Reprinted by permission of the author; **pp. 294–296,** Annie Dillard, "The Fixed" from *Pilgrim at Tinker Creek*, pp. 59–61. Copyright © 1974 by Annie Dillard, renewed in 2002 by Annie Dillard. Reprinted by permission of HarperCollins Publishers, and by permission of Russell & Volkening as agents for the author.

Chapter 7: pp. 305–306, From Rose Castillo Guilbault, "The Conveyor Belt Ladies" in *Farmworker's Daughter: Growing up Mexican in America*, 2005, pp. 153–155. Reprinted by permission of Heyday Books via Copyright Clearance Center, Inc.; **pp. 313–315,** From "A Letter to God," by Gregorio López y Fuentes, translated by Donald A. Yates. Reprinted by permission; **pp. 320–321,** From Art Buchwald, *I Never Danced at the White House.* NY: Putman, 1973. Appeared originally in *The Washington Post*, August 17, 1972. © Tribune Media Services, Inc. All Rights Reserved. Reprinted with permission.

Chapter 8: pp. 334–336, "Prologue," from *Without a Net* by Michelle Kennedy, pp. 1–3. Copyright © 2005 Michelle Kennedy. Originally published by Viking. Reprinted by permission of Viking Penguin, a division of Penguin Group (USA) Inc. and by permission of the Stuart Krichevsky Literary Agency, Inc.; **p. 336,** From Jo Goodwin Parker, "What Is Poverty?" in *America's Other Children: Public Schools Outside Suburbia*, ed. George Henderson, p. 216. University of Oklahoma Press. Copy-right © 1971. Reprinted by permission of University of Oklahoma Press via Copyright Clearance Center; **pp. 336–337,** From Thomas Patterson, *We the People.* From Thomas Patterson, *We the People*, 7th Edition, p. 577. Copyright © 2008 by The McGraw-Hill Companies, Inc. Reprinted with permission; **p. 337,** Excerpt from "Poverty" in *Nickel and Dimed: On (Not) Getting By in America* by Barbara Ehrenreich, p. 214. Copyright © 2001 by Barbara Ehrenreich. Reprinted by permission of Henry Holt and Company, LLC, and by permission of International Creative Management; **pp. 338–341,** "Thank You, Ma'm" from *Short Stories* by Langston Hughes. Copyright © 1996 by Ramona Bass and Arnold Rampersad. Reprinted by permission of Hill and Wang, a division of Farrar, Straus and Giroux, LLC; **pp. 343–345,** Copyright © 1996 by John Daniel from *Looking After: A Son's Memoir.* Reprinted by permission of Counterpoint; **pp. 349–351,** From John W. Santrock, *Child Development: An Introduction*, 11th Edition, pp. 476–78. Copyright © 2007 by The McGraw-Hill Companies, Inc. Reprinted with permission; **pp. 356–359,** "TV," from *The Shelter of Each Other* by Mary Pipher, Ph.D., pp. 89–92, copyright © 1996 by Mary Pipher, Ph.D. Used by permission of G.P. Putnam's Sons, a division of Penguin Group (USA) Inc.

Chapter 9: pp. 374–377, From Wayne Weiten and Margaret A. Lloyd, *Psychology Applied to Modern Life*, 7e. © 2003 Wadsworth, a part of Cengage Learning, Inc. Reproduced by permission. www.cengage.com/permissions; **p. 377,** From 11 Faces Scale, F.M. Andrews and S.B. Withey, *Social Indicators of Well-Being: Americans' Perceptions of Life Quality*, pp. 207 and 306, NY: Plenum, 1976 with kind permission of Springer Science + Business Media; **pp. 380–381,** From James M. Henslin, *Essentials of Sociology: A Down-to-Earth Approach*, 7th Edition, p. 201. © 2007. Reprinted by permission of Pearson Education, Inc., Upper Saddle River, New Jersey; **pp. 386–388,** From Gary Soto, "The Jacket" in *The Effects of Knut Hamsun on a Fresno Boy: Recollections and Short Essays*, by Gary Soto. Copyright © 1983, 1986, 2000 by Gary Soto. Reprinted by permission of Persea Books, Inc., NY, BookStop Literary Agency, and the author. All rights reserved; **pp. 393–397,** From Ronald B. Adler, Russell F. Proctor II, and Neil Towne, *Looking Out, Looking In (with CD-ROM and Info-Trac)*, 11th Edition, p. 229. © 2005 Wadsworth, a part of Cengage Learning, Inc. Reproduced by permission. www.cengage.com/permissions; **pp. 402–405,** John Collier, "The Chaser." Originally appeared in *The New Yorker*, 1940. © 1951 by John Collier. © Renewed 1979 by the estate of John Collier. Permission to reprint granted by Harold Matson Co., Inc.

Chapter 10: pp. 417–419, From Thomas Patterson, *The American Democracy*, 8th Edition, pp. 166–69. Copyright © 2008 by The McGraw-Hill Companies, Inc. Reprinted with permission; **pp. 423–425,** "Ties That Bind" by Alanna Nash, *Reader's Digest*, November 2004. Reprinted with permission from Reader's Digest. Copyright © 2004 by The Reader's Digest Association, Inc.; **pp. 432–434,** From David Bodanis, *The Secret House*, pp. 10–15. Copyright © 2003 by David Bodanis. Reprinted with permission of the Carol Mann Agency.

Chapter 11: pp. 449–450, From David G. Myers, *Social Psychology*, 9th Edition, pp. 555–58. Copyright © 2008 by The McGraw-Hill Companies, Inc. Reprinted with permission; **pp. 454–455,** From Hamilton Gregory, *Public Speaking for College and Career*, 8th Edition, pp. 263–265. Copyright © 2010 by The McGraw-Hill Companies, Inc. Reprinted with permission; **p. 457,** From John Sedgwick, "Goodbye to the Goober," *Newsweek*, October 14, 1996. © 1996 by John Sedgwick. Used with permission; **p. 458,** From Sharon Begley, "Homework Doesn't Help." From *Newsweek*, March 30, 1998. © 1998 The Newsweek/Daily Beast Company LLC. All rights reserved. Used by permission and protected by the Copyright Laws of the U.S. The printing, copying, redistribution, or retransmission of the Material without express written permission is prohibited. http://www.thedailybeast.com/newsweek.html; **p. 459,** From Edward Wong, "New Rules for Soccer Parents: 1) No Yelling. 2) No Hitting Ref." From *The New York Times*, May 6, 2001. © 2001 The New York Times. All rights reserved. Used by permission and protected by the Copyright Laws of the United States. The printing, copying, redistribution, or retransmission of the Material without express written permission is prohibited. www.nytimes.com; **pp. 459–460,** From David B. Ellis, *Becoming a Master Student: Course Manual*, 7th Edition. © 1994 Wadsworth, a part of Cengage Learning, Inc. Reproduced by permission. www.cengage.com/permissions; **p. 461,** From Katherine Brush, "A Birthday Party." Copyright © 1946 Condé Nast Publications. All rights reserved. Originally published in *The New Yorker*, March 16, 1946. Reprinted by permission; **pp. 462–464,** Adapted from material by Alleen Pace Nilsen, *Changing Words in a Changing World*. Washington, DC: Women's Educational Equity Act Program, U.S. Department of Education, 1980, pp. 40, 55; **pp. 465–468,** From Samuel Walker and Charles M. Katz, *The Police in America: An Introduction*, 6th Edition, pp. 122–23, 219, 385, 394, 404–6, 157–58. Copyright © 2008 by The McGraw-Hill Companies, Inc. Reprinted with permission; **pp. 473–476,** "A Hanging" from *Shooting an Elephant and Other Essays* by George Orwell, copyright 1950 by Sonia Brownell Orwell and renewed 1978 by Sonia Pitt-Rivers, reprinted by permission of Houghton Mifflin Harcourt Publishing Company, and (Copyright © George Orwell, 1931) by permission of Bill Hamilton as the Literary Executor of the Estate of the Late Sonia Brownell Orwell and Secker & Warburg Ltd.; **p. 480,** From Sylvia S. Mader, *Human Biology*, 8th Edition, p. 7. Copyright © 2004 by The McGraw-Hill Companies, Inc. Reprinted with permission; **pp. 481–482,** From Stephen E. Lucas, *The Art of Public Speaking*, 8th Edition, pp. 434–35. Copyright © 2004 by The McGraw-Hill Companies, Inc. Reprinted with permission; **p. 482,** From George Rodman, *Mass Media in a Changing World*, p. 432. Copyright © 2006 by The McGraw-Hill Companies, Inc. Reprinted with permission; **p. 482,** From Wayne A. Payne and Dale B. Hahn, *Understanding Your Health*, 6th Edition, p. 545. Copyright © 2000 by The McGraw-Hill Companies, Inc. Reprinted with permission; **pp. 482–483,** From Peg Tyre and Julie Scelfo, "A Car, a Call and a Terrible Crash." From *Newsweek*, May 14, 2001. © 2001 The Newsweek/Daily Beast Company

LLC. All rights reserved. Used by permission and protected by the Copyright Laws of the United States. The printing, copying, redistribution, or retransmission of the Material without express written permission is prohibited. http://www.thedailybeast.com/newsweek.html

Chapter 12: pp. 492–494, From Stanley J. Baran, *Introduction to Mass Communication*, 5th Edition, pp. 363, 385. Copyright © 2008 by The McGraw-Hill Companies, Inc. Reprinted with permission; **pp. 497–498,** From Robert S. Feldman, *Understanding Psychology*, 8th Edition, p. 210. Copyright © 2008 by The McGraw-Hill Companies, Inc. Reprinted with permission; **p. 501,** Reprinted with the permission of Atria Books, a Division of Simon & Schuster, Inc., from *The Other Parent: The Inside Story of the Media's Effect on Our Children* by James P. Steyer, p. 199. Copyright © 2002 James P. Steyer.

Chapter 13: pp. 517–518, From Stephen E. Lucas, *The Art of Public Speaking*, 9th Edition, p. 371, 372. Copyright © 2007 by The McGraw-Hill Companies, Inc. Reprinted with permission; **pp. 521–522,** From "Cannabinoids" in Michael L. Teague, *Your Health Today* Brief, McGraw-Hill 2009, pp. 233–234. Copyright © 2003 by The McGraw-Hill Companies, Inc. Reprinted with permission; **p. 522,** Associated Press, "Medical Marijuana Ruling." Copyright © 2005 by The Associated Press. All rights reserved. Reprinted with permission; **p. 524,** Ethan Nadelmann, "Legalize Medicinal Marijuana," *The American Legion Magazine*, November 2004, p. 10. Copyright © 2004 Ethan Nadelmann. Reprinted by permission of the author; **pp. 524–525,** John P. Walters, "Legalize Medicinal Marijuana," *The American Legion Magazine*, November 2004, p. 10; **pp. 527–528,** From *USA Today*, May 18, 2005, p. A10; Reprinted with permission; **p. 530,** From *USA Today*, May 18, 2005, p. A10; **p. 532,** Gary Storck, Letter to the Editor, *USA Today*, May 2005. Copyright © 2005 Gary Storck. Reprinted with permission; **p. 532,** Letter to the Editor, Unsigned, Drug Free America Foundation; **p. 534,** Mitch Earleywine, Letter to the Editor, *USA Today*, May 2005. Reprinted by permission of Dr. Mitch Earleywine; **p. 535,** Letter to the Editor, *USA Today*, May 2005. Copyright © Kirk Muse. Used with permission.

Chapter 14: p. 541, Reproduced with permission of Taco Bell Corp. The Taco Bell Logo and all related marks are the exclusive property of Taco Bell Corp and are used with permission; **pp. 543–545,** From Alan Brinkley, *American History: A Survey*, 11th Edition, pp. 876–77. Copyright © 2003 by The McGraw-Hill Companies, Inc. Reprinted with permission; **pp. 548–549,** From Sylvia S. Mader, *Human Biology*, 9th Edition, p. 421. Copyright © 2006 by The McGraw-Hill Companies, Inc. Reprinted with permission; **pp. 551–552,** "A Fable for Tomorrow," from *Silent Spring* by Rachel Carson. Copyright © 1962 by Rachel L. Carson, renewed 1990 by Roger Christie. Reprinted by permission of Houghton Mifflin Harcourt Publishing Company and by permission of Frances Collin, Trustee. Any electronic distribution or electronic copying of this text is expressly forbidden; **p. 557,** From William P. Cunningham, *Principles of Environmental*

Science 6e, McGraw-Hill, 2011, Fig 8.13 p. 193 Copyright © 2011 by The McGraw-Hill Companies, Inc. Reprinted with permission; **p. 558,** From Withgott, Jay H.; Brennan, Scott R., *Environment: The Science Behind the Stories* 3rd Edition, © Pearson, 2008, p. 269. Reprinted with permission; **p. 560,** Copyright © 2008 by The Gallup Organization. Reproduced by permission of The Gallup Organization.

Appendices: p. A-6, Dictionary page, "savvy to sayyid" From *The Random House Webster's College Dictionary* by Random House, Inc., pp. 1172–73. Copyright © 1995, 1992, 1991 by Random House, Inc. Used by permission of Random House Reference and Information Publishing, a division of Random House, Inc.; **p. A-7, Definition of "curious"** From *The Random House Webster's College Dictionary* by Random House, Inc., p. 327. Copyright © 1995, 1992, 1991 by Random House, Inc. Used by permission of Random House Reference and Information Publishing, a division of Random House, Inc.; **p. A-8, English Sounds/Non-English Sounds** From *The Random House Webster's College Dictionary* by Random House, Inc., p. xxvi, copyright © 1995, 1992, 1991 by Random House, Inc. Used by permission of Random House Reference and Information Publishing, a division of Random House, Inc.

Photo Credits

Page 1, 2: © Bettmann/Corbis; **8:** © Walter Weissman/Corbis; **15:** © Jean-Régis Roustan/Roger-Viollet/The Image Works; **22:** © Bettmann/Corbis; **44:** © Alex Gotfryd/Corbis; **50:** Photo by Michael Kovac/Getty Images for GQ; **71:** © Porter Gifford/Getty Images; **77, 78:** Courtesy Everett Collection; **116:** © AP Photo/Lynne Sladky; **134:** Paul Kalinian, 1976; **138:** © Roy Stevens/Time & Life Pictures; **143:** © David Young-Wolff/PhotoEdit, Inc.; **150:** © Marc Alcarez; **162:** © George Hall/Corbis;

163: © Hisham F. Ibrahim/RF Getty Images; **169:** Courtesy Everett Collection; **188:** Execution of the Defenders of Madrid, 3rd May, 1808, 1814 (oil on canvas), Francisco Jose de Goya y Lucientes, (1746–1828)/Prado, Madrid, Spain/The Bridgeman Art Library International; **203:** Digital Vision; **213, 214:** © Michael Ochs Archives/Corbis; **214:** © Michael Ochs Archives/Corbis; **215:** © Courtesy of the authors; **224:** © Patrick Fraser/Corbis Outline; **228:** © AP Photo/Douglas C. Pizac; **242:** © Arterra Picture Library/Alamy; **255:** © Tom McHugh/Photo Researchers, Inc.; **258:** © Stephen Saks/Photo Researchers; **263:** © Michael Ochs Archives/Corbis; **277:** © AP Photo; **278:** © 2003 Estate of Pablo Picasso/Artists Rights Society (ARS), New York. Bridgeman-Giraudon/Art Resource, NY; **281:** © AP Photo/Gino Domenico; **295:** © DVL/RF Getty Images; **299:** © Michael Ochs Archives/Corbis; **304:** Photo by Steve Jennings/WireImage; **311:** © Royalty-Free Corbis; **320:** Photo by Frank Capri/Hulton Archive/Getty Images; **325:** © Andrew Ward/Life File/RF Getty Images; **333, 334:** © EMPICS/Landov; **338:** Photo by Robert W. Kelley/Time Life Pictures/Getty Images; **356:** Photo by Keith Philpott/Time Life Pictures/Getty Images; **371:** © EMPICS/Landov; **411, 412, 447:** © 20th Century Fox Film Corp. All rights reserved, Courtesy: Everett Collection; **466:** © Joseph Sohm; Visions of America/Corbis; **471:** © Photo by Hulton Archive/Getty Images; **484:** © 20th Century Fox Film Corp. All rights reserved, Courtesy: Everett Collection; **485:** PRNewsFoto/Minnesota Partnership for Action Against Tobacco; **490:** © Brigette Sullivan/PhotoEdit; **493:** Image Courtesy of The Advertising Archives; **517:** © 20th Century Fox Film Corp. All rights reserved, Courtesy: Everett Collection; **519:** Courtesy of PETA.org; **536:** Office of National Drug Control Control Policy/Partnership for a Drug-Free America; **539, 540:** Photo by Frederick M. Brown/Getty Images; **551:** © Erich Hartmann/Magnum Photos

Index